Crime ~~...~~ ation
The ~~...~~'s

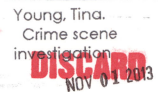

Tina Young, MFS, CBPE
Grossmont College

P. J. Ortmeier, Ph.D.
Grossmont College

Prentice Hall
Boston   Columbus   Indianapolis   New York   San Francisco   Upper Saddle River
Amsterdam   Cape Town   Dubai   London   Madrid   Milan   Munich   Paris
Montreal   Toronto   Delhi   Mexico City   Sao Paulo   Sydney   Hong Kong
Seoul   Singapore   Taipei   Tokyo

Editor in Chief: Vernon Anthony
Acquisitions Editor: Eric Krassow
Development Editor: Elisa Rogers
Editorial Assistant: Lynda Cramer
Director of Marketing: David Gesell
Marketing Manager: Adam Kloza
Senior Marketing Coordinator: Alicia Wozniak
Senior Managing Editor: JoEllen Gohr
Production Editor: Jessica H. Sykes
Senior Operations Supervisor: Pat Tonneman

Operations Specialist: Deidra Skahill
Senior Art Director: Diane Ernsberger
Cover Designer: Suzanne Duda
Media Editor: Michelle Churma
Lead Media Project Manager: Karen Bretz
Full-Service Project Management: Shylaja Gattupalli
Composition: TexTech International
Printer/Binder: Courier/Stoughton
Cover Printer: Lehigh-Phoenix Color/Hagerstown
Text Font: Palatino

Library of Congress Cataloging-in-Publication Data

Young, Tina.
    Crime scene investigation : the forensic technician's field manual / Tina Young, P. J. Ortmeier.
        p. cm.
    Includes bibliographical references and index.
    ISBN-13: 978-0-13-512712-4 (alk. paper)
    ISBN-10: 0-13-512712-2 (alk. paper)
    1. Crime scenes.   2. Criminal investigation.   3. Evidence, Criminal.   I. Ortmeier, P. J.   II. Title.
HV8073.Y683 2011
363.25—dc22

                                                                                2009039107

9 10 V092 16 15 14 13

Prentice Hall
is an imprint of

www.pearsonhighered.com

ISBN 10: 0-13-512712-2
ISBN 13: 978-0-13-512712-4

To Graham, Liam, and Christine

Brief Contents

Contents

Contents

Preface

The field of forensic science expanded dramatically over the past few decades. Technological advancements such as DNA profiling, the Automated Fingerprint Identification System (AFIS), and numerous other scientific breakthroughs greatly enhanced humankind's ability to investigate and solve crimes through applied science.

Forensic science has also been popularized in recent years by the media, movies, and numerous television programs such as *Forensic Files, NCIS,* and *CSI.* The so-called *CSI effect* generates tremendous interest among members of the public and academe. Although fictional accounts of the forensic science operative may not depict reality, those who view the TV programs often identify themselves as amateur sleuths. As a result, many trial jurors expect miraculous results from the application of science to criminal investigations. The interest in forensic science has also led many college students to select a career in the discipline. Publishers responded with forensic science-related textbooks and other learning materials.

CRIME SCENE INVESTIGATION: The Forensic Technician's Field Manual was written in response to the need for a text that addresses the tasks performed by the person who identifies, photographs, documents, collects, preserves, and transports evidence at and from a crime scene. The book is organized as a step-by-step guide for the college student as well as the sworn peace officer or civilian who functions as a crime scene or forensic (evidence) technician. As such, the book is appropriate for basic courses in forensic technology and crime scene investigation and as a field manual or training aid for practitioners. Numerous photographs and diagrams illustrate the techniques discussed.

The protocols and processes suggested are consistent with guidelines established by the American Society of Crime Laboratory Directors (ASCLD) and the International Association for Identification (IAI). Therefore, policies and procedures in a reader's jurisdiction may differ slightly.

Each chapter begins with a set of learning objectives and ends with a summary, a list of key terms, discussion and review questions, a case study, practical lab exercises designed to reinforce skill development, and web-based resources. Included at the rear of the book is a glossary as well as an appendix that lists supplies and equipment needed for a basic crime scene processing kit. The inside front and back covers present measurement conversions and equivalents and trigonometric tables (sine and tangent functions).

ACKNOWLEDGMENTS

The authors wish to express their gratitude to many family members, friends, colleagues, and practitioners who provided encouragement, support, and assistance during the creation of this book. Thanks are extended to many friends at Prentice Hall, including Tim Peyton, Eric Krassow, Elisa Rogers, Adam Kloza, and Alicia Wozniak, JoEllen Gohr, and to Jessica Sykes (production editor), Shylaja Gattupalli (project manager), and Alphonse Fernandez (copy editor) for their keen observation skills and attention to detail. A special thanks to Mary Najjar and Gloria Aldaba for their assistance with the preparation of the manuscript.

The authors are extremely grateful to the manuscript reviewers: Lynne Bell, Simon Fraser University; Katherine M. Brown, Sam Houston State University; Paul H. Clarke Jr., Northcentral Technical College; Michael Emanuel, Northwestern Community College; Paul L. Friedman, Palm Beach Community College; John Hill,

Salt Lake Community College; James R. McDonald, Greenville Technical College; Michael R. Summers, Erie Community College; and David Tate, Purdue University.

Appreciation is also extended to the individuals and agencies that provided assistance and images for the book:

- Dr. Adolfo Gonzales, chief of police, National City, California, Police Department
- Rick Emerson, chief of police (retired), Craig Ogino, crime laboratory manager, Rodrigo Viesca, forensic technician and latent print examiner (retired), Bill Johnson, crime laboratory manager (retired), and the crime laboratory personnel at the Chula Vista, California, Police Department
- Marie Durina, forensic document examiner, and the crime laboratory personnel at the San Diego County, California, Sheriff's Crime Laboratory
- San Diego, California, Police Department Crime Laboratory personnel
- El Cajon, California, Police Department Crime Laboratory personnel
- San Diego County, California, District Attorney's Office
- Dr. Skip Sperber, and the San Diego County Medical Examiner's Office
- Marykay Hunt, certified latent print examiner, Missouri State Highway Patrol and students of the Grossmont College, California, Administration of Justice Department

INSTRUCTOR SUPPLEMENTS

A CourseSmart e-book version of the text (0-13-508975-1) is available and the authors have provided an Instructor's Manual with Test Bank (0-13-512706-8) and PowerPoints (0-13-512707-6) to accompany the text. To access supplementary materials online, instructors need to request an instructor access code. Go to **www.pearsonhighered.com/irc**, where you can register for an instructor access code. Within 48 hours after registering, you will receive a confirming e-mail, including an instructor access code. Once you have received your code, go to the site and log on for full instructions on downloading the materials you wish to use.

ABOUT THE AUTHORS

Tina Young

Tina Young attended The Ohio State University and later graduated cum laude with a bachelor of science in criminal justice and a master of forensic sciences from National University in San Diego, California. She also completed hundreds of hours of forensic science and law enforcement-related training.

In July 2007, Professor Young became a certified bloodstain pattern examiner through the International Association for Identification. She was previously employed as a crime scene specialist with the National City, California, Police Department and an evidence technician with the Chula Vista, California, Police Department.

Currently, Tina Young is an assistant professor in the Administration of Justice Department at Grossmont College in El Cajon, California. Additionally, she provides forensic case consultation and training to public agencies and private entities.

Professor Young published "A Photographic Comparison of Luminol, Fluorescein, and Bluestar" in the November/December 2006 issue of the *Journal of Forensic Identification*. She is a member of the International Association for Identification, the International Association of Bloodstain Pattern Analysts; the California State Division of the International Association for Identification; the Southern California Association of Fingerprint Officers; the California Association of Administration of Justice Educators; and is a member of, and Grossmont College chapter advisor for, the American Criminal Justice Association/Lambda Alpha Epsilon.

Professor Young volunteers to provide forensic science training to disadvantaged youth, children in the foster care system, K-12 math and science teachers, police patrol officers, and at national conferences. In July 2008, she was awarded the *Partner in Law Enforcement Award* by the National City Police Department for her forensic science-related volunteer work.

P. J. Ortmeier

P. J. Ortmeier holds bachelor's and master's degrees in criminal justice and a Ph.D. in educational leadership with an emphasis in public safety training and development. He is a U.S. Army veteran and a former police officer. Dr. Ortmeier developed and implemented numerous courses and degree programs in criminal justice and public safety. As a member of a California Commission on Peace Officer Standards and Training (POST) steering committee, Dr. Ortmeier participated in the integration of leadership, ethics, and community-policing concepts and skill development into the basic academy for entry-level California peace officers.

Currently, Dr. Ortmeier is professor and chair of the 1500-student Administration of Justice Department at Grossmont College in the San Diego suburb of El Cajon, California. He also holds a teaching position at Webster University in San Diego.

Dr. Ortmeier is the author of *Public Safety and Security Administration, Policing the Community: A Guide for Patrol Operations, Introduction to Law Enforcement and Criminal Justice,* and *Introduction to Security: Operations and Management,* as well as numerous articles appearing in journals such as *The Police Chief, The Law Enforcement Executive Forum, California Security, Police and Security News,* and *Security Management.* With Edwin Meese III, former attorney general of the United States, Dr. Ortmeier co-authored *Leadership, Ethics, and Policing: Challenges for the 21st Century.* His writing focuses on professional career education, leadership, ethics, management, police field services, forensic technology, and competency development for public safety personnel.

Dr. Ortmeier is a member of the Academy of Criminal Justice Sciences, the American Society of Criminology, the International Association of Chiefs of Police, the Public Safety Leadership Development Consortium, the California Association of Administration of Justice Educators, and the American Society for Industrial Security. His current interests include homeland defense, forensic science, and the development of leadership skills and career education pathways for law enforcement and other public safety professionals.

The authors encourage and solicit comments regarding this book as well as suggestions for future editions. They are also available to provide technical assistance to anyone who adopts this text for a course. The authors may be contacted directly at:

Tina Young, M. F. S.

Assistant Professor, Administration of Justice
Grossmont College
8800 Grossmont College Drive
El Cajon, CA 92020

P. J. Ortmeier, Ph. D.

Professor/Chair, Administration of Justice
Grossmont College
8800 Grossmont College Drive
El Cajon, CA 92020

1

Overview of Forensic Science

LEARNING OUTCOMES

After completing this chapter, the reader should be able to:

- describe the role of a forensic technician,
- describe the training and education requirements for a forensic technician,
- distinguish a forensic technician from a criminalist,
- describe the role of an investigator,
- articulate the functions of a crime laboratory,
- evaluate safety precautions required of a forensic technician.

INTRODUCTION

In recent years, movie and television producers popularized forensic science and transformed its perception. As a result, forensic science is viewed as adventuresome. Various television dramas, documentaries, and movies with forensic science themes excite viewers. In virtually every episode, an actor portrays a cool and sophisticated forensic science professional who single-handedly solves a major crime. Hollywood portrays the professional as an individual who obtains miraculous results, displays expertise in all areas of forensic science, demonstrates the ability to intimidate criminal suspects, and solves every crime. The portrayal is far from reality.

Fictional accounts of the application of forensic science are often misleading. Thus, the average criminal trial juror forms unrealistic expectations regarding forensic science accomplishments. Many jurors are led to believe that crimes are easily solved. Jurors expect the forensic science results illustrated in television dramas to be replicated in an actual criminal trial.

This chapter realistically examines forensic science, explores the roles of forensic science personnel, and attempts to dispel the myths and misconceptions created by fictional representations. The reader should keep in mind that the primary goal of the forensic science professional is to seek and present the truth based on facts, not to formulate an opinion on an accused person's guilt.

FOUNDATIONS OF FORENSIC SCIENCE

The term *forensic* is derived from the Latin *forensus,* meaning "of the forum." In Ancient Rome, trials took place in the forum. In modern times, **forensic science** refers to the application of science to conflict resolution in a legal environment. Thus, forensic science has been variously defined as the application of science to law (Saferstein, 2007), the sum of the hard sciences as applied in courts of law (Falcone, 2005), and the application of natural, physical, and some social sciences to the investigation of crime (Ortmeier, 2006).

Numerous individuals laid the foundation for modern-day forensic science. Austrian jurist Hans Gross (1847–1915) is widely regarded as the founder of modern criminalistics. In his

Forensic science
The application of science to conflict resolution in a legal environment.

book, *Criminal Investigation* (1893), Gross defined a criminalist as one who utilizes scientific methods to study crime, and identify, apprehend, and prosecute criminals. More recently, the term *criminalist* is often used in reference to a person who engages in forensic biology (serology or DNA), drug or fire debris analysis, or trace evidence (e.g., hairs, fibers, and polymers).

Edmond Locard, an early twentieth century scientist, is another of the first persons identified as a criminalist (Eckert, 1997; Saferstein, 2007). Locard is recognized as the director of the first crime laboratory, established in Lyon, France, in 1910. He is best remembered for the **Locard Exchange Principle,** also known as *Locard's Theory.* Through this principle, Locard proposed that forensic evidence from a crime scene can be linked to a victim and a suspect.

> **Locard Exchange Principle** Principle which proposes that forensic evidence from a crime scene can be linked to a victim and a suspect.

Wherever he steps, whatever he touches, whatever he leaves, even unconsciously, will serve as a silent witness against him. Not only his fingerprints or his footprints, but his hair, the fibers from his clothes, the glass he breaks, the tool mark he leaves, the paint he scratches, the blood or semen he deposits or collects. All of these and more, bear mute witness against him. This is evidence that does not forget. It is not confused by the excitement of the moment. It is not absent because human witnesses are. It is factual evidence. Physical evidence cannot be wrong, it cannot perjure itself, it cannot be wholly absent. Only human failure to find it, study and understand it, can diminish its value.

In concert with Locard's Principle, forensic science involves the application of the sciences to criminal investigations. Thus, scientific methodology is employed in the collection, preservation, examination, and analysis of evidence for possible presentation in a judicial proceeding.

Other notable pioneers in forensic science include the following:

- Mathieu Orfila (Spain)—Orfila is known as the *father of forensic toxicology*. In the early 1800s, Orfila conducted experiments on animals in an effort to detect poisons. He later published his findings and established forensic toxicology as an investigative tool.
- Alphonse Bertillon (France)—Bertillon is known as the *father of criminal identification*. In the late 1800s, he developed the first system for personal identification, utilizing body measurements (anthropometry).
- Francis Galton (England)—Galton is known for his famous book, *Finger Prints,* published

in 1892. Galton was the first to develop a method for classifying fingerprints. His method is still in use.

- Leone Lattes (Italy)—In the early 1900s, Lattes was the first to apply blood typing to criminal investigations.
- Albert Osborn (United States)—In 1910, Osborn established techniques for questioned document examination and published *Questioned Documents*, a reference guide for forensic document examiners that is still in use.
- Calvin Goddard (United States)—In the early half of the twentieth century, while employed by the U.S. Army, Goddard was the first to use a comparison microscope to compare expended firearm projectiles, a technique still in use (Saferstein, 2007).

THE CRIME SCENE UNIT

As the use of forensic science expanded, the discipline divided into three broad categories: medical (coroner, medical examiner), laboratory (criminalistics), and field services (the crime scene unit). The primary focus of this book is on field services, the aspect of forensic science that addresses the identification, collection, preservation, transportation, and preliminary evaluation of evidence. Forensic technicians (civilian field evidence specialists or sworn peace officers) engage in forensic field services. They collect evidence from physical and virtual (cyberspace-based) crime scenes and transport the evidence to the forensic science laboratory.

Photo 1-1. San Diego county sheriffs department forensic evidence technician John Farrell photographing a crime scene.

THE FORENSIC SCIENCE LABORATORY

Forensic science laboratories were established in the United States in the early 1900s. In 1924, Los Angeles police chief August Vollmer established a laboratory within the Los Angeles Police Department (LAPD). Vollmer's lab was directed by Rex Welch, an LAPD officer with a degree in dentistry. In 1929, a crime laboratory was established in Northwestern University's law school in Chicago. The Northwestern lab became the crime laboratory of the Chicago Police Department (Eckert, 1997).

Today, crime labs exist within many local, county, state, and federal law enforcement agencies. Federal crime laboratories include those associated with the Naval Criminal Investigative Service (NCIS), the U.S. Army Criminal Investigations Command (CID), the Federal Bureau of Investigation (FBI), the Drug Enforcement Administration (DEA), the Bureau of Alcohol, Tobacco, Firearms and Explosives (ATF), and the United States Postal Inspection Service.

The services provided by a crime laboratory vary among agencies. Each division or unit within a laboratory may analyze different types of physical evidence. Major divisions within a laboratory are often categorized according to the microscopic (too small for unaided human eye), organic (derived from a living organism), or inorganic (not of biological origin) analysis performed. Typical subdivisions within a large crime laboratory may include the following:

- Arson and Explosives Analysis.
- Biology, encompassing DNA analysis and serology (analysis of seminal and other biological fluids).
- Controlled Substances and Blood-Alcohol Analysis Unit (toxicology).
- Computer Analysis.
- Firearms, focusing on ballistics, trajectory, and firearm tool mark comparisons.
- Forensic Document Examination, encompassing analysis of handwriting, ink, paper, and other questioned documents.
- Friction Ridge Evidence/Fingerprint Analysis.
- Forensic Technology and Photography Unit (Forensic Technicians, Field Evidence Technicians). Photography and evidence collection are the primary duties of the forensic technician.
- Impression Evidence, involving the examination of shoe, tire, and tool mark evidence.

- Trace Evidence Analysis, encompassing testing of items such as hairs and fibers, glass, paint, and soil.

As needed, the services of technicians in anthropology, criminology, forensic odontology, entomology (study of insects), and botany (study of plants) may be solicited also. Many crime scene units and laboratories are certified and contain quality control units that oversee the activities of field and lab personnel. Although crime scene processing rather than lab analysis is the primary focus of this book, the procedures described throughout adhere to American Society of Crime Laboratory Directors (ASCLD) guidelines. Adherence to ASCLD guidelines lends credibility to the crime scene processing protocols used by evidence collection field personnel.

AMERICAN SOCIETY OF CRIME LABORATORY DIRECTORS (ASCLD)

ASCLD is a nonprofit professional organization founded in 1973 by Briggs White, a former director of the FBI Laboratory. Society membership is comprised of crime laboratory managers, directors and supervisors from numerous countries. ASCLD seeks to foster professional interests; assist with the development of laboratory management principles and techniques; acquire, preserve, and disseminate forensic-based information; maintain and improve communications among crime laboratory directors; and promote, encourage, and maintain the highest standards of practice in the field.

ASCLD is not an accrediting organization. However, a laboratory accreditation board was formed within ASCLD and later incorporated as a separate entity. The accrediting body is the American Society of Crime Laboratory Directors/Laboratory Accreditation Board (ASCLD/LAB). Crime lab certification is accomplished through the ASCLD/LAB. The four objectives of the ASCLD/LAB certification program are:

1. Improve the quality of laboratory services provided to the criminal justice system.
2. Develop and maintain criteria that may be used by a laboratory to assess its level of performance and strengthen its operation.
3. Provide an independent, impartial, and objective system by which laboratories can benefit from a total operational review.
4. Offer to the general public and to users of laboratory services a means of identifying

those laboratories which have demonstrated that they meet established standards (American Society of Crime Laboratory Directors/Laboratory Accreditation Board, 2009).

Accreditation helps to ensure that forensic science-related procedures and personnel meet uniform and professionally credible standards. By 2009, all ASCLD/LAB-certified labs fell under ASCLD/LAB–International, which is an International Standards Organization (ISO) program of accreditation. ASCLD/LAB–International defines forensic science as *the exam-*

ination of crime scenes, recovery of evidence, laboratory examinations, interpretation of findings, and presentation of the conclusions reached for investigative or intelligence purposes or for use in court. ASCLD/LAB–International offers accreditation in the following disciplines of forensic science. The list is not exhaustive and additional subdisciplines may be added to the list (American Society of Crime Laboratory Directors/Laboratory Accreditation Board–International, 2009):

Certified crime labs must adhere to strict quality control guidelines and protocols. The ASCLD/LAB–International accreditation process includes the following:

1. A copy of the accreditation manual requested by the laboratory manager.
2. Self-evaluation by applicant laboratory.
3. Application and supporting documents filed by applicant laboratory.
4. On-site inspection by a team of trained ASCLD/LAB inspectors.
5. Inspection report considered by ASCLD/LAB.
6. One year to remedy deficiencies (if any) before final decision by the board.
7. Accreditation review completed by the laboratory annually.
8. Full reinspection required every five years (American Society of Crime Laboratory Directors/Laboratory Accreditation Board, 2009).

ASCLD/LAB-INTERNATIONAL EDUCATION AND TESTING

An ASCLD/LAB-certified laboratory must maintain and document a training program designed to ensure that each individual has the knowledge, skills, and abilities (KSAs) necessary to successfully perform job duties. The laboratory's employee development program can promote knowledge and skill development through active participation with related professional organizations. Attendance must be documented for all organizational meetings, technical training courses, in-house technical meetings, laboratory-sponsored seminars and conferences, and college-level courses.

The ASCLD/LAB educational requirements for individual forensic science disciplines are as follows:

- Analysts working in the controlled substance and trace evidence disciplines of forensic science must possess a baccalaureate or higher degree in a natural science, criminalistics, or a closely-related field.

Discipline	Subdiscipline (Types of Tests)
Biology	• Serology (body fluid identification) • DNA nuclear • DNA mitochondrial
Controlled substances	• General controlled substances
Crime scene	• General crime scene investigation • Crime scene reconstruction • Clandestine laboratory • Bloodstain pattern interpretation
Digital and multimedia evidence	• Computer forensics • Video analysis • Audio analysis • Image analysis
Firearms/tool marks	• Firearms • Tool marks • Impression evidence
Latent prints	• Latent print processing • Latent print comparisons
Questioned documents	• General document examination
Toxicology	• General toxicology • Blood/urine alcohol • Breath alcohol (testing)
Trace evidence	• Fire debris • Explosives • Gun shot residue (instrumental analysis) • Paint • Polymers • Fibers and textiles • Glass • Physical comparisons • Hair (microscopic examination) • Analysis of unknowns • Other materials

- Analysts working in the toxicology discipline of forensic science must possess a baccalaureate or higher degree in a natural science, toxicology, criminalistics, or a closely-related field.
- Analysts working in the biological discipline of forensic science must possess a baccalaureate or higher degree in a natural science, criminalistics, or a closely related field, and, if performing DNA analysis and where applicable, shall meet the education requirements of the quality assurance standards for forensic DNA testing laboratories as well as the quality assurance standards for convicted offender DNA database laboratories.
- Analysts working in the firearm, tool mark, questioned document, or latent fingerprint disciplines of forensic science shall meet the educational requirements specified in the job description.
- All analysts, regardless of academic qualifications or work experience, shall satisfactorily complete a competency test prior to assuming casework responsibility in the laboratory.
- Personnel working with digital evidence and as crime scene specialists (e.g., forensic technicians) shall meet the educational requirements specified in the job description (American Society of Crime Laboratory Directors/Laboratory Accreditation Board–International, 2009).

ROLE OF A FORENSIC TECHNICIAN

In many police agencies in the United States, the forensic technician is a sworn peace officer or case investigator who responds to and processes major crime scenes. However, other agencies employ trained nonsworn civilian personnel as forensic technicians.

Uniformed police officers or sheriff's deputies are often the first officers to respond to a crime scene. The officers secure and protect the crime scene while the forensic technicians process the scene for evidence. Sworn officers (detectives or case investigators) conduct the follow-up investigation.

Many job titles are used to describe a forensic technician: *crime scene technician, forensic specialist, forensic evidence technician, forensic science technician, identification*

> **Forensic technician** A sworn peace officer, case investigator or civilian employee of an agency who responds to and processes major crime scenes. Many job titles are used to describe a forensic technician: *crime scene specialist, crime scene technician, forensic specialist, forensic evidence technician, forensic science technician, identification technician, and crime scene investigator.*

technician, and *crime scene investigator.* **Forensic technician** is the job title used in this book.

A forensic technician should not be confused with a criminalist. Although duties may vary among jurisdictions, the job title of **criminalist** is usually reserved for laboratory analysis personnel who hold bachelors' degrees or higher in fields such as chemistry and biology. Criminalists often begin their careers as forensic technicians.

> **Criminalist** A laboratory analysis person who holds a bachelors degree or higher in fields such as chemistry and biology.

Though fictional crime dramas often portray the forensic technician as a police officer or federal agent who is a self-reliant expert in all areas of forensic science, the forensic technician is more often a support person for the police detective (case investigator). The lead case investigator usually bears the ultimate responsibility for all activities associated with a criminal investigation. A respectful and trusting collaborative relationship between the case investigator and the forensic technician is essential. The forensic technician is not the loner typically portrayed in many popular television shows such as *CSI (Crime Scene Investigation)*. However, the forensic technician is critical to the success of an investigation.

The forensic technician's duties involve responding to a crime scene to document the scene as well as identify, collect, preserve, and transport evidence to the crime lab. Documentation of the crime scene involves a variety of activities including photography, videography, and crime scene sketching. Evidence preservation is conducted through

Photo 1-2. Forensic technician processing a crime scene.

Photo 1-3. Forensic technician processing a crime scene.

photography, evidence collection and storage, and latent fingerprint processing. Follow-up activities may include processing of victims and suspects as well as photography and evidence collection at a postmortem examination (autopsy) of a victim. Other duties include vehicle processing, fingerprint identification and comparison, collecting evidence during the execution of a search warrant, follow-up evidence processing in the crime laboratory, and report writing. Each of these forensic technician duties is discussed in this book.

Ultimately, the forensic technician serves as a human mechanism in search of the truth. Evidence processed by the technician can exonerate the innocent as well as convict the guilty. Therefore, the forensic technician must remain objective, and not formulate and present opinions regarding an accused person's guilt.

EVIDENCE

Evidence Defined

The primary role of a forensic technician is to identify, document, collect, preserve, and transport evidence. Broadly defined, **evidence** is any information or items people use to make a decision. In a judicial proceeding, evidence is used by the fact finder (jury, or judge if a nonjury trial) to make decisions in a criminal or civil case. It is imperative that criminal justice practitioners be knowledgeable regarding the rules of evidence and search and seizure. These rules guide law enforcement personnel, attorneys, judges, and others in the collection,

> **Evidence** Any information or item people use to make a decision. Evidence consists of testimony, writings, material objects, and other items presented in a legal proceeding as proof of the existence or nonexistence of a fact.

preservation, and transportation of evidence as well as the conduct of a judicial proceeding. Criminal cases are sometimes dismissed or reversed on appeal because of violations of evidentiary and procedural rules on the part of the law enforcement, forensic, or prosecutorial staff.

Evidence consists of testimony, writings, material objects, and other items presented in a legal proceeding as proof of the existence or nonexistence of a fact. Proof is the establishment of a requisite degree of belief concerning a fact in the mind(s) of the judge or jurors. Proof is the desired result of evidence. The burden of proof is the obligation to produce evidence sufficient to prove a fact or set of facts.

Evidence is offered in court to establish a fact, to impeach (discredit) a witness, to corroborate or rehabilitate (support) a witness, and to assist in determining an appropriate sentence (i.e., aggravating or mitigating circumstances for sentences, proving no-probation offense elements, and special circumstances in death penalty cases). Evidence must be relevant, competently presented, and legally obtained. The rules of evidence are often described as the rules of exclusion because their language suggests what evidence cannot be used because its use would violate a statutory (law affected by legislative enactment) or constitutional safeguard.

Sources of evidence law include state and federal statutory provisions regarding witness competency, introduction of writings, privileged communications, and hearsay. Sources also include criminal law provisions regarding accomplice testimony, invasion of privacy, and wiretapping; the U.S. Constitution; state constitutions; and case law regarding search and seizure, *Miranda* issues, and interpretations of evidence-related statutes.

Evidence may be excluded from a judicial proceeding if deemed inadmissible because of the *Exclusionary Rule,* a U.S. Supreme Court legal construct based on an interpretation of the Fourth Amendment's prohibition against unreasonable search and seizure. The exclusionary rule provides that otherwise admissible evidence may not be used in a criminal proceeding if it is the product of illegal police activity.

Likewise, evidence considered to be the *fruit of the poison tree* is inadmissible in a criminal proceeding. The concept is based on the premise that once the primary evidence (the tree) is determined to be illegally obtained, then the secondary evidence (fruit) is also poisoned (tainted) and inadmissible. To avoid issues of admissibility of evidence, forensic professionals should be knowledgeable with respect to the rules of evidence established through legislative enactment (statutes) and judicial decisions (case law). Most agencies provide in-service training opportunities that help forensic personnel remain current with statutory and law provisions.

Types of Evidence

Evidence generally falls into four major categories: documentary, physical (real), demonstrative, and testimonial. Although all forms of evidence can be assigned to one of the four major categories, classifications of evidence are often expanded to include the following types:

- Documentary evidence—This type of evidence includes any documented or tangible form of communication offered as evidence in court. Examples of documents include notes, diaries, journals, ledgers, computer-generated data, photographs, audiotapes, and videotapes.
- Physical evidence (material objects)— Examples of physical evidence include fruits (proceeds) of a crime, instrumentalities (tools) of a crime, contraband (items that are illegal to possess), and other physical evidence that establishes the elements of a crime and the identity of the perpetrator.
- Demonstrative evidence—Examples of demonstrative evidence include objects and materials such as maps, models, charts, diagrams, displays, and computer simulations that are meant to demonstrate, portray, or enhance the meaning of evidence presented to the judge or jury.
- Relevant evidence—Evidence that has any tendency to prove or disprove a disputed fact in a case is relevant evidence. Common examples of relevant evidence include motive (reason) for the crime, capacity to commit a crime, opportunity to commit the crime, prior threats or expressions of ill will by the accused, possession of writings or physical evidence linking a suspect to the crime, physical evidence linking a suspect to the crime scene, consciousness of guilt or admissions by conduct evidence, evidence affecting the credibility of a witness, and modus operandi (method of operation) evidence.
- Admissions and confessions—An admission is a statement by a suspect acknowledging some fact relevant to a case. A confession is a statement by a suspect admitting total

liability for a crime. A confession is a full acknowledgment of all elements of an offense, and it negates any defenses. Both are inculpatory (incriminating) and tend to establish the guilt of the accused. Some defendants accuse authorities of coercion and other improper tactics when soliciting an admission or a confession.

- Hearsay evidence—This type of evidence includes any out-of-court statement presented in court by someone other than the original declarant, offered to prove the truth of the matter stated in court. Subject to a few exceptions, hearsay is inadmissible.
- Consciousness of guilt evidence—This type of evidence includes conduct by the accused from which an inference of guilt or an admission can be drawn. Examples include running from the crime scene, assaulting an officer, threatening a witness, providing false information, attempting to destroy or conceal evidence, or refusing to provide personal physical evidence (Ortmeier, 2006; Rutledge, 2007).
- Testimonial evidence (testimony)—Testimony is provided by a witness, including an eyewitness to an event, a victim, or a suspect who has knowledge of the issues being tried in a case. Testimony is also provided by qualified experts in specific disciplines.

Expert Testimony and the Daubert Trilogy

Although forensic science is extremely valuable to the fact finder (jury or judge) in a judicial proceeding, courts still struggle with the admissibility of evidence, especially when presented through the testimony of experts. Acting as *gatekeepers,* judges must differentiate so-called "experts" motivated by financial gain from reliable experts who present relevant testimony.

Until the early 1900s, judges assessed witness expertise by determining if a commercial market existed for the expert knowledge offered. If a person could generate earnings from the knowledge presented, the person was considered an expert. In 1923, a federal court of appeals ruled in *Frye vs. United States* that scientific evidence presented through expert testimony must be relevant as well as generally accepted in the particular field in which it belongs. The Frye case involved admissibility of photographic evidence [*Frye vs. United States*, 293 F. 1013 (DC cir. 1923)]. The *Frye test* (general acceptance rule) remained the standard for evaluating the admissibility of expert testimony in federal courts for 70 years. *Frye* still exists as a standard in many state courts.

In *Daubert vs. Merrell Dow Pharmaceuticals* (1993), the U.S. Supreme Court established a new precedent regarding admissibility of expert testimony in federal judicial proceedings. The court held that federal trial judges must evaluate expert witnesses to determine if their proffered testimony is both relevant and reliable. According to the Court, testimony is relevant if it fits the facts (issues) of the case. Testimony is reliable if the expert derived conclusions through the use of elements of the scientific method (e.g., empirical testing, peer review, publication of results, established standards) as well as general acceptance in the scientific community. In *Daubert,* the U.S. Supreme Court affirmed that nothing in Rule 702 of the 1975 Federal Rules of Evidence indicates that "general acceptance" is the only necessary pre-condition for the admissibility of expert testimony [*Daubert vs. Merrell Dow Pharmaceuticals,* 509 U.S. 579 (1993)].

Daubert was the first in a series of three U.S. Supreme Court decisions that, taken together, comprise the *Daubert trilogy. Joiner* (1997), the second decision of the trilogy, further classified the U.S. Supreme Court's position on admissibility of expert testimony. The Court held that federal appellate courts must affirm the trial court's decision regarding the admissibility of expert testimony unless it can be established that the trial judge abused discretion and rendered a decision that was obviously wrong [*General Electric Co. vs Joiner,* 522 U.S. 136 (1997)]. In *Kuhmo* (1999), the third decision of the Daubert trilogy, the U.S. Supreme Court ruled that the judge's "gatekeeping" function held in Daubert applied to all expert testimony whether scientific or not [*Kuhmo Tire Ltd. vs. Charmichael,* 526 U.S. 137, (1999)].

In essence, the Daubert trilogy proposes that a witness may provide expert testimony if the following questions are considered by the trial court judge when determining admissibility:

- Has the theory or technique been tested under field conditions? Is it falsifiable?
- Does a known or potential error rate exist?
- Has the theory or technique been subjected to peer review and has it been published?
- Do standards exist for control of the methodology?
- Is the theory or technique generally accepted within the field (the Frye test)?

To withstand challenges, forensic technicians and other forensic science professionals should ensure that Daubert trilogy issues and questions are addressed. Such case management strategies are critical to overcoming inadmissibility of testimony challenges as well as preventing unnecessary expenses and delays (Waters & Hodge, 2005).

A CAREER AS A FORENSIC TECHNICIAN

Career Preparation

Most forensic technicians seek employment with a municipal or county law enforcement agency. However, many job opportunities are available in other law enforcement jurisdictions. State and federal agencies also employ forensic technicians and other forensic science personnel. In addition, pre-service and in-service sworn peace officers and others employed in law enforcement can benefit from training and education in forensic science. Most of the approximately 17,000 law enforcement agencies in the United States do not require a college degree of candidates for employment. However, specialized training and education in forensic science is typically required of those employed in the forensics arena.

To work as a federal agent with the FBI, DEA, ATF, U.S. Postal Inspection Service, NCIS, CID, the U.S. Air Force Office of Special Investigations (OSI), or similar agencies, one must possess a bachelor's degree and apply prior to the age of 36. Some of these agencies, such as ATF and NCIS, have evidence response teams that process major crime scenes across the United States and around the world. With specialized training and education in forensic technology, peace officer and federal agent employment opportunities are enhanced.

Training and Education

To prepare for a career as a forensic technician, discipline-related education and training are preferred. Requirements vary among agencies. A few require a high school diploma or equivalency for entry-level positions with no prior experience, training, or higher education. Other agencies require an associate degree in forensic technology or equivalent, with an internship in a crime scene unit or a minimum of one year of experience in law enforcement. Still other agencies will accept a prescribed combination of education and experience, substituting education for a specified period of experience. Most agencies require some formalized training but rarely require formal education beyond an associate degree. As time passes and the use of forensic technicians expands, more agencies will require specialized pre-service training as well as higher education through an accredited college or university.

It is highly desirable that a person pursuing a career as a forensic technician receive training through a practical application-based (laboratory-based) forensic technology program that offers courses presented by current or former forensic technicians, criminalists, and latent fingerprint examiners. Further, practical experience in the form of a forensic science-related internship with a law enforcement agency is extremely worthwhile.

Many forensic technology students obtain volunteer or paid internship positions in an agency's crime laboratory, or within an investigation or crime scene unit. The law enforcement agency benefits by receiving assistance from individuals who are eager to learn. In addition, agency interns provide a valuable pool of potential candidates for paid forensic technician positions. Students benefit by receiving real-life, hands-on experience.

The training and education of a forensic technician never ends because forensic science is a dynamic and evolving field, with new techniques and tools developing almost daily. Continuing education programs are provided through law enforcement agencies, professional organizations, and state-based commissions on peace officer standards and training. A commitment to lifelong learning is necessary to remain current in the field as well as deepen and broaden one's knowledge and skill base.

Many forensic technicians develop expertise in a single area of forensic science and continue their education in the forensic science specialty selected. For example, many latent fingerprint examiners begin their careers as forensic technicians but focus their continuing education and training efforts in the direction of fingerprint examination and comparison. Ultimately, they specialize in a career as a latent fingerprint examiner. Expert latent fingerprint examiners often earn high salaries.

Earning Potential

The salary earned by a forensic technician varies by region within the United States, as do the salaries for most occupations in law enforcement and criminal justice. Depending on local conditions, entry-level salaries for forensic technicians range from $30,000 to $60,000 annually. Many forensic technicians also earn *stand-by (on-call)* pay in addition to the base salary. Stand-by compensation also varies among jurisdictions. Some

Photo 1-4. Forensic students in training.

Photo 1-5. Forensic students in training.

agencies pay a percentage of the base salary, while others pay a flat rate for each week one is on call.

When an off-duty forensic technician is called out, often in the middle of the night, overtime hours may accrue. With callout and overtime pay, a forensic technician can increase earning potential significantly. In busy agencies, extra pay can double the annual salary.

The Pre-employment Interview

Extensive preparation for the interview is critical. Most initial pre-employment interviews for forensic technician positions include technical questions about the job. The applicant should review technical procedures and crime scene processing protocols prior to the interview. The applicant should also conduct research to learn about the job and the employing organization's characteristics:

- What is the population and territory of the agency's jurisdiction?
- What is the crime rate?
- How many sworn and nonsworn personnel are employed with the agency?
- What is the agency searching for in an applicant?
- What is contained in the job description?
- What are the job specifications?
- What are the capabilities of the crime laboratory?

Photo 1-6. Forensic students in training.

• Does the agency outsource any of its crime lab activities?

Most importantly, applicants should be prepared to respond when asked why they applied for the position.

Applicants should mold their experience, education, and training to fit agency needs and desires. A careful analysis of the job description and specifications is essential to learn of the job requirements and prepare for the interview. If allowed, the applicant should participate in a ride-along (or sit-along) with an officer (or lab employee) and tour the agency prior to the first interview. The ride-along and tour will help the applicant learn more about the functions and culture of the agency.

The Background Investigation

As part of the pre-appointment screening process, those applying for volunteer forensic internships as well as paid forensic technician positions must undergo a thorough background investigation. The extent of the background check usually depends on the nature of the position, with candidates for full-time paid positions receiving the closest scrutiny. The background process varies among agencies but typically the applicant completes a background

packet that contains a number of forms requesting the applicant's personal history, including information regarding employment, home addresses, and personal references. In most cases, a background investigator will contact and interview references, former employers, and current and previous landlords to learn more about the applicant. A criminal history records check will be conducted and the applicant's financial history may be examined as well. A poor credit history may be indicative of irresponsible behavior. Some agencies also administer psychological exams and polygraph or voice stress analysis examinations.

The purpose of the background investigation is to determine the applicant's suitability for employment. By reviewing the application and interviewing former employers, coworkers, neighbors, family members, and friends, the background investigator determines if the applicant possesses the knowledge, skills, abilities, ethical orientation, and integrity necessary to work as a forensic technician. If employed, the candidate will have access to and be responsible for confidential information and fragile evidence. The candidate will also be working in a high-stress environment.

If an applicant fails a background check with one agency, it should not be assumed that he or she will fail with another. Some agencies establish strict pre-employment requirements while others do not. Without question, the applicant must be honest in the background investigations process. Dishonesty will most certainly result in disqualification of the applicant.

Pre-employment Polygraph Exams

Although federal and some state laws restrict an employer's ability to require pre-employment polygraph or similar exams, public law enforcement agencies are typically exempt from the statutes. If a legally permissible polygraph or voice stress analysis test is administered, the test will be conducted by a trained agency investigator or a private contractor. The tests are administered in an attempt to verify background information supplied by the candidate. Common questions asked during the test include those related to: information provided by the candidate in the employment application, prior or current drug use, criminal activity, and other subject areas deemed important and appropriate to the employing agency. The questions are reviewed and discussed with the applicant prior to the administration of the test.

The Forensic Technician and Personal Life

Depending on the agency, forensic technicians may work rotating shifts of days and nights, weekdays or weekends as well as holidays, responding to crime scenes while on duty. Others work primarily weekday hours and remain *on call* for any major event that occurs during off-duty hours. A forensic technician may receive overtime or extra pay while on call. The extra compensation may be a salary percentage or a flat hourly rate. When a major crime such as a homicide occurs, overtime hours are often necessary to accomplish tasks in a timely manner.

The work of a forensic technician is more than a career; it is a lifestyle. Rotating shift work, *call outs* in the middle of the night, and *call outs* on weekends impact one's personal life. Anyone with a desire to work as a forensic technician must appreciate that the commitment is beyond that of an average job. Support from family and friends is critical. The work can be demanding and the crimes investigated emotionally draining. Although long hours often accompany a major crime incident, the forensic technician must also maintain a healthy, balanced life. Recreational activities with one's family and friends, a nutritional diet, adequate rest, and exercise help to reduce the high levels of stress that may accompany the forensic technician's career.

OTHER FORENSIC SCIENCE PROFESSIONALS

Many forensic science professionals work in law enforcement or related fields. As discussed earlier, a criminalist is a scientist who applies the principles of the physical sciences, primarily biology, physics, or chemistry, to evidence analysis and crime scene investigation and reconstruction (James and Nordby, 2005). Criminalists analyze evidence collected by forensic technicians to obtain scientific results and place the evidence in the context for a particular crime. Criminalists are typically required to possess a baccalaureate degree in a natural science such as chemistry, biology, or physics. Coursework in mathematics, criminal justice, public speaking, and logic is also desirable.

Criminalists are usually experts in one or more areas of forensic science such as deoxyribonucleic acid (DNA) analysis, bloodstain pattern analysis, toxicology (chemical analysis), trace evidence, analyses involving firearms, or impression (footwear, tire, and tool mark) evidence. Criminalists typically work in a crime laboratory conducting tests on evidence. Some criminalists are also *on call* to respond to major large-scale crime scenes.

Other experts are employed in the forensic science field. An expert on questioned documents is known as a **forensic document examiner.** An expert in the identification and comparison of latent fingerprints is known

> **Forensic document examiner** An expert on questioned documents.

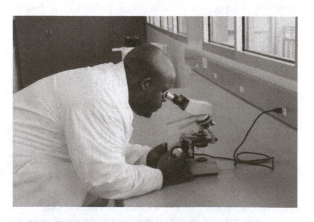

Photo 1-7. Photograph by Chris Nellis.

as a **latent fingerprint examiner**. The **medical examiner/coroner** is typically a medical doctor who performs postmortem examinations (autopsies) to determine cause and manner of death. In some states, the coroner is elected and not required to possess any medical training. In the event that the coroner is elected and not a medical doctor, autopsies are performed by medical doctors under contract to the coroner's office. In addition, medical examiners employ assistants and investigators who are not required to possess a medical degree.

Other experts include the **forensic odontologist**, a dentist with specialized training in forensic dentistry; the **forensic anthropologist**, an anthropologist with specialized forensic training; and the **forensic entomologist**, an expert in the study of insects with specialized forensic training in postmortem (after death) insect activity in and on a human body. A **forensic criminologist** is often an expert in the field of behavioral profiling. Experts in various other fields (accounting, computer science, vehicle collision investigation, etc.) are contracted by law enforcement agencies as the need arises. A forensic technician works with all of these experts on a case-by-case basis.

> **Latent fingerprint examiner** An expert in the identification and comparison of latent fingerprints.

> **Medical examiner (coroner)** Typically a medical doctor who performs postmortem examinations (autopsies) to determine cause, mechanism, and manner of death. In some states, the coroner is elected and not required to possess any medical training.

> **Forensic odontologist** A dentist with specialized training in forensic dentistry.

> **Forensic anthropologist** An anthropologist with specialized forensic training.

> **Forensic entomologist** An expert in the study of insects with specialized forensic training in postmortem (after death) insect activity in and on a human body.

> **Forensic criminologist** An expert in the field of behavioral profiling.

SAFETY PRECAUTIONS AND EQUIPMENT

Crime scene processing safety precautions and equipment is introduced in this chapter because safety should always be one's first consideration. In the early years of a forensic technician's career, a great deal of excitement and adrenalin accompanies the job, especially when one responds to major crime scenes such as homicides. However, excitement and anticipation should never obscure adherence to safety rules.

Safety measures taken are dependent upon the situation. If the forensic technician is employed by an agency that maintains a mobile crime scene unit responding to calls, an initial consideration is to stay away from the crime scene until it is classified as safe. A dangerous suspect may still be present in the incident-affected area. The incident may involve activities that are considered high risk, thus involving an Emergency Services Unit or Specialized Weapons and Tactics (SWAT) team response. In addition, the crime scene may be contaminated with hazardous materials or objects. As exciting as these events might appear, it is not safe for nonemergency personnel, such as forensic technicians, to approach the scene until it is classified as safe by an appropriate authority.

Another unsafe environment is a clandestine illicit drug laboratory, typically located in a home. Specially trained narcotics investigators possess the knowledge and equipment necessary to enter and dismantle these laboratories and render them safe for other personnel. Forensic technicians rarely receive drug lab dismantling training (see Chapter 12 for details).

Yet another unsafe environment is one that may contain an infectious bacteria or virus. Forensic technicians must collect biological fluids (blood, semen, vaginal secretions, urine, feces, saliva, and perspiration) as well as evidence contaminated with these fluids. HIV and Hepatitis C viruses can survive for two weeks outside a living organism (Gammie, 1998). When biological fluids are present, safety precautions include wearing protective (latex) gloves, eye protection, a particle mask, and clothing and shoe protection.

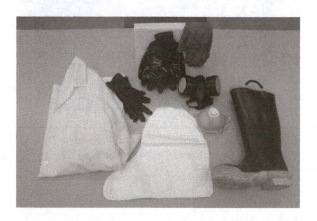

Photo 1-8. Sample of safety equipment for biohazard and fire scenes.

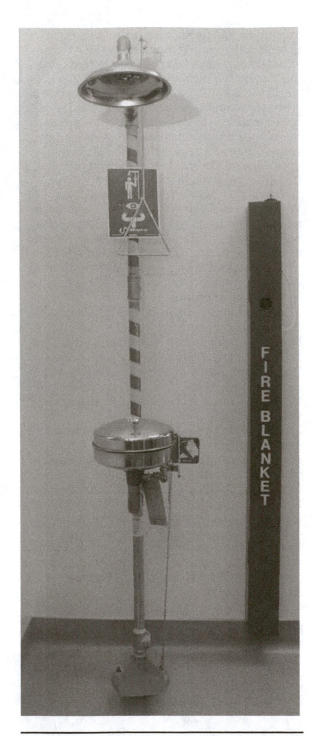

Photo 1-10. Emergency eyewash station, Chula Vista Police Department Crime Laboratory, Chula Vista, California.

Chemicals are used at crime scenes and in crime laboratories to enhance and process some types of evidence, including latent fingerprints and blood. Forensic technicians should read and adhere to instructions contained in the Material Safety Data Sheet (MSDS) prior to using any chemical. Some chemicals are flammable, or may require the use of a fume hood or breathing apparatus during application. The forensic technician should wear eye protection, chemical-resistant gloves, and a long sleeve shirt or laboratory coat to protect the eyes and skin.

If chemicals come into contact with the eyes, the eyes should be rinsed with clean water immediately. In a laboratory setting, the individual should proceed to the nearest eyewash station and rinse the eyes for a minimum of 15 minutes. Safety is the responsibility of every individual.

Photo 1-9. Emergency shower and fire blanket, Chula Vista Police Department Crime Laboratory, Chula Vista, California.

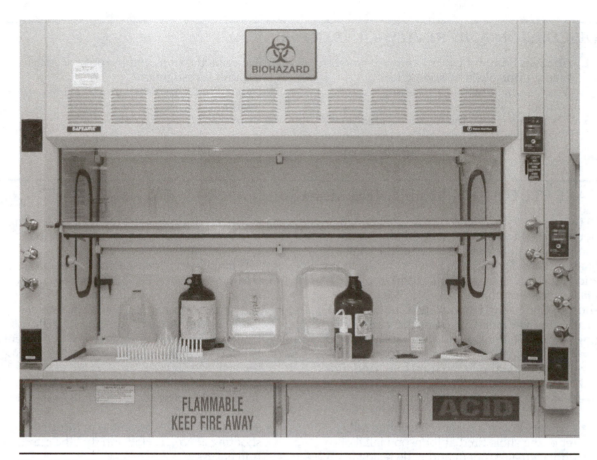

Photo 1-11. Fume Hood, Chula Vista Police Department Crime Laboratory, Chula Vista, California.

SUMMARY

A career as a forensic technician is exciting and rewarding but not as glamorous as portrayed in many television dramas. A career in forensic science requires preparation, hard work, and the ability to perform under stressful and sometimes hazardous conditions. The forensic technician must also possess a high level of integrity and dependability.

There are many forensic science-related career opportunities for those who seek employment at the local, county, state, or federal government levels. Specialized training and education in forensic technology, coupled with practical experience in a crime lab internship, are frequently required to secure a good job in this exciting career. Many forensic technicians continue their education to become criminalists or they may work as an expert in a specific area of forensic science. Regardless of the career path chosen, the field of forensic technology is exciting, challenging, rewarding, and ever-changing.

KEY TERMS

Define, describe, or explain the importance of each of the following:

criminalist	forensic document examiner	forensic technician
evidence	forensic entomologist	latent fingerprint examiner
forensic anthropologist	forensic odontologist	locard exchange principle
forensic criminologist	forensic science	medical examiner

DISCUSSION AND REVIEW QUESTIONS

1. Who was Edmond Locard and what forensic science principle is he known for?
2. What are the functions of a crime laboratory?
3. What is the role of the forensic technician?
4. What professional relationship does a forensic technician have with a case investigator?
5. Describe the steps and purpose of a background investigation?
6. What educational background is typically required of a forensic technician? A criminalist?

CASE STUDY—The Virginia Tech Massacre

In two separate incidents approximately two hours apart, the deadliest single-perpetrator shooting rampage in the history of the United States occurred at Virginia Polytechnic Institute and State University (Virginia Tech) in Blacksburg, Virginia, on April 16, 2007. The shooter, Cho Seung Hui, killed 32 students and faculty and wounded 30 others before committing suicide. Beginning shortly after 7:00 a.m. at West Ambler Johnson Hall, a dormitory on the Virginia Tech campus, Cho used two handguns to kill and wound his victims. The early morning events are summarized as follows:

- 7:15 a.m. Police receive a 911 phone call, reporting shots fired at Johnson Hall. Police find a female student and male resident advisor fatally wounded. Based on witness interviews, police believe the shooting is an isolated domestic incident. Police do not initiate campus-wide security measures. Police focus on the female victim's boyfriend, a student at nearby Radford University. Police later stop and interrogate the boyfriend on a highway in Blacksburg.
- 9:01 a.m. At a nearby post office, Cho mailed a package containing writings and video recordings to NBC News. Cho linked himself to Jesus Christ and expressed hatred for wealthy people.

- 9:26 a.m. Virginia Tech authorities issue first mass email, reporting the 7:15 a.m. shooting and warning students and staff.
- 9:45 a.m. Police receive a phone call about a shooting at Norris Hall, a science and engineering classroom building, about 15 minutes walking distance from West Ambler Johnson Hall. After Cho chained the Norris Hall exterior doors shut, he killed 30 students and faculty in their classrooms before killing himself.
- 9:50 a.m. A second mass email by Virginia Tech officials reports a gunman is loose on the campus.
- 9:55 a.m. A third mass email reports the shooting at Norris Hall and that the gunman is in custody.

Subsequent to the mass killing, it was learned that Cho was treated previously for mental illness.

1. Were any or all of the killings at Virginia Tech preventable?
2. The VA Tech incident involved two crime scenes. Based on the Locard Exchange Principle, how might the forensic technician connect the shooter to both crime scenes?

LAB EXERCISE

Safety precautions and equipment are the subject of this lab exercise. Beginning with the next chapter, students are expected to adhere to safety requirements because laboratory exercises will focus on crime scene processing and evidence collection.

Equipment and supplies required of each student:

- one laboratory coat
- one particle mask

- one pair of latex gloves (or nonallergic vinyl gloves)
- access to the MSDS (if lab setting)
- eyewash station (if available)

1. Review crime scene and laboratory safety procedures.
2. Familiarize yourself with all safety equipment, the location of the equipment, and how to properly apply, wear, and remove masks, coats, and gloves.

3. Practice using the eyewash station.
4. Familiarize yourself with all equipment, including any *on-off* switches or gas valves.
5. Locate the MSDS in the lab and read the chemical safety precautions section. Familiarize yourself with proper storage for chemicals.

6. Divide into pairs and quiz each other about emergency procedures and the proper use of safety equipment relevant to your facility.

WEB RESOURCES

The following is a list of forensic science-related organizations and agencies with accompanying Websites that provide information regarding forensic science career opportunities, skill and educational requirements, and salaries.

Forensic Science Organizations

Academy of Behavioral Profiling: www. profling.org

American Academy of Forensic Sciences: www.aafs.org

American Board of Criminalistics: www.crimi-nalistics.com

Association for Crime Scene Reconstruction: www.acsr.org

The California State Division of the International Association of Identification: www.csdiai.net

California Association of Criminalists: www. cacnews.org

California Commission on Peace Officer Standards & Training (POST): www.post. ca.gov

Canadian Society of Forensic Sciences: www. csfs.ca

Forensic Science Society: www.forensic-science-society.org.uk

Forensic Specialties Accreditation Board: www. thefsab.org

International Association of Bloodstain Pattern Analysts: www.iabpa.org

International Association of Identification: www.theiai.org

International Association of Forensic Nurses: www.forensicnurse.org

Midwest Association of Forensic Scientists: www.mafs.net

New York Police Department: www.ci.nyc. ny.us

Northeast Association of Forensic Scientists: www.neafs.org

Northwest Association of Forensic Scientists: www.nwafs.org

Scientific Working Group for Bloodstain Pattern Analysis: www.swgstain.org

The Southern California Association of Fingerprint Officers: www.scafo.org

Southern Association of Forensic Scientists: www.southernforensic.org

Southwestern Association of Forensic Scientists: www.swafs.us

Law Enforcement Scholarship and Career Information

www.policelink.com

www.policeone.com

Careers with the Federal Government

Bureau of Alcohol, Tobacco, Firearms and Explosives: www.atf.gov

Drug Enforcement Administration: www.dea. gov

Federal Bureau of Investigation: www.fbi.gov or www.fbijobs.gov

U.S. Department of Justice: www.usdoj.gov

Civilian Careers in Military Law Enforcement

Naval Criminal Investigative Service: www. ncis.navy.mil

U.S. Air Force Office of Special Investigations: www.public.afosi.amc.af.mil

U.S. Army Criminal Investigations Command: www.cid.army.mil

Forensic Science Education and Training Information

American Society for Clinical Laboratory Science: www.ascls.org

Career planning: www.careerplanning.about. com

Firearms training: www.firearmsid.com

General crime scene investigation training: www.crime-scene-investigator.net

2

Forensic Photography

LEARNING OUTCOMES

After completing this chapter, the reader should be able to:

- articulate the purposes of forensic photography,
- demonstrate knowledge of the nomenclature and functions of a 35 mm single-lens-reflex (SLR) camera,
- demonstrate ability to manipulate lenses, flash units, and other 35 mm camera equipment,
- demonstrate knowledge of a camera's aperture and shutter speed as well as the ability to manipulate both to change an image's exposure,
- list whole f-stops,
- explain the rule of F-16,
- demonstrate the ability to bracket three photographs,
- demonstrate knowledge of and ability to use bounce flash, fill flash, and indoor and nighttime flash photography,
- demonstrate the appropriate use of white balance.

INTRODUCTION

The purpose of forensic photography is to visually capture, depict, and preserve evidence and facts in photographic images. Forensic photography is not about artistic qualities or displaying an image that is pleasant to view. Nor are forensic photos publicized to elicit emotion from the viewer. Photographing a crime scene with the intent to solicit a horrified response may actually render the images inadmissible in court. A judge may exclude a photograph if it is determined to be too emotional, disturbing, or prejudicial for a jury (fact finder) to view. Therefore, the sole purpose of forensic photography is to accurately capture images of crime scenes and evidence.

Until recently, many courts did not allow color photographs to be viewed in open court. Color photographs of blood, for example, were classified as too grotesque for viewing by the average juror. Today, many courts admit color photographs. The color photos are often enlarged and displayed for the jury. Still, images such as certain autopsy photographs may not be presented in a trial if the judge determines that the images may unduly prejudice jurors against the defendant.

Photographs of a crime scene allow the viewer to visualize the scene. Ideally, the crime scene is photographed in its original condition; that is, photographically documented prior to any evidentiary items being collected or removed. As a result, the viewer will form a mental image of the crime scene and the location of evidence in an original, unaltered state.

Photographs of physical evidence are often presented in court in lieu of the evidentiary item itself. Although most evidentiary items are displayed to the jury, many items are too large or grotesque, pose a threat to health or safety, or emit offensive odors. Therefore, photographs of these items of evidence are presented to the fact finder.

The use of forensic photography is not limited to a crime scene. A police patrol officer often photographs a person encountered during a field interview. A patrol officer may conduct a field interview of the person encountered, obtaining identifying information as well as a photograph of the person for future reference.

If a child or disabled person is reported missing, an officer will obtain a recent photograph of the missing person from a friend or relative. Subsequently, the officer will reproduce or digitize the missing person's photograph for distribution to other officers and the America's

Missing: Broadcasting Emergency Response (AMBER) alert system.

Photographs of a prisoner are also considered forensic photographs. Photographs (mug shots) of persons arrested are stored in databases and used in photographic line-ups for possible victim or witness identification.

Forensic photography has been practiced since photography was invented. This chapter is devoted entirely to forensic photography, an essential tool in the forensic technician's kit. Although some agencies use digital cameras exclusively, many still use traditional film cameras. Familiarity with the basics of film photography also assists with developing skill with a digital camera. Therefore, the fundamentals of film photography are presented in this chapter.

The reader will discover that forensic photography is a common thread woven throughout the remaining chapters of this book. Heavy emphasis is placed on forensic photography because a thorough working knowledge of and an ability to use photography are essential for any crime scene investigator or forensic technician.

FORENSIC PHOTOGRAPHY: A BRIEF HISTORY

The history of forensic photography can be traced to the middle of the nineteenth century. Forensic photography progressed from explosive powder flash units used to photograph horse and buggy accidents to capturing images of evidence using ultraviolet (UV) light and SLR digital cameras. The following is a brief history of forensic photography development:

1841: French police utilize photographs to identify known criminals.

1859: *Luco vs. United* States—A photograph is used in the trial of a forgery case involving a land title dispute.

1875: A photograph of a horse and buggy accident is used to help a jury visualize the scene.

1879: *Reddin vs. Gates*—A photograph of whip mark injuries on a victim's back is admitted as evidence.

1902: *Commonwealth vs. Best*—Photographs are used to identify a firearm. An expended projectile (bullet) from a rifle is compared to photographs of a bullet removed from a deceased victim.

1903: *Leavenworth Prison*—Will West was arrested and taken to Leavenworth Prison. At the time, prisoners were identified

through a photograph as well as a series of anthropological measurements developed by Alphonse Bertillon. West was mistakenly identified as William West, a prisoner already incarcerated at the prison. Fingerprints were obtained from both men to prove their actual identities. The wrongful identification proved that fingerprints are more accurate identifiers than photographs.

1911: *People vs. Jennings*—Photographs of fingerprints are used for identification purposes.

1930: Photoflash bulbs are introduced to the general public.

1934: *State vs. Thorp*—Footprints in blood are recorded using UV photography.

1943: *Green vs. City and County of Denver*—The use of color photographs as evidence is upheld by an appellate court.

1945: Kodak introduces inexpensive automatic cameras.

1963: Polaroid instant photography is introduced to policing and forensics.

1965: The fully automatic electronic flash unit is introduced.

1967: Video recording is used as evidence.

1980s: The fully automatic SLR 35 mm camera is introduced.

1990s: Digital photography is introduced (Miller, 2006).

Forensic photography is vital to evidence collection. A photograph paints a thousand words. It is essential that crime scene investigators and forensic technicians know the basics of photography and are able to apply specific forensic science-related photographic techniques. Before learning how to manipulate the controls of a camera, one must learn how an image is captured and how lighting is used in photography.

CAMERA FILM AND LIGHTING

A photograph is an image created by means of the chemical action of light or other radiation on a sensitive film (Oxford Essential Dictionary, 2008). *Light* is a key term in the definition. Control and manipulation of light determines a photographic result. The human eye views light frequencies within the human visible spectrum. Infrared and UV light are outside the human visible spectrum. Within the visible spectrum are radiations of wavelengths observed by the human eye as various colors. A color is observed when a particular color's light wavelength is abundant. White is observed when all wavelengths within the visible spectrum are equal. The color black is observed when all wavelengths are absent (Miller, 2006).

With film cameras, light enters the camera through the lens (shutter) and an image is recorded on film. The image is latent (invisible) to the unaided human eye. The film must be processed chemically to produce an image visible to humans. The film contains an emulsion consisting of various-sized light-sensitive grains (crystals) of silver halide. The larger the grains of silver halide, the more light sensitive (faster) the film. Faster film requires less light to produce an image. However, the larger the grain (faster the film), the more grainy an image appears, particularly when the image is enlarged.

In 1928, the American Standards Associations (ASA) established film speed designations. Today, film speed (sensitivity to light) is presented as specific rating numbers established by the International Organization for Standardization (ISO). The lower the ISO number, the less sensitive the film is to light. Therefore, the camera's lens must remain open longer to allow more light into the camera. The low ISO produces a crisper (less grainy) photograph. The higher the ISO number, the more sensitive the film is to light (less light is required). The image appears grainy (Fredrickson & Siljander, 1997).

Digital index (DX)-coded film contains a barcode with information that is interpreted automatically by most modern 35 mm cameras. The barcode indicates the ISO of the film so a camera's light meter can automatically determine the amount of light necessary to produce a properly exposed photograph (image). The barcode provides additional information, including the number of exposures (photographs available on the film), when the last image is photographed (for automatic rewind), the exposure range of the film, and other information used for print development (Miller, 2006).

EXPOSURE

Exposure is the effect of light on film. Exposure can be depicted using the following equation:

> **Exposure** The effect of light on film.

Exposure = intensity of light × duration of the intensity (Pekala & Johnson, 2006).

Simply stated, exposure involves allowing light into the camera to create an image. The

Photo 2-1. A manual 35 mm SLR film camera body and lens.

amount of light allowed into the camera is controlled by two elements: aperture (the size of the opening in the lens) and shutter speed (the length of time the light enters the camera through the lens). The amount of light entering the camera is controlled and manipulated by changing either the aperture opening or the shutter speed.

Other factors can change or control how much light enters the camera. The distance between the lens and the film (determined by the *size* of the lens) alters the amount of light that enters the camera. However, longer lenses may contain larger aperture openings to compensate for the distance. Additional information on lenses is presented later in this chapter.

Filters attached to the outside of a lens also alter the amount of light that enters the camera. A filter absorbs a portion of the light. Various types of filters are used in forensic photography. Camera filters are discussed in detail later in this chapter.

SHUTTER SPEED

The **shutter** is located within a camera's body. The shutter controls the length of time that light is allowed to enter the camera and expose the film. The shutter is activated by depressing the shutter release button. The shutter speed (light exposure time) varies from fractions of a second to several seconds or minutes, depending on the shutter adjustments available on the camera. Shutters may be round,

> **Shutter** Located within a camera's body, the shutter controls the length of time that light is allowed to enter the camera and expose the film.

Photo 2-2. View of a square-shaped shutter.

Shutter Speed	Meaning
B	Bulb (shutter remains open until manually closed)
30"	30 seconds
15"	15 seconds
8"	8 seconds
4"	4 seconds
2"	2 seconds
1"	1 second
2	1/2 of a second
4	1/4 of a second
8	1/8 of a second
15	1/15 of a second
30	1/30 of a second
60	1/60 of a second
125	1/125 of a second
250	1/250 of a second
500	1/500 of a second
1000	1/1000 of a second
2000	1/2000 of a second

Figure 2-1. Shutter speed chart.

square, or leafy in appearance, or they may operate as a curtain.

A fast shutter speed allows less light into the camera. For example, a shutter speed of 1/500 of a second allows in twice as much light as a shutter speed of 1/1000 of a second. If too much light enters the camera, the resulting image may be overexposed. An overexposed photograph appears *washed out* (light). If too little light enters the camera, the image may be under-exposed. An under-exposed photograph appears dark.

Shutter speed represents the length of time light enters the camera. A " mark on the LCD screen defines full seconds. If no " mark is observed, it is a fraction of a second (Figure 2.1). A bulb (B) setting speed is typically located next to the slowest shutter speed setting available on a camera. The B setting allows the shutter to remain open until manually closed by the photographer. The term *bulb* heralds from a time when photographers used a squeeze bulb to activate the shutter. The term is still used to describe a **timed-exposure**, referring to the length of time the photographer chooses to keep the shutter open. Timed-exposure photographs are typically obtained at outdoor, nighttime scenes, or in darkened rooms. Timed-exposures will be addressed in various scenarios discussed throughout this book.

> **Timed-exposure**
> The length of time a photographer chooses to keep the shutter open.

When a slow shutter speed is desired, the photographer should place the camera on a tripod to stabilize the camera and prevent camera movement. If the photographer holds the camera without using a tripod, camera movement will occur. Camera movement during film exposure will distort (blur) the photographic image. In

Photo 2-3. Shutter speed dial on a manual 35 mm film camera.

addition, a **shutter release cable** (cable connected to the camera used in lieu of pressing the camera's shutter release button) should be used to prevent accidental movement of the camera.

> **Shutter release cable**
> A cable connected to the camera used in lieu of pressing the camera's shutter release button. Cable is used to prevent accidental movement of the camera.

Photo 2-4. Camera on a tripod.

Photo 2-5. Close-up view of a shutter release cable.

Photo 2-6. Camera and tripod in use.

Photo 2-7. A splash of water at 1/15 shutter speed.

A camera's shutter speed can be adjusted to capture the image of a person or object in motion. If a photographer wishes to capture a person or object moving quickly, a fast shutter speed is selected. Airborne droplets of splashed water can be captured with a fast shutter speed. Likewise, a moving person can be cap-

tured as a distinct clear image if a fast shutter speed is used.

The photographer must determine if shutter speed is an important consideration in capturing an image. Shutter speed is critical when capturing still surveillance photos of a moving criminal suspect. When photographing a dead body at a homicide scene, shutter speed is not an issue.

If a fast shutter speed is used, less light will enter the camera, possibly resulting in an under-exposed photograph. The photographer may compensate for the underexposure and allow

Photo 2-8. A splash of water at 1/2000 shutter speed.

more light into the camera through an adjustment to the aperture.

APERTURE

The **aperture** is the opening in a camera lens that regulates the amount of light allowed to enter the camera. A larger opening allows more light into the camera. The size of the aperture opening also controls depth-of-field.

| Aperture | The opening in a camera lens that regulates the amount of light allowed to enter the camera. |

Depth-of-field is the distance between the point (foreground) directly in front of a photographic subject and the point (background) immediately beyond the photographic subject that is in acceptable focus when the subject is in perfect focus (Redsicker, 2000). Thus, depth-of-field

| Depth-of-field | The distance between the point (foreground) directly in front of a photographic subject and the point (background) immediately beyond the photographic subject that is in acceptable focus when the subject is in perfect focus. |

refers to how much of the area surrounding a photographic subject is in focus. A photographic image with good depth-of-field is one in which relevant material (including the foreground and the background) is in focus. An image with poor depth-of-field is one in which the primary subject matter is in focus, but the surrounding area is out of focus (soft or blurred in appearance). Artistic and forensic depth-of field applications differ. An artist may choose poor depth-of-field in an effort to highlight the primary subject matter. Forensic photographers seek good depth-of-field for clear (in focus) images. Forensic photography depth-of-field applications are discussed throughout this book.

The size of the aperture (lens opening) directly affects the depth-of-field. A larger (wide)

Photo 2-9. Photograph taken at aperture priority F1.7.

Photo 2-10. Photograph taken at aperture priority F22.

Photo 2-11. Photograph taken at aperture priority F1.7.

aperture opening results in poor depth-of-field. A small (narrow) aperture opening results in better depth-of-field. Reducing the size of the

Photo 2-12. Photograph taken at aperture priority F22.

Photo 2-13. Photograph taken at aperture priority F1.7.

Photo 2-14. Photograph taken at aperture priority F22.

aperture to improve depth-of-field is referred to as **stopping down the lens**.

Stopping down the lens Reducing the size of the aperture to improve depth-of-field.

Good depth-of-field (narrow aperture setting) is necessary when three-dimensional photographs are sought for items such as shoe or tire impressions. A wide aperture setting is used to admit more light in photogra-

phy, such as darkened room applications. The forensic photographer may regulate the aperture by selecting a number on the lens that represents the aperture opening size. This number is referred to as an f-stop (f-number).

F-stop (increments of light admission) The f refers to a *factor* that represents a mathematical ratio of the focal length of the lens divided by the diameter of the aperture.

The *f* in **f-stop** (increments of light admission) refers to a *factor* that represents a mathematical ratio of the focal length of the lens divided by the diameter of the aperture. **Focal length** is the distance between the face of the lens and the point inside the lens at which rays of light passing though the lens face converge (Fredrickson & Siljander, 1997). Each f-stop allows one-half the amount of light into the camera as the f-stop immediately preceding it. Full f-stops are as follows:

Focal length The distance between the face of the lens and the point inside the lens at which rays of light passing though the lens face converge. Each f-stop allows half the amount of light into the camera as the f-stop immediately preceding it.

| f1 | f1.4 | f2 | f2.8 | f4 | f5.6 | f8 |
| f11 | f16 | f22 | f32 | f45 | f64 | |

Although f-stops may appear random, each represents the previous f-stop number multiplied by the square root of two (1.4). Every other f-stop number is doubled.

Some cameras can be calibrated for one-third or one-half f-stops. Figure 2.2 illustrates an f-stop incremental chart with full, one-third, one-half, and two-thirds f-stops, ranging from f-1 to f-64.

When using a manually operated camera and lens, depth-of-field settings (scale) are observable on the outside of the lens casing. The scale indicates the acceptable focus range for the f-stop selected.

The photographer must decide which is most critical: time (speed) or depth-of-field. Subsequently, the photographer may compensate for exposure (amount of light) by adjusting either the shutter speed or the aperture opening. For example, if a photographer requires good depth-of-field for the image, the photographer may *stop the lens down* by choosing a higher f-stop. The higher f-stop restricts light entering the camera. The photographer may compensate by slowing the shutter speed, thus allowing more light into the camera.

If the photographer must capture a fast moving object, a fast shutter speed is required. The fast shutter speed also reduces the amount of

Stops	F/Number	Marked on Lens
Full	**1.000**	1.0
1/3	1.122	
1/2	1.189	
2/3	1.260	
Full	**1.414**	1.4
1/3	1.587	
1/2	1.682	
2/3	1.782	
Full	**2.000**	2.0
1/3	2.245	
1/2	2.378	
2/3	2.520	
Full	**2.828**	2.8
1/3	3.175	
1/2	3.364	
2/3	3.564	
Full	**4.000**	4.0
1/3	4.490	
1/2	4.757	
2/3	5.040	
Full	**5.657**	5.6
1/3	6.350	
1/2	6.727	
2/3	7.127	
Full	**8.000**	8.0
1/3	8.980	
1/2	9.514	
2/3	10.079	
Full	**11.314**	11.0
1/3	12.699	
1/2	13.454	
2/3	14.254	
Full	**16.000**	16.0
1/3	17.959	
1/2	19.027	
2/3	20.159	
Full	**22.627**	22.0
1/3	25.398	
1/2	26.909	
2/3	28.509	
Full	**32.000**	32.0
1/3	35.919	
1/2	38.055	
2/3	40.318	
Full	**45.255**	45.0
1/3	50.797	
1/2	53.817	
2/3	57.018	
Full	**64.000**	64.0

Figure 2-2. Lens diaphragm settings.

light allowed into the camera. The photographer can compensate by opening the aperture (selecting a lower f-stop).

LIGHT METERS

A photographer may use a light meter to determine the amount of light necessary to expose the film properly. A *light meter* measures the light reflected from an object, light that falls upon an object, or a flash unit's light output (Fredrickson & Siljander, 1997). The light measurement allows the photographer to choose a camera setting that will produce a properly exposed image. Most forensic photographers utilize the internal light meter that accompanies most 35 mm SLR film and digital cameras.

A camera's *internal light meter* can be viewed by peering through the viewfinder (eyepiece) of the camera. The light meter contains a scale with a minus (–) sign on one end and a plus (+) sign on the other, indicating under- and overexposure.

An arrow or similar character indicates the exposure on the light meter scale. Figure 2.4 illustrates a range of two increments of light underexposed (–2) to two increments of light overexposed (+2). Zero (0) is the optimum exposure. The photographer uses the light meter to calibrate the camera by peering through the viewfinder and adjusting either the f-stop (shutter speed) or aperture (lens opening) until the light meter indicator arrives at the 0 mark.

Other internal light meter scales may display < and > symbols or the terms *under* and *over* to indicate exposure level. The symbols may appear red or blink as a warning to the photographer that the image is under- or overexposed. The camera's operation manual contains specific internal light meter operating instructions.

If a camera is not equipped with an internal light meter, an external light meter is used. If the photographer is outdoors during daylight hours, the *rule of f-16* should be followed. The photographer sets the f-stop at f-16 and adjusts the shutter speed closest to the film ISO being used. For example, if ISO 200 film is used, the shutter speed selection is 1/250. If ISO 100 film is used, the shutter speed selection is 1/125. A proper exposure should result.

Use of an internal camera light meter is not appropriate for indoor forensic applications. Therefore, the rule of f-16 is not used indoors. A flash unit should be used. To ensure that the image is properly exposed, the photographer may wish to take several photos, bracketing

35 MM MANUAL CAMERA LENS

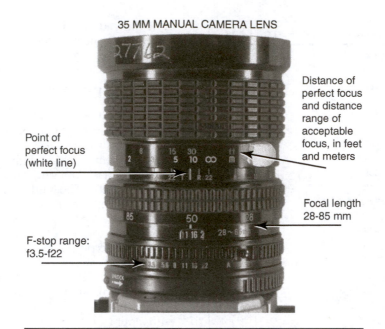

Point of
perfect focus
(white line)

Distance of
perfect focus
and distance
range of
acceptable
focus, in feet
and meters

Focal length
28-85 mm

F-stop range:
f3.5-f22

Figure 2-3. Nomenclature of 35 mm manual camera lens.

−2.1.0.1.2+

Figure 2-4. Light meter scale.

Photo 2-15. Light meter indicates underexposure.

Photo 2-16. Light meter indicates proper exposure.

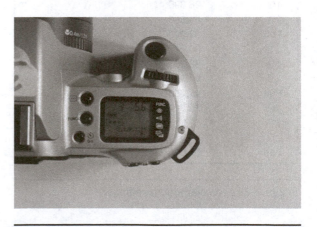

Photo 2-17. Light meter indicates overexposure.

(changing) the camera settings to test exposure settings.

Bracketing is a photographic term that refers to capturing (photographing) the same subject (object) several times, changing the camera settings each time to obtain various exposures.

> **Bracketing** A photographic term that refers to capturing (photographing) the same subject (object) several times, changing the camera settings each time to obtain various exposures.

The photographer changes the f-stop or the shutter speed, purposely creating underexposed and overexposed photographs until an optimum result is achieved. Bracketing applications are discussed later in this book.

Appropriate f-stop, shutter speed, and ISO settings produce optimum results. Additionally, the lens that the photographer selects greatly influences photographic outcomes.

THE CAMERA LENS

A **camera lens** is a transparent material (typically glass) designed to bend light away from (divert) or bend light toward (converge) a point within the lens. A simple lens is similar to a prism. It disperses light and colors, focusing the various color frequencies on different points. An **achromatic lens** contains more than one

> **Camera lens** A transparent material (typically glass) designed to bend light away from (divert) or bend light toward (converge) a point within the lens. A simple lens is similar to a prism that disperses light and colors, focusing the various color frequencies on different points.

element of transparent material. It concentrates light on a point, yielding photographs with true colors (Fredrickson & Siljander, 1997).

Lens Classifications

Camera lenses are classified by focal length and the maximum diameter of the lens aperture. The **focal length** is the distance between the face of the lens and the point at which rays of light converge (Fredrickson & Siljander, 1997). A 50 mm lens will project a sharp image of the photographic subject 50 mm behind the face of the lens.

The *maximum diameter of aperture* refers to the maximum size of the opening of

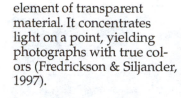

> **Achromatic lens** Lens that contains more than one element of transparent material. It concentrates light on a point, yielding photographs with true colors.

> **Focal length** The distance between the face of the lens and the point inside the lens at which rays of light passing though the lens face converge. Each f-stop allows half the amount of light into the camera as the f-stop immediately preceding it.

Photo 2-18. Underexposed photograph of a fingerprint.

Photo 2-19. Properly exposed photograph of a fingerprint.

Photo 2-20. Overexposed photograph of a fingerprint.

Photo 2-21. The metric ruler adjacent to the 50 mm lens illustrates the point at which the rays of light converge.

the aperture. When comparing lenses, a lens that has a large aperture (small f-stop) is considered *faster* because it allows more light into the lens than one with a small aperture.

Most lenses display the focal length and maximum aperture on the outside casing of the lens.

Zoom lenses offer a focal length range (the focal length can be changed) and a maximum aperture range that depends on the focal length selected.

Lens Categories

Depending on its focal length, a lens will fall into one of four categories: normal, wide-angle, telephoto, or macro.

Normal Lens

A **normal lens** has a focal length that is equal to the diagonal measurement of the image area. The image area of a 35 mm camera is 24 mm × 36 mm, and the diagonal measurement of the image area is 50 mm. Therefore, a normal lens for a 35 mm camera is 50 mm. The photo image angle of a normal lens is 45 degrees, which corresponds to the viewing range of the human eye.

> **Normal lens** Lens with a focal length that is equal to the diagonal measurement of the image area. The image area of a 35-mm camera is 24 × 36 mm, and the diagonal measurement of the image area is 50 mm. Therefore, a normal lens for a 35-mm camera is 50 mm. The photo image angle of a normal lens is 45 degrees, which corresponds to the viewing range of the human eye.

If a forensic photographer wishes to capture the view of a crime scene from the perspective of a witness, the photographer will set the focal length of the camera lens to 50 mm, which is most closely associated with the view from an actual human eye. The human eye engages in peripheral vision. A camera lens does not. Thus, the photographer should maintain the focal length at 50 mm and take overlapping photographs from the witness' vantage point to obtain the best possible photographic depiction of what the witness observed.

Many digital cameras do not have the same image size as a 35 mm camera. Therefore, 50 mm may not be the normal viewing angle for a particular camera. The photographer should refer to the camera's manual to determine the image conversion factor (image size) difference. Digital photography is discussed later in this chapter and throughout the remainder of the book.

> **Wide-angle lens** Lens with a shorter focal length than a normal lens and covers a photo image angle wider than 60 degrees. The large depth-of-field resulting from the short focal length compensates for inexact focusing, which is ideal for wide, overall views of a scene.

Wide-Angle Lens

A **wide-angle lens** has a shorter focal length than the normal lens. The lens covers a photo image angle wider

Photo 2-22. Telephoto, zoom, macro, and normal lens.

Photo 2-23. 35–80 mm lens.

Photo 2-24. The front of the lens indicates: focal length of 35–80 mm, largest aperture range of F4–F5.6, and lens diameter measurement of 52 mm.

than 60 degrees. The large depth-of-field resulting from the short focal length compensates for inexact focusing, which is ideal for wide, overall views of a scene. A subject may appear larger than normal and image distortion may occur. Thus, a wide-angle lens exaggerates the image's perspective.

The shortest focal length typically used by a forensic photographer is 28 mm. A focal length shorter than 28 mm creates too much distortion. Wide-angle lenses are appropriate when photographing buildings, streets, and interiors of homes, especially small rooms such as bathrooms and closets.

Telephoto Lens
A **telephoto lens** (zoom lens) has a long focal length and captures a close-up image of a distant object or subject. The lens captures a small field-of-view and a

Telephoto lens A zoom lens that has a long focal length and captures a close-up image of a distant object or subject. The lens captures a small field-of-view and a shallow depth-of-field. Distant objects are enlarged while near objects do not appear proportionately larger.

Photo 2-25. 50 mm macro lens with largest aperture F2.5.

Photo 2-26. 75–300 mm telephoto lens with largest aperture range F4–F5.6.

Photo 2-27. Normal view taken from an officer's perspective. Courtesy of Chula Vista, California, Police Department.

shallow depth-of-field. Distant objects are enlarged while near objects do not appear proportionately larger. The image magnification is proportional to the focal length. A true telephoto lens (58 mm–200 mm) is different than a long-focus lens (200 mm and beyond). A true telephoto lens has a shorter physical length while achieving the same angle-of-view as the long-focus lens (Miller, 2006).

A telephoto lens is used when the photographer must work at some distance while maintaining the relative size of the photographic subject(s). Surveillance photos are often obtained through the use of a telephoto lens.

Photo 2-28. 18 mm wide-angle view distorts the size of the image.

Photo 2-31. Surveillance photograph. Courtesy of National City, California, Police Department.

Photo 2-29. 18 mm wide-angle view distorts the size of the image.

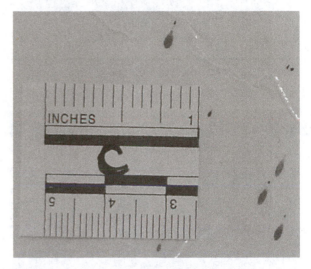

Photo 2-32. Macro view of evidence.

Photo 2-30. Surveillance photograph. Courtesy of National City, California, Police Department.

Camera movement with lenses larger than 200 mm may cause blurry photos and image distortion. Use of a tripod to stabilize the camera and lens is recommended.

Macro Lens

A **macro lens** is used for close-up photography. Though some telephoto lenses contain a macro setting, most macro lenses are normal-view lenses. Macro lenses allow the photographer to obtain close-up and enlarged views of fingerprints, bullet holes, bloodstains or blood drops, tool marks, and other small items of evidence.

> **Macro lens** Lens used for close-up photography that allows the photographer to obtain close-up and enlarged views of fingerprints, bullet holes, bloodstains or blood drops, tool marks, and other small items of evidence.

Detaching and Mounting a Lens

Forensic technicians should inspect all camera equipment prior to an assignment. Cameras and

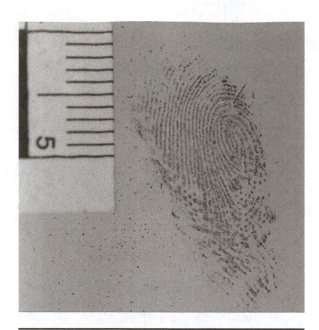

Photo 2-33. Macro view of evidence.

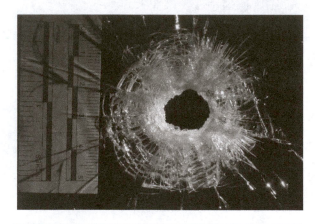

Photo 2-34. Macro view of evidence.

lenses are not always interchangeable. Lenses manufactured to fit Nikon® cameras typically do not fit Canon® cameras.

A camera's lens should not be changed in wet or dusty environments. The inner components of the camera must be protected from dust and moisture. If outdoors and in dusty (high winds with dust) or rainy conditions, the photographer should step inside a vehicle or building to change the camera's lens. If shelter is not available, the lens should be changed inside a plastic bag. To prevent accidental release of the shutter, automatic cameras should be in the *off* position prior to changing the lens.

Photo 2-35. The lens release button is depressed to remove the lens. Align the dot on the lens with the dot on the camera, then twist to lock the lens in place.

To detach a lens from a camera, a release mechanism is activated and the lens is rotated until it detaches from the camera body.

To attach a lens, the distinctive marking on the lens should be aligned with a similar marking on the camera body. After the lens and camera markings are aligned, the lens is rotated until it snaps or screws into place.

LENS FILTERS

A **lens filter** is placed over a lens to change the composition of the light that enters the camera's lens. Filters do not add color. They subtract (remove) color. Filters are also used to increase or decrease contrast. The following filters are commonly used in forensic environments.

> **Lens filter** Device placed over a lens to change the composition of the light that enters the camera's lens. Filters do not add color. They subtract (remove) color. Filters are also used to increase or decrease contrast.

- The *UV haze* filter reduces the amount of UV radiation entering the lens. UV radiation often creates an unwanted hazy appearance. The UV filter also protects the lens from scratching.
- The *polarizing filter* is used when the possibility of extreme reflection exists. To obtain photos near water, on light sand or snow, or near other reflective surfaces, the polarizing filter helps reduce reflection, haze, and glare (Pekala & Johnson, 2006).

Evidence such as a fingerprint may be located on a colored surface. To highlight fingerprint detail for the human eye, a forensic photographer may use a color filter to photograph the fingerprint with black and white film. Many digital cameras are equipped with black and white settings for this purpose.

To remove a background color from an image, a lens filter with the same color as the background is used (e.g., a red filter will remove red from the image). If a particular color must be darkened, a photographic color wheel chart should be examined to determine which colored lens is appropriate. The color on the opposite side of the wheel chart is the filter color used to darken or highlight a particular color. For example, ninhydrin is a chemical used to develop fingerprints on paper. The chemical changes to a purple (magenta) color when activated. To highlight the magenta color, a green color filter is used because green is opposite magenta on the color wheel chart. When using a colored lens filter, black and white film or black and white digital camera settings are used. Otherwise, the entire image will be colored by the filter.

Although colors can be removed from a digital image with Adobe Photoshop® or similar computer software program, the use of a simple color filter on the lens at the time of photography is sufficient.

The size of the filter depends on the diameter of the lens. The lens diameter is usually imprinted on the outside of the lens. One can measure the diameter of the lens face with a metric scale and purchase can filters to fit the lens.

FLASH PHOTOGRAPHY

The best light for photography is natural daylight. However, many crime scenes are indoors or outdoors at night. Indoor scenes typically contain tungsten (artificial light) or fluorescent lighting that distorts the color of the image. Therefore, a forensic photographer should use a flash unit as the main lighting source or as fill flash when additional light is needed in the photograph. A flash unit will override tungsten and fluorescent lighting and provide a photograph with balanced color. Outdoor, nighttime scenes require supplemental lighting.

For nighttime or indoor photography, a flash unit is used as the **main lighting source**, creating light similar to natural daylight. Many 35 mm cameras are equipped with flash units but these units are rarely capable of producing the amount of light necessary for forensic purposes. Therefore, an external flash (strobe) unit is often needed for indoor as well as outdoor, nighttime scenes.

A strobe unit may attach directly to the camera or it may be attached with the use of a **hot shoe** and **flash synchronization (sync) cord**. The hot shoe attaches to the top of the camera. The sync cord attaches to the hot shoe and the other end of the strobe unit. With the strobe unit activated, the photographer presses the shutter release button and a signal is sent from the camera through the hot shoe and sync cord to the strobe unit, causing it to *fire* a flash of light.

Main lighting source A flash unit is used to create light similar to natural daylight.

Hot shoe Attachment connecting a camera with a flash synchronization (sync) cord.

Flash synchronization (sync) Attaches to the hot shoe and a strobe unit. With the strobe unit activated, the photographer presses the shutter release button, and a signal is sent from the camera through the hot shoe and sync cord to the strobe unit, causing the strobe to *fire* a flash of light.

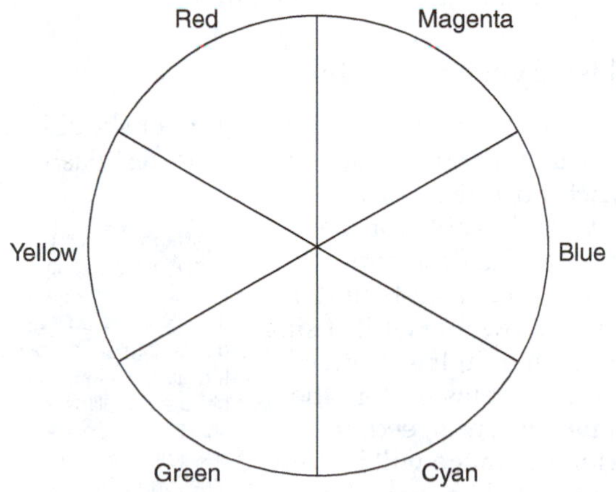

Figure 2-5. A photographic color wheel chart.

Photo 2-36. Camera with hot shoe, synchronization cord, and flash unit.

Photo 2-37. A flash unit can be mounted on a camera.

Photo 2-38. A flash unit can be handheld and used with a synchronization cord.

Photo 2-39. Photograph of a hidden weapon— without a flash.

When outdoor crime scenes are exposed to bright sunlight, **fill flash** is used to eliminate undesirable shadows that may obscure an evidence item in the photograph. Fill flash can be used to eliminate shadows under trees, bushes,

Photo 2-40. Photograph of a hidden weapon— with fill flash.

Photo 2-41. Photograph of a high contrast area with direct sunlight and dark shadows; fill flash was not used. Courtesy of the National City, California, Police Department.

steps, vehicles, and in other outdoor environments that require additional light.

Flash Synchronization

When using a flash, the photographer should set the camera's shutter speed to the fastest flash synchronization (sync speed) allowable for the camera. The flash sync speed is the fastest shutter speed allowable while using the flash unit. If a shutter speed is set faster than the camera's sync speed, the resulting image will be fully illuminated because the shutter is opening and closing faster than the flash unit

Fill flash   Flash used to eliminate undesirable shadows that may obscure an evidence item in the photograph. Fill flash can be used to eliminate shadows under trees, bushes, steps, vehicles, and other environments that require additional light.

is able to fire a flash to illuminate the image. The photographer should refer to the camera's operator manual for information on flash sync speed.

Inverse Square Law

The farther a light source or flash unit is from the subject of a photograph, the more diffused (less bright) the image will appear. At five feet, the light is too bright. At 10 feet, the amount of light is adequate. However, the light from a single flash will not fully illuminate a subject 20 feet away. Why? The light must travel a greater distance, causing it to dissipate. The inverse square law supposes that a single flash located one foot from a subject provides one square-foot of light, but a flash two feet from a subject provides four-square feet of light. Thus, an object 20 feet from the flash reflects only 1/25th of the light than the subject four feet away receives (Miller, 2006).

The inverse square law is an important consideration because photographing at night or in dark places may necessitate overlapping photographs from various sides of the scene to ensure that every view of the scene is captured under good lighting conditions.

In close-up photography that requires a flash, the photographer should hold the flash unit behind and away from the camera to increase the flash unit's distance from the subject, preventing harsh glare that the flash unit may otherwise produce. Photo flash applications are discussed throughout the remaining chapters of this book.

Camera-Mounted Flash versus Hand-Held Flash

A flash unit is mounted on the camera for overall and medium views of a crime scene. For close-up photography, a flash unit mounted on or placed immediately adjacent to the camera produces hard, direct light, and harsh shadows. To avoid harsh shadows, the flash unit should be held away from the camera at a 45 degree angle to the subject. The flash lighting is more effective because shadows drop behind the subject.

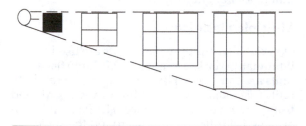

Figure 2-6. Inverse square law diagram.

Diffusing the Flash

Flash intensity can be reduced by considering the inverse square law and increasing the distance between the flash and the photo's subject matter. Light may also be diffused with a filter designed to cover the flash unit. Alternatively, a handkerchief, piece of paper, or any other translucent material or device may be placed between the flash and the subject. Diffusing the flash is desirable when photographing images of people, injuries, and reflective surfaces. It may be necessary to open the aperture or slow the shutter speed to allow more light into the camera because the diffused light can produce an under-exposed photograph.

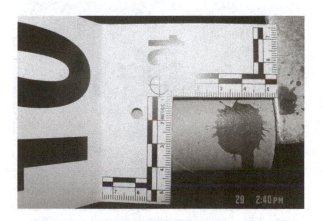

Photo 2-42. View of evidence with a direct flash resulting in glare in the photograph. Courtesy of National City, California, Police Department.

Photo 2-43. View of evidence with a non-direct flash angle resulted in a good exposure. Courtesy of National City, California, Police Department.

Photo 2-44. Built-in diffuser on flash unit.

Photo 2-46. Flash directed into a mirror.

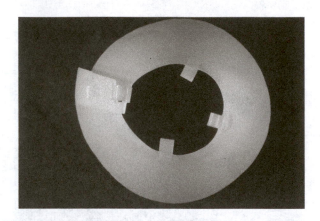

Photo 2-45. Translucent objects such as paper and plastic may be used to diffuse light.

Photo 2-47. Flash directed into a glass case at the end of a hall.

Reflective Surfaces and Bounce Flash

Reflective surfaces include items such as mirrors and glass, walls, and ceilings. If a flash is directed toward a reflective surface, a hot spot (light reflection from the subject surface) will result. The photographer can prevent a hot spot by holding the flash unit at a 45 degree angle to the reflective surface using a diffusion device, or the photographer may bounce the flash.

Bounce flash is a technique used to *bounce* (reflect) light from a white- or light-colored surface rather than allowing the flash of light to hit the subject directly. If the flash unit head is capable of rotation, the flash unit may remain on the camera with the flash head tilted upward. If the flash head is fixed (does not rotate), the photographer must remove the flash unit from the camera and man-

> **Bounce flash** A technique used to *bounce* (reflect) light from a white- or light-colored surface rather than allowing the flash of light to hit the subject directly.

ually tilt the flash unit outward or upward toward the light-colored surface (e.g., a wall or ceiling) and away from the subject.

A photographer should keep the inverse square law in mind because light from a bounced flash must travel to the wall or ceiling, bounce off (deflect), and return to illuminate the subject matter. The amount of light falling on the subject is greatly reduced by the distance it must travel. It may be necessary to open the aperture or slow the shutter speed to compensate for the difference in light exposure.

Multiple Flash Units

Occasionally, multiple flash units are used to illuminate a dark crime scene. Multiple flash units are constructed by connecting several flash units (*slave units*) with synchronization cords and using a remote control device. The flash units are arranged at different angles around the subject (or the scene) to distribute light evenly.

The flash units should not be directed toward the camera lens because the flash of light will create an extremely overexposed image. Neither should the photographer place the flash units or synch cords directly on evidence at the scene. Due to the setup time, expense, and storage necessary for extra flash units, most forensic photographers choose to take multiple photographs or timed exposures rather than use multiple flash units.

Photo 2-48. Flash directed into glass case.

DIGITAL PHOTOGRAPHY

With advancements in photographic technology, many agencies use digital cameras as the primary means of visually documenting evidence. Similar to a traditional film camera, a digital camera utilizes a lens to focus light and a shutter to control exposure time. ISO is also used to control the camera's sensitivity to light, with a higher ISO signifying greater sensitivity. With film cameras, a higher ISO results in a grainy image. With digital cameras, a higher ISO image is referred to as *noisy* rather than grainy.

A digital camera records an image differently than a film camera. Instead of film, the digital camera contains an image sensor that samples light frequencies and converts them to electrical impulses that are transformed into a digital language stored on a memory card.

Digitization (Digitizing)

The image captured by a digital camera contains distinct image elements (units) known as *pixels*. Pixels are square in shape, have specific color values (red, green, or blue) and are continuous (connected to one another). Each pixel contains

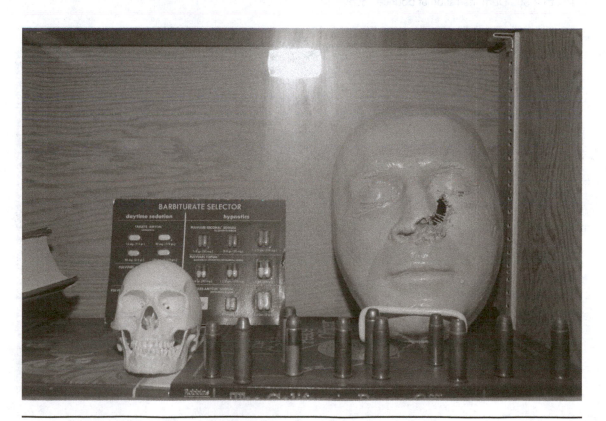

Photo 2-49. Result of direct flash into glass case.

Photo 2-50. Demonstration of bounce flash.

Photo 2-51. Result of bounce flash photograph of glass case.

Photo 2-52. Flash angled at 45 degrees to glass case.

Photo 2-53. Result of flash angled at 45 degrees to glass case.

Photo 2-54. Image photographed with ½ sec shutter, F4, ISO 200.

Photo 2-55. Image photographed with ½ sec shutter, F4, ISO 800.

information (an image element) about the image. When a digital image is stored, each pixel is analyzed for its content. This process is called *sampling*. Pixels are converted into a numeric value (digitized into a certain number of bits) for storage purposes.

In film photography, an image that lacks color is referred to as *black and white*. With digital photography, the image lacking color is called a *grayscale* image. A simple digital black and white photograph, with no depth, is a one-bit image. A grayscale digital image (one with depth but no color) is an eight-bit image. A color digital photograph is a 24-bit image that may contain up to 16 million different colors (Long, 2005).

Resolution

Resolution refers to the ability to capture fine details with a digital image. The number of pixels in an image directly affects resolution. More pixels result in higher resolution. Higher resolu-

tion equates to more pixels per square inch (ppi). An image with poor resolution appears blurry and individual pixels can be observed (pixilation). *Pixilation* is apparent when a digital image with poor resolution is enlarged. An image should be photographed at a high resolution if image enlargements are likely. Many applications in forensic photography require special attention to resolution.

The minimum resolution required to view a digital image of a fingerprint for comparison purposes is 1000 ppi. To maintain 1000 ppi, 2000 × 3000 pixels are necessary to capture the image. A six megapixel digital camera is required to photograph fingerprints. An eight megapixel digital camera is required to photograph an entire hand (palm) or shoe impression. Therefore, a forensic

> **Resolution** Refers to the ability to capture fine details with a digital image. The number of pixels in an image directly affects resolution. More pixels result in higher resolution. Higher resolution equates to more ppi.

Photo 2-56. Image photographed with ½ sec shutter, F4, ISO 1600.

Photo 2-57. Grayscale photograph of a flower.

photographer should use a digital camera with a minimum of eight megapixels to ensure that the camera is appropriate for all forensic science applications (Witzke, 2005).

Photo 2-58. Black and white (bitonal) photograph of a flower.

With traditional film photography, forensic technicians typically photograph fingerprints one-to-one (actual size). In digital photography, the forensic technician should photograph the fingerprint by filling the entire image frame of the camera. If a digital photograph of a fingerprint is taken one-to-one, empty space (wasted pixels) appear around the fingerprint. Resolution is diminished. If a digital photograph of the fingerprint is taken by filling the frame, the majority of the pixels available are consumed by the fingerprint. The digital fingerprint image can be reduced to actual size if necessary and resolution will not be affected. Resolution will be affected only if an image is enlarged. To illustrate the actual size of a fingerprint in a digital photo, a measuring scale is placed adjacent to the fingerprint. Photographing fingerprints and other forensic evidence is discussed throughout the remainder of this book.

White Balance

The human eye can adjust to and detect various colors under different lighting conditions. A digital camera does not possess the same ability. To create a digital image with appropriate colors represented, the digital camera's light setting must be adjusted.

Digital cameras interpret the dominant light in an environment by calculating the dominant light's temperature. The light is measured with a Kelvin light temperature scale. Colors appear different under various light temperatures. For a digital camera to record colors properly, dominant light must be selected within the camera.

The digital camera locates a reference point in an image that the camera detects as the color white and calculates all of the other colors based on the white point. This phenomenon is referred to as **white balance**. Assume, for example, that the main light source in a room is fluorescent and the room contains white walls. If the digital camera chosen to photograph images within the room is set to *daylight white balance* rather than *fluorescent white balance*, the camera may choose the wall color to calculate all colors at an incorrect color temperature, thus producing incorrect colors in the resulting image. To obtain correct colors in the image, the camera should be set to fluorescent white balance so the camera identifies the correct light temperature in the room. The white balance selection is based on the predominant lighting condition. If a flash unit with bright light is used, and the flash dominates all other lighting in the room, the white balance selection should be set to *flash white balance*.

White balance A digital camera locates a reference point in an image that the camera detects as the color white and calculates all of the other colors based on the white point.

If a digital camera is set to automatic white balance, the camera will search for the predominant color in the image and calculate and select the best white balance fit. Automatic white balancing can be a problem, however, if a crime scene or image is dominated by one color and natural light is not present. The automatic camera may erroneously select the wrong white balance setting.

If a photographer is not satisfied with the automatic white balance calculation of the camera, the photographer can use a white card (card that is white in color) to establish the white balance for the desired image. The result is a customized white balance setting. The camera's operator manual should be reviewed for detailed instructions on customized white balance settings.

Light Metering

A digital camera measures the amount of light at a scene and calculates the best exposure based on the light metering mode selected. Three basic types of light metering are available in a digital camera.

- *Matrix metering* analyzes the light across the entire frame of the image and calculates an average light reading. This type of metering is used most frequently. It is effective when

---

Type of Light/Color Temperature Setting in Kelvin

The following is a list of lighting conditions accompanied by the color temperature of the light in the Kelvin light temperature scale:

Candle Flame: 1,500
Incandescent: 3,000
Sunrise, Sunset: 3,500
Midday Sun, Flash: 5,500
Bright Sun, Clear Sky: 6,000
Cloudy Sky, Shade: 7,000
Blue Sky: 9,000

Figure 2-7. Kelvin light temperature scale chart.

---

the image is dominated by bright or dark colors.

- *Center-weighted metering* analyzes the light at the center of the image rather than the entire frame. This type of metering is effective when photographing close-up views (portraits) of a suspect.
- *Spot metering* analyzes the light at the very center (one percent) of the frame. This type of metering is effective when the subject of the photograph is in front of a very bright or dark background.

Special Features

Many digital cameras have settings for artistic photography. The settings permit the camera to determine the type of image the photographer is attempting to capture. The camera chooses depth-of-field, shutter speed, white balance, and exposure for the target image. A fully automatic (point-and-shoot) digital camera works well for the novice photographer. However, it is not appropriate for forensic use because the camera rather than the photographer selects all camera settings.

Shutter Speed/Camera Timings for Point-and-Shoot Cameras

Point-and-shoot (fully automatic) digital cameras must process an image to capture it correctly. Processing consumes time, often referred to as boot time (the amount of time a digital camera requires to prepare itself for photography). Thus, fully automatic digital cameras consume considerable time for pre-focus, shutter lag, and recycling. Pre-focus time is required for the camera to focus, meter the available light, and calculate white balance prior to capturing the image.

Shutter lag is the time delay between activation of the shutter release button and capturing the image. The lag may cause one to miss an important image. Recycling (recovery) time refers to the time it takes for the camera to ready itself to record the next image.

As one might imagine, point-and-shoot digital cameras are not preferred in forensic science. SLR digital cameras are better suited for forensic applications. They are not subject to the lag times. Digital SLR cameras are similar in operation to traditional SLR film cameras.

Playback

A digital camera is advantageous in several respects. An image recorded with a digital camera can be reviewed almost instantly to ensure it was recorded properly. Further, several digitally recorded images can be viewed simultaneously on a single screen. In addition, the zoom feature allows the photographer to enlarge and evaluate the image to determine if appropriate detail was captured.

If appropriate detail is not captured or the settings are not adequate, the photographer should take a second photograph. *At no time should a forensic photographer delete a digital image.* In many jurisdictions, deleting a digital image is considered destruction of evidence. Therefore, a forensic photographer should retain all digital images captured, regardless of their quality.

Digital Image Problems

Digital cameras and the images they produce can be problematic. Utilizing a digital software program, a photographer may choose to view and rotate the image from its original position. Since pixels are square in shape, rotating an image can create a distorted (jagged) effect in the image often referred to as *jaggies*. The jaggies are apparent throughout the image. Jaggies can be prevented by photographing the subject matter without alteration.

Occasionally, digital images exhibit *noise,* which is similar to graininess in traditional film photographs or static on a television. It is most often observed in shadows. Reducing (lowering) the ISO on the camera will prevent or reduce noise in an image. Some software programs used to view or manipulate digital images also reduce noise in the image.

Incorrect (distorted) color in a digital image is another common problem. Distorted color may result from incorrect white balance. To solve this problem, the photographer should ensure the correct white balance and increase depth-of-field.

Lack of detail and sharpness can be problematic with digital images also. Over-sharpness (lines that are too defined in the image) will result in too much contrast while under-sharpness will appear soft. This problem often results from low resolution or poor camera or lens quality.

Compression and Storage

After a digital image is recorded, it must be stored in the camera. **Compression** is used to reduce image file size so the image can be stored, processed, and transmitted to a computer or printer. There are many storage options, but each has limitations. The most common storage option is known as *JPEG* (Joint Photographic Experts Group).

> **Compression** Used to reduce a digital image file size so the image can be stored, processed, and transmitted to a computer or printer.

JPEG is a storage option within a digital camera that compresses the file to conserve storage space. Compression is achieved at the cost of reducing pixels and resolution. When saving in JPEG mode, the camera converts the image data to an eight-bit format, reducing the range of brightness levels. A low-quality JPEG selection will visibly degrade an image while a high-quality selection compresses the image without severe degradation (Long, 2005).

A *raw image (RAW)* contains the original, unprocessed data of the image. The photographer has complete control over the image features and none of the image is lost. RAW is the highest quality image but it requires special software (e.g., Adobe Photoshop®) for viewing. Evidence such as shoe and tire impressions as well as full palm, foot, and fingerprints that may be subjected to comparative analysis should be photographed in RAW.

A *tagged image file format (TIFF)* stores an image without compression. Color values are stored within the camera rather than being added when the image is retrieved. Consequently, more storage space is required in the camera. If RAW is unavailable, TIFF is the next best choice when photographing evidence that may be subject to comparison. If RAW and TIFF are not available, the photographer should photograph the image at the highest-quality resolution JPEG setting.

The image storage process is not the only obstacle to preserving or enhancing image quality. Converting the image to hard copy prints presents additional image quality challenges because of dot-to-pixel equivalencies.

Dot-to-Pixel Equivalents

Digital images are printed in *dots per square inch (dpi)*. Dpi is not the same as ppi. A *dot* is one of eight possible irregularly shaped (not round or square) unique color values. Unlike a pixel, a dot is not of a continuous tone. The quality of the printed image is directly related to dpi and the quality of the printer, ink, and paper, not the camera.

In the hard copy printing process, pixels are converted to dots. Eight dots on a single line equal a single pixel. Twelve hundred dpi is equal to 150 ppi (1200/8 = 150). Plain photo paper contains 360–720 dpi while premium glossy photo paper contains 1400–2880 dpi. Thus, the quality of the print paper is very important. It is recommended that the highest possible dpi and premium glossy photo paper be utilized.

Actual Size versus Filling the Frame

With traditional film photography, forensic photographers capture evidence items such as fingerprints at actual size (1:1 ratio). Photographing at actual size with a digital camera wastes pixels and resolution. Forensic photographers should fill the digital camera's frame when photographing close-up views of evidence such as fingerprints. Filing the frame ensures that the majority of the pixels are used to capture the core of the fingerprint, and that the pixels are not wasted on empty space around the fingerprint.

Due to the loss of resolution with some printing applications, many latent fingerprint examiners (LPEs) compare latent fingerprints obtained from a crime scene to inked fingerprints by utilizing a computer rather than the actual printed image. The LPE will scan the inked fingerprint into a computer and compare it to the digitally captured photograph of the suspect's latent fingerprint. The comparison is completed by viewing the images on a computer monitor rather than the printed images.

FORENSIC PHOTOGRAPHY BASICS

Equipment Maintenance

A photographer will not capture high quality images if the equipment used is not well maintained. A clean camera lens helps produce sharp images. Dirt or debris on the lens will also cause

Photo 2-59. 18 mm horizontal view of an elevated walkway.

scratches, which can affect image quality. Camera equipment should be cleaned and stored properly.

To clean a lens, the photographer should blow on the lens gently and use a camel-hair brush (manufactured for camera lenses) or lens tissue, not a facial tissue or cloth. Lens cleaning solution should not be applied directly to the lens. The cleaning solution should be applied to the lens cleaning tissue. Subsequently, the tissue is applied gently to the lens.

To remove dust from the inner components of a camera, the photographer should use a camera air bulb. When pinched, the bulb releases a stream of air. One should never touch the camera's shutter curtain or mirror when cleaning the camera. Further, compressed air should not be used to clean the inside of a camera because air under pressure contains moisture that may corrode camera components. The internal components of digital cameras should be cleaned by a professional camera technician.

When photographing an outdoor scene during inclement weather (e.g., rain, snow, or dust storm) or a scene containing dust or soot, one should enclose the camera in a plastic bag and cut a hole in the bag for the lens. Further, one should ensure that the camera is protected from dust and moisture before removing or changing the camera's lens. Finally, when camera equipment may be exposed to abrupt temperature changes, the equipment should be placed in a plastic bag or air tight case until the temperature equalizes. Protecting camera equipment during temperature changes helps prevent condensation.

Manipulating the Camera

Camera shake causes blurry photos. To avoid blurred images, the photographer should steady the camera with both hands, regardless of the camera's weight. When photographing large scenes requiring many overlapping photographs, the photographer should stop completely and steady the camera before pressing the shutter release button.

The photographer should peer through the viewfinder to view the entire frame surrounding a subject matter to ensure the desired image is captured. The photographer should ask two questions. What do I wish to photograph? Will the image captured make sense to the viewer?

In forensic science, manual focus of the camera is preferred. When using autofocus, the camera chooses the subject. Therefore, use of autofocus should be limited.

The forensic photographer must position the camera to capture the most relevant view. To photograph an orientation view of a person, doorway, long hallway, or small room (e.g., closet or bathroom), the camera is held to capture a vertical view. Large scenes require horizontally oriented views that capture the breadth of the scene.

Before taking any photograph, all camera settings should be inspected to ensure the best possible image will be recorded. The camera's shutter speed, f-stop, ISO setting, white balance, metering mode, and resolution quality should be reviewed. When photographing a crime scene, evidence, or injuries on a person, the forensic photographer should take overall, medium, and close-up photographs, ensuring that one image leads logically to the next.

Photo 2-60. 18 mm vertical view of an elevated walkway.

Overall Views

When photographing a crime scene, evidence item, or injuries on a person, overall views of the subject matter should be obtained first. Overall views orient the viewer to the subject matter.

Medium (Orientation) Views

Medium (orientation) views of crime scenes, evidence, and injuries follow overall views and precede close-up views. Medium views lead to close-ups. The medium view orients the viewer to the specific evidence item that the close-up views will capture.

Close-Up Views

Close-up views of evidence items and injuries follow the medium views. Close-up views allow the viewer to observe specific details that are not easily observed in the medium views. The face of the camera lens should parallel the evidence item to avoid distortion caused by photographing the item at an angle. Additionally, a scale measure should be placed on the same surface as the evidence item so the actual size of the item can be determined from the photograph. Lastly, the photographer should fill the camera frame with the evidence item, leaving a small amount of space around the item for photograph cropping purposes.

Specific overall, medium, and close-up photographic view applications are discussed throughout the remainder of this book. Crime scene photography techniques are discussed in Chapter 6.

SUMMARY

Artistic photographs call for dramatic compositions that invoke emotion in the viewer. The artistic photographer purposely distorts the point of focus, orients the subject matter to a pre-planned location in the image, and attempts to capture dramatic or humorous images. Artistic photography is not forensic photography. Forensic photographs focus on the depiction of facts, illustrating the exact location of evidence items, avoiding distortion and dramatic images, ensuring the correct depth-of-field, shutter speed, ISO, and exposure balance. One photograph should lead to the next, with overall, medium (orientation), and close-up views of the evidence.

To properly capture images of evidence, knowledge of the nomenclature and application of the various camera settings is essential for a forensic photographer. Thus, fully automatic point-and-shoot cameras are not appropriate in forensic photography. Fully automatic cameras will not properly capture the evidence, rendering photographs virtually useless for forensic purposes. Forensic photography calls for very specific camera settings.

KEY TERMS

Define, describe, or explain the importance of each of the following:

achromatic lens	flash synchronization (sync)	resolution
aperture	cord	shutter release cable
bounce flash	focal length	shutter
bracketing	f-stop	stopping down the lens
camera lens	hot shoe	telephoto lens
compression	lens filter	timed exposure
depth-of-field	macro lens	white balance
exposure	main lighting source	wide-angle lens
fill flash	normal lens	

DISCUSSION AND REVIEW QUESTIONS

1. What is depth-of-field?
2. What is meant by *stopping down the lens*?
3. What is the ISO?
4. When is fill flash necessary?
5. Contrast a normal view with a wide-angle view.
6. What is the inverse square law? Why is it important?
7. What is bounce flash and when is it used?
8. Explain the importance of resolution in digital photography.
9. Why is white balance important in digital photography?

CASE STUDY—Jon Benet Ramsey

On December 26, 1996, Patsy Ramsey discovered that her daughter, Jon Benet, appeared to be missing from their Boulder, Colorado, home. Patsy found a ransom note demanding $118,000 on a kitchen stairway. Despite ransom note instructions to the contrary, Patsy contacted police who subsequently conducted a cursory search of the Ramsey residence. No sign of Jon Benet or forced entry to the home were uncovered in the search. Police allowed friends and family of the Ramsey's to access the home after the kidnapping was reported. No effort was made to secure the home as a crime scene.

Jon Benet's father, John, and two of his friends conducted a second search of the basement late in the day. John discovered Jon Benet's body under a white blanket in the wine cellar. Autopsy results indicated she died from strangulation and a fractured skull.

The Boulder police immediately placed Jon Benet's parents under suspicion. No footprints on the snow-covered ground led to the house and snow on the walkways was removed after the kidnapping was reported. Although the police discovered no sign of forced entry into the residence, a basement window broken before Christmas and a few doors were apparently unsecured before and during the alleged kidnapping.

In December 2003, forensic scientists discovered a DNA profile in a mixed blood sample extracted from an undergarment Jon Benet wore at the time of her death. The DNA profile belonged to an unidentified male. In July 2008, the Boulder, Colorado, District Attorney's office announced that, as a result of newly developed DNA sampling and analysis techniques, Ramsey family members were no longer considered suspects.

1. Develop a crime scene photography plan for the Ramsey case.
2. What evidentiary items are likely to require photographs?

LAB EXERCISES

Shutter speed, f-stop, light metering, and bracketing practice

Equipment and Supplies Required Per Student
one-35 mm film or digital SLR camera
one roll of 24 exposure film (if film camera)
one photo log to record camera settings

Exercise #1—Light Metering (outdoors, during the day)

1. While standing outdoors (not in a shaded area), use a wide-angle lens and peer through the camera's viewfinder at a large open space. With the camera set at manual, use the rule of f-16 to set the shutter speed and f-stop. What are the settings? What does the light meter indicate? Take one photograph of the large space with the wide-angle view.
2. Increase the shutter speed two increments faster than the original setting. Use the light meter to obtain the correct f-stop. What are the settings? Take a photograph of the same view as in Step 1.
3. Reduce the shutter speed two increments below the original setting. Use the light meter to obtain the correct f-stop. What are the settings? Take a photograph of the same view as in Steps 1 and 2.
4. Review the photographs after printing or on a computer monitor (if digital camera used).

Is the lighting of each photo different? Why? Does depth-of-field vary? Why?

Exercise #2—Shutter Speeds (outdoors, during the day, working with a partner)

1. Students form pairs to photograph one another.
2. One student steps back a few feet from the photographer/student and waves hands quickly in front of the face. The photographer/student sets the camera on manual and the shutter speed at 1000, using the light meter to determine the correct f-stop. What are the camera settings?
3. The photographer/student holds the camera in one place and captures three photo images: one at wide-angle, one at 50 mm, and one filling the frame with one of the partner's hands. The light meter setting should be calibrated before each photo because the focal length will change the exposure.
4. Reduce the shutter speed to 500. Use the light meter to determine the f-stop. What are the camera settings? Repeat the three photographs at the same focal lengths as in Step 3.
5. Reduce the shutter speed to 30. Use the light meter to determine the f-stop. What are the camera settings? Hold the camera very still. Movement of the camera at a slow shutter speed may result in blurry photographs. Repeat the three photographs at the same focal lengths as in Step 3.
6. Student-partners trade positions and repeat the exercise.
7. Compare the images. How do the images obtained with the fast shutter speed differ from the slower shutter speeds?

Exercise #3—Depth-of-Field (outdoors, during the day)

1. Locate a row of three trees or plants with straight trunks or stems. Position yourself at one end of the row, focusing on the first tree or plant.

2. Set the camera lens at 50 mm and focus on the first tree or plant. Set the f-stop at 22. Use the light meter to determine the correct shutter speed. What are the camera settings? Peer through the camera's viewfinder at the row and take one photograph.
3. Change the f-stop to eight. Adjust the shutter speed according to the light meter reading. What are the camera settings? Take one photograph of the same image as in Step 2.
4. Change the f-stop to the lowest setting on the camera. Adjust the shutter speed according to the light meter reading. What are the camera settings? Take one photograph of the same image as in Step 3.
5. Compare the images. What differences are observed in the depth-of-field for each f-stop?

Exercise #4—Bracketing (outdoors, during the day)

1. While outdoors, select an outdoor object to photograph. Set the camera lens to 50 mm and the f-stop to eight. Use the light meter to determine the correct shutter speed. What are the camera settings? Take one photograph of the object.
2. Maintain the lens at 50 mm and *stop the lens down* (smaller opening, improved depth-of-field) two full f-stops. Maintain the shutter speed regardless of the light meter reading. What are the camera settings? What does the light meter indicate? Take one photograph of the same object as in Step 1.
3. Reset the f-stop to eight. Maintain the lens setting at 50 mm and open the aperture two full f-stops. Maintain the shutter speed regardless of the light meter reading. What are the camera settings? What does the light meter indicate? Take one photograph of the same object as in Step 2.
4. Compare the images. How do they differ? Which photograph appears to have the correct exposure? Which is under-exposed? Which is overexposed? Why?

WEB RESOURCES

3

Crime Scene Diagrams

LEARNING OUTCOMES

After completing this chapter, the reader should be able to:

- create an overhead (bird's-eye view) sketch,
- create a cross-projection (exploded view) sketch,
- obtain measurements using the coordinate and triangulation techniques,
- explain the baseline measurement technique,
- explain the polar (radial) measurement technique,
- describe the importance and use of the blowup sketch,
- convert a rough sketch to a finished sketch,
- depict a vehicle within a scene,
- depict furniture within a crime scene,
- distinguish between a hand-drawn and computer-aided design (CAD) drawing.

INTRODUCTION

A crime scene diagram (sketch) is a scale drawing of a crime scene. It accurately depicts the location of evidence items within the scene. Although crime scene photography is essential to document (record) the appearance of the scene, the crime scene diagram complements and clarifies photographs of the scene. Photographs depict images of the scene, while the diagram identifies the exact (or near exact) location of all of the evidence items, providing the investigator, prosecutor, defense attorney, witness, judge, juror, and others with a two- or three-dimensional visual of the entire scene. In some court cases, the scene is physically reconstructed for the jury. Without a crime scene diagram, accurate reconstruction is not possible.

Additionally, photographs of crime scenes, particularly indoor scenes, may contain numerous items, such as furniture, clothing, or storage containers, that are not related to the crime. The evidence may be difficult to view in the photograph amongst the irrelevant items. The crime scene diagram need not include irrelevant objects. If depiction of irrelevant objects is necessary to demonstrate a perspective, separate diagrams can be created that simply depict the items of evidence, thus eliminating clutter and confusing artifacts from the visual representation used by investigators and presented in judicial proceedings.

Large crime scenes are often difficult to document photographically. While photographs are taken of large-scale scenes, an overhead (bird's-eye) view diagram is created to accurately depict the overall layout of the scene. An overhead view diagram illustrates the entire scene's appearance as well as the relationship of evidentiary items within the scene.

The crime scene diagram is a tool frequently used in the courtroom. An enlarged display of the diagram allows the defendant, judicial personnel, and the jury to visualize the crime scene. The diagram is also a tool for witnesses to the crime. While presenting testimony, a witness may refer to the diagram to indicate the location of evidentiary items and events. The diagram will also assist those at the scene with recall of details.

The person who creates the crime scene diagram varies among agencies. A small crime scene may be sketched by the uniformed patrol officer investigating a crime, such as a burglary or assault. A large-scale crime scene, such as those often associated with a homicide or officer-involved shooting, may be crafted by someone who is specially trained to create a crime scene sketch. Depending on the agency, this person may be a detective, criminalist, or a forensic technician. The occupational specialty of the person who creates the diagram is not as important as the skill, knowledge, and equipment used to create the diagram.

SKETCHING EQUIPMENT

To measure and sketch a crime scene and evidence items properly, the following equipment and supplies are recommended.

Graph Paper

Graph paper is helpful because the manufactured lines that form squares within the paper assist with sketching the scene to scale. Unlined paper may be used for a rough sketch if graph paper is not available.

Pencil and Eraser

Pencil is preferred so errors are easily erased. Pen or permanent marker may be used if a pencil is not available. If an error is made with the pen, the portion of the sketch containing the error must be redrawn.

Measuring Devices

- one 12 or 24 foot tape measure,
- two 50 or 100 foot cloth tape measure,
- one roll-a-tape measure,
- one laser measuring device (if available).

A tape measure allows the sketcher to obtain short measurements with ease. An assistant is not required. However, it is recommended that a second person be available to verify all measurements, thus avoiding defense counsel accusations of errors in measurements. For long measurements, a 50 or 100 foot cloth tape measure is preferred because it is extremely flexible and can be flattened easily. A long cloth tape measure is also a great tool for the coordinate and baseline measuring techniques discussed later in this chapter. Although not the most accurate measuring device, a roll-a-tape measure is also helpful for approximate measurements of long distances.

A laser measuring device can be used to obtain precise measurements. The sketcher simply holds the device against the surface on

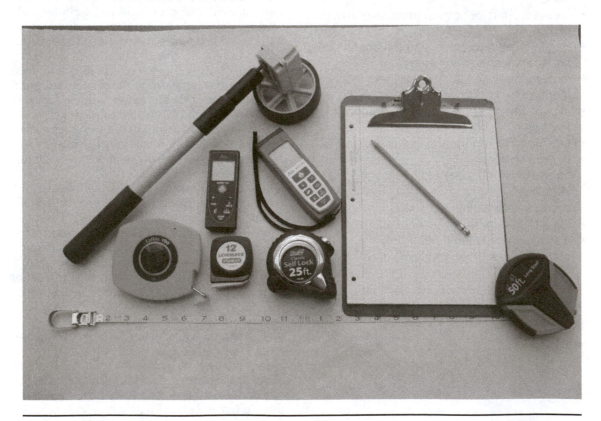

Photo 3-1. Equipment for measuring crime scenes.

which the measurement starts and directs the laser to the end point. However, laser-assisted measurements can be difficult to obtain if the crime scene is outdoors or if the sketcher wishes to obtain measurements at ground level. If either is the case, the sketcher will require an assistant to hold a piece of cardboard or a notebook above the location of the evidence. The cardboard or notebook provides a surface to reflect the laser beam.

Clipboard or Hard Writing Surface

It is difficult to draw a straight line, even on graph paper, if one has no hard surface on which to draw. A clipboard or hard writing surface is a must.

MEASURING TECHNIQUES

With the proper equipment, the forensic technician is ready to create the rough and finished diagrams (sketches) of the crime scene. *Crime scene mapping* (measuring) is a process through which the scene sketcher documents the size of a crime scene and the location of evidence within the scene. By *fixing* the evidence in the scene, an investigator or forensic technician can return to the scene and accurately reposition each evidence item collected.

Based on the nature of the scene, location of evidence items, and the preference of the forensic technician, one or more of the measuring techniques presented here may be applied to a crime scene. Every scene is different. However, measurements should be obtained for rough and finished crime scene sketches and diagrams that will allow others to recreate, as precisely as possible, the location of evidence and other items within the scene. Measurements to and from items of evidence should be taken from relatively permanent structures. It is recommended that measurements be recorded to the nearest quarter inch, though the exact procedure may vary among agencies.

Coordinate Method

The **coordinate sketching method (rectangular coordinate method)** is a measuring technique that uses coordinates from x and y axes to pinpoint evidence items in a crime scene; x

> **Coordinate sketching method (rectangular coordinate method)** A measuring technique that uses coordinates from x and y axes to pinpoint evidence items in a crime scene.

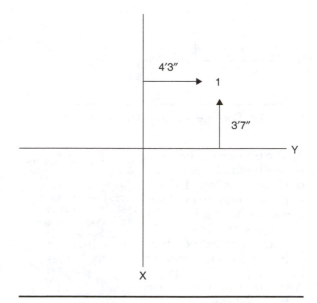

Figure 3-1. Coordinate measuring diagram.

and y can be perpendicular walls, street curb lines, sides of a building, or any stationary north–south and east–west lines, and they should be relatively permanent, stationary, and clearly defined (Gardner, 2005). As Figure 3-1 illustrates, each evidence item is measured to both the x axis and the y axis, so the item's exact location is clearly indicated.

If possible, the location of all evidence items should be measured from the same x axis and the same y axis. For example, if an east–west curb line at an outdoor crime scene is used as the x axis and a north–south curb line is used as the y axis, all evidence items should be measured from the same two curb lines.

Baseline Method

The **baseline sketch method** is most useful at an outdoor scene. It is similar to the coordinate method except that the x or y axis is extended by a line. A tape measure or a chalk line can be used to extend the axis lines. For example, if perpendicular sides of a building provide x and y, the axis can be extended from the building's sides. A 50 or 100 foot cloth tape measure works well in this situation because it will lie flat.

> **Baseline sketch method** Sketch method useful at an outdoor scene. Similar to the coordinate method except that the x or y axis is extended by a line. A tape measure or a chalk line can be used to extend the axis lines. For example, if perpendicular sides of a building provide x and y, the axis can be extended from the building's sides. A 50 or 100 foot cloth tape measure works well in this situation because it will lie flat.

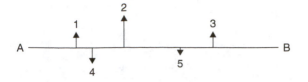

Figure 3-2. Baseline measuring diagram.

The **transecting baseline sketch method** is another outdoor measuring technique that may be used for situations in which there are no x and y axis lines. Instead, two fixed points are chosen and a line is created between the two points. A tape measure can be used as the line. Measurements

> **Transecting baseline method**   An outdoor measuring technique that may be used for situations in which there are no x and y axis lines. Instead, two fixed points are chosen and a line is created between the two points.

to items are taken at 90 degree angles from points along the baseline (Ogle, 2007).

Triangulation

The **triangulation sketch method** can be used at indoor or outdoor crime scenes. Two fixed points are selected. At an indoor scene, corners in a room are typically chosen. The distance between the two points is measured. Next, a measurement is taken from each fixed point to the evidence item. The sketcher can measure to the center of the evidence item or take

> **Triangulation method**   A sketching technique that can be used at indoor or outdoor crime scenes. Two fixed points are selected. At an indoor scene, corners in a room are typically chosen. The distance between the two points is measured. Next, a measurement is taken from each fixed point to the evidence item. The sketcher can measure to the center of the evidence item or take measurements to no more than two of the item's sides or corners.

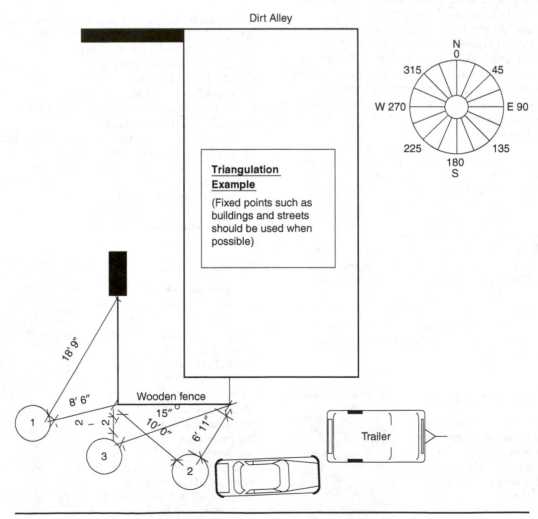

Figure 3-3. Crime scene diagram using triangulation.

measurements to no more than two of the item's sides or corners.

The triangulation method is preferred at outdoor crime scenes when barriers such as ravines or bodies of water separate evidence items. A laser measuring device is also extremely useful in these situations.

Polar (Radial) Method

The **polar (radial) sketch method** is typically used at an outdoor crime scene if evidence is dispersed over a large open area. It is also used if no fixed points from which to measure are available. Open terrain, such as a field, mountain range, desert, or other large area, lends itself to this method. The method is applied as follows:

> **Polar (radial) sketch method** A sketching technique often used at an outdoor crime scene if evidence is dispersed over a large open area. It is also used if no fixed points from which to measure are available. Open terrain, such as a field, mountain range, desert, or other large area lends itself to this method.

1. The sketcher drives a stake into the ground.
2. Using a *global positioning satellite (GPS) tracking device,* the sketcher obtains satellite positioning coordinates for the stake.
3. The sketcher measures the distance from the stake to each evidence item.
4. The sketcher uses a compass and protractor to determine the angle of the evidence item from the stake. The compass is used to determine direction (many GPS devices also have built-in compasses). The protractor is used to calculate the angle of the item in relation to the stake.

Surveying equipment can also be used to obtain extremely accurate measurements. Surveying equipment allows the sketcher to obtain the distance to the evidence item, as well as its elevation angle (Gardner, 2005). Although surveying equipment is very precise and useful, its operation requires many hours of training. Most government engineering or planning departments have surveying equipment. The sketcher may find it necessary to request government surveyor assistance in obtaining measurements. Surveying equipment is also very useful at large-scale traffic collision scenes.

A **total station** is a surveying instrument used by many police agency traffic

> **Total station** A surveying instrument used to obtain horizontal and vertical angle measurements, as well as distance and slope measurements necessary to investigate and reconstruct traffic collision scenes.

units to investigate and reconstruct serious traffic collision scenes. The total station system may be used at large-scale homicide scenes as well. Utilizing the system, an operator can obtain horizontal and vertical angle measurements, as well as distance and slope measurements. The system is automatic, utilizing basic trigonometry to calculate distance from a reference point. An optical prism is placed at a reference point (e.g., location of evidence). The prism reflects light emitted from the total station instrument to the prism.

Two people are required to operate a total station. One person activates the instrument and another holds the optical prism. After all measurements are obtained, the data is downloaded to a computer. The data is converted into an appropriate CAD software program. The use of a total station requires specialized training and many police agencies have adopted the technology because of its accuracy and efficiency (Joice, 2008). Yet, the current high cost of the total station is a deterrent to widespread use.

Furniture

If an item of furniture is located within a crime scene, the sketcher should obtain measurements from at least two corners or two sides of the furniture item to perpendicular walls. Depending on the measuring technique used, additional measurements may be required. For example, if the coordinate method is used, the sketcher must complete two measurements each from the x and the y axis. The measurements are taken from two corners of the furniture, for a total of four

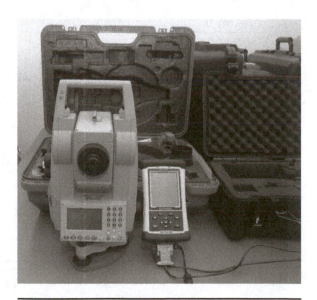

Photo 3-2. Total station equipment.

measurements. If triangulation is used, each point of the triangle requires measurements from two corners of the furniture, for a total of four measurements. If a furniture item is round (e.g., table), a measurement is taken to the center of the item. The diameter of the item is measured as well.

In addition, the sketcher should measure and record the width (or depth), length, and height of furniture items, regardless of the type of crime scene diagram intended. Although the measurements may not be included in the sketch, they may become relevant later. Thus, the measurements should be included in the notes and official report that accompany the sketch.

Evidence

When measuring to or from evidence items, the sketcher can measure to or from the center of the item or two corners or sides of the item, depending on the nature of the item. For example, a bloody tee-shirt lying on the ground may be an evidence item. Measuring to or from the center of the tee-shirt is sufficient. If a coordinate method is used, two measurements (one from the x axis and one from the y axis) to the center of the tee-shirt are obtained. A width measurement should be taken and recorded as well. If the evidence item is a rifle, the sketcher may measure to each end of the rifle. For pools of liquid (e.g., blood), the sketcher should measure to the center of the pool and obtain the length and width (or diameter) of the pool.

Body in a Crime Scene

When a deceased human body is located within a crime scene, the sketcher should obtain measurements of the body and its location prior to removal of the body by the medical examiner, coroner, or other controlling authority. The following measurements are suggested, although additional measurements may be required, depending on the policy of the agency responsible.

If the coordinate or the triangulation method is used, two measurements are obtained from perpendicular lines (e.g., walls) to each of the following:

> top of the head
> each elbow
> tip of the longest finger of each hand
> center of each knee
> tip of the longest toe of each foot
> each shoulder (recommended, not required)

Vehicle in a Crime Scene

Illustrating a vehicle within a crime scene requires measurements from perpendicular lines to the center of one each of the front and rear tires. If the coordinate method is used, x and y axes measurements are obtained to the center of a front and a rear tire, for a total of four measurements (see Chapter 8, for tire treads measurement procedures).

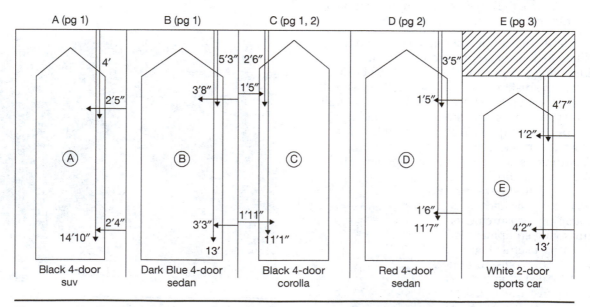

Figure 3-4. Hand-drawn diagram of vehicle measurements. Sketch by Marianne Recasas.

TYPES OF DIAGRAMS

After a detailed search for evidence is completed, and photographs of the crime scene and the evidence are taken, the forensic technician creates a rough diagram (sketch) of the scene, including the location of evidentiary items within the scene. The rough diagram is a crime scene sketch drawn to scale. The type of diagram created is dependent upon the type of crime scene and location of evidence items.

Overhead (Bird's-Eye) View Diagram

The **overhead (bird's-eye) view diagram** is the most common and the simplest sketch to create. It is a view of the crime scene and its evidence as if one was viewing the scene from above. It is a two-dimensional drawing viewed from one direction only. The overhead diagram depicts the overall layout of a scene. For outdoor scenes, the overall view of buildings, streets, parking lots, and vehicles are depicted easily.

> **Overhead (bird's-eye) view diagram** An overhead diagram depicting the overall layout of a scene.

For indoor scenes, the overhead view of rooms, including doors, windows, and furniture, is depicted.

The overhead view diagram also depicts detailed measurements in the scene as long as the evidence is located on the horizontal plane of the two-dimensional sketch. Evidence located on a vertical plane (e.g., wall) cannot be depicted with this type of diagram.

Elevation Diagram

An **elevation diagram** is used to illustrate a vertical plane, such as a staircase or the side of a building.

> **Elevation diagram** A diagram used to illustrate a vertical plane, such as staircase or the side of a building, outdoor terrain, or slope.

The elevation diagram is also used to illustrate outdoor terrain and slopes. If precise measurements of a slope or terrain are necessary, the services of a surveyor may be required (Ogle, 2007).

Cross-Projection (Exploded View) Diagram

The **cross-projection (exploded view) diagram** is ideal for indoor crime scenes with evidence located on the floor, wall(s), or ceiling. The room sketched is thought of as a box, with the floor of the room as the base of the box, the walls as the sides of the box, and the ceiling as the top of the box. If the box is unfolded, the walls will collapse around the floor and the ceiling will connect to one of the walls (Gaensslen, Harris, & Lee, 2008).

The floor is drawn as an overhead (bird's-eye) view diagram. The walls are drawn as attachments to the floor. The vertical elements of the wall, including the location of windows, doors, wall hangings, and evidentiary items are included in the collapsed wall illustrations. The ceiling is drawn as an attachment to one of the walls.

> **Cross-projection (exploded view) diagram** is ideal for indoor crime scenes with evidence located on the floor, wall(s), or ceiling. The room sketched is thought of as a box with the floor of the room represented by the base of the box, the walls by the sides of the box, and the ceiling by the top of the box. If the box is unfolded, the walls collapse around the floor and the ceiling connects to one of the walls.

The cross-projection diagram is created when evidence, such as blood or bullet holes, is discovered on the walls or ceiling.

Blowup Diagram

For some crime scenes, the events that occurred during the incident must be reconstructed. Forensic science experts in bloodstain pattern analysis or bullet trajectory may be consulted. They will view the scene's photographs to aid in analysis. In addition, they require exact measurements and locations of evidence to conduct experiments and reconstruct the crime scene.

A **blowup diagram** is a detailed, enlarged view of evidence such as a bloodstain pattern. It is a detailed sketch of evidence within a larger diagram (Ogle, 2007). The large diagram indicates the location of the enlarged evidence within the crime scene so the evidence can be related to the rest of the scene. The blowup sketch must be precise, with exact measurements, because its purpose is crime scene reconstruction.

> **Blowup diagram** A detailed, enlarged view of evidence such as a bloodstain pattern. It is a detailed sketch of evidence within a larger diagram.

Creating the Rough Sketch

After the forensic technician determines the type of diagram necessary, measurements and creation of the rough sketch may commence. A rough sketch should be created in a systematic and detailed manner.

The first step to sketching a crime scene is to determine direction (e.g., north, south, east, or west). Use of a compass may be necessary. Rough crime scene sketches (as well as finished

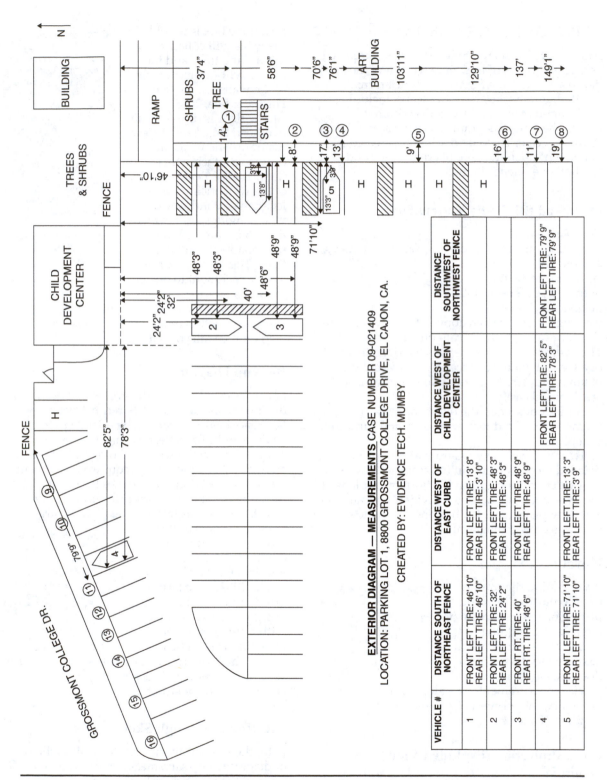

Figure 3-5. Hand-drawn diagram of parking lot and vehicles. Sketch by Christina Mumby.

Figure 3-6. Crime scene diagram of layout of house.

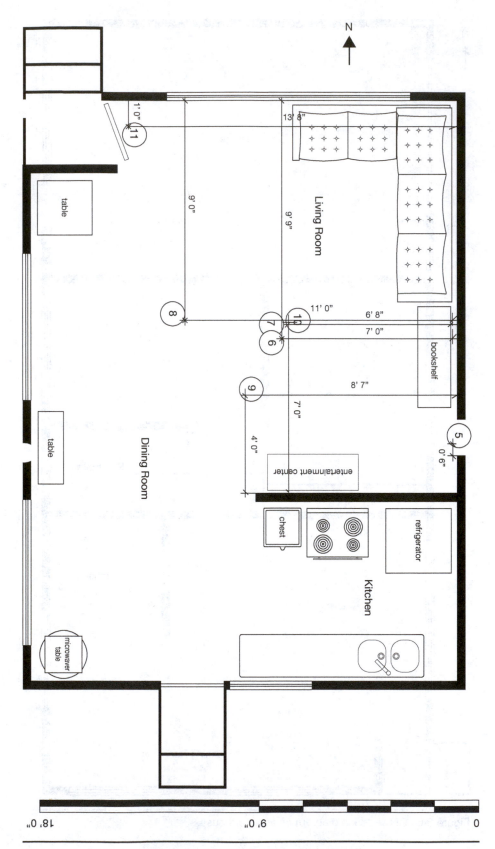

Figure 3-7. Crime scene diagram of bird's-eye view of living room.

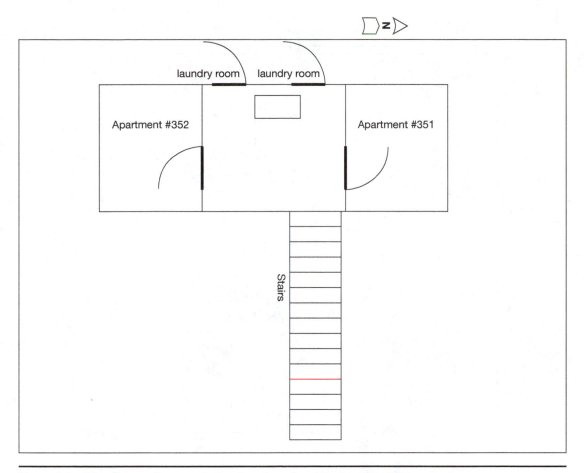

Figure 3-8. Crime scene diagram of elevation view of apartments and stairs.

diagrams) should be created with the direction *north* at the top of the sketch.

After direction is established, the sketcher creates a rough sketch of the overall view of the crime scene. Depending on the size of the scene, the overall view may require several sheets of graph paper. The overall view is typically an overhead (bird's-eye) view sketch.

After the overall view is complete, specific areas within the crime scene are measured and sketched. The location of evidence will determine the type of sketch (e.g., bird's-eye view or exploded view) created.

The sketcher should face *north*, overlooking the entire area to be sketched. It is very difficult to create an accurate sketch while standing in the middle of a crime scene.

Outdoor Scene Rough Sketch
The following procedure is recommended when constructing a rough sketch of an outdoor crime scene:

1. The forensic technician should sketch an overall view of the scene, including any relevant buildings, landscaping (trees and shrubbery), vehicles, and other large items present in the scene. Measurements of large items and evidence are not included in this step.

2. On separate sheets of paper, focus on evidence-relevant areas of the scene. For example, if the evidence is located in a parking lot, only one row of parking stalls need be included in the sketch.

3. Include measurements of the detail area constructed in Step 2. Include the detailed area's length and width, as well as distances between objects such as sidewalks and streets. To obtain these measurements, walk along the perimeter of the detail area, measuring and sketching the length and width of relevant sidewalks, driveway openings, and streets. Do not illustrate evidence in this step.

4. Repeat Step 3 with each area of the scene containing evidence. Obtain measurements of and insert the areas into the sketch.

5. Add evidence items to the sketch. Include measurements from fixed points to evidence

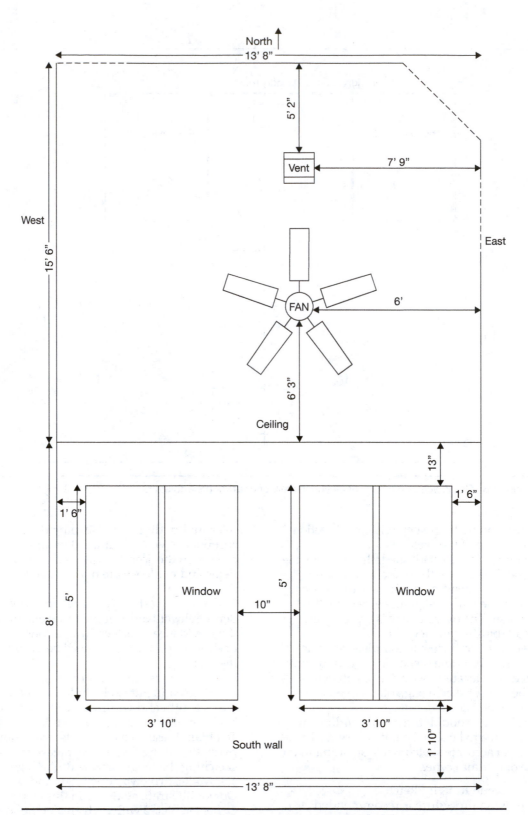

Figure 3-9. Hand-drawn diagram of exploded view of wall and ceiling. Sketch by Jennifer Peterson.

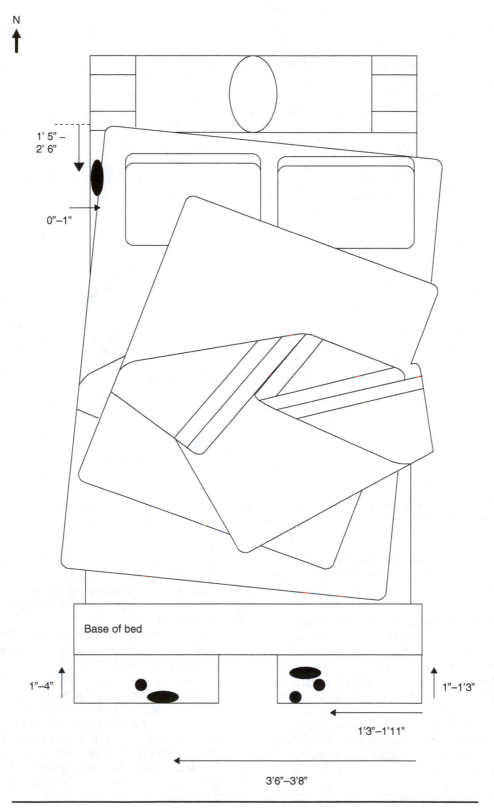

Figure 3-10. Diagram of bloodstains on side and front of bed frame.

N

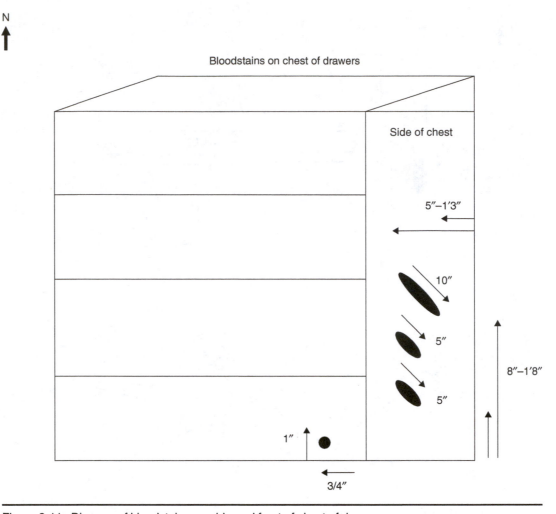

Figure 3-11. Diagram of bloodstains on side and front of chest of drawers.

items. Do not draw images of the evidence. Rather, assign a different number to each evidence item.

Include the evidence item number with an accompanying description of the item in a legend on the sketch. If the rough sketch appears congested, separate sheets of paper can be used to create the rough sketch. In other words, all of the detail need not be drawn on a single page. Another option is to illustrate the location evidence items on a separate sheet of paper using a legend or table (Figure 3-15). Add the exact measurements to the final, computer-generated diagram.

Indoor Scene Rough Sketch
The following procedure is recommended for creating an indoor crime scene rough sketch.

1. Sketch an overall layout of the house or structure. Include all rooms and major furniture items. Do not include measurements of the rooms or furniture. Do not include evidence items in this step.
2. On separate sheets of paper, sketch each room, recording measurements. Measure the length of each wall. Start at a corner of the room and measure from the corner to the nearest opening (e.g., door or window) on the wall. Record the measurement. Measure the width of the opening and record the measurement. Measure from the opening to the next room opening or to the next corner (end of the wall). Continue the process until all perimeter dimensions of the room are measured and recorded.
3. Add major furniture items and measurements from fixed points to each of these items. Include only furniture that are relevant. Assign

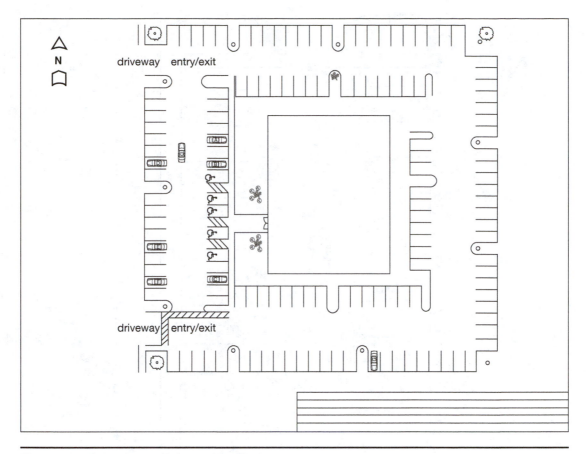

driveway   entry/exit

driveway   entry/exit

N

Figure 3-12. Crime scene diagram of parking lot.

letters to furniture and other nonevidentiary items. Include a description, along with corresponding letters, in a nonevidence item legend or table. Details on how to measure to and from furniture items in a crime scene are described later in this chapter under *Specific Measurement Applications.* Do not sketch evidence in this step.

4. Repeat Step 3 with each room (if relevant) on separate sheets of paper, obtaining and recording measurements on the sketch.

5. Add evidence items to each room sketch and record the measurements to those items on the sketch. Do not draw illustrations of evidence. Rather, assign a number to each item of evidence and insert the number representing the evidence item into the sketch. Include a description of the evidence item in a legend or table.

6. If a single room contains numerous items of evidence, multiple sketches of the room may be necessary. A wall with bullet holes or bloodstain patterns may be sketched separately.

CRIME SCENE SKETCHING TIPS

Considerable time and energy may be conserved if crime scene sketchers follow a few simple guidelines:

- The person responsible for creating the rough sketch of the crime scene as well as the final crime scene diagram should obtain all measurements. Measurements should be verified by a second person as they are obtained. The sketcher should never create a rough sketch or finished diagram from another person's measurements or sketch.

- The sketcher should obtain, record, and present measurements in feet and inches. American jurors are familiar with and can relate to distances in feet and inches. Average jurors do not relate to the metric system or distances measured in inches only.

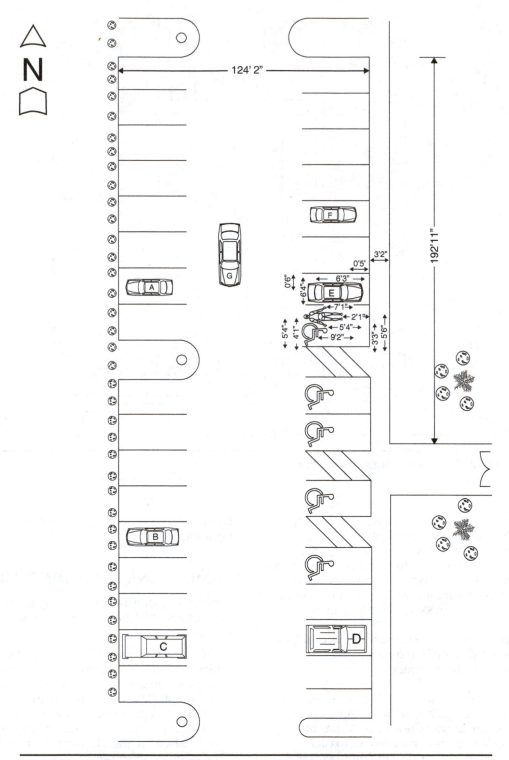

Figure 3-13. Crime scene diagram of parking lot and measurements.

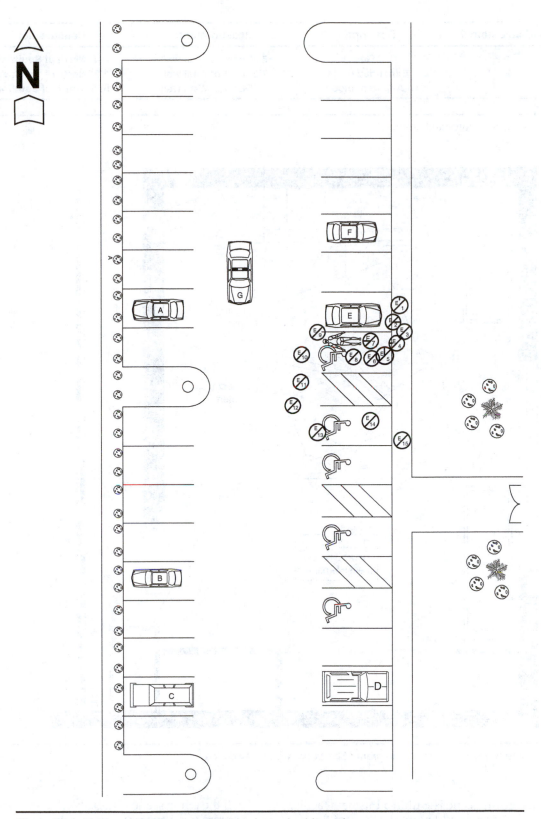

Figure 3-14. Crime scene diagram of parking lot and evidence items.

Evidence Item #	Description	Measurement:	Measurement:
1	Gun	6'3" East of West wall	4'4" North of South wall
2	Expended casing	7'8" East of West wall	1'3" North of South wall
3	Apparent blood	2'3" East of West wall	10'2" North of South wall

Figure 3-15. Measurement chart.

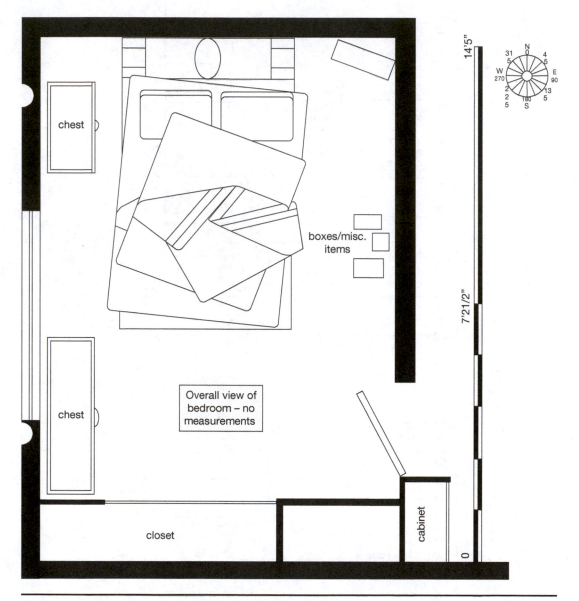

Figure 3-16. Crime scene diagram of bedroom with no evidence.

• If the crime scene is within a business facility, the sketcher should request a copy of the floor plan. If available, the floor plan is a useful tool because it typically displays room dimensions.

• If the crime scene rough sketch and final diagram must contain considerable detail, especially if the crime scene is large, it is advisable to assign personnel to concentrate on measurements and sketching.

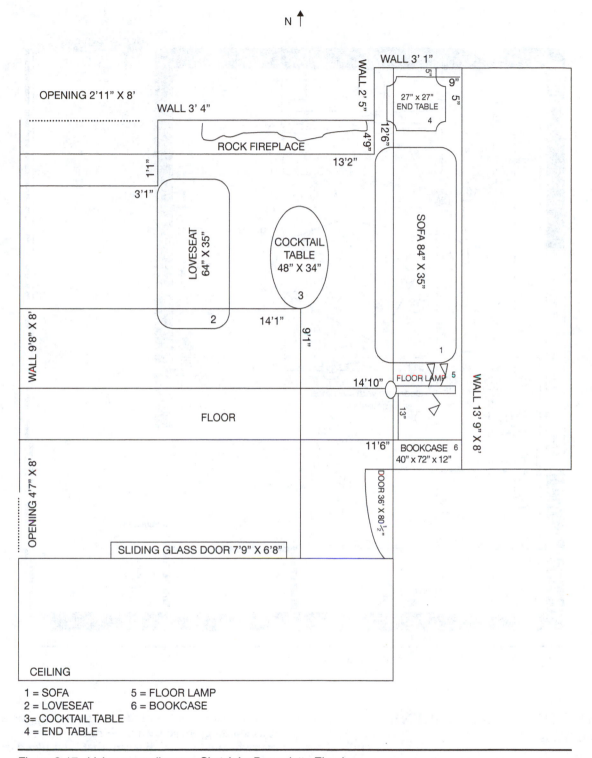

Figure 3-17. Living room diagram. Sketch by Bernadette Elander.

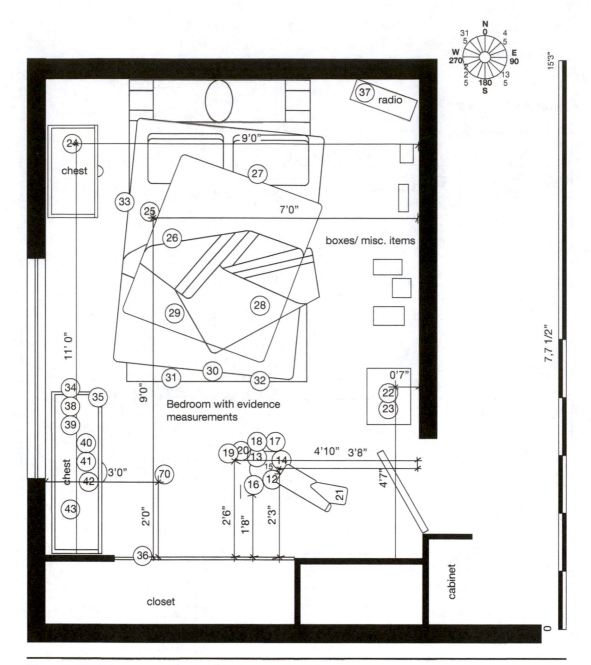

Figure 3-18. Crime scene diagram of bedroom with evidence.

THE FINAL CRIME SCENE DIAGRAM

A *final crime scene diagram* (finished sketch) is prepared from the rough sketch produced at the scene. Final crime scene diagrams may be created by hand with graph paper, a straight edge, templates, and pencils. As discussed earlier, multiple diagrams are often required for large crime scenes. Prosecuting attorneys may wish to include only specific evidence items on a finished diagram so the jury is not overwhelmed with a diagram that is cluttered or confusing.

With the aid of new technology, creating a finished crime scene diagram is faster, easier, more precise, and professional in appearance. Most law enforcement agencies today utilize computers and specialized software to create a finished diagram.

Final Diagram: Required Information

The final crime scene diagram should contain the following information:

- case number,
- type of crime,
- location of crime,
- date of crime,
- name of victim and/or suspect,
- name of sketcher and sketcher's identification number,
- date diagram was prepared,
- scale and disclaimer of *Not to Scale*. A defense attorney may challenge the sketcher during testimony. Technically, only trained experts such as engineers or architects are qualified to prepare scale drawings,
- evidence items are identified numerically,
- nonevidence items, such as furniture, are identified alphabetically,
- legend (or table) that includes all evidence items listed numerically and nonevidence items listed alphabetically. A brief description of each item accompanies its number or letter.

Computer-Aided Drawing (CAD) Programs

Many *CAD programs* designed to produce a finished crime scene diagram are commercially available. The sketcher need not be an artist. Utilizing the computer program, multiple diagrams or layers of a crime scene can be created with relative ease. If a prosecuting attorney requires specific detail in the diagram, the request can be honored.

Most CAD programs contain a quick-draw feature that allows the sketcher to start the drawing at a specific point, and enter measurement and line direction data through the computer's keyboard. The sketcher outlines the perimeter of the scene, adding lines and measurements, simply by inputting instructions via the keyboard. Freehand drawing is eliminated and the outline of the scene is created quickly.

Many CAD programs also include automated indoor and outdoor crime scene templates and illustrations for items such as vehicles, bodies, furniture, landscapes, and other visual representations. The dimensions of these items can be entered for true-to-scale representation. Using the computer software, arms and legs can be adjusted to display the correct positioning of a body at a crime scene. Layering features are available to illustrate multiple layers of the scene, such as an overall view of the scene without evidence, with overlays that include evidence and measurements.

Although many CAD programs are available, popular examples include the following:

Crime Zone—www.cadzone.com
Microsoft Office Visio—www.office.microsoft. com/en-us/visio
Smart Draw—www.smartdraw.com

SUMMARY

The crime scene diagram is essential in criminal investigation. Although it does not replace photographs, it is an equally important aspect of crime scene documentation. It is through the diagram that the exact location of evidence items and measurements of the crime scene are documented. The measurements are crucial to the investigation, crime scene reconstruction, and to judicial inquiry. The scene diagram is used by investigators, prosecutors, defense attorneys, witnesses, jurors, judges, and other participants in the judicial process. The diagram is used by investigators to question suspects and illustrate how suspect statements relate to the evidence. It is used by criminalists to reconstruct events, by forensic technicians to write a report on the description of the crime scene, by prosecutors as a display for the jury, and by witnesses to complement testimony.

Proper equipment and supplies are necessary to create accurate sketches at an incident scene.

In most cases, a measuring tape, paper, pencil, and an eraser are sufficient. Other cases may require a GPS device or sophisticated surveying equipment.

The type of diagram drawn depends on the scene. An overhead (bird's-eye) view diagram is the most common. The scene is viewed from a two-dimensional perspective. An elevated (exploded) view diagram may be necessary to document evidence on vertical surfaces. A blowup view diagram may be used to document evidence on vertical surfaces or enlarge views of evidence such as bloodstain patterns.

The measuring techniques applied depend on the location of the evidence items and available fixed points or surfaces (e.g., walls, streets, and buildings) from which to measure. Common measuring techniques include the coordinate (x, y), baseline, transecting baseline, triangulation, and the polar (radial) methods.

KEY TERMS

Define, describe, or explain the importance of each of the following:

baseline sketch method
blowup diagram
coordinate sketch method (rectangular coordinate method)
cross-projection (exploded view) diagram

elevation diagram
overhead (bird's-eye) view diagram
polar (radial) sketch method
total station

transecting baseline sketch method
triangulation sketch method

DISCUSSION AND REVIEW QUESTIONS

1. Explain the coordinate measuring method.
2. What is an exploded view sketch?
3. When is the polar (radial) measuring method used?
4. What is the most common type of sketch?
5. How is a vehicle illustrated in a crime scene?
6. What is included in a final diagram?
7. When is a GPS device used?
8. Should a sketcher rely on another person to obtain measurements of the scene?
9. What is a blowup sketch and when should it be created?
10. What measurements are necessary to accurately depict the location of a body in a crime scene?

CASE STUDY—Scott Peterson

On Christmas Eve, 2002, fertilizer salesperson Scott Peterson reported his wife, Laci, missing from his Modesto, California, home. Laci was pregnant with their unborn son, Conner. Scott held press conferences and an area-wide search for Laci commenced. Scott initially stated that he was golfing the day Laci disappeared, but later stated he was fishing from his boat at the Berkeley Marina.

Inconsistencies in Scott's statements led police to suspect him in Laci's disappearance. By mid-January 2003, evidence surfaced that Scott engaged in extramarital affairs, including a relationship with message therapist Amber Frey. Amber contacted the police when she learned that she was dating the husband of the missing Laci Peterson. According to Frey, Scott stated that he "lost" his wife 15 days before Laci actually disappeared.

On April 14 and 15, respectively, Conner's fetus and Laci's torso washed ashore in San Francisco Bay, north of the Berkeley Marina where Scott reported he was fishing on the day of Laci's disappearance. The medical examiner could not determine cause of death, but noted that Laci suffered broken ribs prior to her death.

Authorities searched the Peterson home as well as Scott's truck, boat, fertilizer warehouse, and tool box. A single hair believed to be Laci's was discovered in a pliers recovered from the boat.

On April 18, 2003, police arrested Scott in a golf course parking lot in La Jolla (San Diego), California. Scott had grown a goatee and had it and his hair dyed blond. At the time of his arrest, Scott was in possession of nearly $15,000 in cash, camping equipment, four cell phones, credit cards belonging to his family, his brother's driver's license, and a map to Amber Frey's workplace. Police considered Scott's appearance, possessions, and proximity to Mexico as evidence of consciousness of guilt, suspecting that Scott intended to flee into Mexico.

Through the various searches, the police also discovered:

- a homemade cement anchor in Peterson's recently purchased boat that was located in his fertilizer warehouse; prosecutors hinted that Scott constructed a similar anchor to dispose of Laci's body;
- freshly dried cement near the Peterson home driveway;
- a tan tarp that had been drenched in gasoline in Peterson's backyard shed. The prosecutors noted that gasoline can destroy biological material, such as blood and DNA.

Scott Peterson's trial began in June 2004. The case against Scott was based on circumstantial evidence. In addition to the evidence discussed previously, evidence such as taped telephone conversations with Amber Frey and the testimony of a less than adequate defense expert led to a jury finding of guilt on November 12, 2004. Scott was convicted of first-degree murder with special circumstances for Laci's death. He was also convicted of murder in the second degree for the death of his unborn son, Conner. The jury recommended the death penalty.

1. What crime scene sketches are necessary?
2. What should be included in the crime scene sketches?

LAB EXERCISES

Crime Scene Sketching

Equipment and supplies required per student:

one 24 foot measuring tape
five sheets of 8½″ × 11″ graph or plain paper
one pencil with eraser
one clipboard or hard writing surface
one roller tape (if available)
one laser measuring device (if available)
one compass

Exercise #1—Create an overhead (bird's-eye) view of a parking lot
1. Create an overview (bird's-eye view) of a portion of a parking lot.
2. Include two complete horizontal and two complete vertical parking rows in your illustration. If a row is longer than 15 stalls, illustrate 15 stalls only.
3. Measure and sketch the length and width of one standard parking stall and one handicapped stall (if available). Also measure and include loading zones next to handicapped stalls (if available).
4. Measure and sketch walkways and stairs next to the parking lot. Include trees and utility poles next to the parking rows and walkways.
5. Include five vehicles parked in the selected rows and measure the vehicles in place.
6. Measure all the parking rows in place.
7. Include a directional arrow and a legend in your sketch.
8. Create a final diagram from the rough sketch.

Exercise #2—Create a cross-projection (exploded view) sketch of a room
1. Create a cross-projection (exploded view) sketch of a room, such as a classroom or a room within a residence.
2. Include an overhead view of the floor plan with all major furniture items.
3. Explode at least one wall that contains a door or window.
4. Explode (attach) the ceiling to the exploded wall and include any ceiling fixtures (fans or lights) in the sketch.
5. Indicate all furniture items, windows, and doors in the sketch.
6. Include a north arrow and a legend.
7. Create a final diagram from the rough sketch.

WEB RESOURCES

American Board of Criminalistics: www.criminalistics.com
California Association of Criminalists: www.cac-news.org
Association for Crime Scene Reconstruction: www.acsr.org
International Association of Crime Analysts: www.iaca.net
The Forensic Science Society: www.forensic-science-society.org.uk
Canadian Society of Forensic Science: www.csfs. ca
Midwestern Association of Forensic Scientists: www.mafs.net
Northeastern Association of Forensic Scientists: www.neafs.org
Northwest Association of Forensic Scientists: www.nwafs.org
Southern Association of Forensic Scientists: www.southernforensic.org
Southwestern Association of Forensic Scientists: www.swafs.us
Crime Scene Investigation: www.crime-scene-investigator.net

4

Physical Evidence Collection and Analysis

LEARNING OUTCOMES

After completing this chapter, the reader should be able to:

- define physical evidence,
- demonstrate proper techniques for packaging and securing physical evidence,
- conduct a presumptive blood test,
- demonstrate proper techniques for collecting blood and evidence control samples,
- fold paper to form a bindle for trace evidence collection,
- create a sheath for a sharp evidence item, such as a knife,
- explain the difference between class and individual characteristics of evidence,
- describe the proper steps for collecting and processing a questioned document,
- describe the uses of a forensic alternate light source (ALS),
- collect hairs and fibers with a trace evidence lift,
- complete a descriptive evidence report.

INTRODUCTION

As defined in Chapter 1, evidence is used to prove or disprove a disputed fact. Criminal evidence is used to prove, beyond a reasonable doubt, that a crime was committed and that the defendant is the perpetrator. The essential elements of a crime must be demonstrated through facts, circumstances, statements, and information related to that crime. The prosecution must place the defendant, the suspect in the crime, in contact with the crime scene and the victim. The prosecution must identify persons involved in the crime and corroborate the testimony of a victim or witness. The existence of substantial incriminating evidence often leads to a guilty plea by the defendant, limiting the number of cases that actually proceed to trial.

To maintain the integrity of physical evidence for presentation in court, its collection, preservation, transportation, and analysis must be methodical and follow constitutionally and legally permissible processes. These processes are often contrary to fictional forensic science dramas viewed on television. This chapter focuses on proper physical evidence collection techniques. Emphasis is placed on the generally accepted step-by-step process for physical evidence collection and preservation. Readers should consult with local agency personnel for jurisdiction-specific protocols. Further, all forensic science professionals should continue their discipline-related training and education to ensure currency in the field.

CHARACTERISTICS OF PHYSICAL EVIDENCE

The value of each evidence item is dependent upon its characteristics and relationship to the crime. Most physical evidence is associated with a group of similar items with the same or similar properties known as **class characteristics** (Fisher, 2004). Class characteristics of evidence are those characteristics that are common among similar items. For example, two pairs of blue Nike size-12 men's running shoes have the same brand, size, and tread appearance on the sole. These similarities are class characteristics. However, the longer the running shoes are used, the more individual characteristics will appear on them.

> **Class characteristics**
> Physical evidence that possesses the same or similar properties.

Individual characteristics of evidence are those that are unique to that item. If two people wear different shoes with the same class characteristics for a prolonged period of time, each person will create a different wear pattern (individual characteristics) on the sole of the shoe because each person walks differently. Additionally, if one walks across a piece of glass, a unique cut may be created in the sole of the shoe, which would be impossible to replicate in the same manner. These markings are examples of individual characteristics.

> **Individual characteristics** Those that are unique to the item. If two people wear shoes with the same class characteristics for a prolonged period of time, each person will create a different wear pattern (individual characteristics) on the soles of the shoes because each person's stride is unique. Additionally, if one walks across a piece of glass, a unique cut may be created in the sole of a shoe, which would be impossible to replicate in the same manner. These markings are examples of individual characteristics.

Depending on the type or category of evidence, individualization and identification is derived from the evidence available. The remainder of this chapter is devoted to the proper physical evidence collection methodology.

EVIDENCE COLLECTION AND PACKAGING

Crime laboratory accreditation guidelines articulate proper evidence collection and packaging techniques. The evidence collection and packaging techniques presented in this book are consistent with American Society of Crime Laboratory Directors/Laboratory Accreditation Board (ASCLD/LAB) and International Association of Identification (IAI) standards.

Evidence collection is a laborious and tedious task not often depicted accurately in forensic science-related television dramas. Realistic evidence collection may not be exciting to watch or perform, but it is one of the essential tasks performed by a forensic technician. Perishable evidence should be collected first.

Failure to follow approved procedures can be devastating to a criminal prosecution. A major urban city's DNA unit was closed in 2002 and its evidence unit audited due to possible contamination and misplaced evidence. Subsequently, many of the city's criminal court convictions were appealed. Convicted defendants sought new trials, citing the city's sloppy crime lab procedures. Challenged procedures are a crime laboratory's worst nightmare. Many crime laboratories are learning lessons from others'

mistakes as they seek accreditation and certification of their laboratories through ASCLD/LAB. Quality control is viewed as an essential function of crime laboratories today. Quality control and strict standards help to ensure that the guilty are convicted and the innocent are set free. Proper evidence collection and packaging reduces the chances of cross-contamination of evidence.

Cross-Contamination of Evidence

Cross-contamination of evidence may be one of the worst mishaps to occur in a criminal case. A large part of O.J. Simpson's defense in his murder trial was that the evidence from the crime scene was contaminated. Cross-contamination of evidence occurs when the biological or trace evidence from one evidentiary item

> **Cross-contamination of evidence** Occurs when the biological or trace evidence from one evidentiary item contacts and contaminates another piece of evidence, thus destroying the integrity, validity, and credibility of the evidence and its handlers.

contacts and contaminates another piece of evidence, thus destroying the integrity, validity, and credibility of the evidence and its handlers. This transference is based on the Locard Exchange Principle: when something comes into contact with something else, there is an exchange. Cross-contamination of evidence need not happen if proper evidence collection procedures are followed.

First, evidentiary items should always be packaged separately. Second, suspect and victim evidence should be processed separately. The forensic technician is cautioned to exchange contaminated gloves for clean protective (latex or vinyl) gloves between the collection and packaging of different blood evidence samples. Caution must also be exercised when using equipment at a crime scene. For example, setting a camera tripod in blood without protecting the tripod legs and subsequently using the same tripod to photograph a second evidence item may contaminate the second item. Following proper procedures in packaging evidence will also prevent cross-contamination of evidence.

Packaging Evidence

Strict guidelines should be followed when packaging biological evidence, such as blood, semen, vaginal secretions, perspiration, saliva, or hair.

1. The evidence should be completely dry prior to packaging. The evidence can be dried in a secure, sterile room in the crime laboratory. The evidence items should not be dried

together. The drying area should be steril-
ized after each use. If not practical to dry
evidence before packaging, the wet evidence
item may be laid on and rolled in butcher
paper and subsequently dried at the laboratory. Rolling in butcher paper helps prevent
cross-contamination.

2. Once dry, the evidence should be packaged
in paper, not plastic. Plastic provides a habi-
tat for the growth of bacteria that will consume and destroy biological evidence. The
only exception is clothing or other items
containing wet blood. These items should be
transported in plastic to the crime laboratory.
Otherwise, the blood can penetrate the
paper and contaminate other evidence items.
However, upon arrival at the crime lab, the
bloody evidence should be removed from
the plastic bag immediately and laid out to
dry on clean paper in a sterile area of the laboratory or on a clean evidence drying rack.

3. After the item is dried and properly packaged in paper, it is frozen in a long-term
storage container. Vials of blood are kept
refrigerated, not frozen.

The tools most commonly used for packaging
evidence are paper bags and sealing tape.

Virtually any piece of evidence can be placed
in the appropriately sized paper bag for storage,
as long as the bag was not used previously.
An ordinary paper bag can be used or paper
evidence bags with blank labels attached may
be purchased from a crime lab supply company.
The paper bag should be labeled with the following information:

case number,
type of crime,
name and identification number of collector,
date and time of collection,
item number,
brief description of the item.

After the evidence is placed in the bag, a piece
of packing tape or *evidence sealing tape* should be
placed along the fold of the bag. The date and
the collector's initials should be placed across the
seal. It is important that the initials extend from
the bag across the tape as proof that the evidence
bag has not been reopened.

If an evidence bag must be opened after sealing, the person opening the bag should carefully
cut near but not on the original seal. The original
seal must not be broken or cut. Some agencies
prefer that the cut is made at the bottom of the

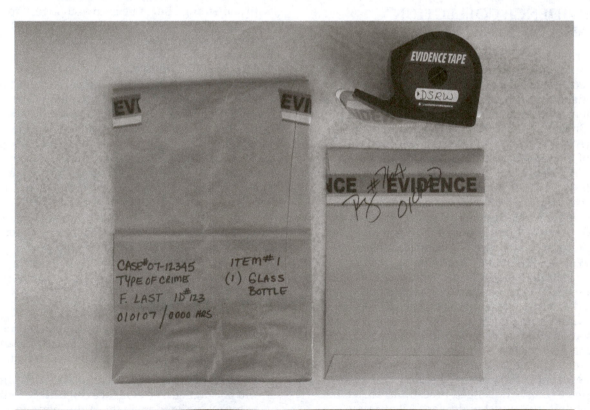

Photo 4-1. Evidence bags.

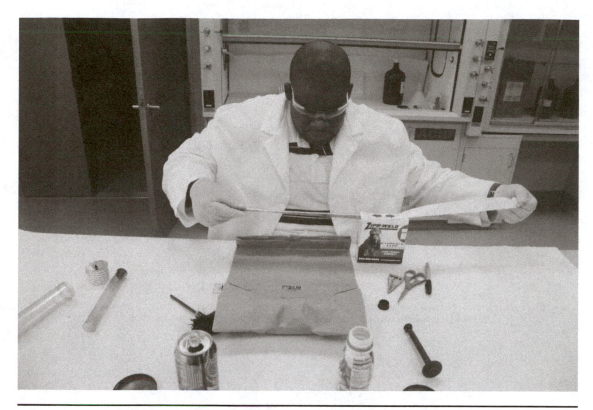

Photo 4-2. Forensic technician sealing an evidence bag. Photograph by Chris Nellis.

Photo 4-3. Signed seal of evidence bag.

bag. Caution must be exercised to ensure that the evidence item in the bag is not damaged. The evidence is removed, analyzed or processed, and returned to the original bag. A new seal is placed over the second cut. The second seal is dated and initialed. This process is repeated for subsequent openings. If no uncut area remains on the bag, a new bag should be used. The original bag is retained and packaged with the evidence in the new bag.

Small items of evidence, such as hair, fibers, or substances on swabs are placed in a **bindle** (druggist fold) before packaging. A bindle is a clean piece of paper that is folded in a manner that prevents damage to or destruction of the trace evidence item. A bindle can be constructed in the following manner:

> **Bindle** A bindle is a clean piece of paper that is folded in a manner that prevents damage to or destruction of a trace evidence item.

1. Wearing a pair of protective gloves, use a sterile knife or scissors to cut a sheet of clean 8½″ × 11″ paper into a square.
2. Fold the paper into a diamond shape.
3. Fold the bottom corners into the middle of the diamond.
4. Fold the bottom edge up and tuck in a top corner.
5. After the bindle is constructed, it should be unfolded. The evidence item is placed in the inside middle of the bindle. The bindle is refolded and placed in a paper bag or manila envelope, sealed, dated, and initialed. Bindles and packaging materials similar to bindles can also be purchased from a supply company.

1. Use a square-shape piece of paper and turn so it appears to be a diamond-shape.

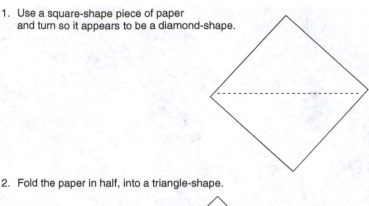

2. Fold the paper in half, into a triangle-shape.

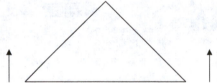

3. Fold the bottom corners in toward the center so the bottom is squared off.

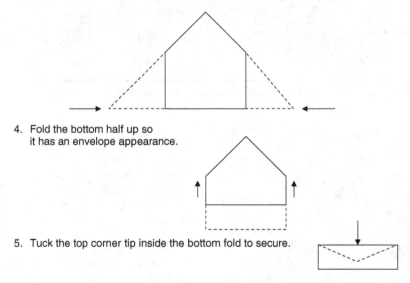

4. Fold the bottom half up so it has an envelope appearance.

5. Tuck the top corner tip inside the bottom fold to secure.

6. Unfold the bindle completely, place evidence in the center, and refold.

Figure 4-1. Bindle folding.

Clothing, bedding, or other evidence items that might contain trace evidence such as hair, fibers, or biological evidence should be dried in a sterile room in the laboratory and wrapped securely in clean, untouched paper, such as craft or *butcher paper*. The trailing end of the paper should be taped to the wrapping to secure the contents of the package. The packaged evidence is placed in a paper bag or a cardboard box and labeled for identification.

A thick plastic bag is used to package controlled substance evidence. After the substance is thoroughly dried and weighed, it is placed in the plastic bag and heat-sealed or sealed with tape if heat-sealing equipment is not available. The person packaging the evidence dates and initials across the seal. Details for collecting and packaging drug evidence are presented in Chapter 12.

When packaging currency or coins, a second person should be present to verify the amount of money placed in the package. Both parties date and initial the sealed bag. This protocol may vary among agencies, but two people are recommended to maintain the money's count integrity.

Large amounts of money are typically handled by detectives, with bank personnel assisting with the count.

Arson evidence typically contains flammable material or chemicals that can evaporate easily. Therefore, arson evidence should be packaged in an airtight container or clean, unused paint can that is manufactured for the purpose of arson evidence collection. The containers are specifically designed to prevent evaporation. The metal or glass containers are manufactured in various sizes. Some containers are manufactured with small openings in the lid for easy access to a sample of the contents. If the evidence is corrosive material, it should be placed in a nonmetallic container. After the evidence is placed inside the container, a rubber mallet is used to secure the lid. A seal should be placed across the container lid. The seal is dated and initialed. Case information can be printed directly on the container.

When packaging a sharp object, such as a knife, a plastic tube with a foam block or a box specifically designed to secure sharp objects can be used. A device provided inside the box is used to secure the item to prevent the sharp edge from puncturing the container.

However, sharp objects may also be packaged in paper bags or envelopes. After processing the sharp object for fingerprints and trace evidence, a container such as a *knife sheath* can be constructed and used to package the object. The sheath will prevent puncturing of the evidence bag as well as injury to others. This very important safety precaution should be followed when packaging sharp objects. A sheath is constructed from cardboard or several sheets of clean paper. The cardboard or paper is folded around the blade and the tip. Tape is placed over the edges of the cardboard or paper.

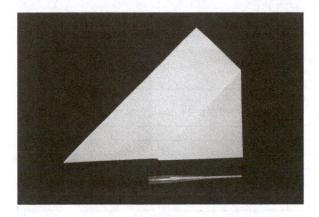

Photo 4-4.   Bindle and swab.

Photo 4-5. Arson can.

Many other types of containers are used for packaging evidence, including but not limited to small pill boxes, gun boxes, and other boxes with see-through windows or openings. See appendix **C** for a list of evidence packaging supplies and Websites of vendors.

Chain of Custody of Evidence

From point of collection to courtroom presentation, criminal justice system personnel must account for the custody of each item of evidence at all times. Many criminal court cases are dismissed or a defendant is acquitted because of defense claims that the evidence was not secured, was compromised, or was subject to tampering.

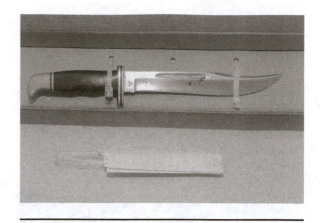

Photo 4-6. Knife inside knife box and knife in sheath.

ITEM	RECEIVED BY	ID NO.	TO	AUTHORIZED BY	DATE	ECA

REMARKS

CASE DISPOSITION:

☐ CASE ADJUDICATED _____   ☐ STATUTE OF LIMITATION
                                               EXPIRED _____

☐ AUTHORIZED BY CASE AGT/SGT_____

_____

EVIDENCE DISPOSITION:

AUCTION ☐ ITEM NO. _____ ECA _____ DATE _____

DESTROY ☐ ITEM NO. _____ ECA _____ DATE _____

Figure 4-2. Chain of custody form.

The **chain of custody of evidence** establishes who had custody of the evidence, on what date and at what time they came in contact with it, under what circumstances, and if any tests were conducted on the evidence. The chain of custody of evidence helps to establish that the evidence collected during an investigation is the same evidence that is submitted to the court (Fisher, 2004).

> **Chain of custody of evidence**
> Establishes who had custody of the evidence, on what date and at what time they came in contact with it, and under what circumstances, and if any tests were conducted on the evidence.

The first link in the chain of custody of evidence is established at the crime scene with the forensic technician. The forensic technician collects, packages, seals, labels, retains custody of, and transports the evidence to the crime laboratory to be processed and analyzed. The forensic technician should not leave the evidence unattended at any time during processing at the crime scene or during transportation to the crime laboratory. The evidence may be stored in a secure room at the crime laboratory or it can be secured (impounded) with the agency's property and evidence unit. Breaking the chain of custody

of evidence jeopardizes the integrity of the evidence and its admissibility evidence in court.

The Property and Evidence Unit

After a forensic technician collects and packages the evidence, it may be transported to a *property and evidence unit*. Property and evidence units are located in almost every law enforcement agency, especially in an agency with a crime laboratory. The unit oversees the custody and proper storage of all evidence for the agency. The unit contains appropriate evidence storage facilities, including refrigeration and freezer compartments. Few people have access to this unit. Access is limited to the employees and supervisor of the unit and the crime laboratory manager. Other persons who wish to enter the property and evidence unit must sign in, be approved for entry, and be escorted. This is an important link in maintaining the integrity and chain of custody of evidence.

Today, most property and evidence units use a computerized database to track evidence items. Barcode stickers are placed on evidence bags and the barcode is scanned into the database. In addition to scanning the barcode, a report is

Photo 4-7. Secured evidence lockers for overnight evidence storage, National City Police Department Property and Evidence Unit, National City, California.

Photo 4-8. Shelf of sealed evidence, National City Police Department Property and Evidence Unit, National City, California.

Photo 4-9. Shelves of sealed evidence, National City Police Department Property and Evidence Unit, National City, California.

Photo 4-10. Walk-in freezer containing sealed evidence, National City Police Department Property and Evidence Unit, National City, California.

Photo 4-11. Secured cage to house vehicles to be processed for evidence, National City Police Department Property and Evidence Unit, National City, California.

completed by each person submitting evidence to or removing evidence from the property and evidence unit. The report describes all the evidence that enters or leaves the unit.

BIOLOGICAL EVIDENCE

With the technological advancements in *DNA* analysis, a very small amount of biological evidence is required for a DNA profile. DNA is a double-stranded molecule held together by hydrogen bonds. It is the genetic material that makes up most living organisms, including human beings. It is found in cells throughout the entire human body, including cells in blood, hair, skin, saliva, perspiration, tears, vaginal and seminal fluid, tissues, and organs. DNA has been extracted from cigarette butts, brims of hats, stamps, the grips of handguns, clothing, and virtually any other surface or material onto which DNA is transferred. In some criminal investigations, the DNA collected is decomposed or deteriorated to some degree. However, with technological advancements in the extraction and analysis of DNA, a contributor profile is still possible.

Combined DNA Index System (CODIS)

With the advancements in DNA technology, cold (dormant) criminal cases are often solved and erroneous convictions reversed. In 1994, the DNA Identification Act (Public Law 103–322) authorized the FBI to establish a national DNA database known as the CODIS. Recovered biological evidence is entered into this database. A section of the database is known as the *forensic index*. It contains the DNA profiles retrieved from crime scene evidence.

Additionally, DNA samples are often taken from offenders who are arrested for major, especially violent, crimes. The DNA profiles from these samples are entered into the CODIS database known as the *offender index*. Forensic and offender indices are compared, possibly linking crime scenes and offenders (U.S. Department of Justice, Federal Bureau of Investigation, 2009).

Although DNA analysis is conducted by a criminalist, collection of DNA evidence is often accomplished by a forensic technician. The specifics of DNA analysis are beyond the scope of this book. However, procedures for locating, collecting, and preserving evidence subject to DNA analysis and profiling is discussed below.

Blood Evidence Collection

Many violent crime scenes contain blood evidence. Keen powers of observation are necessary to locate blood at a crime scene because blood may assume many different color shades depending on its condition and on the surface on which it is deposited. If dry, blood is typically reddish brown in color. However, if the blood is old or decomposed, it may appear grey or black in color. It may appear green if moisture is present in the blood. Blood may also change color if it comes into contact with metal or certain acidic surfaces. Blood may be difficult to locate, particularly at night. Outdoor scenes and dark pavement pose problems. A high-intensity flashlight is essential to locating blood at many scenes. Blood does not reflect light if a forensic ALS (a light using various light frequencies) is used. Rather, it appears dark, almost black in color.

Many types of liquids and other materials appear to be blood, but are not. Such items include ketchup, hot sauce and other food items, drinks such as coffee and soda, and biological evidence such as feces and plant material. To conserve documentation and collection time at a crime scene, questionable blood evidence is subjected to a presumptive blood test.

Presumptive Blood Test

A **presumptive blood test** is used to determine if a substance might be blood. A presumptive blood test does not confirm that a substance is blood, but a positive reaction leads the forensic technician to collect the evidence for further laboratory testing and possible DNA analysis.

> **Presumptive blood test** Test used to determine if a substance might be blood. A presumptive blood test does not confirm that a substance is blood.

A presumptive blood test is not conducted on substances that are obviously blood, such as bloodstains located next to a deceased, bloody victim. Obvious bloodstains are documented and collected regardless. However, a presumptive blood test should be conducted on *questionable substances*. For example, stains located near a toilet might be feces rather than blood. Stains located on clothing in laundry might be plant or food material. Yet, these stains should not be ignored. Blood-like substances present near a toilet and stains on clothing may be indicative of a suspect's attempt to clean bloody surfaces. Analysis of the scene will determine if collection is necessary. However, a presumptive blood test will aid the forensic technician to determine if sample collection is necessary.

When applied, a presumptive blood test will produce an immediate color change if the test

Technical Name	Common Name	Reaction Color	Other Remarks
• Benzidine	• Adler Test	• Blue to dark blue	• Recognized as carcinogen by OSHA
• The Hemastix Test	• Hemastix	• Dark green	• Very sensitive; may produce more false positives comparatively
• Leucomalachite Green (LMG)	• McPhail's Reagent or • Hemident	• Green	
• o-Tolidine or ortho-tolidine		• Blue	• Reported to be carcinogenic; active ingredient in Hemastix
• Phenolphthalein	• Kastle-Meyer Test	• Pink (bright)	• Found most specific for blood comparatively
• Tetramethylbenzidine	• TMB	• Green to blue- green	• Reported to be carcinogenic

Figure 4-3. Presumptive blood test chart.

produces a **positive reaction**. If there is no color change or the color change is not immediate (e.g., taking longer than a couple of seconds), the presumptive blood test produces a **negative reaction**, meaning it is not blood. The change in color depends on the test used (Figure 4-3).

Occasionally, a **false positive reaction** will occur, depending on the presumptive test used. A false positive is a color reaction that appears positive but, after confirmatory laboratory tests, the sample is determined to be something other than blood. Circumstances and materials that might produce a false positive reaction include the amount and quality of the sample, certain food products, plant material, and minerals. Animal blood will react positively to human blood presumptive blood tests. However, tests are available that are specific to human blood. Further, many types of presumptive blood tests used in the past are now considered unsafe and are recognized as carcinogens (cancer-causing agents) by the *Occupational Safety and Health Administration (OSHA)*.

Positive reaction
A presumptive blood test that produces an immediate color change indicating the presence of blood.

Negative reaction
A presumptive blood test that produces no immediate color change indicating the absence of blood.

False positive reaction A presumptive blood test in which the color reaction appears positive but, after confirmatory laboratory tests, the sample is determined to be something other than blood.

Figure 4-3 displays types of presumptive blood tests, the reactive color produced by each, and any additional information that is remarkable or relevant.

The most common presumptive blood tests used currently are Hemastix and phenolphthalein. Hemastix is highly sensitive, producing more false positives. Phenolphthalein is the most specific for blood, resulting in the fewest false positives (Spalding, 2005).

Presumptive blood tests should be administered according to the following procedure:

1. Place a drop of *distilled water* on a *sterile swab*. Distilled water is used to prevent contamination by foreign materials. Sterile swabs are used because they are individually wrapped and not contaminated.
2. Swab a small portion of the suspect substance, but not the entire stain.
3. Place the swab against the presumptive blood test. Do not place the presumptive blood test device against the original stain.
4. An immediate color change should occur if the reaction is positive.
5. If the reaction is negative, the *suspected blood stain* may be ignored. The presumptive test is simply a tool to determine if collection is necessary. However, all work and test results should be retained so a defense attorney cannot claim that the forensic technician or investigator hid results.

6. If the reaction is positive, an evidence number is assigned to the suspected blood and the stain is photographed and measured. Details for photography and measurements are presented in Chapter 2. In a report, the forensic technician should note that the suspected blood was collected because of the positive reaction.

7. The blood is collected and packaged, and the package is sealed and labeled for identification.

The following procedure applies when collecting blood evidence:

1. If the blood is wet, a sterile swab should be rotated in the stain, transferring the blood onto the swab. The swab should be dried thoroughly, packaged in a bindle or a swab container, and stored frozen.

2. If the blood is dry, the forensic technician should scrape the dried blood into a bindle. Alternatively, the technician can place a drop

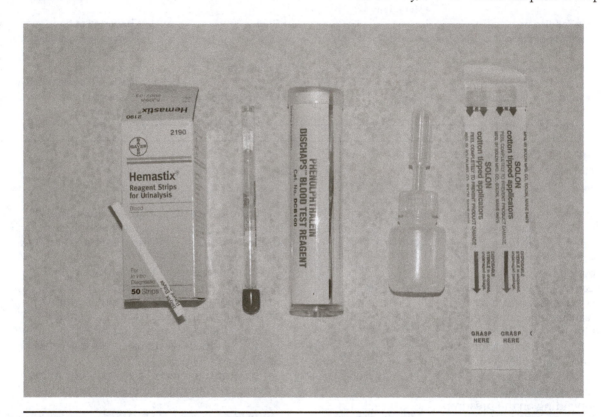

Photo 4-12. Presumptive blood testing supplies.

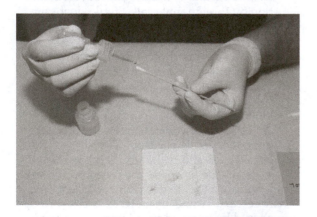

Photo 4-13. Presumptive blood testing with Hemastix.

Photo 4-14. Presumptive blood testing with Hemastix.

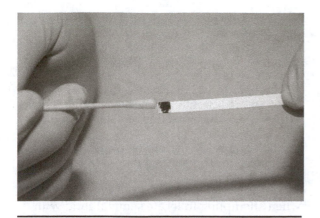

Photo 4-15. Presumptive blood testing with Hemastix.

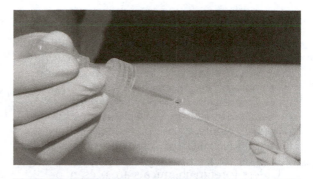

Photo 4-16. Blood collection using a sterile swab and distilled water.

Photo 4-17. Blood collection using a sterile swab and distilled water.

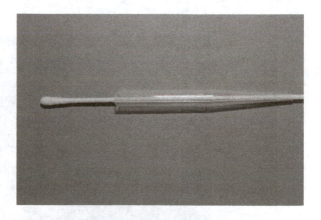

Photo 4-18. Swab and holder.

of distilled water on a sterile swab, swab the bloodstain, dry the swab thoroughly, and package the swab in a bindle or swab holder, and store frozen. The latter method is preferred by most criminalists. Again, distilled water must be used to prevent minerals from contaminating the blood evidence. A sterile swab is also essential to prevent contamination of the evidence.

3. If possible, a *control sample* should be taken from the area adjacent to the blood evidence. A control sample is collected in case the DNA analyst wishes to test the surface contaminants next to the bloodstain. The control sample is collected by following the same procedure used to obtain the blood evidence. Place a drop of distilled water on a sterile swab, swab an area adjacent to blood evidence, dry thoroughly, package in a bindle or swab container, and freeze. This evidence should be labeled as the *control sample* for the blood evidence.

Seminal Evidence Collection

One of the critical types of biological evidence sought in rape or child molestation cases is seminal fluid. This evidence may be located on a carpet, bedding, car seats, clothing, or on other surfaces. However, seminal evidence is difficult to view with the unaided eye. An alternate light source (ALS) is often required to view seminal evidence.

An **alternate light source (ALS)** is an illumination device that is used to locate evidence that cannot be observed with an unaided human eye. The ALS lamp emits light at various

Alternate light source (ALS) An illumination device used to locate evidence that cannot be observed with an unaided human eye.

frequencies inside as well as outside a human's visible spectrum. Depending on the light frequency used, various types of evidence can be observed because the ALS will cause the evidence item to *fluoresce* (glow). One must use a colored filter or colored glasses to observe and photograph the evidence at the different light frequencies. The light frequencies typically available in an ALS range from ultraviolet to infrared. The types of evidence that can be located and observed with an ALS include seminal fluid, fibers, fluorescent fingerprint powders, dye stains, chemicals, inks, erased writings, certain cosmetics, paints, dyes, bones, teeth, tattoos on burned bodies, nearly healed abrasions and bruises on skin, and many other objects.

Unless foreign chemicals are present or added, blood will darken, turning almost black in color, when illuminated with an ALS. Therefore, a bright flashlight or bright white light works best to observe patent (obvious, unobstructed, visible) blood at a crime scene.

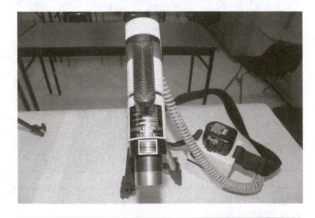

Photo 4-19. ALS.

Most ALS devices are equipped with a white light option. For seminal fluid, an ALS frequency with a 400 nanometer (nm) range is preferred, using yellow or orange goggles to view the evidence.

Photograph 4.22 depicts a ceramic tile with blood and red candle wax near the top of the tile. With an ALS, the blood appears dark, but the candle wax fluoresces.

Photograph 4.23 is clothing containing a seminal fluid stain. The seminal fluid fluoresces when an ALS is applied.

The following procedure is recommended when attempting to locate seminal fluid with an ALS:

1. With a bright white light, conduct a visual search for trace evidence such as hair, fibers, or biological evidence such as blood.
2. Adjust the ALS to 425 mm. With yellow goggles covering the eyes, hold the light source a few inches away from the suspected evidence and scan the evidence until a glow is observed. Seminal fluid glows a yellowish green color under this light frequency. If no seminal fluid is located, adjust the ALS to a higher frequency, such as 485 nm, and use orange goggles to view the evidence.
3. After the evidence is located, the substance should be photographed. See the section on *Photography of Latent Prints and Advanced Lighting Techniques* in Chapter 5.

Photo 4-20. ALS in use.

Photo 4-21. ALS in use.

Photo 4-22. Blood and candle wax viewed with ALS.

An *acid phosphatase* presumptive test for semen may be used if a suspected seminal substance is located. A presumptive test for semen is conducted in a manner similar to a presumptive blood test. The acid phosphatase test is not confirmatory for semen. Rather, it eliminates a substance that is not seminal fluid and it helps the forensic technician determine if further analysis or collection is necessary.

Photo 4-23. Semen stain viewed with ALS.

To conduct a presumptive seminal test and collect seminal fluid, the following procedure is recommended:

1. The forensic technician may conduct an acid phosphatase presumptive seminal fluid test prior to collecting the semen evidence. Wearing protective gloves, place a few drops of distilled water on filter paper that accompanies the presumptive test kit.

2. Place the moist filter paper on the questionable substance and hold in place for one minute. While the filter paper is on the substance, squeeze the two ampoules that are enclosed in the test tube until both break, emptying the contents into the test tube. Shake the test tube for one minute. One

should hold a finger against the lid of the tube to prevent test liquid leakage.

3. Remove the filter paper from the questioned substance. Remove the lid from the presumptive test tube and place the opening of the tube and its contents against the filter paper.

4. If the presumptive test turns a purple color within 30 seconds, it is a positive reaction. Note that the seminal presumptive test may not produce a color reaction immediately. If the color change occurs after 30 seconds, it is considered a negative reaction. If the reaction is positive, the evidence should be collected and submitted to the crime lab for confirmatory testing and DNA analysis. Some laboratories bypass the acid phosphatase presumptive test and require all evidence containing suspected seminal fluid to be analyzed in the laboratory.

5. If the suspected seminal fluid is on clothing or bedding, the entire item should be collected as evidence, dried, wrapped in clean paper, placed in a paper bag or cardboard box, and frozen. The entire evidence item will be subjected to DNA analysis.

6. If the suspected seminal fluid is located on the carpet or a car seat, the affected area should be removed, not swabbed. This procedure will ensure that the entire stain and a sufficient amount of DNA are collected. Approximately half of a person's genetic information is contained in a single sperm cell. Approximately 80 sperm cells are necessary to complete a comprehensive male DNA profile (Greenfield & Sloan, 2005). Therefore, a substantial amount of the suspect substance must be collected. The forensic technician should consult with the case investigator prior to removing carpet or car seat samples.

7. If the questionable substance is located on a hard, nonporous surface, such as a tile floor, the forensic technician should collect the substance in the same manner used to collect blood. Two drops of distilled water should be placed on a sterile swab and the suspect substance should be transferred completely to the swab. Using more than two drops of distilled water may dilute the substance. The swab should be dried, packaged in a bindle or swab holder, and frozen.

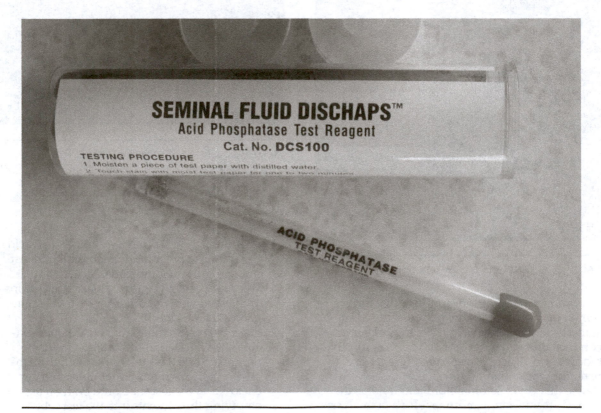

Photo 4-24. Presumptive semen test.

TRACE EVIDENCE COLLECTION

Trace evidence, such as hair and fiber evidence, is often overlooked at crime scenes. However, trace evidence may be crucial to a conviction. The city of San Diego,

> **Trace evidence**
> Evidence, such as hair or fibers, that may be destroyed or disappear if not collected immediately.

California, is very familiar with the importance of trace evidence because it was essential to the conviction of David Westerfield in the kidnapping and murder of seven-year-old Danielle Van Dam in 2002. Westerfield's preliminary hearing and trial were televised on local television channels as well as on CourtTV. Trace evidence in the case included a long, orange acrylic fiber found on the necklace Danielle was wearing at the time of her death. A criminalist from the San Diego Police Department offered testimony that this fiber was similar to fibers located in David Westerfield's sport utility vehicle as well as the laundry room in his home. Other fibers included short blue-gray fibers found on and around Danielle's body that were similar to those located in Westerfield's recreation vehicle. Danielle's body was discovered 25 miles from her home, weeks after she disappeared. Westerfield was convicted and sentenced to death.

Trace evidence is extremely fragile. It may be destroyed or disappear if not collected immediately. The search for trace evidence is an initial step at a crime scene. In cases such as kidnapping, sexual assault, or other crimes involving physical contact between the suspect and victim, trace evidence should be sought. The best tool for locating hairs is *oblique lighting,* a bright white light projected at an oblique angle (an angle of approximately 15 degrees from the surface). A bright flashlight or a white light from an ALS works well for this purpose. The recommended procedure for collecting trace hair and fibers includes the following:

1. If possible, the search area should be darkened. A bright light should be held at a low (15 degrees) angle to the surface. Scan the surface with the light source until hairs or fibers are observed. Some fibers can be located and observed only at different light frequencies. Therefore, an ALS should be used after using a bright white light source, adjusting the ALS to different frequencies.
2. If a hair or fiber is located, the forensic technician should collect the evidence with a protective-gloved hand or with a pair of sterile tweezers. Caution should be exercised when using gloved fingers to collect

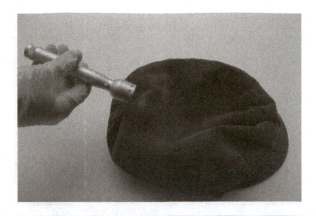

Photo 4-25. Demonstration of oblique lighting used to locate hairs on a hat.

the evidence because hairs and fibers often stick to the glove and are difficult to remove. Tweezers should be used gently, to ensure that the hair or fiber is not stretched in any way.
3. The hair or fiber should be placed in a bindle. The bindle is placed in a paper bag or manila envelope, sealed, and marked for identification. Hairs subject to examination for DNA should be frozen.
4. **Trace lifts** (clear packing tape, Handi-Lifts, or hinge lifters) are used on surfaces where hairs and fibers are not easily observed. The trace lift is pressed against and removed from the suspect surface, and placed

> **Trace lifts** Method of collecting evidence. Clear packing tape, Handi-Lifts, or hinge lifter used on surfaces where hairs and fibers are not easily observed.

on a clean backing. Manufactured trace lifts have the clean backing already attached to the adhesive lift. The backing is removed and the adhesive side of the lift is pressed against the suspect surface, causing hairs and fibers to adhere to the adhesive side. The tape is returned to the backing and the hairs and fibers are safely secured in the lift. The trace lift should be marked for identification (along the edge rather than in the middle of the lift), placed in a paper bag or manila envelope, sealed, and the bag or envelope should be marked for identification. The forensic technician should consult with the trace evidence criminalist for the preferred collection technique.
5. A trace evidence vacuum machine may be used if hairs or fibers are deeply embedded in the surfaces of the crime scene. The vacuum contains filter paper that traps all

Photo 4-26. Trace lift used to collect hairs and fibers from a subject's shoulder.

Photo 4-27. Trace evidence vacuum.

hairs, fibers, and debris vacuumed from the surface. The filter paper is sent to the trace evidence section of the laboratory for analysis. Based on the large volume of trace evidence collected by this method, it is not preferred by most trace evidence criminalists. The vacuum must be cleaned properly after each use to avoid cross-contamination of evidence.

Hairs and fibers may be carried from a crime scene. Because hairs and fibers are fragile in nature, they are typically given a high collection priority. Further, hair and fibers may be subjected to microscopic examination (viewing evidence with a microscope), IR spectroscopy (using IR light to view evidence), or refractive index examination (viewing evidence as light vibrates parallel and perpendicular to it).

Hairs and fibers are not the only types of trace evidence. Virtually any kind of evidence transported to or taken from a crime scene is considered trace evidence. This includes soil, paint

or wood chips, plaster fragments, parts of tools, and buttons. **Fracture match analysis** is used to compare fractured parts of a single item. For example, a questioned tool chip or part may be matched by a criminalist to a known tool.

> **Fracture match analysis** Comparison of fractured parts of a single item.

QUESTIONED DOCUMENT COLLECTION AND EXAMINATION

Questioned documents include suspect checks, contracts, wills, typewritten and handwritten letters, currency, postage stamps, event tickets, receipts, and virtually any other document of evidentiary value. Almost any document that contains handwriting or ink can be analyzed. Inks and paper can be analyzed along with the obliteration and erasure of the inks. Questioned document examination of forged writings is also common. Forgery has been practiced since writing was first used as a form of communication.

> **Questioned documents** Any document of evidentiary value, including suspect checks, contracts, wills, typewritten and handwritten letters, currency, postage stamps, event tickets, receipts, and virtually any other document of evidentiary value.

Albert Osborn testified as an expert witness in the Charles Lindbergh baby kidnapping trial. Osborn's book, *Questioned Documents*, contains methodologies for questioned document analysis that are still practiced. Questioned document examination can provide answers to the following queries: To whom does a signature belong? Is the document genuine? Who wrote the letter? When was the document typed? Is the document a forgery? What does the faded writing communicate? Has the writing been erased or obliterated? Is the writing indented? **Indented writing** is an impression on the document resulting from writing on a paper placed on top of the questioned document (Saferstein, 2007).

> **Indented writing** An impression on a document resulting from writing on a paper placed on top of the questioned document.

Questioned document examination involves procedures such as handwriting and signature comparison, keyboarding and printing device analysis, as well as assessments of alterations and obliterations on documents, suspected forgeries, photocopy manipulation, inks, and paper. Questioned document analysis is often necessary in cases involving fraud, forgery, insurance scams, robbery with a demand note, bomb threats, written communication from terrorists, kidnapping with demand or ransom notes, contract disputes, identity theft, anonymous letters, and extortion.

Questioned (forensic) document examiners do not evaluate a person's personality by analyzing their handwriting. This type of analysis is referred to as *graphology*. Most questioned document examiners refer to graphology as an art, not a science. Graphology is not conducted in forensic crime laboratories. Further, questioned document examiners cannot determine gender, age, race, or exact educational level from a handwriting sample.

To conduct a writing comparison, the questioned document examiner must compare writing exemplars of the suspected writer to the questioned document. If the questioned document is written in print or cursive, pen or pencil, the exemplar should be of the same format and writing instrument type. There are two categories of exemplars: a **nonrequested writing**, which is a spontaneous or undictated writing typically collected from the suspect's home or business;

> **Nonrequested writing** A spontaneous or undictated writing typically collected from a suspect's home or business.

and a **requested writing**, which is dictated writing (i.e., the suspect is told what to write). The suspect should never be allowed to view the questioned document before producing the requested writing.

> **Requested writing** Dictated writing (i.e., the suspect is told what to write).

Types of fraudulent writing include **freehand simulation** (an attempt to copy someone else's writing), **tracing** a signature or writing, and **normal hand forgeries**. With normal hand forgeries, suspects may use their own writing style or they may alter their style to deflect suspicion.

> **Freehand simulation** An attempt to reproduce another person's writing.

> **Tracing** A signature or writing.

Obliterated and erased writing can be detected with IR or UV light. Forensic document examiners typically use a video-spectral comparator (VSC) that allows IR and UR waves to be viewed.

> **Normal hand forgeries** With normal hand forgeries, suspects use their own writing style or they may alter their style to deflect suspicion.

Indented writing (impression left from pressure applied during writing on paper on top of

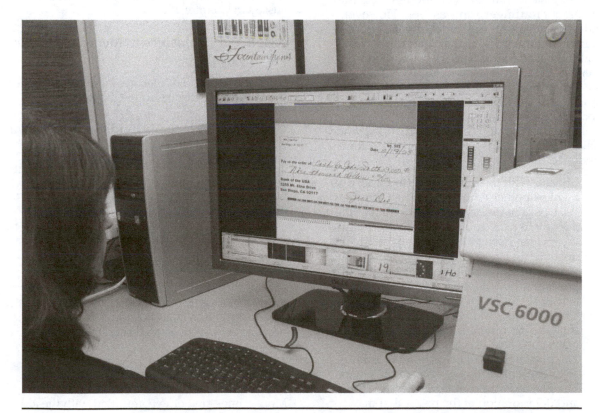

Photo 4-28. Forensic document examiner Marie Durina, San Diego county sheriff's crime laboratory, using the VSC.

Photo 4-29. ESDA located at the San Diego county sheriff's crime laboratory.

indented writing) can be identified with an *electrostatic detection apparatus (ESDA)* (Norwitch & Seiden, 2005). Using static electricity, the ESDA can recover indented writing several pages below the original writing.

A forensic technician usually collects questioned documents and transports them to the questioned document examiner for analysis. The forensic technician will often process the document for fingerprints as well. However, indented writing is destroyed during processing for fingerprints. Further, the solution in acetone-based ninhydrin, used to process documents for fingerprints, will liquify ink, causing the ink to blur. Therefore, fingerprint processing must not be conducted prior to questioned document analysis.

The following steps are recommended when collecting and processing questioned document evidence:

1. Consult with the questioned (forensic) document examiner who will conduct the analysis. Does the examiner wish to analyze the document prior to fingerprint processing?
2. Wear clean latex gloves when handling the document(s).
3. The document should be photocopied and photographed before processing for fingerprints.
4. Unless biological fluid (e.g., blood) is present, the document is best preserved in a plastic bag and sealed in a manila envelope. The plastic bag will help preserve amino acids present in fingerprints on the paper. The plastic bag also retards discoloration and deterioration of the paper that may occur when a document is stored in a paper envelope or bag.

5. Identifying case information should be written on the outside of the evidence container prior to placing the questioned document inside. Otherwise, one may create indented writing on the questioned document.

SPECIALIZED EVIDENCE COLLECTION AND ANALYSIS

Impression Evidence Collection and Analysis

Impression evidence at a crime scene includes footwear and tire impressions, tool marks, and marks on expended projectiles from a rifled firearm. Specific procedures that detail the photography, documentation, and collection of footwear, tire, and tool mark impression evidence are discussed at length in Chapter 9.

Firearm Evidence Collection and Analysis

Firearms are involved in approximately two-thirds of all homicides in the United States. The value of firearm evidence, including the type(s) of firearm(s) and ammunition involved, collection techniques, and trajectory analysis is discussed in Chapter 10.

Arson and Explosives Evidence Collection and Analysis

Specific arson and explosives evidence collection procedures are discussed in Chapter 7.

Controlled Substance Evidence Collection and Analysis

Toxicology (the analysis of toxins, controlled substances, and blood-alcohol content) is conducted by a criminalist in a crime laboratory. Blood or urine sample collection is accomplished by a forensic nurse or phlebotomist. The forensic technician is not typically involved in the collection of this type of evidence. However, forensic technicians do collect narcotics and other controlled substances at crime scenes. Therefore, a forensic technician must be able to recognize drugs and drug paraphernalia and conduct presumptive narcotic tests. Details are discussed in Chapter 12.

Computer Evidence Collection and Analysis

More crimes are being committed with the aid of a computer. In Chapter 7, forensic computer analysis is discussed along with the procedures for collecting computers and computer-generated evidence.

Friction Ridge Evidence Collection and Analysis

Friction ridge evidence is skin ridge detail from the hands and feet. Friction ridge evidence has been used longer than any other type of forensic evidence to identify criminal perpetrators. Friction ridge evidence recognition and collection techniques are discussed in Chapter 5.

DESCRIBING EVIDENCE IN REPORTS

Each item of evidence submitted to the property and evidence unit should be described in an evidence report. As discussed previously, the evidence bag or container is labeled with the evidence item number and a brief description of the bags or container's contents. In the accompanying evidence report, the description of the evidence item is more detailed. Any identifying and remarkable information regarding the evidence item should be included in the report. At a minimum, the evidence report should include the following information for each item:

item number
brand, make, or model (if any)
serial number (if applicable)
size
color
remarkable characteristics

When evidence is processed and analyzed, a follow-up processing report should be completed, describing the processing techniques used as well as the results of any analysis. The format for the follow-up processing report is based on each crime laboratory's policies and procedures. Some crime laboratories utilize forms with check-off boxes specifying the processing and testing procedures to be followed. Other crime laboratories require a narrative report format.

Regardless of the format utilized, the follow-up processing report should contain information such as case number, type of crime, location of crime, investigator's name, forensic technician's and analyst's names, the dates and times that processing and analysis occurred, methods used, the results of the analysis, and the chain of custody of the evidence. Additional information on report writing is presented in Chapter 15.

SUMMARY

Documentation, collection, preservation, and analysis of forensic evidence lie at the foundation of a forensic technician's job. If a material error is made in the process, the evidence may be inadmissible in court and the victim, the victim's family, and society will not be served. It is absolutely crucial that the forensic technician knows and adheres to guidelines established for the proper documentation and collection of evidence. The ASCLD/LAB was created to ensure that proper guidelines are established and publicized.

Agencies accredited by ASCLD/LAB require employees to follow the guidelines.

In this chapter, the discussion focused on guidelines for collecting, preserving, packaging, sealing, and documenting evidence. Though some requirements may vary among agencies, adherence to established procedures is critical. Those who come in contact with evidence are responsible and accountable for ensuring that all evidence is properly managed and that chain-of-custody rules are followed.

KEY TERMS

Define, describe, or explain the importance of each of the following:

Alternate light source (ALS)	false positive reaction	normal hand forgery
bindle	fracture match analysis	positive reaction
class characteristics (of evidence)	freehand simulation	presumptive blood test
chain of custody of evidence	indented writing	questioned document
	individual characteristics (of evidence)	requested writing
cross-contamination of evidence	negative reaction	trace evidence
	nonrequested writing	trace lift
		tracing

DISCUSSION AND REVIEW QUESTIONS

1. What is chain of custody of evidence?
2. What is cross-contamination of evidence?
3. What information should be included on an evidence bag or container?
4. What is the difference between class and individual characteristics of evidence?
5. What is the purpose of a presumptive blood test?
6. What are some of the applications of a forensic/alternate light source?
7. Should biological evidence be packaged in plastic? Why or why not?
8. What is the difference between a questioned (forensic) document examination and graphology?
9. What is the difference between a freehand simulation and a normal hand forgery?
10. Explain why one must conduct indented writing analysis prior to processing a document for fingerprints?

CASE STUDY—O.J. SIMPSON

Late in the evening of June 12, 1994, Nicole Brown Simpson, the ex-wife of O.J. Simpson, and Nicole's friend, Ronald Goldman, were found fatally stabbed outside Brown's Bundy Drive condominium in the Brentwood area of Los Angeles. Subsequently, O.J. Simpson was charged in connection with the killings. Simpson pled *not guilty* and his 134-day televised murder trial began on January 25, 1995.

The prosecution called dozens of expert witnesses on subjects such as DNA profiling, bloodstain pattern analysis, and shoe prints. Evidence against Simpson included blood droplets found at his home that matched Brown's and Goldman's. An LAPD criminalist testified that results of DNA analyses of blood drops found at the crime scene revealed that the blood was Simpson's, placing Simpson at his ex-wife's condominium at the time of the killings.

During cross-examination by the defense, it was learned that the forensics person who collected the blood samples from Simpson that were compared with blood evidence from the crime scene was actually a trainee who carried the vial of Simpson's blood in his lab coat pocket for nearly a day before submitting it to the crime lab. The defense argued that Simpson was the victim of sloppy investigative procedures.

On October 3, 1995, after deliberating nearly three hours, the trial jury returned a verdict of *not guilty*. During posttrial interviews, a few jurors suspected that Simpson committed the murders, but they believed the police and the prosecution bungled the case, thus creating reasonable doubt.

1. How should blood samples be collected and transported? How soon after collection should the samples be secured in a crime lab or police evidence facility?
2. How can a forensic technician ensure that evidence collection and preservation procedures are not challenged in a judicial proceeding?
3. How do chain-of-custody errors help to produce reasonable doubt?

LAB EXERCISES

Evidence Collection and Packaging

Equipment and Supplies Required Per Student
one Hemastix
one bottle of distilled water (water need not be distilled if practice exercise)
three sterile swabs
one tape lift or Handi-Lift
one pair of disposable tweezers
four bindles (students may make their own)
one 8½" × 11" sheet of paper (for sheath)
one 2ft × 2ft sheet of butcher (craft) paper (to wrap clothing)
six small-sized paper bags
one medium-sized paper bag
one large-sized paper bag
one large-sized manila envelope
one gallon reclosable plastic bag
two pairs of clean latex or vinyl gloves
one roll evidence sealing tape or packing tape
one marking pen

"Evidence" to package
one article of clothing per student
one tile with blood (or blood substitute) on its surface (students can share). Blood can be

obtained (by the instructor) using a diabetic blood tester if no other source is available
one soda can
one plastic disposable knife

Exercise #1—Presumptive blood test; blood collection and packaging
1. Students share a blood-stained tile. Each should wear protective gloves.
2. Each student conducts a presumptive blood test using the Hemastix. Follow the instructions presented in this chapter.
3. Swab a blood (or blood substitute) stain and obtain a control swab following the instructions in this chapter. Place each swab in a separate bindle.
4. Package both bindles together in a small paper bag.
5. Label the bag with the case information provided by the instructor. Seal and label the bag for identification.

Exercise #2—Packaging soda can
1. Each student will grasp a soda can, transferring latent fingerprints to the can.
2. Cover hands with clean protective gloves.
3. Use a swab containing one or two drops of distilled water to swab the mouth opening of the can for DNA material.
4. Place the DNA swab in a bindle, properly package the bindle in a small paper bag, seal the bag, and label for identification.
5. Package the soda can in a medium paper bag, seal, and label for identification. The soda can will be used later in the latent fingerprint processing laboratory.

Exercise #3—Packaging bloody, sharp knife
1. Using paper, each student will create a knife sheath. Assume that the knife has been processed for DNA material and latent fingerprints prior to packaging.
2. Package the knife in a small bag, seal, and label for identification.

Exercise #4—Trace evidence collection
1. Students work in pairs to obtain hairs and fibers from one another using a protective-gloved hand, tweezers, and tape lift. Collect hairs from your partner's back, not the front. Do not remove clothing in the process.
2. Using the gloved hand and tweezers, place the hairs collected in a single bindle, package the bindle in a paper bag, seal, and label for identification.
3. Compress the tape lift to your student partner's back, remove, and place the tape onto a clear backing. Place the tape lift in a small manila envelope or paper bag, seal, and label for identification.

Exercise #5—Packaging "bloody" clothing
1. Each student should wrap a piece of clothing in craft paper, place the wrapped clothing in a large paper bag, seal, and label the bag for identification.

Exercise #6—Packaging a demand note
1. Each student will write a "demand note" and place it in a reclosable plastic bag.
2. Label a manila envelope for identification prior to placing the demand note inside to prevent indented writing on the demand note.
3. Place the reclosable plastic bag containing the demand note inside the manila envelope, seal, and label for identification.

WEB RESOURCES

DNA Resource Websites:
    Armed Forces Institute of Pathology: www.atip.og
The Joint POW/MIA Accounting Command Central Identification Laboratory: www.jpac.pacom.mil
International Association of Crime Analysts: www.iaca.net
The Forensic Science Society: www.forensic-science-society.org.uk
Canadian Society of Forensic Science: www.csfs.ca
Midwestern Association of Forensic Scientists: www.mafs.net

Northeastern Association of Forensic Scientists: www.neafs.org
Northwest Association of Forensic Scientists: www.nwafs.org
Southern Association of Forensic Scientists: www.southernforensic.org
Southwestern Association of Forensic Scientists: www.swafs.us
The President's DNA Initiative: www.dna.gov
International Association for Microanalysis: www.iamaweb.com

5

Fingerprint Classification and Processing

LEARNING OUTCOMES

After completing this chapter, the reader should be able to:

- identify three basic fingerprint patterns and their subcategories,
- explain the purpose of the Automated Fingerprint Identification System (AFIS),
- articulate the role of pre-transfer, transfer, and post-transfer in the recovery of latent fingerprints,
- demonstrate the ability to process and lift a fingerprint using standard black and magnetic powders,
- demonstrate the ability to photograph a fingerprint.

INTRODUCTION

A fingerprint is a print or impression caused by the friction ridges of a finger. A **friction ridge** is the raised portion of a human's epidermis on digits (fingers and toes), palmer (palms), or plantar (foot sole) skin. Personal identification through the friction ridge of the fingers, palms, and feet has been accepted as evidence in court proceedings for nearly a century. In 1911, an Illinois court was the first to recognize the validity and reliability of print evidence (Southern California Association of Fingerprint Officers, 1998). Subsequently, friction ridge evidence survived scrutiny in numerous court proceedings and has proven to be reliable evidence. Latent print examiners (LPEs) are respected in the courtroom and their profession is recognized as a specialty within the field of forensic science.

A **fingerprint** is created when contaminants (e.g., natural secretions, ink) are transferred from the peaks of friction ridges to a relatively smooth surface (e.g., firearm, bottle, fingerprint card). Using the fingerprints of a human's 10 fingertips (digits), the prints may be classified, providing a unique individualized personal identifier.

A **latent fingerprint** is one that is observable after being processed with a powder or chemical. *Latent* means hidden or concealed. Latent prints are retrieved from evidence or crime scenes.

> **Friction ridge** The raised portion of a human's epidermis on digits (fingers and toes), palmar (palms) or plantar (foot sole) skin.

> **Fingerprint** Created when contaminants (e.g., natural secretions, ink) are transferred from the peaks of friction ridges to a relatively smooth surface (e.g., firearm, bottle, fingerprint card). Using the fingerprints of a human's 10 fingertips (digits), the prints may be classified, providing a unique individualized personal identifier.

> **Latent fingerprint** A fingerprint that is observable after processing with a powder or chemical.

LATENT PRINT EXAMINER EDUCATION AND TRAINING

The education, training, and job requirements of the LPE vary among agencies. Some LPEs are sworn peace officers or forensic technicians who receive advanced training and perform numerous tasks related to latent print comparison. Others begin their careers as interns or aides in latent print units. The latter are mentored by seasoned professionals until they develop the skills of an expert LPE. Some possess a bachelor's degree in criminal justice or related field, while others complete some college but hold no degree. Some LPEs respond to crime scenes and autopsies to process fingerprints. Others examine evidence items in the laboratory to identify and collect latent fingerprints. Still other LPEs limit their activities to searching fingerprint databases to locate and compare prints.

Regardless of the personal background, each LPE should receive continuous training and mentoring from more experienced examiners. Advanced courses that address complex techniques are recommended as well. Training in courtroom testimony is also helpful. Many LPEs, testifying in court as experts, face Daubert challenges (see Chapter 1).

To upgrade skills, the LPE may attend seminars and conferences relevant to the field. The LPE may also obtain memberships in professional organizations. The Southern California Association of Fingerprint Officers (SCAFO) is one such professional organization. Another is the Scientific Working Group on Friction Ridge Analysis, Study and Technology (SWGFAST), established by the FBI in 1997 to assist LPEs with providing the highest-quality service to the criminal justice system.

The International Association for Identification (IAI) offers a certification program for print examiners. To obtain the IAI title of *Certified Latent Print Examiner (CLPE)*, the applicant must submit the courtroom testimony and charted fingerprint enlargements of an actual case completed by the LPE to the IAI Latent Print Certification Board. In addition, the applicant must provide evidence of good moral character, high ethical standards, and professional standing, and must meet the following application requirements:

- Have a minimum of 80 hours of formal training in latent print matters.
- Have a minimum of two years of full-time experience in the comparison and identification of latent print material and related matters.
- Have a bachelor's degree plus two years of full-time latent print experience or an associate degree (or documentation of 60 semester or 90 quarter units of college credit) and three years of full-time experience as an LPE or four years of full-time experience as an LPE.
- Provide two letters of reference from supervisors or professionals in the field of forensic science. The letters must accompany the application.
- Submit an application fee.

If the application is accepted by the IAI certification board, the applicant must pass an eight-hour, three-part written examination as well as an oral board review consisting of the following:

Part A. Comparison of 15 latent prints with inked prints. Must correctly identify 12 of the latent prints. Passing score: 80 percent.

Part B. Pattern interpretation of 35 inked impressions. Passing score: 90 percent.

Part C. True/false and multiple choice questions relative to the history of fingerprints, pattern interpretation, and latent prints. Passing score: 85 percent.

If the applicant has not presented expert testimony in a court of law, the applicant is required to undergo questioning before a board. The oral board addresses latent prints, inked prints, charted enlargements, and court-qualifying interrogatories.

Upon successful completion of the application and testing process, certification is granted for five years. Subsequently, the CLPE may apply for recertification (International Association for Identification, 2008).

Although preferred, certification as an LPE is not an industry standard currently. Yet, periodic proficiency testing of LPEs helps to ensure validity, reliability, and consistency. Documented proficiency testing may also help defend against Daubert challenges when testifying in court.

For details on LPE certification, contact the IAI at http://www.theiai.org.

FINGERPRINT PATTERNS AND CLASSIFICATION BASICS

Fingerprint classification involves the application of a process of individualization to the prints of a human's 10 fingers. The resulting classification is a unique identifier. The process for classifying fingerprints is time-consuming, is extremely detailed, and requires extensive training. Thus, a detailed account of fingerprint classification technique is beyond the scope of this book. However, the forensic technician should be familiar with fingerprint patterns and the basics of fingerprint classification. Fundamental knowledge helps one to appreciate the need to collect fingerprints that are classifiable.

> **Fingerprint classification** The application of a process of individualization to the prints of a human's ten fingers.

In the commonly used Henry system of classification, three basic types of fingerprint patterns exist. Each type contains general characteristics (arch, loop, or whorl) as well as subcategories. The basic fingerprint pattern types and their subcategories include the following:

Arch (5 percent of all fingerprints)
   a. plain arch
   b. tented arch
      1. angular tented arch
      2. upthrust tented arch
      3. loop type tented arch
Loop (65 percent of all fingerprints)
   a. radial loop
   b. ulnar loop
Whorl (30 percent of all fingerprints)
   a. plain whorl
   b. central pocket loop whorl
   c. double loop whorl
   d. accidental whorl

Regardless of the basic fingerprint pattern type, each contains ridge formations. A **ridge formation (minutiae)** is a characteristic observed in all types of fingerprints. Ridge formations include the following (Figure 5.1):

Ridge formation (minutiae) A characteristic observed in all types of fingerprints.

FINGERPRINT MINUTIAE

1.	Short Ridge	14.	Bifurcation
2.	Bifurcation	15.	Bifurcation
3.	Bifurcation	16.	Island
4.	Bifurcation	17.	Island
5.	Bifurcation	18.	Bifurcation
6.	Ridge	19.	Bifurcation
7.	Ending Ridge	20.	Ending Ridge
8.	Bifurcation	21.	Dot
9.	Bifurcation	22.	Ridge
10.	Ridge	23.	Island
11.	Ending Ridge	24.	Island
12.	Ridge	25.	Ending Ridge
13.	Short Ridge		

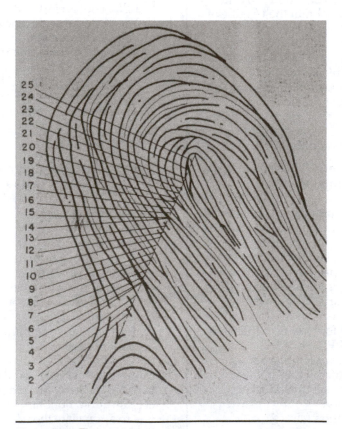

Figure 5-1. Fingerprint minutiae.

- short ridge,
- bifurcation,
- ending ridge,
- island,
- dot.

Arch

A fingerprint with a **plain arch fingerprint pattern** contains ridge flow that enters the pattern area at one end, flows upward slightly in a wavelike appearance, then flows downward and out to the opposite end of the pattern. Ridge formations (minutiae) may be observed in the center of the print.

A **tented arch fingerprint pattern** is similar to a plain arch. However, the top (highest point) of the arch is more pronounced (the peak's ridge flow changes direction abruptly).

Plain arch fingerprint pattern Fingerprint containing ridge flow that enters the pattern area at one end, flows upward slightly in a wavelike appearance, then flows downward and out to the opposite end of the pattern. Ridge formations (minutiae) may be observed in the center of the print.

Tented arch fingerprint pattern Similar to a plain arch. However, the top (highest point) of the arch is more pronounced (the peak's ridge flow changes direction abruptly).

Other variations of the arch pattern include an **angular tented arch fingerprint pattern,** one in which ridge incline is 90 degrees or less. An **upthrust tented arch fingerprint pattern** contains ridges that form an upthrust, with ridgeline angles of 45 degrees or more. A **loop-type tented arch fingerprint pattern** appears similar to a loop pattern but it lacks a recurring ridge between the delta and the core of the print. A **delta** is an area on a ridge nearest the center of type lines in the fingerprint pattern. The **core** is the center of the fingerprint.

Loop

In a **loop fingerprint pattern,** the ridgelines enter the pattern area from the left or right side of the finger, recurve and reverse direction, exiting the pattern area

Angular tented arch fingerprint pattern Variation of the arch pattern that contains ridge incline of 90 degrees or less.

Upthrust tented arch fingerprint pattern Fingerprint that contains ridges that form an upthrust, with ridgeline angles of 45 degrees or more.

Loop-type tented arch fingerprint pattern Similar to a loop pattern but it lacks a recurving ridge between the delta and the core of the print.

Photo 5-1. Plain arch fingerprint.

Photo 5-2. Tented arch fingerprint.

in the direction of the entry point. Three characteristics (requirements) designate a loop fingerprint pattern: sufficient ridgeline recurve, a delta, and a ridge count across a looping ridge.

If all three loop requirements are not met, the fingerprint is typically a loop-type tented arch pattern.

A **sufficient recurve** is a ridgeline that enters and exits the pattern area at nearly the same point. It does not contain a sharp, right-angle ridge or appendage on the outside of the ridgeline.

Type lines are the two innermost (closest to the center) ridges of the fingerprint pattern that start out parallel, then diverge and begin to surround the pattern. Some type lines are continuous ridges that surround the pattern area, but most are broken lines that contain but do not completely surround the pattern. In a loop pattern, the delta is located on the side opposite the ridgelines' entry/exit point (Figure 5-2).

In the loop pattern, the core is a specific point at the innermost recurve line of the pattern. In fingerprint classification, the ridges of a loop pattern are counted. **Ridge count** refers to the number of ridgelines between the delta and the core of the loop pattern. A fingerprint examiner counts ridges by placing an imaginary line between the delta and the core.

A loop with ridgelines that enter and exit (start and end) the pattern area in the direction of the radial bone (thumb) is called a **radial loop.** A loop with ridgelines that enter and exit the pattern area in the direction of the ulna bone (little finger) is called an **ulnar loop.** When examining a fingerprint from a crime scene, it is not readily apparent if the fingerprint is from the left or right hand. Therefore, it may be difficult to ascertain which bone the fingerprint ridges flow to or from. Thus, the loops are referred to as right or left slant loops (indicating the direction of the ridge flow).

Delta   An area on a ridge nearest the center of type lines in the fingerprint pattern.

Core   The center of the fingerprint.

Loop fingerprint pattern   Fingerprint in which the ridge-lines enter the pattern area from the left or right side of the finger, recurve, and reverse direction, exiting the pattern area in the direction of the entry point. Three characteristics (requirements) designate a loop fingerprint pattern: sufficient ridgeline recurve, a delta, and a ridge count across a looping ridge.

Sufficient recurve   Fingerprint in which a ridgeline enters and exits the pattern area at nearly the same point. It does not contain a sharp, right-angle ridge or appendage on the outside of the ridgeline.

Type lines   The two innermost (closest to the center) ridges of the fingerprint pattern that start out parallel, then diverge, and partially surround the pattern. Some type lines are continuous ridges that surround the pattern area, but most are broken lines that contain but do not completely surround the pattern. In a loop pattern, the delta is located on the side opposite the ridgelines' entry/exit point.

Ridge count   The number of ridgelines between the delta and the core of the loop pattern.

Radial loop   A loop with ridgelines that enter (start) and exit (end) the pattern area in the direction of the radial thumb bone.

Ulnar loop   A loop with ridgelines that enter and exit the pattern area in the direction of the ulna bone (little finger).

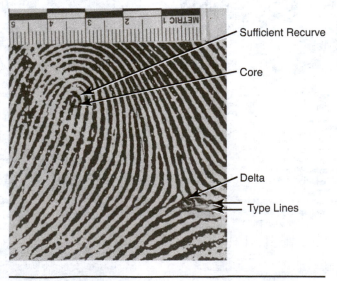

Figure 5-2. Nomenclature of loop fingerprint—sufficient recurve, delta, core, etc.

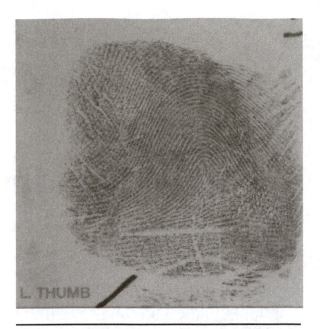

Photo 5-3. Left-slanted loop.

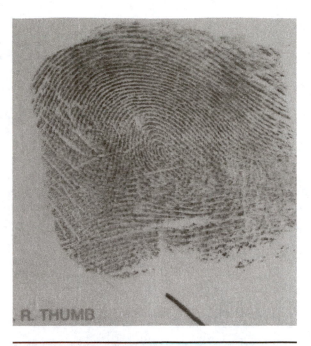

Photo 5-4. Right-slanted loop.

Whorl

A **whorl fingerprint pattern** appears circular, spiral, or oval in shape and contains at least two deltas with a recurving ridge in front of each delta. Each type of whorl pattern (plain, central pocket loop, double loop, and accidental) contains specific characteristics.

The characteristics of the **plain whorl fingerprint pattern** include:

- two deltas,
- at least one complete circuit of ridge flow,
- at least one recurving ridgeline in the inner pattern area if an imaginary straight line is drawn between the two deltas.

A **central pocket loop whorl fingerprint pattern** is a plain whorl pattern in which a line drawn between the two deltas does not cross a recurving ridgeline.

A **double loop whorl fingerprint pattern** is a

Whorl fingerprint pattern Appears circular, spiral, or oval in shape and contains at least two deltas with a recurving ridge in front of each delta. Each type of whorl pattern (plain, central pocket loop, double loop, and accidental) contains specific characteristics.

Plain whorl fingerprint pattern Contains characteristics that include two deltas, at least one complete circuit of ridge flow, at least one recurving ridgeline in the inner pattern area if an imaginary straight line is drawn between the two deltas.

Central pocket loop whorl fingerprint pattern A plain whorl pattern in which a line drawn between the two deltas does not cross a recurving ridgeline.

Photo 5-5. Plain whorl fingerprint.

pattern with two separate loop formations and two deltas. The two separate loops need not be joined by a sharing ridge. The ridgelines in the loops are not counted.

An **accidental whorl fingerprint pattern** is a pattern that contains a

Double loop whorl fingerprint pattern A pattern with two separate loop formations and two deltas. The two separate loops need not be joined by a sharing ridge. The ridgelines in the loops are not counted.

Photo 5-6. Central pocket loop whorl fingerprint.

Photo 5-8. Accidental whorl fingerprint.

Whorl Tracing

In fingerprint classification, tracing is conducted on each whorl pattern. Both deltas are located. The ridge starting at the left delta is traced until it reaches the right delta. If the ridge being traced passes above the right delta and three or more ridgelines lie between the traced ridge and the right delta, the tracing is referred to as an **inner tracing.** If there are less than three ridgelines above or below the traced ridge and the right delta, the tracing is referred to as a **meet tracing.** If the traced ridge passes below the right delta and three or more ridgelines lie between the traced ridge and the right delta, the tracing is referred to as an **outer tracing** (Federal Bureau of Investigation, 1984; Leo, 2004; Scott, 2007).

> **Inner tracing** The ridge traced passes above the right delta and three or more ridgelines lie between the traced ridge and the right delta.

> **Meet tracing** Less than three ridgelines above or below the traced ridge and the right delta.

> **Outer tracing** The traced ridge passes below the right delta and three or more ridgelines lie between the traced ridge and the right delta.

Photo 5-7. Double loop whorl fingerprint.

combination of two separate types of fingerprint patterns. Yet it is not a plain arch with two or more deltas or a pattern that conforms to one of the basic fingerprint patterns.

> **Accidental whorl fingerprint pattern** A pattern that contains a combination of two separate types of fingerprint patterns.

Fingerprint Classification

A fingerprint collected at a crime scene is not classifiable. To classify a subject's fingerprints, prints of all 10 digits (fingertips) must be available. The classification usually occurs after a person (subject) has been fingerprinted.

Fingerprint classification involves several detailed steps. The first step is to identify the fingerprint pattern type for each finger. Second, ridge counting for loop patterns and trace counting for whorl patterns is conducted. A formula similar in appearance to a fraction in mathematics is used to present a person's 10-print classification. The classification is based on the types of patterns, the finger containing the pattern, loop ridge counts, whorl tracings, and other factors. The formula contains letters and numbers presented above or below a line to identify the fingerprint classification for the subject's 10 prints.

Fingerprint classification is a manual process, unless one uses automated (computerized) fingerprint identification software. Although the rules and steps of the manual classification process provide foundational information for LPEs, most manual classification processes have been replaced with automated fingerprint classification, storage, and retrieval systems.

Automated Fingerprint Identification System

The **AFIS** is a computerized database containing millions of known and unknown fingerprints

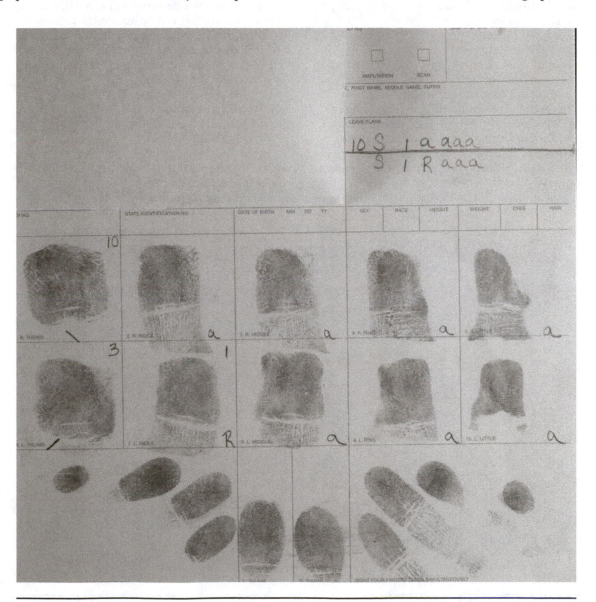

Photo 5-9. 10-Print chart.

and palm prints. AFIS stores fingerprints by pattern type and the relationship of the minutiae in the fingerprints. The AFIS computer program does not catalog loops, arches, whorls, bifurcations, or ridge endings. Rather, it utilizes programmed algorithms and identifies relationships associated with the physical features of a fingerprint pattern.

AFIS also contains electronic 10-print cards of individuals. A *10-print card* is a standardized personal fingerprint identification card. Traditionally, 10-print cards have been used to obtain a person's fingerprints. Ink is applied to the fingertips (digits) and the tip is rolled over a square on the card, producing an inked fingerprint. Subsequently, the inked cards are scanned into AFIS. Fingerprints may also be captured electronically through a digital scanning device. *LiveScan* is an automated digital scanning system through which fingerprints are captured by an optical scanner and recorded in a computer data-

> **Automated Fingerprint Identification System (AFIS)** A computerized database that stores fingerprints by pattern type and the relationship of the minutiae in the fingerprints. The AFIS computer program does not catalog loops, arches, whorls, bifurcations, or ridge endings. Rather, it utilizes programmed algorithms and identifies relationships associated with the physical features of a fingerprint pattern.

base. The subject's hand is pressed against the LiveScan high-speed computer scanning device. Users can immediately determine if the prints are classifiable. If not classifiable, the fingerprints can be rescanned.

To conduct a fingerprint search and compare an unknown print to a known print in the AFIS database, the unknown fingerprint is scanned into the system. The unknown print must have enough clarity for the computer to conduct a search. Additionally, the basic fingerprint type for the unknown print must be provided. If pattern type is uncertain, a possible fingerprint type (called a reference) is entered. The orientation (directionality or correct positioning) of the print must be provided as well, although multiple searches with different orientations may be conducted if the orientation is uncertain. AFIS can search local, state, and national fingerprint databases. Although automation enhances search capabilities, a considerable amount of time, effort, and human involvement are still necessary.

The FBI's **Integrated Automated Fingerprint Identification System (IAFIS)** contains fingerprints of over 50 million of

> **Integrated Automated Fingerprint Identification System (IAFIS)** The FBI's computerized database containing fingerprints of over 50 million individuals.

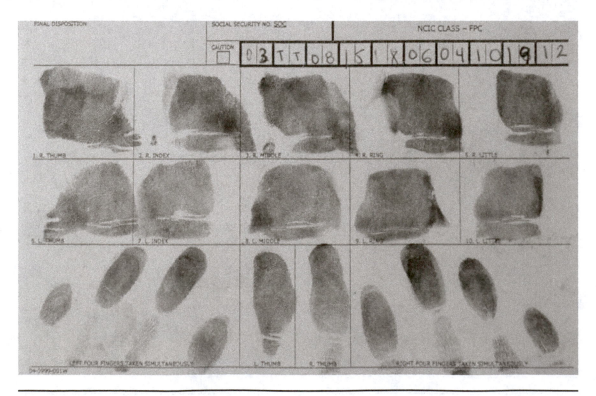

Photo 5-10. NCIC classification chart.

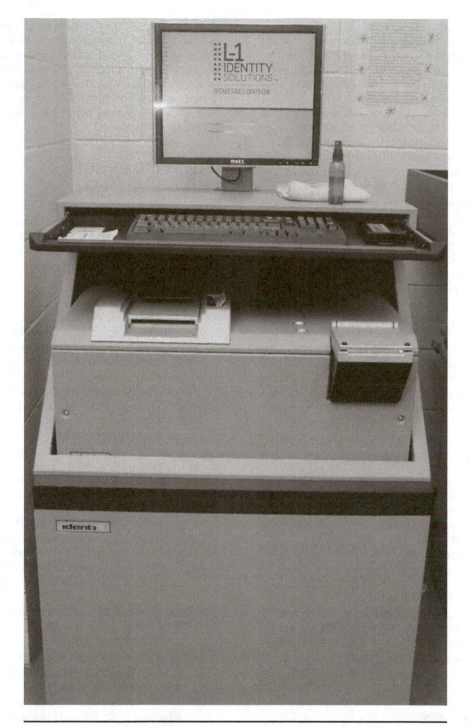

Photo 5-11. LiveScan Machine, Chula Vista, California, Police Department.

individuals. IAFIS offers five key services to participating agencies.

1. 10-Print-based fingerprint identification services: Criminal 10-prints are submitted electronically or by mailing inked 10-print cards of subjects arrested for crimes. The inked cards are scanned into an electronic medium. Civil 10-print submissions are 10-print cards related to employment, licensing, and other non-criminal activities.

2. Latent fingerprint services: Electronic and hard copy submissions of latent fingerprints are accepted and compared with prints in the IAFIS database. If no match is found, the prints are placed in the unsolved latent fingerprint file.
3. Subject search and criminal history services: Millions of criminal histories are stored nationally and by participating states. The histories are searched upon request.
4. Document and imaging services: Documents involving arrests, dispositions, expungements, and other miscellaneous updates are organized and available through this service. Electronic images of fingerprints are provided to agencies upon request. The photo services section accepts, stores, and distributes photographs submitted and requested by participating agencies.
5. Remote 10-print and latent fingerprint search services: Upon request, the FBI will provide remote fingerprint editing software packages to law enforcement agencies at no charge. The software performs searches of IAFIS from remote locations and it supports IAFIS transactions, including image and feature-based searches for latent and 10-print fingerprints.

Fingerprint Identification

Fingerprint classification is not the same as fingerprint identification. **Fingerprint identification** involves the process of comparing questioned and known friction skin ridge prints and impressions. Although a fingerprint pattern may be observed and AFIS matches a known with an unknown print, the prints may not be identical. Many minutiae points or class characteristics may be similar, yet not the product of the same finger. The fingerprint must undergo careful analysis, evaluation, and identification by a trained LPE. The print match must be verified by a second LPE before a fingerprint identification is confirmed positive.

> **Fingerprint identification** The process of comparing questioned and known friction skin ridge prints and impressions.

When comparing a questioned with a known fingerprint, three levels of friction ridge detail are reviewed. The first level is the ridge flow (pattern) of the fingerprint. Identification cannot be made at this level because a pattern is considered a class characteristic. The second level involves examining and comparison of the minutiae in the fingerprints. Identification can be made at the second level. The third level of friction ridge detail comparison focuses on individual ridge appearance, which involves examination and comparison of skin pores, individual ridge shapes, and the appearance of ridge endings. Identification can be made at the third level. An LPE examines and compares a questioned with a known print or impression through a procedural, scientific guide, entitled the ACE-V process.

THE ACE-V PROCESS

ACE-V is an acronym that refers to the four-step *analysis, comparison, evaluation,* and *verification* process used to identify a fingerprint. ACE-V provides guidance and structure based on scientific principles and it assures the reliability of conclusions. The ACE-V process includes the following steps.

1. Analysis—This first step involves a thorough examination of the latent print to determine the clarity of the print and identify any distortions of the friction ridges as well as any external factors such as surface or deposition factors, or processing techniques used that may influence the print's appearance. During the analysis step, the following are considered:
   a. clarity of the print/impression,
   b. distortion assessment (based on surface or transfer),
   c. deposition factors of the print/impression,
   d. value and usability of the print/impression. Can it be compared?
2. Comparison—If the questioned print/impression is identified as valuable and usable, it is compared with a known print.
   a. Friction ridges from the known print are compared to the questioned (unknown) print.
   b. Level one detail, print orientation, pattern type, ridge flow, and focal points are examined and compared.
   c. Level two detail, shape, location, orientation, and relationship of the minutiae are examined and compared.
   d. Level three detail, pores, and friction ridge endings are examined and compared.
3. Evaluation—The evaluation step is similar to the experimental stage of scientific methodology. A hypothesis is tested to form a conclusion. The following factors are considered:
   a. A tentative conclusion is drawn that the questioned (unknown) print is derived from the same source as the known print.

b. Both prints are examined in their totality. Friction ridge details and features are examined to test the tentative conclusion.

c. A final conclusion (individualization, non-identification, or inconclusive) is drawn.

4. Verification—The final step involves an independent examination of the questioned and known prints by a second LPE:

a. The second LPE repeats the ACE-V process.

b. The second LPE draws an independent conclusion.

c. The first and second LPEs discuss the independent preliminary conclusions and arrive at consensus on a final conclusion.

d. The final conclusion is recorded.

e. Disagreements, if any, are resolved by following the agency's conflict resolution procedure.

Learn more about the ACE-V process through the Chesapeake Bay Division of the International Association for Identification (CBDIAI) at www.cbdiai.org.

An LPE may draw one of the three conclusions when comparing a questioned (unknown) to a known print.

- Individualization (Identification)—The two prints are derived from the same source.
- Elimination—The two impressions are not derived from the same source.
- Inconclusive—Not enough detail is present to identify or eliminate the print (U.S. Department of Justice. Federal Bureau of Investigation, 1984; Leo, 2004; SWGFAST, 2004).

SWGFAST publishes standards for arriving at conclusions from comparisons of questioned (unknown) and known prints. The SWGFAST standards are summarized as follows:

- Individualization (Identification): Agreement is reached that sufficient friction ridge detail exists in sequence.

A. Conditions:
1. A determination is made by a competent examiner.
2. Application is made to a common area in both prints.
3. Basis is made on sufficient quantity and quality of friction ridge detail.
4. No discrepancy exists.
5. Conclusions are reproducible.

B. Basic principles:
1. No pre-determined number of corresponding friction ridge details exist.

2. Individualization is supported by theories of biological uniqueness and permanence.

- Exclusion: Disagreement of friction ridge details exists.

A. Conditions:
1. A determination is made by a competent examiner.
2. Application is made to all comparable anatomical areas.
3. A discrepancy exists.
4. Determination is based on sufficient quantity and quality of friction ridge details.
5. Reproducible conclusions.

B. Basic principles:
1. The presence of one discrepancy is sufficient to exclude.
2. A distortion is not a discrepancy and may not be used to exclude.
3. The exclusion is supported by theories of biological uniqueness and permanence.

- Inconclusive: Sufficient ridge detail is absent. A conclusion of individualization or exclusion cannot be supported.

A. Conditions:
1. A determination is made by a competent examiner.
2. The determination is based on quantity and quality of friction ridge detail.
3. Insufficient agreement (disagreement) between friction ridge details exists.
4. Conclusion is reproducible.

B. Basic Principles:
1. Not applicable (SWGFAST, 2004).

LATENT, PATENT, AND PLASTIC PRINTS

Friction skin is unique and individualized. Therefore, no two fingerprints are identical. Friction skin is also permanent. Fingerprint patterns are formed in the womb and they remain the same throughout a person's life. The only exception is permanent damage (e.g., scar from a deep cut) that may be sustained to a person's friction ridge skin (Ashbaugh, 1999).

When searching for fingerprints at a crime scene, the forensic technician should start at any suspected point of entry, and search in locations the subject may have traveled. Consultation with the case investigator or the victim (if alive and able to communicate) will assist with the identification of fingerprint search locations. Disturbed areas are searched as well as any location where a struggle may have occurred.

Friction skin ridges contain perspiration glands and the pores are arranged uniquely. The body's secretion of oil and water from the glands through the pores creates a film on the friction ridges. When a person's fingertip contacts a surface, the film is transferred, producing a latent (hidden) print of the fingerprint pattern on the surface contacted.

A **patent print** is a fingerprint that is visible to the unaided human eye. A substance or contaminant (substrate) on the individual's fingertips causes the transfer of visible ridge characteristics. Bloody or inked fingerprints are two examples of patent prints. The fingerprint image deposited by the substance is visible to the human unaided eye. Blood-enhancing chemicals can highlight additional ridge detail in bloody fingerprints. Blood-enhancing chemicals are discussed in detail in Chapter 9.

> **Patent print** A fingerprint that is visible to the unaided human eye. A substance or contaminant (substrate) on the individual's fingertips causes the transfer of visible ridge characteristics. Bloody or inked fingerprints are two examples of patent prints.

A **plastic print** is a three-dimensional fingerprint that is visible to the human unaided eye. Fingerprints in putty, wax, and other substances are examples of plastic prints. Recovery of plastic prints is accomplished through photography or the application of a casting material (see Chapter 9).

> **Plastic print** A three-dimensional fingerprint that is visible to the human unaided eye. Fingerprints (impressions) in putty, wax, and other substances are examples of plastic prints. Recovery of plastic prints is accomplished through photography or the application of a casting material.

Law enforcement agencies utilize various latent fingerprint processing techniques to highlight, collect, and preserve latent fingerprints. A few agencies use the reflected ultraviolet imaging system (RUVIS), a device designed to highlight latent fingerprints on nonporous surfaces. RUVIS is not affected by ambient light and can be used in daylight or complete darkness. Some camera manufacturers provide accessories that attach to the RUVIS system so the fingerprint, once highlighted, may be photographed.

Although RUVIS is useful, successful recovery of latent fingerprints is not automatic. A fingerprint is not always recoverable. Many factors determine latent fingerprint recoverability.

Latent Fingerprint Pre-transfer Factors

A person's age may affect the quality and clarity of a fingerprint transfer. The fingerprint of an infant or small child has very fine friction ridges that may not deposit a well-defined fingerprint. An elderly person may have dry skin that will not secrete sufficient oil to facilitate the deposit of a fingerprint.

Latent fingerprints deposited by men generally contain more clarity than do women's prints because men have thicker, well-defined ridges. Men often secrete more oil as well. A person's occupation may also affect the transfer of fingerprints. Some occupations require frequent hand washing, while other jobs involve the use of various substrates that contaminate a person's skin. Workers whose occupations require use of abrasives (e.g., construction workers, those who handle a large volume of paper) may temporarily wear down the ridges of the friction skin.

Latent Fingerprint Transfer Factors

Although a person may possess outstanding fingerprint pretransfer capabilities (the skin secretes sufficient oil and the ridge detail is clear), other factors may prohibit the recovery of a latent fingerprint. Contaminants on the subject's skin may inhibit transfer. Further, a subject may smear the print with a swiping motion, causing distortion of the details of the latent fingerprint.

Finally, the surface contacted by the subject may not be conducive to receipt of a quality latent fingerprint. The surface may be too rough to accept a full print deposit, or the surface may contain contaminants, such as dirt, that inhibit transfer (Ashbaugh, 1999).

Latent Fingerprint Post-transfer Factors

A quality latent fingerprint may be successfully transferred onto a conducive surface, yet post-transfer factors may destroy the fingerprint before it is recovered. Hot weather quickly dries the oil and water in the latent fingerprint. If a latent fingerprint is deposited on a handgun and the weapon is subsequently discharged, the heat from the handgun's discharge may dry the fingerprint. Further, humidity can add moisture to the latent fingerprint and cause it to smear.

Finally, latent fingerprints deposited on an individual evidence item collected for subsequent processing may be destroyed if the item is not handled and transported properly. If the item is handled too much or swiped with gloved hands or evidence bags, latent fingerprints can be destroyed.

LATENT PRINT PROCESSING TECHNIQUES

Forensic technicians, LPEs, investigators, police officers, and other trained law enforcement personnel are frequently involved with searching and processing evidence and crime scenes for latent fingerprints. For the purposes of this book, the title *forensic technician* is used when describing any person involved in latent print development.

A variety of processing techniques, colored powders, and chemicals are available for latent fingerprint development. The decision regarding which processing technique, powder or chemical to use is typically left to the discretion of the forensic technician processing the item. Training and availability of equipment are determining factors as well. With improvements in technology, safer and more sophisticated fingerprint processing techniques are anticipated.

One must first acquire a thorough working knowledge of techniques and available latent fingerprint development powders and chemicals. The forensic technician should never test a new latent print developing technique on actual evidence. If the technique has not been tested, experimentation on fictitious evidence is preferred until skill with the technique is realized. Many crime laboratories publish written guidelines for latent print development. Many also provide training and require a competency exam before application of latent print development techniques.

Perishability (shelf life) of chemicals is also a consideration. If the chemical's shelf life is uncertain, a control test on fictitious evidence should be conducted prior to using the chemical on an actual evidence item.

Sequential processing is another consideration when developing a latent fingerprint. **Sequential processing** involves the use of more than one technique to enhance and develop the latent fingerprint. If sequential processing is used, the processing steps must be followed in the appropriate sequence. Altering the steps' sequence may destroy the fingerprint.

> **Sequential processing** Involves the use of more than one technique to enhance and develop a latent fingerprint.

Publications that accompany fingerprint development chemicals and powders provide instructions on their use. In addition, professional organizations such as the CBDIAI publish information on chemicals and their specific uses. CBDIAI provides the following for chemical reagents (reactants).

- Surfaces on which the reagent may be used.
- Substrates (e.g. amino acids) the reagent interacts with or is incompatible with.
- Common names for the reagent.
- Application procedure.
- Documentation requirements.
- Sequential techniques.
- Error rate of reagent.
- Formula (recipe to produce the reagent).
- Shelf life.
- Storage information.
- Safety precautions (fume hood, protective gear required).
- Additional recommendations (Chesapeake Bay Division—International Association for Identification, 2003).

A forensic technician should wear latex or vinyl protective gloves when handling evidence and processing surfaces to develop latent fingerprints. Gloves protect the forensic technician's skin and prohibit transfer of additional latent prints onto the applicable surface. If chemicals are used, chemical-resistant gloves, eye protection, and other safety apparel should be worn.

Before applying a powder or chemical to a surface, a visual inspection for trace evidence adhering to the evidence item as well as a search for visible (patent) fingerprints should be conducted. Use of oblique (an angle less than 90 degrees) lighting or holding the evidence item at various angles under good lighting conditions will reveal trace evidence and visible fingerprints.

The forensic technician should consider all the types of forensic evidence that may be present on the item, rather than processing for latent fingerprints only. Trace evidence, such as hairs, fibers, or saliva, should be properly collected prior to latent print development. To process drink containers, such as bottles, soda cans, and glassware, the forensic technician should swab the mouth contact area for DNA-related material prior to developing latent fingerprints. Some latent fingerprint processing techniques destroy DNA. Therefore, recommended sequential steps must be followed. Patent (visible) fingerprints should be photographed prior to enhancement.

Several latent fingerprint processing techniques and supplies are commonly used. The powders and chemicals referenced here may be purchased through forensic science supply companies such as those listed in Appendix C.

Processing Fingerprints with Powder

Fingerprint processing powder clings to friction ridge skin oil and residue deposited (transferred from the skin) on a surface. Fingerprint powder can be created by rubbing pencil lead (graphite) on fine sand paper. Commercial fingerprint powder is available in various colors. The fine powder is applied with a brush. When the powder clings to the oil and residue, the details of the ridgeline formations appear (Keppel, Brown, & Welch, 2007). Over-processing (applying too much powder) can destroy ridge detail and cause several individual ridges to appear as one.

Traditional fingerprint powders are used on smooth, nonporous surfaces such as glass, marble, tile, and some metals. Fingerprint powder is applied as follows:

1. Pour a small amount of powder on a working surface, such as a table covered with craft paper.
2. Dip the tip of the brush into the powder.
3. Tap the brush on the craft paper-covered table surface to remove excess powder.
4. Carefully brush the powder onto the evidence item, with light, circular motions. Some forensic technicians prefer to twirl the brush between the index finger and the thumb. Whether a circular or twirling motion is used, it is important to contact the evidence item lightly rather than rub the brush against the item's surface or poke the surface with the brush.
5. When the ridge detail is observable, continue processing (brushing) the fingerprint, following the ridge flow of the print and exercising caution not to over-process with too much powder.
6. After the fingerprint is satisfactorily processed (clearly visible), blow the excess powder from the evidence item, so that the fingerprint lifting tape will adhere properly. Some agencies dispose of any unused powder rather than returning it to its original container. Discarding excess powder helps prevent cross contamination of DNA or trace evidence.
7. The forensic technician may choose to photograph the fingerprint prior to lifting it. This step is dependent upon the crime laboratory's policy as well as the discretion of the forensic technician.
8. Although ordinary household adhesive cellophane tape will lift a print, commercial fingerprint lifting tape is available in various textures, sizes, and adhesive qualities. Some tape is specifically designed to stretch and bend around and within curved or textured surfaces. One learns which tape is most suitable through experimentation, use, experience, and knowledge of surfaces.

The tape's end is pulled away from the roll. The forensic technician should attach the end of the tape (adhesive side down) at one edge of the developed latent fingerprint and carefully place the tape over the print. If the print is on a curved surface, the center of the tape should be placed in contact with the core of the fingerprint pattern. The remainder of the tape is applied outward toward the perimeter of the print. This tape application procedure prevents wrinkles and air pockets from forming under the tape.

9. After the tape is applied across the fingerprint, the tape is carefully peeled (lifted) from the evidence item and placed on a 3″ × 5″ card or the glossy side of a commercial latent fingerprint card. The best practice is to anchor one end of the tape to the card and roll the tape onto the card.
10. If wrinkles occur in the tape during the lifting process, it is best to press the lifted fingerprint portions of the tape against the card. If wrinkles occur while pressing the tape against the fingerprint card, do not attempt to smooth the wrinkles. In doing so, the friction ridges overlap, causing analysis of the latent fingerprint to be more difficult for an LPE.
11. Trim excess tape from the edges of the latent print card. Record case information, describing the evidence item from which the print was lifted and sketch the evidence item, including an arrow indicating the position of the tape on the evidence item, on the back of the latent print card.
12. Some agencies require that the location of the print on the evidence item be photographed or marked and initialed.

Magnetic Powder

Similar to traditional powder, magnetic powder adheres to bodily secretions that are transferred from friction ridge skin to an object's surface. Magnetic powders are available in various colors and are similar in composition to traditional powders, except that they contain minute particles of metal. The metal particles in the powder adhere to a magnet, which is located inside a magna wand used to apply the powder to evidence. The magna wand is equipped with a device that allows the user to release powder from the wand. Magna wands are available in various sizes.

A fingerprint brush should not be used with magnetic powder because the metal particles will embed in the bristles of the brush. If the brush is reused, the metal particles will scratch evidence. In addition, a magna wand may

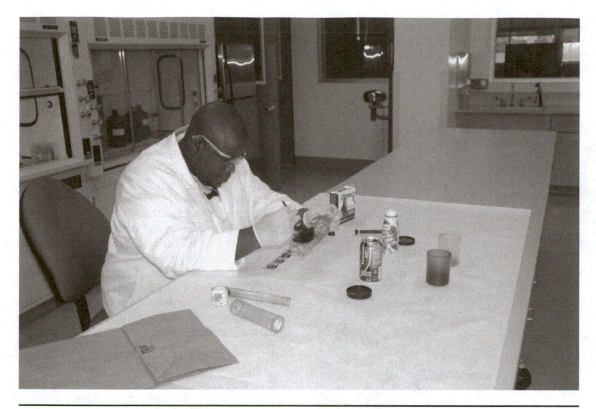

Photo 5-12. Forensic technician processing evidence. Photograph taken by Chris Nellis.

Photo 5-13. Black powder applied to evidence.

scratch evidence if the forensic technician allows the wand to contact the evidence item. Magnetic powders can be used on nonporous, glossy surfaces, plastics, leather, walls containing oil-based or glossy paints, and many other surfaces. Magnetic powder is applied as follows:

1. Pour a small amount of powder on a working surface, such as a table covered with craft paper.

2. Dip the magna wand in the magnetic powder until a small amount of the powder adheres to the end of the wand.
3. Carefully release the powder onto the evidence item containing the latent fingerprint. Do not brush or rub the wand against the evidence. If the wand contacts the evidence item, scratch marks can be created on the latent fingerprint and evidence item (Keppel, Brown, & Welch, 2007).
4. As the latent fingerprint develops, use the wand to follow the ridge flow with the powder until processing is complete. Do not over-process the fingerprint.
5. Blow the excess powder off and apply tape in the same manner used with traditional fingerprint powder.
6. Remove the tape and apply it to the fingerprint card, recording relevant case information on the reserve side of the card.
7. Dispose of the excess powder (if agency protocol requires).

Magnetic powder requires more time to apply than traditional powder because the amount of powder that adheres to the magna wand is typically less than the amount of traditional powder that adheres to a brush. It may be beneficial to use traditional powder to locate prints, and then highlight the ridge detail with magnetic powder.

Photo 5-14. Fingerprint lifting tape applied to powdered prints on evidence.

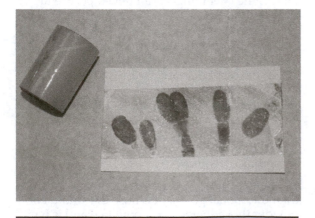

Photo 5-15. Lifted black powdered fingerprints.

Magnetic Powder on Textured Surfaces

Latent fingerprints are often located deep within textured surfaces because of the pressure applied when the surface is touched. The latent fingerprint powder must reach the lower points to adhere to the oils. Magnetic powder is very effective on textured surfaces because the powder can penetrate the grooves, whereas traditional powder only coats the surface. By applying magnetic powder in the same manner as applied on nonporous evidence, the forensic technician can visualize the fingerprint located within the textured surface. However, traditional tape lifting methods may not lift the fingerprint from the grooves. Instead, the following procedure is recommended when lifting a powdered fingerprint from a textured surface.

After developing the latent fingerprint with magnetic powder, one should photograph the print and use clear school glue or casting putty such as Mikrosil® or Forensic Sil® to process and remove the fingerprint.

1. Squeeze a small amount of clear school glue (or putty) onto the base of the fingerprint.
2. Using a straw, carefully blow a thin layer of glue across the fingerprint. One may also use a 3″ × 5″ card to slowly spread the glue over the fingerprint. Fast motions may alter the fingerprint powder and destroy the fingerprint. The glue must be allowed to dry completely.
3. After the glue has dried, place clear fingerprint lifting tape over the glue. Tape with a strong adhesive quality is best.
4. Carefully lift the tape from one end. The glue containing the fingerprint will lift as it adheres to the tape. If a portion of the glue does not adhere to the tape, use a pencil point or sharp pointer to assist with lifting the glue.
5. The fingerprint should appear through the clear fingerprint tape. The tape is mounted on a fingerprint card.

Fluorescent Powder

Fluorescent powder adheres to oil transferred from friction ridge skin. The powder's adherence qualities are much greater than traditional or magnetic powders. Very little fluorescent powder is required. A soft feather brush (designed for fluorescent powders) is used for application. Traditional fingerprint brushes are not used because they over-process the evidence.

Fluorescent powders are manufactured in various colors. After the powder is applied, the fingerprint can only be viewed with an ALS. Fluorescent powder is often used on nonporous

Photo 5-16. Magnetic powder applied to evidence.

Photo 5-17. Magnetic powder applied to evidence.

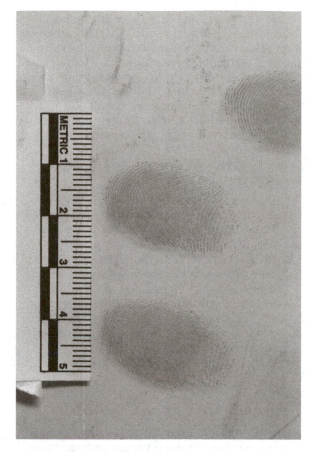

Photo 5-18. Latent fingerprints developed with magnetic powder.

surfaces because of its great adherence qualities. Based on one of the authors' experiences, fluorescent powder works well on wood and worn laminate furniture.

The ALS is used during the fluorescent powder's application. One must observe the fingerprint as it is developing to ensure that over-processing does not occur. Applying additional powder with the feather brush often leads to over-processing. The fingerprint should be photographed. After photography, a forensic technician may view the fingerprint with an ALS, lift the fingerprint, and place it on a fingerprint card.

Sticky-Side Powder

Occasionally, a forensic technician is tasked with processing a fingerprint located on the adhesive side of tape or a label. Lifting fingerprints from such adhesives can be accomplished in several ways, including application of sticky-side powder. *Sticky-side powder* is a nontoxic powder that does not require the use of safety gear

Photo 5-19. Fluorescent powder and brush.

(beyond protective gloves) or a fume hood. However, over-processing is possible with some adhesive surfaces. Black electrical tape, paper labels, and tapes with dried adhesives usually generate poor results.

Superglue fuming (discussed later) does not inhibit the use of sticky-side powder. However, superglue fuming should be accomplished prior to using sticky-side powder. The forensic technician should experiment with nonevidence tape to ascertain which method yields better results. The crime laboratory should keep samples of various adhesive tapes and labels so that the experiments can be performed when needed.

Sticky-side powder should be applied in the following manner:

1. Place one teaspoon of sticky-side powder into a mixing bowl. Combine equal parts of Photo-Flow® (liquid used to develop film) and water. Stir until a liquid paste forms.
2. Brush the paste onto the sticky side of the tape. Alternatively, the tape may be immersed in the paste.
3. Wait 30 to 60 seconds and rinse under a light stream of cold tap water. Do not allow the paste to remain on the tape longer than 60 seconds.
4. Allow the tape to air dry completely.
5. Photograph the developed fingerprints.

Fingerprint Developing Chemicals

Many porous and nonporous surfaces contain contaminants that inhibit the use of fingerprint processing powders. Chemicals are used on these surfaces and substrates.

When using any chemical for fingerprint development, the forensic technician should wear eye protection and chemical-resistant gloves. In many situations, a fume hood is necessary as well. The material safety data sheet (MSDS) that accompanies a chemical should be read prior to using the chemical.

Cyanoacrylate ester (Superglue®) Fuming

Cyanoacrylate ester fuming is a common chemically-enhanced fingerprint processing technique. Cyanoacrylate ester is the generic name for fast-acting glue sold under the trade names *Superglue®* and *Krazy Glue®*. Superglue fuming works well on nonporous surfaces and it can be used prior to the application of most powders and chemicals. Other than visual examination, the technique is often the first step in fingerprint development. The process utilizes heat and humidity

> **Cyanoacrylate ester fuming**
> A common chemically-enhanced fingerprint processing technique. Cyanoacrylate ester is the generic name for fast-acting glue sold under the trade names *Superglue®* and *Krazy Glue®*.

Photo 5-20. Sticky-side powder.

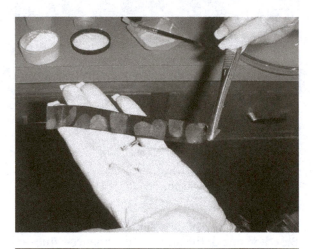

Photo 5-21. Fingerprints developed on the sticky side of black electrical tape.

to cause the Superglue® to fume. The particulates in the gaseous mixture released by the heat and humidity adhere to the oil and residue in the fingerprint, producing a white glued print.

Inhaling Superglue® fumes may irritate the lungs. Additionally, the fumes can cause contact eyewear to adhere to a person's eye. Therefore, fuming should occur in a clear glass chamber that does not release fumes into an inhabited space. A simple fish tank with a tight lid will suffice, as long as a heat source and humidity are inside the tank. The process is safest when accomplished inside chamber units designed specifically for Superglue® fuming. The units are equipped with controls designed to release the correct amount of heat and humidity. When the fuming is complete, environmental filters clear the chamber of life-threatening particulates and toxic gases.

Superglue® fuming occurs as follows:

1. Place evidence items inside the fuming chamber (container). Labels (tags) are placed near the evidence items. Masking tape works well as a labeling tool.
2. Place known (control) fingerprints on a dark-colored surface such as the glossy side of a black fingerprint card. This allows the forensic technician to verify that the Superglue® processing is working and helps prevent over-processing.
3. Place a ½" diameter drop of superglue on a piece of aluminum foil and place the foil on top of the heat source. A heat plate works well for this purpose. If liquid superglue is not available, a gel packet of superglue may be used. Superglue gel packets commence fuming as soon as they are opened. A heat source is not required.
4. Place a water source (bowl of hot, steamy water) near the heat source.
5. Seal the chamber (container) and monitor the fuming, which is usually complete within 8–10 minutes.
6. Allow the fumes to escape through the filter or into an uninhabited environment. If a fish tank is used, the fumes should be expelled through a fume hood.
7. Examine the evidence for fumed fingerprints. Oblique lighting may be used.
8. Depending on agency protocol, the fingerprints are photographed or processed with powder, dye stain, or chemicals.

Superglue fuming is not limited to use in the laboratory. A *cyanowand* is a portable superglue fuming wand that may be used at crime scenes. The wand is held next to the object of interest and superglue fumes are released. The forensic technician must take care not to overfume the object.

Cyanoacrylate packets may be used to fume small compartments such as the interior of a vehicle. The packet is opened and fumes are slowly released. The chemical in the packet dries within several hours, causing the fuming to cease. When fuming a vehicle interior, two packets are usually enclosed in the vehicle overnight. The chemical in the packets dries before over-fuming occurs.

Fluorescent Dye Stain

Fluorescent dye stain adheres to superglue-fumed prints on nonporous surfaces. Superglue fuming must precede dye stain application. Dye-stained prints are observable only with an ALS. The ALS light frequency setting depends on the dye stain used. Photography is the only means of preservation. Photographic documentation should take place within 24 hours of dye stain application. Some dye stains are purchased in premixed solutions. Some require a rinse solution while others do not. The forensic technician should be familiar with the types of dye stains and conduct an experiment with a dye stain on a nonevidence surface prior to use on actual evidence. Protective eyewear, chemical-resistant gloves, and a fume hood should be used regardless of the dye stain selected. All dye stains are applied according to the following:

1. Fume the evidence with Superglue.
2. Dip the fumed evidence in the dye stain and rinse according to the directions that accompany the dye stain.
3. Allow the evidence to air dry.
4. Photograph developed fingerprints.

Liqui-drox

Liqui-drox is a mixture of Liqui-nox, Ardrox (a fluorescent dye stain), and distilled water. It is used to develop latent fingerprints on the adhesive and nonadhesive sides of dark-colored tapes, such as black electrical tape. The mixture is applied after superglue fuming and the results are preserved photographically. The application process is as follows:

1. Superglue the tape.
2. Mix 200 ml of Ardrox, 400 ml of Liqui-nox, and 400 ml of distilled water. The resulting solution should appear milky-yellow.
3. Apply the solution onto both sides of the tape with a camel hair brush and allow to dry for 10 seconds.
4. Rinse under a light stream of cold tap water.
5. Allow to air dry.
6. Examine with an ALS at ultraviolet setting.
7. Photograph results.

Gentian Violet

Gentian violet (crystal violet) is a stain that is used on nonporous surfaces, especially the adhesive side of tape. It works particularly well on duct tape. It does not work well on tape coated with a water-soluble adhesive. Gentian violet is available in crystals that are dissolved in distilled water. The tape can be stained and rinsed repeatedly until optimum results are achieved. The results are preserved photographically.

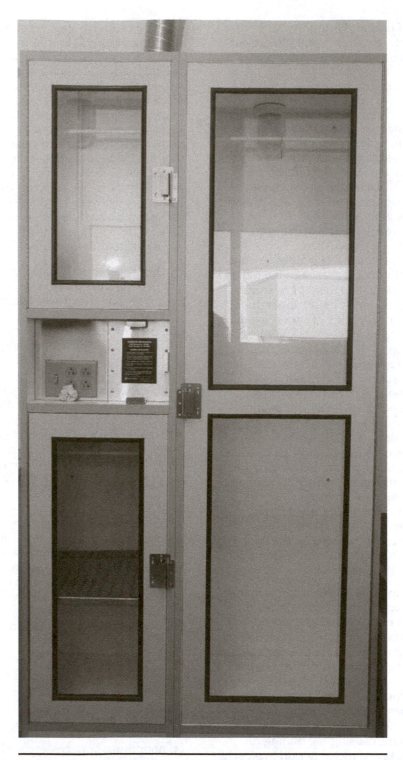

Photo 5-22. Superglue fuming tank, Chula Vista, California, Police Department.

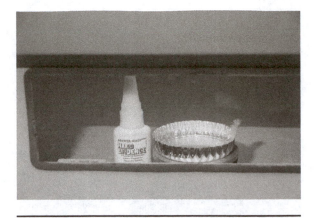

Photo 5-23. Superglue is placed on tray and heated.

Photo 5-26. Use of handheld ALS to view prints.

Photo 5-24. Superglued prints on plastic.

Photo 5-25. Demo fluorescence dye stain on evidence.

Photo 5-27. Fluorescent fingerprints.

Gentian violet is extremely toxic and should not be allowed to contact human skin. The forensic technician should wear eye protection, a laboratory coat, and chemical-resistant gloves when using Gentian violet. A fume hood is not necessary. The application process is as follows:

1. Mix 1 g of gentian violet crystals with 1000 ml of distilled water.
2. Pour solution into a tray until the bottom of the tray is covered with the solution. Dip the tape into the solution for one to two minutes.
3. Rinse the tape for 30 seconds with cold tap water. Repeat dipping and rinsing until desired results are achieved.
4. The results can be observed with the unaided eye or with an ALS at 505–570 nm with red goggles.
5. Photograph results.

Wetwop®

Wetwop® is a stain that is used on the adhesive side of tapes and labels. The forensic technician should wear eye protection, a laboratory coat, and chemical-resistant gloves when using wetwop. A fume hood is not necessary. The application process is as follows:

1. Shake the premixed solution of wetwop thoroughly.
2. Pour a small amount of wetwop into a clean dish.
3. Use a camel hair brush to apply wetwop to the adhesive side of the evidence item. Cover the surface completely.
4. Wait 15–30 seconds.
5. Rinse the solution from the evidence with a gentle stream of tap water.
6. Allow the evidence to air dry.
7. Photograph the results.

Ninhydrin

Ninhydrin is a chemical commonly used to develop latent fingerprints on porous surfaces such as paper. Ninhydrin reacts with the amino acids in perspiration, turning dark purple in color (Keppel, Brown, & Welch, 2007). Because it reacts to amino acids, ninhydrin will also react to blood. However, ninhydrin is not typically used to enhance bloody fingerprints because it often overdevelops the ridge detail of the prints.

Ninhydrin can be used on virtually any porous surface, including wallpaper, unpainted walls, or walls with a matte finish. A fume hood must be used when dipping evidence into ninhydrin. One must wear a breathing apparatus while painting or spraying ninhydrin on walls at a crime scene.

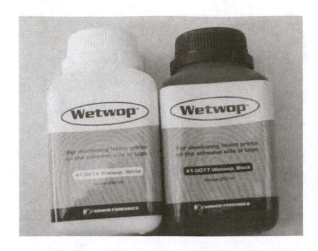

Photo 5-28. Wetwop.

Photo 5-29. Duct tape processed with wetwop. Photo by Allen Brogdon.

Additionally, ninhydrin is highly flammable. If used at a crime scene, the pilot light of any gas appliance should be off. Eye protection and chemical-resistant gloves should be worn. The fumes should not be inhaled.

Mixing instructions accompany ninhydrin. The chemical is also available in a premixed, ready-to-use solution. Heat and humidity accelerates the reaction time of ninhydrin. Without ample heat and humidity, reaction time can take days. Ninhydrin is applied as follows:

1. Dip porous evidence directly into a tray of ninhydrin solution, or spray the solution onto the evidence.
2. Remove the evidence and air dry (usually a few seconds to minutes).
3. To accelerate development, place the ninhydrin-treated evidence between two sheets of craft paper and steam iron the top sheet.

Alternatively, one may hold the iron a few inches above the evidence so the heat and steam radiate onto the evidence. The iron must not contact the evidence. Some forensic technicians use a heat press to heat ninhydrin-treated evidence. Adding heat and humidity will usually develop fingerprints within a few minutes.

4. The evidence should be photographed for permanent recording. Ninhydrin-treated prints dissipate quickly.

5. Unless biological fluid is present on the evidence, ninhydrin-processed evidence is best stored in a plastic bag. The plastic bag will preserve the ninhydrin-developed prints for a considerable period of time.

Precautions Regarding Ninhydrin

An acetone-based ninhydrin reacts well with amino acids, but acetone will cause ink to run. Evidence containing writing should be photocopied prior to applying the chemical.

If a document is processed with ninhydrin, indented writing on the document is not recoverable. If indented writing on the document must be retrieved, the document should first be processed by a forensic document examiner.

Ninhydrin should never be used on polystyrene plastic (e.g., Styrofoam®). Although polystyrene is porous, the chemicals in ninhydrin will cause it to disintegrate. It should be processed for fingerprints using Superglue® fuming or magnetic powder.

Ninhydrin Technique on Thermal Paper

Thermal paper (paper with a glossy coating often used in ATMs) will turn black in color if dipped in ninhydrin. In lieu of dipping, one can place thermal paper in a plastic bag containing ninhydrin crystals (not liquid ninhydrin). Additionally, publicized experiments indicate that applying dry heat while simultaneously processing an item with ninhydrin will usually result in developed fingerprints. Dry heat may be applied by holding a heated clothes iron a few inches over the document. Alternatively, placing the processed evidence over a container of hot water and simultaneously applying dry heat will usually develop prints (Scott, 2008).

Physical Developer

Physical developer is a chemical that can be used on an item after it is processed with ninhydrin. While ninhydrin reacts with the amino acids found in fingerprints, Physical developer reacts to the lipids or oils in the fingerprint. Physical developer may highlight more detail of the fingerprint if ninhydrin development is not satisfactory. Physical developer can also be used on

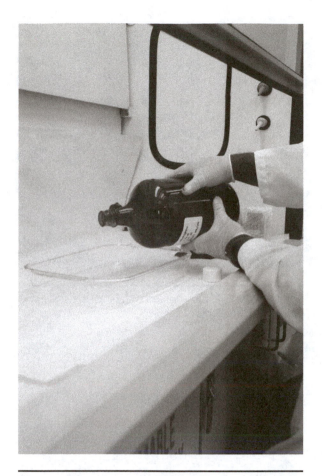

Photo 5-30. Ninhydrin being poured. Photo by Chris Nellis.

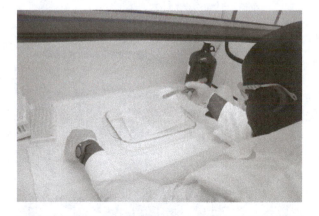

Photo 5-31. Evidence dipped in ninhydrin. Photo by Chris Nellis.

wet, unprocessed documents and natural wood. It should not be used on thermal paper. Eye protection, a laboratory coat, and chemical-resistant gloves should be worn. The solution should not

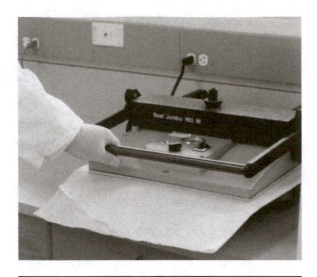

Photo 5-32. Evidence heated with heat process. Photo by Chris Nellis.

be used in direct sunlight. A fume hood is not necessary. Physical developer processing steps include a prewash, a working solution, and two rinse solutions. Results should be photographed.

Sudan Black
Sudan Black is a chemical used on nonporous surfaces that are contaminated with grease, food, and other substances. The chemical may also be used on the inside of latex gloves subsequent to superglue fuming. Eye protection, a laboratory coat, and chemical-resistant gloves should be worn. Although there are no known respiratory health hazards associated with sudan black, use of a fume hood is recommended. The application process is as follows:

1. Dissolve 15 g of Sudan Black powder in 1000 ml of ethanol, and then add 500 ml of distilled water.
2. Immerse the evidence in the solution for two minutes.
3. Rinse the evidence with cold tap water to remove excess solution.
4. Dry at room temperature.
5. Photograph results.

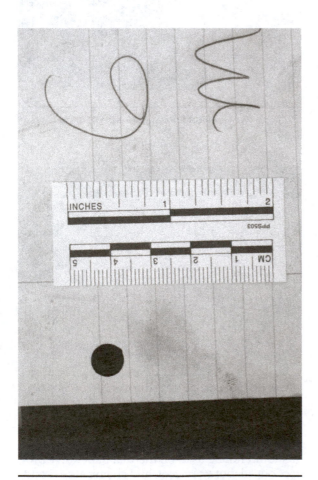

Photo 5-33. Evidence processed with ninhydrin.

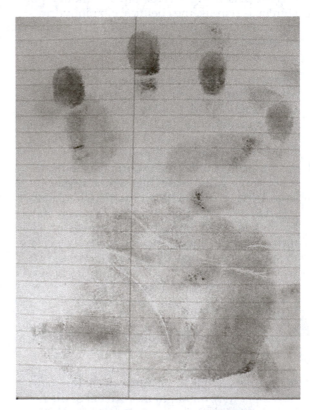

Photo 5-34. Evidence processed with ninhydrin.

Small Particle Reagent

Small particle reagent (SPR) contains the active ingredient *molybdenum disulfide (Moly-B)*. The chemical is used on nonporous, wet surfaces, typically surfaces exposed to rain or snow. SPR can be applied after Sudan Black, superglue fuming, or dye staining. SPR is available as a ready-to-mix material as well as a premixed solution. Protective clothing and gloves should be worn. A fume hood is not necessary. The SPR application process is as follows:

1. Spray SPR directly on the evidence.
2. Rinse evidence with tap water for 15 seconds.
3. Allow the evidence to dry at room temperature.
4. Photograph results or lift developed fingerprints with fingerprint lifting tape.

Gun Blueing

Gun blueing is a chemical reagent used on firearm cartridge cases made of brass. The reagent erodes the brass not coated by oils from latent print residue, revealing the un-eroded portion (latent fingerprint) on the cartridge casing. Gun blueing does not work well on steel cartridges or those with a plastic jacket. Although not required, the chemical works best when the brass cartridge case is fumed with Superglue®.

Gun blueing can overdevelop easily and must be monitored continuously while processing. Acidified hydrogen peroxide is used to remove the chemical. Protective clothing and gloves are worn and a fume hood should be used. The gun blueing application process is as follows:

1. The gun blueing reagent is mixed with distilled water according to instructions that accompany the reagent.
2. After superglue fuming the cartridge casing lightly, immerse the casing in the reagent. Rotate the casing in the solution, monitoring the casing for print development.
3. As soon as a print appears, stop processing immediately by immersing the casing in distilled water for two minutes.
4. Allow casing to air dry.
5. Photograph the results.

Precaution Regarding Gun Blueing

Treating a brass cartridge casing with gun blueing can produce a negative side effect. Gun blueing creates a coating on the cartridge case that may interfere with examination of certain firearm tool marks.

Iodine Fuming

Iodine fuming is used to retrieve fingerprints from porous as well as nonporous surfaces. Commercial iodine fuming kits include application procedures instruction.

Iodine is extremely toxic and the fumes are very hazardous. Iodine fume inhalation or skin contact may lead to birth defects or death.

The results of iodine fuming must be photographed immediately. The fumes should not be allowed to contact camera equipment. Due to the health risks associated with iodine fuming, many crime laboratories ban its use.

Blood-Enhancement Chemicals

A variety of chemicals enhance bloody fingerprints and impressions, including bloody shoeprints. The chemicals are available in a variety of colors and several application techniques (see Chapter 9). Regardless of the chemical used, specific protocol should be followed:

Photo 5-35. Wetprint.

Bloody Fingerprints—Protocol

1. If a bloody fingerprint contains ridge detail, photograph the fingerprint prior to development and processing.
2. Collect a blood sample for DNA analysis by swabbing a portion of the fingerprint. If coagulated (thickened) blood has collected in portion of a fingerprint, collect the coagulated portion. If possible, avoid the core of the print and any minutiae points.
3. Apply the appropriate blood-enhancement chemical and rinse (if applicable).
4. Take a second photograph of the fingerprint.
5. Apply blood-enhancement chemically a second time (if applicable).
6. Take a third photograph of the fingerprint.

Vacuum Metal Deposition

Vacuum metal deposition (VMD) is a process by which evidence is placed in a vacuum and metal fragments are transferred onto the evidence, revealing latent fingerprint residue. The process may be used on smooth, nonporous surfaces such as plastic bags and packaging, leather, plastic, glass, some fabrics, and other smooth surfaces. Due to its expense, VMD is not commonly used.

FINGERPRINT PHOTOGRAPHY

General Guidelines

A forensic technician must photograph fingerprints on various surfaces and under various lighting conditions. Although fingerprint powder and lifting techniques are used, the fingerprint should be photographed prior to lifting. In many criminal cases, photography is the only means of documenting the fingerprint evidence. The steps to photographing a fingerprint include the following:

1. Place a camera on a tripod. The face of the camera lens must be parallel with the fingerprint.
2. If using a digital camera, it should be eight megapixels or above and should be set at the maximum resolution available.
3. Take orientation photos of the location of the fingerprint with an evidence placard in place.

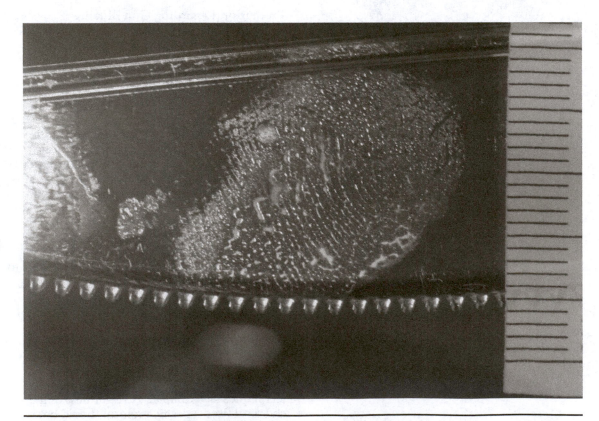

Photo 5-36. Bloody fingerprint on plastic knife.

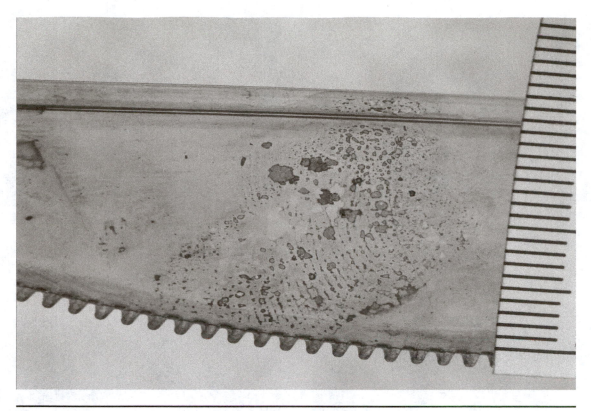

Photo 5-37. Bloody fingerprint after chemical enhancement.

4. Place an adhesive-backed scale on the surface next to the fingerprint. Many agencies require that photographs be taken without and with a scale.
5. Using a macro lens, fill the frame of the viewfinder with the scale and fingerprint.
6. Set the white balance to the dominant lighting in the room.
7. Auto metering may be used.
8. The depth-of-field may require adjustment. F-11 will generally produce sufficient depth-of-field. Adjust the shutter speed to obtain the appropriate exposure.
9. If a flash unit is necessary, position the unit at a 45-degree angle to the print to avoid hot spots. Take a control photograph without the flash to ensure that the flash does not obscure detail of the fingerprint.
10. Side (continuous) lighting positioned at 45 degrees to the evidence may be used. Adjust the white balance accordingly.

Fingerprints on Low-Level Vertical Surfaces

Fingerprints on low-level vertical surfaces will require inverse mounting of the camera on a tripod. Viewfinder accessories that attach to the camera and operate like a periscope accompany some cameras. The periscope helps the photographer peer through the viewfinder when the camera is in an awkward position. If such accessories are not available, it may be necessary for the photographer to lie in a prone position to peer through the camera's viewfinder. To avoid contact with contaminates that may be present, the forensic technician should place craft paper or plastic sheeting on the surface before lying down.

Fingerprints on Curved Surfaces

Photographing fingerprints on curved surfaces such as bottles or cans requires excellent depth-of-field, preferably F-22. Alternatively, one may capture multiple, overlapping images of the fingerprint and layer the photographs with a software program (e.g., Adobe Photoshop®).

Fingerprints on Mirrors

Photographing a fingerprint on a mirror can be problematic because a reflective (duplicate) image of the fingerprint will be observed in the

Photo 5-38. Photographic setup with print on a
vertical surface.

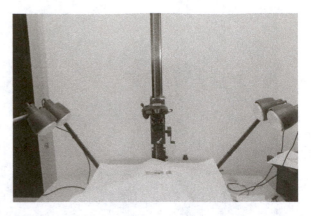

Photo 5-40. Photographic setup with print on
horizontal surface.

Photo 5-41. Filters may be used to remove background colors.

Photo 5-39. Photographic setup with print on a
vertical surface.

Photo 5-42. Photographic setup for evidence on low
vertical surface.

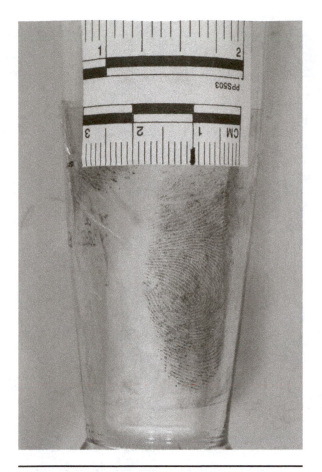

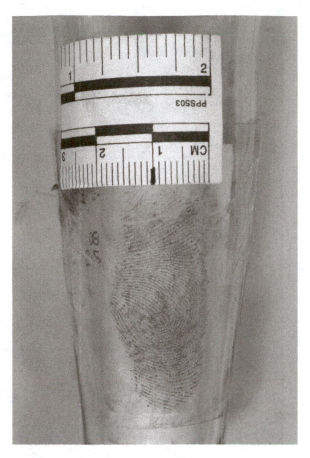

Photo 5-43. Fingerprint on curved bottle.

Photo 5-44. Fingerprint on curved bottle.

photo. If good depth-of-field is used, the duplicate image is enhanced. Therefore, the photographer should use poor depth-of-field, which minimizes the duplicate image reflected by the mirror.

The photographer should bracket images of the print, using multiple f-stop settings, starting with the poorest depth-of-field setting and increasing the f-stop with each subsequent photograph. The shutter speed may be adjusted to compensate for exposure changes with each photograph. One of the photographs should produce little or no duplicative image but provide enough depth-of-field for comparison purposes.

Fingerprints on Vehicle Windows

Photographing fingerprints on vehicle windows can be challenging also. Reflection and objects on the opposite side of the window can distort the fingerprint image. A sheet of paper may be taped

to the opposite side of the window to prevent reflections or obscure distracting objects. Diffused lighting may help if the window is reflective. Reducing depth-of-field will also help diminish distracting images on the opposite side of the glass.

Alternate Light Source Photography

An ALS, also referred to as a forensic light source, is used in a variety of forensic applications. To photograph evidence being viewed with the assistance of an ALS, one should follow a simple rule: *The ALS filter used by the photographer to observe the evidence should be of the same color as the filter used in the camera.* The steps to photographing evidence viewed with an ALS are as follows:

1. Place the camera on a tripod or copy stand. If photographing a fingerprint, the face of the camera lens must be level with and parallel to the fingerprint. The same procedure is followed

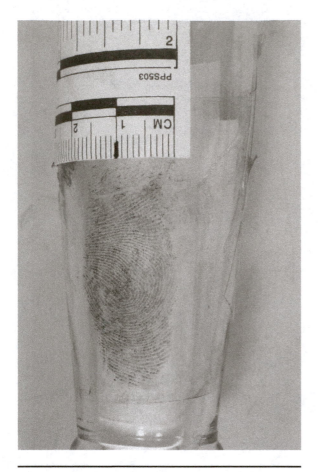

Photo 5-45. Fingerprint on curved bottle.

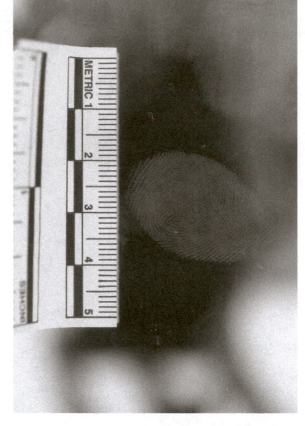

Photo 5-46. Fingerprint on mirror; poor depth of field was used to minimize reflection and double image.

for shoe impressions, bite marks, or any type of evidence subject to comparisons. When photographing evidence such as biological fluids for documentation (not comparison) purposes, the face of the camera lens need not be level or parallel with the evidence.

2. The same filter color used on the ALS is used on the camera. A glass or plastic filter is connected to the front of the camera lens. In lieu of a camera lens filter, a square plastic filter can be held in front of the lens.

3. The ALS and the square plastic filter should be stationary. A stand with clamps can be used to hold the ALS and plastic square in place. The ALS should be positioned at an oblique (less than 90 degree) angle a few inches from the fingerprint.

4. Depth-of-field depends on the surface. F-8 is usually sufficient. If the surface is curved, the depth-of-field should be increased.

5. ISO 400 film is recommended and the shutter speed is adjusted for proper exposure.

6. Auto white balance is recommended.

7. A scale is placed next to the fingerprint. The camera's photo frame is filled. Photographs without and with a scale should be taken.

8. The photographer should bracket the exposure, even if photographing digitally. Although the image may appear satisfactory on the LCD screen, the actual fingerprint image may be too bright. Therefore, the photographer should take underexposed and overexposed images two full f-stops in both directions. Underexposed images are usually best for fingerprints viewed with an ALS.

Advanced Lighting Techniques

Lighting conditions are problematic when photographing a fingerprint located on reflective evi-

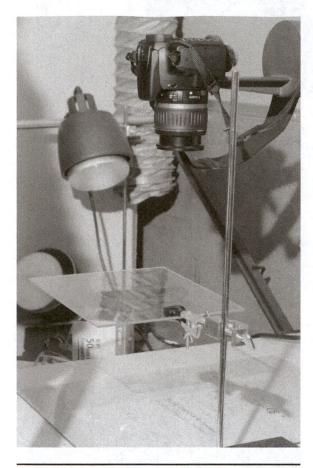

Photo 5-47. ALS photography setup with a copy stand.

dence. Diffusing the light or controlling its angle may solve the problem. The light may be diffused with translucent paper, a white cloth, or a plastic diffuser. A black shield works well also.

Black Shield

Black shield can be used to prevent hot spots in a photograph. The following steps are recommended:

1. Place the evidence item on a table or stand and position continuous lighting (photographic flood lamps) at a 45 degree angle to the evidence.
2. Position a camera equipped with a macro lens directly above the evidence. The face of the camera lens must be parallel with the evidence. Attach a shutter release cable.
3. Using a piece of black cardboard or other black shield with a hole large enough

to accommodate the camera lens, position the shield in front of the camera with the lens protruding through the hole of the shield. Hold the shield in place with clamps connected to the stand.
4. The shield should prevent excess light from entering the camera lens and creating hot spots.
5. Use the appropriate camera settings, starting with a poor depth-of-field (for mirrors), ISO 200 or 400, tungsten white balance, and adjust the shutter speed for proper exposure. Bracket camera settings. Take macro photographs with and without a scale in the image.

Vertical Illumination (Axial Lighting)

Vertical Illumination (Axial Lighting) is a photographic technique used to refract (bend) light. The technique is often used for patent (visible) fingerprints observable only when light at a particular angle is reflected from the print. The following is recommended.

> **Vertical illumination (axial lighting)** A photographic technique used to refract (bend) light. The technique is often used for patent (visible) fingerprints observable only when light at a particular angle is reflected from the print.

1. The vertical illumination technique should be used in dark or near dark conditions.
2. Place the evidence item on a horizontal surface.
3. Place a camera equipped with a macro lens on a tripod directly above the evidence. The camera lens must be parallel with the evidence. Attach a shutter release cable.
4. Place a continuous light source (e.g., photographic flood lamp) to the side of and slightly above the evidence and direct the light beam to the side and just above the evidence.
5. Adjust the camera to the appropriate settings (good depth-of-field such as F-11, tungsten white balance, ISO 200 or 400), and adjust the shutter speed for proper exposure.
6. Hold a piece of glass between the evidence and camera lens at a 45 degree angle to the light source.
7. Peer through the camera's viewfinder while holding the shutter release cable with one hand and tilting the glass slightly with the other hand. The fingerprint is observable when the light refracts (bends) at the appropriate angle to the evidence. Take the photograph when the fingerprint is visible through the viewfinder. Take macro photographs with and without a scale (Siljander & Fredrickson, 1997).

Photo 5-48. ALS photography setup with a quadrapod.

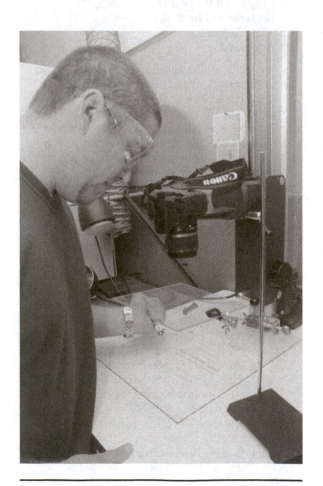

Photo 5-49. Forensic technician preparing for ALS photo.

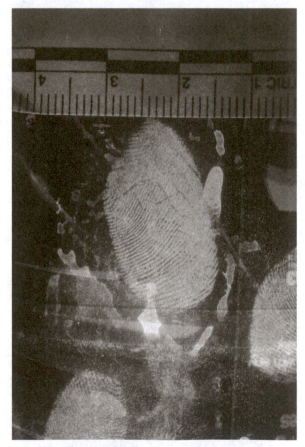

Photo 5-50. Photo taken with ALS.

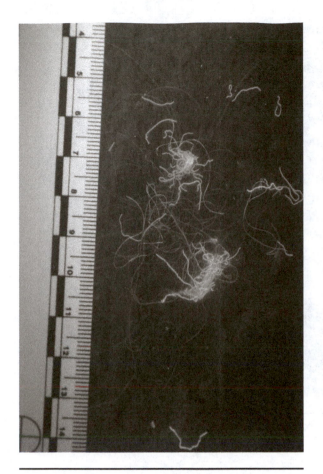

Photo 5-51. Photo taken with ALS.

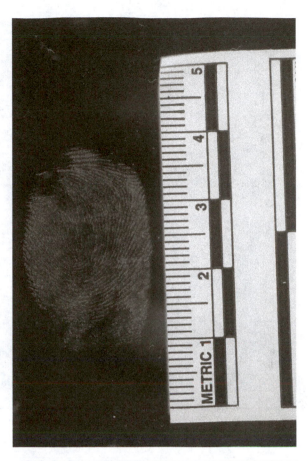

Photo 5-53. Resulting photograph of black shield photography.

Photo 5-52. Photographic setup using a black shield.

Photo 5-54. Photographic setup vertical illumination/axial lighting.

Photo 5-55. Photographic setup vertical illumination/ axial lighting.

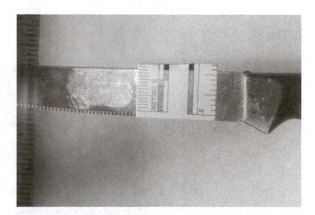

Photo 5-56. Resulting photograph of vertical illumination/axial lighting photography.

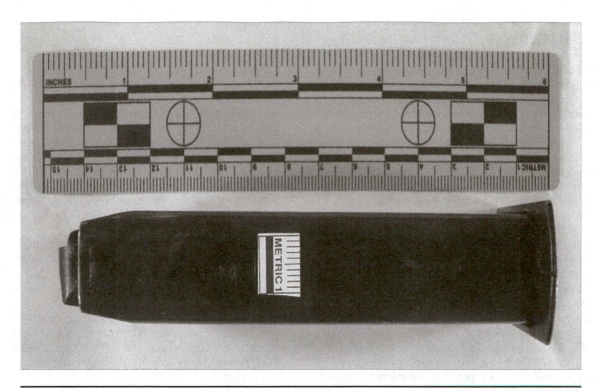

Photo 5-57. Orientation and close-up photographs of a fingerprint on the magazine of a handgun. The fingerprint was photographed using vertical illumination/axial lighting. Courtesy of the Chula Vista, California, Police Department.

Photo 5-58. Orientation and close-up photographs of a fingerprint on the magazine of a handgun. The fingerprint was photographed using vertical illumination/axial lighting. Courtesy of the Chula Vista, California, Police Department.

Photo 5-59. Orientation and close-up photographs of a fingerprint on the magazine of a handgun. The fingerprint was photographed using vertical illumination/axial lighting. Courtesy of the Chula Vista, California, Police Department.

SUMMARY

An LPE may be a sworn peace officer, forensic technician, or other public safety professional. Although the training and education requirements vary among agencies, each LPE must have advanced training in friction ridge analysis and comparison. Practical training coupled with a mentorship with a seasoned LPE is essential.

The first step to analyzing a fingerprint is to determine the print's basic pattern type: arch, loop, or whorl. Each type includes subcategories.

The LPE must possess a working knowledge of the friction ridge characteristics that determine each pattern type. The fingerprint's classification is based on individual characteristics of the pattern. With the development of AFIS technology, manual classification of fingerprints is nearly obsolete.

To identify a fingerprint, the LPE follows the ACE-V method, which involves a thorough analysis of the print, comparison of the questioned to the known print, evaluation of the ridge characteristics and findings made, and verification by a second examiner. The ACE-V's scientific method helps prevent errors.

Evidence items and crime scenes may contain latent, patent, or plastic fingerprints. Retrieval of a fingerprint from evidence is dependent upon many pretransfer and transfer factors associated with the human subject of the print and the surface on which the print is deposited. Fingerprint processing and documentation methods depend on the type of print as well as substrates, surface conditions, lighting, and other factors.

Many fingerprint powders, chemicals, and processing techniques are available. An experiment on a nonevidence item should be conducted prior to using an untested technique or chemical.

Many fingerprints must be photographed for preservation purposes. The photographic technique used depends on the lighting conditions and the surface on which the fingerprint is deposited.

KEY TERMS

Define, describe, or explain the importance of each of the following:

accidental whorl fingerprint
  pattern
Automated Fingerprint
  Identification System (AFIS)
angular tented arch fingerprint
  pattern
central pocket loop whorl
  fingerprint pattern
core
cyanoacrylate ester fuming
delta
double loop whorl fingerprint
  pattern
fingerprint
fingerprint classification

fingerprint identification
friction ridge
inner tracing
Integrated Automated
  Fingerprint Identification
  System (IAFIS)
latent fingerprint
loop fingerprint pattern
loop-type tented arch fingerprint pattern
meet tracing
outer tracing
patent print
plain arch fingerprint pattern
plain whorl fingerprint pattern

plastic print
radial loop
ridge count
ridge formation (minutiae)
sequential processing
sufficient recurve
tented arch fingerprint pattern
type lines
ulnar loop
upthrust tented arch fingerprint
  pattern
vertical illumination (axial
  lighting)
whorl fingerprint pattern

DISCUSSION AND REVIEW QUESTIONS

1. What are the three basic fingerprint patterns and their subcategories?
2. What is a ridge count?
3. Describe the technique used to conduct a whorl tracing.

4. Explain the importance of ACE-V methodology.
5. How do latent, patent, and plastic fingerprints differ?

6. Describe the difference between standard black and magnetic powders.
7. How are dye stains used to develop latent fingerprints?
8. Describe safety precautions regarding ninhydrin.
9. List the steps for documenting and preserving a bloody fingerprint.
10. Describe the basic steps in photographing a fingerprint.

CASE STUDY—PHOTOGRAPHING FINGERPRINTS

At approximately 7:00 a.m., on January 29, 2003, a nine-year-old girl was walking to school in the 400 block of L Street in Chula Vista, California. A gold Jeep Grand Cherokee drove in front of her and an unknown, large male jumped out and grabbed the young girl. The male forced the girl into the vehicle through the right rear passenger door. The little girl quickly crawled across the seat and attempted to open the left rear passenger door, but it was locked. The male entered the back seat, closed the right rear passenger door behind him and proceeded to fondle and physically molest the little girl. When he finished, the male released the girl from the vehicle and drove away. The girl ran home, told her family, and police were notified. Chula Vista police detectives and patrol officers searched for the vehicle and the suspect. Patrol activity was also increased during school hours.

At approximately 12:50 p.m., on March 24, 2003, a 12-year-old girl was accosted while walking home from school in the 200 block of G Street in Chula Vista, California. An unknown male attacked the 12-year-old in a manner similar to that of the nine-year-old victim on January 29th. This time, the man held a knife to the victim's throat and he was much more violent. After the attack, the male released the victim who ran to a nearby house to telephone the police. Vehicle and suspect descriptions were similar to the January 29th incident.

At approximately 5:10 p.m., on March 24, Chula Vista police agent Adkins was driving a marked police vehicle in the area where the crimes had occurred when he observed a vehicle that matched the victims' descriptions. The driver was speeding in a school zone. Agent Adkins stopped the vehicle and asked the driver for identification. The driver did not have identification in his possession. However, he claimed to have a valid Georgia driver's license and provided a fictitious name to the officer. A records check on the vehicle's registration revealed a Florida driver's license with the driver's true identity as Domenico Diaz-Granados.

Diaz-Granados was arrested for providing false information to an officer and for an outstanding arrest warrant. Case detectives Hinzman and Hinkledire interviewed Diaz-Granados at the police station. From a photo lineup, the victims positively identified Diaz-Granados as their assailant. Subsequently, a physical lineup was conducted. In separate viewings, both victims positively identified Diaz-Granados as the assailant.

A media release was issued and a third victim, aged seven, came forward and stated she was similarly victimized on January 12, 2003, while walking home from school. The third victim also positively identified Diaz-Granados as her assailant. The detectives noticed that the perpetrator became more violent with each successive attack.

The detectives obtained a search warrant for Diaz-Granados and his vehicle. One of the authors of this book, Tina Young, was employed as an evidence technician with the Chula Vista Police Department at the time of the incidents. Young photographed Diaz-Granados and processed him for forensic evidence. Hair samples, fingernail scrapings, DNA swabs, and fingerprints were collected.

The suspect's vehicle was photographed and searched for forensic evidence. A strong odor of men's cologne was noticeable in the vehicle. One of the victims had previously confirmed that there was a strong odor of men's cologne inside the vehicle in which she was assaulted. Hairs and fibers were collected from the seats and floors.

While processing the vehicle with black fingerprint powder, Young developed a hand print on the exterior of the right rear passenger door. The print appeared to be the size of a child's hand. Near the child-sized handprint was a large print that appeared to be the size of a man's hand. Young photographed the handprints and each individual fingerprint. After photographing the hand and finger prints in detail, Young lifted the developed prints. However, some of the fingerprint powder did not adhere completely to the fingerprint tape.

The forensic evidence was analyzed by criminalists at the San Diego County Sheriff's

Department crime laboratory. No DNA or trace evidence that could link any of the victims to the vehicle was discovered. Identification could not be made from the fingerprint lifts because some of the powder did not adhere to the appropriate minutiae points. Chula Vista Police Department LPEs Hunt and Viesca used the photos of the prints to identify a fingerprint on the small handprint as belonging to one of the victims. A fingerprint on the large handprint was linked to Diaz-Granados. The identification was made from the photographs taken of the hand and fingerprints.

A jury convicted the suspect. He received a 100 years-to-life sentence for his crimes. Jury members later told investigators that the photographs of the prints were the primary reason for the guilty verdict.

1. Why is it important to photograph hand or finger prints prior to lifting?
2. Develop a plan to search for and collect prints from a suspect vehicle.
3. Why should the forensic technician utilize sequential steps in evidence documentation?

LAB EXERCISES

Fingerprint Processing and Photography

Equipment and Supplies Required Per Student:

- one 35-mm camera (film or digital)
- one 24 exposure roll of film (if film camera is used)
- one macro camera lens
- one light source (photographic flood lamp, if available)
- one shutter release cable
- one tripod or stand
- one adhesive-backed scales
- one bottle or beverage can, and used compact disk (CD)
- one pair of vinyl or latex gloves
- one container of black fingerprint powder
- one powder fingerprint brush
- one roll of fingerprint lifting tape (or fingerprint lifter)
- 10–15 fingerprint cards
- fingerprint ink and slab
- fingerprint roller
- 10-print card (one per student)
- fingerprint ink remover
- paper towels

Exercise #1—10-Print Ink Cards
1. While working in pairs, each student creates a 10-print inked fingerprint card from the other.

2. The owner of the fingerprints should save the card for future exercises.

Exercise #2—Fingerprint Processing
1. Each student will place fingerprints on a CD and a bottle or can.
2. Wearing a pair of gloves, process the CD and bottle or can for latent fingerprints using the black fingerprint powder technique discussed in this chapter.
3. After fingerprints are developed, stop and proceed to Exercise #3.

Exercise #3—Photograph Fingerprint on a Curved Surface
1. Each student will use photography techniques discussed in this chapter to photograph one fingerprint that was developed on the CD and bottle or can.
2. After photography is complete, continue processing the evidence by lifting the fingerprint.

Exercise #4—Latent to Inked Fingerprint Comparisons
1. Compare the processed latent fingerprints to the 10-print card.
2. Identify the fingers on the latent prints

WEB RESOURCES

International Association for Identification: www.theiai.org

Southern California Association of Fingerprint Officers: www.scafo.org

Chesapeake Bay Division—International Association for Identification: www.cbdiai.org

Integrated Automated Fingerprint Identification System: www.fbi.gov/hq/cjisd/iafis

Evidence crime scene products: www.evidence-crimescene.com

Sirchie Fingerprint Laboratories: www.sirchie.com

6

Crime Scene Processing

LEARNING OUTCOMES

After completing this chapter, the reader should be able to:

- describe the role of the first responding officer,
- articulate the steps to processing a crime scene,
- demonstrate the ability to photograph a crime scene,
- describe evidence search techniques,
- demonstrate the ability to locate and photograph evidence at a crime scene,
- explain the requirements for obtaining a search warrant.

INTRODUCTION

The individual technical skills associated with photography, crime scene sketching, evidence collection, and fingerprint processing are integrated and collectively utilized to perform the primary task of the forensic technician—processing a crime scene. The task is approached systematically. The goal is to properly document the scene and the evidence.

This chapter presents the systematic approach and the methodical steps necessary to correctly process a crime scene. The approach may be adapted to fit the unique needs of each scene. This chapter also addresses the challenges faced when processing a crime scene.

ROLE OF THE FIRST RESPONDING OFFICER

When a crime occurs, victims and witnesses often telephone 9-1-1. This is especially true if the crime involves violence. The 9-1-1 calls are received by police, sheriff, state police, highway patrol, and other emergency dispatchers. The dispatchers quickly obtain information regarding the crime and its location, the status of the victim, and the suspect. Through radio communication the dispatcher relays the information to officers in the field who respond to the incident scene.

The first priority for the responding officer(s) is safety, confirming that the suspect is no longer in the immediate area or is not a threat to the officer or citizens at the scene. Secondly, priority is given to preservation of human life. Peace officers often arrive at a scene prior to emergency medical personnel. Therefore, the first responding police officer will initiate lifesaving measures such as CPR and first aid. Other officers search the area for the suspect while an officer secures and restricts access to the scene with police barrier tape. Other available officers obtain preliminary information from witnesses. After the scene is secured, investigators and forensics personnel arrive to process the scene.

CALL-OUT AND BRIEFING

Investigators and forensics personnel are notified (called out) to respond to an incident scene. The forensic technician should record the date and time the *call-out* is received. The forensic technician proceeds to the scene, typically in an agency crime scene vehicle stocked with appropriate forensic science supplies and equipment. The forensic technician meets the investigator(s) at the crime scene, where a *briefing* about the incident typically occurs.

The forensic technician should record arrival time at the incident scene and the time the briefing commences. All investigators and forensics personnel responsible for processing the crime scene should be present at the briefing. The briefing is typically conducted by a patrol sergeant or the first responding officer at the crime scene. The person conducting the briefing provides personnel with the details of the case based on available information. The forensic technician should also document the names and identification numbers of all personnel present.

Although a designated crime scene may be identified with police barrier tape, all personnel should exercise caution when approaching the crime scene briefing area. Evidence may be located outside the perimeter of the barrier tape.

During the briefing, the forensic technician inquires about case specifics. Responses to questions relative to the position of the suspect and the witnesses are very helpful in determining appropriate scene processing protocol. Asking if any fragile evidence or area within the scene has been disturbed is also important. The forensic technician should be made aware of any such disturbances at the scene (e.g., tracked blood, shoe or tire impressions from first responder activity). For example, emergency medical personnel or police officers may have stepped in the victim's blood while conducting lifesaving measures and transported the blood through the scene.

After the briefing, the forensic technician is prepared to process the scene. Challenges unique to a scene may cause the specialist to adjust processing priorities.

INITIAL SEARCH FOR EVIDENCE

The **initial search for evidence** occurs after the briefing. Typically, the forensic technician(s) and crime scene investigator (if one is assigned) survey the scene to determine and prioritize tasks. The patrol sergeant or first responding officer at the scene may assist in the scene survey if important items must be identified and located. Fragile evidence, such as shoe impressions, observed by the first responding officer is protected during the survey.

The forensic technician records the date and time the initial search for

Initial search for evidence Search conducted by the forensic technician(s) and crime scene investigator (if one is assigned) to survey the scene to determine and prioritize tasks.

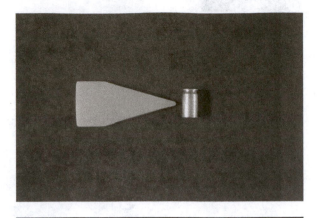

Photo 6-1. Bullet casting and first responder triangle marker.

evidence commences. During the initial search, the forensic technician records notes on areas of interest and location of evidence. The specialist also notes environmental and premises conditions: lighting, open doors or windows, unusual arrangements, point of entry or exit by the suspect, and areas that appear disturbed.

The forensic technician should proceed slowly. During the initial search, the forensic technician's senses (sight, smell, hearing, and touch) are most alert. At outdoor, nighttime crime scenes, evidence such as blood drops on black pavement may be difficult to observe, and expended firearms casings and projectiles in grass or under bushes will be difficult to locate.

The forensic technician should carry reflective first responder triangle markers during the initial search of the scene, placing a marker near each evidence item located. The markers also alert other crime scene personnel to the location of difficult-to-observe evidence.

After a careful survey (initial search) of the scene, the forensic technician proceeds with photographic documentation of the scene and the evidence.

GENERAL CRIME SCENE PHOTOGRAPHY

The forensic technician records the date and time that crime scene photography begins. When photographing a crime scene, indoors or out, the forensic technician should start outside the perimeter of the scene and work toward the middle. Some agencies require that the forensic technician write the case (incident) number, location of the incident scene, and name and identification

NORTH ↑	
CASE NUMBER	
TYPE OF CRIME	
LOCATION OF CRIME	
VICTIM	
DATE / TIME	
PHOTOGRAPHER	

Figure 6-1. Blank photo card.

number of the photographer on a 3″x 5″ card, which is photographed. The card or its photograph accompanies the photos taken of the scene.

If the scene is located in an urban setting, the forensic technician should take overlapping photographs of the nearest street, street sign, and the house or building street number. The overlapping photographs are later aligned in a fashion similar to panoramic photography, so the photos illustrate the entire view of the scene.

For outdoor scenes, the forensic technician should photograph overlapping views from each side of the scene and work toward the middle. Medium views of evidence are photographed. If buildings are located next to the scene, photographs of each side of each building are taken if relevant to the scene. Relevant vehicles within an outdoor crime scene are photographed as well. If possible, all four sides of a vehicle are photographed to illustrate the location of the vehicle within the scene. Additional details on vehicle photography are presented in Chapter 8.

Camera settings depend on lighting conditions. For outdoor, daytime scenes, the best depth-of-field is utilized, ensuring that the shutter speed is not slow. Fill flash is used in shadowed areas. The white balance is selected according to the lighting conditions (e.g., *shady* if a cloudy day or *daytime bright sun* if in direct sunlight). A low (100 or 200) ISO is selected if daytime. A digital camera's resolution is set to JPEG, although some agencies require that all crime scenes be photographed in RAW.

For nighttime outdoor scenes, the camera settings are quite different. Overall wide-angle views should be taken from various sides of the scene. Because light emitted from a flash unit is limited to within 30 feet, timed exposures should be taken to photographically document overall views of the nighttime scene.

Timed-Exposure Photography

Timed-exposure photography may be necessary at night or in the dark areas. Timed-exposure photographs are obtained as follows:

1. The forensic technician is positioned at a side of the scene, overlooking the scene. Vehicles parked facing the camera should have headlights off. The camera is mounted on a tripod, and a shutter release cable is attached.
2. The focal length is set to wide-angle and infinity focus. The white balance is set to *automatic* or *custom*, depending on the camera. The shutter speed is set to bulb, the f-stop to F-8, and the ISO to 400, depending on the available light (e.g., street lights, illumination from nearby businesses or residence).
3. The forensic technician activates the shutter release cable and, depending on the intensity of available light, determines the length of time the shutter should remain open.
4. The forensic technician brackets (takes photos at different exposures) the timed exposure, depending on the intensity of the available light.

Photo 6-2. Timed exposure of scene. Courtesy of National City, California, Police Department.

If the available light is extremely uneven (very bright on one side of the scene and very dark on the other) or the entire scene is extremely dark, the forensic technician may choose to utilize a painting-with-light procedure instead of timed exposures.

Painting-With-Light Photography

Painting-with-light is a process through which one adds light to a timed-exposure photograph. Painting-with-light photography proceeds as follows:

> **Painting-with-light**
> A process through which one adds light to a timed-exposure photograph.

1. The forensic technician is positioned at one side, overlooking the scene. Vehicles facing the camera have headlights off. The camera is mounted on a tripod, and a shutter release cable is attached to the camera.
2. The focal length is set to wide-angle and infinity focus. The white balance is set to flash white balance. The shutter speed is set to bulb, the f-stop to F-8, and the ISO to 400.
3. Ideally, two people paint with light. One person is positioned at the camera and covers the lens with a black card or dark object. The second person is positioned behind an obstruction (e.g., tree or parked car) and aims a detached flash unit (set on manual flash) toward the scene (away from the camera).
4. The flash unit person signals the camera person to activate the shutter. The camera person removes the black card covering the camera lens and activates the shutter. The flash unit person releases a burst of light from the flash unit. As soon as the burst of light is observed, the camera person covers the lens with the black card.
5. The flash unit person moves to another location within the scene, again hiding behind an object, and signals the camera person to remove the black card. The black card is removed, and the flash unit person releases a burst of light from the flash unit, highlighting another area of the scene.
6. The process is repeated until all areas of the scene are exposed to light. The camera person deactivates the shutter release cable, ending the exposure.

When painting with light, the person activating the flash unit must not aim the flash unit toward the camera. The entire exposure will be overexposed (washed out).

Photo 6-3. Painting-with-light of scene. Courtesy of National City, California, Police Department.

Painting-with-light is not conducted if evidence items can be destroyed as the flash unit person traverses the scene. In lieu of painting-with-light, one may utilize multiple flash units (slaves) that are placed strategically throughout the crime scene. The units are synchronized to flash simultaneously when the shutter is released.

Although not recommended, painting-with-light can be accomplished by a single person. The photographer releases the shutter and quickly runs through the scene, stopping behind objects and activating the flash unit at each stop. The photographer quickly returns to the camera and deactivates the shutter, ending the exposure.

Outdoor Nighttime Flash Photography

After painting-with-light or obtaining timed exposures, overall views of the scene should be photographed with a flash unit. Subsequently, several medium views should be taken with the camera set to flash white balance and the ISO to 200 or 400. The shutter speed should not be faster than the flash synchronization speed of the camera. A flash unit with camera settings at F-5.6 and shutter speed of 1/125 or F-8 and shutter speed of 1/60 are good choices. The resolution should remain the same.

The photographer should repeat overall view photography of the scene during daylight hours. Although many of the evidence items may have been removed, it is advantageous to have overall views of the area with good lighting. If a high-elevation location exists near the scene (e.g., hilltop or roof of a building), it is recommended that the photographer take pictures of the scene from the higher vantage point.

DETAILED SEARCH FOR EVIDENCE

After overall views of the crime scene and medium views of apparent evidence are photographed, the forensic technician conducts a **detailed search**. The date and time the detailed search for evidence commences are recorded in the field notes. The search for evidence starts at the perpetrator's point of entry to the crime scene, if known, and continues systematically throughout the scene.

Detailed search A search for evidence that starts at the perpetrator's point of entry (if known) to the crime scene and continues systematically throughout the scene.

Photo 6-4. Overall views of outdoor night scene. Courtesy of National City, California, Police Department.

Photo 6-5. Overall views of outdoor night scene. Courtesy of National City, California, Police Department.

Photo 6-6. Overall views of outdoor night scene. Courtesy of National City, California, Police Department.

Photo 6-7. Overall views of outdoor night scene. Courtesy of National City, California, Police Department.

Photo 6-8. Overall views of outdoor night scene. Courtesy of National City, California, Police Department.

Photo 6-9. Overall views of outdoor night scene. Courtesy of National City, California, Police Department.

Photo 6-10. Overall views of outdoor night scene. Courtesy of National City, California, Police Department.

Photo 6-11. Overall views of outdoor night scene. Courtesy of National City, California, Police Department.

Photo 6-12. Overall views of outdoor night scene. Courtesy of National City, California, Police Department.

Photo 6-13. Overall views of outdoor night scene. Courtesy of National City, California, Police Department.

Photo 6-14. Overall views of outdoor night scene. Courtesy of National City, California, Police Department.

A numerical evidence placard is placed near each evidence item. Many placards contain measuring scales that illustrate the length of the evidence item. All placards should face the photographer so the item numbers are observed in a photograph.

The detailed search for evidence should be systematic, utilizing an accepted crime scene search method. Ideally, a scene is searched at least twice, with different individuals conducting each search. Multiple searches by different personnel help to ensure that evidence is not overlooked (Michelson, 2004).

Spiral Search Method

Utilizing the **spiral search method,** the searcher begins at the center of the crime scene and proceeds outward in a circular fashion to the outer edge. Alternatively,

Spiral search method Search that begins at the center of the crime scene and then proceeds outward in a circular fashion to the outer edge.

the searcher may begin at an outer edge of the scene and spiral inward. The spiral search method is best suited to indoor scenes.

Strip Search Method

The **strip search method** is ideal for large outdoor crime scenes (e.g., field or parking lot). It may also be applied in a street to search for small items such as expended firearm cartridge casings and projectiles. The strip search involves one or more persons walking in a linear fashion, reversing directions at the outer edge of the scene to search an unsearched strip.

> **Strip search method**
> A strip search involves one or more persons walking in a linear fashion, reversing directions at the outer edge of the scene to search an unsearched strip.

Line Search Method

The **line search method** is similar to the strip search. The line search is used in large, outdoor areas, but instead of reversing directions, a line of searchers walk side by side in one direction only. The location of evidence is marked. The line search method is not recommended unless search personnel are available in sufficient numbers.

> **Line search method**
> The line search is used in large, outdoor areas. Instead of reversing directions, a line of searchers walk side-by-side in one direction only.

Grid Search Method

The **grid search method** is appropriate for large outdoor crime scenes. The grid search is similar to a strip search except that it requires a search

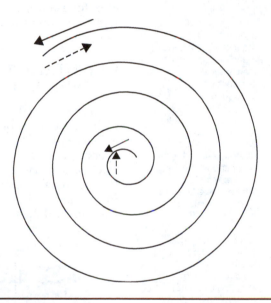

Figure 6-2. Spiral search diagram.

Figure 6-3. Strip search diagram.

Figure 6-4. Line search diagram.

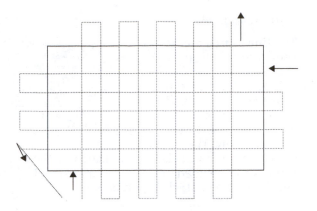

Figure 6-5. Grid search diagram.

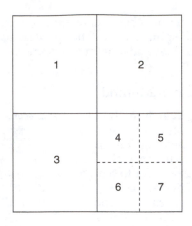

Figure 6-6. Quadrant search diagram.

in four directions rather than two. After the searcher weaves through the scene from two directions (e.g., north–south), the searcher repeats the search from the opposite direction (e.g., east–west) and weaves back and forth through the scene in search of evidence (Gardner, 2005).

Grid search method Appropriate for large outdoor crime scenes. The grid search is similar to a strip search except it requires a search in four directions rather than two. After the searcher weaves through the scene from two directions (e.g., north-south), the searcher repeats the search from opposite directions (e.g., east-west) and weaves back and forth through the scene in search of evidence.

Quadrant (Zone) Search Method

The **quadrant (zone) search method** involves dividing the search area into four quadrants (zones). Each quadrant is searched separately, until the entire scene is searched.

The quadrant search method is appropriate indoors or out, and is often used to search inside vehicles. Each major section of the vehicle is identified as a zone (e.g., driver's area, front passenger area, rear passenger area, trunk, and engine compartment). Details for searching a vehicle are discussed in Chapter 8.

The zone search method is also used to search large mass casualty or disaster scenes (e.g., aircraft crashes or bombing scenes). The large area is isolated and subdivided into quadrants or zones. A searcher is assigned to each subdivided area.

Search methods can be used interchangeably at a variety of crime scenes, depending on the

Quadrant (zone) search method A search that involves dividing the search area into four quadrants (zones). Each quadrant is searched separately, until the entire scene is searched.

preference of the forensic technician. The methods can also be used simultaneously. A large search area, for example, may be subdivided into zones, with each zone searched using the line search method.

ORIENTATION PHOTOS OF EVIDENCE

After the detailed search for evidence is complete, crime scene photography resumes with evidence placards in place. Depending on agency policy, a compass or "North" arrow indicator card is placed near each evidence placard. Photos are taken from the perimeter of the scene toward the evidence and from the evidence outward toward the perimeter.

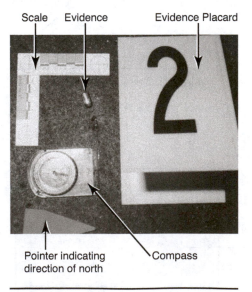

Figure 6-7. Evidence, evidence placard, scale, compass, north direction.

Photo 6-15. Medium views of evidence with yellow placards. Courtesy of National City, California, Police Department.

Photo 6-16. Medium views of evidence with yellow placards. Courtesy of National City, California, Police Department.

Photo 6-17. Medium views of evidence with yellow placards. Courtesy of National City, California, Police Department.

The photography resumption time is recorded in the field notes. The photographer focuses on evidence items, capturing medium views (within 10 feet) of the objects with accompanying placards observed in the photos. Multiple images of each item from several viewpoints are photographed so the relational distance between evidence items can be observed.

The photographer may choose to take a series of medium views from various perspectives, followed by close-up views of evidence items that are in close proximity to one another. Subsequent to each medium and close-up series, the photographer relocates to another evidence item, repeating the medium and close-up view photo series. Alternatively, the photographer may choose to photograph medium (orientation) views of all evidence items first, returning later to photograph close-up views of

the evidence items. Either procedure is acceptable. However, special attention must be given to close-up photography.

CLOSE-UP PHOTOS

When photographing close-up views of evidence, the photographer must ensure that a numerical evidence placard and a measuring device (e.g., ruler) are near the evidence item in the photo. A separate measuring device is not required if the placard contains a built-in measurement scale. The photographer should fill the frame of the photograph with the evidence item, the placard, and measuring device (if applicable), and photograph the item with the camera lens casing perpendicular to the evidence. The face of the camera lens should be parallel with the evidence. Some agencies require that a close-up image without a placard or measuring device be captured as well.

Photo 6-18. Medium views of evidence with yellow placards. Courtesy of National City, California, Police Department.

Photo 6-19. Medium views of evidence with yellow placards. Courtesy of National City, California, Police Department.

Photo 6-20. Medium views of evidence with yellow placards. Courtesy of National City, California, Police Department.

Photo 6-21. Medium views of evidence with yellow placards. Courtesy of National City, California, Police Department.

Photo 6-22. Close-up view of evidence with yellow placards. Courtesy of National City, California, Police Department.

Photo 6-25. Close-up view of evidence with yellow placards. Courtesy of National City, California, Police Department.

Photo 6-23. Close-up view of evidence with yellow placards. Courtesy of National City, California, Police Department.

Photo 6-26. Close-up view of evidence with yellow placards. Courtesy of National City, California, Police Department.

Photo 6-24. Close-up view of evidence with yellow placards. Courtesy of National City, California, Police Department.

Photo 6-27. Close-up view of evidence with yellow placards. Courtesy of National City, California, Police Department.

Photo 6-28. Close-up view of evidence with yellow placards. Courtesy of National City, California, Police Department.

Photo 6-31. Close-up view of evidence with yellow placards. Courtesy of National City, California, Police Department.

SUSPECT AND VICTIM PATHWAY PHOTOS

A suspect or a victim may flee a crime scene, dropping or discarding evidence along the escape route. The pathway may proceed down alleys or through backyards, parking lots, or other areas. The pathway is considered part of the crime scene and should be photographed and processed for evidence.

When photographing a pathway, the photographer should set the camera's focal length at 50 mm, the focal length closest to what is observed by the human eye. The photographer should follow the path, taking photographs every 20 feet until the pathway is completely photographed. The pathway is photographed in both directions (to and from the incident scene). When a pathway direction changes (e.g., evidence indicates that the suspect or victim turned a corner or ran behind a building), the photographer should photograph each direction change separately. When evidence is observed along the pathway, the evidence is photographed in the same manner as other items of evidence located at the incident scene.

Photographs of a suspect or victim pathway can be accomplished day or night. Camera settings vary depending on the lighting conditions. During daylight hours, the photographer should choose good depth-of-field, yet set the aperture to allow ample light to enter the camera. F-11 and F-16 are typical daylight aperture settings. The photographer should use a light meter to calculate an appropriate shutter speed, ensuring that the shutter speed is not too slow for the focal length. The white balance is based on lighting conditions (e.g., *shade white balance* if photographing in the shade). The photographer may use *fill flash* for shadowed areas.

Photo 6-29. Close-up view of evidence with yellow placards. Courtesy of National City, California, Police Department.

Photo 6-30. Close-up view of evidence with yellow placards. Courtesy of National City, California, Police Department.

During nighttime hours, the photographer should choose an aperture setting that will allow enough light into the camera yet provide depth-of-field. A flash unit is also used, and flash white balance is selected.

INDOOR CRIME SCENE PHOTOGRAPHY

For indoor crime scenes, photography starts outside the structure with an image of the street address captured in a photo. Next, photographs are taken facing the scene from opposite directions. If the premises contain a front or back yard, overall views should be taken of the yard(s) as well. If apparent evidence is located in a yard, medium views (five to ten feet) of the evidence should be taken during the initial photography stage. The forensic technician proceeds to the interior of the structure, capturing overlapping views from each corner of each room. Medium views of apparent evidence are obtained.

A camera flash is used for indoor scenes. Flash white balance is selected. The ISO is dependent on the ambient (artificial) light. If the indoor scene is well lit, ISO 200 is sufficient. If the scene is dark, ISO 400 is preferred. A camera setting of F-5.6 and shutter speed of 1/125 or F-8 and shutter speed of 1/60 are good choices. The resolution remains the same.

The same basic photographic steps are followed for an indoor scene as with an outdoor scene. Overall and medium views are photographed, followed by a detailed search for evidence. Evidence placards are set in place, and orientation and close-up view photos are taken of the evidence items.

Photo 6-32. Indoor crime scene photos. Courtesy of National City, California, Police Department.

THE CRIME SCENE DIAGRAM

After the crime scene and evidence items are photographed, the forensic technician should measure and sketch the scene. The time sketching begins is recorded in the field notes. Details on crime scene sketching and diagrams are discussed in Chapter 3.

EVIDENCE COLLECTION

After the scene is sketched, the forensic technician collects and preserves the evidence. The collection time is recorded in the field notes. Details of evidence collection and packaging are discussed in Chapter 4.

DEAD BODY PROCESSING

Overview

If a dead human body is located at the scene, it will typically remain at the scene until a medical examiner or coroner arrives to retrieve or release the body. The medical examiner or coroner has jurisdiction over the body. Therefore, the body

Photo 6-33. Indoor crime scene photos. Courtesy of National City, California, Police Department.

Photo 6-34. Indoor crime scene photos. Courtesy of National City, California, Police Department.

Photo 6-35. Indoor crime scene photos. Courtesy of National City, California, Police Department.

Photo 6-36. Indoor crime scene photos. Courtesy of National City, California, Police Department.

Photo 6-37. Indoor crime scene photos. Courtesy of National City, California, Police Department.

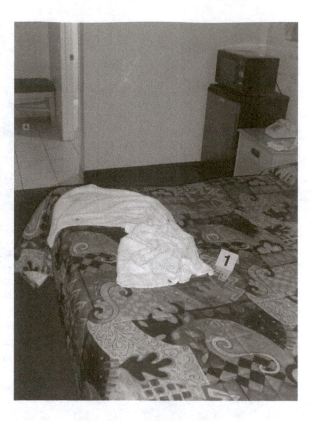

Photo 6-38. Indoor crime scene photos. Courtesy of National City, California, Police Department.

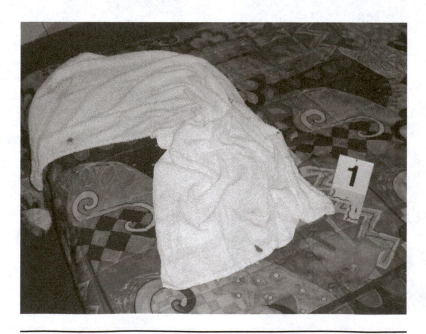

Photo 6-39. Indoor crime scene photos. Courtesy of National City, California, Police Department.

Photo 6-40. Indoor crime scene photos. Courtesy of National City, California, Police Department.

Photo 6-42. Indoor crime scene photos. Courtesy of National City, California, Police Department.

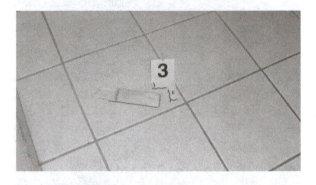

Photo 6-43. Indoor crime scene photos. Courtesy of National City, California, Police Department.

Photo 6-41. Indoor crime scene photos. Courtesy of National City, California, Police Department.

Photo 6-44. Indoor crime scene photos. Courtesy of National City, California, Police Department.

Photo 6-45. Indoor crime scene photos. Courtesy of National City, California, Police Department.

Photo 6-46. Indoor crime scene photos. Courtesy of National City, California, Police Department.

Photo 6-47. Indoor crime scene photos. Courtesy of National City, California, Police Department.

Photo 6-48. Indoor crime scene photos. Courtesy of National City, California, Police Department.

Photo 6-49. Indoor crime scene photos. Courtesy of National City, California, Police Department.

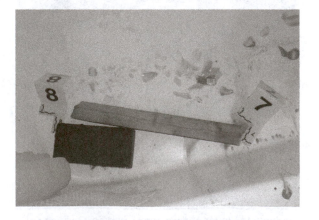

Photo 6-50. Indoor crime scene photos. Courtesy of National City, California, Police Department.

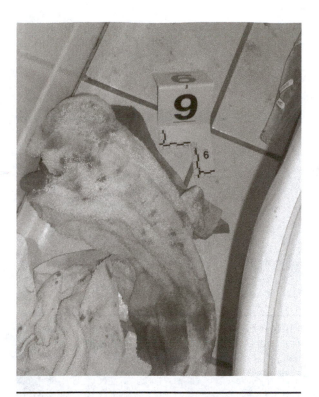

Photo 6-51. Indoor crime scene photos. Courtesy of National City, California, Police Department.

Photo 6-52. Indoor crime scene photos. Courtesy of National City, California, Police Department.

should not be moved prior to the arrival of the medical examiner or coroner staff. The roles of the medical examiner and coroner are discussed in Chapter 14.

Photographs of the Body

Before the body is moved by appropriate staff, the forensic technician must measure and photograph the deceased. Specific measurements obtained from the body at the crime scene are discussed in Chapter 3. The forensic technician should photograph the body from various angles so the body's position is well documented. The following photographic views are recommended.

Overall Views

- From the head, peering down the length of the body to the toes.
- Head to toes, from the right side of the body.
- From the feet, peering up the body toward the head.
- Head to toes, from the left side of the body.

Photo 6-53. Body in outdoor crime scene. Courtesy of National City, California, Police Department.

Photo 6-54. Body in outdoor crime scene. Courtesy of National City, California, Police Department.

Segmented Views

Segmented views of the body are photographed as well. The segmented views are photographed at a 50-mm focal length. Segmented views (head to mid-chest, mid-chest to thighs, thighs to feet) are photographed for each of the following:

- Right (or back) side of the body.
- Left (or front) side of the body.
- Top of the body (upward- or outward-facing portion of the body).

Close-Up Views

Close-up views of the sides of the head and both hands are photographed.

Other Photos

When the medical examiner or coroner arrives at the scene, the arrival time is documented, and the name(s) and identification number(s) of arriving personnel are recorded. Medical examiner staff will examine and rotate the body to expose the underside. Subsequently, the forensic technician should photograph overall and

segmented views of the underside of the body. If the body was face down in its original position, the forensic technician will photograph the face after the body is rotated onto its back.

Photo 6-57. Body in outdoor crime scene. Courtesy of National City, California, Police Department.

Photo 6-55. Body in outdoor crime scene. Courtesy of National City, California, Police Department.

Photo 6-58. Body in outdoor crime scene. Courtesy of National City, California, Police Department.

Photo 6-56. Body in outdoor crime scene. Courtesy of National City, California, Police Department.

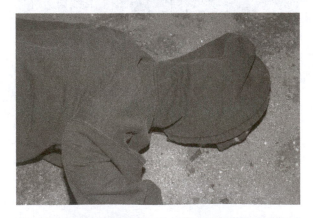

Photo 6-59. Body in outdoor crime scene. Courtesy of National City, California, Police Department.

Photo 6-60. Body in outdoor crime scene. Courtesy of National City, California, Police Department.

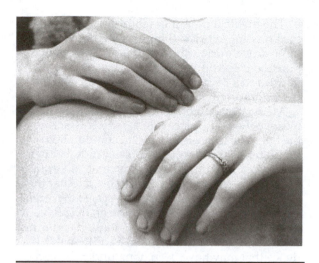

Photo 6-63. Close-up of deceased victim's hands. Courtesy of National City, California, Police Department.

Photo 6-61. Body in outdoor crime scene. Courtesy of National City, California, Police Department.

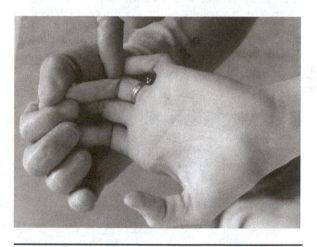

Photo 6-64. Close-up of deceased victim's hands. Courtesy of National City, California, Police Department.

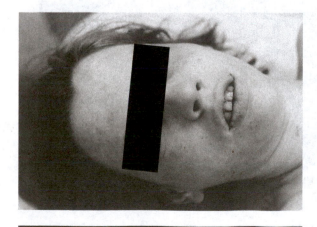

Photo 6-62. Close-up of a deceased victim's face. Courtesy of National City, California, Police Department.

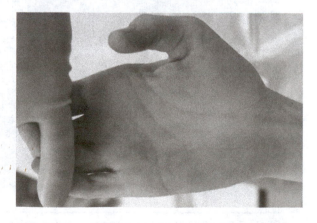

Photo 6-65. Close-up of deceased victim's hands. Courtesy of National City, California, Police Department.

The medical examiner (coroner) may search the body for injuries. If injuries are observed, the forensic technician should photograph orientation and close-up views of each injury. The injuries will be photographed in more detail at the postmortem examination (see Chapter 14).

Medical examiner (coroner) personnel will retrieve the body, place it in a body bag, and seal the bag. The forensic technician should photograph the seal and record the seal's number in the field notes. The time the body is removed from the scene is recorded in the field notes. After the body is removed from the crime scene, the forensic technician should photograph an overall view of the area where the body was located and conduct a search of the area for any additional evidence that may have been lying under the body.

High-Vantage-Point Views of Scene

At outdoor crime scenes, if possible, the forensic technician should take overall views of the scene from a high vantage point. Locations such as the roof of an adjacent building or the balcony of a nearby multilevel residence provide good locations from which one can take such photographs.

The photographs must be taken during the day, using good depth-of-field and no flash. If the crime scene is processed at night, the forensic technician should wait until sunrise to take high-vantage-point photographs.

LATENT FINGERPRINT PROCESSING

The last step in crime scene processing is typically fingerprint identification and collection. The forensic technician will record the time fingerprint collection begins. Details of latent fingerprint processing and collection techniques are discussed in Chapter 5.

FINAL WALK-THROUGH

Prior to leaving the crime scene, the forensic technician should conduct a final walk-through of the crime scene to ensure that all evidence and equipment are collected. Subsequently, the crime scene processing completion date and time are recorded in the field notes.

Photo 6-66. View of parking lot from 15th floor balcony. Courtesy of Chula Vista, California, Police Department.

EVIDENCE TRANSPORTATION AND PROCESSING

After processing the crime scene, the forensic technician transports all of the collected evidence to the property and evidence unit of the crime laboratory. Evidence items must be secured, and the chain of custody of evidence maintained at all times. Evidence such as bloody clothing should be laid out to dry in a secure and sterile blood-drying room or chamber. The remaining evidence should be prioritized for crime lab processing.

Some evidence may be transported directly to relevant sections (e.g., DNA, trace, or firearms) of the crime laboratory for analysis. The evidence must be properly packaged and the chain of custody must be maintained as the evidence is transported and distributed to relevant sections of the laboratory. Other evidence items may require detailed photography or may be processed for latent fingerprints. The forensic technician should verify the prioritization of evidence processing with the case investigator.

AERIAL PHOTOGRAPHY

Aerial views of the crime scene may be necessary as well. However, the aerial views are usually photographed weeks after the incident. Their purpose is to provide a birds-eye view of the scene's location.

Aerial photographs are best taken from a helicopter on a clear day. The photographer should sit behind the pilot so their side views are identical. The photographer can point out areas of interest, and the pilot can hover over or circle the area until the photographer captures all necessary images. The camera settings are as follows:

- Fast shutter speed of 1/500 is ideal.
- The light meter should be used for the f-stop.
- The ISO is adjusted as needed.
- The white balance is set for the type of lighting (daylight).
- To avoid vibration, the photographer should not allow the camera lens to contact the frame or window (if any) of the aircraft. The photographer should capture wide-angle, normal, and telephoto views of the scene.

For police pursuit or suspect pathways, the photographer will ask the pilot to fly the aircraft along the path. A helicopter's pilot can rotate and tilt the aircraft slightly so the photographer captures a full view of the pathway. A helicopter pilot can also fly the aircraft sideways along the path so the photographer can obtain unobstructed images along the pathway. The photographer should keep the focal length set (not alter it) until the entire pathway is photographed.

Photo 6-67. Aerial photo. Courtesy of Chula Vista, California, Police Department.

Photo 6-68. Aerial photo. Courtesy of Chula Vista, California, Police Department.

Photo 6-69. Forensic technician in helicopter.

REPORT WRITING

All tasks completed by the forensic technician are documented in various types of reports. The crime scene description and its processing, vehicle and suspect processing, and all follow-up work on evidence is documented. Some agencies provide pre-printed forms for report writing purposes. Others prefer a written narrative format for most reports. Agencies vary on the requirements for report writing. Regardless of the format, the forensic technician should keep detailed and accurate field notes on all work completed. The information contained in the notes is used to complete the appropriate report. The forensic technician should write in the first person and document events and processes chronologically. Agency report writing protocol should be followed. Additional information on report writing is presented in Chapter 15.

SEARCH WARRANTS

To process an indoor crime scene, a suspect's home, vehicle, business, or live body, a search warrant may be required. The case investigator is usually the person who writes and files the affidavit (application) for the search warrant.

Reasons for a Search Warrant

Reasonable searches and seizures are permitted under the Fourth Amendment to the U.S. Constitution. In public law enforcement, a **search** involves a governmental intrusion into an area in which a person has a reasonable expectation of privacy. The purpose of the search is to discover evidence that may be used in a criminal prosecution. A **seizure** occurs when a person's freedom of movement is restricted or when property is taken into custody by the government. A seizure involves meaningful governmental interference with a person's movement or property interest. Subject to several exceptions discussed later, a search warrant is required for any governmental intrusion.

Search A search involves a governmental intrusion into an area in which a person has a reasonable expectation of privacy. The purpose of the search is to discover evidence that may be used in a criminal prosecution.

Seizure Occurs when a person's freedom of movement is restricted or when property is taken into custody by the government.

Probable cause involves facts that would lead a person of ordinary care and prudence to believe that there is a fair probability that evidence or contraband will be found in or at a particular location. A public peace officer may seek a search warrant or conduct a warrantless vehicle search based on probable cause.

Probable cause Involves facts that would lead a person of ordinary care and prudence to believe that there is a fair probability that evidence or contraband will be found in or at a particular location.

The *scope of a probable cause search* is limited by the circumstances under which the search is being conducted. The two elements for determining the legal scope of a search include, first, what the officer is looking for (e.g., evidence, contraband, weapons, victims, or suspects) and, second, where the officer is likely to find the items or people (e.g., reasonable chance for the officer to find the object or person in the area being searched). Evidence or contraband recovered outside the lawful scope of a search may be inadmissible in a judicial proceeding.

Any evidence obtained by the government or its agents in violation of the Fourth Amendment must be excluded at trial. The purpose is to deter misconduct by peace officers by eliminating the incentive for unconstitutional searches and prohibit the admission of evidence that is obtained illegally, and to maintain the integrity of the judiciary by excluding tainted evidence from the trail. Not only is illegally seized evidence inadmissible in court, but any evidence that directly stems from this evidence is also inadmissible because it is the *fruit of the poisonous tree.*

A **search warrant** is an order issued by a judge and directed to peace officers, commanding a search of a described location for described evidence or contraband. The grounds for issuance of a search warrant must be specified in the application (affidavit) for a search warrant. Search warrants are not required in all search and seizure situations (e.g., vehicles with probable cause; probation or parole searches). However, subject to limited exceptions, some search and seizure situations (e.g., residential search, body intrusion) will almost always require acquisition of a search warrant. Specific rules regarding search warrants include the following:

Search warrant An order issued by a judge and directed to peace officers, commanding a search of a described location for described evidence or contraband.

- A search warrant requires probable cause or facts that would lead a reasonable person to believe that evidence or contraband will be found at a specific location. Probable cause can be established through a police officer's personal observations, reliable information received from citizens or other informants, and information received through official channels. Probable cause is communicated to a judge through a written or telephonic affidavit (sworn application).
- Once issued, a search warrant is valid for 10 days and is usually limited to service between 7:00 a.m. and 10:00 p.m., unless endorsed by the judge on good cause to be served at anytime of the day or night.
- Knock and notice rules apply to the service of search warrants. A police officer serving a search warrant must knock (or otherwise signal to possible occupants), identify and announce purpose, demand entry, and give

the person(s) inside reasonable opportunity to allow access. A factual exigency (emergency circumstance), such as danger to officers, destruction of evidence, or escape of a suspect, may excuse knock and notice or permit a contemporaneous entry if an exigency arises. Failure to comply with knock and notice provisions can result in the suppression of evidence seized under the authority of the search warrant.

- The scope of the search under a search warrant is limited to items and the location listed in the search warrant. Any additional evidence or contraband located in plain view or within the scope of the warrant may be legally seized as fortuitous finds. If additional evidence or contraband (e.g., drugs) observed during the warrant service causes an officer to believe there is more of the same at the premises or location, a second search warrant may be necessary to legally search further for more evidence.

- Although the requirements for search warrant returns (e.g., timing, format) vary somewhat among the states, officers are required to maintain an inventory of evidence and contraband removed from the search location and file a return (accounting of the inventory) with the issuing court (California Commission on Peace Officer Standards and Training, 2008; Gardner & Anderson, 2004; Ortmeier, 2006).

Exceptions to the Search Warrant Requirement

Several exceptions to the search warrant requirement exist. The **plain-view doctrine** holds that anything in plain view is not constitutionally protected. There are two elements to the plain-view doctrine. First, the officer must possess legal authority to be in the position from which the observation is made. Second, the officer must have probable cause to believe that the object or property observed constitutes evidence of a crime. A plain-view observation can serve as the basis for seizure of the evidence observed or can prompt a legal basis to search for more evidence or contraband. The plain-view doctrine has been

> **Plain View Doctrine** Holds that anything in plain view is not constitutionally protected. There are two elements to the plain-view doctrine. First, the officer must possess legal authority to be in the position from which the observation is made. Second, the officer must have probable cause to believe that the object or property observed constitutes evidence of a crime.

expanded to include sensory observations beyond those associated with visual recognition. Examples include plain feel (touch) and plain smell (of distinctive odor).

A **consensual encounter** is any interaction between a police officer and another that does not involve formal police restraint of the other person's freedom of movement. A consensual encounter does not involve seizure of the person under the Fourth Amendment. During a consensual encounter, a person is under no obligation to cooperate with an officer or answer questions, and is free to leave at any time. Permissible officer actions during a consensual encounter include walking up to a person or a parked vehicle and making inquiries about the subject's presence in the area; using a flashlight or spotlight for illumination; requesting, examining, and returning identification; and general follow-up conversation on a person's responses to the officer's questions. Officer actions that convert the encounter into a restriction of a person's freedom of movement include using a red light, directing or ordering a person to stop or remain, demanding identification, and retaining identification to conduct an arrest warrant check. Many police officers refer to the consensual encounter as a *contact*, a reference that is erroneous. To the average juror, contact means touching. This misunderstanding may lead a juror to believe that the officer made physical contact with the subject.

> **Consensual encounter** Any interaction between a police officer and another that does not involve formal police restraint of the other person's freedom of movement.

A **frisk** is cursory search (pat-down) of a legally detained subject for the purpose of discovering deadly or dangerous weapons that could be used to assault a police officer or other person legally authorized to arrest. A frisk can be conducted lawfully when a person is detained and the frisk is for a crime involving weapons or instrumentalities that may be used as weapons or for an offense that threatens violent conduct. The frisk's purpose is discovery of weapons to ensure officer safety. A frisk may also be conducted with consent of the subject during an encounter or nonviolent detention. The scope of a frisk is limited to objects that could reasonably be defined as weapons. The objects can be retrieved, examined, and retained during the detention.

> **Frisk** A cursory search (pat-down) of a legally detained subject for the purpose of discovering deadly or dangerous weapons that could be used to assault a police officer or other person legally authorized to arrest.

If the object is contraband, probable cause for a police officer to arrest exists. The stop and frisk of a subject cannot be based solely on an anonymous tip that the subject may be carrying a weapon.

A police officer may conduct a **search incidental (contemporaneous) to a lawful custodial arrest**. The search is limited to the arrestee and the area within the arrestee's immediate control for possible evidence, weapons, or contraband. This search includes pockets and containers in the possession of the arrestee. When a person is arrested inside a residence, a police officer may, incidental to the arrest, search the person of the arrestee and any object or area (cabinets, drawers, furniture, containers, and closets within leaping distance of the arrestee) within the arrestee's immediate control.

> **Search incidental (contemporaneous) to a lawful custodial arrest** A search limited to the arrestee and the area within the arrestee's immediate control for possible evidence, weapons, or contraband.

When a person is arrested inside or very close to a motor vehicle, a police officer may, incidental to the custodial arrest, search all compartments and containers within the passenger area of the vehicle. The passenger area is considered to be within arm's reach of the person being arrested. The search of a vehicle incidental to a lawful arrest is not authorized if the arrestee's ability to access the vehicle is restricted (e.g., the arrestee is handcuffed and cannot access the vehicle).

If a police officer has probable cause to believe evidence or contraband is in a vehicle that is mobile and accessible to a roadway, the police officer may conduct a warrantless search of the vehicle, including all compartments and containers. This type of search is referred to as the **fleeting targets exception** to the search warrant requirement.

If a vehicle is abandoned, the owner loses the reasonable exception of privacy, and the abandoned vehicle may be searched by the police without a search warrant or requirement of probable cause. Further, one may conduct an inventory search of a vehicle that has been impounded by the police. The inventory search must be in good faith and not a pretext to search without consent or probable cause. Finally, a

> **Fleeting targets exception** (to the search warrant requirement) If a police officer has probable cause to believe evidence or contraband is in a vehicle that is mobile and accessible to a roadway, the officer may conduct a warrantless search of the vehicle, including all compartments and containers in the vehicle.

vehicle that has been legally repossessed may be searched with the permission of the repossession agency.

A **consent search** is one in which a person knowingly and voluntarily waives Fourth Amendment rights after having been given a request-choice by an officer. Consent allows a police officer to conduct an exploratory investigation of the area or property to which the consenting party has possessory rights.

> **Consent search** A search in which a person knowingly and voluntarily waives Fourth Amendment rights after having been given a request-choice by an officer. Consent allows a police officer to conduct an exploratory investigation of the area or property to which the consenting party has possessory rights.

An officer may also conduct a warrantless entry into an area when necessary to protect life, health, or property, to prevent the imminent escape of fleeing suspects, or to prevent the imminent destruction of evidence. These warrantless entries are referred to as *exigency searches*. An **exigent circumstance** is an emergency that requires swift and immediate action. Any evidence or contraband an officer discovers in plain view while searching for victims or suspects is admissible.

> **Exigent circumstance** An emergency that requires swift and immediate action.

A parolee is in the *constructive custody* of the government after release from prison and is subject to conditions supervised by a parole officer or agent. A parolee waives Fourth Amendment rights during the parole period. In some states, a **parole search** may be conducted without a trigger or reasonable (particularized) suspicion, as long as the search is not arbitrary, capricious, or harassing. Thus, a search conducted under the auspices of a properly imposed parole search condition does not intrude on any reasonable expectation of privacy.

> **Parole search** Search that may be conducted without a trigger or reasonable (particularized) suspicion, as long as the search is not arbitrary, capricious, or harassing. Thus, a search conducted under the auspices of a properly imposed parole search condition does not intrude on any reasonable expectation of privacy.

In other states, a parole search by a police officer requires a trigger or reasonable suspicion of renewed criminal activity or a violation of a parole condition. In these situations, it is recommended that a police officer attempt contact with a parole officer (agent) for authorization to conduct a parole search. The parole officer reviews the reasonable suspicion information gathered by the police officer and makes an independent decision that the search is necessary to enforce parole conditions. If contact with a parole officer is impractical or unsuccessful, and a reasonable suspicion trigger otherwise exists, the search should be conducted. Case law supports parole searches under these circumstances.

A **probation search** is possible because of the supervised release of a probationer into the community. When a search clause or Fourth Amendment waiver is attached to probation conditions, a probation search may be conducted without a trigger or reasonable suspicion of renewed criminal activity. The purpose of a probation search is to ascertain if the probationer is complying with the terms of probation. For a police officer to conduct a probation search, prior authorization from a probation officer is not required. A probation search can be routinely conducted by any law enforcement officer as long as the search is not conducted in an arbitrary or harassing manner.

> **Probation search** A search to ascertain if the probationer is complying with the terms of probation.

An **administrative search** is based on a compelling governmental interest embodied in statutory or case law. Under these circumstances, the interests of society take precedence over the privacy interests of the individual. Administrative searches include searches associated with custodial institutions, booking searches, vehicle inventories, fish and game code enforcement, immigration and border inspections, U.S. immigration and customs enforcement, airport and courthouse searches, and driving-under-the-influence (DUI) sobriety checkpoints. Probation and parole searches are also forms of administrative searches.

> **Administrative search** is based on a compelling governmental interest embodied in statutory or case law. Under these circumstances, the interests of society take precedence over the privacy interests of the individual. Administrative searches include searches associated with custodial institutions, booking searches, vehicle inventories, fish and game code enforcement, immigration and border inspections, U.S. immigration and customs enforcement, airport and courthouse searches, and driving under the influence (DUI) sobriety checkpoints.

If a suspect swallowed evidence, stomach pumping or the administration of an emetic to induce vomiting can legally occur if the suspect expressly consents to such procedures. If the ingested substance presents a clear and immediate threat to the suspect's life, as independently determined by medical personnel, recognized life-saving procedures, including stomach pumping or the use of emetics may take place over the objection of the suspect. A physician may not act as an agent of the police. Evidence recovered fortuitously during an emergency procedure is admissible, however. Although it is legally possible to have a judge issue a search warrant for an emetic procedure, such circumstances are rare.

Taking a blood sample from a suspect involves a body intrusion. A separate search and seizure basis is required in addition to the suspect's being lawfully under arrest. If a blood sample is needed as a biological control in a homicide, rape, or assault case, a police officer must obtain consent from the suspect or seek a search warrant from a judge for the seizure. The suspect's blood type will not change. Therefore, there is no exigency. If a blood sample is needed for under-the-influence evidence in a driving-while-intoxicated or vehicular manslaughter case, a police officer may seize the blood sample pursuant to an exigency because of the possibility of destruction of evidence. The alcohol or drug levels will metabolize in the suspect's body during the time it takes to seek a search warrant.

There is no constitutional privilege to refuse to be fingerprinted or provide exemplar evidence (e.g., handwriting, voice, photographic) incident to a lawful arrest. This evidence is nontestimonial in nature and does not violate a suspect's Fifth Amendment privilege to be free from self-incrimination. An officer may use reasonable force to obtain such evidence, although the level of resistance by the suspect may well mitigate the quality of the exemplar evidence obtained. A resistant or uncooperative suspect should be advised that the suspect has no right to refuse to provide this evidence. Any refusal or resistance can be argued later in court as evidence of consciousness of guilt (Acker & Brody, 1999; California Commission on Peace Officer Standards and Training, 2008; Gardner & Anderson, 2004; Ortmeier, 2006).

Search Warrant Scenes

On occasion, a forensic technician is asked to assist investigators during the execution of a search warrant. Unless the forensic technician is an armed officer, entry to the scene should not be made until it is safe to do so. For an indoor scene, such as a suspect's residence, the forensic technician may photograph the overall view outside the premises prior to the indoor search for evidence. A diagram of the residence may be necessary as well.

When the search begins, evidence may be located by investigators. The forensic technician is often directed to photograph each evidence item, with orientation and close-up views, and collect and preserve each item. A sketch with the exact location of each evidence item is not typically required. The purpose of the search warrant is simply to collect evidence that may link the suspect to criminal activity. The search warrant scene is not usually the scene of the crime to which the evidence collected is linked. However, each evidence item collected must be inventoried as one of the search warrant requirements.

Receipt and Inventory

The **receipt and inventory** is a list of all evidence items collected as the result of the execution of the search warrant. The items seized are listed on a form that produces duplicate copies. One copy (a receipt) is left with those who occupy the premises. Another copy is forwarded to the judge who signed the search warrant. The original is retained in the records of the agency serving the warrant.

> **Receipt and inventory** A list of all evidence items collected as the result of the execution of the search warrant.

Dominion and Control Evidence

Dominion and control evidence is documentation that links a person to a residence or business. The documentation may be a utility bill or some other document that establishes that a person or persons exercise dominion and control over the property (e.g., residence) searched. Dominion and control evidence is a subject of a search at crime and warrant scenes.

> **Dominion and control evidence** Documentation that links a person to a residence or business.

CRIME SCENE CHALLENGES

Due to environmental (e.g., weather) and security issues, outdoor crime scenes often present more challenges than do indoor scenes. Although photography of a scene usually precedes evidence collection, circumstances may dictate that evidence collection occur prior to photography. For example, rain can deteriorate blood evidence, and wind may disperse evidence. Snow and dew can destroy latent fingerprint and trace evidence. Thus, in some situations, evidence must be collected before it is destroyed or displaced by inclement weather.

If inclement weather is probable, the forensic technician should use reflective chalk or a grease pencil to mark the location of evidence. The forensic technician can photograph the marked area after the evidence is removed. The chalk or grease pencil markings indicate the location of each evidence item.

Security issues arise at an outdoor crime scene because police barrier tape defines a scene perimeter but does not prevent access. If a victim's body is lying within the crime scene, the victim's friend or relative, overwhelmed with grief and emotion, may attempt to enter the crime scene to access the victim. In this situation, the forensic technician should immediately summon a police officer or investigator for assistance to calm the friend or family member and restrict access to the crime scene. Other interested parties such as transients, the media, or citizens who attempt access to the scene should be dealt with by sworn peace officers. The forensic technician should photograph, measure, and collect evidence near the body immediately so the body can be removed from the crime scene as soon as possible.

SUMMARY

When processing a crime scene, the following steps are taken, ideally in the order presented.

1. Call-out and briefing
2. Initial evidence search
3. General crime scene photography
4. Detailed evidence search (including assignment of numbers to evidence items)
5. Orientation photos of evidence
6. Close-up photos
7. Suspect and victims pathway photos
8. Crime scene diagram
9. Evidence collection
10. Body processing
11. Latent fingerprint processing
12. Final walk-through

Evidence collected at a crime scene is transported to the agency's property and evidence unit or to a crime laboratory. The evidence must be packaged properly, and the chain of custody of evidence must be maintained. On occasion, aerial photography of a crime or incident scene may be necessary.

All actions taken by the forensic technician must be documented through effective field note taking and report writing. Forensic technicians are also involved with collection of evidence as investigators execute search warrants.

There are many situations in which a specific crime scene protocol cannot be followed. If inclement weather may destroy evidence, collection will precede photography. A human body may require immediate removal, especially at scenes involving security issues. These and other circumstances may cause the forensic technician to alter a crime scene processing plan. As long as the evidence is properly collected and preserved, subsequent admission of evidence in a judicial proceeding should not be jeopardized.

KEY TERMS

Define, describe, or explain the importance of each of the following:

administrative search
consensual encounter
consent search
detailed search
dominion and control evidence
exigent circumstance
fleeting targets exception
frisk
grid search method

initial search (for evidence at a
    crime scene)
line search method
painting-with-light
parole search
plain-view doctrine
probation search
probable cause
quadrant (zone) search method

receipt and inventory
search
search warrant
search incidental (contemporaneous) to a lawful custodial
    arrest
seizure
spiral search method
strip search method

DISCUSSION AND REVIEW QUESTIONS

1. What is the role of the first responding officer at a crime scene?
2. What information should the forensic technician collect at a briefing?
3. What series of photographs are taken at a crime scene?
4. Describe crime scene search methods. When should the forensic technician apply a search method?
5. What is the purpose of a search warrant?

CASE STUDY—Danielle Van Dam

On the Friday evening of February 1, 2002, Brenda Van Dam and a few of her friends relaxed at Dad's Bar in the San Diego suburb of Sabre Springs. Brenda's husband, Damon, remained at home to care for their 7-year-old daughter, Danielle, and her two brothers. Damon sent the children to bed around 10:00 p.m. and fell asleep. Brenda returned home about 2:00 a.m. with four of her friends. Damon awoke to visit with Brenda and her friends. Around 3:00 a.m., the friends departed and the Van Dams went to sleep, believing their daughter was sleeping safely in her room. The next morning, Danielle was missing. The Van Dams called the police at 9:39 a.m.

The police interviewed neighbors, and forensic technicians collected evidence from the Van Dam home. Police officials soon discovered that a neighbor, David Alan Westerfield, was not at home the Saturday morning of Danielle's disappearance. Westerfield was placed under 24-hour police surveillance on February 4, after authorities became suspicious when he was observed cleaning his RV. Westerfield claimed he had been driving through the desert, at the beach, and in the mountains.

During questioning, Westerfield appeared nervous, citing 13 different destinations for his weekend RV trip. Detectives also observed small cuts on Westerfield's hands. Search warrants were obtained for his home and RV. In Westerfield's home computer files police discovered pornographic images of young girls. In his RV, police located blood, hair, and a fingerprint matching Danielle's. (It was later revealed that days after Danielle disappeared, a haggard and barefoot Westerfield stopped at a dry cleaning store to drop off two comforters, two pillow covers, and a jacket with stains that would later yield Danielle's blood.)

On February 22, police arrested Westerfield for Danielle's kidnapping. On February 27, Danielle's decomposed naked body was discovered under a cluster of oak trees 20 feet from a busy road east of San Diego. Murder was added to the charges against Westerfield. He was subsequently convicted and sentenced to death.

1. On the basis of the facts presented, what might be considered the scene(s) of the crime(s)?
2. How should a forensic technician process the crime scene(s) identified in Question 1?

LAB EXERCISE

Outdoor Crime Scene Processing

Equipment and supplies required per student team:

- one 35-mm camera (film or digital) and film (if film camera is used)
- gloves (latex or vinyl)—one pair per student
- one measuring tape or laser measuring device
- ten evidence placards
- ten medium paper bags
- one roll-packaging tape
- one marking pen
- one flashlight (depending on lighting)
- mock evidence (supplied by instructor)

The students are divided into teams of four to six. Using the techniques discussed in this chapter, each team will process an assigned outdoor mock crime scene and collect no more than 10 evidence items. The team shall prioritize the most forensically important evidence to be collected. Each team member will assist in the search for evidence (for practice purposes). Each team will designate the following assignments to the team members:

- Photographer: takes photographs and prepares photograph list report.
- Evidence collector(s): collects and packages evidence and prepares evidence list report.
- Sketcher: sketches and obtains measurements of the scene and evidence, and prepares a rough and final crime scene diagram.
- Note taker and final report writer: takes field notes indicating individual assignments, date and times; completes a narrative description of the crime scene.

Students submit all field notes, reports, packaged evidence, and scene diagrams and photographs to the instructor by the date due.

WEB RESOURCES

International Association for Identification: www.theiai.org

American Academy of Forensic Sciences: www.aafs.org

Association for Crime Scene Reconstruction: www.acsr.org

Canadian Society of Forensic Science: www.csfs.ca

Naval Criminal Investigative Service: www.ncis.navy.mil

U. S. Army Criminal Investigation Command: www.cid.army.mil

U. S. Air Force Office of Special Investigations: www.public.afosi.amc.af.mil

Crime Scene Investigation: www.crime-scene-investigator.net

7

Special Case Crime Scenes

LEARNING OUTCOMES

After completing this chapter, the reader should be able to:

- describe processing techniques used at an officer-involved shooting scene,
- explain the investigative focus at an arson scene,
- describe the role of Federal Disaster Mortuary Operational Response Team (DMORT),
- explain the cycle of violence,
- describe the types of evidence typically located at the scene of child neglect,
- explain the importance of entomological evidence.

INTRODUCTION

As a forensic technician approaches a crime scene, the unexpected should be anticipated. No two crime scenes are alike. Although standardized procedures exist to ensure that the scene and evidence are properly documented and preserved, every case and each scene present a unique set of circumstances. The tasks performed depend on the nature of the crime scene.

Several special case crime scenes are addressed in this chapter—although one cannot predict or plan for every conceivable type of incident. Yet investigators and forensic technicians can utilize their education, training, and experience to approach unusual cases in an informed and systematic manner. Additionally, experienced investigators and forensic technicians are quick to realize when it is necessary to summon additional assistance, perhaps from an agency that is better equipped to handle unusual circumstances and crime scenes.

This chapter is intended as a guide for many types of special cases. Although the list of special cases and their investigative procedures are not intended to be exhaustive, the special case crime scene discussions present a brief glimpse into the many unique types of cases a forensic technician may encounter. The forensic technician is cautioned to remember that absolutely nothing is routine in investigations.

OFFICER-INVOLVED SHOOTING (OIS) SCENES

One of the most unique crime scenes a forensic technician will process is one at which an officer injures or kills another human being. If death occurs as a result of officer actions, a homicide investigation as well as an agency internal affairs review will determine if the homicide is justifiable. The future of the officer's career and personal life is at stake. The officer as well as the employing agency may face tremendous civil liability. The officer will also be challenged by the media and scrutinized by the public.

Especially troubling are situations in which disturbed individuals chose to end their lives through violent confrontations with the police. Referred to as *suicide by cop*, the phenomenon appears to have increased in recent years. The death of the suicide-by-cop victim exacts a heavy emotional toll on the victim's family and friends as well as the officer(s) involved.

An OIS case is intense, with a lot of pressure placed on the investigators and forensic technicians involved. As with other types of cases, the forensic technician must perform each task with the utmost caution, paying close attention to detail. The forensic technician must not succumb to pressure to produce a predetermined result. The evidence must speak for itself. Objective documentation and evidence collection procedures will ensure that the facts are uncovered and presented.

The OIS Scene Briefing

The forensic technician must ask relevant questions at the OIS scene briefing: "Where was the officer when the shooting occurred?" "Where was the suspect?" "Where were the witnesses, if any?" To obtain photos of participants' viewpoints, the forensic technician must know the position of all parties involved.

OIS Scene Photography

The forensic technician should photograph an OIS scene by following the same procedure used when photographing any other incident scene. However, additional views are photographed:

- The forensic technician should position the camera at the involved officer's viewing level at the time of the shooting. The camera's focal length should be set at 50 mm. Overlapping, panoramic views of the incident area are photographed. A tripod is used to ensure that the overlapping images are photographed at the same observation level.
- The forensic technician should repeat the panoramic photography process from the victim's and witnesses' observation levels. Overlapping, panoramic photographs at 50-mm focal length should be obtained for each person's viewpoint.

OIS Scene Trajectory

If available, a firearms examiner or criminalist is summoned to the OIS scene to identify and analyze the bullet trajectory. The forensic technician will photograph trajectory results. Trajectory measurements and the photographic procedures used to document the trajectory are discussed in Chapter 10.

Processing the Officer Involved in the Shooting

Detailed photographs of the officer involved in the shooting are obtained to ensure that the officer was clearly identifiable (e.g., visible uniform, badge) as a peace officer. Overall, medium,

Photo 7-1. Officer-involved shooting outdoor scene. Courtesy of National City, California, Police Department.

Photo 7-2. Officer-involved shooting outdoor scene. Courtesy of National City, California, Police Department.

Photo 7-3. Officer-involved shooting outdoor scene. Courtesy of National City, California, Police Department.

Photo 7-5. Officer-involved shooting outdoor scene. Courtesy of National City, California, Police Department.

Photo 7-4. Officer-involved shooting outdoor scene. Courtesy of National City, California, Police Department.

Photo 7-6. Officer-involved shooting outdoor scene. Courtesy of National City, California, Police Department.

Photo 7-7. Officer-involved shooting outdoor scene. Courtesy of National City, California, Police Department.

Photo 7-8. Officer-involved shooting outdoor scene. Courtesy of National City, California, Police Department.

and close-up photographs of the officer are taken from the front, back, and side view perspectives. Photographs taken of the officer are very similar to those obtained of a suspect. The details for photographing live individuals are addressed in Chapter 13.

Photo 7-10. Officer and equipment. Courtesy of National City, California, Police Department.

Photo 7-9. Officer and equipment. Courtesy of National City, California, Police Department.

Photo 7-11. Officer and equipment. Courtesy of National City, California, Police Department.

Photo 7-12. Officer and equipment. Courtesy of National City, California, Police Department.

Photo 7-13. Officer and equipment. Courtesy of National City, California, Police Department.

Photo 7-15. Officer and equipment. Courtesy of National City, California, Police Department.

Photo 7-14. Officer and equipment. Courtesy of National City, California, Police Department.

Photo 7-16. Officer and equipment. Courtesy of National City, California, Police Department.

Photo 7-17. Officer and equipment. Courtesy of National City, California, Police Department.

Photo 7-18. Officer and equipment. Courtesy of National City, California, Police Department.

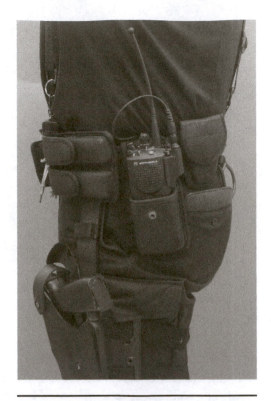

Photo 7-19. Officer and equipment. Courtesy of National City, California, Police Department.

Photo 7-20. Officer and equipment. Courtesy of National City, California, Police Department.

Additionally, the forensic technician should photograph any damage to the officer's clothing or uniform as well as any injuries sustained by the officer during the event.

Depending on agency protocol, the officer's firearm is inspected by a firearms examiner or criminalist, or a forensic technician photographs the officer's firearm. Prior to photographing a firearm, it should be rendered safe (unloaded).

If the handgun is a semi-automatic, the weapon, its magazine, and its bullets are photographed separately. Additional details for photographing firearms are discussed in Chapter 10.

GANG-RELATED HOMICIDES

Many assaults and homicides are related to gang activity, especially in large urban settings. If gang activity is suspected, the forensic technician should photograph any graffiti (tagging) located at or near the scene. Graffiti is applied with spray paint or any type of writing instrument. Graffiti is a form of gang communication that is used to mark and display a gang's name or a member's moniker (nickname).

As graffiti is photographed, the forensic technician should examine the markings. If the marking is recent, the time of the incident and the graffiti application may be linked.

Photo 7-21. Graffiti. Courtesy of Chula Vista, California, Police Department.

Photo 7-22. Graffiti. Courtesy of Chula Vista, California, Police Department.

Photo 7-23. Graffiti. Courtesy of Chula Vista, California, Police Department.

Photo 7-24. Graffiti. Courtesy of Chula Vista, California, Police Department.

Photo 7-25. Graffiti. Courtesy of Chula Vista, California, Police Department.

Photo 7-26. Graffiti. Courtesy of Chula Vista, California, Police Department.

Photo 7-27. Graffiti. Courtesy of Chula Vista, California, Police Department.

Additionally, the forensic technician should search the area for spray paint cans or markers that can be processed for latent fingerprints. The surface containing graffiti as well as handrails or surfaces adjacent to the graffiti may be processed for latent prints as well. Shoe prints or impressions near graffiti may also link a suspect to a crime scene.

ARSON INVESTIGATION

A fire is caused by the convergence of fuel, oxygen, heat, and an uninhibited chemical chain reaction. The fuel can be solid (e.g., wood), liquid (e.g., gasoline or kerosene), or a gaseous vapor (e.g., natural gas). The normal atmosphere contains approximately 21 percent oxygen. A fire requires a 15 percent oxygen level. As the temperature rises, less oxygen is necessary for combustion. A fire consumes oxygen and releases carbon monoxide, a toxic gas. Heat is produced:

- chemically, through rapid oxidation,
- mechanically, as the result of friction,
- electrically, due to an electrical malfunction,
- in a compressed gas, because molecular activity is greatly increased,
- through a nuclear reaction, the splitting of atomic particles.

Heat is transferred through **conduction** (direct contact), **convection** (super-heated gases), and **radiation** (invisible waves that travel at the same speed as visible light). Radiant heat travels in a direct line from the source until it strikes an object.

A fire expands horizontally and vertically from its point-of-origin. It follows the path of least resistance through ceilings, doorways, windows, stairways, and other openings. Unless restricted or suppressed, a fire will grow and spread in four stages (Redsicker, 2005).

Conduction A situation in which heat is transferred through direct contact.

Convection Heat transfer through fluid or superheated gases.

Radiation Invisible waves that travel at the same speed as visible light. Radiant heat travels in a direct line from the source until it strikes an object.

1. *Incipient stage.* The earliest stage of a fire. The duration may be a fraction of a second to hours, depending on the fuel available and the ignition source.
2. *Emergent smoldering.* Combustion activity increases.
3. *Free burning.* The rate and intensity of the fire increases. The intensity of the heat doubles with each 18 degree Fahrenheit temperature rise. The fire builds from the

point-of-origin and spreads to upper areas of a structure. Additional heat is transferred through conduction and radiation. A *flashover* may occur if all combustible items in an area reach ignition temperature.

4. *Oxygen-regulated smoldering.* Oxygen-enriched air in an area or a room is depleted, causing combustion to cease. Dense smoke and superheated gases, including carbon monoxide, may be forced from the room. The temperature may exceed 1000 degrees Fahrenheit. If oxygen is re-introduced to the fire, a *backdraft* (explosive ignition) may occur.

Fire Investigation Focus

Other than police officers, local firefighters are typically the first responders to a fire scene. After life safety measures are applied and the fire is suppressed, a fire investigation commences with a cause analysis as its primary focus. The investigation is often a cooperative effort between the police and fire marshals or fire agency investigators. The causes of fire are reduced to four basic classifications.

- natural (e.g., lightning),
- accidental (e.g., unintentional or negligent, but explainable human action),
- incendiary (e.g., intentional),
- undetermined (unknown).

To determine the cause of the fire, an arson investigator will inspect fire safety and early warning systems; electrical wiring, including light fixtures and appliances; and heating, ventilation, and air-conditioning equipment. Candles, smoking materials, chemicals, and possible accelerants located on the premises are examined as well. If the cause is identified as intentional, law enforcement personnel are summoned, and the fire scene is treated as a crime scene. Although not an element of the crime, the motive (reason) for an intentional fire is an important consideration (Redsicker, 2005).

Motive

A motive for the crime of arson may include:

- concealment of another crime, such as a homicide,
- defrauding an insurance company for economic gain,
- destruction of evidence from another crime,
- revenge (e.g., against a spouse or former lover),
- intimidation (e.g., to extort money from another),

- terrorism or hate (e.g., hate crime),
- pyromania (a mental disorder that leads the arsonist to receive pleasure from setting fires).

A motive may be obvious, such as an attempt to conceal a homicide. Alternatively, identification of a motive for an intentional fire may require considerable investigative resources. Regardless of the motive, the fire scene must be processed for evidence. An important aspect of arson scene processing is the determination of the fire's point-of-origin.

A Fire's Point-of-Origin

A fire's *point-of-origin* yields valuable information. It usually contains the heaviest fire damage because it is the point at which the fire started. The areas of the structure that are not damaged or are less affected by the fire are evaluated first. Investigators follow a trail through more severely burned areas toward the fire's point-of-origin.

Fire damage patterns observed in the most intensely burned areas include melting and distortion of items as well as severe charring, often referred to as *alligator patterns* because of their rough, scaled appearance. The point-of-origin may be located on the exterior or the interior of a structure. A fire typically travels vertically and horizontally from its point-of-origin. The burn is often a V-shaped fire damage pattern, which indicates direction of the fire's movement. The fire continues to travel in a path of least resistance (e.g., through stairways, doorways, and window openings).

To determine the origin of a fire, the areas of the structure that were not damaged or are less affected are analyzed. The areas of heaviest damage are near the area of origin. Fire patterns, charring, and melting, as well as physical evidence, are analyzed to determine the location of the origin of the fire (Redsicker, 2005).

Safety at the Fire Scene

A fire scene can be dangerous because fire damage to a building can lead to structural collapse. Moreover, the fire can reignite. Nails and other sharp objects may pose a threat to safety, and toxic gases, such as carbon monoxide, may linger in the area.

A forensic technician should wear a hard hat, protection clothing, and a breathing apparatus at a fire scene. If a breathing apparatus is not available, a particle mask should be worn. The forensic technician must have a flashlight available to illuminate darkened pathways and assist with photography. Self-contained portable lighting equipment can also be used to illuminate darkened areas.

Fire Scene Photography

If fire suppression is still in progress when the forensic technician arrives on the scene, video-recording of the scene is recommended. The video should capture the fire, the people and vehicles in the area, and fire suppression activities. If a video-recorder is not available, photographs are taken. After the fire is suppressed, still photographs of the following views are obtained.

Exterior Views

- all sides and the roof of the structure (if the fire consumed grassland or forest rather than a structure, photograph the area first affected by the fire),
- burn patterns on the exterior of the structure,
- all windows and doors,
- broken glass (burned and undamaged),
- exposed wiring outside the structure,
- evidence of forced entry,
- V-shaped burn patterns on doors, windows, and other openings,
- melting of siding, window frames, and doors,
- suspicious impressions and containers,

- exterior utility equipment (service/circuit breaker boxes), wiring, and evidence of tampering,
- the scene from witnesses' perspectives,
- other views specified by the fire investigator.

Photo 7-28. Residential arson scene. Courtesy of National City, California, Police Department.

Photo 7-29. Forensic technician at arson scene. Courtesy of National City, California, Police Department.

Photo 7-30. Vehicle arson. Courtesy of Chula Vista, California, Police Department.

Photo 7-31. Vehicle arson. Courtesy of Chula Vista, California, Police Department.

Photo 7-33. Vehicle arson. Courtesy of Chula Vista, California, Police Department.

Photo 7-32. Vehicle arson. Courtesy of Chula Vista, California, Police Department.

Photo 7-34. Vehicle arson. Courtesy of Chula Vista, California, Police Department.

Interior Views

The darkened interior of an arson scene absorbs light and can be difficult to photograph. The photographer should increase the camera's ISO to 400 or higher, open the aperture to F4 use or F5.6, 1/60 shutter speed (depending on the focal length of the lens), and utilize a flash. The following views should be photographed:

- the point-of-origin, if known,
- all rooms, hallways, stairways, and closets,
- overlapping photographs of the ceiling, walls, and floor of each room,
- furnishings and contents, including location and arrangement,
- V-shaped patterns,
- alligator patterns,
- evidence of forced entry or exit,
- interior wiring,
- gas appliances that appear out of place,
- severed gas lines,
- fire suppression equipment (extinguishing systems) and alarms,
- fire damage indicating direction to point-of-origin (melted light bulbs, glass, plastic, and candles),
- clocks,
- all fuel and heat sources,
- all flammable materials,
- anything that appears out of place or foreign to the area,
- other views specified by the fire investigator (Siljander & Fredrickson, 1997; National Fire Protection Association, 2008).

Evidence Collection

Contamination and destruction of biological and trace evidence are common in a fire scene. The fire, along with water, suppression agents, and firefighter activity, usually destroys most if not all biological, trace, and latent fingerprint evidence. Additionally, evidence is difficult to locate and observe at indoor fire scenes due to the absorption of light by the blackened and charred interior. The search for evidence is also labor intensive because ash and fire debris must be sifted for evidence.

A fire scene can be searched if any of the following conditions apply:

- Exigent (emergency) circumstance. Fire personnel may enter the scene for life safety and fire suppression purposes. Any evidence relating to the fire cause in plain view is not protected under the Fourth Amendment, and it can be seized and removed. No search warrant or consent from the property owner or lessee is required.
- Consent. Authorization from the property owner or lessee.
- Search warrant. A legal document issued by a competent court, based on an affidavit (application) articulating probable cause for the search.

If flammable liquids, fabric, or containers containing accelerants are present at a fire scene, they are collected immediately. Typical accelerants include gasoline, kerosene, charcoal lighter fluid, paint thinner, turpentine, and alcohol. The accelerants or materials (e.g., wood, debris, carpet, rugs, rags, or other fabrics) containing the accelerant are collected and placed in evidence cans designed to prevent evaporation. The evidence cans are similar in appearance and operation to gallon-size paint cans. The containers should not be filled beyond two-thirds of their capacity.

If the point-of-origin is determined, samples of burned materials from the surrounding area are collected. Control samples some distance away from the suspected point-of-origin are collected as well. Metal cans, glass jars, and special fire scene evidence bags are used to collect the burned and control samples. A fire investigator should be present at the fire scene to guide the evidence collection process and respond to inquiries about items to be collected. Effective communication between the forensic technician and the fire investigator will ensure that all evidence is properly documented and collected.

Explosive Fire Scenes

A fire may be the result of a low- or high-velocity explosion. A low explosion contains a velocity of less than 1,000 meters per second detonation. Examples include those caused by black or smokeless powder. A high explosion contains a velocity of greater than 1,000 meters per second detonation (e.g., dynamite).

A person can create an explosive device with items purchased at a gun store. Recipes for these destructive devices are accessible through the Internet. If a forensic technician is assigned to process a suspected explosion scene, U.S. Bureau of Alcohol, Tobacco, Firearms and Explosives (ATF) investigators should be summoned to the scene. ATF agents are trained in the identification and recovery of explosives. ATF agents also have the appropriate training and equipment to effectively and safely process the crime scene.

MASS CASUALTY SCENES

On September 11, 2001, America was attacked by terrorists who hijacked and flew four commercial jetliners, one each into the north and south towers of New York City's World Trade Center, one into the Pentagon, and one into a field in Pennsylvania. The World Trade Center site represents the largest crime scene in the United States to date, with nearly 2,800 deaths. Only 20 people were rescued from the rubble alive. Among others, deaths at the World Trade Center included:

- 343 New York City firefighters,
- 84 New York Port Authority employees, 37 of whom were Port Authority police officers,
- 23 New York City police officers.

The World Trade Center site required a laboriously exhaustive crime scene investigation as well as meticulous procedures to identify the deceased. A federal DMORT was dispatched to the scene to assist local officials. The three core units within a DMORT include the following.

- Disaster Portable Morgue Unit (DPMU). The DPMU is responsible for the logistics of a response to a disaster, including the supply of forensic equipment, instrumentation, and administrative and support services necessary to operate a temporary field morgue or support a local morgue facility.
- Family assistance. This unit is responsible for working directly with families of loved ones involved in a mass casualty incident. The unit supplies antemortem (before death) and postmortem (after death) victim information.
- Weapons of Mass Destruction (WMD) Team. The WMD team is responsible for decontamination of human remains subsequent to a chemical, biological, or nuclear event.

A DMORT unit is located in each of ten regions in the United States. Each unit employs the services of:

- medical examiners and coroners,
- forensic pathologists,
- forensic odontologists,
- forensic anthropologists,
- fingerprint specialists,
- DNA specialists,
- investigative personnel,
- forensic technicians,
- funeral directors and embalmers,
- dental assistants,
- X-ray technicians,
- photographic specialists,
- heavy equipment operators,

- computer specialists,
- mental health specialists,
- medical records technicians,
- transcriptionists,
- administrative support staff,
- security personnel,
- facility maintenance personnel,
- other forensic scientists and assorted specialists.

The services provided by a DMORT include:

- mobile morgue operations,
- forensic examination,
- DNA acquisition,
- remains identification,
- search and recovery,
- scene documentation,
- medical and psychology support,
- embalming and casketing,
- family assistance,
- antemortem data collection,
- postmortem data collection,
- records data entry,
- database administration,
- personal effects processing,
- release of remains coordination,
- liaison with the U.S. Public Health Service (USPHS),
- communications equipment and support,
- safety and security.

A DMORT responds only when requested. Jurisdictions in need of assistance must contact their local office of the Federal Emergency Management Agency (FEMA) for departmental procedures (DMORT, 2009).

SEXUAL ASSAULT AND RAPE

Sex crimes are more common than many other types of crime (e.g., arson). Further, many sex crimes may go unreported because of a victim's fear or embarrassment. In most cases, the victim and the perpetrator know each other.

Generally, the crime of rape (first-degree sexual assault in some states) requires proof of an intentional act constituting nonconsensual penetration of a penis or other body part (e.g., finger) or an object manipulated by the perpetrator into an intimate body cavity of another. Proof of penetration can be established through DNA analysis or the presence of seminal fluid. However, the assailant may have worn a condom. Thus, the absence of DNA or seminal fluid should not be construed to mean that penetration did not occur.

Lack of consent may be established through the victim's statement or evidence of physical trauma to the victim. Bruising or tearing inside the vagina or anus may be present. Bruises, injury to the scalp (from severed hair), or other injuries may be apparent on the victim. Evidence of a struggle as well as soiled clothing can be located at the incident scene.

In most jurisdictions, the victim of an alleged rape is transported to an area hospital, where a forensically trained **sexual assault nurse examiner (SANE)** searches the victim for evidence. A **Sexual Assault Response Team (SART)** member may be available to assist and counsel the victim and the victim's family. The SANE photographs the victim's external injuries, collects and preserves the victim's clothing, and conducts a search for trace evidence. The SANE also combs genital hair for trace evidence, obtains fingernail scrapings and oral swabs (if oral copulation occurred), conducts a body cavity exam for signs of trauma, and swabs for the assailant's biological material. The victim is provided with alternate clothing upon release.

A young or immature victim who experiences a traumatic event such as a rape often minimizes the experience or expresses emotions in an uncustomary manner. The victim may laugh as a means of coping with the traumatic experience. Although the victim may not appear to take the event seriously, a criminal investigator should not assume that the alleged crime did not occur. The unorthodox behavior demonstrated can be characterized as the victim's way of dealing with the situation.

Although the SANE often locates and documents internal trauma and injuries sustained by the victim, some sex crime victims are unable or reluctant to provide physical evidence of an assault. Most sex crime victims can identify their assailants because the latter are family

Sexual assault nurse examiner (SANE) A forensically trained nurse. The SANE photographs the victim's external injuries, collects and preserves the victim's clothing, and conducts a search for trace evidence. The SANE also combs genital hair for trace evidence, obtains fingernail scrapings and oral swabs (if oral copulation occurred), conducts a body cavity exam for signs of trauma, and swabs for the assailant's biological material. The victim is provided with alternate clothing upon release.

Sexual Assault Response Team (SART) Available to assist and counsel the victim and a victim's family.

members, friends, or acquaintances. However, a victim may have unsuspectingly ingested a date rape drug and be unable to identify the assailant.

Date Rape Drugs

Rohypnol (flunitrazepam) is a benzodiazepine drug that operates as a depressant on the central nervous system. Also known as *Rophies, Roofies,* and *Roach,* Rohypnol was a common party and date rape drug in the mid-1990s. The drug is placed into the drink of an unsuspecting victim. The drug is designed to incapacitate, release inhibitions, and overcome resistance. The drug often causes victim memory loss which may lead to non-reporting of the rape.

Gamma hydroxybutyric acid (GHB) produces a euphoric sensation. It is used as an anabolic (sleep aid) agent. GHB is often used to carry out a sexual assault. If consumed with alcohol, the effects of GHB are compounded and may result in an overdose. Like Rohypnol, GHB causes depression that may result in victim memory loss. The drug dissipates rapidly so detection is difficult (U.S. Drug Enforcement Administration, 2005).

Locating and processing the scene of an alleged date rape can be challenging. Victims rarely recall details. However, if the incident occurred at a private party, witnesses may provide corroborating statements.

The Sex Crime Scene

A rape or sexual assault can occur almost anywhere. Common venues include vehicles, hotel rooms, residences, and outdoor areas. Trace evidence such as hair and fibers may be present and seminal fluid may be located if the perpetrator ejaculated and did not wear a condom.

Regardless of the setting, the forensic technician should consult with the lead investigator about known facts of the case before processing the scene. Most importantly, the exact location of the alleged attack should be identified. Victim statements are most helpful in this regard.

In a residence or hotel room one should not assume that the sexual assault occurred on a bed. If bedding is collected, the forensic technician should label the bedding (for orientation purposes) prior to collection. Using a marking pen, a mark indicating the top-right corner (or any other corner) should be identified so the bedding's orientation is known. Each item of bedding should be packaged separately, wrapped carefully in clean evidence paper.

The forensic technician must not restrict the search for trace and biological evidence to the bedding. The assault may have occurred in a bathroom or on a floor. Moreover, environments such as hotel rooms often contain numerous unrelated biological specimens on the outer bedding and the floor. If the exact location of the attack is identified, fewer biological material specimens need be collected.

As described in Chapter 4, an alternate (forensic) light source should be used to locate fibers, hairs, and seminal fluid. The acid phosphatase presumptive seminal fluid test may be performed as well, depending on agency protocol.

Signs of a struggle are usually apparent unless the victim was passive or other people disturbed the scene after the alleged incident occurred. The forensic technician should photograph and document evidence of an apparent struggle, such as a damaged door, lock, or door frame as well as furniture or other items in disarray. Evidence that links the victim, suspect, and location (e.g., soil) is collected. Beverage containers, cigarette butts, or other evidence that could yield a suspect or victim biological specimen or latent fingerprints should be collected as well.

Photo 7-35. Rape crime scene. Courtesy of National City, California, Police Department.

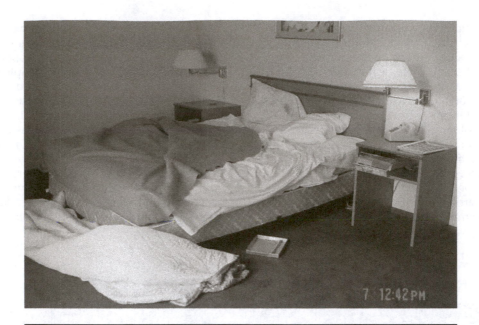

Photo 7-36. Rape crime scene. Courtesy of National City, California, Police Department.

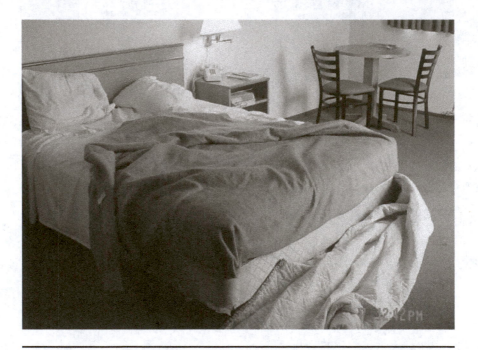

Photo 7-37. Rape crime scene. Courtesy of National City, California, Police Department.

DOMESTIC VIOLENCE

Domestic violence can lead to a killing or a suicide. In some states, laws related to domestic violence authorize a police officer to arrest a domestic violence suspect without the victim's cooperation. Most domestic violence statutes apply to those who were previously or are currently involved in a relationship of an intimate sexual nature. The laws were created to address psychological as well as physical injuries upon a victim.

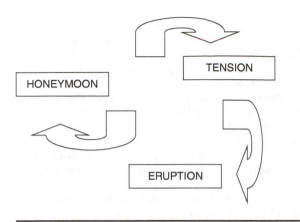

Figure 7-1. Cycle of domestic violence.

Repeat domestic violence perpetrators often engage in a cycle of violence that includes three developmental stages: tension building, eruption or explosion, and the honeymoon (Meadows, 2006).

Unfortunately, a domestic violence perpetrator often becomes more violent with each successive cycle, until the victim seeks assistance, the perpetrator is incarcerated, or someone is killed. In most domestic homicide situations, the police responded previously to reported domestic disturbances at the home.

A domestic violence incident is one of the most potentially dangerous encounters for a police patrol officer. Therefore, more than one patrol officer should respond to a report of domestic violence. The perpetrator as well as the victim may be combative and the situation is emotionally charged. If a forensic technician is summoned to a domestic violence scene, the cycle of violence has probably ended in a homicide. The site is processed according to established homicide crime scene protocol.

CHILD NEGLECT, ABUSE, AND MOLESTATION

Children are often unable or unlikely to report neglect or incidents of abuse, either because of their underdeveloped communication skills or because of emotional and mental trauma associated with the abuse. Symptoms of neglect or abuse include injuries or bruises on a child's body, malnourishment, severe diaper rash, and burn marks. Head injuries account for the greatest number of deaths due to child abuse.

Symptoms of child sexual abuse (molestation) include bleeding in the genital or anal area;

bruising on the breasts, thighs, or genitals; soiled, bloody, or torn undergarments; venereal disease; and chronic infections. However, little or no evidence exists in many cases.

Infant abuse or infanticide (killing of an infant) may result from exposure, dehydration, starvation, abandonment, concussion (due to head injury), suffocation, stabbing, scalding, or shaken baby syndrome. With *shaken baby syndrome*, the perpetrator shakes the baby repeatedly, causing a whiplash effect that often leads to death. The perpetrator may report that the baby fell. However, physical trauma to the infant suggests otherwise. The trauma observed on a shaken baby syndrome victim often includes bruises on the abdomen, arms, or shoulders caused by the perpetrator's fingertips. Other signs of injury include bleeding, swelling, ruptured blood vessels in the brain, retinal hemorrhaging, and cervical (spine) fracture (Spitz & Platt, 1993). The victim of shaken baby syndrome rarely exhibits scalp contusions, which would be consistent with a fall.

Ten percent of child abuse victims suffer burns. Children are burned with substances such as cigarettes, cigars, stoves, curling irons, hair dryers, radiators, portable heaters, and scalding water. An impression of the object used to cause the burn may be apparent on the child's skin. Hot water scalding is the most common type of burn injury inflicted on a child. Water at 130 degrees Fahrenheit will produce a second-degree burn within 30 seconds (Spitz & Platt, 1993). The suspect typically claims that the burn was an accident; that the child fell into the water. However, signs of immersion often appear on the buttocks, thighs, and waist, but not the hands or backs of the knees. The backs of the knees are spared because the child reflexively bends the knees in an attempt to escape the scalding.

In burn cases, the forensic technician should attempt to locate and collect any object that could have been used to burn the child. In a suspected scalding incident, the forensic technician should record the temperature of the water available immediately upon arrival at the scene. If probable that the hot water used was released from a faucet, the forensic technician should record the temperature of the water from the suspect faucet. The forensic technician should also determine the temperature of water in the water heater.

The Crime Scene

The home of a chronically abused or neglected child is typically an environment filled with trash, fecal matter, and vermin (e.g., insects, rats). Spoiled food is often located throughout the home. Very little wholesome food is available. Sanitary facilities may not be operational. Fecal matter may be found in a bathtub used as a toilet. Children may be unclothed and malnourished. A child's sleeping area is often infested with urine and fecal matter. Drugs and drug paraphernalia may be scattered throughout. In extreme cases, children are restrained in closets or other areas of the home.

If a forensic technician is called to a child abuse or molestation scene, overall photographs of the entire residence should be taken, with additional photographs depicting the living conditions. The refrigerator and kitchen cabinets should be opened and photographed to document the lack of food. Insect activity and any child's sleeping area should be photographed as well. Soiled clothing and bedding as well as restraints and weapons should be collected as evidence.

Processing a Child Victim

Chapter 13 describes the photographs taken and evidence collected from a live victim, including a child. In addition to standard evidence collection procedures, the forensic technician may wish to use an alternate light source to locate and document bruises on the victim that are no longer visible to the unaided human eye. In sexual assault (child molestation) cases, a forensic nurse documents and collects evidence from the child.

ELDER ABUSE

The three basic categories of *elder abuse* are domestic, institutional, and self-neglect. As with children, the elderly are often targets of abuse because of their vulnerability. In most cases, the perpetrator of elder abuse is a family member (spouse or adult child) of the victim. The abuse can be passive (neglect) or active (physical) (Meadows, 2006).

Symptoms of physical abuse of an elder include injuries (e.g., bruises) at various stages of healing, welts, rope abrasions, restraint marks, fractures, untreated injuries, dislocated bones and joints, broken eyeglass frames, and other signs of abnormality. Symptoms of sexual abuse include bruises on or near the breasts or genitals, venereal disease or infection, unexplained anal or vaginal bleeding, stained or bloody undergarments, or the elder's report of sexual abuse. Symptoms of emotional abuse

include an elder's sudden behavioral change such as sucking, biting, or rocking back and forth. The elder may appear emotionally upset, agitated, withdrawn, or non-communicative, or refuse to receive visitors.

The elderly are victims of financial exploitation as well. Symptoms of financial abuse include sudden changes in the elder's bank account balances, increased withdrawals or ATM use, changes in the elder's legal documents (e.g., will), and relatives or friends who suddenly appear interested in the elder.

Symptoms of neglect include dehydration, malnutrition, poor hygiene, untreated bedsores, poor health care, prescription medicine not refilled, unsafe or unclean living conditions, or the elder's report of such phenomenon or activities. Elder neglect may be self-inflicted. As an adult, the elder may voluntarily withhold medication or nourishment, or refuse to bathe or live in a clean environment. Reports of elder neglect or abuse are handled individually and investigated thoroughly to determine if the abuse is self-inflicted or the result of a criminal act. State and county adult protective service (APS) agencies work with law enforcement to investigate reports of elder abuse. Medicare and Medicaid fraud control units (MFCU) also assist law enforcement agencies with the investigation of finance irregularities.

Crime scene processing techniques used in suspected elder abuse cases are similar to those employed at child abuse scenes. The living conditions are documented in the same manner. Additionally, investigators should collect empty prescription medicine containers and search for unfilled prescription documents. Financial statements also should be collected if relevant to the nature of the investigation.

BURGLARY

Under modern statutes, the offense of burglary is generally defined as the entering of a structure with the intent to commit a felony or steal property of any value. Thus, a person commits a burglary upon entering a residence with the intent to kill an occupant. The burglary is complete upon entry with the requisite intent. If the intended victim is not home, the burglary is still complete. Most burglaries, however, involve intent to steal property.

In small agencies, patrol officers as well as forensic technicians may be involved with processing burglary scenes. The investigative focus of a burglary is on the points of entry and exit, area(s) of attack, and items stolen. Evidence such as latent fingerprints is sought at entry/exit points and attack areas.

A burglar may sustain an injury while on the premises. Therefore, an investigator or forensic technician should search for blood evidence in areas most likely encountered by the intruder. Additionally, shoe impressions or prints may be located at a point of entry or exit.

Burglary scene processing is typically limited to photographs of the entry/exit sites and attack areas, a search for shoe impressions and prints as well as blood evidence at points of entry/exit, and the processing of relevant areas for latent fingerprints. Items may be collected for latent fingerprint processing at a later time. A crime scene sketch is often characterized as optional.

Most burglaries are committed by individuals seeking money or items to sell. Drug addicts often commit residential and vehicle burglaries to finance the purchase of drugs. To avoid detection, most burglars attack targets that are unoccupied at the time of the incident.

Although rare, the *hot prowl burglar* enters a residence when the occupants are home and often asleep. The hot prowl burglar may enjoy the adrenaline rush associated with the high risk of detection. These burglars may steal items from the room in which an occupant is sleeping. A hot prowl burglary is considered dangerous by police because the event can transform into violent crime such as rape or murder. Apprehending the hot prowl burglar is a high priority for law enforcement agencies.

ROBBERY

Generally, robbery is taking property in the victim's presence through the use of force or the threat of force. Interviewing the victim and any witnesses to a robbery is critical to obtaining a description of the suspect. If a surveillance camera covered the scene during the incident, reviewing the camera's recording may prove helpful in obtaining the perpetrator's description. If the victims or witnesses indicate that the perpetrator touched surfaces at or near the location of the robbery, the investigator or forensic technician should search the surfaces for latent fingerprints.

With robberies of federally insured financial institutions (e.g., banks, credit unions), the FBI and the local agency have concurrent jurisdiction. If a forensic technician is called to the scene, the surveillance video should be reviewed to identify surfaces the suspect may have touched. Some robbers climb onto the

teller counter to intimidate to the victim(s). The forensic technician may retrieve shoe prints from dust on the counter. Details for locating and preserving shoe prints and impressions are discussed in Chapter 9.

SPECIAL WEAPONS AND TACTICS RESPONSE SCENES

High-risk law enforcement activities often require the use of highly trained personnel such as those assigned to a *Special Weapons and Tactics (SWAT)* unit or similar *Emergency Response Team (ERT)*. Circumstances that may require the services of SWAT or ERT include but are not limited to hostage situations, an armed person threatening the public, and the execution of a high-risk search warrant. Subsequent to SWAT team activity, a forensic technician may be summoned to process the crime or search warrant scene.

A forensic technician must never enter a high-risk scene until it is declared safe by the controlling authority. The forensic technician should process the scene as any other scene, taking overall photographs of the scene as well as photographs of any facility damage caused the SWAT team. Photographically documenting the damage helps to ensure proper reporting of the damage.

The extent to which the forensic technician processes the scene depends on the situation. If a perpetrator held hostages and someone was killed, the area is treated as a homicide scene. If the situation involved the execution of a high-risk search warrant, documentation may be limited to photography and evidence collection. The responsible person in charge (e.g., investigator, commanding officer) will determine the level of forensic technology applied to the scene.

COMPUTER SEIZURES

Computers connected to the Internet are located in most homes and businesses. As computer technology advances, the ability to commit cybercrime increases. Computers are also used to document and organize data in criminal enterprises such as white collar crime and illegal drug activities, or to view child pornography. Regardless of the type of crime, the data contained in the computer's hard drive is vital to a criminal investigation.

An investigator trained in computer-based crimes should be consulted. An untrained investigator should never attempt to retrieve data from a computer. However, an investigator or forensic technician may be required to seize,

Photo 7-38. SWAT team. Courtesy of National City, California, Police Department.

Photo 7-39. Hostage rescue simulation. Courtesy of National City, California, Police Department.

secure, and deliver a computer to a trained professional who will search the hard drive for data.

If a computer is collected as evidence, the investigator or forensic technician should photograph the computer and document the location of each wire and attached device. The computer should not be *shut down* or turned off. Rather, the electric power cord supplying the computer should be disconnected at the electrical receptacle (outlet) in case the computer criminal installed a virus designed to destroy data if the computer's power supply is intercepted by normal means. If the computer is connected to a network with other computers, a professional should be summoned to properly disconnect and seize all the computers.

CLEANED CRIME SCENES

Occasionally, a perpetrator will attempt to disguise a crime. The cover-up may include activities such as cleaning the crime scene, destroying the scene with fire, or disposing of a body or weapon.

Traces of latent blood may be detected at cleaned crime scenes through the application of blood-enhancing chemicals such as Luminol® or Bluestar®. Each is highly sensitive to diluted blood and will chemiluminesce (glow) in reaction to the presence of blood. Neither requires the aid of a forensic light source. Fluorescein®, another blood-enhancing chemical, requires the use of a forensic light source to view the reaction.

When an investigator receives information regarding the possible location of latent blood, a blood-enhancing chemical may be used to identify the exact location. However, prior to using any blood-enhancing chemical, a forensic technician should attempt to locate visible blood. The specialist should search the underside of carpet and carpet pads. A mattress may be rotated in search of blood stains. The undersides of furniture and stair hand railings are also inspected for possible blood evidence.

If visible blood is not located, Luminol, Bluestar, or Fluorescein is applied. Complete darkness is preferred when using any of these chemicals. The blood evidence should be photographed and collected according to the following protocol.

- Place a camera on a tripod and attach a shutter release cable to the camera. Take a flash photograph of the suspect area prior to application of the chemical. The following camera settings are recommended.
  - 800 ISO,
  - the widest aperture (lowest f-stop) possible for the camera's lens,
  - "bulb" shutter speed.
- Luminol or Bluestar is sprayed on the suspect area. At the first sign of a reaction, the camera's shutter release cable should be activated, opening the shutter. The shutter should remain open until the reaction disappears. If the reaction continues for three minutes or longer, the shutter is closed.
- If Fluorescein is chosen, an alternate (forensic) light source set to 450 nm is used. An orange filter is placed over the camera lens before photography begins. To prevent overexposure of the photograph, the shutter should not remain open longer than one minute (Young, 2006).

After Luminol, Bluestar, or Fluorescein is applied and the chemical's reaction is photographed, the forensic technician should not repeat the process in an attempt to obtain better photographic results. Over-application of a chemical to the suspect area may dilute the biological evidence, rendering it useless for DNA analysis. Rather, the affected area should be removed or swabbed, depending on the nature of the surface, and transported to the DNA lab for analysis.

Luminol, Bluestar, and Fluorescein are used for presumptive blood testing only. The tests are not confirmatory for blood. The chemicals can produce false positive reactions when placed in contact with some other chemicals and certain organic (e.g., plant) materials.

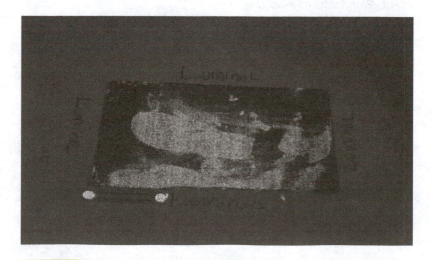

Photo 7-40. Luminol timed exposure.

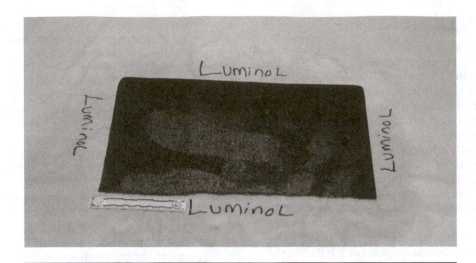

Photo 7-41. Luminol with bounce flash.

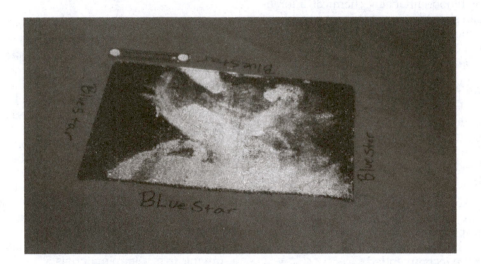

Photo 7-42. Bluestar timed exposure.

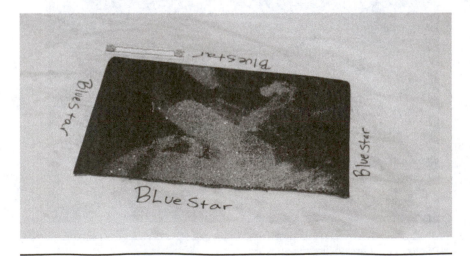

Photo 7-43. Bluestar with bounce flash.

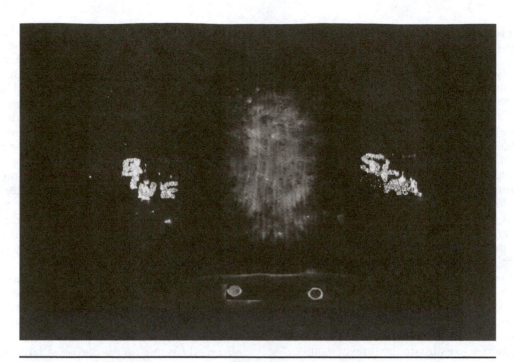

Photo 7-44. Bluestar timed exposure with words "Blue star" written in latent blood.

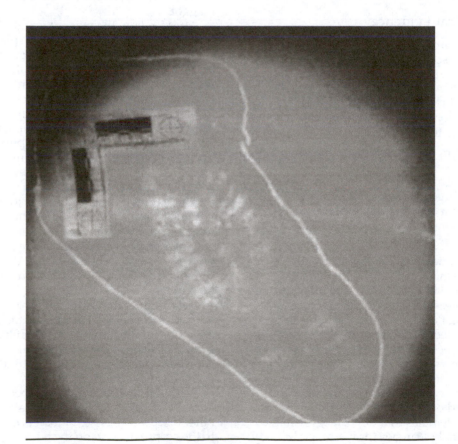

Photo 7-45. Fluorescein timed exposure.

DISCARDED BODIES (BODY DUMPS)

If the body of a homicide victim is discovered in a remote area, it is highly unlikely that the body's location is the site of the homicide. Still, the body's location contains important associative (trace) evidence that can link the killer to the body's location as well as the scene of the homicide.

The forensic technician should search the body dump site for shoe and tire impression evidence. If located, this evidence is photographed and a cast of the impression is obtained (details in Chapter 9). Trace evidence (e.g., hair or fibers from the perpetrator) may be located on or near the victim's body. If a struggle occurred, biological material containing the perpetrator's DNA may be located under the victim's fingernails. If the case involved a sexual assault, seminal fluid may be present as well.

An extremely important aspect of a homicide investigation is to estimate the time of death. At body dump sitescenes, entomological (insect) evidence may assist investigators with determination of the approximate time of death.

Entomological Evidence

Forensic entomology is the study of the insect activity associated with a dead body. Insect activity is used to approximate time since death (Anderson, 2005). In addition, insect activity can be used to determine:

> **Forensic entomology**
> The study of the insect activity associated with a dead body.

- postmortem body movement (based on the type of insects on the body),
- the presence and position of wound sites (maggots may be present at these sites),
- if the victim consumed drugs or was poisoned (insects can be analyzed for the drugs or poisons).

The time of death estimation is usually based on two main factors: the predictable development of larval Diptera (the blow fly), and the predictable successive colonization of carrion (decomposing flesh) insects in the body. Blow flies are attracted to a body immediately after death. The insects are large, metallic blue-colored flies often observed near food, refuse containers, or feces. Both male and female blow flies require protein for ovary or testis development. Adult blow flies feed on the dead body. The majority of blow flies are females that deposit eggs on the body. The female searches for warm, moist body areas on which the eggs are deposited.

After blow fly eggs are laid, they hatch into the first instar (first larval stage). As the environmental temperature increases, the larvae's developmental time decreases. At the first-instar stage, the larvae are delicate and unable to penetrate the skin of the corpse. However, they require a liquid protein source. Thus, the adult female fly searches for a moist area of the body (wound site, genital area, nose, or mouth) on which to lay eggs.

Eventually, the first-instar larvae molt (shed cuticle) into a second-instar stage. The second-instar larvae are slightly larger and less delicate than the first. They can penetrate the corpse's skin by secreting enzymes and engaging in rasping actions with their newly developed mouthparts.

The second-instar larvae molt into third-instar larvae (maggots) as they shed the cuticle and mouthparts of the second instar. The third-instar larvae have an insatiable appetite. Masses of third-instar larvae are frequently observed feeding on the corpse. A large amount of tissue is consumed quickly, and maggot temperature increases. A dark-colored food-storage organ (crop) can be observed through the translucent outer membrane of each maggot.

After feeding, the maggot wanders from the food source in search of a safe place to pupate (become inactive). The maggot may travel into the hair or clothing of the corpse or wander several meters away from the corpse into the surrounding soil or carpet. The third-instar cuticle hardens, darkens, and forms a puparium. Inside, the maggot pupates into an adult fly and breaks open the pupal case. The newly created dull gray fly emerges with crumpled wings. Although the newborn fly is weak and unable to fly, it can run quickly. The fly will hide until it dries and is able to fly, usually within 24 hours. Newborn flies should be collected at a body dump site because a forensic entomologist can estimate the age of a newborn blow fly. After the fly is airborne, the fly's age cannot be determined, and it cannot be linked to the human remains.

Determining the age of a blow fly associated with a corpse helps to determine the approximate time of the human's death. If blow flies in the initial stage of development are located, each succeeding stage is identified until further development is not observed.

As the corpse decomposes, it becomes less attractive to blow flies and more attractive to other insects. The types of insects attracted to the corpse depend on the body's stage of decomposition and environmental conditions (geographical region, season, temperature, and climate) (Anderson, 2005; Haglund, 2005).

A forensic entomologist should be consulted if insect activity is observed at a body dump site. If an entomologist is unavailable, the forensic technician should proceed according to crime scene processing protocol. Entomological evidence should be collected as well.

- A butterfly net is used to capture insects flying near the body. The net containing the flies is closed and submerged in ethyl alcohol, which will kill and preserve the flies.
- Collect crawling insects from different locations on and near the body. Do not mix insects from different locations (e.g., do not mix insects from the head area with insects from the pubic area). Different insect types can be collected together as long as they are from the same body location. Place the crawling insects in a jar containing ethyl alcohol.
- Obtain temperature readings from the following locations: air, ground surface, four inches below the ground, the exposed surface of the body, under the body, and the center of any maggot masses.
- Search for maggots and pupa shells within a 25-feet radius of the human remains. Collect maggots from the maggot masses located on the body. Preserve some of the maggots in ethyl alcohol and keep some alive. Prior to preservation in alcohol, maggots should be submerged in hot water to prevent shrinkage. Live maggots are placed in a jar containing damp soil and a teaspoon of wet cat food. The maggots are secured in the jar with a perforated lid. Collect at least 50 maggots from each site, but do not integrate maggots from different locations. Use a separate jar for each site.
- Collect soil samples from maggot and insect collection sites.
- All entomological evidence is transported to a forensic entomologist for analysis.

Photo 7-46. Maggots.

Shallow Grave Excavation

If a corpse is buried in a shallow grave, a forensic anthropologist should be summoned for excavation assistance. If a forensic anthropologist is not available, the forensic technician should process the gravesite and excavate the remains in the following manner:

1. Take overall photographs of the scene.
2. Carefully remove litter and vegetation from the grave while examining the debris for evidence. Examine the scene for coloration distortions that may indicate a mixing of topsoil and subsoil.
3. Using stakes and a string, isolate the grave area to be excavated. Connect the string to each stake 8–10 inches above the ground. Sketch the area with references to directional coordinates and major, relatively permanent points of reference (large trees, buildings, fences). Use a global positioning system (GPS) device, if available.
4. Locate the grave outline. Scrape the soil surface horizontally with a flat shovel until the topsoil is removed. Photograph, measure, and sketch the grave outline. Carefully remove and sift the soil. Search for relevant items such as cigarette butts, trash, weapons, projectiles, bullet and bullet casings, rope, hair, bags, and bits of clothing.
5. Successively scrape away thin layers of soil, maintaining a flat horizontal work surface. Caution must be exercised to ensure that human body fragments and bones are not damaged by the tools. For better control, a trowel may be used in lieu of a flat shovel. Use the trowel to gently lift the soil from the site.
6. As evidence is discovered, stop, photograph, measure, collect, and preserve the evidence.
7. Stop when the corpse is contacted. Remove enough soil to determine the position of the body. Do not move or remove any portion of the corpse.
8. Circumscribe (pedestal) the corpse by removing soil from its perimeter. In other words, dig a trench around the corpse. As soil is removed around the corpse, the corpse is elevated in relation to its immediate surroundings. The process is referred to as **pedestaling**, a technique that allows one to observe and work near the corpse without disturbing it.

   Pedestaling A technique that allows one to observe and work near a corpse without disturbing it.

9. Expose more of the human remains, using a soft brush and small tools. Do not use a

brush on fabric because it may destroy fiber evidence. Examine the soil near the skull for hair.

10. If the remains are of an adult female, one should search for the presence of a fetal skeleton in the pelvic area.

11. Document the condition of the remains and measure the remains in place. Place a paper bag around each hand and foot. Collect detached hair and fingernails. Examine the mouth and collect detached teeth.

12. Photograph, measure, and collect all associative evidence and artifacts, including jewelry and clothing.

13. The remains are removed from the grave and placed in a body bag.

14. Continue excavation until unstained, undisturbed soil is reached. Sift loosened soil for evidence.

15. Return sifted soil to the grave opening and clean the area. Take final photographs of the gravesite (Burns, 2006; Sorg, 2005).

Photo 7-47. Students performing a shallow grave excavation.

Photo 7-48. Students performing a shallow grave excavation.

Photo 7-49. Students performing a shallow grave excavation.

Photo 7-50. Skeletal remains crime scene. Courtesy of Chula Vista, California, Police Department.

Photo 7-51. Skeletal remains crime scene. Courtesy of Chula Vista, California, Police Department.

Photo 7-52. Skeletal remains crime scene. Courtesy of Chula Vista, California, Police Department.

Photo 7-53. Skeletal remains crime scene. Courtesy of Chula Vista, California, Police Department.

Photo 7-54. Skeletal remains crime scene. Courtesy of Chula Vista, California, Police Department.

Photo 7-55. Skeletal remains crime scene. Courtesy of Chula Vista, California, Police Department.

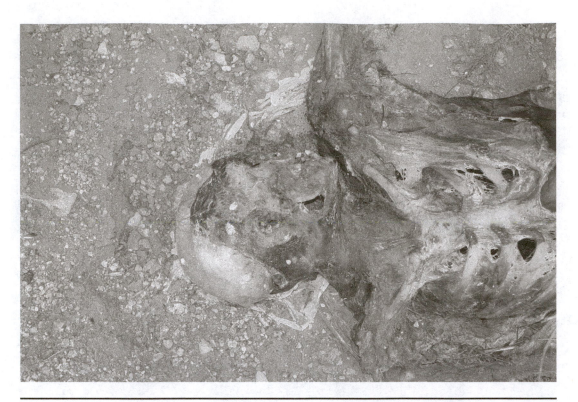

Photo 7-56. Skeletal remains crime scene. Courtesy of Chula Vista, California, Police Department.

Photo 7-57. Skeletal remains crime scene. Courtesy of Chula Vista, California, Police Department.

Photo 7-58. Skeletal remains crime scene. Courtesy of Chula Vista, California, Police Department.

SUMMARY

Some crime scenes are unique. They require the services of someone who is a qualified expert in a specific forensic science field to ensure that safety measures are enforced and proper documentation and collection techniques are implemented. The forensic technician or case investigator will call upon a network of forensic experts when necessary.

Specific photography techniques are employed at OIS scenes. The services of a firearms examiner may be necessary. Documenting graffiti and consulting with gang investigators is important for gang-related crime scenes.

Arson investigations require specific photography and evidence collecting techniques that are overseen by an arson investigator. Mass casualty scenes require the use of multiple experts. A DMORT is an organized group of forensic experts dispatched to mass casualty and disaster scenes.

Rape and sexual assault cases may involve trained SART personnel to assist the victim. A SANE examines and obtains evidence from the victim. Specific evidence collection techniques depend on the nature of the crime.

Cases involving child and elder abuse are highly sensitive. Specially trained investigators and social workers are usually involved. The specific evidence collection procedures depend on the details of the individual case.

Evidence collected at burglary and robbery scenes depend on the manner in which the crime is accomplished. Forensic technicians are not involved in SWAT operations but may photograph and process SWAT-related scenes after the site is rendered safe.

Sophisticated technology and chemical applications are used to process crime scenes cleaned by the perpetrator or others. Body dump sites often involve the use of entomology, anthropology, and excavation measures.

KEY TERMS

Define, describe, or explain the importance of each of the following:

conduction   radiation   Sexual Assault Response Team
convection   sexual assault nurse examiner   (SART)
forensic entomology   (SANE)
pedestaling (of a dead body)

DISCUSSION AND REVIEW QUESTIONS

1. Describe the photographs obtained at an OIS scene?
2. Why is *tagging* at a gang-related crime scene photographed?
3. Explain the three most common forms of heat transfer.
4. Why is the point-of-origin important at a fire scene?
5. What is the role of DMORT?
6. What are date rape drugs?
7. How should the victim of a sexual assault or rape be processed?
8. How does a forensic technician document a child abuse scene?
9. What are the developmental stages of the blow fly? Why are the stages important?

CASE STUDY—Caylee Anthony

Caylee Marie Anthony was born on August 9, 2005, and was reported missing to the police by her grandmother, Cindy Anthony, on July 15, 2008. Cindy became suspicious when her daughter, Casey Anthony, the mother of Caylee, could not produce the child. Cindy had not seen her grandchild in weeks. Cindy also detected an odor in the trunk of Casey's car, an offensive odor that was similar to that of a "dead body."

When police questioned Casey Anthony regarding the whereabouts of her daughter, Casey's account of Caylee's disappearance raised suspicion. Casey claimed to have seen Caylee last on June 9, 2008, although Caylee's disappearance was not reported until July 15. Casey claimed that Caylee was with a babysitter, Zenaida Fernandez-Gonzalez. When police contacted a local woman named Zenaida Gonzalez on July 17, the woman provided credible evidence that she did not know Casey or Caylee Anthony.

Other statements offered by Casey Anthony revealed additional discrepancies. For example, Casey claimed she worked at Universal Studios, Orlando. However, during a visit to the theme park accompanied by police, Casey admitted that she was no longer employed by Universal Studios. Casey also claimed to be investigating Caylee's disappearance on her own, although family and friends were unaware Caylee was missing. Subsequently, photos surfaced that depicted Casey partying while Caylee was missing.

Police discovered hair matching Caylee's, an apparent blood stain, and chloroform in the trunk of Casey's car. Casey's computer revealed that she had searched the Internet for instructions on the use of chloroform. An "air test" of Casey's car trunk suggested that a corpse had been in the trunk.

On October 14, 2008, Casey Anthony was indicted for first-degree murder. On December 11, 2008, scattered skeletal remains of a young child were discovered by a utility worker in a swampy wooded area within a half mile of Caylee's home. Subsequent DNA tests confirmed that the remains were Caylee's. However, since Caylee's skeletal fragments were small and scattered throughout the body dump site, the cause of death could not be determined by the medical examiner. Apparently, Caylee's remains were not discovered earlier by search teams because the body dump site was submerged by the summer's heavy rains.

1. What changes did Caylee's body undergo as a result of its exposure to the body dump site's environment?
2. Caylee's remains were scattered throughout the dump site. How should the site be processed by forensics personnel?

LAB EXERCISE

Indoor Crime Scene Processing

Equipment and supplies required per student:

- one 35-mm camera (film or digital)
- one roll, 24 exposure film (if film camera)
- one pair of gloves (latex or vinyl)
- one measuring tape or laser measuring device
- ten evidence placards
- ten paper bags (four small, four medium, two large)
- one roll packaging tape
- one marking pen
- one flashlight (depending on lighting)
- mock evidence (supplied by instructor)

The students are separated into teams of at least four students. Each team will process an assigned indoor crime scene. For practice purposes, every team member will assist in the search for evidence. Although more than 10 evidence items may be present at the mock crime scene, each team will collect no more than 10 evidence items. The team must determine which evidence items are most important forensically. Each team will determine the following assignments:

- Photographer—takes photographs and prepares photograph list report, if required.
- Evidence collector(s)—collects and packages evidence and prepares evidence list report.
- Sketcher—sketches the crime scene, obtaining measurements of the scene and the evidence; prepares rough and final crime scene diagrams.
- Note taker and final report writer—takes field notes indicating individual assignments and records times; completes a narrative description of the crime scene.
- Students submit all field notes, reports, packaged evidence, scene diagrams, and photographs to the instructor by the due date.

WEB RESOURCES

Computer Crime and Intellectual Property Section (CCIPS) of the U.S. Department of Justice:
www.cybercrime.gov
Computer Forensics, Inc.:
www.forensics.com
Federal Bureau of Investigations:
www.fbi.gov
U. S. Postal Inspection Service:
www.postalinspectors.uspis.gov
Naval Criminal Investigative Service:
www.ncis.navy.mil
U. S. Army Criminal Investigation Command:
www.cid.army.mil
U. S. Air Force Office of Special Investigations:
www.public.afosi.amc.af.mil

American Board of Criminalistics:
www.criminalistics.com
California Association of Criminalists:
www.cacnews.org
International Association of Crime Analysts:
www.iaca.net
Association for Crime Scene Reconstruction:
www.acsr.org
The Forensic Science Society:
www.forensic-science-society.org.ukwww.csfs.ca
Terrorism, Transnational Crime and Corruption Center (TraCCC): www.policy-traccc.gmu.edu
Forensic Anthropology Center:
www.utk.edu/~anthrop/index.htm

8

Vehicle Processing

LEARNING OUTCOMES

After completing this chapter, the reader should be able to:

- describe the steps to processing a motor vehicle used in a crime,
- articulate the investigative measures taken while processing a motor vehicle involved in a rape or child molestation,
- describe the photographs obtained at a multi-vehicle collision scene,
- explain the importance of photographing a stolen motor vehicle's exterior locks and ignition area.

INTRODUCTION

With the mobility available through automobiles in America, it is no surprise that motor vehicles are often used as instrumentalities (tools) to carry out a crime. Vehicles are often stolen and used as transportation to commit crimes such as burglaries, robberies, rapes, and homicides. A vehicle may be used to transport and discard a body at some distance from a crime scene. The vehicle can also be the scene of the crime itself. The steps that a forensic technician takes when processing a vehicle are determined by the relevance of the vehicle to the crime. It is essential that one consult with the case investigator prior to processing any suspect vehicle. The forensic technician must have knowledge of how the vehicle is associated with the crime. Further, forensics personnel as well as investigators must have legal authority to search the vehicle (see *Exceptions to the Search Warrant Requirement* in Chapter 6).

VEHICLE PROCESSING: INSIDE A CRIME SCENE

A perpetrator may drive a vehicle to the scene of a crime. Subsequently, the perpetrator may flee from the scene on foot, become incapacitated, or be arrested at the scene. If a vehicle relevant to a crime is parked within the crime scene, the forensic technician should process the vehicle before it is removed. In officer-involved shooting incidents, a police vehicle involved in the shooting should remain at the scene until it is processed by a forensic technician.

The forensic technician should take the following photographs of a vehicle within a crime or officer-involved shooting scene.

- Overall views of the area in which the vehicle is located, photographed in the same manner as overall views of any other outdoor crime scene.
- Orientation views of any evidence items near the vehicle, photographed in the same manner as an outdoor crime scene.
- The four sides of the vehicle, if possible, filling each photo frame with one side of the vehicle.
- A close-up photograph of the vehicle's license plate and **vehicle identification number (VIN)**. The VIN is usually located on the dash near the driver's side. If

> **Vehicle identification number (VIN).** A unique identifier assigned to a vehicle when manufactured and is usually located on the dash near the driver's side.

Photo 8-1. Overall view of black Expedition.

Photo 8-2. Overall view of black Expedition.

Photo 8-3. Overall view of black Expedition.

Photo 8-4. Overall view of black Expedition.

the vehicle has front and rear license plates, the forensic technician should check both plates to verify that they display the same number and that the plate number corresponds to the VIN for the vehicle. If the license plate number is foreign to the VIN, the vehicle may be stolen. In most cases, an investigator or patrol officer on the scene will verify the license plate and VIN information.

- Photograph of any evidence on the exterior of the vehicle, with orientation and close-up views captured, with a scale (measuring device) in place. The forensic technician should search for any fragile evidence (hairs, fibers) on the exterior of the vehicle. The forensic technician should place an evidence placard near each evidence and photograph orientation and close-up views of the evidence with the placard in the photo's frame. Subsequently, the location of the evidence is documented and the evidence is collected.

Photo 8-5. Medium view of evidence and yellow placard. Courtesy of National City, California, Police Department.

Photo 8-6. Close-up view of evidence and yellow placard. Courtesy of National City, California, Police Department.

After exterior photographs are obtained, the forensic technician should measure and sketch the vehicle into the crime scene diagram as described in Chapter 3. It may be necessary to process the vehicle's interior at the crime scene. However, crime scene processing often requires many hours of exhaustive work. If practical, the forensic technician should have the vehicle towed to the agency impound facility prior to processing. Removal of the vehicle allows the forensic technician to concentrate on processing the reminder of the crime scene first, which is usually the highest priority.

Before removal, the vehicle's exterior and driver area within the vehicle should be processed to prevent destruction of evidence during vehicle transportation. The decision to process the vehicle at the crime scene or at the agency's impound facility is dependent upon the relevance of the vehicle to the crime. If a body is located inside the vehicle, for example, photographs and measurements of the body must be obtained prior to removal of the vehicle from the scene (Ogle, 2007). The forensic technician should consult the case investigator if unsure of processing priorities.

VEHICLE PROCESSING

A forensic technician may be assigned to process a motor vehicle that was previously impounded from a crime scene or a vehicle that was otherwise impounded by an investigator or patrol officer. The vehicle is usually stored at an impound facility. Typically, an investigator is assigned to the case involving the vehicle. Regardless of the nature of the crime, the forensic technician should consult with the case investigator prior to processing the vehicle to learn of the vehicle's relevance to the crime. Knowledge of the nature of the crime and the vehicle's role helps to determine vehicle processing protocol.

Processing the Vehicle's Exterior

The forensic technician should record information about the vehicle, including the year of manufacture, make (manufacturer), model, color, number of doors, license plate and VIN numbers, and any remarkable damage to the vehicle. Some agencies provide check-off lists (vehicle processing forms) to be completed during processing.

Next, the forensic technician should photograph the vehicle. The camera settings used are dependent upon the lighting situation. If the vehicle is inside a building, a flash unit should be used. The following photographs and evidence should be obtained.

1. Overall photographs of the four sides of the vehicle.
2. A close-up photograph of the license plate(s) and VIN number.
3. Medium and close-up views of any damage to the vehicle, with a scale (measuring device) placed next to the damage.
4. Evidentiary items on the vehicle's exterior such as bullet holes or blood. An orientation photo should be taken to show the location of the evidence on the vehicle.
5. An evidence placard should be assigned and placed next to each evidence item. An orientation photo is taken with the evidence placard in place.
6. A close-up view of each evidence item is photographed, with a scale in place. The photographer should fill the camera's frame with the evidence, placard, and the scale, ensuring that the face of the camera lens is directly in front of and parallel to the evidence.

Photo 8-7. Overall view of green Lebaron.

Photo 8-8. Overall view of green Lebaron.

Photo 8-9. Overall view of green Lebaron.

Photo 8-10. Overall view of green Lebaron.

7. Depending on the forensic technician's preference or the agency's protocol, the technician may collect evidence from the exterior of the vehicle or photograph the interior of the vehicle before evidence collection occurs. The forensic technician should swab the undersides of the door handles to collect material for possible DNA analysis. Two drops of distilled water are placed on a sterile swab, and the undersides of the door handles are swabbed for DNA evidence. The forensic technician should photograph the locations swabbed. The swabs are packaged appropriately.

8. The forensic technician may process the exterior of the vehicle for latent fingerprints, following the latent fingerprint collection procedures discussed in Chapter 5. The forensic technician should photograph the developed fingerprints prior to lifting (depending on agency protocol and the forensic technician's discretion). It is advisable to photograph the fingerprint's location on the vehicle. Agency policy will dictate the exact procedure.

Processing the Vehicle's Interior

After processing the exterior of the vehicle, the forensic technician should photograph the vehicle's interior. A flash unit should be used, indoors or out. To avoid reflection, the flash should not be directed toward window glass. To avoid distorted shadows, the flash should not be pointed toward a door jam or car seat. The following overall interior views should be photographed.

1. With all doors except the driver's closed, the forensic technician should stand outside the open door and photograph an overall view of the front seat and floor from the driver's viewpoint.
2. The driver's seat is photographed, followed by the driver's floor area.
3. The door pocket (if applicable) of the driver's door is photographed.
4. The ceiling over the driver's seat is photographed.
5. The forensic technician will close the driver's door and open the right-front passenger door, repeating the photographic

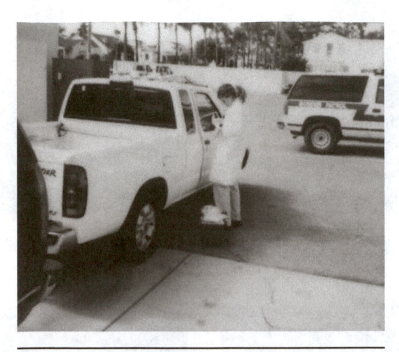

Photo 8-11. Forensic specialist processing vehicle exterior for latent prints.

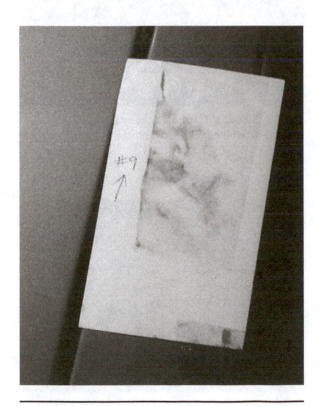

Photo 8-12. Latent prints developed on the exterior of a vehicle. Courtesy of Chula Vista, California, Police Department.

procedure used to obtain photos of the driver's area.

6. The center console (if any) and the glove compartment should be opened and photographed.

7. The forensic technician will close the right-front passenger door and move in a clock-wise direction, taking photographs of the interior from each remaining vehicle door, including overall views of the seats and floors as well as applicable door and seat pockets.

8. An overall view of the trunk, hatch, or back area is photographed.

9. An overall view of the interior of the engine compartment should be photographed.

The forensic technician may be required to search for trace evidence such as hairs or fibers. To avoid loss or destruction of trace evidence, all vehicle compartment doors should remain closed except for the doorway used to gain access to the area being processed for evidence. Further, the forensic technician should wear a hat or other hair covering to avoid contamination of the vehicle.

• A flashlight with a bright light should be used and held at an oblique (less than 90-degree) angle when searching for hairs

Photo 8-13. Interior views of vehicle.

Photo 8-16. Interior views of vehicle.

Photo 8-14. Interior views of vehicle.

Photo 8-17. Interior views of vehicle.

Photo 8-15. Interior views of vehicle.

Photo 8-18. Interior views of vehicle.

Photo 8-19. Interior views of vehicle.

Photo 8-20. Interior views of vehicle.

Photo 8-21. Interior views of vehicle.

Photo 8-22. Interior views of vehicle.

Photo 8-23. Interior views of vehicle.

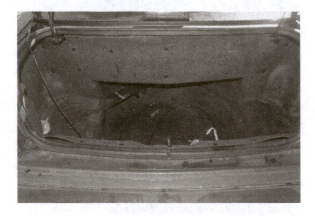

Photo 8-24. Interior views of vehicle.

and fibers. A suspect hair or fiber should be placed in a bindle. The bindle is placed at the site where the hair or fiber was discovered.

- The forensic technician will search for additional evidence within the vehicle. The search focuses on evidence related to the crime (e.g., fruits or instrumentalities of the crime) or evidence that may provide a forensic link to the suspect or the victim. The forensic technician should divide the passenger compartment of the vehicle into quadrants (sections) and search each quadrant thoroughly. The forensic technician must search under the seats, floor mats, and carpet, and within every other cavity in each quadrant. Caution must be exercised to prevent personal injury from broken glass or needles that may be hidden within recessed areas.

Quadrant 1 may include the driver's seat, floor, door pocket, sun visor, cup holder,

and center console. Quadrant 2 may include the right-front passenger's seat, floor, door pocket, sun visor, glove compartment, cup holder, and ash tray. Proceed to the right and left rear passenger areas (if any), designated quadrants 3 and 4, respectively.

- If an evidence item is located, the forensic technician will place a numbered evidence placard near the item. Evidence numbers should be assigned systematically throughout the vehicle. If an item of trace evidence was located earlier and placed in a bindle, a numbered evidence placard is placed near the bindle. Some agencies also require the forensic technician to take close-up photographs of all evidence items without the evidence placard in place.
- The trunk area (if applicable) is searched and evidence placards assigned as appropriate.
- The engine compartment is searched if appropriate.
- The forensic technician will obtain orientation photographs showing the evidence items within the vehicle, followed by close-up views with a scale (measuring device) in place. If an evidence item is located under a seat, it may be removed from its location to be photographed.
- For genetic (DNA) profiling purposes, the forensic technician should swab the steering wheel, gear shift lever or knob, and other surfaces that may reveal DNA evidence. The swabbed surfaces are photographed as well.
- If blood is located on a seat, the floor, or upholstery of the vehicle, a portion of the fabric or carpet containing the blood evidence should be removed. Blood located on hard surfaces of the vehicle may be swabbed. The forensic technician should also examine seatbelts for possible blood or trace evidence.
- It may be necessary to collect trace evidence lifts from the seats or floors. A trace evidence vacuum may be used as well (Gardner, 2005).
- Measurements to identify the exact location of evidence items inside a vehicle are not obtained unless reconstruction of the vehicle interior scene is a possibility. Policies and procedures in this regard depend on the type of case and the agency's protocol. Scene reconstruction within vehicles is usually limited to a determination of a bullet's trajectory or bloodstain pattern analysis. In either case, a subject matter expert is usually consulted.
- The evidence is collected and packaged appropriately.
- Finally, the forensic technician will process the interior of the vehicle and the trunk

Photo 8-25. Medium and close-up views of evidence and placards.

Photo 8-26. Medium and close-up views of evidence and placards.

Photo 8-28. Medium and close-up views of evidence and placards.

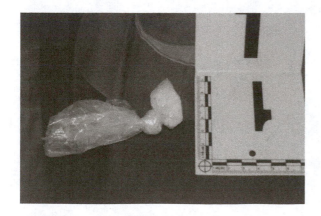

Photo 8-27. Medium and close-up views of evidence and placards.

Photo 8-29. Medium and close-up views of evidence and placards.

Photo 8-30. Medium and close-up views of evidence and placards.

Photo 8-31. Medium and close-up views of evidence and placards.

Photo 8-33. Medium and close-up views of evidence and placards.

Photo 8-32. Medium and close-up views of evidence and placards.

Photo 8-34. Medium and close-up views of evidence and placards.

Photo 8-35. Medium and close-up views of evidence and placards.

Photo 8-36. Medium and close-up views of evidence and placards.

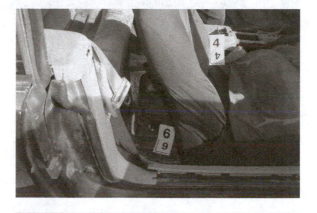

Photo 8-38. Medium and close-up views of evidence and placards.

Photo 8-37. Medium and close-up views of evidence and placards.

Photo 8-39. Medium and close-up views of evidence and placards.

Photo 8-40. Medium and close-up views of evidence and placards.

Photo 8-42. Medium and close-up views of evidence and placards.

Photo 8-41. Medium and close-up views of evidence and placards.

Photo 8-43. Medium and close-up views of evidence and placards.

Photo 8-44. Medium and close-up views of evidence and placards.

Photo 8-45. Medium and close-up views of evidence and placards.

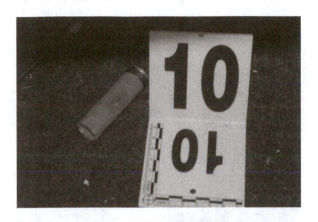

Photo 8-46. Medium and close-up views of evidence and placards.

interior (if applicable) for latent fingerprints. The forensic technician should photograph the developed fingerprints as well as the locations from which the latent prints are lifted. Vehicle surfaces that typically yield classifiable latent fingerprints include windows, interior door frames, smooth door finishes, seatbelt buckles, smooth instrument panel surfaces, door handles, and rearview and vanity mirrors. Surfaces unlikely to yield classifiable fingerprints typically include textured dashboards and steering wheels, and other rough surfaces. In some cases, however, special fingerprint processing techniques can be employed to locate and lift fingerprint evidence from rough surfaces. Special fingerprint processing techniques are discussed in Chapter 5.

VEHICLE PROCESSING: SPECIAL CASES

Some crimes that occur inside a vehicle require special forensic tools and investigative measures to locate relevant forensic evidence. A few of these crimes and special procedures are discussed here.

Rape or Child Molestation inside a Vehicle

In addition to the vehicle processing protocol discussed previously, the forensic technician should search for the following evidence when an alleged rape or molestation occurs inside a vehicle.

- An alternate light source (ALS) should be used to search for seminal fluid (if applicable). Chapter 4 presents a detailed procedure for the use of an ALS. If a suspect stain is located on vehicle seat fabric or a carpeted floor, it should be photographed without and with a numbered evidence placard. Further, the forensic technician should remove the stained portion of the fabric rather than swab the stain.
- When processing the inside surface of a vehicle window for fingerprints, smears indicative of a struggle from a hand or a foot may be observed. Although the detail of the print may not be sufficient for comparison purposes, the friction skin smears may be valuable evidence to validate movement and possibly corroborate a victim's statement. The forensic technician should take overall and medium view photographs of the smeared print as well as a close-up view with a scale to illustrate the location of the print.
- After all evidence is collected, the forensic technician should examine (test) child safety door locks (if applicable) and document window obstructions and seat positioning. Child safety locks are often located on the interior rear doors of vehicles. Their purpose is to prevent a child from opening the door of a moving vehicle. Some child safety locks are activated with an upward or downward movement of a button, while others are activated with a key. If the victim was attacked in the rear seat and the vehicle contains child safety locks, the forensic technician should photograph and process the locks for fingerprints. The victim may have attempted an escape by accessing the locks. Orientation and close-up views of the locks are obtained.

Photo 8-47. Forensic technician processing interior of vehicle for latent prints.

The lock can be tested by sitting in the back seat of the vehicle, with the doors closed, and attempting to open the doors from the inside. If the doors remain secured, the child safety lock is activated. The forensic technician should document the results of the test in the final report.

• In some child molestation cases, perpetrators attempt to obstruct an outside person's view through the vehicle's window. Dark tint may be installed on the windows, sunshades may be placed throughout, or curtains (if any) are lowered. If the vehicle was parked in a public area when the incident occurred, the forensic technician should determine the type of lighting (e.g., day or night, artificial light inside a parking structure) that illuminated the vehicle when the alleged incident occurred. If possible,

Photo 8-49. Child safety lock—medium view.

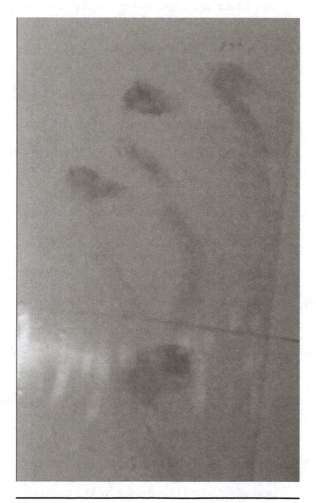

Photo 8-48. Smeared handprint in sexual assault case, developed with black powder. Courtesy of Chula Vista, California, Police Department.

Photo 8-50. Child safety lock—close-up view.

the forensic technician should place the vehicle in similar lighting and take photographs from outside the vehicle toward the inside, thus documenting one's ability to view the interior of the vehicle. The forensic technician may ask another technician or an investigator to sit inside the vehicle to determine if a person inside the vehicle can be observed from outside. The results are documented in the final report. If sunshades were placed over the window interiors or window curtains were lowered when the incident occurred, the forensic technician should attempt to replicate the same conditions and photograph the results.

- In some vehicles, seats recline or can unfold into a prone position. Seats should be positioned in the same manner as reported by the victim. The results should be documented and photographed.

Stolen Vehicles

A vehicle may be stolen and used as an instrumentality (tool) to commit another crime (e.g., robbery). The stolen vehicle is often abandoned after the criminal transaction is complete. The manner in which the vehicle is stolen depends on the auto thief's skill, knowledge, and preferred method of operation (MO). Some car thieves use *shaved* keys to unlock car doors and activate vehicle ignitions. Others use a slim-jim (lock-out tool; thin strip of metal) to open vehicle doors and a screwdriver to replace a key in the ignition. Still others severely damage the exterior

door locks and hotwire (short-circuit) the ignition to start and steal the vehicle. If the vehicle was reported stolen, the forensic technician should take orientation and close-up photographs of the exterior door locks and the ignition switch area.

Body Dumps

If a vehicle may have been used to transport and dump a body, the forensic technician will search for evidence beyond that which is normally sought during standard vehicle processing procedures. Although the vehicle may not contain visible evidence of the presence of blood, the forensic technician should apply chemicals such as Luminol®, Bluestar®, or Fluorescein® in an attempt to locate latent (not visible to the unaided human eye) blood. Application and photographic techniques used with blood-enhancing chemicals are discussed in Chapter 7.

In many body dump cases, foreign material (trace evidence) from the body dump scene may adhere to the vehicle. Therefore, the forensic technician should collect soil samples from the vehicle's tires and search for plant material in and on the vehicle.

VEHICLE COLLISIONS

Many police agencies operate specialized traffic management units staffed with investigators who receive vehicle collision reconstruction training. Most of the investigators are trained in forensic photography, scene sketching,

Photo 8-51. Exterior door lock.

Photo 8-52. Damaged ignition.

and evidence collection. Therefore, collision investigators may not require the services of a forensic technician at a collision scene. However, a forensic technician's assistance may be sought for multi-vehicle collision scenes, especially for photography and evidence collection purposes.

The forensic technician will follow the lead investigator's direction when assisting at a major vehicle collision scene. If the collision occurred at an intersection subject to heavy vehicular traffic, the scene must be processed quickly. The following photographs are taken of a **motor vehicle collision (MVC)** within an intersection:

> **Motor vehicle collision (MVC)** A situation in which a motor vehicle comes into contact with another vehicle, person, or object.

1. Photograph the location of the intersection (street signs associated with intersection).
2. Consult with the investigator to learn how each driver should have viewed the intersection upon approach. The forensic technician will take multiple photographs with the focal length set at 50 mm (closest to the human eye), documenting each driver's approach to the intersection.
3. Photograph traffic control devices (signs and signal lights) as well as any obstructions

(e.g., trees, fences, buildings) from each driver's viewpoint, facing the intersection.
4. Photograph tire skid marks (if present) from the vehicles. See Chapter 9 for details on tire mark and impression photography.
5. At the intersection, photograph overlapping views from each approach to and each corner of the intersection. Take overall views away from each side and each corner of the vehicles involved (Siljander & Fredrickson, 1997).
6. Photograph the **point of impact** (location where vehicles collided). Photograph the position and relationship of any debris resulting from the collision.

> **Point of impact** The location at which vehicles collide.

7. Photograph overall, orientation, and close-up views of collision damage to and the point of impact on each vehicle, with measurement scales placed near the damage on each vehicle.
8. Consult with the investigator regarding evidence to be collected. Place evidence placards near the evidence. Photograph orientation and close-up views in the same manner as in outdoor crime scenes.
9. Search for and photograph vehicle speedometers, which may indicate the speed of the vehicles at the time of impact. Alcohol

containers in the vehicles should be photographed and collected as evidence. The vehicle ignition area is photographed to document a key in place. If no key is in the ignition, the vehicle may be stolen.

10. If assisting with the sketch and diagram of the collision scene, consult with the investigator regarding necessary measurements. Record measurements of the width of the streets, the intersection, the vehicles involved, and the location of evidence (including the vehicles) within the scene.

11. If the collision resulted in fatalities and bodies are present, photograph and measure the location of the bodies in the same manner as in a homicide scene.

12. If it is nighttime, photograph each view of the scene, using timed exposures. Reflective chalk may be used to highlight evidence items within the scene. Additionally, the forensic technician should examine the headlight switch inside each vehicle to determine if the lights were on at the time of the collision (Sullivan, 2007).

If a person involved in a collision flees the scene on foot or in a vehicle, the collision is referred to as a **hit-and-run**. At hit-and-run collision scenes, the forensic

Hit-and-run A vehicle collision from which a person involved in a collision flees the scene.

technician will search for evidence that links the fleeing person or vehicle to the scene. Broken glass, headlamps, reflectors, grillwork and other debris from the missing vehicle are photographed and collected. Skid marks from the suspect's vehicle tires are photographed as well. Vehicles at the scene should be examined for paint from the suspect's missing vehicle that transferred upon impact to vehicles at the scene (Fisher, 2004). After the suspect vehicle is located, it is usually processed by a forensic technician. The technician will process the vehicle in the same manner as any other vehicle used in a crime, with special attention directed toward the following:

- If the suspect vehicle hit a pedestrian, the forensic technician should search for clothing fibers, fabric impressions, hair, blood, and biological evidence as well as fingerprints on the vehicle's hood, undercarriage, or any other part of the vehicle that may have come in contact with the victim's body.
- If the suspect vehicle hit another car, paint transfer from the victim's vehicle should be photographed and collected using a clean scalpel or razor blade. The paint can be analyzed to determine its origin.
- The forensic technician should confer with the investigator for directives on any other forensic procedures required.

Photo 8-53. Traffic collision scene. Courtesy of Chula Vista, California, Police Department.

Photo 8-54. Traffic collision scene. Courtesy of Chula Vista, California, Police Department.

Photo 8-55. Traffic collision scene. Courtesy of Chula Vista, California, Police Department.

Photo 8-56. Traffic collision scene. Courtesy of Chula Vista, California, Police Department.

Photo 8-57. Traffic collision scene. Courtesy of Chula Vista, California, Police Department.

Photo 8-58. Traffic collision scene. Courtesy of Chula Vista, California, Police Department.

Photo 8-59. Traffic collision scene. Courtesy of Chula Vista, California, Police Department.

Photo 8-60. Traffic collision scene. Courtesy of Chula Vista, California, Police Department.

Photo 8-61. Traffic collision scene. Courtesy of Chula Vista, California, Police Department.

Photo 8-62. Overhead view of high-speed single vehicle collision. Courtesy of Chula Vista, California, Police Department.

Photo 8-63. Photos of traffic collision scenes. Courtesy of National City, California, Police Department.

Photo 8-64. Photos of traffic collision scenes. Courtesy of National City, California, Police Department.

Photo 8-65. Photos of traffic collision scenes. Courtesy of National City, California, Police Department.

Chapter Eight

SUMMARY

Vehicles may be used as tools to commit crime. The investigative measures and evidence processing techniques utilized will depend on the nature of the offense. If a vehicle is located within a crime scene, the vehicle is photographed and measured within the scene. In summary, the following protocol is appropriate when processing a vehicle.

1. First, consult with the case investigator.
2. Photograph the exterior of the vehicle(s), including its four sides, the license plates and VIN.
3. Photograph medium and close-up views of the damage to the vehicle.
4. Photograph, measure, and collect evidence on the exterior of the vehicle.
5. Obtain swabs for DNA analysis of the undersides of the door handles.
6. Process the exterior for latent fingerprints.
7. Photograph overall views of the interior, including the trunk and engine compartment.
8. Search for evidence in the interior, including the trunk and engine compartment.
9. Assign placards to all evidence items.
10. Take orientation photographs of evidence items.
11. Take close-up photographs of each evidence item with and without the placard and a measurement scale in place.
12. Take measurements of the evidence to identify its location within the scene.
13. Collect all evidence.
14. Obtain trace evidence lifts (if applicable).
15. Obtain swabs from the steering wheel, gear shift lever, and other applicable surfaces for possible DNA analysis.
16. Use an ALS if necessary.
17. Process the interior of the vehicle and the trunk (if any) for latent fingerprints.

KEY TERMS

Define, describe, or explain the importance of each of the following:

hit-and-run
motor vehicle collision (MVC)

point of impact
vehicle identification number (VIN)

DISCUSSION AND REVIEW QUESTIONS

1. What interior photographs should be taken of a vehicle involved in a crime?
2. What is the purpose of photographing and processing child safety locks inside a vehicle?
3. Describe the photographs obtained at a multi-vehicle collision scene.
4. In a hit-and-run pedestrian collision, what evidence should the forensic technician attempt to locate on the suspect vehicle?
5. Why is it important to inspect the license plate and VIN of a vehicle involved in a crime?

CASE STUDY—The Oklahoma City Bombing

In April 1995, Timothy McVeigh parked a Ryder rental truck laden with explosives in front of the multi-story Alfred P. Murrah federal building in downtown Oklahoma City and walked away from the scene. Subsequently, the truck exploded, shattering the morning calm. The blast destroyed most of the building and killed 168 people.

Later that morning, McVeigh was stopped outside the city by an Oklahoma Highway Patrol officer. McVeigh was driving a 1977 Mercury Marquis without a license plate. The officer discovered that McVeigh was in possession of a loaded firearm. McVeigh was subsequently arrested for illegally transporting a firearm.

Portions of the exploded rental truck revealed unique information that was used to identify the rental company and a rental agreement signed by McVeigh, who used the alias Robert Kling. The address on McVeigh's driver's license matched the address written on the rental agreement. The address was that of McVeigh's friend and co-conspirator, Terry Nichols.

Later, forensic experts located detonation cord residue on clothing McVeigh wore the day of his arrest by the highway patrol officer. Investigators also linked McVeigh's fingerprints to a fingerprint recovered from a receipt for 2,000 pounds of ammonium nitrate, a chemical used to create explosives.

1. What role did forensic science play in the investigation of the Oklahoma City bombing?
2. How would one process the vehicle McVeigh was driving?

LAB EXERCISE

Vehicle Processing

Equipment and supplies required per team of four or five students:

- one motor vehicle volunteered by a student or offered by a vehicle impound facility
- one 35-mm camera (film or digital)
- one roll of 24 or 36 exposure film (if film camera)
- protective gloves (latex or vinyl); minimum of one pair per student
- ten numerically sequenced evidence placards
- three small paper bags
- four medium paper bags
- three large paper bags
- one roll packaging tape
- one marking pen
- one flashlight (depending on lighting)
- mock evidence (supplied by instructor)
- one for each team—black fingerprint powder, powder brush, fingerprint lifting tape
- ten latent fingerprint cards per team

Using the techniques described in this chapter, students will separate into teams of four or five. Each team will process an assigned vehicle. There may be more than 10 mock evidence items in or on the vehicle. Each team will identify and collect 10 evidence items that are the most forensically important. Each team member will search for evidence (for practice purposes). Each team will decide which members are assigned to the following roles:

- Photographer. Takes photographs and prepares photograph list report if needed.
- Evidence collector(s). Collects and packages evidence and prepares evidence list report.
- Note taker and final report writer. Takes notes indicating individual assignments, records times and measurements, completes narrative description of the crime scene.
- Latent print processor(s). Processes latent prints on the exterior and the interior of the vehicle.
- Sketcher (optional). A sketch of the interior of the vehicle is not usually required unless it contains blood spatter or bullet holes.

Students submit all rough notes, reports, packaged evidence, latent print cards, photographs, and sketch (if applicable) to the instructor by the due date assigned.

WEB RESOURCES

International Association of Crime Analysts: www.iaca.net

The Forensic Science Society: www.forensic-science-society.org.uk

Canadian Society of Forensic Science: www.csfs.ca

Association for Crime Scene Reconstruction: www.acsr.org

Crime Scene Investigation: www.crime-scene-investigator.net

Northwestern University: www.nucps.northwestern.edu

9

Impression Evidence

LEARNING OUTCOMES

After completing this chapter, the reader should be able to:

- photograph a three-dimensional shoe or tire impression,
- photograph a dusty shoe impression lifted with polyester film (e.g., Mylar®),
- lift shoe impressions in dust using rubber-gelatin lifters,
- demonstrate the ability to use an electrostatic lift,
- measure parallel tire impressions,
- cast a three-dimensional shoe impression,
- document and collect bloody shoe impressions,
- cast a tool mark impression.

INTRODUCTION

Impression evidence includes objects or materials that assume the characteristics of other objects or materials through direct physical contact (Bodziak, 2000). Impression evidence commonly encountered at crime scenes includes two- and three-dimensional shoe, tire, and tool mark impressions. The value of impression evidence is based on physically matching the random and individual characteristics of the impression at the scene to a specific shoe, tire, or tool that made the impression. The exact age of an impression cannot be determined. However, a suspect may be linked to the crime scene through the impressions. In addition, impression evidence may indicate any of the following:

- point of entry to or exit from the scene,
- path of the suspect through and away from the scene,
- brand name of a shoe or tire,
- shoe or tire impression pattern,
- approximate size of a shoe or tire,
- types of shoes worn within the scene,
- number of suspects.

Although impression evidence is valuable, documentation and collection is time consuming and labor intensive. The process requires patience and attention to detail because the evidence is fragile and can be destroyed easily.

Impression evidence may be destroyed inadvertently prior to the forensic technician's arrival at the scene. First responding police officers, paramedics, and firefighters may walk, drive, or roll a gurney over an impression. In addition to inadvertent first responder or investigator activity, impression evidence is often destroyed or overlooked because:

- unauthorized or untrained personnel are allowed into the scene,
- environmental conditions (e.g., rain, snow, wind) destroy evidence,
- crime scene personnel may not suspect impression evidence is present,
- crime scene personnel do not aggressively search for impression evidence,
- crime scene personnel perform an incomplete search or fail to determine points of entry and exit,
- the surface on which the impression is located may not be conducive to impression identification or collection because of background (e.g., color) distortion.

Impressions need not be overlooked or destroyed if all crime scene personnel collaborate to identify and protect the evidence. On-scene personnel should:

- protect the crime scene, including a wide perimeter surrounding the scene,
- search for shoe impression evidence often located near or under a victim's body,
- exhaust all efforts to determine points of entry and exit,
- focus on areas where impression evidence may be destroyed if not secured and collected immediately,
- search for latent (invisible to the naked human eye) shoe impressions within the crime scene,
- not discard partial impressions,
- photograph impressions prior to enhancing or developing,
- conduct a methodical search of the scene, including a visual search with existing light to locate patent (visible) impressions and use of oblique lighting indoors to locate latent prints in dust.

IMPRESSION EVIDENCE AT OUTDOOR CRIME SCENES

Shoe and Tire Impressions

Shoe and tire impression evidence is commonly located at outdoor scenes. Shoe impressions in soil (not mud) are easily disguised by direct sunlight. The sun can eliminate shadows, *washing out* highlights of the impressions. If soil is present in or around a crime scene, the forensic technician should block direct sunlight while searching for impressions.

As first responders walk through a scene, they may deposit shoe impressions. The forensic technician wastes valuable time when photographing and collecting impressions left by officers and paramedics. If confusion exists as to which impressions were deposited by first responders or possible suspects, the forensic technician should digitally photograph the shoe soles of each first responder who entered the scene. This will aid the forensic technician in discerning which impression is evidence.

Forensic technician and other crime scene personnel may deposit shoe impressions at the scene as well. Therefore, it is advisable that crime scene personnel wear shoe covers to distinguish non-relevant shoe impressions from suspect impressions. Another option is to place evidence markers near suspect impressions so they are not overlooked, destroyed, or mistaken for first responder impressions.

After shoe or tire impression evidence is located within a scene, the forensic technician should alert other crime scene personnel present to avoid walking on or near the evidence. If numerous shoe or tire impressions are located within a scene, a personnel pathway should be designated. The forensic technician(s) assigned the task of photographing and collecting evidence should be the only personnel allowed near the impression(s).

If environmental conditions make destruction of impression evidence likely, the forensic technician should obtain close-up photographs and collect the impression evidence quickly, prior to taking overall photos of the scene. If the impression is not likely to be compromised, the forensic technician may continue with normal crime scene procedures.

After photographing overall and medium views of the scene, the forensic technician will assign evidence placards to the shoe or tire impression evidence as well as other items of evidence. Orientation views of the items in relation to one another should be photographed from various viewpoints, followed by close-up views of each evidence item with a scale (measuring device) in place. If a shoe or tire impression is to be collected, the impression is assigned a numbered evidence placard. If the impression is photographed, but not collected, the evidence typically receives a letter placard. The procedure depends on agency policy. Some agencies collect all impressions while others allow the forensic technician to determine which impressions are relevant. Regardless of agency policy, all impressions should be photographed prior to casting.

Three-Dimensional Shoe Impression Photography

The following procedure is recommended when photographing close-up views of a three-dimensional shoe impression in dirt or mud:

1. Remove debris (e.g., sticks, leaves) that is not part of the impression.
2. Place a camera on a tripod (inverse mount preferred).
3. Use a level to ensure that the face of the camera lens is parallel with the impression. If the impression is on an incline, use an angle finder to determine the angle of the surface that contains the impression. Next, place the angle finder on the back of the camera and adjust the camera mount on the tripod until the face of the camera lens is at the same angle as the impression.

Photo 9-1. Overall view of shoe and tire impression evidence within a crime scene. Courtesy of National City, California, Police Department.

Photo 9-2. Camera being leveled.

4. Use a normal view or telephoto focal length. Do not use a wide-angle focal length because it distorts detail. For description of a normal view focal length, see Chapter 2.
5. Use the best depth-of-field. F22 is recommended.
6. For clarity, 100 ISO is preferred.

7. Black and white is recommended; color is acceptable.
8. An FBI scale (a thin, rigid, L-shaped, 7" × 13" ruler designed by the FBI) is placed on the same plane and at the lowest point of the shoe impression. The scale may be pressed into the soil next to the impression.
9. A compass or other device indicating direction and an evidence marker are placed near the impression.
10. Fill the frame of the image with the impression, scale, compass, and evidence marker.
11. Focus on the bottom (deepest area) of the impression.
12. Shade the impression, eliminating direct sunlight. If possible, use a large (3' × 3') black fabric or cardboard to shade the impression. An assistant may be necessary to hold the shading material.
13. Hold a flash unit connected to the camera at a 15 degree angle approximately five feet above the impression.
14. Take the photograph.
15. Repeat the procedure with the flash unit at 30 and 45 degree angles.

Photo 9-3. An assistant shading a shoe and tire impression with a black cloth.

Photo 9-4. Demo of flash angle use for shoe and tire impression photo.

16. Relocate the flash unit to illuminate another portion of the impression and take photographs with the flash at 15, 30, and 45 degree angles above the impression.

17. Repeat the process (if possible) until all four sides of the impression are photographed with the flash unit at 15, 30, and 45 degree angles above and light evenly dispersed across the impression. At a minimum, the impression should be photographed with the flash unit positioned at three different locations around the impression.

Flash photos from all sides of the impression will highlight different details of the impression. Footwear examiners prefer to view multiple photographs at different flash angles to ensure that all of the details of the impression can be observed and compared (Bodziak, 2000; Staggs, 2005).

Three-Dimensional Tire Impression Photography

The following procedure is recommended when photographing close-up views of three-dimensional tire impressions in soil (or mud):

1. Place a lettered evidence marker at each end of the tire impression to illustrate the front (leading edge) and back (trailing edge) of the impression. Assign an evidence number if the

Photo 9-5. Shoe impression evidence photographed at various flash angles. Courtesy of National City, California, Police Department.

Photo 9-6. Shoe impression evidence photographed at various flash angles. Courtesy of National City, California, Police Department.

Photo 9-7. Shoe impression evidence photographed at various flash angles. Courtesy of National City, California, Police Department.

Photo 9-8. Shoe impression evidence photographed at various flash angles. Courtesy of National City, California, Police Department.

tire impression is to be cast. The exact procedure may vary among agencies.

2. Extend a measuring tape beside and along the entire length of impression with the front of the tape measure placed at the leading edge of the impression.

3. Without touching the impression or concealing the tape measure, place a scale (ruler) beside the portion of the impression to be photographed on the same plane as the lowest portion of impression. If an L-shaped ruler is used, ensure that the ruler does not contact the impression.

4. The tripod and camera setup and settings are the same as three-dimensional shoe impression photography. The forensic technician must avoid placing one of the tripod legs on the impression. A quadripod (four-leg camera stand) may be used to straddle the impression.

5. The tire impression is photographed in one-foot (12″) sections. The photographer must ensure that each foot of the impression photographed is observed through the viewfinder with a one- to two-inch overlap between the one-foot sections. Photograph the impression using the same flash angles used in three-dimensional shoe impression photography, taking a total of 12 photographs for each one-foot tire impression section.

6. With the measuring tape remaining in place, move the camera, tripod, and ruler to the next one-foot section of the tire impression, ensuring overlap of the photographs. Repeat the photographic steps.

7. Repeat the process until at least one rotation of the tire is photographed.

Two-Dimensional Tire Mark Photography

Two-dimensional tire tread skid marks may be present on pavement at a crime or vehicle collision scene. The close-up photography for a two-dimensional tire mark is similar to the three-dimensional method except that the camera flash angle is 45 degrees to the side of the mark. There is no need to photograph the tire tread mark with flash angles of 15 and 30 degrees. Neither is it necessary to take multiple flash photos from the sides of the mark. However, at least one entire tire rotation should be photographed, utilizing the three-dimensional tire impression photography procedure described earlier.

Photo 9-9. Photographs of a complete tire rotation.

Photo 9-10. Photographs of a complete tire rotation.

Photo 9-11. Photographs of a complete tire rotation.

To determine the starting point of a skid, locate the end that is the thickest (darkest) portion of the skid mark (where most tire rubber is gathered). The thinnest (lightest) portion of the skid is typically the end of the skid.

Tire Impression and Mark Measurements

In addition to photography, the forensic technician should record the following measurements of parallel tire impressions and tread marks at a crime or vehicle collision scene:

- tread width (outside edge to inside edge of each tread) for each impression or mark,
- center of first tread to center of second tread,
- outside edge of first tread to outside edge of second tread,
- inside edge of first tread to inside edge of second tread.

Three-Dimensional Shoe and Tire Impression Casts

All photography of the impression must be complete prior to casting. The forensic technician has one opportunity to cast an impression successfully.

A three-dimensional shoe or tire impression cast preserves the crime scene impression for subsequent comparison and analysis by a footwear or tire impression expert. Casting materials include substances such as plaster of Paris, silicone, or *dental stone* (Traxtone®). Experiments and studies have revealed that dental stone is preferred for casting three-dimensional shoe and tire impressions (Bodziak, 2000).

Dental stone, a gypsum-based powder, hardens when mixed with water. Pre-measured dental stone can be purchased in plastic bags through many forensic supply companies. The forensic technician simply adds water, mixes, and pours.

The following steps are recommended to cast a three-dimensional shoe impression.

1. If the impression is located in fine soil, the forensic technician may first spray liquid hairspray directly above (not directly into) the impression. The hairspray particles descend onto the impression, causing the soil particles to adhere and form a mold.

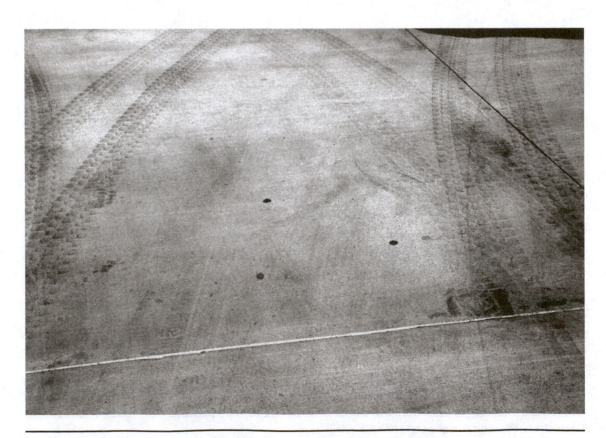

Photo 9-12. Photograph of multiple tire skid marks.

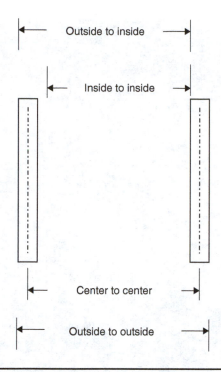

Figure 9-1. Tire track measurements diagram.

Photo 9-13. Hairspray sprayed on dirt.

2. A retaining ridge (wood, cardboard, or metal reinforcement brace) is placed around the impression to restrain the liquefied casting material. The retaining ridge may not be necessary when using dental stone. However, if the impression is located on an incline, a brace prevents progression of the liquid dental stone beyond the impression.
3. Prepare the casting material or mix a pre-measured dental stone casting package. The pre-measured casting powder package will indicate the amount of water needed, typically eight ounces. The forensic technician pours the water into the plastic bag, closes the bag, and immediately mixes the powder and water by massaging the plastic bag and its contents. A common error in impression casting is improper mixing of the powder and water. Many powders contain colored beads that disappear when the powder is completely saturated with water. The forensic technician should ensure that no colored beads or lumps remain within the mixture.
4. Gently pour the mixture within the retaining ridge and next to the impression, allowing the liquid to flow over and onto the impression. Do not pour the mixture directly onto the impression because the force of the pour may destroy detail in the impression. Continue to pour until the mixture flow covers the entire impression.
5. A spatula may be used to spread the mixture over the impression, exercising caution to ensure that no impression detail is disturbed. Do not push the mixture across the impression.
6. Wooden tongue depressors or craft sticks may be gently submerged into the mixture as it hardens, to reinforce and strengthen the cast. Dental stone, however, has proven to be strong and does not require reinforcement material.
7. The cast is allowed to harden for approximately 45 minutes. In damp climates, cast drying may take longer. Once dry, the forensic

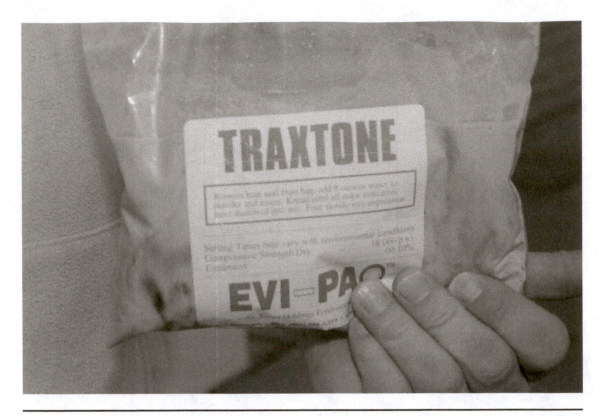

Photo 9-14. Traxtone shoe impression casting.

Photo 9-15. Casting poured into shoe impression.

Photo 9-16. Casting drying.

technician should slide fingers under the cast and carefully dislodge the cast from the soil. The cast may break if removed by the edges. The cast is removed carefully and placed in a box. The cast will remain soft and fragile for approximately 48 hours. Therefore, the cast should remain undisturbed in the box for at least 48 hours. The forensic technician may clean the cast after it is completely dry and hardened.

8. If an impression contains water, such as an impression in mud, the forensic technician may add casting powder to the water.

9. Tire impressions are cast in the same manner as shoe impressions except that tire impressions require additional casting material because one complete tire rotation should be cast. A bucket may be used to mix appropriate amounts of casting powder and water. After the tire impression cast is dry, it is slid onto an

unfolded cardboard box. The box is re-folded over the cast, and transported.

Shoe and Tire Impressions in Snow

Photographing shoe or tire impressions in snow is challenging. The photography setup is the same as any other three-dimensional impression photographic procedure. However, reflective white snow often poses photo exposure challenges. A camera's internal light meter will identify the snow's reflection and calculate the image's exposure inappropriately, resulting in an underexposed photograph. To compensate, the photographer may use an 18 percent gray card to obtain the light meter reading and adjust the camera settings accordingly. Alternatively, one may purposely allow more light into the camera by opening the lens two f-stops or slowing the shutter speed by two full settings. The photographer should bracket the settings and take several photographs (Staggs, 2005).

Another problem with shoe and tire impressions in snow is the difficulty with casting the impressions. As the casting mixture hardens, it radiates heat that can melt the snow, destroying the impression.

The difficulties encountered with photographing and casting three-dimensional shoe and tire impressions in snow can be overcome with the aid of a wax coating such as *Snow Print Wax®*, a substance that is sprayed onto the impression deposited in the snow. The wax maintains the shape of the impression because the snow is insulated by the wax, preventing loss of detail from heat radiation caused by the casting process. The wax is dark red in color, which allows the forensic technician to photograph the impression without the reflection and underexposure challenges caused by untreated white snow.

To apply the wax, the forensic technician simply sprays a thin wax coating onto the impression and allows the wax to dry. Two additional thin wax coatings are applied, allowing each coat to dry before adding another. The impression is photographed, followed by casting according to the recommended procedures.

IMPRESSION EVIDENCE AT INDOOR CRIME SCENES

Impression evidence at indoor crime scenes includes dusty shoe impressions or marks; latent or patent (visible) foot or shoe prints in blood, grease, and other substances; and tool mark impressions. Depending on the type of crime and the scene, the forensic technician will perform various photographic and collection procedures to preserve the impression evidence.

Bloody Shoe Impressions and Prints

Violent crimes frequently result in bloodshed. When a victim's blood is shed at a crime scene, it is common for the perpetrator to walk through the blood. Bloody foot or shoe prints may be located near or under a body, throughout the crime scene, or leading away from the scene. Some prints are patent (visible), while others are very faint or latent (invisible to the naked eye). Specific chemicals are used to enhance bloody prints. However, proper documentation and collection steps must be followed because the chemicals used may interfere with DNA analysis. Further, over-processing or destruction of a print may occur if the chemical is not applied correctly.

Dried blood can flake easily. Therefore, a blanket or other covering should not be placed over bloody shoe prints or impressions unless environmental conditions (e.g., rain, snow) dictate. If the blood is dry, it may flake and disperse when the covering is removed. Additionally, dried blood flakes and disperses easily if unauthorized personnel walk through the scene.

The following procedure is recommended for documenting and collecting bloody shoe prints and impressions at an indoor crime scene:

1. Assign an evidence number to the print or impression to be documented and collected.
2. Take orientation photographs of the print or impression in relation to the crime scene.
3. Take close-up photographs of the print or impression with the same camera setup used for three-dimensional shoe impressions, except that the flash angle need not be 15 or 30 degrees. A depth-of-field of F-11 or F-16 is sufficient. A camera tripod, level, L-shaped scale, and compass are used. The photo's frame is filled with the impression, scale, compass, and evidence marker.
4. Prints and impressions are photographed, even if they are located in blood or other liquid or substance. Further enhancement or collection of the blood evidence is dependent upon the substance. If the substance is blood (obviously, or determined through a presumptive blood test), a small portion of the blood is collected on a swab for subsequent DNA analysis. One should not swab an area that contains

Blood-Enhancing Chemical Name	Resulting Color Change Upon Reaction
Leucocrystal violet (LCV)	Violet or purple
Amido black	Dark blue, almost black
Hungarian red dye	Dark red
Patent blue	Aqua-blue
Fuschin acid dye	Fuschia pink
Tartazine	Yellow
Diaminobenzidine	Brown

Figure 9-2. Chart of blood-enhancement chemicals.

detail of the print or impression. Instead, one may swab an area on the edge of the print or impression or a location where the blood is thickest. Two drops of distilled water are placed on the swab before the blood evidence is collected.

5. Blood-enhancing chemicals can be used to enhance print and impression detail. Because the chemicals can cause blood to change color, the surface on which the print or impression is deposited must be considered when choosing which blood-enhancing chemical to apply. Typically, chemicals that produce dark-colored reactions are applied after a light-colored reaction chemical is applied. The impression is photographed.

One should not confuse blood-enhancing chemicals with presumptive blood test or latent blood detection chemicals. Blood-enhancing chemicals are used to enhance the details of visible, known bloody prints or impressions. Figure 9.2 lists different types of blood-enhancing chemicals and each chemical's corresponding color reaction.

Bloody Shoe Impressions on a Red Surface

The forensic technician should choose a blood-enhancing chemical that will provide the best contrast. For example, amido black will provide a good contrasting color (dark blue) against a red background. Hungarian red dye (dark red) will not. If foot or shoe prints and impressions in blood are located on red surfaces, such as red brick, they may be difficult to observe and photograph prior to chemical enhancement. Use of an alternate light source provides a visual contrast: the blood appears dark against the red surface. The forensic technician should follow

Photo 9-17. Patent (visible) bloody shoe print.

the alternative light source photography steps presented in Chapter 5 to photograph a print or impression in blood prior to chemical enhancement. Further, a sample of the blood should be collected for DNA analysis before blood-enhancing chemicals are applied.

Foot and Shoe Prints and Impressions in Dust

Foot or shoe prints or impressions may be deposited on numerous surfaces at indoor crime scenes. A burglar may enter through a window and step onto a counter or chair to gain access to a residence or business. A bank robber may jump onto a teller's countertop to frighten bank employees. A killer may walk across a floor next to the victim's body or kick a door during a violent attack. In each of these incidents, trace elements and dust may be transferred from the perpetrator's foot or shoe onto a surface. Footprint evidence is often overlooked at a crime scene because it is not easily observed with the unaided human eye.

To locate foot or shoe prints or impressions one should first inquire if the perpetrator walked within the scene. Next, the forensic technician should turn off ambient lights and use a flashlight with a bright light, a light-emitting diode (LED) directional light, or a white light held at an oblique (low to the surface)

Photo 9-18. Flashlight held at an oblique angle.

angle to search the area for dusty shoe prints or impressions.

After print or impression evidence is located, it is photographed according to the following procedure:

1. Place a camera on a tripod (inverse mounting preferred) directly over the print or impression.
2. Use a level to ensure that the face of the camera's lens is parallel to the print or impression.
3. Use a normal view or telephoto focal length. Do not use a wide-angle focal length because it distorts the detail.
4. Good depth-of-field is required. F-11 or F-16 is sufficient.
5. A low ISO creates a crisp photograph, but a low-light situation may require a higher ISO. An ISO of 200–400 is recommended.
6. Black and white photography is recommended. Color photography is acceptable.
7. An FBI L-shaped scale and an evidence placard are placed near the impression.
8. Fill the frame of the image with the impression, L-shaped scale, and evidence placard.
9. Focus on the print or impression rather than the scale.
10. A continuous light source is held at an oblique (low) angle of approximately 10 degrees, with the light passing over the surface of the print or impression. Auto or tungsten white balance is selected if a digital camera is used.
11. The camera is set on aperture priority ("A" or "AV"). If a manual camera is used, the camera's light meter is used to calculate the appropriate shutter speed. If the lighting is dim, the shutter speed will be slow. Therefore, the photographer should use a shutter release cable to prevent camera movement. Several photographs are taken to ensure that at least one photograph is properly exposed.

Electrostatic Lift

After photographing a foot or shoe print or impression in dust, the print or impression can be collected with an **electrostatic lift.** The lift produces static electricity that assists with collecting the print or impression in dust. A thin piece of polyester film (e.g., Mylar), usually black in color, is placed on top of the dust print or impression. A metal probe connected to the lift is placed against the Mylar. A grounding plate is placed next to the Mylar. The electrostatic lift is activated, sending static electricity through the Mylar. The static charge causes the dust to adhere to the Mylar. Subsequently, the grounding unit is disconnected, and the Mylar is collected and transported to the crime laboratory where the dust print or impression is photographed. Details of the procedure include the following:

> **Electrostatic lift** An electrostatic lift produces static electricity that assists with collecting a print or impression in dust.

1. Locate the dusty foot or shoe print by disconnecting all ambient lights and using oblique lighting from a flashlight, LED light, or white light.
2. Place a piece of Mylar, black side down, silver side up, over the print in dust.
3. Place the metal grounding unit adjacent to but not in contact with the Mylar.
4. Hold half of the electrostatic lift one to two inches above the Mylar and the other half over the metal grounding plate. A single metal probe is located at one end of the electrostatic lift, and two parallel metal probes are located on the opposite end. Place the single metal probe on the Mylar. The two parallel probes located at the opposite end of electrostatic lift are placed on top of the metal grounding plate.
5. Set the voltage on low and activate the electrostatic lift. Slowly increase the voltage to high. The Mylar will charge with static electricity and adhere to the surface of the dusty foot or shoe print. To prevent static electric shock, keep hands away from the Mylar.
6. Use a rubber roller to remove air pockets between the Mylar and the print while the device is activated. The rubber on the roller functions as an insulator and will prevent the static charge from shocking a person using the roller.

   Lower the voltage and deactivate the electric lift. Wait a few seconds before removing the metal probes from the Mylar. Remove the metal grounding plate and the Mylar to view the dusty foot or shoe print with oblique lighting.

Photo 9-19. Electrostatic dust lifter.

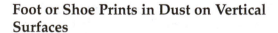

Photo 9-20. Demo of electrostatic dust lifter.

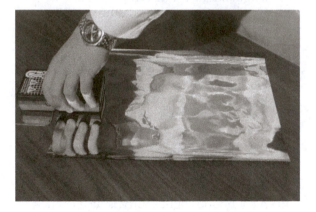

Photo 9-21. Demo of electrostatic dust lifter.

Foot or Shoe Prints in Dust on Vertical Surfaces

Foot or shoe prints on a vertical surface (e.g., door or wall) can be collected in the same manner as prints located on a horizontal surface. Using the electrostatic lift, the Mylar and metal grounding plate are taped to the vertical surface. Masking tape is preferred because it does not restrict the static electricity charge flow. Duct

tape should not be used because it prohibits the flow of the static charge. The electrostatic lift is held in place by crime scene personnel.

Transporting the Print on Polyester Film (Mylar)

When Mylar is charged, it attracts dust that may contaminate the print. For this reason, Mylar should be transported in a dust-proof container.

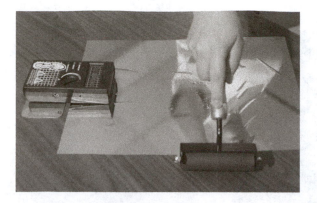

Photo 9-22. Demo of electrostatic dust lifter.

A plastic rectangular-shaped container works well because it can be cleaned after each use. The Mylar is placed in the container face up (dust print up). Tape is used to secure the Mylar in place. Caution must be exercised when removing the Mylar from the container so the dust print is not compromised.

Photographing the Print on Polyester Film (Mylar)

When Mylar loses its static electricity charge, dust particles disconnect from the Mylar, and the print is destroyed. Therefore, the print is photographed as soon as possible. The photographic technique is very similar to the process used when photographing other dusty prints at the crime scene.

1. The camera is placed on a tripod (inverse mounting preferred) directly over the print or impression.
2. An appropriate level must be used to ensure that the face of the camera's lens is parallel with the print or impression.
3. A normal view or telephoto focal length should be used. Do not use a wide-angle focal length because it distorts the detail.
4. Good depth-of-field is required. F-11 or F-16 is sufficient.
5. A low ISO creates a crisp photograph, but a low-light situation may require a higher ISO. An ISO of 200–400 is recommended.
6. Black and white photography is recommended. Color photography is acceptable.
7. An FBI L-shaped scale and an evidence placard are placed near the impression.
8. The frame of the image is filled with the impression, L-shaped scale, and evidence placard.

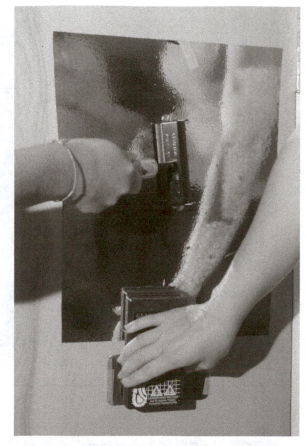

Photo 9-23. A dusty shoe impression is obtained from a door with an electrostatic lift. The Mylar and grounding plate is secured with tape while the electrostatic unit is held in place.

9. The photographer should focus on the print or impression rather than the scale.
10. A continuous light source should be held at an oblique (low) angle of approximately 10 degrees, with the light passing over the surface of the print or impression. The continuous light can be a floodlight flashlight with a bright bulb, LED light, or white light. Auto or tungsten white balance is selected if a digital camera is used.
11. The camera is set on aperture priority ("A" or "AV"). If a manual camera is used, the camera's light meter is used to calculate the appropriate shutter speed. If the lighting is dim, the shutter speed will be slow. Therefore, the photographer should use a shutter release cable to prevent camera movement. Several photographs are taken to ensure that at least one photograph is properly exposed.

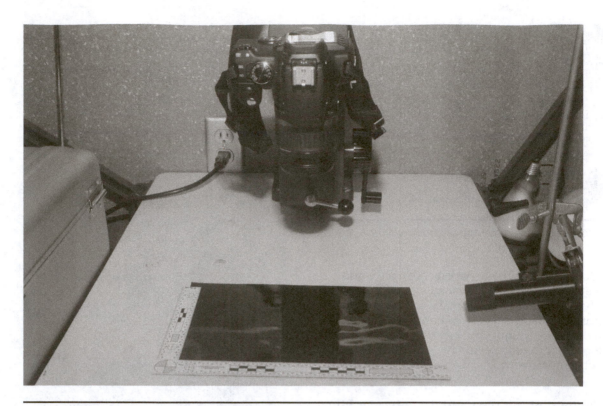

Photo 9-24. Photographic setup for an electrostatic lift.

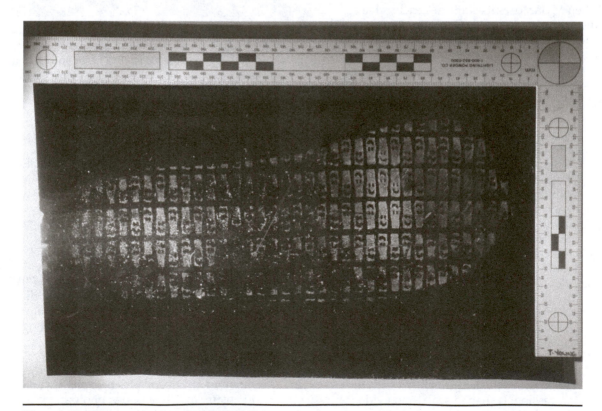

Photo 9-25. Photograph of an electrostatic lift.

Rubber-Gelatin Lifters

If an EDL is not available, one may use a **rubber-gelatin lifter** to collect prints in dust. The lifter is made of thick, low-adhesive gelatin designed to lift and collect finger- and foot-prints, marks, and other trace evidence in dust. Lifters are available in various sizes and colors. A black lifter is preferred for a foot or shoe print in dust, so the contrast in the print can be observed.

> **Rubber-gelatin lifter**
> A material made of thick, low-adhesive gelatin designed to lift and collect finger- and footprints, marks, and other trace evidence in dust.

The print is identified and located with ambient light off and oblique light on. If a print cannot be observed but the forensic technician suspects a print is present in the dust, use of a rubber-gelatin lifter is recommended.

1. Locate the foot or shoe print or identify the area where a suspected latent print may be located.
2. Place the lifter on its back adjacent to the print or suspect area. Remove the protective cover sheet from the lifter. The adhesive side of the lifter should be face up.
3. Carefully roll the adhesive side of the lifter over the print or suspect area. Start at one end of the print and place the lifter over the print by slowly rubbing the lifter with fingers or with a rubber roller until the lifter completely covers and adheres to the surface.
4. Slowly remove the rubber-gelatin lifter from the surface, starting at one end. The dusty foot or shoe print should adhere to the lifter.
5. The print on the lifter is photographed in the same manner as a Mylar lift, without the protective cover sheet in place. The print is photographed as soon as possible because prints in dust may deteriorate over time (Lightning Powder Co., Inc., 2000). The photography can be completed at the scene or in the laboratory.
6. After photographs are obtained, the lifter's cover sheet should be cleaned and replaced (returned to the lifter's adhesive surface) to protect the dust print.

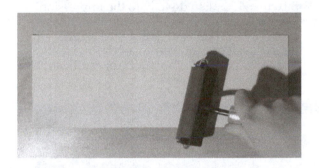

Photo 9-26. Demo of gel lifter.

Photo 9-28. Demo of gel lifter.

Photo 9-27. Demo of gel lifter.

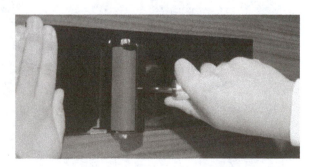

Photo 9-29. Demo of gel lifter.

Tool Mark Impressions

Tool mark impressions are often located at a scene of a forced entry (e.g., burglary). Tools used to open a door or window may leave marks or impressions. The impressions are often apparent at the point of entry, typically a door frame, or other surface adjacent to a door or window. The impression is photographed and cast for preservation. In addition to the tool's impression, fragments of the tool, chipped paint, wood, and other trace evidence should be collected.

Photography

Tool mark impressions are photographed according to the following procedure:

1. Photograph orientation views of the impression in relation to the scene.
2. Mount the camera on a tripod and use a level to ensure that the face of the camera lens (film plane) is parallel to the impression.
3. Place a scale near the tool mark. An adhesive-back scale works best because it adheres to the surface on which the impression is located.
4. Appropriate depth-of-field is critical because the impression is three-dimensional. Use F-22.
5. Use oblique angle lighting from a continuous light source (e.g., flashlight with a bright light, LED light, or white light). A flash unit should not be used because it may wash out the detail of the impression. While positioning the light at oblique angles, the photographer should peer through the camera's viewfinder until the detail of the impression is observed.
6. Fill the frame with the impression and the scale, and take the photograph. Move the light source to different positions in relation to the impression and repeat the photographic process.

Tool Mark Impression Casting

After photography, the tool mark impression can be cast with a **casting putty** material.

Casting putty
Used to lift magnetic power-developed fingerprints from textured surfaces.

Casting putty is available in a variety of colors, and it can be used to lift magnetic powder-developed fingerprints from textured surfaces.

Mikrosil® and *Forensic Sil*® casting putty are commonly used to cast tool marks. The putty is mixed and applied directly to the impression. The putty dries within a few minutes and is peeled away. The result is a rubbery three-dimensional cast impression of the tool mark. The cast is packaged in a plastic or cardboard box.

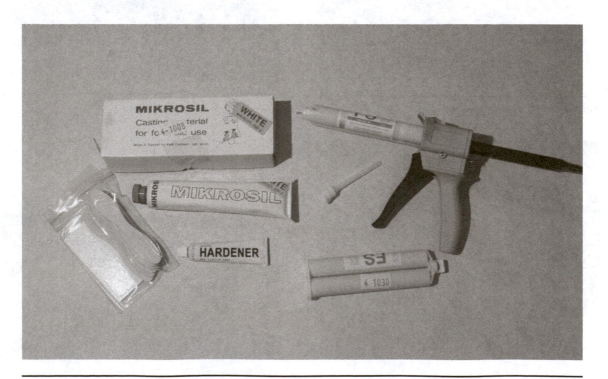

Photo 9-30. Mikrosil casting putty and Forensic Sil.

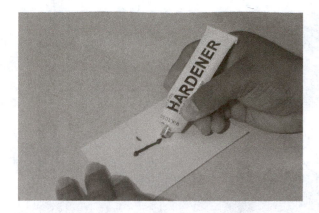

Photo 9-31. Mikrosil hardener placed on a card.

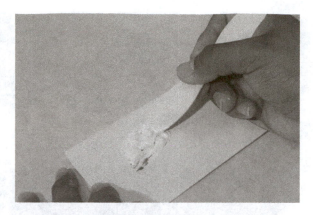

Photo 9-33. Putty and hardener mixed together.

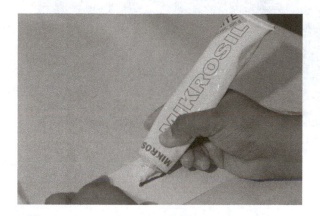

Photo 9-32. Mikrosil casting putty placed next to hardener.

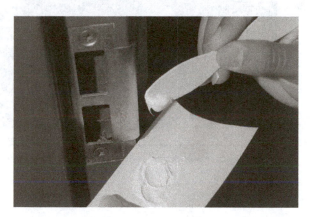

Photo 9-34. Mikrosil ready for application to tool mark.

DOCUMENTING A SUSPECT'S SHOE AND TIRE EVIDENCE

Shoe or tire impression evidence is valuable only if there is a known source for comparison. When shoe or tire impression evidence is collected at the crime scene, one must ensure that a suspect's shoes are collected and suspect vehicle tires are inspected. Photographs and impressions of a suspect's shoes or tires provide a basis for comparison with photos and castings collected at a crime scene.

Photographing Suspect Shoes

After a suspect in custody is photographed and processed, the suspect's shoes are collected and the shoe soles are photographed.

1. Photograph overall views of the sides and top of each shoe.

2. Use a clamp to secure the shoe with the sole level and facing up.
3. Place an L-shaped scale next to the shoe sole, framing the shoe's outer edge. The scale should be on the same plane as the shoe sole.
4. Mount the camera on a stand or inverted tripod directly above the shoe sole with the camera facing the sole. Ensure that the camera is level and the face of the camera's lens is parallel with the shoe sole.
5. Use good depth-of-field. F-22 is recommended.
6. Use oblique angle lighting from a continuous light source.
7. Fill the photo frame with the shoe sole and scale, and obtain the photograph.

The forensic technician examines the shoes for trace evidence relevant to the case. If broken glass was found at the scene, the forensic technician will search the exterior and interior

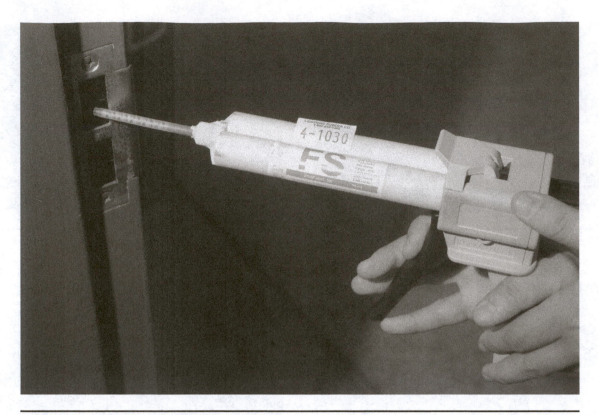

Photo 9-35. Forensic Sil ready to apply by pulling trigger.

of the shoe for broken glass. If bloody shoe prints were located at the crime scene, the forensic technician will search for patent and latent blood on the shoes. The forensic technician should swab the shoes for biological material if DNA analysis is a possibility. The forensic technician will also obtain casts of the shoes' soles after they are searched for trace evidence.

Casting a Suspect's Shoe Sole

A forensic technician must obtain a cast impression of the suspect's shoes if shoe sole cast impressions were obtained at the crime scene. The forensic technician should place the suspect's shoe sole in a foam material (e.g., Bio-foam®) designed to replicate three-dimensional shoe impressions. After placement of a shoe in the foam, the foam is allowed to harden. Subsequently, the shoe is removed, and a shoe casting material such as dental stone is mixed and poured directly into the foam cast. After the casting material hardens, the foam is brushed away, resulting in a three-dimensional casting of the shoe.

Suspect Shoe Sole Prints

A two-dimensional print of the suspect's shoe can be obtained and compared to photographs of shoe prints collected at the crime scene. One applies a thin coat of fingerprint ink to the entire shoe sole. The inked shoe sole is placed on clear plastic (transparency) sheeting. Alternatively, one can apply fingerprint ink to a sheet of thin cardboard, place the shoe sole on the inked surface, and then place the shoe sole on a clear plastic (transparency) sheet. The transparency sheeting onto which the inked shoe print is transferred is superimposed on and compared to photographs taken of the shoe print at the crime scene.

Photographing Suspect Tires

Similar to shoe prints or impressions, tire impressions photographed at the crime scene can be compared to suspect tires in police custody. The tires are photographed and inspected for trace evidence. Tires are manufactured with identifying letters and numbers issued by the U.S. Department of Transportation (DOT).

Photo 9-36. Photograph of a shoe sole. Photograph by Justin Smith.

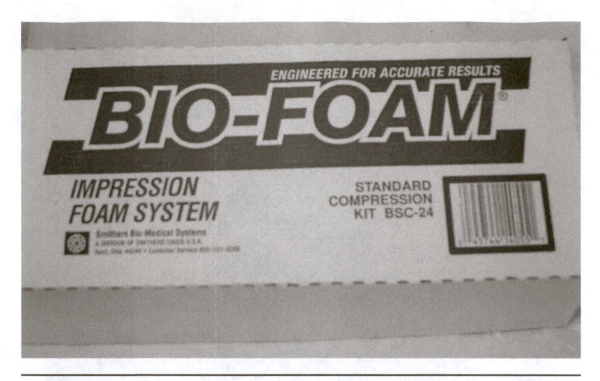

Photo 9-37. Bio-foam.

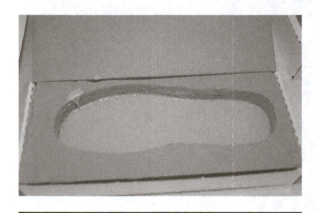

Photo 9-38. Bio-foam.

The letters and numbers identify the location and date of a tire's manufacture.

The identifying information is included in the forensic technician's report. Measurements of the tire tread widths and the distance between the tires should be taken and compared to similar measurements obtained at the crime scene. The following procedure applies to photography of vehicle tires:

1. To photograph a vehicle's rear tire tread, the tire should be removed from the vehicle.

Tires on the front of a vehicle can be turned to the extreme left or right to expose the tire tread.

2. A card containing case information, tire position (e.g., *right front, left front*), the tire identifier (serial number), and the photographer's name is placed near and photographed with the tire tread.

3. A measurement scale is held near the tire on the same plane as the tire's tread.

4. A camera is held directly over the tire, scale, and case information card, with the face of the camera lens (film plane) parallel with the tire tread.

5. Use F-22 depth-of-field and a continuous light source held at an oblique angle.

6. Because the tire is round, the forensic technician can accurately photograph only a few inches of the tire tread at a time. Markings are placed on the tire indicating the area photographed. The tire is rotated to expose and photograph additional sections of tread. The process is repeated until the entire length of the tire tread is photographed. If the tire was removed for photography, it is returned to the relevant vehicle hub after photography is complete.

Photo 9-39. Photographs of shoe impression casts obtained from soil and Bio-foam.

Printing Suspect Tires

The procedure for obtaining tire prints is similar to obtaining shoe sole prints:

1. The tire is inspected for trace evidence.
2. Approximately eight feet of clean white cardboard (or art board) is laid flat and coated with fingerprint ink.
3. Eight feet of clear plastic sheeting is placed on a white paper backing.
4. The eight-foot length of plastic on white backing is placed end-to-end with the inked cardboard.
5. The tire is driven or rolled over the inked cardboard and the clear plastic sheeting, creating an inked print of the entire tire tread on the plastic.

Tire tread prints can be produced with black fingerprint powder instead of fingerprint ink.

Aerosol cooking spray is applied to the tire tread, followed by black fingerprint powder. Subsequently, the tire is rolled over clear plastic, transferring the fingerprint powder to the plastic. The plastic sheeting with the tire tread print is placed over and compared to tire tread photographs taken at the crime scene (Nause & Souliere, 2008).

FOOTWEAR AND TIRE PRINT AND IMPRESSION ANALYSIS

Footwear Print and Impression Analysis

By design, shoes and other footwear share *class characteristics* (characteristics common to more than one) such as size, shape, style, and pattern design. *Individual characteristics* unique to a shoe include cuts, scratches, impeded debris, tears, shoe-repair material, holes, and air pockets formed during the manufacturing process.

Additionally, a shoe can be unique because of individual *wear characteristics*, areas of a shoe that are worn or damaged due to use of the shoe. Two important considerations when inspecting a shoe for wear characteristics are the position and degree (extent) of the wear. Factors that affect wear include individual human foot type and function (stride, occupation, habits, body weight and type). Wear characteristics also depend on the shoe sole material and the surfaces walked upon. All class, individual, and wear characteristics are analyzed by a forensic footwear examiner (Bodziak, 2000).

Tire Print and Impression Analysis

An *original equipment (OE)* tire is placed on a vehicle at the time of vehicle manufacture. Thousands of tires of the same size and brand are placed on vehicles of the same make and model. These tires possess the same class characteristics, including make and model, tread design, dimension (size), and noise treatment (tread designed to reduce the noise produced by tires in motion) (Bodziak, 2005).

A replacement tire is substituted for a worn or damaged OE tire. As tire tread wears through use, individual characteristics become apparent. The individual tire characteristics include thinning of the tire tread as well as damage caused by scratches, cuts, tearing, abrasions, and embedded debris.

Known and Questioned Shoe and Tire Evidence

When submitting questioned shoe or tire print or impressions obtained from a crime scene for comparison to known prints or impressions obtained from a suspect or suspect's vehicle, the forensic technician must ensure that the print and impression expert receives all evidence pertaining to the questioned and known items, including all photographs, casts, and inked prints. The forensic technician must not attempt to determine which items are the best evidence for analysis. Rather, all evidence is submitted for the expert's review. Additionally, the forensic technician should not formulate opinions or conclusions based on the evidence. The analysis is conducted and conclusions are developed by a print and impression evidence expert.

Photo 9-40. Photo of suspect tire. Courtesy of National City, California, Police Department.

Photo 9-41. Partial tire impression at crime scene. Courtesy of National City, California, Police Department.

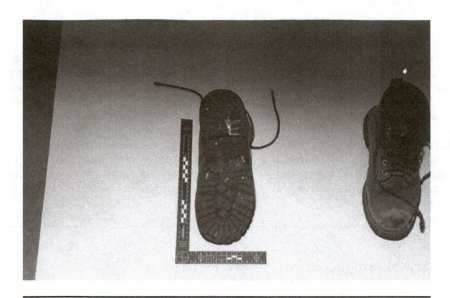

Photo 9-42. Overall view of suspect boot sole. Courtesy of National City, California, Police Department.

Photo 9-43. Partial boot impression at crime scene. Courtesy of National City, California, Police Department.

SUMMARY

Shoe, tire, and tool mark prints and impressions are valuable evidence. Random, individual characteristics of prints and impressions obtained from a crime scene can be linked to known prints and impressions obtained from a suspect or a suspect's possessions.

Print and impression evidence at a crime scene must be located, protected, documented, and collected carefully because it is fragile and easily destroyed. Questioned prints and impressions are photographed, documented, and preserved for comparison purposes.

The forensic technician is often the individual who photographs and collects both the questioned and the known print and impression evidence. Footwear, tire, or tool mark prints and impressions are compared and analyzed by an expert who determines the linkage, if any, between the questioned and known prints or impressions.

KEY TERMS

Define, describe, or explain the importance of each of the following:

casting putty
electrostatic lift
rubber-gelatin lifters

DISCUSSION AND REVIEW QUESTIONS

1. In addition to linking a suspect to a crime scene, what additional information may shoe or tire print or impression evidence provide?
2. What activities and conditions lead to the destruction of shoe and tire prints and impressions at crime scenes?
3. What precautionary measures are implemented to protect print and impression evidence at a crime scene?
4. List and describe the steps to photographing a three-dimensional shoe or tire impression.
5. Why should a forensic technician cast a shoe or tire impression at the crime scene?
6. List and describe the steps to preserving bloody shoe prints.
7. List four blood-enhancing chemicals and the color reaction of each.
8. What procedure is followed when searching for shoe prints in dust at a crime scene?
9. What is an electrostatic lift and how is it used?
10. How should a tool mark located at a crime scene be photographed and preserved?
11. How should a suspect's shoe be photographed?

CASE STUDY—Impression and Print Evidence

Dorka Lisker, age 66, was beaten and stabbed to death in her Sherman Oaks, California, home on March 10, 1983. Police and paramedics were summoned to Dorka's home by her 17-year-old adopted son, Bruce, who stated that he returned home to find his mother near death.

Authorities found Dorka lying near the front entry of her home. She had a crushed skull, a broken right arm, stab wounds in her back, and a contusion in the shape of a shoe impression behind her right ear. Police also located bloody shoe prints in and around the Lisker home.

Bruce was under the influence of meth, and his hands were covered with blood.

Bruce, who had a history of drug abuse and conflict with his mother, became the prime suspect. Although some evidence suggested the possibility of a former friend as an alternate suspect, Bruce was charged with his mother's death. At one point, Bruce confessed in a plea bargain for a reduced sentence. He later recanted his confession but was ultimately convicted and sentenced to prison in 1985. At Bruce's trial, a Los Angeles Police Department (LAPD) detective testified that key evidence in the form of bloody shoe prints closely resembled Bruce's sports shoe.

Nearly two decades later, Bruce Lisker is seeking a new trial, still maintaining his innocence. Footwear impression expert analysis from the FBI and LAPD crime labs bolster Bruce's case. Experts from both labs confirmed that the shoe impression on Dorka's head and the bloody shoe prints at the scene were not made by Bruce Lisker's shoes. The shoe impression and prints were not examined by a forensic footwear expert during the original investigation.

1. To the untrained eye, is it possible for a shoe impression to closely resemble a shoe sole pattern when the impression was in fact created by a different shoe?
2. Why is it important for qualified, trained experts to analyze shoe impression evidence?
3. Why are independent verifications of forensic evidence analyses important?

LAB EXERCISES

Print and Impression Evidence

Equipment and supplies required per each pair of students:

- one digital or film camera (with film)
- one camera tripod
- one camera shutter release cable
- one camera level
- one L-shaped ruler (measuring device)
- one camera flash unit
- one 3' × 3' black cardboard or black fabric
- one measuring compass
- one electrostatic lift (e.g., Pathfinder)
- one 6″ × 12″ sheet of Mylar
- one fingerprint roller
- one black rubber-gelatin lifter
- one flashlight with a bright bulb (or LED light)
- one standard size (14″ × 6″ × 2¼″) box of Bio-foam
- two packages of casting material (e.g., dental stone)
- two 8-ounce cups of water
- two shallow cardboard boxes
- one 2-ounce bottle of liquid hairspray
- one casting putty (e.g., Mikrosil or Forensic Sil kit)
- one 2' × 4' × 6' block of wood
- one Philips-head screwdriver

Exercise #1—Shoe Impression Photography

1. Students form pairs. Each pair creates a shoe impression in soil.
2. Students photograph the shoe impression.
3. One student will shade the impression while the second student photographs it. After appropriate photographs are obtained, the students switch roles and repeat the exercise.

Exercise #2—Collecting Shoe Prints in Dust

1. Students work in pairs.
2. One student will place a shoe sole on a dusty desk or other smooth, dusty flat surface in a room.
3. The students will darken the room and view the impression using oblique angle lighting.
4. The students will use an electrostatic lift, Mylar, and a fingerprint roller to collect the shoe print in dust.
5. The students will create a second shoe print in dust on a smooth surface and collect the print using a rubber-gelatin lifter.

Exercise #3—Casting Three-Dimensional Shoe Impressions

Each pair of students will create a three-dimensional cast of a shoe impression in soil.

1. Create a shoe impression in soil.
2. Spray liquid hairspray directly above the impression.
3. Mix the casting powder (e.g., dental stone) with water.
4. Pour the casting material next to the impression, allowing the casting material to flow into the impression.
5. While the cast dries, the students will use the same shoe to create an impression in Bio-foam.
6. Mix a second batch of casting powder. Pour the casting material into the Bio-foam impression (mold) of the shoe.
7. After both castings harden, collect the castings from the soil and the Bio-foam impression. Place the castings in separate shallow boxes. The castings are allowed to dry for 48 hours, after which the impressions are cleaned of foreign material and Bio-foam.

8. The students compare the shoe sole castings made from the impression in the soil (questioned impression) with the casting made with Bio-foam (known impression).

Exercise #4—Three-Dimensional Tool Mark Impressions
1. Using a Philips-head screwdriver, the student pairs will create a three-dimensional tool mark impression in a block of wood.

2. Mix casting putty and hardener (e.g., Mikrosil or Forensic Sil).
3. Apply putty to the tool impression.
4. After the cast hardens, peel the casting putty away, revealing the cast of the tool mark impression.

WEB RESOURCES

American Board of Criminalistics: www.criminalistics.com

California Association of Criminalists: www.cacnews.org

Midwestern Association of Forensic Scientists: www.mafs.net

Northeastern Association of Forensic Scientists: www.neafs.org

Northwest Association of Forensic Scientists: www.nwafs.org

Southern Association of Forensic Scientists: www.southernforensic.org

Southwestern Association of Forensic Scientists: www.swafs.us

10

Firearm Evidence

LEARNING OUTCOMES

After completing this chapter, the reader should be able to:

- explain the importance of criminal investigation,
- describe procedures for the safe handling of firearms discovered at crime scenes,
- use rods to determine bullet trajectory,
- determine bullet trajectory using a laser beam,
- photograph a laser beam using photographic fog or a white board,
- document and collect cartridges from a revolver or a semiautomatic pistol,
- describe the information that can be obtained from an examination of an expended firearm cartridge casing or projectile,
- articulate how bullet holes and cracks in glass are analyzed to determine the sequence of shots fired.

INTRODUCTION

Firearms can be used to commit a multitude of crimes, including robbery, assault, and murder. The forensic value of firearm and ballistics evidence is associated with the ability to link the firearm to the crime and the shooter. Firearm marks and striations on expended cartridge casings and projectiles discovered and collected at a crime scene are compared to known, test-fired bullets. By checking national databases, a firearm may be linked to several crimes. DNA and fingerprint evidence obtained from a firearm may also be linked to the shooter.

Crime scene reconstruction (the re-creation of the sequence of events at a crime scene) may be determined through **ballistics** (scientific study of the dynamics of projectiles) and bullet trajectory (the path of a bullet). The shooter's location and the sequence of shots fired may also be determined through bullet trajectory analysis.

> **Ballistics** The scientific study of the dynamics of projectiles and bullet trajectory (the path of a bullet).

Analysis and comparison of firearms evidence depends on the type of firearm used. An expert firearms examiner possesses in-depth knowledge of firearms and ammunition as well as the forensic evidence that can be obtained from both. A forensic technician must document a firearms-related crime scene, and safely and correctly collect firearm evidence for comparison by a firearms expert.

FIREARM EVIDENCE COLLECTION AT CRIME SCENES

Handguns (e.g., semiautomatic pistols and revolvers) are the firearms most commonly used to commit crimes. Shoulder-operated firearms such as shotguns or rifles (also referred to as long guns) are used by perpetrators less frequently. Occasionally, fully automatic and other types of firearms are used. If unfamiliar with the type of firearm discovered at a crime scene, the forensic technician should seek assistance from a firearms expert. Many firearms used by criminals are inexpensive and poorly constructed, posing a risk to the handlers.

Semiautomatic Pistols

A **semiautomatic pistol** fires a bullet and automatically reloads a cartridge (ammunition) each time the *trigger* is pulled. It contains a *magazine* that holds and advances the cartridges. By pulling back on the slide of the pistol, a cartridge from the top of the magazine is chambered. Simultaneously, the firing mechanism is cocked and ready to fire (Rowe, 2005). When the shooter pulls the trigger, the *firing pin* strikes the primer on the base of the cartridge, igniting the gunpowder, which causes the bullet to be sent through the barrel.

Due to **rifling** (grooves bored into the barrel during manufacturing), the bullet spins, enhancing accuracy of the bullet's trajectory. The portions of the rifling cut into the barrel are known as **grooves**. The portions of the barrel not cut away are called **lands**. Microscopic marks are created by the rifling on the bullet as it spins through the barrel. While the bullet travels through the rifled barrel of a semiautomatic firearm, the *expended cartridge casing* is simultaneously pushed against the *breechblock*, stripped away by the *extractor*, and ejected from the pistol by the *ejector* (Saferstein, 2007). An unfired cartridge from the magazine is automatically loaded into the firing chamber, and the firing mechanism is rearmed. The firing and reloading cycle occurs within fractions of a second.

> **Semiautomatic pistol** Fires a bullet and automatically reloads a cartridge (ammunition) each time the trigger is pulled.

> **Rifling** Lands and grooves bored into the barrel during manufacturing which cause the bullet to spin, enhancing accuracy of the bullet.

> **Groove** The portion of the rifling cut into the barrel.

> **Land** The portion of the interior of a firearm's barrel not cut away when manufactured.

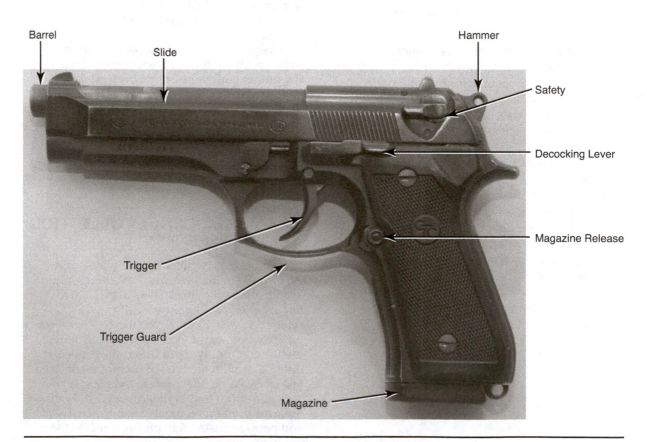

Figure 10-1. Nomenclature of semi-auto handgun.

Photo 10-1. Beretta .40 cal.

Photo 10-3. Beretta .22 cal.

Photo 10-2. Beretta 9 mm.

Photo 10-4. Glock .40 cal with magazine, ammunition, and laser.

Semiautomatic Pistol Collection

If any firearm, especially a semiautomatic pistol, is discovered at a crime scene, it should be rendered safe immediately. Safety is the first priority. If possible, assign an evidence number to the firearm, photograph orientation and close-up views, and take measurements of the firearm's location prior to collecting it. To render a semiautomatic pistol safe, the forensic technician should wear latex or vinyl gloves and unload the semiautomatic pistol as follows:

1. Grasp the pistol at the grip, pointing the pistol downward and away from people.
2. Avoid contact with smooth surfaces that may contain latent fingerprints.

3. Press the magazine release button to dislodge the magazine. Place the magazine inside a paper bag or firearms box.
4. Pull the pistol's slide back and eject any cartridge present in the chamber. Place the ejected cartridge in a coin envelope or pill-box for preservation. Steps 3 and 4 must not be reversed. If the slide is pulled back prior to removal of the magazine, a new cartridge will be chambered, and the pistol will be loaded with a live cartridge.
5. Pull the pistol's slide back until it locks into place, ensuring that no cartridges remain in the pistol. Place a plastic zip-tie or similar device through the slide opening. Place the firearm in a box or paper bag.
6. Mark the magazine, cartridge, and firearm containers for identification.

Revolvers

Revolvers are handguns with rotating cartridge cylinders. A **single-action revolver** operates by pulling the handgun's hammer back (cocking) and by pulling the trigger to release the hammer. The hammer activates a firing pin that contacts the primer on the cartridge. A **double-action revolver** can be operated in a single-action mode or by pulling the trigger. The double-action mode requires a longer and often heavier trigger pull than single-action (Rowe, 2005). The cylinder rotates as the hammer is pulled back or the trigger is pulled, moving the next cartridge into position to ready it for firing. Typical revolver cylinders contain five to nine cartridges, depending on the revolver's manufacturer and model. The expended cartridge cases, however, are not automatically ejected from a revolver.

Like semiautomatic pistols, the barrels of revolvers are rifled. Lands, grooves, and striation markings are cut into the expended projectile in the same manner as semiautomatic pistols. **Striations** are fine scratches inside a firearm's rifled barrel that are produced by imperfections created during the manufacturing process.

> **Single-action revolver** Operates by pulling the handgun's hammer back (cocking) and pulling the trigger to release the hammer. The hammer activates a firing pin that contacts the primer on the cartridge.

> **Double-action revolver** Can be operated in a single-action mode or by pulling the trigger. The double-action mode requires a longer and often heavier trigger pull than single action.

> **Striations** Fine scratches inside a firearm's rifled barrel that are produced by imperfections created during the manufacturing process.

Photo 10-5. Revolver and ammunition. Courtesy of National City, California, Police Department.

Revolver Collection

A revolver discovered at a crime scene should be rendered safe immediately. Assign an evidence number to the revolver, photograph orientation and close-up views, and take measurements of the firearm's location prior to collection. To render a revolver safe, the forensic technician should wear latex or vinyl gloves and unload the revolver. As discussed earlier, if the revolver is unfamiliar, the forensic technician should seek the assistance of a firearms expert.

1. Grasp the revolver at the grip, pointing the handgun downward and away from people.
2. Hold the revolver by the handgrip and avoid contact with smooth surfaces that may contain latent fingerprints.
3. Using a permanent black marking pen with a fine tip, place a small line on the cylinder on either side of the revolver's top strap. This will ensure that the forensic technician can return the cylinder to its original position after opening.
4. Press the cylinder release button and carefully open the cylinder. (Cylinder release mechanism may vary depending on manufacture of revolver.)

Photo 10-6. Revolver.

Photo 10-7. Revolver with open cylinder.

5. Press the cartridge release ejector and carefully remove each cartridge, expended or not, in a clockwise manner. The cartridges are removed in sequential order. The cartridge in line with the barrel is labeled cartridge #1. The cartridge immediately clockwise is labeled #2, and so on. Draw a diagram of the cylinder, with the appropriate number of cartridge holes in the field notes. Label each hole with the corresponding cartridge number. The cartridges are packaged separately in coin envelopes or pillboxes and the packaging of each is marked for identification.

6. Place a plastic zip-tie or similar device through the revolver frame (under the top strap) to render the revolver safe. Place the firearm in a box or paper bag and mark for identification.

Shoulder Firearms

Shoulder firearms include a vast array of single-action, pump, semiautomatic, and fully automatic rifles and shotguns. Semiautomatic rifles

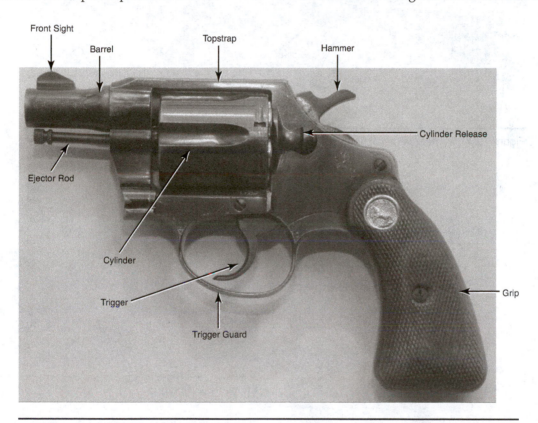

Figure 10-2. Nomenclature of revolver.

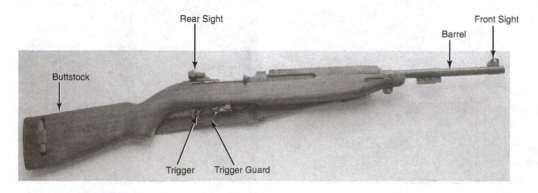

Figure 10-3. Nomenclature of rifle.

and shotguns automatically eject expended cartridges from the firearm.

Although rifle ammunition cartridges vary in size and caliber, the tool mark and barrel rifling evidence provided by spent rifle cartridge casings and bullets are similar to handguns.

Unlike a rifled-barrel handgun or shoulder firearm, the interior surface of a shotgun's barrel is smooth and does not impress typical tool markings (lands, groves, striations) onto expended projectiles. Shotgun ammunition (shot shell) is also quite different. It consists

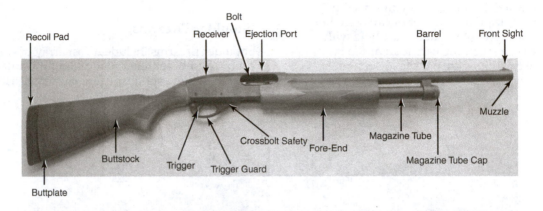

Figure 10-4. Nomenclature of shotgun.

Photo 10-8. Rifle.

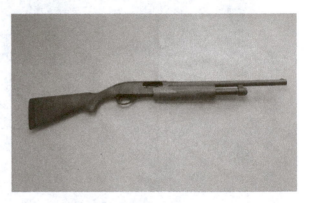

Photo 10-9. Shotgun.

Photo 10-10. Shotgun ammunition.

of projectiles of small lead balls, pellets or metal slugs, gunpowder, and paper or plastic wadding encased in paper or plastic cover and metal base. Although rifling impressions are not present on the projectiles fired, a firing pin impression can be located on the base of the expended shotgun shot shell casing.

Shoulder Firearm Collection

As with any firearm, a shoulder firearm (long gun) located within the crime scene should be rendered safe immediately. Rendering the firearm safe depends on its mechanism. If a forensic technician is uncomfortable or unfamiliar with unloading a firearm, a firearms

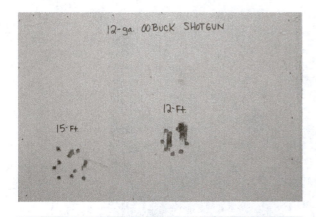

Photo 10-11. Target shot with 12-gauge shotgun at distances of 12 and 15 feet.

Photo 10-12. Spread of shotgun pellets at shooting crime scene. Courtesy of National City, California, Police Department.

Photo 10-13. Firearms collected from a police/SWAT (special weapons and tactics) shootout with robbery suspect. Courtesy of National City, California, Police Department.

expert, firearms range master, or knowledgeable officer or investigator on scene can render the firearm safe. It is recommended that all forensic technicians complete a firearms safety course and obtain any available firearms safety protocol training from the agency's firearms expert or range master.

Assign an evidence number, photograph orientation and close-up views of the long gun in place, and take measurements of the firearm's location prior to collection. The forensic technician should hold the firearm by the grip or stock and avoid contact with smooth surfaces that may yield latent fingerprints. Point the firearm downward and away from people.

When collecting any firearm, objects should not be placed inside the barrel. The object may scratch the barrel or contaminate trace or DNA evidence located within the barrel.

Photo 10-14. Firearms collected from a police/SWAT (special weapons and tactics) shootout with robbery suspect. Courtesy of National City, California, Police Department.

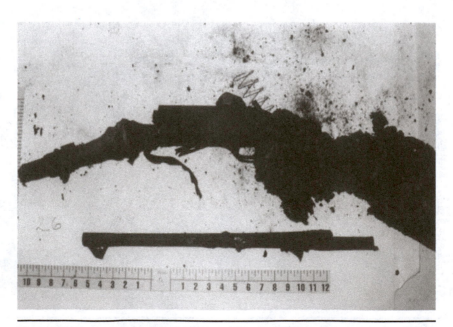

Photo 10-15. Firearms collected from a police/SWAT (special weapons and tactics) shootout with robbery suspect. Courtesy of National City, California, Police Department.

Photo 10-16. Firearms collected from a police/SWAT (special weapons and tactics) shootout with robbery suspect. Courtesy of National City, California, Police Department.

Collecting Expended Projectiles and Cartridge Casings

Each expended cartridge casing, projectile, and remnants of shotgun ammunition located at a crime scene should be assigned a separate evidence item number, photographed, and measured for placement in the crime scene diagram. Subsequently each item is collected and packaged in a small pillbox or coin envelope. The individual evidence containers are placed into larger envelopes or bags, depending on the agency's protocol. An imbedded projectile should not be pried from a wall or similar surface because striation marks on the projectile may be damaged. Instead, the portion of the wall or surface containing the projectile should be removed and transported to the laboratory.

FIREARM EVIDENCE ANALYSIS AND PROCESSING

To link a firearm cartridge casing or projectile from a crime scene to a suspect firearm, the same type of ammunition is test-fired from the suspect firearm into a water or gelatin tank. Using a comparison microscope, the tool marks (striations) on the expended projectile and cartridge casing are compared. A firearms expert compares the questioned (crime scene) cartridge casing or projectile evidence to the known (test-fired) cartridge casing or projectile

evidence. If the suspect firearm is not located, firearm class characteristics and databases may provide clues to the type of firearm used.

Analysis of Expended Projectiles

Expended projectiles provide valuable evidence even if the suspect firearm is not located. Class characteristics provide information regarding the make and model of the firearm used to fire the projectile. Class characteristics include:

- weight of the projectile,
- direction of twist of the rifling,
- degree of twist of the rifling,
- number of lands and grooves,
- width of lands and grooves.

In addition to class characteristics, trace evidence such as fibers, paint, patterned markings from clothing, and chips of concrete, brick, wood, window screens, or other surfaces may be located on the expended projectile. Rifling marks imprinted on the bullet (expended projectile) include the lands and grooves as well as striations. As discussed earlier, striations on the projectile are caused by imperfections in the steel created during the barrel manufacturing process. Striations are often located along the length of the lands and grooves. They are unique and impossible to duplicate between or among firearm barrels (Saferstein, 2007).

**FIREARM TEST-FIRE
WORKSHEET**

CASE #: _____ ANALYST: _____ DATE: _____

ITEM #: _____ TYPE OF FIREARM: _____

MAKE: _____ MODEL: _____ CALIBER: _____

SERIAL # _____ LOCATION: _____

HAMMER: COCKED ☐   UNCOCKED ☐

SAFETY: ON ☐   OFF ☐

TYPE OF FINISH: _____ CONDITION: _____
STOCK/GRIPS:_____
OVERALL LENGTH: _____ BARREL LENGTH: _____
BORE: # LANDS: _____ TWIST: _____ CONDITION: _____
CYLINDER CAPACITY: _____ CYLINDER ROTATION: _____

CYLINDER CONTENT:

1.	2.	3.
4.	5.	6.
7.	8.	9.

MAGAZINE CAPACITY: _____

MAGAZINE CONTENT:

CHAMBER	6.	12.
1.	7.	13.
2.	8.	14.
3.	9.	15.
4.	10.	16.
5.	11.	17.

TRACE EVIDENCE: _____ BARREL SWAB: YES ☐   NO ☐

TEST FIRE: # / TYPE OF CARTRIDGES USED: _____

OPERABILITY: OPERABLE ☐   INOPERABLE ☐

ACTION: SINGLE ☐   DOUBLE ☐

TRIGGER PULL: SINGLE _____ LB   DOUBLE _____ LB

OPERATING CONDITION: _____ EJECTION PATTERN: _____

NOTES:

_____

_____

Figure 10-5. Sample firearm test-fire worksheet.

Photo 10-17. Crime lab personnel test-firing a pistol. Photograph by Chris Nellis.

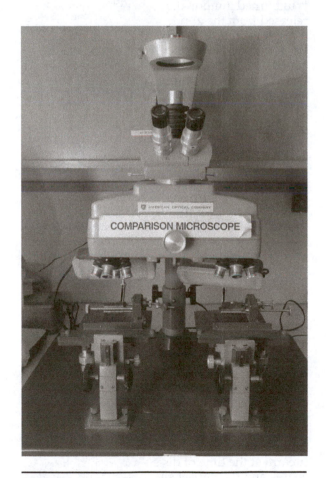

Photo 10-18. Comparison microscope.

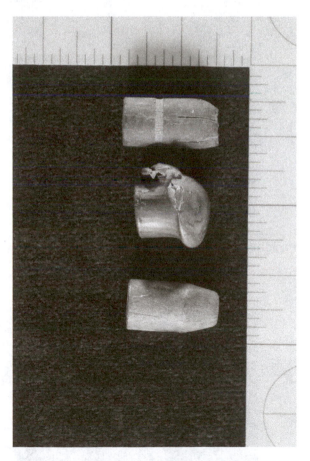

Photo 10-19. Expended projectiles.

Analysis of Expended Cartridge Casings

Class characteristic information obtained from the expended cartridge casings include:

- *headstamp* information (manufacturer, make, and caliber stamped on the base of the cartridge case),
- size and shape of the firing pin,
- location of the firing pin,
- size and geometric relationship of an extractor or ejector.

A firearms examiner will use a stereo binocular microscope to view details of the markings on the expended cartridge casing as well as a comparison microscope to compare the markings of the known to the questioned cartridge casing evidence.

Automated Firearms Databases

In the early 1990s, the FBI and the Bureau of Alcohol, Tobacco, Firearms and Explosives (ATF)

Photo 10-20. Headstamp of cartridge casing.

Photo 10-21. Headstamp of cartridge casing.

created databases that contain information relative to expended projectiles and cartridge casing marks. The FBI created *DRUGFIRE,* a database that focuses on markings from cartridge casings. ATF created the *Integrated Ballistic Identification System (IBIS),* a database that contains markings from expended cartridge casings as well as projectiles. The markings are entered into the databases through the use of a microscope and digital imaging.

In 1999, the FBI and ATF merged the databases to create the *National Integrated Ballistics Information Network (NIBIN),* used to assist federal, state, and local crime laboratories with comparison of expended projectiles and cartridge casings. Using NIBIN, a single firearm may be linked to multiple crimes (Saferstein, 2007).

Gunshot Residue

Gunshot residue (GSR) is unburned gunpowder released from the gun when it is fired. GSR may be located on the shooter's hands, the victim's clothing, or surrounding surfaces. Elements of GSR include lead, barium, and antimony. The elements can be viewed under magnification with a scanning electron microscope. The presence of these elements indicates that a firearm was discharged nearby. Collecting GSR from a suspect's hands supports the contention that the suspect discharged a firearm recently. Details for the steps to collecting GSR from a suspect are discussed in Chapter 13.

> **Gunshot residue (GSR)** Unburned gunpowder released from a firearm when it is discharged. GSR may be located on the shooter's hands, the victim's clothing, or surrounding surfaces.

The evidentiary value of GSR may be limited in court if a defendant can establish a legitimate reason (e.g., recent hunting or target practice) for the presence of GSR. Yet its presence as well as the amount and pattern of the residue deposited on a surface can provide clues to the proximity of a firearm to a shooting victim. A comparison of the GSR concentration and the pattern aids a firearms examiner in determining distance. **Distance determination** involves a calculation of the approximate distance between the firearm at the time of discharge and the impact site of the projectile and GSR. This evidence is critical to

> **Distance determination** A calculation of the approximate distance between the firearm at the time of discharge and the impact site of the projectile and GSR. This evidence is critical to determining *near* versus *far* discharge (e.g., suicide versus homicide).

determining a *near* versus *far* discharge (e.g., suicide versus homicide). By evaluating the concentration and pattern of GSR located on a victim's clothing, a firearms examiner can determine the approximate distance the gun was from the victim at the time it was fired, thus determining if the victim could have fired the gun.

The concentration of GSR depends on the distance as well as the caliber and type of firearm. Therefore, the only means through which a firearms examiner can determine distance is to test-fire the suspect weapon into the same type of material, fabric, or surface under examination. The original surface (wall, fabric, skin) is never fired upon. Rather, similar material and ammunition is used during the test fire. After the GSR concentration and pattern is replicated, the firearms examiner can determine the approximate distance between the firearm and projectile impact area at time of discharge.

GSR on clothing may not be visible to the unaided human eye. The fabric's color, contrast, or blood covering can disguise GSR. Infrared light is used to highlight the elements of GSR. Nitrates in the GSR may also be located and tested positive with the *Griess Test,* a chemical analysis technique used by firearms examiners to develop a GSR pattern (Saferstein, 2007).

When clothing or fabric suspected of containing GSR is collected, the item is photographed in detail, with a scale present in orientation and close-up photos. The clothing is packaged in layers, with each clothing layer and fold separated with craft or butcher paper. Clothing should not be folded onto itself because the GSR may transfer to other parts of the material.

Processing Firearms

When processing a firearm, a forensic technician should first confirm that the firearm is safe to handle. One should never assume a firearm is not loaded. Next, a visual inspection is conducted. The forensic technician will search for trace evidence such as hairs, blood (especially in close-range shootings), and visible fingerprints. A bright white light and magnifier may be used to assist in the search. An alternate light source may be used as well. Trace evidence is photographed, collected, and packaged. Visible fingerprints are photographed. If the grip of the firearm is textured, obtaining comparable fingerprints from the grip is unlikely. However, the textured grip may be a good source of DNA material. Therefore, the forensic technician should use a sterile swab containing a drop of distilled water to collect biological material from a firearm's grip. The swab is packaged appropriately.

Finally, the forensic technician will process the firearm for latent fingerprints. The forensic technician should follow the standard protocol established by the agency's crime laboratory. Some fingerprint development techniques, such as dye staining, may rust the metal portions of the firearm. A less caustic technique is preferred. The forensic technician should also process the magazine (if any) and any unused cartridges.

Serial Number Restoration

In an attempt to conceal a firearm's unique registry, some criminals purposely destroy the visible serial numbers stamped onto firearms by the manufacturer. Although the serial number may be destroyed at the surface level, the number is actually imbedded in metal crystals a short distance beneath the original serial number stamp. A metal etching agent that dissolves the damaged area may reveal the serial number. However, if the serial number area is destroyed beyond its lowest depth or if a new number is stamped over the original, recovery is not possible (Saferstein, 2007).

TRAJECTORY AND BALLISTICS ANALYSIS

Trajectory refers to a bullet's path from the moment of discharge from a firearm until it comes to rest (Ogle, 2007). Analyzing trajectory at a crime scene may help determine the dynamics and events surrounding a shooting. The following information may be obtained from trajectory analysis:

> **Trajectory** A bullet's path from the moment of discharge from a firearm until it comes to rest.

- path of the bullet (projectile),
- location of the shooter,
- sequence of shots fired,
- which bullet holes or impressions are entry, exit, or ricochet.

The forensic technician should photograph and measure bullet holes and trajectory approximations at a shooting crime scene. Although trajectory approximations can be determined, reconstruction of the scene and conclusions regarding the dynamics of events are left to the firearms expert. A firearms expert may be summoned to the crime scene in cases involving extensive trajectory analysis or officer-involved shootings.

Bullet Entry and Exit Points

In most cases, bullet entry and exit points on surfaces are easily differentiated by their appearance. Bullet entry points are usually smoother and smaller than exit points. The bullet entry point is often indented while the exit point typically displays surface material protruding out and away from the exit. A bullet soot and dirt smudge ring is sometimes observed at the bullet entry point. If the bullet entered the surface at an oblique (less than 90 degree) angle, the hole may be oval in shape. In these cases, the leading edge of the hole will often appear smoother.

In addition to an evaluation of a bullet hole's appearance, a forensic technician can conduct a

Photo 10-24. Bullet entry holes.

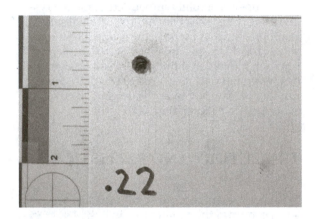

Photo 10-22. Bullet entry holes.

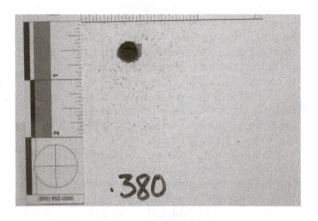

Photo 10-25. Bullet entry holes.

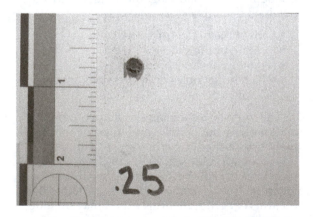

Photo 10-23. Bullet entry holes.

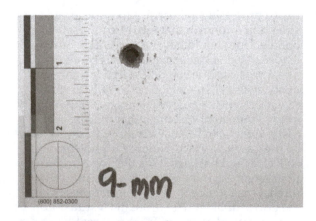

Photo 10-26. Bullet entry holes.

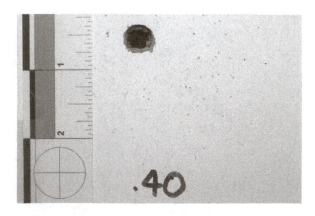

Photo 10-27. Bullet entry holes.

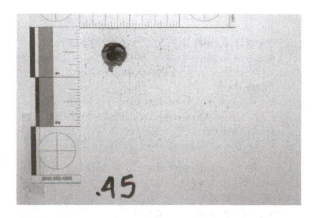

Photo 10-28. Bullet entry holes.

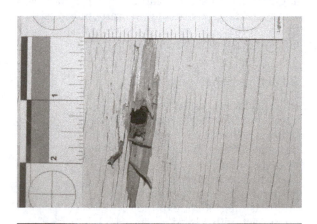

Photo 10-29. Bullet exit hole.

chemical test to verify the presence of copper or lead from a bullet. Two commercially available tests can be used: the Plumbtesmo test for lead and the Cuperotesmo test for copper. Each utilizes pretreated filter papers that are moistened with distilled water and pressed against the suspect bullet hole. Each test reacts with a reddish violet color as a positive indicator of the presence of copper or lead (Gardner, 2005).

Bullet Holes in Glass

The cracks surrounding bullet holes in a pane of glass may be analyzed to determine sequencing of slots (which occurred first, second, and so on). **Radial cracks** radiate out and away from a bullet hole as jagged, sharp lines. **Concentric cracks** appear in a circular shape around a bullet hole. Sequencing of impacts can be determined by viewing the radial cracks. A radial crack will terminate on its own (when the inertia terminates) or when it collides with another crack.

A forensic technician or trace evidence expert can also determine which side of the glass a bullet impacted first by viewing the edge of the damaged area's radial cracks. The fractured

> **Radial cracks** The cracks surrounding bullet holes in a pane of glass which radiate out and away from a bullet hole as jagged, sharp lines.

> **Concentric cracks** The cracks surrounding bullet holes in a pane of glass that appear in a circular shape around a bullet hole.

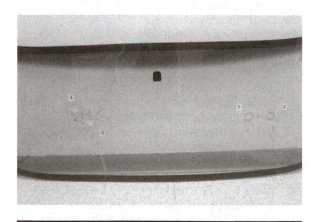

Photo 10-30. Bullet holes in glass numbered by sequential shots. Determining sequential shots fired in vehicular windshield glass is difficult because of the multiple layers of glass.

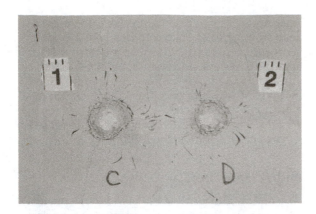

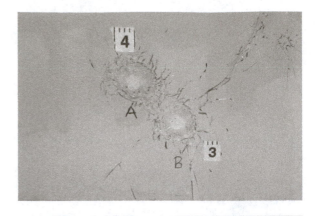

Photo 10-31. Bullet holes in glass numbered by sequential shots. Determining sequential shots fired in vehicular windshield glass is difficult because of the multiple layers of glass.

Photo 10-32. Bullet holes in glass numbered by sequential shots. Determining sequential shots fired in vehicular windshield glass is difficult because of the multiple layers of glass.

glass will exhibit **conchoidal lines** which originate on the side of the initial impact, curve, then straighten, and end perpendicular to the opposite (inside) edge of the glass (Saferstein, 2007).

> **Conchoidal cracks**
> Cracks in glass which originate on the side of the initial impact, curve, then straighten, and end perpendicular to the opposite (inside) edge of the glass.

    Darkfield illumination is a photographic technique used to document bullet holes in glass. The technique highlights the details of the fracture lines and removes distracting features located beyond the glass. To achieve optimum results, the darkfield illumination technique must be conducted under dark conditions.

> **Darkfield illumination** A photographic technique used to document bullet holes in glass. The technique highlights the details of the fracture lines and removes distracting features located beyond the glass.

1. Take orientation photographs of the glass and bullet holes. Include a measuring scale to indicate the height and location of the holes.
2. Take medium and close-up photographs of the individual bullet holes with and without a scale in place near the holes.
3. Obtain close-up (macro) photos of the bullet holes by placing the camera on a tripod. Position the tripod on the outside of the glass. Ensure that the face of the camera lens is parallel to the glass containing the bullet hole.
4. If nighttime, place a continuous light source (such as a photographic lamp) inside the glass (the side opposite of the camera and tripod). Direct the light source toward the glass at a 45 degree angle. The interior lights should be off, and the outside should be fairly dark.
5. Use good depth-of-field. F-11 is sufficient. ISO 200 or 400 is used. Adjust the shutter speed for proper exposure.
6. Press the shutter release button.

    The resulting image should accurately depict the bullet holes with a dark background. The forensic technician may choose to take additional photos, bracketing the f-stop, shutter speed or ISO, until the desired exposure is obtained.

    The technique may be used with vehicle windows, though the placement of the continuous light source and tripod may be challenging. An angle finder is used on slanted surfaces such as windshields to ensure that the camera is positioned at the same angle as the windshield (Siljander & Fredrickson, 1997).

Bullet Ricochet

Bullet ricochet occurs when a bullet in flight strikes and deflects rather than penetrates a surface. Heavy, low-velocity bullets are more likely to ricochet while lighter, high-velocity bullets often disintegrate or expand on impact with a hard surface (Girard, 2008). One can often determine the

> **Bullet ricochet**
> Occurs when a bullet in flight strikes and deflects rather than penetrates a surface. Heavy, low-velocity bullets are more likely to ricochet while lighter, high-velocity bullets often disintegrate or expand on impact with a hard object.

Photo 10-33. Light source at an angle of 45 degrees to the bullet hole.

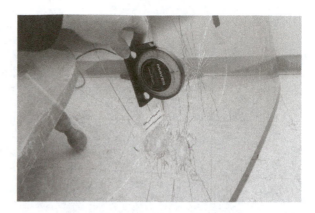

Photo 10-35. Angle finder to ensure that camera lens is parallel.

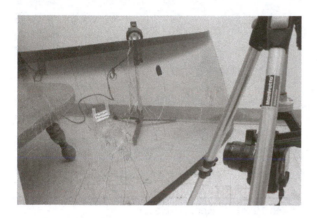

Photo 10-34. Camera set parallel to the hole.

Photo 10-36. Resulting photograph illuminating cracks with darkened background.

direction of travel of a ricochet bullet, especially on surfaces such as a painted vehicle.

1. Photograph the bullet's impression. Overall, medium, and close-up photographs of the impression are taken, without and with a measurement scale in place.
2. Swab the ricochet impression for GSR.
3. Dust the ricochet impression and surrounding area with fingerprint powder. The fingerprint powder may highlight fine lines around the impression. The lines will arch in the direction the ricochet bullet traveled.
4. Repeat the sequence of photographs after the fingerprint powder is applied. The details (fine lines) of the ricochet impression may be lifted with fingerprint lifting tape. The lift of the ricochet impression will be

used by a firearms trajectory expert to examine the appearance of the ricochet and determine directionality.

Bullet Trajectory Documentation

Specific photographs and measurements are obtained when a bullet penetrates a surface. The procedure may occur with the guidance of a firearms expert. A trajectory kit is used to determine the projectile's impact angle. The kit contains trajectory rods, screws, spacer cones, rubber washers, an angle finder, a protractor, and preferably a laser pointer and tripod stand. Access to a caliper (an instrument with two hinged legs used for measuring internal and external dimensions) or a loupe (magnified measuring device) is extremely helpful.

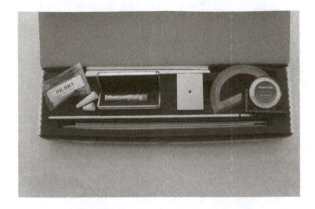

Photo 10-37. Trajectory kit.

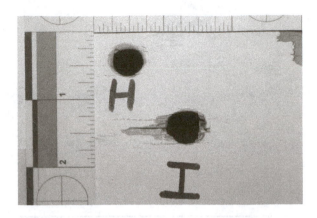

Photo 10-38. Bullet holes marked H and I.

To document bullet trajectory, the following procedure is suggested:

1. Photograph overall, medium, and close-up views of all bullet entry and exit points without and with a scale in place. For close-up views, place an adhesive-backed scale and an evidence number or letter on the same plane and next to the entry and exit points. Fill the frame of the camera lens with the hole, evidence number or letter, and scale.
2. Swab the bullet hole(s) for GSR.
3. Measure and record the size of the bullet hole(s) with a caliper or loupe.
4. Measure and record the location of each bullet hole in relation to the crime scene. Measure the distance of each hole from the ground or floor to the hole and from an adjacent perpendicular wall or surface edge.
5. Assemble an appropriate number of trajectory rods using the screws provided. Place a spacer cone inside the entry bullet hole. A spacer cone is used because the trajectory rod is too thin for most calibers. The spacer cone ensures a snug rod fit and proper trajectory determination. Place a rubber washer over the trajectory rod opposite the leading tip to prevent slippage. Insert the trajectory rod into the entry point and through the spacer cone and bullet hole until the rod protrudes from the bullet exit hole.
6. Take a photograph of the trajectory rod at both the entry and exit hole points. Take side-view photographs of the trajectory rods with the face of the camera lens parallel to the intersection of the rod and the bullet hole. Photographs are also taken from either the top or bottom view of the trajectory rod with the camera lens facing down or up toward the intersection of the rod and bullet hole (Ogle, 2007).

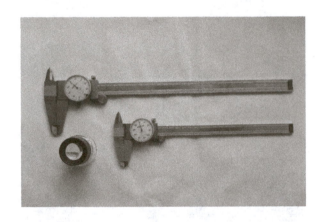

Photo 10-39. Caliper and loupe.

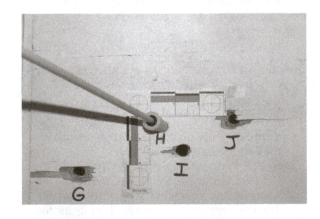

Photo 10-40. Views of trajectory rod in place.

7. The vertical (up-down) angle of the trajectory is determined with the angle finder. The angle finder is placed on top of the trajectory rod and held upright (not tilted). The upward or downward angle of the

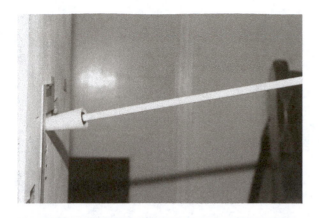

Photo 10-41. Views of trajectory rod in place.

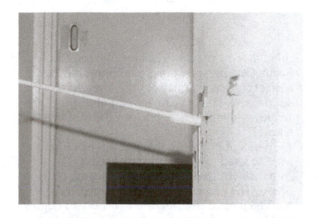

Photo 10-42. Views of trajectory rod in place.

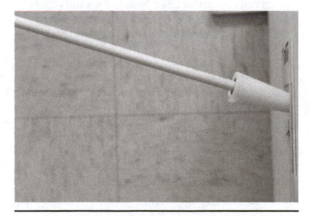

Photo 10-43. Views of trajectory rod in place.

Photo 10-44. Angle finder used for up-down angle determination.

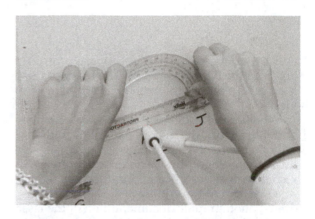

Photo 10-45. Protractor used for azimuth angle determination.

trajectory rod. The angle the rod's center line crosses is the approximate azimuth angle of the bullet's trajectory.

Trajectory Documentation with a Laser

If a laser beam device is available, it can be used to determine a bullet's trajectory or provide a visual of the bullet's path through the crime scene. Using the laser to determine bullet trajectory, the forensic technician should mount the laser on a tripod and direct the laser beam toward the bullet's exit hole. The laser beam is positioned to pass through the bullet exit point and out the entry opening. The point at which the laser beam strikes a surface is documented using coordinate or triangulation measurements (Ogle, 2007).

The laser beam can also be used to assist the forensic technician with locating the expended projectile. In this case, the laser is

trajectory rod (bullet's path) is indicated on the angle finder.

8. The *azimuth* (horizontal, side-to-side) *angle* is determined using a protractor. The zero point of the protractor is aligned with the

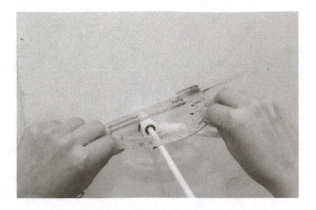

Photo 10-46. Protractor used for azimuth angle determination.

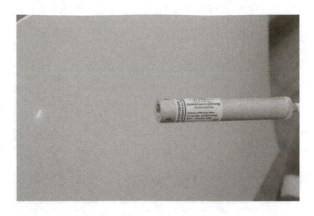

Photo 10-47. Laser beam reflecting from a white card.

attached to the end of a trajectory rod protruding from the bullet exit point. The beam of the laser is traced until the expended projectile is located.

Whether the laser beam is used to determine bullet trajectory, the overall path of the bullet, or both, the laser beam path is documented through photography. Darkness is required to visualize the laser's beam. If indoors, all lights must be off and the windows darkened. If outdoors, photographic documentation of the laser beam must occur during nighttime hours. To photograph a laser's beam, the following steps are recommended:

1. The camera is mounted on a tripod with a shutter release cable attached to it. A flash photograph of the area is taken prior to the laser beam photograph, ensuring that the camera is in the same position for both photographs. Later, specialized computer software (e.g., Adobe Photoshop) can be used to superimpose the flash photograph over the laser beam photograph to illustrate the laser beam (trajectory) path relative to the crime scene.

2. For the laser photograph, the shutter speed is set to bulb, F-5.6, with ISO 400 and auto white balance.

3. If the scene is indoors, or outdoors with no wind, photographic fog (an aerosol

mist) may be used to visualize the laser beam. One person sprays photographic fog along the laser beam, from the laser light source to the laser beam's point of impact, while a second person releases the camera's shutter.

4. In lieu of photographic fog, a white board may be used to reflect the laser beam. The camera settings are the same as described in Step 2. The camera operator activates the shutter. The person holding the white board begins at the laser light beam source and walks along the path of the laser beam, allowing the beam to reflect off the board. The board is angled so it does not block the laser beam from the camera's view. After the entire path of the laser is reflected off the white board, the shutter is released.

5. Instead of superimposing a flash photograph of the scene over the laser beam photograph, a forensic technician may also take a single photograph that captures the scene as well as the laser beam. The camera's flash unit is activated. The shutter is left open as the laser beam is captured (Sullivan, 2007). However, the forensic technician must adjust the ISO and f-stop to prevent overexposure of the photograph.

Photo 10-48. Timed-exposure photograph with a laser beam. Courtesy of National City, California, Police Department.

SUMMARY

Firearm evidence is common at the scene of many violent crimes. Safe collection of the firearm is a high priority. However, evidence preservation is also essential. Further, the firearm used to commit the crime may not be discovered at the scene. Yet cartridge casings and expended projectiles may be present and provide information about the type of firearm used. After a suspect firearm is retrieved, its identification is possible because distinctive tool marks on the expended casings and bullets can be linked to the firearm.

The events surrounding a shooting may be reconstructed by identifying and analyzing the trajectory of a bullet. Distance determination is possible if a GSR pattern is present. The forensic technician must follow photographic, measurement, and firearm evidence collection protocols to ensure items are preserved for analysis. Conclusions regarding trajectory, distance determination, and comparison of evidence to a suspect firearm are most often accomplished by a trained firearms expert.

KEY TERMS

Define, describe, or explain the importance of each of the following:

ballistics	double-action revolver	semiautomatic pistol
bullet ricochet	groove	single-action revolver
concentric cracks	gunshot residue (GSR)	striations
conchoidal cracks	land	trajectory
darkfield illumination	radial cracks	
distance determination	rifling	

DISCUSSION AND REVIEW QUESTIONS

1. What is GSR? Distance determination?
2. What are striations on expended projectiles and why are they forensically valuable?
3. What are the class characteristics of cartridge casings and expended projectiles? How are they analyzed?
4. How can a firearm's serial number be restored?

5. Explain the difference between radial and concentric cracks in glass?
6. How is a bullet ricochet documented? How can it be enhanced?
7. What is an azimuth angle and how is it determined?

CASE STUDY—Beltway Sniper Attacks

In October 2002, ten people were killed and three critically injured during a three-week spree-killing rampage throughout southeastern Maryland and northern Virginia (the Washington, DC, area). John Allen Muhammad and Lee Boyd Malvo were responsible for the shootings. Their rampage began a month earlier, with three murders and a robbery in Louisiana and Alabama.

Early eyewitness accounts of the shooting cited a white box truck as the suspect sniper vehicle. The police stopped numerous white box trucks in search of the suspect(s) and the .223 caliber rifle used in the attacks.

The sniper(s) communicated with authorities by leaving cryptic notes and Tarot cards at several shooting scenes. A call from the suspect(s) was traced to a pay telephone in Henrico County, Virginia. Police arrived minutes after the suspects terminated the call and fled the area. During the phone call, the sniper alluded to an unsolved murder at a liquor store in Montgomery, Alabama.

Media coverage of the shootings was widespread. By mid-October, many networks provided live coverage after each new sniper attack. *America's Most Wanted* devoted an entire episode to the killings.

Police discovered New Jersey vehicle license plates issued to one of the snipers (Muhammad) on a dark blue 1990 Chevrolet Caprice stopped for questioning near several shooting locations in various jurisdictions. Police immediately publicized a description of the suspect vehicle. Previously, however, police were focused almost exclusively on a white box truck (van) as the suspect vehicle.

On October 24, an observant truck driver (Whitney Donahue) noticed the suspect vehicle at an Interstate 70 rest stop near Myersville, Maryland. Donahue blocked the exit to the rest stop with his truck while he notified police. Authorities arrested Muhammad and Malvo, who were found sleeping in the 1990 Caprice. Ballistics tests on a .223 caliber rifle recovered from the car conclusively matched the rifle to bullets recovered at sniper attack scenes.

1. Describe the importance of ballistics to this case.
2. Which ballistics test(s) are used to match a firearm to a bullet?

LAB EXERCISES

Firearms Evidence Collection and Analysis

Equipment and supplies required per student or group of students:

- one expended firearm projectile
- one expended firearm cartridge casing

- one magnifier
- one gram scale
- one metric scale
- one vernier (dial or digital) caliper or a 10-power metric loupe
- one stereo binocular microscope (if available)

- one large box containing bullet hole(s) or simulated bullet hole(s)
- one trajectory kit (laser beam not necessary)
- six handguns of various calibers and models (if available)

Students may work individually, with a partner, or in a group, and rotate through the following exercises until all exercises are complete.

Exercise #1 Firearms Safety
1. Practice safe handling procedures with various handguns.
2. Using the Internet, research safe firearms handling procedures (e.g., Google "unload AK47").

Exercise #2 Bullet Trajectory Determination
1. Use a trajectory kit (rods, angle finder, and protractor) to develop responses to the following questions, recording the response directly below the question:

Bullet path direction— up or down?	Bullet path direction— left to right or right to left?	Up or down bullet angle?	Azimuth (side-to-side) bullet angle?

Exercise #3 Class Characteristics of Expended Projectile and Casing
1. Use a gram scale to weigh the expended projectile. Record the weight in the chart below.
2. Use a magnifier to determine the direction (right or left) of the rifling twist (direction of twist toward the nose of the projectile) of the expended projectile. Count the number of lands and grooves. Use a caliper or loupe (and a stereo binocular microscope, if available) to measure the width of the lands and grooves. Record your measurements in the chart below.
3. Use a metric scale to measure the length and diameter of each expended cartridge casing. Record your measurements in the chart below.

Projectile weight	Rifling twist— left or right?	Number of lands/grooves	Width of lands/grooves	Casing length	Casing diameter

4. Examine the headstamp of the expended cartridge casing and record the headstamp information in the first circle below.

5. Use a stereo binocular microscope (if available) to examine the firing pin mark on the base of the cartridge casing. Sketch the location of the mark in the second circle below. Use a caliper or a loupe to measure the dimensions of the firing pin mark and record the dimensions next to the second circle.

WEB RESOURCES

Association of Firearm and Tool Mark Examiners: www.afte.org

Bureau of Alcohol, Tobacco, Firearms and Explosives: www.atf.gov

Forensic Firearm Identification: www.firearmsid.com

International Association for Identification: www.theiai.org

American Academy of Forensic Sciences: www. aafs.org

American Board of Criminalistics: www.criminalistics.com

Canadian Society of Forensic Science: www.csfs.ca

California Association of Criminalists: www.cacnews.org

Midwestern Association of Forensic Scientists: www.mafs.net

Northeastern Association of Forensic Scientists: www.neafs.org

Northwest Association of Forensic Scientists: www.nwafs.org

Southern Association of Forensic Scientists: www.southernforensic.org

Southwestern Association of Forensic Scientists: www.swafs.us

11

Bloodstain Pattern Documentation and Analysis

LEARNING OUTCOMES

After completing this chapter, the reader should be able to:

- describe the education and training that a bloodstain pattern expert must obtain,
- determine the directionality of a blood spatter,
- demonstrate the steps for photographing bloodstain patterns,
- describe the three basic bloodstain pattern classifications and the sub-categories of each,
- demonstrate the steps for reconstructing an impact mechanism bloodstain pattern using the tangent and stringing techniques.

INTRODUCTION

Bloodstain pattern analysis (BPA) is a unique area of forensic science through which the dynamics or actions occurring in a crime scene may be analyzed and interpreted. Through a detailed analysis of the bloodstain patterns at the crime scene, the **bloodstain pattern expert (BPE)** formulates a theory regarding the sequence of events that occurred at the scene of a crime. Obviously, the sequence of events is vital information for any criminal investigation, but particularly so for scenes that pose serious circumstantial questions. *Is this the scene of a homicide or suicide? Was this a case of self defense or was it a brutal attack?* A BPE may be able to answer these and other questions by analyzing the bloodstain pattern evidence. BPA assists the BPE in determining the following:

> **Bloodstain pattern analysis (BPA)** Area of forensic science through which the dynamics or actions occurring in a crime scene are analyzed and interpreted.

> **Bloodstain pattern expert (BPE)** Through detailed analysis of the bloodstain patterns at a crime scene, a BPE develops a theory regarding the sequence of events that occurred.

- type of force inflicted on the victim,
- approximate number of times the victim was struck,
- damage to a victim's artery,
- struggles occurring at the scene,
- sequence of events at the scene,
- determination of homicide or suicide,
- determination of self-defense or murder,
- type of weapon involved,
- corroboration of eye witness statements.

BPA may assist the case investigator with the following:

- interrogation of the suspect(s),
- exoneration of an accused suspect,
- determination of sequence of events (crime scene reconstruction).

Although BPA may be an integral part of a criminal investigation, the analysis is never all encompassing. The BPE relies upon DNA results, bullet trajectory analysis, postmortem examination analysis, and other relevant evidence when formulating the final interpretation of the bloodstain pattern evidence. If a BPE limits the final interpretation to the bloodstain patterns alone, errors will most certainly occur. For example, if the perpetrator stabs a resistant victim multiple times, it is common that the perpetrator sustains knife wounds during the attack. Without a DNA report, a BPE may erroneously determine that blood patterns contain blood from the victim when in fact the blood source is the perpetrator. The BPE must also consider the victim's injuries. A BPE may determine that a bloodstain pattern is a result of a gunshot when the victim sustained blunt force injuries and no gunshot wounds. The postmortem examination report must corroborate the bloodstain pattern interpretation.

The BPE must also possess a working knowledge of crime scene investigation. Especially important for the BPE are skills associated with the creation and interpretation of crime scene diagrams, scene and evidence photography, evidence collection procedures, and blood enhancement techniques.

BPE EDUCATION AND TRAINING

BPE education and training varies among agencies. BPEs can be sworn officers or forensic technicians who received advanced training in BPA. Others may have a medical background or be criminalists with physical science degrees who received specialized crime scene processing and BPA training. Some are certified experts while others are not. Although the formal education and background may vary greatly, most BPEs are well-informed and diverse, with expertise in multiple areas of forensic science. Although a BPE may not possess a physical science degree, knowledge of geometry, trigonometry, and basic physics are valuable to one involved with BPA (James, Kish, & Sutton, 2005).

Regardless of the formal education or training, it is very important that a BPE receive practical training in the field. Practical field experience usually begins with attending a BPA course involving laboratory experiments that allow the student to learn the dynamics and mechanics of bloodstain pattern creation. The student is involved in creating, interpreting, and reconstructing bloodstain patterns.

Advanced training and a practicum are also recommended. The advanced training typically involves review of crime scene reconstruction techniques. Advanced analysis also involves bloodstain pattern interpretations based on case photographs, bloodstains on clothing and other evidence, documentation procedures, computer analysis, and courtroom testimony techniques.

On a regular basis, the BPE should attend seminars and conferences relevant to BPA. Membership in related professional organizations is also helpful. The International Association of Bloodstain Pattern Analysts (IABPA) requires members to complete a basic

40-hour BPA course. In addition the Scientific Working Group for Bloodstain Pattern Analysis (SWGSTAIN), established by the FBI in 2002, convenes meetings of BPEs to discuss and evaluate BPA techniques, terminology, protocols, education, and research related to the field. SWGSTAIN subcommittees address the subject areas of education and training, legal aspects, quality assurance, research, and terminology (James, Kish, & Sutton, 2005).

Several professional organizations and licensing boards offer certification programs in BPA. A notable organization, the International Association for Identification (IAI), offers certification in various fields of forensic science, including BPA. To obtain the title of Certified Bloodstain Pattern Expert (CBPE) through IAI, the applicant must be of good moral character, demonstrate integrity and high ethical standards, be in good professional standing, and must successfully complete the following:

- minimum of 40 hours of education in an approved BPA workshop,
- minimum of three years of practical experience within the discipline of BPA, following the 40-hour training course,
- minimum of 240 hours of instruction in fields of study relating to BPA,
- a 40-hour photography course,
- certification application with proof of training and experience [two reference letters from supervisors or professionals in the field of forensic science must accompany the application along with a fee (International Association for Identification, 2008)].

After an application is accepted by the IAI certification board, the applicant must successfully pass (with a score of 75 percent or higher) a written examination involving the following areas of BPA:

- BPA terminology,
- documentation, photography, illustration, and sketching of bloodstains and bloodstain patterns,
- wound pathology,
- investigative procedures,
- crime scene processing,
- history of BPA,
- BPA theory and logic,
- mathematics (basic math related to BPA),
- bloodstain and pattern recognition.

The IAI CBPE certification is granted for five years. Subsequently, the CBPE may apply for recertification, providing proof of involvement and training in the field of BPA. Additional information may be obtained from IAI at www.theaia.org

Beyond formal education, training, and certification, professional growth for the BPE is obtained at crime scenes, preferably working side by side with a seasoned expert who may serve as a mentor. No amount of education or training can replace a BPE mentor with extensive crime scene BPA experience.

Prior to responding to and interpreting bloodstain patterns at crime scenes, one must obtain foundational knowledge in BPA. A basic knowledge of the properties of blood and the physics involving blood in flight (when acted upon by a source of energy) is foundational to analyzing and interpreting complex bloodstain patterns.

PROPERTIES OF BLOOD—DROPS AND IN FLIGHT

Before a BPE can analyze and reconstruct a bloodstain pattern, foundational knowledge regarding blood and blood in flight must be gained. Blood constitutes approximately 8 percent of the total body weight of human beings: five to six liters of blood in most males and four to five liters in most females. Blood's **viscosity** (resistance to flow) ranges between 4.4 and 4.7. In comparison, water's viscosity is one. Therefore, blood is nearly five times more resistant to flow than water. Additionally, blood possesses adhesive qualities and may transfer and adhere to surfaces it contacts. Wiping blood from a surface is much more difficult than wiping water because of blood's viscosity and adhesive qualities (Bevel & Gardner, 2008).

> **Viscosity**
> Resistance to flow.

The size and volume of a blood droplet is also dependent upon the object from which the droplet is released. An open, dripping wound will release droplets of a different volume than blood dripping from a weapon. A droplet forming on a large surface will cover more surface area and possess more surface tension, resulting in higher blood droplet volume than a droplet that forms on a small surface. For example, blood dripping from a baseball bat will have more surface area and greater surface tension, resulting in a larger blood drop than blood dripping from a smaller surface area such as a narrow knife blade (James, Kish, & Sutton, 2005). To better understand how object and weapon

surface affect the formation of blood drops, one should experiment with the formation of blood drops on various types of objects.

Free-falling blood droplets (blood drops that are dripping due to gravity and are not in flight) average 4.56 mm in size (while in the air) and are .05 ml (milliliters) by volume (Bevel & Gardner, 2008). As a blood droplet of a constant volume descends, the diameter of the blood droplet increases as the distance it falls increases because the droplet travels faster as it falls. However, the blood droplet will reach a maximum diameter, regardless of the distance or height. The maximum blood droplet diameter occurs when terminal velocity is reached. At this point, gravity and air resistance are balanced so the droplet falls at a constant rate.

At a crime scene, the distance a blood droplet fell cannot be determined because the volume of the blood drop is not known. Further, the size of the blood drop stain on a surface provides few clues to its volume because surface characteristics vary. Some surfaces absorb or distort the blood droplet as it contacts the surface (Wolson, 2000). To better understand how various surfaces affect the appearance of a blood droplet after contact, one should experiment with releasing droplets of identical volume the same distance onto different types of surfaces.

Blood in Flight

Blood droplets fragment upon impact with a surface. The fragments form smaller droplets that are placed in flight. The distance the newly formed blood droplets travel depends on their ability to overcome air resistance, based on their velocity (speed) and the size of the droplet. If two blood droplets of different sizes travel at the same speed, the larger drop possesses the capacity to travel farther because it has greater mass and can overcome air resistance more easily than the smaller blood droplet.

When analyzing bloodstain patterns, the BPE examines the overall pattern and how the various sized blood drops are dispersed. The very small (mist-sized) drops do not possess the mass that allows them to travel far. Obviously, drops travel farther at higher speeds, but if the drops are very small, the distance traveled is limited.

Directionality of Blood Drops

When a blood droplet descends at 90 degrees to a surface, the bloodstain resulting from the drop's impact is circular and symmetrical. As a blood droplet impacts a surface from an acute angle (angle less than 90 degrees), the droplet

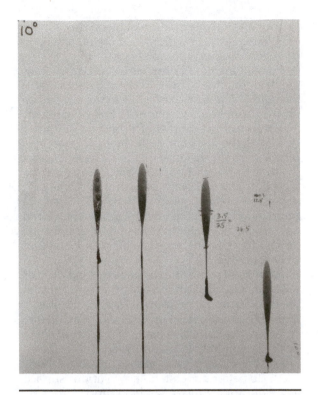

Photo 11-1. Blood dropped at 10 degrees. Note the inverted "bowling pin" appearance of the drops at more acute angles.

Photo 11-2. Blood dropped at 20 degrees. Note the inverted "bowling pin" appearance of the drops at more acute angles.

Photo 11-3. Blood dropped at 30 degrees.

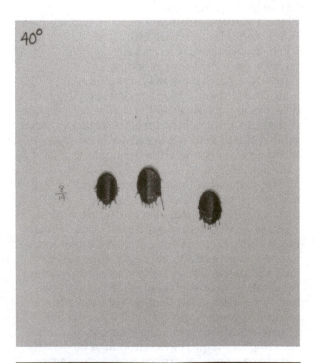

Photo 11-4. Blood dropped at 40 degrees.

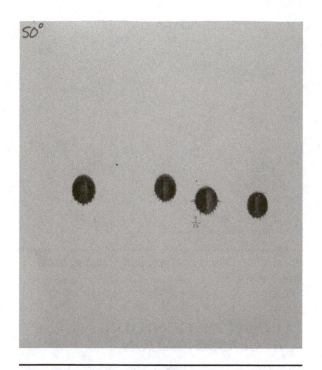

Photo 11-5. Blood dropped at 50 degrees.

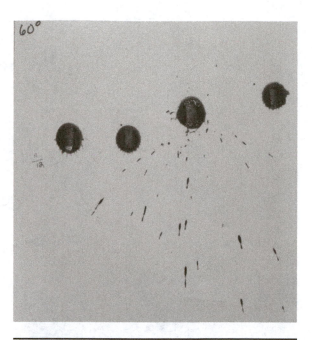

Photo 11-6. Blood dropped at 60 degrees.

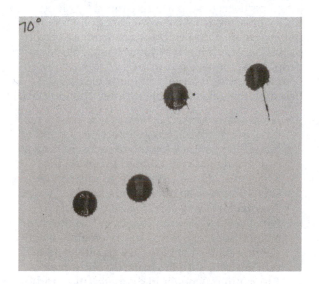

Photo 11-7. Blood dropped at 70 degrees.

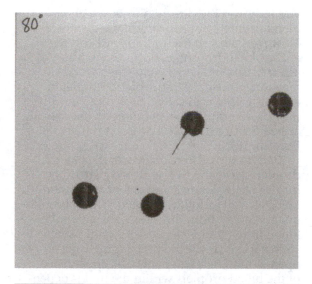

Photo 11-8. Blood dropped at 80 degrees. Note the inverted "bowling pin" appearance of the drops at more acute angles.

first contacts the surface, then continues to travel along the surface, often forming a tear-shaped stain. The steeper the surface impact angle, the more elongated the tear-shaped drop. To determine the direction the drop traveled,

the BPE examines the irregularly shaped end (jagged or tear drop shape) of the blood drop stain. The irregular end indicates the direction the blood was traveling at time of impact with the surface. Therefore, the uniformed (regular)

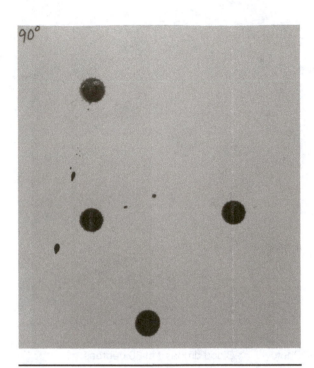

Photo 11-9. Blood dropped at 90 degrees.

Photo 11-10. Photo of directionality of blood; blood drop marked D.

end indicates the direction from which the blood droplet contacted the stained surface. However, the surface itself may distort the entire blood drop stain. Surfaces such as asphalt, concrete, brick, and some wood surfaces may cause the entire blood droplet to appear irregular in shape. Still, directionality may be determined, depending on the overall appearance of the blood drop stain (Laber & Epstein, 1998).

Determining directionality of the blood droplet assists the BPE with reconstructing human struggles and movement within the scene as well as following blood trails throughout and away from the scene. The amount of blood in the trail is dependent upon the blood source itself. (Is the blood dripping from an open wound or a weapon?) The appearance of the blood droplets within the trail is dependent upon the velocity (speed) and the type of surface the droplets impact. The BPE examines the entire blood trail to determine the movements of the wounded person or bloody object.

Determining the directionality of blood drops is also one of the first steps in reconstructing an impact bloodstain pattern. A basic knowledge of bloodstain pattern recognition techniques and classification is helpful to reconstructing an impact bloodstain pattern.

PATTERN RECOGNITION AND CLASSIFICATION

The classification of bloodstain patterns has been debated among BPEs for many years. Originally, bloodstains were grouped as transfer patterns (e.g., a bloody object contacts a surface), projected patterns (e.g., patterns caused by blood under pressure from a severed artery), cast-off patterns (e.g., blood is dislodged from an object or weapon), and impact patterns (e.g., blood droplet fragments upon impact).

Impact patterns were originally classified based on the velocity of the droplet upon impact.

- A *low-velocity impact pattern* is one in which a force of approximately five feet per second hits a blood source (open wound), creating a converging pattern of blood drops on the adjacent surfaces, with the majority of the stains 4 mm or larger in diameter.
- A *medium-velocity impact pattern* is one in which a force of up to 25 feet per second hits a blood source (open wound), creating a converging pattern of blood drops on the adjacent surface, with the majority of the stains 1 to 3 mm or smaller in diameter, plus additional drops larger and smaller.
- A *high-velocity impact pattern* is one in which a force of 100 feet per second or greater hits a blood source (victim), sending blood in flight that subsequently hits an adjacent surface, creating a converging pattern of blood drops on the adjacent surfaces, with a majority of the stains less than 1 mm in diameter. Some mist droplets (those 0.1 mm or smaller in diameter) may be present. High-velocity impact patterns are associated with gunshot

wounds. The velocity of an object that creates this pattern type may not require an open wound to create the pattern. The object often contains enough energy to simultaneously break the skin and send blood in flight.

However, classifying impact patterns simply as low-, medium-, or high-velocity is often problematic because appearances can be deceiving. For example, a bloodstain pattern may appear to be caused by a high-velocity impact, and may be interpreted as a pattern caused by a gunshot. Subsequently, one discovers that a blunt force object created the pattern. By classifying bloodstain patterns based on apparent velocity, the BPE may report erroneous findings (James, Kish, & Sutton, 2005).

A more holistic and generally accepted bloodstain pattern classification approach analyzes patterns based on the physical features of stain size, shape, location, concentration, and distribution. As illustrated in Figure 11.1,

the modern approach classifies bloodstain pattern stains into three main categories (passive, spatter, and altered), with sub-categories contained within each main category (James, Kish, & Sutton 2005).

PASSIVE BLOODSTAIN PATTERNS

A **passive bloodstain pattern** is affected by gravity and secondary contact with blood at the crime scene. Patterns affected by gravity include drops, blood flow, and a large volume of blood. Patterns affected by secondary contact include those that are caused when an object or person contacts blood and transfers it to another object or surface.

Passive bloodstain pattern Created by gravity and secondary contact with blood at the crime scene. Patterns affected by gravity include drops, blood flow, and a large volume of blood. Patterns affected by secondary contact include those that are created when an object or person contacts blood and transfers it to another object or surface.

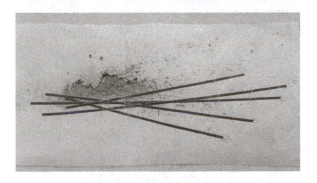

Photo 11-11. Pattern appears to be that of high velocity, but is not.

Passive Patterns	Spatter Patterns	Altered Patterns
Transfer	Impact Mechanism (gunshot, beating, stabbing, power tools)	Clotted
Drop(s)	Secondary Mechanism (satellite spatter)	Diluted
Flow	Projection Mechanism (cast-off, arterial, expired)	Diffused
Large Volume		Insects Sequenced Voids

Figure 11-1. Categories of bloodstain patterns.

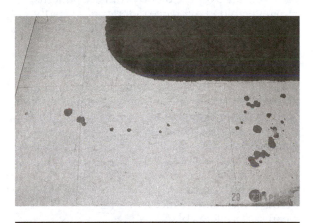

Photo 11-12. Blood drops on a tiled floor. Courtesy of National City, California, Police Department.

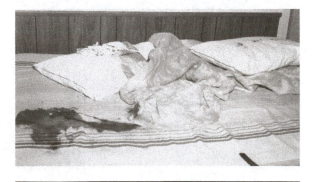

Photo 11-13. Blood flow pattern on a bed. Courtesy of National City, California, Police Department.

Transfer Patterns

A **transfer bloodstain pattern** may be a non-motion or a motion stain pattern. A non-motion transfer pattern occurs when a bloody object contacts a clean surface (e.g., bloody weapon placed on a clean surface; a bloody shoe pressed against a clean floor). Individual characteristics may be present in the pattern. If the bloodstain pattern is caused by a weapon, the bloodstain pattern evidence may provide investigators with information on the size and type of weapon used. If the pattern reveals a sole print of a shoe, individual characteristics of the shoe (e.g., size, tread design) may be present. The forensic technician must properly photograph and measure blood pattern evidence of this nature.

> **Transfer bloodstain pattern** A non-motion or a motion stain pattern that occurs when a bloody object contacts a clean surface (e.g., bloody weapon placed on a clean surface; a bloody shoe pressed against a clean floor).

In an attempt to preserve evidence, first responders to a crime scene may place blankets or coverings over the bloody transfer patterns. However, blood evidence deteriorates rapidly and may be destroyed if covered. Blood flakes after drying. Removal of the coverings may cause the blood evidence to flake and lose its pattern and evidentiary value. Protect the blood evidence by minimizing the number of people allowed into the scene and ensure that all crime scene personnel are aware of the location of blood transfer patterns.

A motion transfer pattern may be caused by a **blood swipe**, which occurs when a bloody object moves along a clean surface (e.g., bloody

> **Blood swipe** Occurs when a bloody object moves along a clean surface (e.g., bloody hair moving across a clean wall or floor).

hair moving across a clean wall or floor). Or, it may be a **blood wipe**, which occurs when a clean object moves against a bloody surface (e.g., a hand or cloth moving through a pool of blood). Motion transfer patterns are indicative of movement within the crime scene and may provide clues regarding movement of the victim, attempts to clean the crime scene, struggles within the scene, and other valuable criminal event information.

> **Blood wipe** Occurs when a clean object moves against a bloody surface (e.g., a hand or cloth moving through a pool of blood).

Blood Drops

If the perpetrator was injured and bled, drops of blood may be observed on or around the victim. A trail of blood may depict the perpetrator's movements and lead away from the crime scene. Thus, the forensic technician must photograph, document, and collect all blood drop stains within the scene.

Photo 11-15. Wipe transfer pattern.

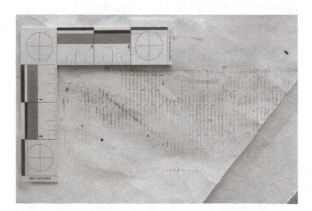

Photo 11-14. Transfer pattern.

Photo 11-16. Wipe transfer pattern.

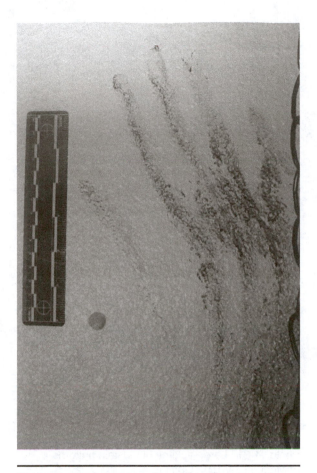

Photo 11-17. Swipe transfer pattern. Courtesy of National City, California, Police Department.

Photo 11-18. Blood trail leading away from crime scene. Courtesy of National City, California, Police Department.

Blood Dripping into Blood

If a person bleeding from an open wound is stationary for a period of time, drops of the person's blood will fall onto a surface area. As each drop of blood impacts the surface, the blood gathers into a pool. Each subsequent drop of blood adds to the pool. As drops land in the pool of blood, tiny fragments of each drop may break away and land outside the pool.

These tiny fragments of blood are referred to as **satellite spatter**. Satellite spatter is included in the category of *spatter patterns*, but it may be observed in any type of bloodstain pattern. Satellite spatter may be misinterpreted by an investigator who is new to analyzing bloodstains because it is easily mistaken for an impact spatter pattern or projected blood.

Satellite spatter
Tiny fragments of blood. Satellite spatters are small blood spatter stains created when blood droplets detach from a larger blood drop as it impacts an object.

Photo 11-19. Blood trail leading away from crime scene. Courtesy of National City, California, Police Department.

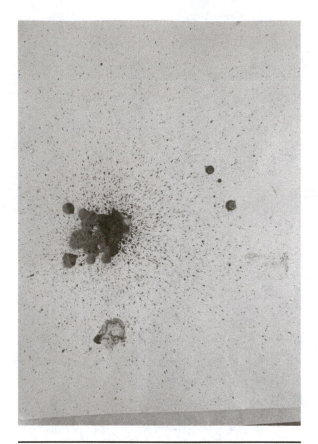

Photo 11-20. Blood dripped into blood.

Photo 11-21. Large-volume bloodstain patterns. Photograph by Todd Griffiths.

Flow Patterns

A blood **flow pattern** is created when a large volume of accumulated blood flows from one area to another based on gravity and the contour of the surface. A flow pattern may be observed on a vertical surface (e.g., wall) or on a victim's body as blood flows downward along the contour of the body. If the body was moved after blood flow began, the BPE may observe a blood flow that changed direction and is contradictory to gravity. The observation is vital to determining movement of the body after blood flow commences.

> **Flow pattern**
> Created when a large volume of accumulated blood flows from one area to another based on gravity and the contour of the surface. A flow pattern may be observed on a vertical surface (e.g., wall) or on a victim's body as blood flows downward along the contour of the body.

Large-Volume Patterns

A **large-volume pattern** is indicative of extensive bleeding in a fixed position. A person's body will *bleed* from an open wound while the person is alive. Bleeding is a function of cardiac (heart) activity. When a person dies, the wound no longer bleeds because the heart has ceased to function. After death, blood will drain rather than bleed from the open wound.

A large volume of blood will pool on a non-absorbent surface and saturate an absorbent surface. If the volume of blood is large enough, blood can penetrate carpet, carpet padding, or several layers of bedding. A perpetrator may clean a bloodstained carpet or rotate a bloody mattress. If an investigator, forensic technician, or BPE suspects that bloodshed occurred on a carpeted floor or on a bed, it is wise to search under the carpet and carpet padding or mattress for blood evidence. The search for

> **Large volume pattern**
> Indicative of extensive bleeding in a fixed position. A person's body will *bleed* from an open wound while the person is alive. Bleeding is a function of cardiac (heart) activity. When a person dies, the wound no longer bleeds because the heart ceased to function. After death, blood will drain rather than bleed from an open wound.

continued to bleed or blood drained from the corpse, a large volume of blood may flow over the original pattern.

SPATTER BLOODSTAIN PATTERNS

A **spatter bloodstain pattern** results when blood is placed in flight because of action upon it. Determination of the action that created the resulting spatter pattern is essential. Actions that may create spatter bloodstain patterns include gunshots, beatings, stabbings, satellite (secondary mechanism) spatter, projection mechanisms (cast-off patterns from blood, object in motion), and arterial and expirated blood (blood forced from a live human body through arterial pressure or coughing action).

> **Spatter bloodstain pattern** Results when blood is placed in flight because of action upon it. Actions that may create spatter bloodstain patterns include gunshots, beatings, stabbings, satellite (secondary mechanism) spatter, projection mechanisms (cast-off patterns from blood, objects in motion), and arterial and expirated blood (blood forced from a live human body through arterial pressure or coughing action).

Training, experimentation, crime scene experience, and mentoring are critical to accurate BPE interpretation of spatter bloodstain patterns. To draw the proper conclusion regarding the type of mechanism involved in creating the spatter pattern, the pattern is analyzed to determine the size, quantity, distribution, and shape of individual spatters within the pattern as well as the surface on which the pattern appears.

Impact Mechanism Bloodstain Patterns

An **impact mechanism bloodstain pattern** is created when an action such as blunt force or a gunshot fragments a blood source (victim), creating a converging pattern of individual blood spatter on nearby surfaces. Using basic physics and mathematics, the con-

> **Impact mechanism bloodstain pattern** Created when an action such as blunt force or a gunshot fragments a blood source (victim), creating a converging pattern of individual blood spatters on nearby surfaces.

verging pattern may be analyzed and measured to determine the force's area of origin, or where the impact occurred. The size and distribution of spatter within the impact pattern is dependent upon the volume of blood impacted and velocity and mass of the force. The more blood available, the larger the spatter pattern is likely to be. The greater the force, the more fragmented the individual spatter will appear.

Photo 11-22. Large-volume bloodstain patterns. Photograph by Todd Griffiths.

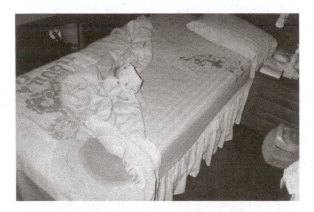

Photo 11-23. Large-volume bloodstain patterns. Photograph by Todd Griffiths.

observable blood should always precede the use of latent blood-enhancing chemicals.

A large-volume bloodstain pattern may conceal another bloodstain pattern. Impact transfer blood patterns may be present, but as the victim

The BPE analyzes the overall pattern as well as individual spatters within the pattern. The shape of the individual spatters will depend upon the flight path of the spatter droplets as well as the texture, shape, and angle of the impact surface (James, Kish, & Sutton, 2005).

Gunshot Bloodstain Patterns

Gunshot bloodstain patterns typically appear cone shaped. The individual spatter within the cone consists of very fine drops of blood, which are mist-like in appearance. Medium- and large-sized drops of spatter may be observed within the pattern also. However, the mist-sized spatter is most indicative of a gunshot because of the high velocity required to fragment blood into very small particles. The higher the velocity of the bullet, the greater its impact and blood fragmentation. Injuries resulting from power tools and motor vehicle collisions also fragment blood into a mist-like spatter.

The resultant spatter pattern from a gunshot depends on the caliber of the weapon, the velocity of the projectile, and the distance the projectile travels, as well as victim clothing, hair, or position that may obstruct blood droplets on flight. With contact and close-contact gunshot wounds to the head, for example, brain matter, spinal fluid, and fragments of skull or teeth may be observed within the spatter pattern.

Though uncommon, a **backspatter pattern** may be observed as well. A backspatter (blood particles released toward the weapon) pattern may result when a projectile contacts the body. Backspatter is not as symmetrical as forward spatter because it is traveling in the opposite direction of the projectile. The small droplets located in backspatter do not travel more than four or five feet. The presence of backspatter on a firearm or a perpetrator is dependent upon the distance between the firearm and the victim (Bevel & Gardner, 2008).

> **Backspatter pattern**
> A backspatter (blood particles released toward a weapon) pattern may result when a projectile contacts the body. Backspatter is not as symmetrical as forward spatter because it is traveling in the opposite direction of the projectile. The small droplets located in backspatter do not travel more than four or five feet.

Beating Bloodstain Patterns

The impact mechanism action that generates the largest amount of individual spatter usually involves a blunt force instrument. Common blunt force instruments (weapons) include hammers, bricks, baseball bats, golf clubs, pipes, wrenches, and other blunt objects.

Photo 11-24. Shotgun bloodstain pattern and volume blood flow. Courtesy of National City, California, Police Department.

The spatter pattern typically radiates from the impact site, which is indicative of the direction of the blood spatter blow. The distribution and size of the impact spatter is dependent upon the shape and size of the weapon, the amount of force, the direction of the force, the amount of blood available at the wound site, and the movements of the victim and perpetrator during the attack.

An impact spatter pattern is created when the blunt force weapon connects with a blood source. Typically, the first blow of the weapon will not create a bloodstain pattern. Rather, the first blow exposes the blood source. Subsequent blows create impact spatter patterns as the weapon contacts the blood source (open wound), causing blood to radiate from the wound site.

The amount of blood backspatter an assailant receives is directly related to the positions of the

Photo 11-25. Impact spatter pattern.

assailant and the victim, the direction of the force, and the location of the blow(s). In many beating incidents, perpetrators receive very little blood (backspatter). Assailants who deliver blows with overhead swings to a victim who is lying down will often receive blood spatter on their lower legs and hand (or hands) nearest to the victim's wound(s). Blows delivered at a relatively horizontal angle in a direction away from the assailant will usually result in less blood spatter on the assailant. Still, the forensic technician should search for blood in or on objects (shoe soles, belts and belt buckles, eyeglasses, watches and other jewelry, and hats) worn by the assailant.

Stabbing Bloodstain Patterns

Most do not associate a stabbing mechanism with an impact spatter pattern. Although less frequent, the bloodstain pattern created by stabbing depends upon the force applied to an open blood source. In a case involving multiple stab wounds, a violent attack may occur as the perpetrator uses great force to thrust the sharp edge of the weapon into the victim. After multiple stab wounds, the victim is often bloodied. With each thrust of the edged weapon, the perpetrator's fist and the weapon impact that blood source, resulting in an impact spatter pattern. Since the mass of the edged weapon and perpetrator's fist are often not as large as many blunt force weapons, the resulting edged weapon impact bloodstain pattern is usually smaller in overall pattern size. Less spatter is visible throughout an edged weapon bloodstain pattern than is observed with most blunt force weapons.

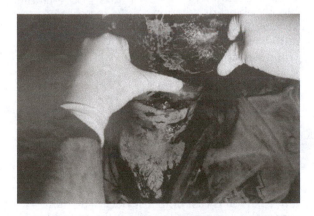

Photo 11-26. Bloodstain patterns from a stabbing. Courtesy of National City, California, Police Department.

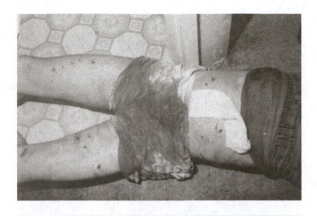

Photo 11-27. Bloodstain patterns from a stabbing. Courtesy of National City, California, Police Department.

Secondary Mechanism Spatter

As discussed under *Blood Drops* earlier in this chapter, satellite spatters are small blood spatter stains created when blood droplets detach from a larger blood drop as it impacts an object. A satellite spatter is named a **secondary mechanism spatter** because it is produced by a second impact. Satellite spatter can occur in virtually any bloodstain pattern involving blood in flight or dripping blood. Satellite spatter is noted for what it is: a fragmented portion of an original drop of blood. But satellite spatter can pose a problem if misinterpreted as an original impact mechanism. If several satellite spatters are observed in a larger bloodstain pattern, they usually radiate from a pool of blood or several drops of blood in a symmetrical fashion. All of the individual satellite spatters are quite uniform in appearance. Uniformity of appearance is not present in an impact spatter pattern. Individual spatters from an impact mechanism are not usually symmetrical. They vary in size and converge on an area.

> **Secondary mechanism spatter** An alternative reference to satellite spatter because it is produced by a second impact. Satellite spatter can occur in virtually any bloodstain pattern involving blood in flight or dripping blood.

Even more confusing are satellite spatters on vertical surfaces. If a bleeding victim walks through a hallway and stops momentarily near a wall, the victim may bleed several drops of blood onto the floor. Each drop that lands on another blood drop may create satellite spatter against the base of the wall. One might interpret that satellite spatter as an impact mechanism

Photo 11-28. Secondary mechanism spatter (satellite surrounding) drops of blood. Courtesy of National City, California, Police Department.

pattern that occurred low on the wall. However, if the analyst examines the entire hallway wall, a motion transfer (swipe) of blood from the victim onto the wall may be visible. A blood trail on the hallway floor showing directionality of the victim's movements may be apparent as well. The forensic technician (or BPE) may then conclude that the satellite spatter near the base of the wall was not created by an impact mechanism. To avoid an erroneous bloodstain pattern interpretation, one must examine the entire scene while analyzing bloodstain patterns.

Projection Mechanism Bloodstain Patterns

A **projection mechanism bloodstain pattern** is created by blood placed in flight and projected by a force other than an impact. The sub-categories of projection mechanism include cast-off, arterial, and expired blood, all of which are created differently.

> **Projection mechanism bloodstain pattern** Created by blood placed in flight and projected by a force other than an impact.

Cast-Off Bloodstain Patterns

A **cast-off bloodstain pattern** is created when blood is dislodged from a bloody object or weapon as it is being swung. This type of pattern is often observed in beating and stabbing cases. The pattern can be linear or arc-shaped, with individual

> **Cast-off bloodstain pattern** Created when blood is dislodged from a bloody object or weapon as it is being swung. This type of pattern is often observed in beating and stabbing cases.

blood spatters parallel to each other, or teardrop-shaped, indicating directionality of the swing. Cast-off bloodstain patterns are frequently located on a ceiling, wall, or floor. They may overlap impact patterns and other bloodstain patterns as well as other cast-off patterns. They may be located on a victim as well as an assailant. Cast-off bloodstain patterns are typically 4–8 mm, but may be larger or smaller in size.

The amount of blood present in a cast-off pattern is dependent upon the type and size of weapon used, how well blood adheres to the weapon's surface, the blood source, the blood available from the source, and the force applied by the assailant. The more force applied in the swing, the smaller the drops and the higher the number of drops released. Because of these variables, the overall width of a cast-off pattern may not help identify the weapon that created it. The forward swing toward a victim is usually more forceful than a backward swing. As an assailant changes weapon direction with each swing, blood is dislodged from the weapon, depositing circular or oval-shaped stains on nearby surfaces.

When multiple cast-off patterns are observed, the BPE should analyze the directionality of the swings to generalize the number of swings made. One swing is added to the number of determined swings because at least one blow is required to create a blood source. Further, some swings of a weapon may not result in contact with the victim. If the victim is deceased, reviewing postmortem examination findings will assist with determination of the number of weapon-body contacts.

A **cessation cast-off pattern** occurs when a bloody object or weapon strikes another object or surface and comes to a complete stop. Blood is dislodged from the object previously in motion and cast-off in the same direction the weapon or object was swung.

> **Cessation cast-off pattern** Occurs when a bloody object or weapon strikes another object or surface and comes to a complete stop. Blood is dislodged from the object previously in motion and is cast-off in the same direction the weapon or object is swung.

Arterial Bloodstain Patterns

An **arterial bloodstain pattern** is created when blood under pressure from a punctured artery of a live person is cast onto a surface. The more severe the damage to the artery, the more blood volume discharged from the artery. Arterial damage can result from a sharp instrument, blunt force, or a gunshot wound. Sharp objects

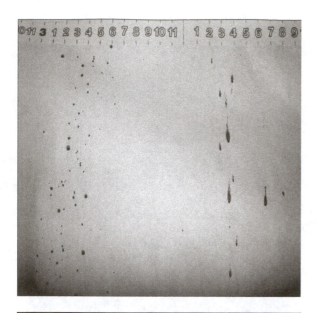

Photo 11-31. Multiple cast-off patterns from police dog bite on an armed robbery suspect. Courtesy of National City, California, Police Department.

Photo 11-29. Minimal of two cast-off patterns; left pattern has a downward directionality and right pattern has upward directionality.

Photo 11-30. Multiple cast-off patterns from police dog bite on an armed robbery suspect. Courtesy of National City, California, Police Department.

puncture or cut an artery. Blunt force can crush an artery. A firearm projectile will puncture an artery.

The diameter of arterial bloodstain patterns range from less than 1 mm to more than 1 cm. Elongated spines (bloodstain with a long appearance) or satellite spatter around arterial

Arterial bloodstain pattern Created when blood under pressure from a punctured artery of a live person is cast onto a surface. The more severe the damage to the artery, the more blood volume discharged from the artery.

pattern may be visible as well. The arterial bloodstain pattern may be circular, oblong, or irregular in shape. If the blood is discharged onto a vertical surface, a downward flow of blood may be observed. An arterial bloodstain pattern on a horizontal surface will often have an elongated spine around the stain. The elongated spine results when blood under pressure impacts the surface. Movement and positioning of the victim as well as the surface will greatly affect the appearance of the pattern. Other factors that affect arterial bloodstain pattern appearance include location of the artery within the body, severity of the injury, additional injuries, and medical intervention. Because arterial damage often results in significant blood loss, high-volume blood flows can mask arterial bloodstain patterns.

Venous Hemorrhaging

In some natural death cases, the decedent's vein may rupture and release blood, creating a bloodstain pattern that appears arterial in nature. Transfer stains resulting from swiping motions or movement by the decedent before death may add to the confusing nature of the scene. What is actually a natural death from a ruptured vein may be viewed as a homicide. Closer inspection of the scene and bloodstain patterns should reveal a cause of death other than homicide. A struggle associated with a violent attack will not be observed at a natural death scene. Impact mechanism or cast-off bloodstain patterns are not present. Although the decedent may have touched the injury site and flung some of the blood in a cast-off motion, the totality of the scene will not be consistent with a violent attack. Additionally, a

Photo 11-33. Expirated blood from a natural death. Photograph by Todd Griffiths.

Photo 11-32. Venous hemorrhaging from cut wounds in suspect's hands. Suspect stabbed victim multiple times. Courtesy of National City, California, Police Department.

postmortem examination of the decedent should reveal a pre-existing medical condition that led to the hemorrhaging of the vein.

Expirated Bloodstain Patterns

An **expirated bloodstain pattern** is created when a victim coughs, sneezes, or expels blood from the mouth. Expirated bloodstain patterns may be associated with a homicide or natural death. The decedent may have blood in the mouth because of a disease or internal hemorrhaging and may cough up and deposit blood throughout

> **Expirated bloodstain pattern** Created when a victim coughs, sneezes, or expels blood from of the mouth. Expirated bloodstain patterns may be associated with a homicide or a natural death. The decedent may have blood in the mouth because of a disease or internal hemorrhaging and may expel and deposit blood throughout a scene. Conversely, a victim may sustain a stab wound that results in injury to a lung or some other violent injury may force blood through the mouth.

a scene. Conversely, a victim may sustain a stab wound that results in injury to a lung, or some other violent injury may force blood to the mouth. Blood throughout the scene may be indicative of survival time after the injury was inflicted. Regardless of underlying cause for the release of the blood, any resulting bloodstain pattern may be confused with an impact mechanism pattern caused by a violent assailant.

Expirated bloodstain patterns can be large, medium, small, or mist-like. The stains should not be confused with gunshot or other impact mechanism bloodstain patterns. The presence of air bubbles and mucus within the bloodstain pattern is indicative of expirated blood.

If the presence of expirated blood is the result of a natural phenomenon such as a disease, the scene may still appear as though a violent attack occurred. A large volume of blood as well as transfer patterns are often observed in conjunction with expirated blood. The color and odor of the blood may vary, however, because of disease. As with any other apparent natural death, the forensic technician should examine the entire scene for signs of a struggle, forced entry, and other crime-based indicators. Additionally, the postmortem examination results will clarify the cause and manner of death.

ALTERED BLOODSTAIN PATTERNS

Virtually any bloodstain pattern located at a crime scene may be classified as an **altered bloodstain pattern** if it changed due to environmental conditions, first responder activities, and other actions. As blood dries, oxygen is expelled from the red blood cells, resulting in a color change to the blood. When blood is exposed to direct sunlight, it darkens quickly. As a bloodstain ages, its color change progresses from red to reddish brown, green, dark brown, and black. The drying time for blood varies greatly, depending on volume of blood, temperature, humidity, air flow, and the target surface. Small stains may dry within minutes while high-volume stains may require long periods of time.

> **Altered bloodstain pattern** Any bloodstain pattern located at a crime scene that is altered due to environmental conditions, first responder activities, or other actions.

Clotted Blood

As blood clots, the liquid portion of blood (serum) and the platelets and fibrinogen separate. The serum separation phase may consume an hour or more, depending on blood volume, temperature, humidity, and the target surface. With normal, healthy individuals, the time between bloodshed and clotting is 3–15 minutes. However, diseases causing platelet deficiencies as well as anticoagulants (blood thinning medications) may increase clotting time. Additionally, clotting time may be extended if blood continues to flow as a victim continues to sustain injuries. With head injuries, cerebrospinal fluid may be released, which causes blood to clot faster.

Since blood clotting and serum separation surrounding the clotted blood are approximate time indicators, they should be photographed and documented at a crime scene. Actions may occur after the clotting process begins. A bloodstain pattern containing partially clotted blood is indicative of a time interval between the original bloodshed and the subsequent action that produced the bloodstain pattern. This evidence is crucial to the investigation because it may indicate the sequence of events at the scene.

Diluted Blood

Diluted (thinned) blood may result from environmental conditions, such as rain, snow, or other water source; bloodshed that occurred indoors in a bathtub full of water; or an attempt to clean blood from a surface or object. Diluted blood is usually light brown in appearance, with a darker coloration around the rim and a lighter coloration in the center of the stain.

Diluted blood on clothing may be the result of perspiration or urine mixed with the blood. Blood diluted with saliva can result from expiration. Head trauma may cause spinal fluid to dilute blood.

Diffused Blood

Blood diffusion (separation) is frequently observed when a large volume of bloodstains and saturates bedding and clothing. As blood is absorbed by the fabric, the outer edges of the stain appear lighter and less concentrated than the center of the stain. The diffusion action of the blood should not be confused with diluted blood (blood mixed with fluid).

Insect Activity

Insect activity in or on blood can distort bloodstain pattern appearance. Fly activity within a

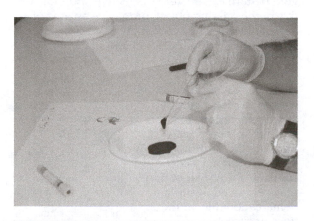

Photo 11-34. Clotting blood.

Photo 11-35. Diluted blood on a sink. Courtesy of National City, California, Police Department.

bloody crime scene can produce tiny stains, often referred to as **fly specks**, that may be misinterpreted as spatter stains. Flies consume blood within the scene and regurgitate the blood onto other surfaces. The fly's enzymes cause the blood to disintegrate. The fly returns to consume a portion of the regurgitated blood. The regurgitated blood may appear as a small bloodstain often 1 mm or less in diameter. The fly speck can be confused with a spatter stain involving an impact mechanism. The fly speck, however, will be inconsistent with actual bloodstains throughout the scene and will not converge with an overall impact bloodstain pattern. Cockroaches and similar insects crawl through blood and leave transfer stains as they transport the blood throughout the scene (James, Kish, & Sutton, 2005).

> **Fly specks** Fly (inspect) activity within a bloody crime scene can produce tiny stains that may be misinterpreted as spatter stains. Flies consume blood within the scene and regurgitate the blood onto other surfaces.

Sequenced Bloodstain Patterns

A **sequenced bloodstain pattern** is one of several overlapping bloodstains frequently located at crime scenes. A determination must be made regarding the sequence of the stain patterns. Motion transfer bloodstains (swipes and wipes) are often observed in sequenced bloodstain patterns. High-quality, sharp photographs make the task of determining sequence much easier.

> **Sequenced bloodstain pattern** Overlapping bloodstains frequently located at crime scenes. A determination must be made regarding the sequence of the stain patterns. Motion transfer bloodstains (swipes and wipes) are often observed in sequenced bloodstain patterns.

Photo 11-36. Sequenced impact and transfer bloodstain patterns.

Photo 11-37. Skeletonized bloodstains with wipe and transfer pattern.

Some bloodstains are deposited and begin to dry within a few minutes. Drying may cause the blood to flake, revealing an outline of the original pattern. Motion through the original, partially dried blood may occur as well, leaving the original outline plus the motion transfer (wipe) at the scene. The outline of the original stain is referred to as a **skeletonized bloodstain**.

> **Skeletonized bloodstain** The outline of an original bloodstain prior to drying or motion transfer.

Void Bloodstain Patterns

A **void bloodstain pattern (ghost)** occurs when an object containing a portion of the bloodstain is removed leaving an outline of the voided pattern behind. The outline lacks blood spatter within the area once occupied by the object. The void pattern can also be caused by the victim or perpetrator blocking the blood spatter from hitting a target surface. The void pattern can be very distinctive and indicative of the missing object, or may be an area of an apparently missing bloodstain. The void pattern is dependent upon the object and the amount of blood surrounding the object.

> **Void bloodstain pattern (ghost)** Occurs when an object containing a portion of the bloodstain is removed leaving an outline of the voided pattern behind. The outline lacks blood spatter within the area once occupied by the object.

An abrupt end to a blood spatter pattern is referred to as a **demarcation line**. It is indicative of an object blocking the continuation of the blood spatter. A door containing a partial pattern may be moved, leaving a demarcation line on the floor or carpet.

> **Demarcation line** An abrupt end to a blood spatter pattern that is indicative of an object blocking the continuation of the blood spatter. A door containing a partial pattern may be moved, leaving a demarcation line on the floor or carpet.

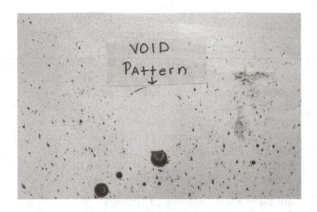

Photo 11-38. Circular void pattern.

DOCUMENTING AND RECONSTRUCTING BLOODSTAIN PATTERNS

After examining and categorizing bloodstain patterns within a crime scene, documentation and reconstruction of events take place. The BPE may not be able to formulate complete answers to questions associated with the dynamics of the scene without conducting laboratory experiments, reading postmortem examination and DNA reports, and thoroughly analyzing all aspects of the crime scene. However, the forensic technician or BPE (if trained in photography) should photograph and document all bloodstain patterns within the crime scene prior to reconstruction of impact mechanism patterns. This ensures a record for subsequent analyses by other BPEs.

Photographic Documentation

The following steps are recommended when photographing bloodstain patterns located within a crime scene:

1. Overall photographs are taken of the entire crime scene, including overall views of the bloodstain patterns within the scene. Use the appropriate camera settings based on the lighting conditions available.
2. If multiple bloodstain patterns cover a large surface area (e.g., wall, floor, ceiling), the area can be subdivided into zones or a grid. A ruler with an adhesive backing can serve as a measuring device as well as a divider to separate the zones or grids. Alternatively, thin art tape can be applied or straight lines may be drawn with the use of a level and marking pen.

Subdivide the affected area into two-foot squares (or other designated square size). Designate each square with a letter. If a bloodstain pattern type overlaps into two or more squares, use the same letter for each square but add a number. For example, if the first square contains a portion of an impact mechanism pattern, label the square A1. If the second square contains another portion of the same impact pattern, label the second square A2. If the pattern continues into a third square, label the third square A3. If the fourth square does not contain a portion of the impact pattern, but contains a different pattern type, the fourth square is labeled B1, and so on.

3. Take overall photographs of the entire surface area, followed by orientation photographs of each square within the surface area.
4. If an adhesive-backed measuring device (ruler) was not used to create the grid, measuring devices illustrating vertical and horizontal distances from the base and side of the affected area are set into place so the location of the square is observed in the photograph. The square is photographed a second time, with the ruler in place, illustrating the location of the square.
5. Take close-up photographs of each square with the measuring device in place. The face of the camera lens must be parallel to the bloodstain pattern. As with any close-up evidence photograph, wide-angle should not be used because it distorts the image. A normal lens (50 mm) or macro views should be used for all close-up photographs.

Close-Up Photography of Transfer Pattern

Non-motion transfer patterns such as bloody shoe prints and fingerprints are assigned an evidence number. Orientation photographs of the evidence in relationship to the rest of the crime scene (or grid) are taken. Close-up photographs with a scale in place are taken with the face of the camera lens parallel to the evidence, and the photo frame filled with the pattern. If the transfer evidence contains an identifying mark (e.g., a shoe print or fingerprint), a small portion of the blood is swabbed for DNA purposes. The print is enhanced with a blood-enhancing chemical and photographed a second time. (See Chapter 9 for a list of blood-enhancing chemicals.)

Motion transfer patterns (swipes and wipes) are assigned an evidence number and the overall pattern is photographed with a scale in place. With drag mark or extremely long motion transfer patterns, the forensic technician should place a measuring tape or an adhesive-backed ruler along the entire length of the pattern. An overall view is photographed with the measuring tape in place.

Next, the camera is inversely mounted on a quadripod (four-legged camera stand) or a tripod. The camera is positioned with the face of the lens parallel to the bloodstain or print. The photographer takes one-foot-section photographs of the entire pattern, overlapping each photograph by one inch. The process is very similar to tire mark photography: a lengthy impression (or print) is captured in one-foot increments.

Close-Up Photography of Cast-Off Patterns

Cast-off patterns vary in length but are usually elongated linear or arc-shaped patterns. Similar to lengthy motion transfer patterns and tire impressions, the entire pattern must be photographically captured in increments. An adhesive-backed ruler is placed along the entire

pattern. If the pattern is arc-shaped, the ruler may be cut into sections to curve with the pattern. An overall view with the ruler in place and orientation views of the pattern in relationship to the rest of the crime scene are photographed. The camera is mounted on a tripod with face of the camera lens parallel to the pattern. With the ruler in place, overlapping one-foot increments of the pattern are photographed until the entire cast-off pattern is photographed. The photographs should overlap by one inch to ensure that every portion of the pattern is photographed.

Close-Up Photography of Impact Mechanism Patterns

A BPE may use basic physics and mathematics to determine the area of origin of impact mechanism patterns. Due to the nature of the calculation, close-up photography must be precise so BPEs can analyze and reconstruct the pattern from the photographs. Additionally, many BPEs process digital photographs of impact patterns

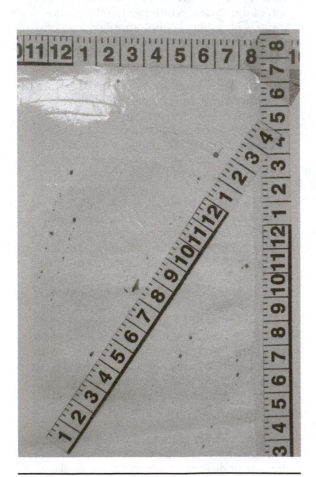

Photo 11-39. Cast-off pattern photographed in four-inch segments.

Photo 11-40. Cast-off pattern photographed in four-inch segments.

Photo 11-41. Cast-off pattern photographed in four-inch segments.

Photo 11-42. Cast-off pattern photographed in four-inch segments.

Photo 11-43. Cast-off pattern photographed in four-inch segments.

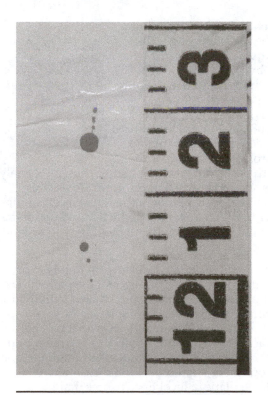

Photo 11-44. Cast-off pattern photographed in four-inch segments.

using BPA software. If close-up images are photographed in RAW format only, the software processing time is slowed considerably. However, some agencies require forensic technicians to digitally photograph evidence in the RAW format. If the RAW format is required, it is recommended that the photographer set the digital camera to RAW plus JPEG. The camera saves the image twice: as a RAW image and as a JPEG image. The photographer should review the camera's operating manual to learn how to use this setting. The RAW images are used by the crime laboratory and the JPEG images are used for bloodstain pattern software program processing. They are the same images, but JPEG has lower resolution and does not consume as much memory in the bloodstain pattern software.

If a bloodstain pattern is located on a wall, adhesive-backed rulers are strung from the floor and an adjacent wall across the entire impact pattern. The rulers are placed from at least two directions (up/down and right/left) across the pattern. An overall photograph of the impact pattern is obtained, and orientation photos of the surrounding area are taken. Either of two techniques (roadmapping or quadrant/grid) may be utilized to take close-up photographs of an impact mechanism bloodstain pattern.

Roadmapping Technique

The **roadmapping technique** was developed by Toby Wolson, a criminalist with the Metro-Dade Police Department in Miami, Florida (Bevel & Gardner, 2008). The technique utilizes scales strategically placed throughout the impact pattern based on the blood spatter chosen for analysis and reconstruction purposes. To use this technique, the photographer must receive training in BPA to determine which individual stains should be selected. The photography technique proceeds as follows:

> **Roadmapping technique** Utilizes measurements placed strategically throughout the impact pattern; based on the blood spatter chosen for analysis and reconstruction purposes.

1. Small scales are labeled with numbers or letters and placed throughout the pattern. The scales are strategically placed next to individual blood spatters selected for analysis.
2. If the bloodstain pattern is on a vertical surface such as a wall, a level line is drawn under the scale and blood spatter. Although the photographer should position the camera on a level plane, a level line ensures that the analyst is aware of the proper orientation of each photograph.

3. Orientation photos of the pattern are taken, including several photos of the scales in the same photograph. Scales are overlapped in subsequent photographs so an orientation to the overall pattern can be created.
4. Close-up photographs of the scale and selected bloodstains are taken. The camera must be on a quadripod or tripod and level, with the face of the camera lens parallel to the bloodstain pattern. Each close-up photograph is taken from the same distance as all previous and subsequent close-up photographs. The process ensures that proper analysis and reconstruction can be conducted from the photographs at a later time. To ensure that each photograph is taken at the same distance from the pattern, the camera's focal length must not change. If the bloodstain pattern is on a vertical surface, such as a wall, the photographer may either hold the camera quadripod and press its legs against the surface of the wall or place a tripod on the floor, ensuring that the tripod legs are the same distance away from the wall with each photograph taken.
5. Step 4 is repeated until all scales and selected blood spatter have been photographed.

Quadrant (Grid) Technique

The **quadrant (grid) technique** is a method for ensuring that all areas of an impact bloodstain pattern are photographed. The photographer does not require specialized training in BPA to use this technique. However, some view this technique as intrusive to the pattern. The photography technique proceeds as follows:

> **Quadrant (grid) technique** A method for ensuring that all areas of an impact bloodstain pattern are photographed.

1. A quadrant or grid of 6"×6" (or other determined size) squares is created throughout the impact pattern. The quadrant or grid can be created by using a level and string, thin tape, or straight lines drawn with a marking pen.
2. Scales are placed in each square. The vertical columns of the scale are labeled with letters. The horizontal rows receive numerical designations; the first column's markings are labeled A1, A2, A3, etc. The second column's markings are labeled B1, B2, B3, and so on.
3. After the label markings are placed within the grid, overall and orientation photos are taken of the entire pattern.
4. Each square (grid) is photographed individually. The camera must be level with the face

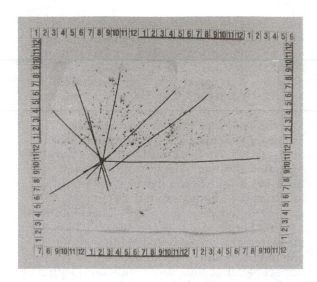

Photo 11-45. Roadmapping technique.

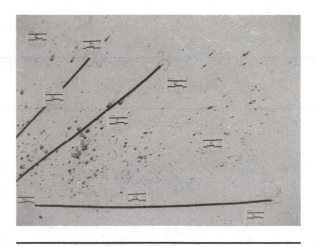

Photo 11-48. Roadmapping technique.

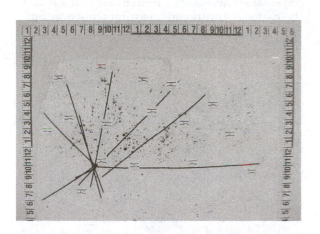

Photo 11-46. Roadmapping technique.

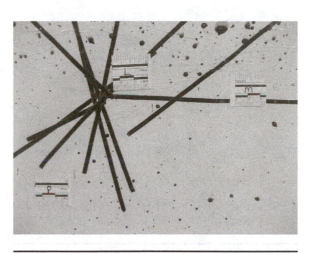

Photo 11-49. Roadmapping technique.

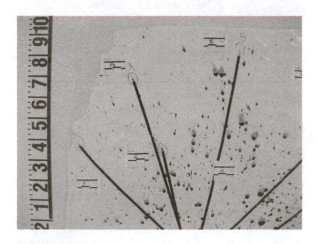

Photo 11-47. Roadmapping technique.

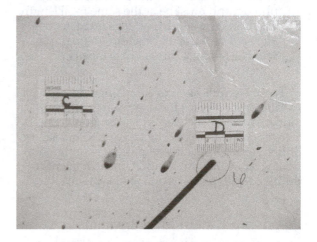

Photo 11-50. Roadmapping technique.

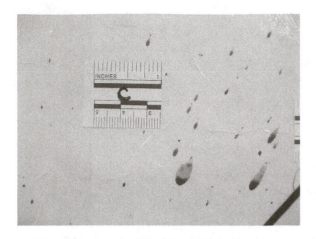

Photo 11-51. Roadmapping technique.

Photo 11-52. Roadmapping technique.

of the lens parallel to the pattern, and each photograph must be at the same focal length. The tripod or quadripod legs must not be adjusted because all close-up photographs must be taken at the same distance from the pattern.

There are pros and cons to using the roadmapping versus the quadrant (grid) technique. The method selected is based on the preferences and training of the forensic technician or BPE involved in the investigation. In addition to photographic documentation, measurements of the bloodstain patterns and stains are taken.

Bloodstain Pattern Measurements

As part of (or in addition to) the crime scene diagram, the forensic technician will obtain detailed measurements of the bloodstain patterns within a crime scene. A pattern's overall width, length, and circumference (if applicable) should be measured and recorded. The exact location of the pattern within the scene is recorded through triangulation or rectangular coordinate techniques. The crime scene diagram should include the pattern measurement's start and end points.

For transfer patterns, the overall dimensions are recorded. For drag mark and motion transfer stains, the overall length and width is recorded. For cast-off patterns, the overall length and width is recorded, along with the size of predominate (majority) stains within the pattern. For arterial patterns, the overall pattern measurements are recorded along with the circumference of any predominate stains. For impact patterns, the overall width and length of the pattern is recorded, along with the size of any predominate individual stains as well as the smallest and largest individual stains within the pattern. Additional measurements may be taken at the discretion of the forensic technician or BPE.

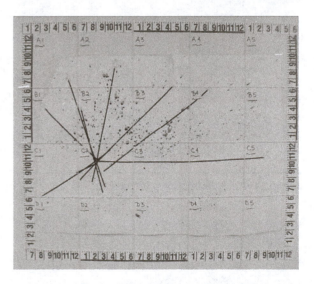

Photo 11-53. Grid technique.

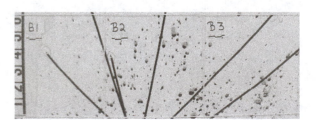

Photo 11-54. Grid technique.

Photo 11-55. Grid technique.

Photo 11-56. Grid technique.

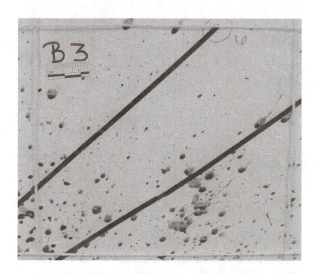

Photo 11-57. Grid technique.

Impact Pattern Reconstruction

As discussed previously, an impact mechanism pattern is the only pattern for which basic physics and mathematics are used to determine the *area of origin* of the impact. The area of origin is three-dimensional. Prior to determining the three-dimensional area of origin, the two-dimensional origin, known as the *area of convergence* is determined. Analysis and reconstruction of the impact pattern proceeds as follows:

1. The area of convergence is determined by examining several (8–10) individual blood spatters that have a directionality that radiates from the overall pattern. The individual spatter stains selected are based on the following:
   - Size and shape of the spatter—the spatter's length and width must be discernable and measurable with the use of magnification.
   - Spatter location—the spatter should be located within the pattern area.
   - Directionality—the spatter should not have a downward direction as gravity will have added to the parabola (rise and fall) of the spatter trajectory. The spatter should have an upward direction or a direction to the right or left of the overall pattern.
   - Singularity of spatter—ensure that the spatter is a single spatter stain, and not several overlapping spatters.
2. A letter or number marker (or other indicator) is placed near each selected blood spatter

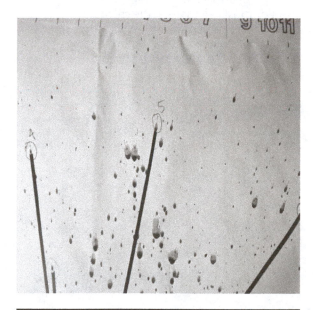

Photo 11-58. Drops marked "4" and "5" in pattern are circled for selection.

to avoid confusion. Small self-adhesive tabs are useful markers. After identifying individual spatter stains, a line is constructed with use of string or non-adhesive tape. The line starts at the spatter termination point and travels in the opposite direction of the individual spatter. The process is repeated for each identified and selected spatter pattern until the lines intersect (converge). The intersection represents the convergence or two-dimensional origin of the pattern stains. The lines must continue past rather than stop at the intersection to observe the overall parabola of the spatter's trajectory.

3. Examine the point at which the lines converge (the area of convergence) and locate the point of intersection. Mark the center point. The mark is the *area of convergence* for the pattern and is used later for reconstruction measurement purposes.

4. Using a **loupe** (a magnifier with a built-in metric scale), measure and record the length and width of each selected blood spatter. The width is the widest part of the spatter stain. The length is the base of the stain at the beginning of the tail or the irregular part of the stain. The tail is not counted as part of the length.

> **Loupe**   A magnifier with a built-in metric scale used to measure and record the length and width of each selected blood spatter.

5. Measure and record the width and length of each spatter stain selected.

6. The following mathematical formula is used:

$$\text{Impact angel} = (W/L)\ \text{sine}^{-1}$$

For most calculators, the calculation sequence proceeds as follows:

   a. Enter the width of the stain.

   b. Press the divide ($\div$) button.

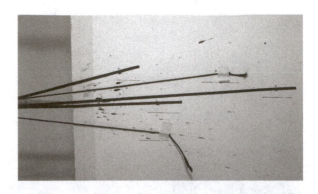

Photo 11-60. Tape or string is used to display two-dimensional convergence of bloodstains.

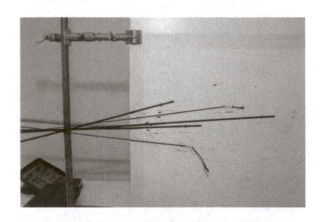

Photo 11-61. Tape or string is used to display two-dimensional convergence of bloodstains.

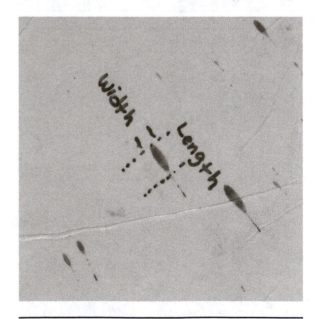

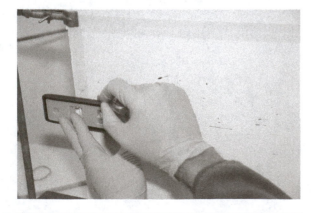

Photo 11-59. Level lines are created under individual stains.

Photo 11-62. Width and Length measurement of blood drop.

c. Enter the length of the stain.

d. Press the equal (=) button.

e. Press the *Inv* (inverse) or *2nd* button.

f. Press the Sin (sine) button.

The calculator should respond with a number that is the *impact angle* for the spatter stain pattern calculated. If a scientific calculator is not available, the analyst may stop after step "d" and use a trigonometric sine function table to determine the impact angle (see Appendix B).

7. The three-dimensional area of origin is determined. The area of origin is the location of the impact. Computer software programs are available for determining the area of origin. The tangent or the stringing method may be used as well.

Tangent Method

1. Measure and record the distance from the base of each selected spatter stain to the area of convergence (the center mark).

2. Use the tangent formula (TAN I = H/D) for each individual spatter stain.
   Tangent the Impact angle = Height/Distance of the stain to the area of convergence
   Height is the unknown measurement that, once calculated, identifies the area of origin.
   Alternative method:
   TAN of impact angle × (distance to area of convergence) = height of origin

3. For most calculators, the command execution sequence is as follows:
   a. Enter the impact angle (previously obtained) for the stain.
   b. Press the TAN (tangent) button.
   c. Press the multiplication (×) button.
   d. Enter the distance to the area of convergence (previously obtained) for the stain.
   e. Press the equal (=) sign.
   f. Repeat the process for each individual spatter stain.
   g. Obtain the average (mean) of all of the selected stains. The average is obtained by adding all of the height measurements and dividing the sum by the number of stains calculated.

Stringing Method

In lieu of trigonometry, a stringing method may be used to calculate the area of impact. Although the stringing method provides a visual of the area of origin, the method can be quite cumbersome and difficult to accomplish at a crime scene.

1. A protractor and string are required. In lieu of string, cord that will not sag is preferred.

2. The protractor should have a zero baseline. In other words, the extra measuring increment at the base of the protractor should be removed if necessary so the zero may be placed on the same surface as the bloodstain.

3. The protractor's zero base line is aligned with the convergence line and base of the individual spatter stain.

4. The string is placed at the base of the blood spatter and aligned with the protractor at the impact angle for the spatter stain.

5. The opposite end of the string is connected to a pole set up at the area of convergence. Alternatively, the string can be extended across the room and connected to another surface.

6. Repeat Steps 1–5 with all selected spatter stains. The area where all the strings intersect (converge) in the three-dimensional plane is the area of origin.

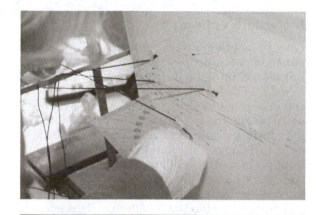

Photo 11-63. Demo use of protractor.

Photo 11-64. Area of origin string in same place.

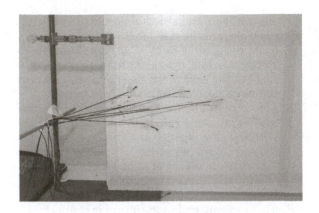

Photo 11-65. Area of origin string in same place.

7. Measure and record the distance from the wall and the floor to the intersection of the strings. The forensic technician should photograph the intersection with a measuring device in place. Frontal and side views of the strings are photographed as well.

Bloodstain Collection

After photography, measurements, and reconstruction of the bloodstain patterns are complete, samples of the blood from the patterns are collected for DNA analysis and profiling. One should never assume that blood within a crime scene is from the victim only. The perpetrator may sustain injuries and bleed within the scene as well. If the victim struggled with the assailant, multiple bloodstain patterns from the victim as well as the perpetrator may be present. Therefore, the forensic technician should collect blood samples from each bloodstain pattern at the scene.

BPA on Clothing

Bloodstain patterns can appear on victim or suspect clothing. If possible, the forensic technician should photograph the stain patterns while the victim or suspect is wearing the clothes. Overall, medium, and close-up photographs are taken. Detailed photographs of the clothing are taken after the clothing is removed. Forensic personnel should exercise caution when removing the clothing to ensure that bloodstain patterns do not overlap or contact other areas of clothing. Bloodstained clothing should not be folded prior to examination. If it must be folded, the bloodstains should first be allowed to dry. Clea wrapping paper should be placed on both sides of the garment before it is folded to avoid fabric-to-fabric contact.

When photographing bloodstained clothing in a laboratory setting, the forensic technician should place a measuring device next to the clothing and take overall photographs of the clothing. The roadmapping technique is beneficial when photographing bloodstains on clothing because the measuring scales may be strategically placed on the clothing. Medium and close-up views of the scales and bloodstain patterns are taken, with the face of the camera lens parallel to the patterns. If the color or pattern of the clothing obscures or prohibits viewing of the details of the bloodstain pattern, an alternate light source can be used to illustrate the bloodstained area.

The forensic technician or BPE should also sketch and record measurements of the clothing and any bloodstain patterns on the clothing. For trousers, measurements may be taken from the inseam and bottom of the trouser leg to the bloodstain pattern. The entire bloodstain pattern and individual stains are measured as well.

Only BPEs with advanced training in BPA on clothing should attempt to interpret stain patterns on fabrics. Transfer stains have been erroneously interpreted as impact mechanism patterns. To view individual blood spatter in greater detail, a stereo binocular microscope can be used to observe the spatter within the weave of the fabric. If possible, fabric of a similar weave should be obtained for control testing. Experiments can be conducted on the control fabric to determine if a suspected pattern is an impact mechanism, transfer, or another type of bloodstain pattern (James, Kish, & Sutton, 2005).

BPA on clothing should precede DNA analysis and profiling because portions of the bloodstained clothing may be cut for DNA testing. Some DNA experts are also trained in BPA and crime scene reconstruction because the two areas of forensic science are interrelated.

Photo 11-66. Impact bloodstain patterns on various dry fabrics.

Photo 11-67. Impact bloodstain patterns on various dry fabrics.

Photo 11-68. Impact bloodstain patterns on various dry fabrics.

Photo 11-69. Impact bloodstain patterns on various dry fabrics.

Photo 11-70. Impact bloodstain patterns on various dry fabrics.

Photo 11-71. Impact bloodstain patterns on various dry fabrics.

Photo 11-72. Impact bloodstain patterns on various dry fabrics.

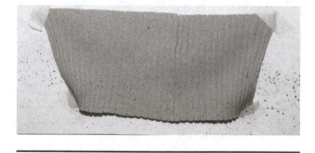

Photo 11-73. Impact bloodstain patterns on various dry fabrics.

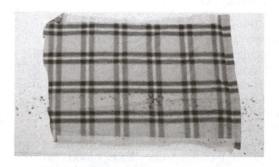

Photo 11-74. Impact bloodstain patterns on various fabrics previously wet.

Photo 11-75. Impact bloodstain patterns on various fabrics previously wet.

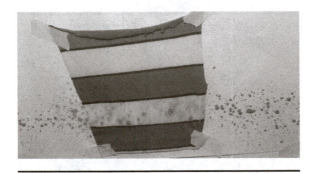

Photo 11-76. Impact bloodstain patterns on various fabrics previously wet.

Photo 11-77. Impact bloodstain patterns on various fabrics previously wet.

SUMMARY

A BPE may have a diverse background ranging from experience as a sworn peace officer or a forensic technician to formal education in the physical sciences or medicine. However, all BPEs must receive specialized training and continuing education as well as crime scene experience and a mentorship, working with a seasoned expert, to be successful in the field of BPA.

When analyzing bloodstain patterns, a basic knowledge of the properties of blood and how blood responds to movement is critical. The knowledge will aid the BPE in classifying the relevant bloodstain patterns. After classification

is determined, the BPE or forensic technician will properly photograph, measure, and record the pattern. Impact mechanism patterns may be reconstructed to determine the area of origin (location of the impact). Finally, blood samples should be collected from each bloodstain pattern located at the crime scene.

Proper photography, measurement, and collection of bloodstain patterns ensure that the criminal investigation may proceed to an appropriate conclusion. Following established procedure also ensures that subsequent analysis of bloodstain evidence can be conducted properly.

KEY TERMS

Define, describe, or explain the importance of each of the following:

altered bloodstain pattern	expirated bloodstain pattern	roadmapping technique
arterial bloodstain pattern	flow pattern	satellite spatter
backspatter pattern	fly specks	secondary mechanism spatter
blood swipe	impact mechanism bloodstain	sequenced bloodstain pattern
blood wipe	pattern	skeletonized bloodstain
bloodstain pattern analysis	large-volume pattern	spatter bloodstain pattern
(BPA)	loupe	transfer bloodstain pattern
bloodstain pattern expert (BPE)	passive bloodstain pattern	viscosity
cast-off bloodstain pattern	projection mechanism blood-	void bloodstain pattern (ghost)
cessation cast-off pattern	stain pattern	
demarcation line	quadrant (grid) technique	

DISCUSSION AND REVIEW QUESTIONS

1. Why are the low-, medium-, and high-velocity classifications of impact blood patterns rarely used today?
2. Why are 90-degree angle bloodstains relevant to crime scenes?
3. How is directionality of a bloodstain determined?
4. Explain how satellite spatter can be misinterpreted as an impact mechanism pattern.

5. Explain the difference between blood swipes and blood wipes.
6. How can expirated blood be identified?
7. What is a skeletonized bloodstain?
8. How is a cast-off pattern photographed? Impact pattern?
9. Utilize the trigonometry technique to reconstruct an impact mechanism bloodstain pattern.

CASE STUDY—Bloodstains Point to Killer

Molly Wright, aged 73, was bludgeoned to death in her home on September 27, 2006. Soon thereafter, Ms. Wright's son-in-law and business partner, David Hill, was charged with her murder. Hill claimed that he discovered Wright on her kitchen floor and that he attempted to revive her.

At Hill's trial, BPE Samantha Warna testified that evidence of blood spatter was located on the shoes, jeans, and denim jacket that Hill was wearing at the time Hill stated he found Ms. Wright. Further, Warna testified that the distribution and condition of Wright's blood on Hill's clothing was consistent with repeated blows with a heavy object. On the basis of her BPA, Warna stated that the blood spatter could not be accounted for with David Hill's version of events. Hill was convicted.

1. How important was BPE Warna's testimony?
2. What types of blood evidence may be located on an assailant who bludgeons someone to death?

LAB EXERCISE

Bloodstain pattern analysis

Equipment and supplies required per team of four to six students:

- one 35-mm camera (film or digital)
- one roll 24 exposure film (if film camera)

- twelve ounces animal blood (may be ordered from forensic supply company or pig's blood may be obtained from a local butcher shop for BPA experiments)
- one laboratory coat, protective gloves, and safety goggles (one pair per student)

- one disposable blood container (one container per team of students)
- one disposable pipette (one per team of students)
- nine 12″ square white cards (targets)
- three 11″ × 17″ or larger white poster boards (non-glossy) (per team of students)
- one disposable shoe, wig, knife, and other items to create transfer patterns
- one rubber mallet
- one sponge
- one paper plate
- one large plastic sheet (to protect any walls, floor or ceiling)
- one 24″ string or cord
- one graphic art tape
- one protractor
- one scientific calculator
- one loupe
- one marking pen, paper, and pen

The laboratory area (floor, wall, and ceiling) should be protected with plastic sheeting.

Exercise #1—Blood Dripped at Various Angles

1. Students work in teams of four to six, wear gloves, and draw a pre-determined amount of blood (or blood substitute) into a pipette. The amount is determined by the instructor based on the amount of blood available.
2. Place one of the 12″ square white cards flat on the floor.
3. Hold the pipette one foot above the 12″ square white card and release the blood onto the card.
4. Using a protractor to determine the angle, hold a second 12″ white card at an angle of 10 degrees to the floor. Repeat Steps 1–3, using the same amount of blood with the same distance (one foot), and release the blood.
5. On new 12″ white cards, repeat Steps 1–3 at 20, 30, 40, 50, 60, 70, and 80 degree angles to the surface.
6. Analyze the blood drop spatters after they dry. Practice measuring the width and length of each spatter and calculate the impact angle.

Exercise #2—Blood Dripping into Blood

1. Wearing protective gloves, students work in teams. Draw a pre-determined amount of blood into a pipette.

2. Place a piece of white poster board flat on the floor.
3. Using the pipette, release a drop of blood onto the poster board.
4. Using the pipette, release another drop of blood directly on top of the original drop.
5. Continue to release drops of blood, one on top of the other, until satellite spatter is visible on the perimeter of the pool of blood drops.
6. Record and submit notes on your observations.

Exercise #3—Transfer Pattern Creation

1. Wearing laboratory coats and protective gloves, students work in teams.
2. Use a disposable shoe, wig, knife, or other object to create non-motion and motion (swipe and wipe) transfer patterns on poster board.
3. Record and submit notes on your observations.

Exercise #4—Impact Mechanism Pattern Creation

1. Wearing laboratory coats and protective gloves, students work in teams.
2. Place a designated amount of blood on a sponge or paper plate (use the plate if the sponge absorbs too much of the blood).
3. Tape a poster board to a wall or surface (designated target).
4. Place or hold the blood-soaked sponge (or paper plate) near the poster board.
5. Strike the blood-soaked sponge (or paper plate) with a rubber mallet, creating an impact pattern on the poster board.
6. Allow the blood on the poster board to dry.
7. Analyze the impact pattern.

Exercise #5—Impact Pattern Photography and Reconstruction

1. Students work in teams
2. Teams exchange poster boards that contain impact patterns.
3. Use the techniques discussed in this chapter to photograph and reconstruct the impact pattern. Use both tangent and stringing techniques for reconstruction.

WEB RESOURCES

International Association of Bloodstain Pattern Analysts: www.iabpa.org

Scientific Working Group on Bloodstain Pattern Analysis: www.swgstain.org

International Association for Identification: www.theiai.org

American Academy of Forensic Sciences: www.aafs.org

American Board of Criminalistics: www.criminalistics.com

Association for Crime Scene Reconstruction: www.acsr.org

The Forensic Science Society: www.forensic-science-society.org.uk

Canadian Society of Forensic Science: www.csfs.ca

Midwestern Association of Forensic Scientists: www.mafs.net

Northeastern Association of Forensic Scientists: www.neafs.org

Northwest Association of Forensic Scientists: www.nwafs.org

Southern Association of Forensic Scientists: www.southernforensic.org

Southwestern Association of Forensic Scientists: www.swafs.org

The President's DNA Initiative: www.dna.gov

12

Controlled Substance Recognition

LEARNING OUTCOMES

After completing this chapter, the reader should be able to:

- describe CSA drug schedules and classifications,
- describe the paraphernalia used with various types of drugs,
- articulate the hazards encountered at a clandestine methamphetamine laboratory,
- describe evidence that is collected at a drug-related crime scene,
- explain the dangers of poly-drug use,
- demonstrate the steps to conducting surveillance photography.

INTRODUCTION

Many crimes of violence are associated with illicit drug activity. Crimes such as robbery, assault, and murder may result from drug trafficking, while other equally violent crimes are committed by those under the influence of controlled substances. Due to the connection between violent crime and illegal drugs, forensic technicians must be knowledgeable in the subject areas of drug identification and paraphernalia, indications of drug use at a crime scene, and personnel safety at drug production sites.

Forensic technicians and investigators should also be aware of street terminology (*slang*) as it relates to the illicit drug culture. The types of drugs produced and used as well as *slang* vary throughout the United States. Additionally, forensic technicians and investigators must stay current with respect to drugs introduced to the illicit drug market. Controlled substances may be grown, mixed or manufactured in clandestine laboratories, or synthesized from legal drugs.

Knowledge of controlled substances and their trafficking is one thing, proving the crime is another. Surveillance photography is an important tool for gathering information and providing evidence through a narcotics investigation. This chapter will provide information on the techniques and recommended camera settings for capturing surveillance images. For the sake of expediency, controlled substances addressed in this chapter are referred to simply as *drugs*.

DRUG SCHEDULES AND CLASSIFICATIONS

All controlled substances can be abused. Drugs alter a person's mood and feelings, relieve pain and anxiety, or provide a sense of euphoria. The degree to which a person's body, emotions, or mind is altered is correlated with the amount of abuse. The initial stage of drug abuse is commonly referred to as the honeymoon stage, when feelings of euphoria are experienced without the effects of chemical dependence. Eventually, however, excessive drug use results in physical and psychological dependence upon the drug abused. While physical dependence may be overcome after a period of abstinence, psychological dependence can linger for a lifetime.

The **Controlled Substance Act (CSA) of 1970** categorizes each drug

Controlled Substance Act (CSA) of 1970 Legislation that categorizes each drug into one of five schedules based on the substance's medical use, potential for abuse, and dependence liability.

into one of five schedules based on the substance's medical use, potential for abuse, and safety or dependence liability. The five schedules, as well as their drug descriptions and examples, are presented here.

Schedule I

- high potential for abuse,
- no accepted medical use in the United States,
- no medical safety regulations,
- examples: heroin, lysergic acid diethylamide (LSD), marijuana, gamma hydroxybutyric acid (GHB), Ecstasy, methaqualone.

Schedule II

- high potential for abuse,
- accepted medical use in the United States,
- abuse of drug may lead to severe psychological or physical dependence,
- examples: morphine, phencyclidine (PCP), cocaine, methadone, methamphetamine.

Schedule III

- less potential for abuse compared to drugs in Schedules I and II,
- accepted medical use in the United States,
- abuse may lead to moderate or low physical dependence or high psychological dependence,
- examples: anabolic steroids, codeine, and hydrocodone with aspirin or Tylenol®; some barbiturates.

Schedule IV

- low potential for abuse compared to drugs in Schedule III,
- currently accepted medical use in the United States,
- abuse may lead to limited physical or psychological dependence compared to drugs in Schedule III,
- examples: Rohypnol, Darvon, Talwin, Equanil, Valium, Xanax.

Schedule V

- low potential for abuse compared to drugs in Schedule IV,
- currently accepted medical use in the United States,
- abuse may lead to limited physical or psychological dependence compared to drugs in Schedule IV,
- examples: cough medicines with codeine.

The CSA regulates five classifications of drugs based on distinguishing properties and effects of the drugs:

- narcotics
- stimulants
- depressants
- hallucinogens
- anabolic steroids

NARCOTICS

Except for those produced through synthetic (artificial) or semi-synthetic means, narcotics such as opium, morphine, codeine, and thebaine are derived from the poppy plant. Semi-synthetic narcotics, derived from opium and artificial means, include heroin, hydromorphone, oxycodone, and hydrocodone. Synthetic narcotics, those produced within a laboratory, include meperidine, dextropropoxyphene, fentanyl, pentazocine, and butorphanol.

A **narcotic** dulls human senses, relieves pain, and reduces tension, anxiety, and aggression. If used for medical purposes, narcotics may induce anesthesia. The effect of the drug depends on the dose, how it is administered, and the human subject's tolerance level. The side effects of narcotic use include but are not limited to drowsiness, inability to concentrate, feelings of indifference, flushing of the face and neck, constipation, nausea, vomiting, and respiratory depression. Major medical problems that can occur include abscesses on the skin or in the lung or brain, inflammation of the lining of the heart (endocarditis), or death.

Narcotic A narcotic dulls human senses, relieves pain, and reduces tension, anxiety, and aggression.

Narcotics are administered by sniffing, smoking, or injection with needles. Drug abusers who inject narcotics with previously used needles subject themselves to diseases such as hepatitis and HIV/AIDS.

There are two major types of narcotics abusers. One type includes those who first used the drug in the context of medical treatment and continued their use through fraudulent prescriptions. The second type includes those who first used the narcotic recreationally or through drug experimentation.

Physiological dependence on the drug increases with chronic use. Physical withdrawal symptoms may occur as the drug dissipates from the body. Withdrawal symptoms include a runny nose, yawning, perspiration, watering eyes, restlessness, irritability, loss of appetite, nausea, tremors, drug craving, and severe depression. If the drug is not ingested, withdrawal symptoms also involve elevation in heart rate and blood pressure, chills, excessive sweating, pain in the bones, muscles, and back, and muscle spasms.

An alternate narcotic, such as methadone, may be administered to reduce the symptoms. Methadone is a drug commonly used to treat heroin addiction. It assists the user in detoxifying while blocking the side effects of heroin withdrawal. However, methadone is addictive and subject to abuse as well.

Psychological dependence on narcotics may affect the addict after the physical dependence has subsided. The addict may think about the drug and feel overwhelmed with everyday life. The addict may speak about the drug and its effects. If an environmental or emotional situation is challenging, the addict may relapse into drug use.

Heroin

Heroin is a semi-synthetic narcotic derived from morphine. Heroin was used as a pain remedy in the late 1800s. Today, it has no recognized medical use in the United States, but it is a common illicit street drug with remarkable addictive qualities. Some chemicals used to create heroin include acetic anhydride, sodium carbonate, activated charcoal, ethyl alcohol, acetone, and ether.

> **Heroin**   A semi-synthetic narcotic derived from morphine.

A bag (small amount of heroin for personal use) contains approximately 30–50 mg of powder, of which less than 10 percent is heroin. The remaining 90 percent of powder contains **cutting agents** (additives designed to add weight to the amount of heroin sold). Cutting agents include sugar, starch, acetaminophen, procaine, benzocaine, quinine, or other types of additives. A drug that contains cutting agents to create volume is referred to in street slang as *stepped on* (U.S. Office of National Drug Control Policy, 2003; U.S. Department of Justice. Drug Enforcement Administration, 2005).

> **Cutting agents**   Additives designed to add weight and dilute a drug. Cutting agents include sugar, starch, acetaminophen, procaine, benzocaine, quinine, or other types of additives.

Heroin addicts on the East Coast usually prefer a white or brown powder form of heroin. The white-colored heroin is commonly referred to on the street as China White or *smack*. In the Southwest region of the United States, the most common form of heroin is a tar-like substance commonly referred to as Mexican black tar heroin. West Coast users refer to heroin as *chiva*.

Black tar heroin is typically sold in one-tenth of a gram per use portions and packaged in plastic wrap or wax paper. Heroin users refer to these plastic or wax paper heroin bindles as *tadpoles* because of the tadpole appearance of the packaging. The heroin drug dealer may place the tadpoles inside a balloon. The balloon is folded tightly and tied. Heroin dealers prefer balloon packaging because balloons can be transported inside the mouth and quickly ingested if the carrier encounters law enforcement officers. The balloons proceed through the carrier's digestive system without breaking. After the police encounter, the carrier can either self-induce vomiting or defecate to retrieve the balloons and sell or deliver the drugs.

Prior to the late 1990s, most addicts administered heroin through injection. Addicts who inject drugs are commonly referred to as *hypes*. Since the late 1990s a trend toward snorting or smoking heroin has been observed. The fear of HIV/AIDS and hepatitis as well as the social stigma attached to syringe use are the primary reasons for the decline in popularity of injections. Many new users ignorantly believe that snorting or smoking heroin reduces the risk of addiction. Some areas of the world still experience a major problem with injection of heroin. To minimize the spread of HIV/AIDS and hepatitis, needle exchange programs have been implemented in many of these countries (Publishers Group, 2006).

Heroin Paraphernalia

A *hype kit* (drug paraphernalia) typically used by heroin addicts includes a syringe or set of syringes, tourniquet or belt, water dropper, spoon, lighter or matches, and heroin, possibly in a tied balloon. If the heroin is smoked, a pipe is part of the paraphernalia kit.

STIMULANTS

Stimulants produce exhilaration, reduce fatigue from both mental and physical activity, increase alertness, and decrease appetite. Stimulants such as nicotine contained in tobacco products, caffeine in chocolate and many drinks, as well as non-prescription medicines, are commonly used in American society. Many other stimulants are regulated by the CSA and are available only by prescription for legitimate medical use to treat various conditions such as attention deficit disorder, narcolepsy, and obesity.

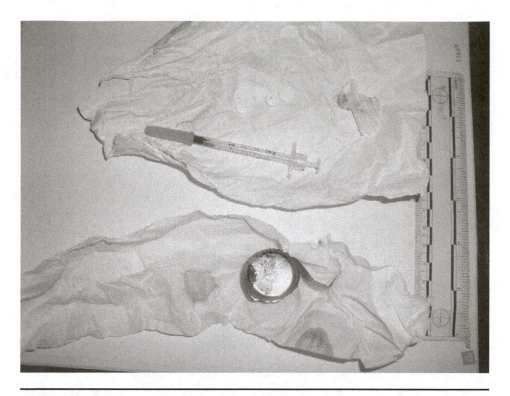

Photo 12-1. Hype kit. Photographs by Officer Jared Madsen. Courtesy of National City, California, Police Department.

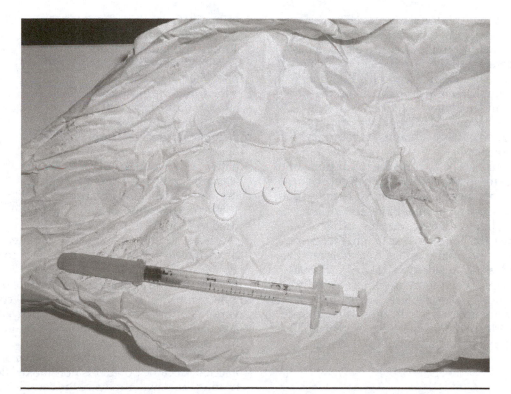

Photo 12-2. Hype kit. Photographs by Officer Jared Madsen. Courtesy of National City, California, Police Department.

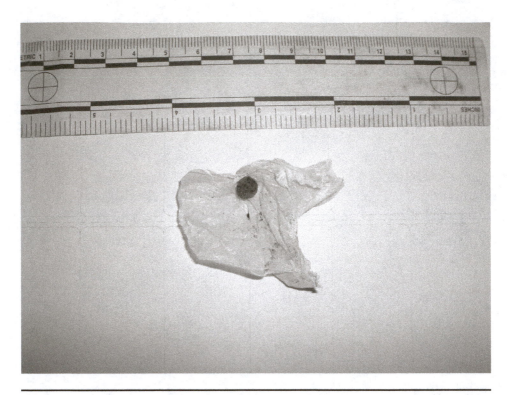

Photo 12-3. Heroin tadpole. Photograph by Officer Jared Madsen. Courtesy of National City, California, Police Department.

Dependence on stimulants develops as the user increases dosage to maintain the same level of benefit from the drug. To increase the drug's potency, the composition of the drug is enhanced in clandestine (concealed) illegal laboratories. Later, the drug is sold on the street. Stimulants may be snorted, smoked, injected, or taken orally. Binge use (sporadic consumption of large amounts) is common among abusers.

Frequent users may continue to consume until the drug supply is depleted or physical exhaustion or mental psychosis develops. The physical side effects of long-term or binge use include dizziness, body tremors, seizures, extreme headaches, flushed skin, chest pain, excessive perspiration, vomiting, and abdominal cramping. An overdose can result in a stroke or cardiovascular collapse. Long-term use can also produce negative psychological effects leading to thoughts or behaviors associated with aggression, suicide or homicide, paranoia, auditory or visual hallucinations, panic, and anxiety.

Cocaine

Cocaine is derived from the coca plant grown in the Andean mountains in South America,

primarily Colombia. The coca leaves are mixed with gasoline or kerosene to form an alkali that is mashed in a pit. Other chemicals are added, and the mash is filtered, producing a paste. The mash paste is dried, yielding a powdered form of cocaine. South American natives chew the coca plant leaves or brew them into a tea to relieve fatigue. In the 1880s, pure cocaine was used as a local anesthetic for eye, nose, and throat surgery. Subsequently, safer drugs have been developed to replace cocaine as an anesthetic.

Cocaine Derived from the coca plant grown in the Andean mountains in South America, primarily Colombia. The coca leaves are mixed with gasoline or kerosene to form an alkali that is mashed in a pit. Other chemicals are added and the mash is filtered, producing a paste. The mash paste is dried, yielding a powdered form of cocaine.

Illicit cocaine appears as an off-white or white chunky or powdery substance. It contains various cutting agents (additives) such as sugar and pain killers such as lidocaine. Cocaine hydrochloride, the water-soluble form of cocaine, is usually snorted or dissolved in water and injected. Cocaine powder is not smoked because heating the powder reduces the cocaine's effect.

Crack, the rock form of cocaine, can be heated and is smoked through a crack pipe. While the effects of cocaine can be experienced in three to five minutes through snorting, smoking crack produces intense, immediate results.

> **Crack** The rock form of cocaine that can be heated and smoked through a crack pipe.

The intense high quickly subsides, producing fatigue and depression as the user crashes (comes down off the high). Ingestion of crack is repeated frequently to avoid the crash. On the street, crack users are commonly referred to as crack heads.

In comparison to cocaine in the powdered form, crack cocaine is inexpensive, and its use is widespread. Smoking crack produces respiratory problems, including chronic cough, severe chest pains, difficulty breathing, lung trauma, and respiratory failure. As crack cocaine use increased in the United States, so did drug-related violence.

Cocaine Paraphernalia

The paraphernalia associated with cocaine use varies. When snorting cocaine was widespread in the 1980s, a razor, mirror or glass, and a rolled dollar bill were used. If injected, a syringe kit is used. Pipes for smoking crack cocaine are often part of the crack user's paraphernalia.

Khat

Khat is an evergreen found in East Africa and the Arabian Peninsula. Khat contains cathinone and cathine, both of which are stimulants. The khat leaves are chewed or eaten to obtain a stimulating effect similar to that of caffeine. Fresh leaves contain cathinone, which is a Schedule I drug. Thirty-six hours after harvesting, the chemical composition in the plant disintegrates, producing cathine, a Schedule IV drug.

The common side effects of Khat use include insomnia, hypertension, and gastric intestinal problems. Chronic use may result in anorexia, fatigue, suicidal thoughts, manic behavior, violence, and hallucinations (Publishers Group, 2006).

Methamphetamine

Amphetamine (a stimulant) was introduced in the early 1930s and later marketed as Benzedrine®, an over-the-counter inhaler used to treat nasal congestion. In the late 1930s, amphetamine was available in tablet form by prescription and was used to treat narcolepsy and attention deficit hyperactivity disorder (ADHD). During World War II, soldiers were given

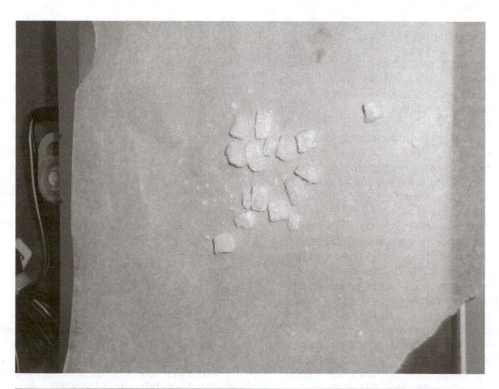

Photo 12-4. Crack cocaine. Photograph by Officer Jared Madsen. Courtesy of National City, California, Police Department.

dextroamphetamine and amphetamine to increase stamina in battle. In the 1960s, amphetamine was used by truck drivers to keep them awake during long trips, by athletes to increase stamina and performance, and by others to control appetite and weight gain. In 1965, amendments to federal food and drug laws were passed to combat the black (illegal) market of amphetamines. Despite the federal government's efforts, increasing demand for amphetamine resulted in the production of methamphetamine in clandestine drug laboratories.

Methamphetamine (meth) remains in the central nervous system much longer than cocaine. Meth's effects are similar to those of cocaine but develop slowly and last longer. Long-term, chronic methamphetamine users are commonly referred to as *tweakers*. Young female users in their teens or twenties often ingest meth in an effort to lose weight. While weight loss may occur, the consequences and long-term negative side effects of meth use are severe.

> **Methamphetamine (meth)** A stimulant that remains in the central nervous system much longer than cocaine. Meth's effects are similar to cocaine but develop slowly and last longer. Long-term methamphetamine use results in a psychosis with characteristics similar to schizophrenia. The user becomes paranoid, is preoccupied with delusional thoughts, may have auditory or visual hallucinations, and may pick at skin. Violent, unpredictable behavior is common among long-term meth users.

Long-term methamphetamine use results in a psychosis with characteristics similar to those of schizophrenia. Users become paranoid, are preoccupied by delusional thoughts, may have auditory or visual hallucinations, and may pick at their skin. Violent, unpredictable behavior is common among long-term meth users. The psychotic symptoms and characteristics may continue for months or years after the user discontinues use of the drug. Many homicide detectives, forensic technicians, and other forensic professionals can testify to the extreme violence associated with methamphetamine use. Many police agencies are extremely cautious when hiring personnel who may have chronically abused methamphetamine.

Just as *crack* is the rock form of cocaine, *ice* is the crystal form of methamphetamine. Ice is smoked. All forms of methamphetamine are highly addictive and destructive to the user.

Methamphetamine is manufactured by combining ephedrine with numerous other chemicals, and applying heat to vaporize the liquid and yield a crystal substance. Many chemicals used in methamphetamine production are common household products that serve as

Chemical Needed	Household Product Substitute
Ephedrine	Sudafed or other sinus medicine
Sulfuric acid	Drain cleaner
Lye	Drain opener
Ether	Engine starting fluid
Lithium	Alkaline batteries
Ammonium nitrate	Fertilizer
Red phosphorus	Matches
Salt	Rock salt or table salt
Methanol	Car fuel system cleaner
Alcohol	Paint thinners
Veterinarian products (cutting agent)	Allergy suppression products

Figure 12-1. Chart of chemicals used to make meth.

substitutes for other chemicals. Figure 12-1 lists the chemicals used in methamphetamine production along with the household product substitute.

Methamphetamine Paraphernalia

The paraphernalia associated with methamphetamine use varies. If injected, a syringe kit is used. Yet smoking the drug is most common. Abusers may use a pipe commonly referred to on the street as a *pizzle* to smoke meth. The pipe is constructed from a light bulb, medical test tube, or other glass tubing. The barrel of a gun can also serve as a pizzle. The drug is placed inside the pipe, heated, and smoked. A fragment of scrubbing pad (e.g., Brillo® Pad) normally used to clean dishes may be placed inside the tube to hold the drug in place. The scrubbing pad also acts as a filter, so the user does not inadvertently inhale all of the drug at one time.

Clandestine Laboratories

The most common clandestine drug laboratory in the United States is one used to manufacture methamphetamine. The ease with which the drug is made and its tremendous profit potential resulted in a dramatic increase in meth's availability. Meth labs can be located virtually anywhere: a hotel room, a residential bathroom or garage, or outdoors.

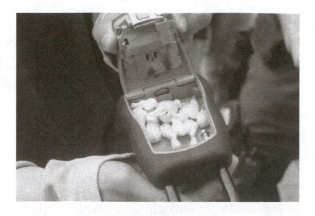

Photo 12-5. Methamphetamine packaged for sale. Courtesy of National City, California, Police Department.

Photo 12-6. Meth lab response team in safety suits.

Significant dangers exist in or near a clandestine methamphetamine laboratory. The chemicals mixed and heated can produce a chemical chain reaction that may cause an explosion or emit poisonous gases that pose threats to safety and health. The laboratory may be equipped with an anti-personnel weapon (e.g., explosive device, vicious dog, poisonous reptile) designed to injure or kill law enforcement personnel. Other weapons within the lab may include dangling fish hooks positioned to puncture the face of an unsuspecting officer, and light switches connected to flammable liquid or explosive devices.

As one opens a door to enter a clandestine lab, a fresh supply of oxygen entering the facility may react with the burning chemicals, causing an explosion or igniting flammable materials. Exposure to the toxic chemicals can lead to skin problems, eye irritation or blindness, reproductive organ damage, and respiratory ailments, including lung cancer. Under no circumstances should an untrained forensic technician enter a clandestine lab until it is deemed safe by trained first responders or hazardous materials personnel.

Typical signs of a clandestine methamphetamine laboratory include:

- a supply of chemicals needed to manufacture methamphetamine,
- pots or containers used for cooking,
- a heat source such as stove, or camp cooking equipment,
- filters and funnels to separate the finished product from waste material.

Clean-up of a methamphetamine laboratory requires a team trained in hazardous materials disposal procedures. It is estimated that for every pound of methamphetamine produced, five to seven pounds of toxic waste is created. Clean-up costs can approach hundreds of thousands of dollars, depending on the size of the clandestine laboratory (Publishers Group, 2006). In some jurisdictions, government funds and regional hazardous materials teams are available to assist with clean-up of methamphetamine laboratories.

DEPRESSANTS

Depressants are drugs that depress (slow) the central nervous system. Depressants are used throughout the world to induce sleep, relieve anxiety, and alleviate stress. Alcohol is one of the oldest and most widely used depressants, though many pharmaceutical depressant drugs are available today. Depressants are rarely produced in clandestine laboratories. Instead, legally manufactured pharmaceutical depressants are obtained fraudulently for illicit use. The two major groups of depressant drugs are barbiturates, which became popular during the first half of the twentieth century, and benzodiazepines, introduced in the 1960s.

Depressant drugs are taken orally and produce a state of intoxication that is similar to the effects of alcohol. The symptoms of depressant use include slurred speech, loss of motor skills, and mental impairment. Tolerance can develop rapidly, depending on dose and frequency of use. As tolerance to the drug develops, the user

> **Depressants** Drugs that depress (slow) the central nervous system. Depressants are used throughout the world to induce sleep, relieve anxiety, and alleviate stress.

must increase the drug's dosage to obtain similar effects.

As dosage and frequency of use increases, physical and psychological dependence may develop. While increasing the dosage of barbiturates significantly increases the risk of overdose, large doses of benzodiazepines are rarely fatal unless combined with alcohol or other drugs.

Chronic high-dose usage may result in toxicity to the central nervous system, resulting in headaches, confusion, memory impairment, irritability, and depression. Withdrawal symptoms include insomnia, anxiety, tremors, weakness, seizures, and delirium (hallucinations). Abrupt non-medical withdrawal can be fatal.

Rohypnol

Flunitrazepam, commonly called Rohypnol, is a benzodiazepine that is not legal in the United States. It is often smuggled into the United States. Rohypnol is legal and frequently prescribed in over 70 countries, including many countries in Europe and Latin America. Rohypnol is ten times stronger than the prescription drug *Valium*, and it is the third most prescribed sleeping sedative in the world. The drug is tasteless and odorless, and it may be injected or taken orally in a tablet form (Publishers Group, 2006).

Common street names for Rohypnol include *rophies, roofies,* and *roach*. The drug gained the attention of law enforcement personnel because of its use as a date rape drug. A **date rape drug** is a depressant that is inconspicuously placed into the drink (typically an alcoholic drink) of the unsuspecting victim. The date rape drug is used to incapacitate or lower the inhibitions of the victim, overcoming resistance to a sexual encounter. The victim is typically removed to a clandestine location by the perpetrator. Proving this type of crime is difficult. The victim often has no recollection of what happened because the drug produces memory impairment. Thus, incidents of *date rape* are rarely reported to authorities.

> **Date rape drug**
> A depressant that is inconspicuously placed into the drink (typically an alcoholic drink) of the unsuspecting victim. The date rape drug is used to incapacitate or lower the inhibitions of the victim, thus overcoming resistance to a sexual encounter. The victim often has no recollection of what happened because the drug produces memory impairment.

Gamma Hydroxybutyric Acid

GHB is a depressant also used as a date rape drug. Like Rohypnol, it is slipped into the drink of an unsuspecting victim. The victim is rendered helpless, has little memory of the attack, and the drug is quickly eliminated from the victim's body, rendering detection of GHB very difficult. Some voluntarily consume the drug for its euphoric effects, while others abuse the drug to enhance muscle growth or aid with sleep.

The effects of GHB include drowsiness, dizziness, nausea, amnesia, visual hallucinations, hypotension, respiratory depression, and coma. Mixed with alcohol, the effects are enhanced dramatically and are frequently fatal. A rapist using GHB as an assault tool can easily commit a murder in addition to a rape. Forensic technicians and homicide detectives involved with investigating GHB-related sex crimes must act quickly to obtain a urine sample from the victim. The container the victim drank from is collected as evidence. Witnesses at the crime scene must be interviewed as well.

HALLUCINOGENS

Hallucinogens are some of the oldest known drugs used to alter human sensory mechanisms. A **hallucinogen** appears in natural form in some plants and fungi, or it can be produced synthetically (artificially). Synthetic hallucinogens are more potent than the naturally occurring drug. While the term *hallucinogen* may cause one to assume that a user will hallucinate under its influence, not all drugs in this classification produce hallucinations. Most will, however, produce changes in mood, perception, and thought patterns.

Physiologically, some hallucinogenic drugs produce an elevated heart rate, dilated pupils, and increased blood pressure. Psychologically, some produce time and space distortion. Colors may appear exaggerated or more significant, and the passage of time may appear to slow. The user's perception and mood may change. The drug use experience can vary, from very pleasurable to incredibly frightening. Further, the effect of the drug trip (experience under the influence of a hallucinogen) may vary with each use. Additionally, the user may experience recurrences of the drug use experience weeks or months after ingesting the drug. The reoccurring drug experiences are called flashbacks.

> **Hallucinogen** A hallucinogen appears in natural form in some plants and fungi, or it can be produced synthetically (artificially). Synthetic hallucinogens are more potent than the naturally occurring drug. While the term *hallucinogen* may cause one to assume that a user will hallucinate under its influence, not all drugs in this classification produce hallucinations. Most will, however, produce changes in mood, perception, and thought patterns.

Lysergic Acid Diethylamide

The most potent hallucinogen known to science, LSD, was created by Dr. Albert Hoffman in 1938. Intended as a research drug to study mental illness, Dr. Hoffman inadvertently discovered its effects when he accidentally ingested some of the drug. Taken orally, 25 micrograms (equivalent to one to two grains of salt) produces vivid hallucinations.

LSD abuse was most popular in the 1960s and was typically sold on blotter acid paper that contained colorful designs. The drug was also sold in microdot tablets, thin gelatin squares, and sugar cubes. All forms were administered orally. The typical effects include those listed in Figure 12-2.

Psilocybin, Psilocyn, Peyote, and Mescaline

Psilocybin and *psilocyn* are natural hallucinogens found in certain mushrooms grown in tropical and subtropical regions of South America, Mexico, and the United States. *Peyote* is a natural hallucinogen found in a cactus common to Northern Mexico and the southwestern United States. *Mescaline* is extracted from peyote but is also produced synthetically. Parts of the peyote plant or fungi can be dried and eaten or brewed into a tea. Peyote is commonly used in Native American cultural activities. The effects of these hallucinogens include relaxation of the muscles and visual, auditory, and emotional distortions.

Phencyclidine

PCP was developed in the 1950s. It was used in the 1960s as a veterinary anesthetic under the trade name Sernylan®. Its use was discontinued in the 1970s. Today, virtually all illegal PCP is produced in clandestine laboratories. Common street names for PCP include *angel dust, supergrass, killer weed, embalming fluid,* and *rocket fuel.* The drug may appear white, tan, or brown and is sold in powder or gum form. PCP is most commonly smoked after applying it to leafy material such as marijuana or herbs.

The effects of PCP vary with each use. The user may feel separated from physical surroundings or experience loss of coordination, numbness, slurred speech, or a sense of great strength and invincibility. The PCP abuser may also experience auditory hallucinations, image distortion, and extreme mood changes. Behaviorally, the user may stare, demonstrate rapid involuntary eye movements, engage in an unusual or exaggerated walk, or be hostile or violent. Psychologically, the user may experience extreme anxiety, paranoia, or psychosis that is medically indistinguishable from schizophrenia.

KETAMINE

Ketamine (*Special K, Super K*), is a general anesthetic most frequently used in veterinary medicine. Ketamine's pharmacological profile is very similar to PCP's. Ketamine is often distributed illicitly in powdered form. It may be administered orally or can be snorted or injected. Effects are experienced within 15 minutes, while the effects through intravenous injection are almost immediate.

Ketamine can act as a depressant, or it may produce psychedelic, euphoric, or hallucinogenic effects similar to PCP. Users exhibit less confusion and less violent behavior than PCP users. The negative side effects include dizziness, slow reaction time, disorganized thoughts, amnesia and, in high doses, coma.

First Hour after Ingesting LSD	Hallucinatory State of LSD	After LSD Trip
• Visual changes • Extreme mood change	• Impaired depth and time perception • Distorted perception of object sizes and shapes, movements, color, sound, touch, self body image • User may *hear* colors and *see* sounds • Sense of danger impaired	• May experience extreme anxiety • May suffer from depression • May experience flashbacks

Figure 12-2. Chart of LSD body reactions.

(U.S. Drug Enforcement Administration, 2005)

ECSTASY

Methylenedioxymethamphetamine (MDMA), also known as *ecstasy*, was first developed in 1912 but did not become popular until the 1980s. Its popularity increased dramatically at the end of the twentieth century. By 2000, an estimated two million ecstasy tablets were smuggled into the United States each week.

Ecstasy is commonly abused by young people at *rave parties* (parties that usually involve music, laser lights, and drugs of abuse). The drug is usually administered orally. It is available in tablets of various colors. The tablets are imprinted with graphic or commercial designs. Ecstasy produces stimulation similar to amphetamine. It also produces mild hallucination and increased sensual arousal. The effects usually appear within 45 minutes of administration, peak within 90 minutes, and subside within four to six hours.

Although many users falsely believe that ecstasy is safe to ingest, the side effects can be severe. Nerve cell damage, including damage to the brain, can result, creating long-term cognitive impairment, psychiatric problems, muscle tension, tremors, blurred vision, and hyperthermia (increased body temperature) that can lead to organ failure or death. Symptoms of overdose include rapid heart rate, high blood pressure, panic attacks, muscle cramps, faintness, unconsciousness, and seizures. Abuse of the drug can result in permanent damage to the user's neurotransmitter (serotonin) in the brain. Serotonin regulates a person's ability to sense joy, to sleep, and to experience pain and increased appetite. Ecstasy abuse also results in chronic depression and anxiety.

Unbeknownst to the user, many ecstasy tablets contain a mixture of other drugs and analogs. *Analogs* are chemicals that have a similar structure but differ slightly in composition. The following is a list of chemicals that have been discovered in ecstasy tablets:

- AMT: a hallucinogenic stimulant
- BDMPEA: an illicit variation of chemicals
- BZP: an illegal stimulant drug
- caffeine
- codeine
- DMT: a hallucinogenic stimulant
- DOB: hallucinogen that is grouped with the most powerful psychoactive substances known
- dextromethorphan (DXM)
- ephedra: Chinese herbal stimulant
- ephedrine: derivative of ephedra

- MBDB: an amphetamine
- MDA: a substance related to amphetamine, LSD, and mescaline
- MDE: similar to MDMA but less intensity
- MMDA: a hallucinogen from the phenethylamine family
- phenylpropanolamine: a stimulant with hallucinogenic effects
- PMA: a stimulant with hallucinogenic effects; more toxic than ecstasy
- pseudoephedrine
- TFMPP: an illegal drug with hallucinogenic effects
- 4-MTA: an amphetamine causing powerful serotonin release; considered more deadly than ecstasy
- 5-methoxydimethyltryptamine (5-Meo-DMT): stimulant more powerful than DMT
- 2C-1: a stimulant with hallucinogenic effects
- 2-CT-2: a stimulant with hallucinogenic effects
- amphetamine
- cocaine
- heroin
- ketamine
- methamphetamine
- PCP

The following chemicals are commonly used to produce ecstasy (Publishers Group, 2006):

- benzylmethylketone (BMK)
- piperonylmethylketone (PMK)
- safrole
- isosafrole
- acetone
- ethanol
- methanol
- ether
- methylamine
- isopropanol
- hydrogen gas
- hydrochloric acid
- sulfuric acid
- ammonium formamide
- formic acid
- sodium
- hydroxide
- caustic soda
- magnesium stearate
- magnesium gluconate
- lactose
- sorbitol

ANABOLIC STEROIDS

Anabolic steroids are hormonal substances that advance muscle growth and are pharmacologically related to testosterone. Anabolic steroids do

Anabolic Steroid Side Effects in Men	Anabolic Steroid Side Effects in Women	Anabolic Steroid Side Effects in Adolescents
Shrinkage of testicles	Facial hair growth	Growth prematurely halted
Sperm count reduced	Male-pattern baldness	Premature skeletal maturity
Infertility	Disruption of menstrual cycle	Increased changes in puberty
Baldness	Clitoris enlargement	
Breast development	Deepened voice	
Prostate cancer risk		

Figure 12-3. Chart of steroid body reactions.

(U.S. Drug Enforcement Administration, 2005)

not include estrogens, progestins, or corticosteroids. Steroids have been legally prescribed to treat patients with low testosterone levels, AIDS, and many other diseases. Steroids are also used illegally and abused by athletes and body builders to improve physical endurance and appearance. Most illicit steroids are sold at gyms and athletic competitions, or through mail order trafficking.

Steroids may be ingested orally or injected intravenously. Periodical doses over a period of time is referred to as *cycling*. Users often combine a variety of steroids to maximize effectiveness. Consuming different steroids simultaneously is referred to as *stacking*.

The major side effects of anabolic steroid abuse include cancer of the liver, tumors in the kidneys, jaundice (yellowish coloration of the skin), high blood pressure, an increase in bad cholesterol or a decrease in good cholesterol, retention of bodily fluids, severe acne, and trembling. Gender-specific side effects are presented in Figure 12-3.

CANNABIS (MARIJUANA)

Cannabis (marijuana) is the most commonly used illicit drug in the world. Derived from the cannabis plant, which grows naturally in many tropical and temperate regions of the world, it is the cannabinoid chemical called *delta-9-tetrahydrocannabinol (THC)* inside the plant that is responsible for the psychoactive effects. Although marijuana is the natural form of THC, synthetic THC is legally manufactured in pill form to control nausea and vomiting in chemotherapy patients and increase appetite in AIDS patients.

> **Cannabis (marijuana)** The most commonly used illicit drug. Derived from the cannabis plant, which grows naturally in many tropical and temperate regions of the world. The cannabinoid chemical named *delta-9-tetrahydrocannabinol (THC)* inside the plant is responsible for the psychoactive effects.

The potency and effects of marijuana will vary depending on the THC level. *Sinsemilla* (Spanish for "without seed") is marijuana developed from un-pollinated female cannabis plant.

Marijuana is usually smoked in rolled cigarettes known as *joints* or hollowed-out commercial cigars referred to as *blunts,* or from large pipes (typically glass) called *bongs*. Joints and blunts may be laced with other drugs, including PCP. Common street names for marijuana include *pot, grass, weed, Mary Jane,* and *reefer*. The effects of the drug are usually experienced within minutes, peak in 10–30 minutes, and last for two to three hours. Feelings of well-being, relaxation, and vivid sight, smell, taste, hearing, thoughts, and expressions are often experienced. Distortion of time and space, impaired memory, fantasies, loss of personal identity, hallucinations, and paranoia may be experienced as well.

While many believe marijuana is safe, the effects on the user's health can be long-term and severe. The same toxins and carcinogens (cancer-causing chemicals) contained in tobacco are found in cannabis. Side effects include bronchitis, emphysema, asthma, increased heart rate, mouth dryness, reddening of the eyes, impairment in motor skills and concentration, and a craving for sweets. Long-term use increases health risks to the user's lungs, reproductive system, and immune system. Long-term use may also cause **amotivational syndrome,** a condition through which the user experiences indifference, impairment of judgment (makes bad decisions), memory loss, inability to concentrate, diminished attractiveness, and lack of achievement.

> **Amotivational syndrome** A condition created by long-term use of cannabis through which the user experiences indifference, impairment of judgment (makes bad decisions), memory loss, an inability to concentrate, diminished attractiveness, and lack of achievement.

Photo 12-7. Marijuana seizures. Courtesy of National City, California, Police Department.

Photo 12-10. Marijuana seizures. Courtesy of National City, California, Police Department.

Photo 12-8. Marijuana seizures. Courtesy of National City, California, Police Department.

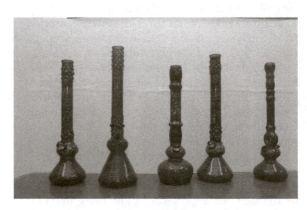

Photo 12-11. Marijuana bongs and pipe.

Photo 12-9. Marijuana seizures. Courtesy of National City, California, Police Department.

Photo 12-12. Marijuana bongs and pipe.

Many law enforcement drug investigators view marijuana as a **gateway drug,** one that can lead to use of more potent and dangerous drugs. Long-term marijuana use impairs the user's ability to make informed choices. The user may also experiment with new drugs as they are introduced, or mix various drugs with marijuana.

> **Gateway drug**
> Many law enforcement drug investigators view marijuana as a drug that can lead to use of more potent and dangerous drugs.

INHALANTS

Inhalant abuse involves sniffing or breathing fumes from many household products and solvents such as glue, spray paint, aerosol, cream, gasoline, nitrous oxide, nail polish remover, air freshener, butane fuel, wax remover, analgesic spray, deodorant, lighter fluid, cement, rubber, cleaning fluid, and degreaser. The common terminology associated with inhalant abuse is *sniffing, snorting, bagging,* and *huffing.*

The inhalant abuse produces intoxicating effects that usually last a few minutes but may last several hours if a large amount of the substance is ingested. With successive inhalations, the user feels less inhibited and may lose consciousness. Inhalants can cause severe damage to the brain and nervous system. Side effects also include an erratic heart rate. High concentrations may cause death from suffocation as the toxic substance displaces oxygen in the lungs.

OVER-THE-COUNTER AND PRESCRIPTION DRUGS

The fastest growing categories of drugs of abuse are over-the-counter and prescription drugs. According to the National Institute on Drug Abuse (NIDA), an estimated 48 million people in the United States have used prescription drugs for non-medical reasons. Certain prescription drugs can affect brain activity and lead to addiction. It is believed that easy access to these drugs is the most likely contributing factor to increase of abuse among adolescents. Not only are drugs obtained from household medicine cabinets, some online pharmacies distribute medication without appropriate identification verification or without a physician's prescription.

The prescription drug most commonly abused by teenagers is *OxyContin.* Its tablets are the oral consumption form of oxycodone hydrochloride, an opium derivative. The tablets are taken legitimately for the purpose of managing moderate to severe pain. The tablet is formulated to control release of the drug. If crushed or chewed, the drug is released rapidly and may be fatal.

Common negative side effects of oxycodone include constipation, nausea, fatigue, headache, dizziness, anxiety, euphoria, and dry mouth. If high doses are absorbed or if the subject is not tolerant of opiates, side effects may include shallow breathing, pupil constriction, respiratory arrest, or death.

Withdrawal symptoms may occur if oxycodone use is terminated suddenly. Typical withdrawal symptoms include muscle pain, fever, nausea, insomnia, and anxiety.

POLY-DRUG ABUSE

With chronic drug abusers, the tolerance level may increase greatly. At this stage of drug abuse, many use multiple drugs simultaneously to increase the euphoric potential and reduce the negative side effects.

Mixing alcohol (a depressant) with drugs is common. A depressant such as benzodiazepine may be mixed with a narcotic. The chronic abuser purposely mixes drugs to reduce the side effects of over-stimulation or withdrawal symptoms.

Another common practice is combining marijuana with psilocybin (*mushrooms*). Marijuana helps alleviate nausea while adding to the euphoria (high) experienced with the mushrooms.

An incredibly dangerous and often fatal drug combination is referred to as *speedballing,* a term used to describe the combination of morphine or heroin with cocaine, a stimulant. The desired effect is a greater high without overdosing. The heroin or morphine slows the heart rate, thus preventing overdose from the high dosage of cocaine. After the cocaine dissipates, the full effects of the heroin or morphine are experienced. Another potentially fatal practice is *five-way,* which involves snorting heroin, cocaine, methamphetamine, and flunitrazepam and drinking alcohol.

Common drug combinations include but are not limited to those listed in Figure 12-4.

Drug Combinations	Street Name
Cocaine + Heroin or Morphine	*Speedball*
Cigarette laced with Cocaine + Heroin	*Flamethrower*
Cocaine + Marijuana	*Cocoa Puff*
Crack + PCP	*Space Basing or Parachute*
Ecstasy + Viagra (prescription sexual stimulant drug)	*Sextasy*
Ecstasy + Ketamine	*Kitty Flipping*
Ecstasy + Mescaline	*Love Flipping*
Ecstasy + Methamphetamine	*Hugs & Kisses*
Ecstasy + PCP in pill form	*Pikachu*
Ecstasy + PCP	*Elephant Flipping*
Ecstasy + LSD	*Tripping & Rolling or Trolling*
Ecstasy + Psilocybin (mushrooms)	*Hippie Flipping or Flower Flipping*
3+ Ecstasy tablets together	*Stacking*
Heroin + Benadryl (over the counter allergy medicine) or Heroin alone	*Cheese*
Marijuana + Alcohol	*Green Dragon*
Marijuana + Coffee	*Hippie Speedball*
Marijuana + PCP	*Wet Daddy*
PCP + Crack	*Beam me up Scottie*

Figure 12-4. Chart of Poly drug use.

(U.S. Drug Enforcement Administration, 2005)

EVIDENCE COLLECTION AT A DRUG CRIME SCENE

Many violent crimes are related to drug abuse or drug trafficking. Items at drug-related crime scenes that should be collected include the following:

- Dominion and control evidence. Any item, such as a utility bill with a person's name, that establishes who owns or leases (exercises domination and control over) the property.
- Pay and owe records. Any type of documentation that indicates drug transactions, such as names, amount of drug, or money paid or owed. The pay and owe record may be a small piece of paper, a ledger, or a computer-generated document. Computers should be seized because a computer's hard drive may contain drug trafficking information.
- Scales to measure drugs.
- Drug paraphernalia.
- Drugs.

An initial presumptive drug test should be conducted to determine the type of drug collected. Presumptive drug tests are not confirmatory, but they establish probable cause for arrest. Confirmatory tests are conducted in a forensic laboratory by a trained criminalist. Presumptive drug test chemicals are distributed in hard plastic pouches containing one or two glass ampules. The presumptive test pouch is opened, the suspected drug is placed inside the pouch with the ampules, the pouch is closed, and the ampules are crushed. The test pouch is shaken to blend the test liquid from the ampules with the suspected drug. A color change (positive reaction specified on the pouch packaging) will indicate if the substance tested is the suspected drug. If a positive reaction occurs, the substance should be collected.

Gross and net weight calculations for the suspect substance are obtained at a laboratory. The drug is weighed while in the collection pouch, revealing the gross weight. The drug is removed from the pouch and placed in a separate package while the pouch is weighed. The pouch's weight is subtracted from the gross weight, revealing the net weight of the suspect substance.

Subsequent to weight calculations, the suspected substance is stored. *Marijuana and other plant-type drugs are typically packaged in paper to prevent deterioration (rotting).* All other drugs are placed in thick plastic bags and heat-sealed.

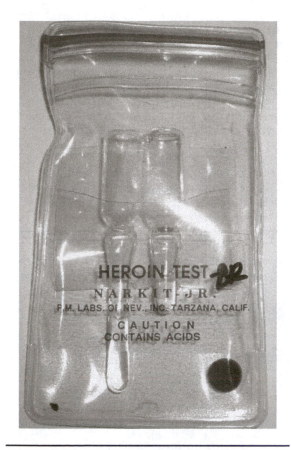

Photo 12-13. Heroin presumptive drug test with positive reaction. Photograph by Officer Jared Madsen. Courtesy of National City, California, Police Department.

Photo 12-14. Crack cocaine presumptive drug test with positive reaction. Photograph by Officer Jared Madsen. Courtesy of National City, California, Police Department.

Photo 12-15. Crack cocaine weighed in its original packaging. Photograph by Officer Jared Madsen. Courtesy of National City, California, Police Department.

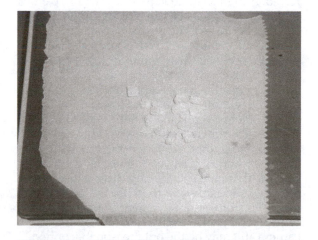

Photo 12-16. Crack cocaine weighed outside its original packaging. Photograph by Officer Jared Madsen. Courtesy of National City, California, Police Department.

SURVEILLANCE PHOTOGRAPHY

Detectives who investigate homicides and drug-related crimes frequently conduct surveillance as part of the investigation. Arguably, drug crime investigators conduct more surveillance and take more photographs during surveillance activity than any other investigator in law enforcement. Rarely do forensic technicians conduct surveillance activities because of the potential danger it imposes.

Law enforcement personnel must be skilled in the art of surveillance photography so clear, defined photographs of criminal activity are obtained. For the benefit of the reader who may be a drug investigator, photographic techniques for surveillance activities are presented here.

The investigator may wish to photographically capture a suspect's face, a hand-to-hand drug and money exchange between a drug dealer and a buyer or informant, or capture the license plate of a suspect's car. A rapid shutter speed is often necessary. The shutter setting depends on the speed of the object. A speeding car, for example, will require a much faster shutter speed than a hand-to-hand exchange of drugs for money.

Additionally, an investigator will likely conduct surveillance at a remarkable distance from the subject. A telephoto (zoom) lens is required to capture necessary detail. Use of the zoom lens is necessary to capture normal lens views as well as telephoto (close-up) views. A zoom lens with a focal length range of 70–200 mm is recommended, while a lens with the capacity to reach beyond 200 mm (e.g., 300 mm) is preferred. A digital single-lens-reflex (DSLR) camera with a 200-mm lens has an effective zoom of 300 mm because of the sensor's small size. Most DSLR cameras are also equipped with an optical image stabilizer in the camera's body or in the lens.

The longer the focal length, however, the more likely camera shake and low light will present problems. While many authors recommend the use of a camera tripod or stand for surveillance photography, most investigators will confirm that there is rarely enough time to mount a camera. Criminal activity and drug transactions are often sudden, and tripod use inhibits investigator flexibility and movement. A telephoto lens with an anti-shake mechanism for holding the camera still may be the only reasonable option.

While engaged in surveillance, the investigator is often seated inside a vehicle equipped with tinted windows that restrict lighting and exposure. Therefore, the camera's aperture should be opened as much as possible, and the ISO should be increased in low light situations.

Due to limited lighting and the relative speed of the subject, camera settings will vary greatly in surveillance photography. With this in mind, the following digital camera operating procedure is recommended during surveillance photography activities.

- Use a telephoto (zoom) lens, preferably equipped with an anti-shake mechanism.
- Set the camera to manual operation. Open the aperture to a low f-stop number. Allowing abundant light into the camera is more critical than good depth-of-field. Focus on the subject or object (e.g., vehicle license plate). The area surrounding the subject or object need not be in focus. In rare circumstances, the surrounding area must be in focus, and the depth-of-field should be increased accordingly.
- Choose a high ISO (e.g., 400) if daytime. If dusk or dawn, an ISO of 800 is recommended. If nighttime, ISO higher than 800 may be necessary. Graininess (noise) resulting from the increase in ISO is acceptable to capture the details of the criminal event.
- If daylight, and time permits, meter the outside light, not the lighting inside the investigator's vehicle. Choose the fastest shutter speed possible, while maintaining a good exposure. A slightly underexposed photograph can be adjusted easily with any photo software program.
- Take a test photograph before any relevant activity commences. View the test photo on the LCD screen, and adjust the camera settings if necessary.
- Manual versus auto focus. Due to time constraints, manual focus may not be practical during a drug crime transaction. If the camera is equipped with an infinity focus setting and the subject (object) remains in focus, a manual focus operation is appropriate. If the camera's zoom feature is used, time may not allow for manual focus. Therefore, auto focus is often used for surveillance photography. However, the camera's auto feature will choose the point of focus. If the camera's auto feature cannot locate the subject (object) in a timely fashion, the event may not be captured photographically. If using auto focus, the photographer may wish to aim the camera

Photo 12-17. Surveillance photographs. Courtesy of National City, California, Police Department.

Photo 12-19. Surveillance photographs. Courtesy of National City, California, Police Department.

Photo 12-18. Surveillance photographs. Courtesy of National City, California, Police Department.

at a large object near the subject (object) to provide a focal point for the camera. If possible, the photographer should take a few test (control) photographs prior to the relevant criminal activity to determine if manual or auto focus is appropriate.

Surveillance photography is one of the most difficult tasks in forensic photography because of the challenges associated with light, speed, and focus. If a desired subject (object) is not photographically captured, valuable documentary evidence may be foregone. The investigator should practice with the assigned camera equipment before attempting to capture desired images during actual surveillance work.

SUMMARY

The United States CSA of 1970 categorizes drugs into five separate schedules based on the drugs' medical use, potential for abuse, and health and safety concerns. The schedules act as a guide for law enforcement personnel relative to the severity of the different types of drugs encountered on the street and at crime scenes.

In addition to categorizing drugs into schedules, the CSA separates drugs into five classifications based on the drugs' properties and effects. The five classifications (narcotics, stimulants, depressants, hallucinogens, and anabolic steroids) also assist law enforcement personnel with identifying drug user symptoms and behaviors associated with each of the controlled substances. The CSA also identifies possible hazards one may

encounter during a confrontation with a person under the influence of a particular substance.

Paraphernalia used with a drug of choice varies, depending on the method of ingestion and type of drug. Familiarization with the appearance and physical characteristics of drugs and drug paraphernalia will assist investigators and forensic technicians in determining if the drugs or items are related to the activity under investigation or the crime scene being processed. Types of drugs used, administration preferences, and street slang associated with each drug varies throughout the United States.

Clandestine laboratories, particularly methamphetamine labs, are volatile and potentially dangerous for first responders who encounter the labs. Awareness of the characteristics of a laboratory and the chemicals typically used to produce methamphetamine will assist first responders in ascertaining if the scene is a clandestine laboratory. Hazardous materials-trained personnel should be summoned to the scene to dismantle the laboratory and render the scene safe for investigators and forensic personnel.

Surveillance photography is a crucial aspect of most, if not all, drug investigations. Camera film exposure and speed are the two areas of concern when photographically capturing drug transactions. The photographer must use a telephoto (zoom) lens, high ISO film (or high digital camera ISO settings), and proper camera settings to capture an image. An investigator who conducts surveillance photography must have a working knowledge of the assigned camera equipment and should practice surveillance photography in fictitious situations prior to actual case work.

KEY TERMS

Define, describe, or explain the importance of each of the following:

amotivational syndrome	crack	hallucinogen
cannabis (marijuana)	cutting agent	heroin
Controlled Substance Act	date rape drug	methamphetamine
(CSA) of 1970	depressant	(meth)
cocaine	gateway drug	narcotic

DISCUSSION AND REVIEW QUESTIONS

1. What criteria cause a drug to be included in CSA Schedule I?
2. What are the five CSA classes of drugs?
3. Explain the difference between physiological and psychological dependence on a drug.
4. What is *speedballing* and why is it dangerous?
5. What is the difference between cocaine and crack? Methamphetamine and ice?
6. What chemicals are used to manufacture methamphetamine?
7. What is a date rape drug and how does it affect a victim?
8. List five multiple drug use combinations and the street names for each.
9. What is the goal of surveillance photography?
10. What camera settings should be used in surveillance photography?

CASE STUDY—Meth Lab Dangers

Methamphetamine (meth) can be manufactured practically anywhere one can connect a hot plate to an electrical circuit: RVs, homes, garages, hotel rooms. Meth labs are extremely dangerous. The volatile chemical ingredients used (e.g., iodine, nail polish remover, hydrogen peroxide, drain cleaner, rubbing alcohol, non-prescription pseudoephedrine) produce toxic vapors that spread over countertops and into furniture and carpeting, setting the stage for an explosion. If the chemicals in liquid form are stored in a refrigerator before cooking, the vapor from the chemicals can penetrate wrapped food.

In spite of their danger, many meth labs are constructed and operated when children are present. Children can easily ingest the drug through contact with contaminated surfaces, materials, and food. As a result, the children may become addicted and lose their lives.

In one notorious California case, Ivan and Veronica Gonzales, both meth addicts and the uncle and aunt of four-year-old Genny Rojas, tortured and scalded their niece in a bathtub with water so hot that Genny's skin peeled. Ivan and Veronica left Genny to die. Subsequently, they were convicted in Genny's death. They represented the first husband-and-wife couple sentenced to California's death row.

1. What safety precautions must a forensic technician follow when processing a meth lab crime scene?
2. Develop a plan for processing a meth lab crime scene.

LAB EXERCISES

Drug Presumptive Testing

Equipment and supplies required per student:

- one 35-mm camera (film or digital)
- one 24 exposure roll ISO 400 film (if film camera)
- one telephoto (zoom) lens
- one gram scale
- one tsp of salt in a plastic bag (one bag per pair of students)
- one tsp of sugar in a plastic bag (one bag per pair of students)
- non-prescription (over-the-counter) anti-itch skin ointment (e.g., Lanacain)
- pseudoephedrine over-the-counter nasal congestion medicine
- one presumptive drug test kit for cocaine (if available) (one per pair of students)
- one presumptive drug test kit for methamphetamine (if available) (one per pair of students)

Exercise #1 – Surveillance Photography

1. Students may work individually or with a partner. Students can photograph each other as part of the assignment. Keep a photo log (list) of each photograph taken, recording the camera settings for each photograph.
2. Use the appropriate camera settings to photograph the following:
   - a driver in a moving vehicle,
   - the license plate on a moving vehicle,
   - a person walking.
3. Submit the photo log and photographs to the instructor.

Exercise #2 – Gross and Net Weight of Drugs

1. In pairs, students obtain the gross and net weights of a substance. Record the findings and submit to the instructor.

Exercise #3 – Presumptive Drug Testing

1. Working in pairs, students open the cocaine presumptive drug test kit.
2. Place a small amount of skin ointment (e.g., Lanacain) inside the presumptive test pouch and follow the presumptive test manufacturer's instructions to obtain results.
3. Repeat Step 2 with pseudoephedrine tablets, using the methamphetamine presumptive drug test kit.

WEB RESOURCES

Drug Identification Bible:
www.drugidbible.com
National Institute on Drug Abuse (NIDA):
www.drugabuse.gov
Office of National Drug Control Policy
(ONDCP): www.whitehousedrugpolicy.gov

Street Drugs Info: www.streetdrugs.org
U.S. Drug Enforcement Administration:
www.usdoj.gov/dea/

13

Suspect and Live Victim Processing

LEARNING OUTCOMES

After completing this chapter, the reader should be able to:

- describe the legally permissible procedure to identify, collect, preserve, and document evidence from a crime suspect or victim,
- demonstrate the steps for photographing, measuring, and documenting injuries on a live victim,
- describe suspect processing safety precautions.

INTRODUCTION

Forensic technicians respond to crime scenes to search for, photograph, measure, collect, and preserve evidence. Evidentiary samples are also obtained from the crime's victim as well as a suspect to link the crime scene, the victim, and the suspect, completing the cycle according to the Locard Exchange Principle. As discussed in Chapter 1, the Locard Exchange Principle supposes that anytime a person contacts an environment, the person exchanges trace evidence with that environment. The Locard Exchange Principle provides the basis for linking suspects and victims to each other and to the scene of the crime. It is the basis for forensic evidence collection. The principle emphasizes the need for great care and precision when collecting evidence from a suspect, a victim, or a crime scene.

SUSPECT PROCESSING

A crime suspect may be arrested at the time of the incident or several months later. Hopefully, evidence collected from a suspect is linked directly to a crime scene. In most cases, a forensic technician is summoned to collect evidence from a suspect involved in a major crime, such as an unlawful homicide, rape, child molestation, or other violent crime against a person. Detailed forensic photography and evidence collection procedures must be followed when processing a suspect of a major crime. The forensic technician must collect evidentiary items that are necessary for comparison and analysis purposes. The type of evidence sought is determined by the length of time between the incident and the suspect's apprehension. Trace evidence such as soil, fibers, hair, and blood from the crime scene, for example, may not be present on the suspect if the incident occurred several months before the suspect is apprehended.

A forensic technician should keep in mind that a crime suspect may be innocent. The forensic technician's job requires objectivity and a search for the truth.

Communicating with the Case Investigator

Before evidence is collected from a suspect, the forensic technician should confer with the case investigator. The investigator will inform the forensic technician if a "full work-up" is necessary or if collecting certain evidence is irrelevant based on the date of the alleged crime versus the date of arrest. Further, the investigator should share any case information or clues that pertain to the evidence sought, such as scratch marks that the suspect may have sustained during an attack or other information that the investigator obtained while interviewing victims or witnesses. An investigator may obtain new information while interviewing the victim. The victim may report scratching the perpetrator on an obscure body location. It is imperative that the investigator share this information with the forensic technician, so scratch marks on the suspect are searched for and, if located, photographed. Conversely, the forensic technician should notify the case investigator if significant or remarkable evidence is discovered during suspect processing. The forensic technician may locate relevant evidence, such as bloodstains, on the suspect's clothing. Shared findings are critical to proper follow-up and evidence analysis.

Communicating with the Suspect

A critical issue that often arises during the processing of a suspect is the forensic technician's legal authority to obtain evidence from the suspect. The case investigator should communicate the legal authority for the search to the suspect. Another legal issue arises if the suspect discusses the incident with the forensic technician. The suspect may volunteer information or make self-incriminating statements relevant to the case. The forensic technician should include any unsolicited comments made by the suspect in the final report and inform the case investigator of any statements made. Further, the forensic technician should not initiate questioning of the suspect about the incident because such questioning may violate the suspect's rights under the Constitution. However, unsolicited self-incriminating statements made voluntarily by a suspect are admissible in court after invocation of constitutional rights. Additional information on admissions, confessions, and search and seizure is presented in Chapter 7.

The suspect may also question the forensic technician about the search process. Suspect questions may include, "Why are you doing all of this to me?" or "Why am I here?" A suggested response is, "You must speak with the investigator for answers to those questions." However, the forensic technician may explain processing steps to the suspect. For example, at the photographic stage of the processing, the forensic technician may state:

Please stand in front of this wall with your hands to your side, facing me, eyes looking straight ahead. I will take three photographs. After each I will request that you rotate your body a quarter turn to the right.

I will take three more photographs and ask you to turn your body again, a quarter turn to the right. We will continue this process until I photograph all four sides of you. Okay?

Explaining the process in advance will reduce suspect stress and foster cooperation. In addition, it is best to refer to the alleged crime as the *incident*, a term that is neutral and less accusatory. A crime suspect may be more cooperative if approached by the forensic technician from a position of neutrality.

Gunshot Residue Collection

Suspects should not be allowed to wash their hands prior to evidence collection. Hand washing may destroy or remove microscopic evidence such as gunshot residue (GSR) or biological evidence, such as a victim's DNA. Further, many knowledgeable suspects discard their clothing quickly, especially if they suspect a GSR test is possible. Hopefully, a suspect's clothing is seized immediately upon arrest by arresting officers.

If the suspect is accused of involvement in a shooting, a GSR test will be conducted in most jurisdictions. GSR is fragile evidence and dissipates easily. The GSR test should be conducted immediately, prior to removal of the suspect's clothing, because GSR may transfer to clothing when removed.

Detailed processing instructions accompany standard GSR kits. The kits contain four vials with adhesive tabs. The vials are labeled RIGHT BACK, RIGHT PALM, LEFT BACK, and LEFT PALM, indicating the area of the hand to which the adhesive tab is to be applied.

1. Wearing latex or similar protective gloves, the forensic technician should remove the adhesive tab from the RIGHT BACK vial and press the tab several times against the back of the suspect's right thumb and forefinger, and against the web of the hand, the area between the thumb and forefinger. GSR will adhere to the tab as the tab is pressed against the skin. The tab is removed and returned to the vial.
2. The tab must be removed from the RIGHT PALM vial. The tab is pressed against the right palm and returned to the RIGHT PALM vial.
3. Using the LEFT BACK vial tab, the tab is pressed against the back of the index finger and thumb and the web of the thumb. Return the tab to the LEFT BACK vial.
4. Using the LEFT PALM vial tab, the tab is pressed against the left palm. Return the tab to the LEFT PALM vial.

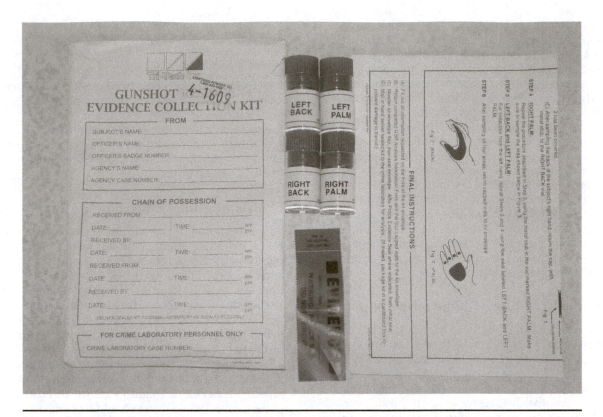

Photo 13-1. Gunshot residue kit.

Photo 13-2. Gunshot residue vials.

Subsequently, the vials are transported to the trace evidence section of a crime laboratory. At the laboratory, a scanning electron microscope is used by a criminalist to identify the presence of GSR.

Suspect Photography

After fragile evidence such as GSR is removed from the suspect, the next phase in suspect processing is photography. If the case investigator requests trace evidence collection, the suspect is asked to stand on a large sheet of clean evidence paper for the photographic process. Standing on the paper ensures that any trace evidence (e.g., hair, fibers) dislodged from the suspect will fall onto the paper for subsequent collection rather than the floor, where it could be lost or contaminated.

Preferably, the forensic technician should photograph a suspect standing in front of a plain background (light gray or white wall) to prevent reproduction of reflections, distractions, or imperfections in the photograph backdrop. A light gray wall, which reflects less light, is preferred. If a gray wall is not available, a plain, white wall will suffice. The suspect is asked to step approximately one foot away from the wall, so harsh shadows produced by the camera's flash unit drop behind the suspect's body and are not depicted in the photograph.

Numerous images are photographed, each capturing a different view of the suspect for possible witness or victim identification. Several photographs are taken, including overall, medium, and close-up images in order to capture scars, injuries, or tattoos that a victim or witness may have observed and described. The following procedure is recommended for suspect photography:

1. With the suspect facing the photographer, arms at sides, looking straight ahead, the forensic technician will take one overall photograph of the entire body, head to toe. The camera should be positioned vertically, flash unit on top, avoiding a wide angle.
2. A medium-range photograph of the suspect from head to chest is taken. The camera should be rotated to its normal position (horizontal) for this image.
3. A close-up of the suspect's face is taken next. At close range, the forensic technician should position the flash unit at a 45-degree angle to the suspect's face to prevent a hot spot (overexposure) of the suspect's face.
4. The suspect is asked to complete a quarter turn to the right, exposing the suspect's left

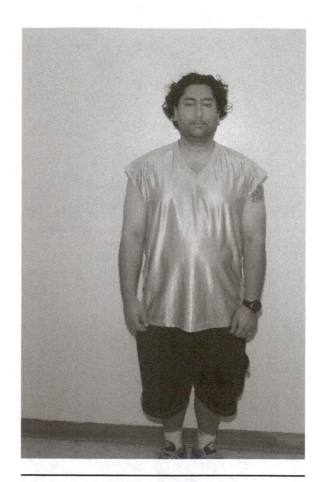

Photo 13-3. Model posing as a suspect.

Photo 13-4. Model posing as a suspect.

profile, and the photographic process is repeated: head to toe, head to chest, and close-up of the left side of the head.
5. The suspect is asked to complete a second quarter turn to the right. After the quarter

Photo 13-5. Model posing as a suspect.

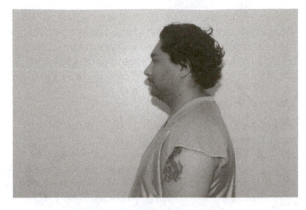

Photo 13-7. Suspect photos.

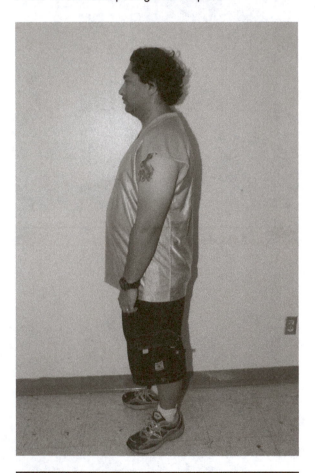

Photo 13-6. Suspect photos.

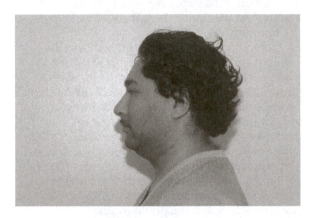

Photo 13-8. Suspect photos.

turn, the suspect should be facing the wall, with the suspect's back to the photographer. The photographic process is repeated: head to toe, head to chest, and close-up of the back of the head.

6. The suspect is asked to complete a third quarter turn, exposing the right side, and the photographic process is repeated: head to toe, head to chest, close-up of the right side of the head.

7. The suspect is seated and asked to place both hands on a table. Photographs are taken of the front and back of the suspect's hands.

8. If a victim's blood was shed during the incident, the victim's blood may have contacted and adhered to the suspect's clothing. With the suspect in a standing position, the forensic technician should search for traces of blood evidence and take an orientation photograph (a photograph showing the location of the evidence), followed by a close-up photograph of the suspected blood evidence with a measurement scale in place within the photo's frame. If the suspect is wearing shoes or boots that might have been worn during the incident under investigation, orientation and close-up views of the tops and soles of the suspect's footwear should be photographed as well.

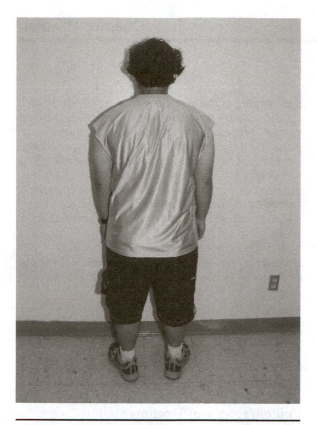

Photo 13-9. Suspect photos.

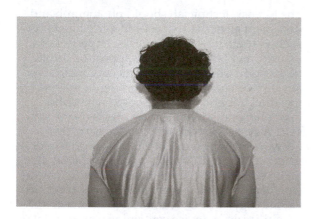

Photo 13-10. Suspect photos.

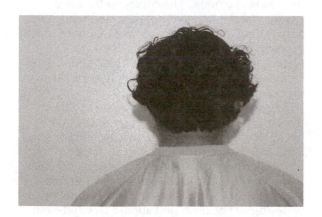

Photo 13-11. Suspect photos.

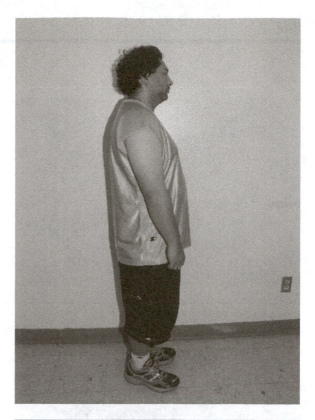

Photo 13-12. Suspect photos.

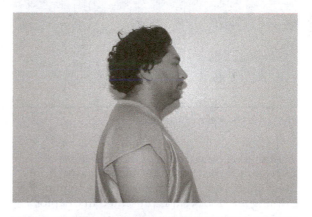

Photo 13-13. Suspect photos.

Photo 13-14. Suspect photos.

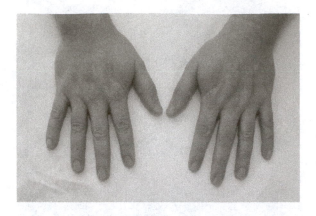

Photo 13-15. Back of hands.

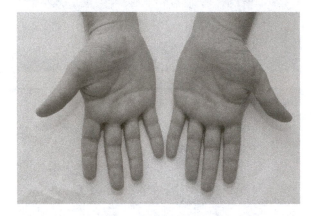

Photo 13-16. Palm of hands.

Detailed photographs of the clothing and footwear will be taken later, after removal from the suspect. More information on photography of clothing and footwear is presented in Chapter 9.

Clothing Collection

After general photographs of the suspect are taken, each item of the suspect's clothing is collected. Alternative clothing is provided for the suspect. The clothing collected may be searched later for trace evidence (e.g., hair and fibers). Therefore, each item of clothing should be wrapped separately in clean evidence packaging paper (commonly referred to as *butcher or craft paper*) and placed in a clean paper bag. Each bag should be sealed, labeled for identification, and stored with the property and evidence unit.

If the incident under investigation is an alleged sex crime, the forensic technician may be required to repeat all of the photographic steps of the suspect, including overall, head-to-chest, and close-up views of the suspect's head, after the clothing is removed. The forensic technician should consult with the case investigator prior to suspect processing to inquire if nude photographic images are necessary. If the suspect does not consent to the nude photos, the forensic technician must also ensure that photos taken without the suspect's consent are legally permissible. In some jurisdictions, photographing a nude suspect without consent may be considered an illegal strip search.

If nude images are required, the suspect should be photographed by a forensic technician of the same gender. If a forensic technician of the same gender is not available, an agency employee of the same gender as the suspect should be present during the photo session. The suspect's clothing should be removed according to the procedures necessary to protect and preserve relevant trace evidence that may be present on the clothing.

Photography and Documentation of Scars, Injuries, and Tattoos

The forensic technician should photograph and document all of the suspect's identifying marks such as scars, moles, birthmarks, imperfections, injuries, and tattoos that may appear on the suspect's body. The forensic technician should follow a systematic protocol, working from head to toe, front to back, and left to right when photographing and documenting marks on the suspect. A systematic approach will ensure that every identifying mark is photographed. An orientation (medium) view is photographed first, followed by a close-up without and with a measurement scale. An American Board of Forensic Odontology (ABFO) Number 2 photomacrographic scale (a device containing a gray scale and circles) should be used to accurately depict the size of the mark. The circles on the scale ensure that the image is not distorted while the gray portion on the scale ensures that the correct exposure is taken of the image. The scale is placed on the skin, next to the mark, and included in the photo to accurately depict the precise measurement of the mark.

The surface of the camera lens should be at the same level and perpendicular to the mark, not at an angle to it. The forensic technician may bend at the knees or squat while photographing the mark to ensure that the lens is perpendicular to the mark. To avoid distortion, photographs should be taken at 50 mm or closer but not at wide angle. The flash unit should be hand-held at an angle of 45 degrees to the identifying mark being photographed.

Photo 13-17. Orientation view of tattoo.

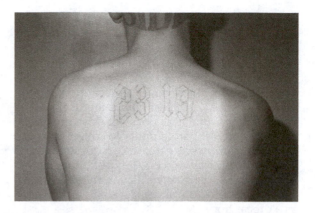

Photo 13-20. Orientation view of gang member's tattoo. Courtesy of Chula Vista, California, Police Department.

Photo 13-18. Close-up view of tattoo without scale.

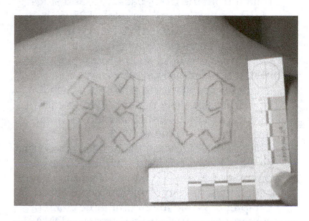

Photo 13-21. Close-up view of gang member's tattoo. Courtesy of Chula Vista, California, Police Department.

orientation and one close-up photograph with and without a scale, and describe the mark in the field notes and final report. The location and length of the scratch mark should be included in the documented description. The forensic technician should repeat the process with all scars, injuries, tattoos, and birthmarks on the suspect's body.

Collecting Hair

Head hair samples are often collected from a crime suspect. Subsequently, the head hair sample is examined and compared to hairs collected from the crime scene and from the victim. A victim or witness may report that the suspect's head was shaved. Yet the suspect has head hair at the time of arrest and processing. Forensically speaking, it is not necessary to collect a sample

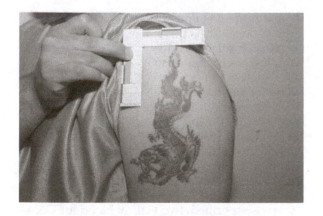

Photo 13-19. Close-up view of tattoo with scale.

The forensic technician should measure and describe each identifying mark in a report after photographing it. For example, if the suspect has a scratch mark on the back, the forensic technician should photograph the scratch with one

from a suspect in this situation. If the suspect was bald or the head was shaved at the time of the incident, it is extremely unlikely that any of the suspect's head hair was deposited at the crime scene. Thus, there is nothing to compare a sample hair to. However, as a precaution, it is wise to search for suspect hair at the crime scene. A more opportune time does not exist. Further, some case investigators prefer to collect suspect head hair samples as a defense to questioning during the judicial process. If questioning by the defense in a subsequent judicial proceeding is a possibility, collecting a suspect's hair is viewed as a precaution.

The following procedure is recommended for collecting a suspect's head hair:

1. Using tweezers, five to ten hairs should be pulled from the front, back, top, and sides of the suspect's head—a total of 25–50 hairs. Depending on its location, head hair can vary in appearance. Collecting hair from all head areas provides an appropriate sample of hair for comparison purposes.
2. The hairs are placed in a bindle, which is a small piece of clean paper folded to ensure that trace evidence, such as hairs or fibers, are not lost or contaminated.
3. The bindle containing the hairs is placed in a clean paper bag or large envelope. The bag or envelope is sealed and labeled for identification with case information as described in Chapter 4. While maintaining the chain of custody, the hair sample is frozen if DNA analysis is a possibility.

Buccal Epithelial Cell Collection

Buccal epithelial (oral cheek) cells are collected from the suspect's mouth and later used to obtain the suspect's DNA profile. The following procedure is recommended for obtaining buccal epithelial samples:

1. The forensic technician should wear clean protective latex gloves and use two sterile swabs to wipe an inner cheek of the suspect's mouth, thus transferring epithelial (cheek) cells from the suspect's mouth onto the swabs.
2. The swabs are placed in a bindle or a swab container, air dried, and packaged in a clean paper bag or large envelope marked for identification, sealed, and frozen, while maintaining the chain of custody. Subsequently, the cells on the swabs are used for DNA analysis and comparison.

Fingernail Scrapings and Clippings

Fingernail scrapings and clippings are often collected from a suspect involved in a crime. DNA from the scrapings and clippings are compared to a victim's DNA, especially in incidents (e.g., rape) in which transfer of this type of evidence is most probable. If a suspect is arrested several months after the alleged incident occurred, one may conclude that securing a victim's DNA from a suspect's fingernails is highly improbable. However, an investigator may view this evidence collection measure as a precaution against judicial scrutiny (queries by a defense attorney, prosecutor, or judge). The following procedure is recommended for obtaining fingernail scrapings or clippings from a suspect:

1. A bindle is unfolded, and one of the suspect's hands is placed in the middle of the bindle.
2. A clean toothpick or similar device is used to scrape under each fingernail of the hand. Sterile fingernail clippers may also be used to clip each fingernail.
3. The fingernails, scrapings, and toothpick are kept in the bindle. The bindle is folded and packaged in a clean paper bag or large envelope. The bag or envelope is marked for identification, sealed, and frozen. The process is repeated with the other hand. When applicable, this evidence is analyzed and compared to the victim's DNA.

Blood Draw

A **phlebotomist** (a medical professional who is trained to extract human blood samples) is summoned to draw vials of the suspect's blood for subsequent DNA analysis and profiling. If it appears that the suspect is under the influence of alcohol or drugs, an additional vial of blood should be drawn for toxicology (foreign or poisonous substance) analysis. The number of vials of blood drawn is dependent upon the guidelines and protocol of the laboratory that will test the blood. Unless otherwise specified, two vials of blood for DNA analysis and one vial of blood for toxicology testing are usually sufficient. To ensure that the required number of blood samples is available for analysis, crime laboratory personnel should be consulted prior to sample collection. The vials containing the blood are labeled for identification and packaged in a padded envelope, sealed,

> **Phlebotomist**   A medical professional who is trained to extract human blood samples.

and the envelope marked for identification. Blood in liquid form should be refrigerated, not frozen.

Suspect Fingerprints and Major Case Prints

When a suspect is arrested, the finger digits (fingertips) are inked and rolled onto a ten-print fingerprint card by the intake (booking) officer. Alternatively, the fingers, palms and sides of each hand may be scanned through the use of LiveScan. The inked prints are electronically scanned, or the LiveScan fingerprints are incorporated into AFIS. The data scanned is that of the ridge detail from the fingertips, and the palms and sides of each hand.

Often, latent fingerprints obtained from a crime scene are those of the suspect's palms or entire fingers, not just the tips of the fingers. However, only ridge detail of the fingertips can be used to compare and classify fingerprints obtained from a crime scene. To compare all of the latent palm prints and fingerprints collected from the crime scene, "major case" prints are obtained from the suspect. In other words, all friction skin on the palm and fingers is recorded (U.S. Department of Justice. Federal Bureau of Investigation,1984).

Major case prints are recordings of all of the ridge detail of the suspect's hand, not the fingertips alone. The tips, sides, and lower joints of the fingers are printed. An inked surface or magnetic powder and pre-printed fingerprint cards or paper are used. When using fingerprint ink, the front of each individual finger is inked from side to side and rolled onto the fingerprint card or paper. Thus, the sides, front and tip of the finger are inked. The inked fingers are rolled, one at a time, onto the appropriate square on the 8-inch × 8-inch fingerprint card or plain cardstock paper. If a pre-printed fingerprint card is not available, the print is identified (labeled) on the card or paper.

Next, the entire palm and front of all fingers as well as the outer edges of the hand are inked with a fingerprint ink roller. A second piece of 8-inch × 8-inch plain cardstock paper is placed on a rounded surface, and the hand is placed on the paper, starting with the wrist, and rolled forward, ending with the fingertips. Next, the outer sides of the little finger and the thumb are pressed onto the paper, and the appropriate finger is identified (labeled) on the cardstock paper.

> **Major case prints**
> The recordings of all of the ridge detail of a suspect's hand, not the fingertips alone. The tips, sides, and lower joints of the fingers are also printed.

Photo 13-22. Demo of obtaining known hand prints.

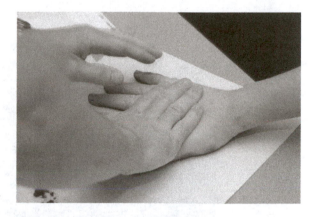

Photo 13-23. Demo of obtaining known hand prints.

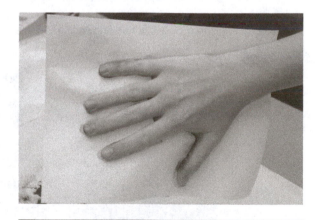

Photo 13-24. Demo of obtaining known hand prints.

If using black magnetic powder instead of ink, the palm and front and sides of the fingers are covered with a light coating of the powder. The forensic technician should not apply an excessive amount of powder because too much powder

Photo 13-25. Demo of obtaining known hand prints.

will inhibit transposition of the pattern ridge detail. After the entire palm, all fingers, and sides of the hand are covered with black magnetic powder, excess powder can be removed by blowing lightly over the hand. A piece of 8-inch × 8-inch adhesive fingerprint lifting paper is placed against the palm, and the forensic technician presses the paper around the palm and the fingers. Next, each finger is printed separately, utilizing small (approximately 2-inch × 3-inch) adhesive fingerprint lifting tabs or paper.

The recorded major case prints should be identified (labeled) with the case number, the suspect's name and signature, and the forensic technician's name and identification number.

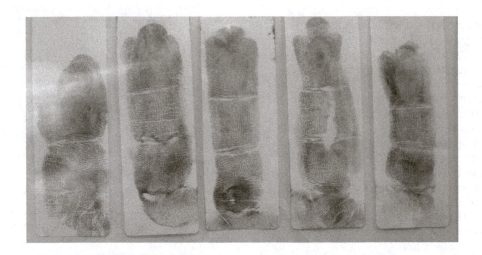

Photo 13-26. Lifted known finger prints.

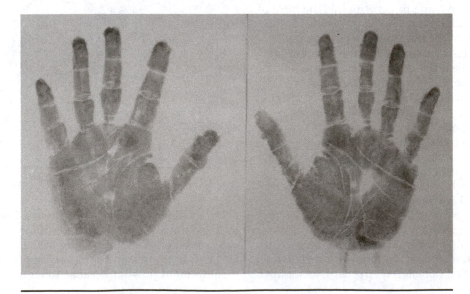

Photo 13-27. Lifted known hand prints.

The hands should be labeled left or right. The thumb, index, middle, ring, and little fingers should be labeled as well. The recorded major case prints are placed in a large manila envelope and packaged according to the agency's policy.

Safety Precautions

Processing any suspect is potentially dangerous. Close proximity to a suspect places the forensic technician at risk of serious injury, especially if the forensic technician is not a sworn peace officer with specialized training in defensive tactics and prisoner restraint techniques. Processing a crime suspect involves rolling or scanning of fingerprints and an array of evidence collection and photographic procedures. Tools such as tweezers, pencils, pens, and fingernail clippers can be used as weapons. These items should be kept out of reach of the suspect.

A forensic technician often processes unrestrained suspects. Thus, the forensic technician is placed in vulnerable and unsafe positions. For this reason, it is recommended that a sworn peace officer or investigator be present during suspect processing. The presence of a sworn officer does not ensure that a suspect will be civil, compliant, or non-threatening. In situations in which physical aggression is likely, restraints can be applied to a suspect to protect personnel while evidence is collected. Although cooperation is never assured, civility and respect on the part of the forensic technician may encourage suspect cooperation and promote forensic technician safety.

LIVE VICTIM PROCESSING

Forensic technicians are required to photograph injuries of and collect evidence from victims of a variety of crimes. Live victims of child or elder abuse, domestic violence, sex crimes, and other violent offenses must be processed. Victims of violent crime are often vulnerable, fearful, and anxious. During the victim interview and processing, the forensic technician and other law enforcement personnel involved should be empathetic and assist the victim in any manner professionally possible. Victim advocates as well as specialists (e.g., sexual assault nurse examiners) are available in many jurisdictions.

If the victim is not of the same gender as the forensic technician, personnel of the victim's gender should be present during processing, especially if evidence or injuries are located in or near intimate parts of the victim's body. Personnel of the victim's gender should collect clothing from and provide alternate clothing for the victim. Further, a sign that reads "victim being processed" should be displayed outside the processing room, so no one inadvertently enters during the evidence collection process.

Victims often sustain injuries to areas of the body that are covered with clothing. If the victim's apparel is not collected for evidence, the victim need only remove that portion necessary to expose the injury for photographic purposes. If a victim is wearing a long-sleeve shirt (or blouse) and sustained an injury high on an arm, it may not be possible to access the injury by simply moving the shirt's sleeve up. Alternatively, the victim can be asked to remove the arm from the shirt, rather than remove the shirt completely. If the victim sustained an injury on the back, the back of the shirt can be lifted to expose the injury. Complete removal of the shirt may not be necessary.

If the victim sustained an injury to a leg and is wearing tight pants, the pants must be lowered. The victim should be provided with a lab coat or other covering to protect the victim's privacy and personal dignity whenever an intimate body part might be exposed.

Live Victim Photography

The procedure for live victim photography is similar to suspect processing. The following procedure is recommended when photographing a crime victim:

1. Trace evidence from the suspect may be located on the victim's clothing or body. The victim is asked to stand on a large sheet of clean paper so any hair or fibers that fall away from the victim's clothing or body are collected on the paper and are not contaminated.
2. The victim is asked to stand approximately one foot in front of a plain light gray or white wall, with hands to the side, facing the photographer. An overall, head-to-toe view is photographed.
3. A close-up view of the victim's face is photographed for identification purposes. Unlike suspect photography, the victim is not asked to turn sideways for profile photographs.
4. If the victim sustained any physical injuries, the injuries are photographed following the same procedure used when photographing a suspect. The victim is photographed head to toe, front to back, left to right until every injury is photographed. Orientation and close-up photographs without and with an

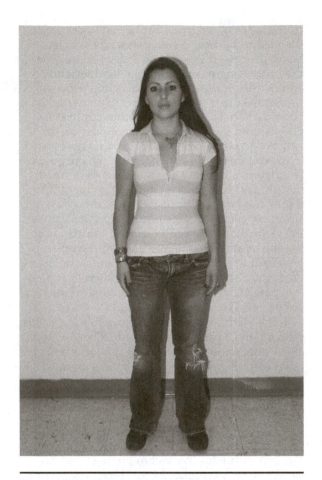

Photo 13-28. Model posing as a victim.

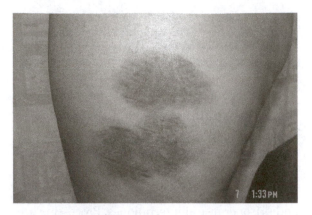

Photo 13-30. Orientation and close-up photographs of a victim's bruise. Courtesy of National City, California, Police Department.

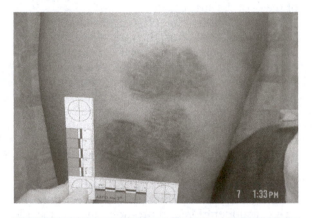

Photo 13-31. Orientation and close-up photographs of a victim's bruise. Courtesy of National City, California, Police Department.

Photo 13-29. Model posing as a victim.

L-shaped measuring device should be obtained. Each injury should be measured, described, and documented. Refer to the suspect photography section discussed previously for details.

Along with photographing, describing, and documenting bruises, scratches, and other injuries, the forensic technician should photograph petechial hemorrhaging that might be visible in the eyes. **Petechial hemorrhaging** is the pinpoint hemorrhaging (or rupture) of small blood vessels often observed in the eyes of a victim of an attempted strangulation or other events related to breathing airway obstruction (DiMaio & DiMaio, 2001). Evidence of petechial hemorrhaging and its exact cause is best verified by a trained medical professional.

> **Petechial hemorrhaging** The pinpoint hemorrhaging (or rupture) of small blood vessels often observed in the eyes of a victim of an attempted strangulation or other events related to breathing airway obstruction.

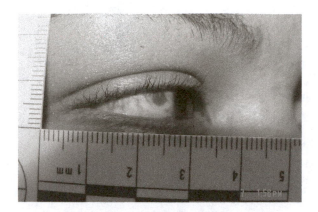

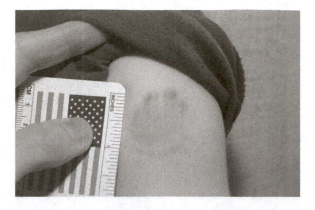

Photo 13-32. Petechial hemorrhaging. Courtesy of National City, California, Police Department.

Photo 13-33. Bite mark injuries on a child.

Bite Mark Photography

In some sex crime and child abuse cases, victims sustain bite mark injuries from the perpetrator. Bite mark evidence is fragile and should be photographed as soon as possible, but no later than 24 hours after the injury is sustained. Prior to photography, the injured area should be swabbed to collect any saliva deposited by the perpetrator when the injury was inflicted. The saliva sample is subject to DNA analysis and profiling. Two drops of distilled water should be placed on a sterile swab. The swab is rubbed on the bite mark, thus collecting epithelial (cheek) cells that may have been transferred to the victim from the perpetrator. The swab is placed in a bindle or swab holder, dried, packaged in paper, labeled for identification, and frozen.

To photograph a bite mark, the following procedure is recommended:

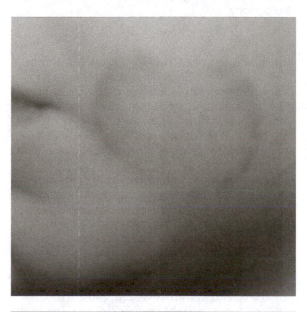

Photo 13-34. Bite mark injuries on a child.

1. An orientation (medium) view of the bite mark should be taken first so the viewer of the photo(s) is aware of the location of the bite mark on the victim. A close-up photo of the bite mark is taken after completion of Steps 2–10.
2. The camera should be secured on a tripod.
3. The camera should be placed directly in front of the bite mark with the surface of the camera lens parallel to (facing) the mark.
4. An L-shaped ruler (measuring device) should be placed against the skin, next to the bite mark.
5. The camera's aperture setting should provide the best depth-of-field possible. An F-stop setting of F-22 is recommended.
6. If using a digital camera, the frame should be filled with the details of the bite mark as well as the ruler, rather than photographing

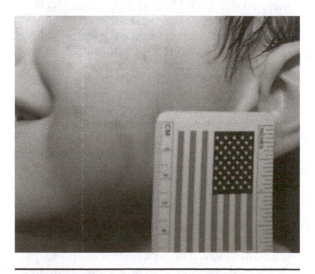

Photo 13-35. Bite mark injuries on a child.

Photo 13-36. Photographic setup for bite mark photography.

Photo 13-37. Demo of forensic technician conducting bite mark photography.

the bite mark one to one (life size). It is important that the pixels in the image are used to capture the detail of the bite mark and ensure the best resolution. Photographing the image one to one (a film camera technique) wastes pixels, thus reducing resolution. The image can be printed later, at life size, for comparison purposes.

7. The camera's flash unit should be held at a 45 degree angle to the bite mark. A series of photographs should be taken, bracketing (using different shutter speeds to allow in different amounts of light) if necessary.

8. An alternate light source (ALS) may be used to view and photograph the bite mark so details of the bite mark not normally observed by the naked eye are revealed. Most ALS devices provide light frequencies ranging from ultraviolet (UV) to infrared (IR). It is recommended that both UV and IR frequencies be used. The forensic technician should experiment with different colored goggles (typically orange, yellow, and red) to determine which color highlights most of the observable detail of the bite mark. The victim should be provided with protective goggles to prevent damage to the eyes during the ALS photography process.

9. The lens filter or shield used on the camera should be the same color as the goggles used by the forensic technician to view the bite mark. If orange goggles produce the best results when viewing the bite mark, then an orange lens filter or shield should be used on the camera. The photographer should connect the appropriate colored lens filter to the camera or clamp the appropriate colored shield to the front of the camera lens if no lens filter is available.

10. The ALS is held at an angle (approximately 45 degrees), with the light beam shining

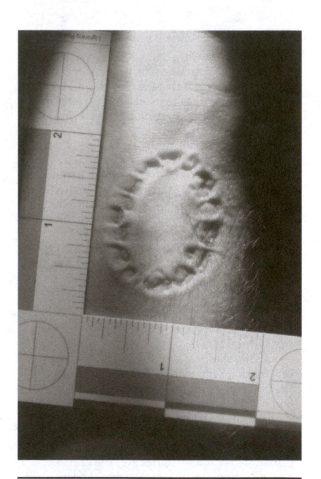

Photo 13-38. ALS photograph of a bite mark. Photograph by Todd Griffiths.

directly on the bite mark. The L-shaped ruler and a good depth-of-field should also be used. A series of photographs should be taken, bracketing the exposure.

ALS photography does not replace color photographs of a bite mark. Color photographs reveal moles and marks on the skin that could be misinterpreted as part of the bite mark in an ALS (black and white) photograph (Sperber, 2009).

Photographs of the victim's bite mark injury are crucial evidentiary items. When the suspect is arrested, bite mark impressions will be obtained from the suspect by a forensic odontologist who will compare the bite mark photographs secured by the forensic technician to the suspect's dental impressions. If available, the forensic technician/ investigator may wish to consult with a forensic odontologist to ensure that the details of victim's bite mark injury were photographically captured for comparison purposes. Since bite marks can change appearance within 24 hours of infliction, a forensic odontologist should review the images as soon as possible.

Evidence Collection

Evidence collected from a victim is often similar to that collected from a suspect. Clothing, hair, oral cheek cells, fingernail scrapings, and fingerprints are collected. Collecting these items from the victim requires adherence to the same procedures as is followed during suspect processing.

Rape and Sexual Assault Cases

In suspected rape or sexual assault cases, the victim should be transported by officials to a health care facility that employs forensically trained nursing staff. A forensic medical professional photographs the victim. Microscopic images of internal trauma (trauma to the anus or vaginal cavity) are collected. The victim's clothing is collected according to established procedure, and DNA evidence is collected with oral, anal, or vaginal swabs.

Biological evidence, (e.g., blood, semen, saliva) located on clothing should be stored in paper, not plastic, to prevent accelerated deterioration. The chain of custody of evidence is not broken if a law enforcement officer is not physically present to observe collection of evidence by a sexual assault nurse examiner or similar medical professional. However, the evidence must be transferred to law enforcement personnel immediately for impoundment with the agency's property and evidence unit.

A forensic technician is rarely involved in evidence collection from a rape victim because the evidence is usually collected by the forensically trained medical professional. The protocol varies among jurisdictions, depending on the policies and procedures of individual agencies. The forensic specialist is summoned for follow-up photography of the victim's external injuries only.

Many rape or other sex crime victims transport themselves to a hospital without notifying police. Subsequently, hospital personnel record the incident and notify law enforcement authorities.

Child Abuse Cases

In child abuse cases, an investigator and a representative for the child victim, such as a social worker, should be present during victim processing. The victim's parent should not be present. The emotional reaction of the parent may impact the child negatively, and interfere with evidence collection. The forensic technician should demonstrate compassion and use language that helps reduce the victim's fear and anxiety. Distractions help reduce anxiety in children. Demonstrating how ALS reveals clothing fibers not normally seen with the naked human eye, or explaining the use of magnetic powder, works well as distraction techniques. Magnetic powder and ALS are discussed in Chapters 5 and 7, respectively.

Photographic and evidence collection procedures with a child-victim are similar to any other live victim. In suspected child molestation cases, a forensic medical professional (e.g., forensic pediatrician) often collects appropriate evidence and photographs internal injuries. If evidence is collected by the forensic technician, unsolicited statements of the child that are relevant to the case should be documented.

SUMMARY

The goals of the criminal justice system include the apprehension of the crime perpetrator and justice for victims of crime. To accomplish these tasks, evidence must be located, documented, collected, compared, and proven to link the suspect, the victim, and the crime scene. Communication between the forensic specialist and case investigator is vital to ensure that a comprehensive, legally permissible process is followed.

Photographs must be taken of the victim and the suspect, including all injuries to the victim as well as all injuries, birthmarks, scars, and tattoos on the suspect. A thorough search for trace evidence such as hair and fibers must be conducted along with the collection of samples for DNA analysis. Collecting an array of evidence for comparison increases the likelihood of suspect, victim, and crime scene linkage.

When processing the victim of a violent crime, the forensic specialist should demonstrate compassion, care, respect, and patience. Treating a crime suspect with respect and demonstrating patience with a suspect is often more challenging, but equally important. The forensic specialist should keep an underlying goal in mind: to objectively obtain evidence essential to a successful case disposition. The forensic specialist's primary objective is to seek the truth.

KEY TERMS

Define, describe, or explain the importance of each of the following:

major case prints   petechial hemorrhaging   phlebotomist

DISCUSSION AND REVIEW QUESTIONS

1. What photographs are taken during the processing of a suspect?
2. What photographs are taken of a live crime victim?
3. Describe the procedure for photographing a bite mark.
4. What evidentiary items are collected during suspect processing?
5. Why is it important to treat a suspect with respect?
6. If you were sexually assaulted, how would you wish to be treated by a forensic technician?

CASE STUDY—Stephanie Crowe

The radio alarm clock sounded and went unanswered at 6:30 a.m. on January 21, 1998, in the bedroom of 12-year-old Stephanie Crowe. Judith Kennedy, Stephanie's grandmother, went into the bedroom to investigate. Judith discovered Stephanie dead and bloodied. Stephanie had been stabbed nine times through her bedding.

Police briefly detained Richard Raymond Tuite, a schizophrenic transient often observed in the Crowe's Escondido, California, neighborhood. Police ruled Tuite out as a suspect, exchanged his clothes for a sweatsuit, and released him.

The police investigation soon turned in the direction of Stephanie's 14-year-old brother, Michael, and two of his teenage male friends. The boys were arrested and after lengthy interrogations, they provided self-incriminating information, including a detailed confession.

During the pre-trial phase of the case in early 1999, a judge ruled that the teenagers' incriminating statements were coerced and the murder charges against the boys were dismissed upon the prosecutors' motion. Subsequently, the case languished until Escondido police transferred the case to the San Diego County Sheriff

Department's homicide unit. Prosecution of the case was transferred to the California Attorney General's Office, which charged Richard Tuite in 2002.

Tuite's trial began in 2004. Jurors learned from sheriff's forensics personnel that Stephanie's blood was located on two items of Tuite's clothing that were exchanged for the sweatsuit when he was released by Escondido police. After eight days of deliberation, jurors found Tuite guilty of voluntary manslaughter.

1. How might Stephanie's blood on Tuite's clothing have been overlooked when the police detained Tuite originally?
2. Outline the protocol for processing a crime suspect.

LAB EXERCISE

Suspect Processing

Equipment and supplies required per student:

- one 35-mm camera (film or digital)
- one roll of 35-mm film, 200 or 400 ISO (if using film camera)
- one L-shaped ruler (measuring device)
- one pair of disposable latex gloves (or alternate gloves if latex allergic)
- one pair of disposable tweezers
- two sterile cotton swabs
- two toothpicks
- four bindles
- one fingerprint ink and roller, or magnetic powder and powder wand
- four 8" × 8" cardstock paper or adhesive fingerprint lifting paper
- four envelopes or small bags
- one 8½" × 11" manila envelope
- one roll of packing tape
- one marking pen
- hand cleaner

1. Using the techniques learned in this chapter, students form pairs and alternate roles as a forensic specialist and a suspect, processing each other as a suspect arrested for a crime.
2. Obtain the evidence listed in the check-off sheet below and make notes, including date and time of collection. Write a final report of the processing steps taken.
3. If your suspect utters a self-incriminating statement (admission or confession), document the statement in your report.
4. Clothing will not be collected. Assume your suspect is in a jail suit and the clothing was collected previously. A blood draw will not be conducted.
5. Check off each box below after completion of the accompanying activity. Upon completion of the exercise, submit the check-off sheet, notes, report, and all properly collected, packaged, and labeled evidence and photographs to the instructor.

Photographs   Date: Time:

- ☐ Overall views, all four sides
- ☐ Medium views, all four sides
- ☐ Close-up views, all four sides
- ☐ View of hands, front and back
- ☐ Orientation view of injury, scar or tattoo

Create a mark if none is apparent. Do not remove clothing.

- ☐ Close-up view of mark without an L-shaped ruler
- ☐ Close-up view of mark with an L-shaped ruler

Evidence Collection	Date:	Time:

☐ Head hair sample

One hair is enough for practice. Package properly.

☐ Oral swabs

Obtain oral skin cell samples from an inner cheek using two swabs. Package properly.

☐ Fingernail scrapings

Collect fingernail scrapings using a separate clean toothpick for each hand. Package each toothpick separately and label properly.

Fingerprinting	Date:	Time:

☐ Fingerprints

Collect fingerprints using either the ink or magnetic powder method.

Label the fingerprint card properly and place in manila envelope.

WEB RESOURCES

Department of Justice:
  www.usdoj.gov
Federal Bureau of Investigations:
  www.fbi.gov
Minority Nurse:
  www.minoritynurse.com
National Center for Missing and Exploited
  Children:
  www.missingkids.com
National Online Resource Center on Violence
  against Women (VAWNET):
  www.new.vawnet.org

National Sexual Violence Resource Center
  (NSVRC):
  www.nsvrc.org
Naval Criminal Investigative Service:
  www.ncis.navy.mil
Office for Victims of Crime:
  www.ovc.gov
United States Army Criminal Investigation
  Command:
  www.cid.army.mil
United States Air Force Office of Special
    Investigations: www.public.afosi.amc.af.mil

14

The Postmortem Examination

LEARNING OUTCOMES

After completing this chapter, the reader should be able to:

- describe the role of the forensic pathologist,
- distinguish cause, mechanism, and manner of death,
- list the five categories of manner of death,
- describe the characteristics of a sharp force injury,
- describe the characteristics of a blunt force injury,
- describe the characteristics of contact, close-range, and distant gunshot entry wounds,
- define asphyxia,
- list the categories of traumatic death caused by asphyxia,
- define algor mortis, livor mortis, and rigor mortis,
- articulate the biological processes that accompany decomposition,
- describe the photographs taken and evidence collected during a postmortem examination.

INTRODUCTION

An unexpected death of a human being, or one caused by an injury or suspected poisoning, usually requires a *postmortem examination (autopsy)*. Postmortem means *after death* and autopsy means to *look at oneself*. If the deceased was under a physician's care and the doctor signs a death certificate that specifies the cause and manner of death, the deceased typically does not undergo an autopsy.

In most states, a coroner or a medical examiner system is in place. The coroner system developed in England before the tenth century. The coroner was an inquisitional judge who conducted investigations. In the United States, a **coroner** is an elected official, not necessarily a medical doctor, who oversees **forensic pathologists** (medical doctors who perform autopsies). In the medical examiner system, a **medical examiner** (a medical doctor trained in pathology) oversees the pathologists in the jurisdiction (James & Nordby, 2005).

> **Coroner** An elected official (not necessarily a medical doctor) who oversees **forensic pathologists** (medical doctors who perform autopsies).

> **Medical examiner** A medical doctor trained in pathology who oversees the pathologists in the jurisdiction.

This chapter addresses the role of the forensic pathologist as well as the categories of traumatic death and the basic types of injuries associated with each category. The information presented is not all inclusive, but it addresses the most common injuries associated with violent crimes. The chapter also discusses the role of and tasks performed by the forensic technician at a postmortem examination.

FORENSIC PATHOLOGIST EDUCATION, TRAINING, AND DUTIES

A forensic pathologist's formal education begins with a baccalaureate in one of the physical sciences, such as biology or microbiology, and is followed with four years of medical school plus four years of post-medical school training in pathology. A fifth year of paid pathology training takes place at a coroner or medical examiner office. In addition to the extensive formal education, a forensic pathologist usually completes forensic science training in toxicology, serology, tool mark examination, firearms examination, crime scene analysis, anthropology, odontology, and criminal law. To become certified by the

American Board of Pathology, a forensic pathologist must pass an exam.

In conjunction with an autopsy, the forensic
pathologist may:

- review the medical history of the deceased,
- ascertain if death was sudden, unexpected
  (not involving a known pre-existing condition), or due to delayed effects of a previous
  injury,
- determine if visible injuries are a result of life
  saving attempts by paramedics or other first
  responders,
- determine the deceased's activity prior to
  death,
- review any witness statements obtained by
  the police,
- review crime scene photos, sketches,
  evidence, and reports,
- visit the crime scene prior to the autopsy
  (Wright, 2005b).

The pathologist may also consult with other
professionals, such as a forensic anthropologist
or a forensic odontologist.

THE POSTMORTEM EXAMINATION (AUTOPSY)

The **postmortem examina-
tion (autopsy)** is the primary duty of the forensic
pathologist. The autopsy is
conducted to determine the
cause, mechanism, and
manner of death of a
human being. While the forensic pathologist
may employ an investigator to visit and evaluate
a crime scene and review scene evidence, photos,
and reports, the forensic pathologist cannot dele-
gate performance of the autopsy. However, non-
medical personnel often assist the pathologist
with various aspects of the autopsy.

During the autopsy, the forensic pathologist
conducts a thorough examination of the exterior
of the body, noting measurements of injuries
and remarkable conditions of the body. Clothing
is removed from the deceased, typically by an
assistant, and collected by a forensic technician.

After examining the exterior of the body, a
Y-shaped incision is made in the chest area. The
incision is made from each shoulder to the middle of the chest and from the chest down through
the abdomen. The chest cavity is opened, and
internal organs are examined and removed.
Samples of the internal organs may be preserved
for toxicology and microscopic analysis.

**Postmortem exami-
nation (autopsy)** An
examination conduc-
ted to determine the
cause, mechanism,
and manner of death
of a human being.

After the internal organs of the chest cavity
are examined and removed, an incision is made
to the back of the head from ear to ear. The scalp
is peeled up and forward over the face, and the
skull is opened with precise electric saw cuts.
Trauma caused by the saw to the skull cap is
documented, and the skull cap is removed,
revealing the brain. The brain is removed from
the skull and analyzed for trauma. Portions of
the brain are fixed (preserved) in a chemical for
future analysis.

Analysis of other portions and organs of
the body is dependent upon the nature of the
investigation. The neck and spinal cord will
receive special attention in strangulation cases.
Incisions may be made into tissue to view
bruises that are not readily observable on the
surface of the skin.

After the autopsy, organ specimens are examined and tested for drugs, alcohol, and poisons.
DNA analysis may be conducted as well. The
tests and analyses may be conducted in the
autopsy laboratory or specimens may be forwarded to another laboratory. The protocol
varies among jurisdictions.

The forensic pathologist prepares final written
reports of the postmortem examination findings.
The **gross report** is based on
information obtained and
observations made during
the autopsy. The
microscopic report contains
information obtained and
observations made from
specimens viewed under a
microscope. The final
reports will include any
determination of the cause,
mechanism, and manner of
death.

Gross report
Written report contain-
ing information
obtained and obser-
vations made during
the autopsy.

Microscopic report
Written report contain-
ing information
obtained and obser-
vations made from
specimens viewed
under a microscope.

CAUSE, MECHANISM, AND MANNER OF DEATH

Cause of death is a conclusion drawn by the
forensic pathologist that identifies the injury or
disease that led to the biological chain of events
resulting in death. Example
of causes of death determi-
nations include a gunshot
wound to the head or a stab
wound to the heart.
Mechanism of death is the
determination of the forensic pathologist that identifies the biochemical or

Cause of death A
conclusion drawn by
the forensic patholo-
gist that identifies the
injury or disease that
led to the biological
chain of events result-
ing in death.

physiological abnormality that causes the death. Hemorrhaging as a result of a gunshot wound is an example of the mechanism-of-death determination (DiMaio & DiMaio, 2001).

Mechanism of death The determination of the forensic pathologist that identifies the biochemical or physiological abnormality that caused a death.

Manner of death is the determination made by the forensic pathologist that concludes how the cause of death came to be. The five broad categories of manner of death are easily remembered through the acronym *S-H-A-U-N*:

Manner of death The determination made by the forensic pathologist that concludes how the cause of death occurred.

- Suicide—the death is self-inflicted.
- Homicide—death was the result of the actions of another human being. The homicide may be excusable (e.g., self-defense), justifiable (e.g., court-ordered execution), or criminal (e.g., murder or manslaughter).
- Accidental—the actions that resulted in death are determined to be accidental.
- Undetermined—the cause of death is unknown.
- Natural—the cause of death is based on a disease or a biological abnormality.

TRAUMATIC DEATH

A traumatic death is classified into one of four basic categories:

- Mechanical trauma—includes sharp object injuries, blunt force trauma, firearms injuries, and occasional asphyxia.
- Chemical trauma—includes drugs, poisons, and occasional asphyxia.
- Thermal trauma—includes hypothermia, hyperthermia, and occasional asphyxia.
- Electrical trauma—includes injuries involving electricity.

Investigations and autopsies are routinely performed in traumatic death cases (Wright, 2005a).

Mechanical Trauma Injuries

A **mechanical trauma injury** results from the application of an object such as a sharp or blunt force instrument or a firearm trajectory. Mechanical trauma wounds are the most

Mechanical trauma injury Injury resulting from the application of an object such as a sharp or blunt force instrument or a firearm trajectory.

common injuries encountered by law enforcement personnel. Identifying the weapon that inflicted the injury is very important in a criminal investigation. Sometimes the type of weapon used is obvious. Other times, the source of the injury is not readily apparent and may not be determined until an autopsy is performed.

In most cases, pathologists can determine the type of weapon used to inflict an injury. Special cases may require consultation with a weapon-to-injury comparison expert. A bite mark impression, for example, may require consultation with a forensic odontologist.

Identifying the type of weapon used helps the pathologist determine cause and manner of death. Knowing the type of weapon also helps the case investigator during suspect and witness interviews and assists the bloodstain pattern expert in reconstructing the crime scene.

Sharp Object Injuries

A **sharp object injury** includes cutting, stabbing, and chopping wounds. Weapons used to produce cuts and stab wounds include knives, swords, scissors, ice picks, or any other sharp or pointed instrument, tool, or weapon. Weapons used to produce chopping wounds are sharp and heavy, including axes, meat cleavers, heavy swords, machetes, and other large sharp weapons (Spitz, 1993e).

Sharp object injury Injury resulting from cutting, stabbing, and chopping wounds.

Cut (slash) wounds may be identified through the following appearance criteria:

Cut (slash) wound Wound created by a cutting action with a sharp instrument. The wound typically has even, defined edges.

- The wound is created by a cutting action with a sharp instrument.
- The wound typically has even, defined edges.
- The wound is deepest where the instrument was first applied.
- Determination of suspect left- or right-handedness is possible.
- The wound is longer than it is deep.
- There is little abrasion (scraping) and minimal bruising around the wound.
- The wound appearance offers little information about the weapon.

Stab wounds puncture the skin and tend to penetrate more deeply than cut wounds. They typically appear as follows:

Stab wound Wound that punctures the skin; tends to penetrate more deeply than a cut.

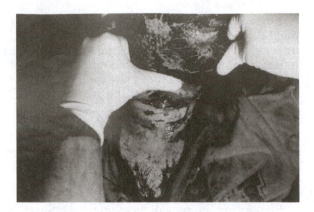

Photo 14-1. Cut (slash) wound. Courtesy of National City, California, Police Department.

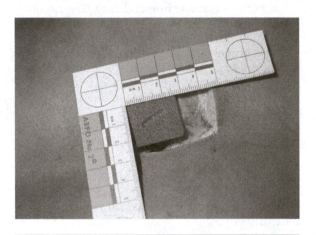

Photo 14-2. Stab wound. Courtesy of Chula Vista, California, Police Department.

- The wound is deeper than it is wide because the weapon is thrust into the body.
- Vital organs may be damaged because of the force of the weapon and the depth of the wound.
- Internal bleeding may be severe.
- Wound appearance may indicate if the weapon was single sharp edged, double sharp edged, square shaped, or rounded.
- Few abrasive (scraping) marks exist around the wound.
- A cutting action as well as a thrust may have been applied. Therefore, the wound may be longer than the width of the blade, making it difficult to determine the width of the blade from the appearance of the surface wound.

Chopping Wounds typically appear as follows:

> **Chopping wound**
> Wound caused by a heavy, sharp instrument, tool, or weapon.

- Chopping wounds are caused by heavy, sharp instruments, tools, and weapons. The injuries are incised wounds combined with blunt force, crushing wounds.
- Wound appearance is a combination of sharp object cuts and blunt force abrasions.

Hesitation wounds typically appear as follows:

> **Hesitation wound** A self-inflicted injury caused by an indecisive suicidal person. The hesitation may be due to fear, anticipation, or uncertainty of the level of force necessary to carry out the suicide.

- Hesitation wounds are self-inflicted injuries caused by an indecisive suicidal person. The hesitation may be due to fear, anticipation, or uncertainty of the level of force necessary to carry out the suicide.

Photo 14-3. Stab wound. Courtesy of Chula Vista, California, Police Department.

- If the victim is attempting to cut or slice at the wrist or throat, the hesitation wound may be one or several cuts that are often parallel and vary in depth. The hesitation marks typically appear on the wrist or under the ear opposite the suicidal person's strong hand.
- If the victim is attempting to stab at the heart or other organ, the hesitation wound may be one or several stab wounds that vary in depth, with the fatal wound typically deepest.
- Investigators should never rule out the possibility that an apparent suicide may actually be a homicide that is staged by the suspect to appear suicidal. Evidence at the crime scene and injury analysis during the autopsy can assist investigators with the determination of the actual manner of death.

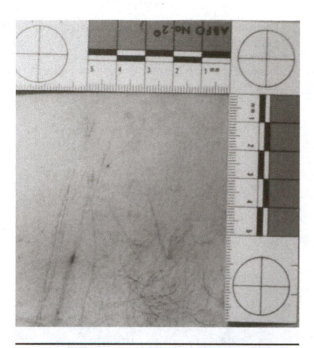

Photo 14-4. Hesitation wounds. Courtesy of National City, California, Police Department.

Paired injuries appear as follows:

- Paired injuries are those that occur simultaneously (at the same time and in the same manner). More than one injury is produced because of multiple sharp edges on the weapon. For example, a pair of scissors or a fork may produce more than one injury per thrust.

> **Paired injuries**
> Injuries that occur simultaneously (at the same time and in the same manner). More than one injury is produced because of multiple sharp edges on the weapon. For example, a pair of scissors or a fork may produce more than one injury per thrust.

- The number of wounds exceeds the number of thrusts.

Penetrating and perforating injuries appear as follows:

- **Penetrating injuries** are caused by instruments that enter the body but do not exit.

> **Penetrating injury**
> Injury caused by instruments that enter the body but do not exit.

- **Perforating injuries** are caused by instruments that enter and pass through the body, exiting the body at another point.

> **Perforating injury**
> Injury caused by instruments that enter and pass through the body, exiting the body at another point.

Blunt Force Injuries

Blunt force injuries are wounds that cause tearing or shearing of the skin, tissue, or muscles, as well as crushing of bones. Weapons used to produce blunt force injuries include objects and activities such as hammers, bricks, baseball bats, pipes, golf clubs, a person's fist, and stomping actions. The three basic injuries resulting from blunt force trauma include contusions (bruises), abrasions (scrapes), and lacerations (tearing of the skin, muscle, or tissue). (Spitz, 1993b).

> **Blunt force injury**
> Wound that causes tearing or shearing of the skin, tissue, or muscles, as well as crushing of bones.

Contusion wounds appear as follows:

- A contusion is a bruise that results when a blunt force weapon impacts the body, crushing tissues, and rupturing blood vessels. The skin is discolored but not broken.

> **Contusion** A bruise that results when a blunt force object impacts the body, crushing tissues, and rupturing blood vessels. The skin is discolored but not broken.

- As the contusion heals, the color of the wound may change, from red to bluish red, dark purple, green, yellow, and brown. The extent of the color change and the speed of healing depend on the victim's blood circulation, health, age, and other factors. Pathologists can usually determine if a contusion was inflicted ante- (before), peri- (during), or post- (after) death.
- The width of the weapon may be determined, depending on the angle of the weapon's impact on the skin.
- A contusion around an eye (black eye) may not be due to a direct blunt force. Rather, a black eye may result from trauma to the back of the head, the forehead, or a fracture at the base of the skull.

Abrasion wounds typically appear as follows:

- An abrasion results from the scraping and removal of layers of skin when a blunt force instrument strikes the body.

> **Abrasion** An abrasion results from the scraping and removal of layers of skin when a blunt force instrument strikes the body.

- The injury may display distinctive characteristics of the weapon's impact surface.
- The injury indicates the site of impact and the direction from which the force was applied. The skin is pushed in the same direction as the force.
- The injury will form a scab and heal if the victim is alive. The injury will darken if the victim dies immediately.

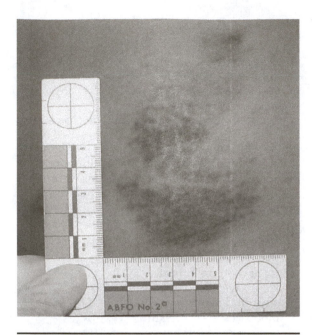

Photo 14-5. Contusion. Courtesy of National City, California, Police Department.

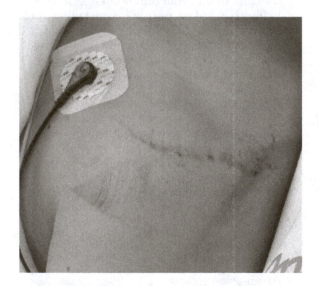

Photo 14-6. Photograph of an abrasion. Courtesy of National City, California, Police Department.

Laceration wounds appear as follows:

- Lacerations are produced by the tearing, ripping, crushing, bending, pulling, stretching, and shearing of skin, muscle, or tissue when a blunt force object is applied to the body.

> **Laceration** Injury produced by the tearing, ripping, crushing, bending, pulling, stretching, and shearing of skin, muscle, or tissue when a blunt force object is applied to the body.

- Lacerations may be the result of direct and glancing (indirect) blows.
- The injury appears abraded and jagged because the skin is split. Bridges of tissue may be observed. The injury is not sharp and defined like an incised wound.
- The injury may contain foreign material such as wood chips, fibers, paint chips, glass, grease, or other material from the instrument.
- The term *laceration* is sometimes misused by investigators and forensic personnel to describe an incised wound (cut). Lacerations are blunt force injuries, not injuries created by sharp objects.

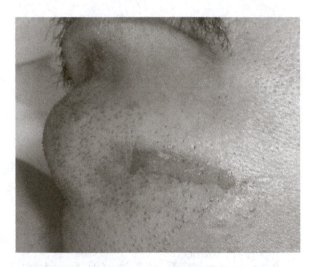

Photo 14-7. Laceration. Courtesy of National City, California, Police Department.

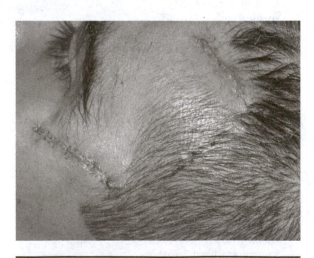

Photo 14-8. Laceration. Courtesy of National City, California, Police Department.

Defense wounds appear as follows:

- Defense wounds often result when victims defend themselves against attacks from sharp and blunt force weapons. The injuries occur when the victim attempts self-defense with arms or legs, blocking the weapon from hitting the body or head.
- Defense wounds are usually located on the victim's hands, arms, legs, or feet (Spitz, 1993e).

> **Defense wound**
> Wound that often results when victims defend themselves against attacks from sharp and blunt force weapons. The injuries occur when the victim attempts self-defense with arms or legs, blocking the weapon from hitting the body or head.

Coup and contrecoup injuries appear as follows:

- A coup injury is an injury to the brain caused by blunt force trauma. The injury results from the skull bone pressure against the brain. The injury can be observed on the brain at the weapon impact site.
- A contrecoup injury to the brain is also caused by blunt force trauma. The injury is caused by the brain moving and impacting the inside of the skull opposite the weapon impact site.

> **Coup injury** An injury to the brain caused by blunt force trauma. The injury results from skull bone pressure against the brain. The injury can be observed on the brain at the weapon impact site.

> **Contrecoup injury** A contrecoup injury to the brain is caused by blunt force trauma. The injury is caused by the brain moving and impacting the inside of the skull opposite the weapon impact site. The injury appears on the side of the brain opposite the impact site.

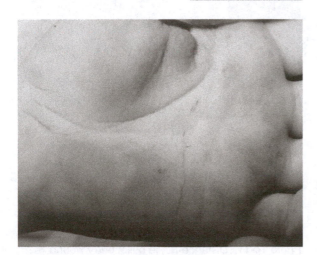

Photo 14-9. Defense wound. Courtesy of National City, California, Police Department.

The injury appears on the side of the brain opposite the impact site. Coup and contrecoup injuries are uncovered by a pathologist at an autopsy (DiMaio & DiMaio, 2001).

Pattern Injuries

Pattern injuries are those indicative of the object or surface that produced the injury. An impression of the weapon may be observed.

> **Pattern Injury** A pattern injury is indicative of the object or surface that produced the injury.

Pattern of Injuries

A **pattern of injuries** relates to the distribution of external and internal injuries that suggest a sequence of events or the order in which the injuries were inflicted. The determination is made by a pathologist or a forensic injury-to-weapon expert.

> **Pattern of Injuries** A pattern of injuries relates to the distribution of external and internal injuries that suggest a sequence of events or the order in which the injuries were inflicted.

Firearm Injuries

A **firearm injury** is a wound inflicted as a firearm's projectile enters and injures the body. The severity of the wound depends on the type of weapon and its ammunition. Wound appearance will also vary depending on the distance the firearm was from the victim. Entry and exit wounds caused by projectiles also vary greatly (Spitz, 1993d).

> **Firearm injury** A wound inflicted as a firearm's projectile enters and injures the body. The severity of the wound depends on the type of weapon and its ammunition.

Handgun or Rifle Contact Entrance Wounds

- If the muzzle of a handgun or rifle is pressed against the skin and fired, gunpowder and soot as well as the bullet fired from the muzzle will enter the body.
- A smudge ring or stippling (tattooing) from the gunpowder and soot may be observed around the perimeter of the wound.
- Scorching of hair and skin may appear around the wound.
- The contact wound may be jagged in appearance because gases discharged by the firearm are forced under the skin, forming a star-shaped wound.
- Soot, metal particles, and gunshot residue are located within the wound.

Handgun or Rifle Close-Range Entrance Wounds

- If a handgun or rifle is fired at close range (within 18 inches), the resulting wound's appearance is different from a contact wound's. Incompletely burned gunpowder residue may be observed on the victim's skin and clothing around the entry wound. The amount of residue depends on the weapon and type of ammunition.
- The bullet wound may appear round or oblong, depending on the bullet's entry angle. If the bullet entered at a 90 degree angle to the body, the hole will usually appear round. As the angle of entry increases or decreases, the wound will appear more oblong. The entry wound area may have skin abrasions resulting from the bullet's penetration of the skin. The wound may also have a smudge from soot transferred from the bullet as it contacts the skin.
- Hairs and fibers surrounding the wound may be burned if the muzzle of the weapon is within 6 inches of the body.
- **Stippling (tattooing)** (the embedding of unburned gunpowder and metal particles into the skin) may be observed around the wound. The tattooing is most pronounced at the point where the bullet entered the body. The

> **Stippling (tattooing)**
> The embedding of unburned gunpowder and metal particles into the skin around an entrance wound. The tattooing is most pronounced at the point where the bullet entered the body.

pattern and density of the tattoo helps firearms examiners determine the range (distance) between the firearm and the victim at the time of the firearm's discharge. The forensic technician must take detailed photographs of the unburned gunpowder around the entry wound so firearms examiners can examine the powder pattern and compare test fires of suspect weapons.

Handgun or Rifle Distant-Range Wounds

- If a handgun or rifle is fired at a distant range (greater than 18 inches), tattooing related to unburned gunpowder and soot around the wound may not be apparent. Usually, gunshot residue will not travel more than 18 inches.
- The entrance wound is usually circular or oval shaped unless the bullet ricocheted from an object before entering the body.
- Handgun and rifle distant-range entry wounds appear similar, but the internal damage may be much greater with large caliber ammunition as well as small caliber ammunition with a high muzzle velocity.

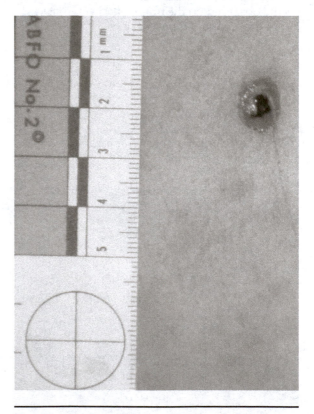

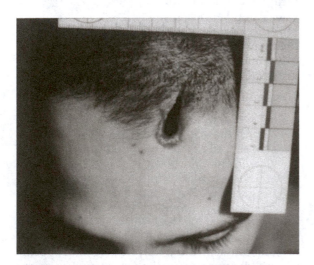

Photo 14-10. Close-range bullet entry wound. Courtesy of National City, California, Police Department.

Photo 14-11. Distance-range bullet entry wound. Courtesy of National City, California, Police Department.

Handgun or Rifle Exit Wounds

- An exit wound will appear at the point where the projectile is expelled from the body.
- Exit wounds from a handgun or rifle vary in size and appearance, depending on the weapon, caliber, ammunition, and area of the injured. Exit wounds in the head are typically star-shaped (jagged) due to skull fragment.
- Exit wounds contain no unburned gunpowder, stippling, or tattooing.
- Tissues and bone fragments pushed by the bullet may cause a large exit wound.
- A bullet may tumble after it enters the body, resulting in an exit wound that appears linear. Some linear exit wounds resemble stab or cut wounds.
- If the exit wound area is pressing against a hard surface when the bullet exits, an abrasion caused by the surface may appear on the body as well.

Shotgun Entrance Wounds

- Shotgun ammunition creates severe and traumatic injuries that are often fatal. Entry wound appearance depends on the proximity to the shotgun, the shotgun's choke (pattern) and barrel length, and the ammunition's gunpowder load, size of the shot, and gauge. Contact and near-contact wounds to the head are usually fatal and often result in mutilation of the head. Close-range discharges to

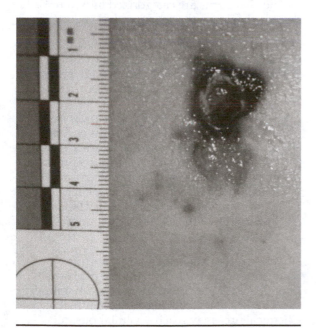

Photo 14-12. Bullet exit wound. Courtesy of National City, California, Police Department.

Photo 14-13. Shotgun wound to the head. Courtesy of National City, California, Police Department.

the head often cause fragmentation or disintegration of skull and brain tissue.
- Contact and near-contact shotgun wounds usually result in massive hemorrhaging. The size of the entry wounds depends on the gauge of the weapon and the ammunition.
- A close-range discharge (within five feet) will result in minimal scalloping (spreading) of the shot.
- Unburned gunpowder and soot may be observed on the victim's clothing and skin.
- The nature of long-range shotgun wounds also varies depending on the weapon and ammunition. Scalloping (spreading) of the shot is apparent. A firearms examiner will test-fire the shotgun to determine distance relative to scalloping.
- Shotgun exit wounds are rare except for shots to the head. Shot (pellets) are usually embedded in the body. Large shot or slugs may pass through the body because of their mass and the kinetic energy they carry (Spitz, 1993f).

Suicide Shootings

Suicidal shootings can be accomplished with virtually any type of firearm. The muzzle of the firearm is usually held against the victim's forehead, temple, roof of the mouth, or chest near the heart. Questions asked relative to a suspected suicide include the following:

- Was it physically possible for the victim to fire the weapon?
- Is the victim left- or right-handed?

- Did the recoil of the weapon cause injury to the victim's head?
- Is blood spatter on the victim consistent with a suicide?
- Does the victim have gunshot residue on a hand or other body surface? It is possible for gunshot residue to transfer from one person to another.
- Is the firearm nearby? The wound may not be immediately fatal. Thus, the victim may move after the shooting (Spitz, 1993d).

Chemical Trauma

A **chemical trauma death** occurs primarily through the ingestion of toxins such as drugs, alcohol, or poison. Fifty percent of all chemical trauma deaths involve the ingestion of ethyl alcohol (ethanol) contained in beer, wine, or distilled spirits. Ethyl alcohol is a central nervous system depressant. At levels of less than 0.03 percent blood-alcohol concentration (BAC), reaction time slightly improves because inhibitory neurons are slowed. However, BAC levels greater than 0.03 percent result in slowing of mental processes and reaction time. A BAC of 0.40 percent may result in loss of consciousness. A BAC of 0.45 percent is fatal in approximately 50 percent of the population.

> **Chemical trauma death** Occurs primarily through the ingestion of toxins such as drugs, alcohol, or poison. Fifty percent of all chemical trauma deaths involve the ingestion of ethyl alcohol (ethanol) contained in beer, wine, or distilled spirits.

Although usually accidental, carbon monoxide (CO) poisoning is also a common cause of chemical trauma death. Carbon monoxide is odorless and colorless, and is a gas produced by the incomplete combustion of fuels containing carbon. Death occurs because CO binds to the hemoglobin in the body 300 times more strongly than oxygen, thus restricting the oxygen supply to the brain. Victims who survived carbon monoxide poisoning state that they experienced a severe headache. Persons trapped in a fire may have CO concentration blood levels of up to 90 percent. However, a 20 percent CO concentration can be fatal. Tobacco smokers typically have CO levels of 2–10 percent. A person who dies from CO poisoning usually displays a cherry red skin coloration.

Cyanide is sometimes used as a tool for homicide because it is easily placed in an unsuspecting victim's food or drink. Similar to CO, cyanide interferes with oxygen flow to the brain. Cyanide emits an almond-like odor. However, half of the human population is unable to detect the odor. Cyanide is available in a potassium salt used in polishing metals. If a person swallows potassium cyanide, a gas may build up in the stomach. If the stomach is cut open during the autopsy, the gas is released and may be fatal to attending personnel.

Thermal Trauma

Thermal trauma is caused by hypothermia, hyperthermia, and burns as well as electrical and asphyxia phenomena. A **hypothermia death** results from exposure to excessively cold temperatures. A **hyperthermia death** is caused by exposure to excessive heat. Hyperthermia is common among the elderly and children left in vehicles during hot weather. The temperature inside a vehicle can reach 140 degrees Fahrenheit in 10 minutes (Wright, 2005a; Spitz, 1993g).

> **Hypothermia death** Death caused by exposure to excessively cold temperature.

> **Hyperthermia death** Death caused by exposure to excessive heat.

Thermal burns are wounds produced by contact with an object with a temperature of 150 degrees Fahrenheit. Exposure to high temperatures from hot liquid or fire leads to death caused by organ failure. A thermal burn is life threatening if it exceeds 20 percent of a child's body surface. Thermal burns on adults exceeding 40 percent of body surface are life threatening.

Thermal burns are categorized into four degrees, based on the severity of the injury:

- First-degree burn—damage to the outer layer of skin; no blisters; some peeling of skin.
- Second-degree burn—the upper layers of the skin are destroyed; blisters and scarring appear.
- Third-degree burn—the entire thickness of the skin, including the epidermis and dermis, are damaged; pain is absent because nerve endings are destroyed; scarring occurs; skin grafting (skin replacement) is necessary.
- Fourth-degree burn—the skin is charred, with complete destruction of the skin and underlying tissues. Damage to bones is possible.

The severity of a burn injury depends on the intensity of the heat and the exposure time. The average house fire may reach temperatures higher than 1300 degrees Fahrenheit. Chemical fires may reach several thousand degrees Fahrenheit. Figure 14.1 illustrates the level of damage to an adult in a house fire at

EXPOSURE TIME – 1200 degrees F	LEVEL OF DAMAGE – ADULT BODY
20 minutes	Rib cage, arm and facial bones exposed
25 minutes	Legs and shin bones exposed
35 minutes	Complete burning of all flesh

Figure 14.1. Burn injury severity.

1200 degrees Fahrenheit. Skin under tight belts and within shoes and tight clothing may be less affected because oxygen is unable to reach these areas.

If a flammable liquid was poured on the victim, disproportionate burned and patchy charring will be observed on the body. Chemical analysis of burned skin and clothing may reveal the presence of an accelerant.

The weight and length of a charred body is significantly less than normal. Skin may shrink to two-thirds of normal size. Scars and tattoos may be visible after upper layers of burned skin are removed by the pathologist. Gender determination is made by examining internal organs. In extreme situations, a determination of race can be made only by an anthropologist or odontologist.

Cremation of an adult human body in a gas-fired chamber at 1500 degrees Fahrenheit takes 1–1.5 hours. A child's body can be cremated completely in an average house fire. A newborn infant can be incinerated in an ordinary kitchen stove in less than two hours.

To determine if a victim was alive prior to a fire, pathologists search for several clues, including the concentration of CO in the blood (though absence of CO does not confirm that death occurred before the fire). The absence of thick white foam at the nostrils or mouth is indicative of the victim's breathing while the fire was in progress. The foam is created by fluid released from the lungs. Flash fires, such as those in chemical plants or an explosion, usually result in instant death due to the inhalation of superheated toxic gases that cause swelling in the airway, leading to suffocation (Spitz, 1993g).

Electrical Trauma

Although relatively rare, electrical trauma deaths can occur from low- or high-voltage electricity. Low voltage may cause the heart to quiver, leading to death. Electrical burns on the skin usually require several seconds of exposure to low voltage.

High voltage (in excess of 1,000 volts) does not typically cause a heart to quiver. However, electrical burns can occur within fractions of a second with high voltage. Additionally, high-voltage contact creates holes within tissue cell membranes, which can result in loss of limbs (Wright, 2005a).

High-voltage electrocutions are relatively easy for forensic pathologists to determine because extensive burns are often present on the body of the deceased. An electrocution is often suspected if an individual falls while near a charged electrical source. The victim's back may arch while falling, and the victim may scream during the electrocution. An electrocution can occur when the following event occurs simultaneously: A charged device sends an electric current through a pathway in the victim's body to a grounding source (metal pipe, faucet, metal part of an electrical outlet, radiator, grounded appliance, other metals).

If the electrical current flows through the spinal cord or the brain, the central nervous system is damaged, causing respiration to cease. If the current flows through the heart, cardiac arrest may result. A low-voltage current is more likely to cause a fatal heart attack. Blood is less resistant to electrical current than tissue. Thus, a large amount of electrical current may flow through the blood vessels. The heat from the current may disintegrate red blood cells and damage blood vessel lining.

Many electrocutions occur at home, often when a charged electrical appliance (e.g., hair dryer, shaver) falls into the bathtub while the victim is bathing. Even if the appliance is off, the attached cord is still charged with electricity if connected to the electrical receptacle (outlet). Children, for example can place extension cords into their mouths, leading to electrocution (Wright, 2005a).

Police Taser devices utilize low-voltage electricity to induce involuntary muscle spasms. The electrical current persists for a few seconds, but is an effective less-than-lethal weapon.

Asphyxia

Asphyxia is defined as interference with the oxygenation of the brain. Asphyxia can occur as a result of chemical, thermal, or mechanical trauma. With chemical trauma, a toxin such as carbon monoxide causes asphyxia when the toxin binds to hemoglobin and interrupts the flow of oxygen to the brain. In carbon monoxide poisoning, the victim's skin often appears cherry red in color. With thermal trauma such as one resulting from a superheated fire, a person's airway (and breathing) is obstructed, thus leading to asphyxia. With mechanical traumas such as strangulation or a hanging, oxygenated blood flow to the brain is cut off, resulting in asphyxia.

> **Asphyxia** Death caused by interference with the oxygenation of the brain. Asphyxia can occur as a result of chemical, thermal, or mechanical trauma.

Hanging versus Strangulation

A **hanging** can be the result of an accident, a suicide, or a homicide. Most commonly, hangings are accidents or suicides. Complete suspension of the body need not occur for a person to die from a hanging. Asphyxia occurs as oxygenated blood flow to the brain is restricted. A ligature on the neck with minimal pressure applied to arteries servicing the brain can restrict blood flow.

Babies and toddlers have been victims of accidental hangings, resulting from baby monitor cords in a baby's crib and from window blind cords hanging low to the floor. If the cord is accidentally wrapped around the child's neck, pressure on the carotid artery may cause the child to lose consciousness, leading to asphyxia and death.

> **Hanging** Can be the result of an accident, a suicide, or a homicide. Most commonly, hangings are accidents or suicides. Complete suspension of the body need not occur for a person to die from a hanging. Asphyxia occurs as oxygenated blood flow to the brain is restricted. A ligature on the neck with minimal pressure applied to arteries servicing the brain can restrict blood flow.

Strangulation is a purposeful act involving the placement of hands or a ligature around a victim's neck, restricting oxygenated blood flow to the brain. This act is violent, and a great amount of pressure is applied. The hyoid bone located within the neck is often fractured. Hemorrhaging in the neck muscles is often observed. As oxygen is depleted in the

> **Strangulation** A purposeful act involving the placement of hands or a ligature around a victim's neck, restricting oxygenated blood flow to the brain.

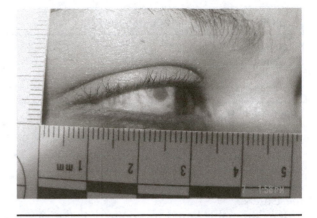

Photo 14-14. Petechial hemorrhaging. Courtesy of National City, California, Police Department.

brain, blood vessels may burst. Pinpoint hemorrhaging known as **petechia** (plural: petechiae) is often observed in the eyes. Petechia can occur throughout the body. In strangulation or attempted strangulation cases, petechia is often observable within the white area of the victim's eyes (DiMaio & DiMaio, 2001; Spitz, 1993a).

> **Petechia** (plural: petechiae) Pinpoint hemorrhaging often observed in the white area of the victim's eyes. Petechia can occur throughout the body.

Accidental Asphyxia

Asphyxia may occur by accident. Popular yet very dangerous thrill-seeking activities can lead to asphyxia. Some children and teenagers deliberately sniff glue or aerosol fumes, or manually choke each other to obtain a *head rush* (instant high). By placing or spraying glue or toxins into a plastic bag and sniffing (*huffing*) the fumes, the participant experiences a high. The toxic fumes displace oxygen in the brain, creating the *head rush*. Children may also use hands or ligatures to purposely restrict oxygenated blood flow to the brain. Children sometimes fasten a ligature around the neck or place a plastic bag over the head and inadvertently lose consciousness, causing death.

Autoerotic asphyxia (autoerotic death) is an accidental hanging caused by the victim's attempt at sexual arousal. The victim ties a noose or other ligature around the neck and the hands with the intent to gain sexual pleasure from oxygen restriction to the

> **Autoerotic asphyxia (autoerotic death)** An accidental hanging caused by the victim's attempt at sexual arousal. The victim ties a noose or other ligature around the neck and the hands with the intent to gain sexual pleasure from oxygen restriction to the brain during masturbation.

brain during masturbation. The binding may be elaborate, but careful examination will reveal that the victim was able to create the binding without help from another person. The death is usually not intentional. However, an equipment malfunction or too much pressure against a carotid artery can restrict the oxygen supply to the brain. The victim loses consciousness and eventually dies. Most victims are male and are often found nude or partially nude, although they may be wearing female clothing. Pornographic literature and sex paraphernalia are often located near the victim (DiMaio & DiMaio, 2001).

Drowning

Drowning is a type of asphyxia that may be caused by homicide, suicide, or accident:

1. The person struggles to keep the head above water, increasing the need for oxygen.
2. During the struggle to keep the airway open, water enters the back of the victim's throat and is inhaled.
3. Water in the upper air passages triggers coughing as well as an inhalation reflex.
4. Water enters the smaller air passages and the muscles that protect the alveoli in the lungs begin to spasm. Alveoli exchange carbon dioxide in the bloodstream with oxygen.
5. The spasms create an acute asthma attack, trapping air in the lungs.
6. Involuntary inhalation of water, vomiting, and a loss of consciousness soon follow.
7. The heart stops within a few minutes.

Signs of drowning in the body include:

- hemorrhaging in the air passages,
- water in the sinuses and the stomach,
- hyperinflation of the lungs,
- diatoms found throughout the body.

A diatom is a small unicellular degradation-resistant organism located in fresh- and saltwater. In the latter stages of drowning, the victim's heart circulates diatoms throughout the victim's body and into various organs. Diatoms differ based on water type and seasonal conditions. Locating diatoms in a victim's body helps to prove that a drowning occurred. They also assist with determining the approximate time and place of the drowning (Wright, 2005a; Spitz, 1993c).

POSTMORTEM CHANGES

Antemortem refers to *before death*. **Perimortem** is a term meaning *during death*.

> **Antemortem** Before death.

Postmortem means *after death*. When performing an autopsy (postmortem examination), the pathologist attempts to determine which injuries were sustained ante-, peri-, and postmortem. Determining the approximate time of death is also an important consideration in death investigations. Unless another person was present or the death was recorded, it is impossible to determine the exact time of death.

> **Perimortem** During death.

> **Postmortem** After death.

A variety of sources, investigative protocols, and biological factors aid in determining the approximate time of death. Investigative protocol involves determining and tracing the victim's actions and whereabouts before death. The investigator can review credit card and automatic teller machine (ATM) use history. Interviewing the person who last saw the victim alive may also assist the investigator with determining approximate time of death.

Various postmortem changes occur in the body after death. By analyzing these changes collectively, the pathologist can assist the investigator with determining approximate time of death (Perper, 1993).

Algor Mortis

Algor mortis is the cooling of the body after death. Under normal atmospheric conditions, the rate of cooling occurs as follows:

> **Algor mortis** The cooling of the body after death.

- 2–2.5 degrees Fahrenheit loss per hour for the first two hours,
- 1.5–2 degrees Fahrenheit loss per hour 2–14 hours after death,
- 1 degree Fahrenheit loss per hour 26–32 hours after death until ambient (atmospheric) temperature is reached.

The pathologist obtains the deceased's body temperature measurement by placing a thermometer into the victim's liver.

Several factors determine the rate of temperature loss, including the victim's body temperature at the time of death. If the victim was running at the time of death, the body's temperature may be higher than normal. The temperature of the environment also affects the body's temperature. Further, the thickness and insulation qualities of the deceased's clothing as well as the victim's weight are determinative when calculating the rate of cooling of the body.

Livor Mortis

Livor mortis (lividity) is the pooling of blood within the body caused by gravity after cardiovascular circulation ceases. When the heart stops, the person no longer bleeds. Rather, blood drains to the lowest parts of the body. As the blood pools at the lowest extremities of the body, a discoloration appears under the skin. The discoloration may appear purple, blue, or red, depending on the victim's skin pigmentation. Lividity is observed on the back and buttocks if the deceased was lying in a supine (face-up) position after death. Conversely, lividity may be observed on the face and front of the body if the victim was lying in a face-down position. Lack of lividity (pale appearance) is observed in areas where the body pressed against a hard surface. This is due to the inability of the blood to drain into the blood vessels.

> **Livor mortis (lividity)**
> The pooling of blood within the body caused by gravity after cardiovascular circulation ceases. When the heart stops, the person no longer bleeds.

Lividity can be observed within approximately one hour after death and is fully developed within three to four hours. If lividity begins to form and the body is moved, the position of the lividity may change. However, the original position of the lividity is often apparent, indicating that the body was moved or rotated three to four hours after death. In extreme blood loss situations, such as those involving arterial damage, little or no lividity may be apparent (Wright, 2005a).

Rigor Mortis

Rigor mortis (rigidity) results from the biochemical changes that occur in the muscles after death. Initially, rigor mortis causes the muscles of the body to stiffen. When the chemicals begin to decompose and deteriorate, the muscles become flaccid (lack firmness). Rigor mortis appears within 2–6 hours after death and is usually complete (full rigor) within 12 hours. All of the body's muscles are stiff (rigid) at full rigor. Full rigor mortis remains for approximately 12 hours and gradually disappears as the muscles become flaccid in the next 12 hours. A simple expression for the rigor mortis timeline is *12-12-12*. It takes approximately 12 hours for rigidity to become pronounced. Full

> **Rigor mortis (rigidity)** Results from the biochemical changes that occur in the muscles after death. Initially, rigor mortis causes the muscles of the body to stiffen. When the chemicals begin to decompose and deteriorate, the muscles become flaccid (lack firmness).

rigor continues for 12 hours and subsides in the last 12 of the 36-hour period.

Some investigators mistakenly believe that rigor mortis starts at the head and progresses through the body to the toes. This is not the case. The rigidity develops and subsides equally in all muscles. Yet rigor mortis appears more pronounced in the smaller muscles first, because of their size. This information is helpful when determining time of death based on the stage of rigidity. For example, if the hand muscles are stiff but the leg muscles are not, one might assume that the body is in the first 12 hours of rigor mortis. Conversely, if the leg muscles are stiff but the hand muscles are not, one can assume that the body is in the last 12 hours of rigor.

A different phenomenon, cadaveric spasm, can be mistaken for rigor mortis. A **cadaveric spasm** is a rare form of instantaneous muscle stiffening that occurs at death. The cause is unknown, but it usually occurs in conjunction with deaths associated with great excitement or emotion. Cadaveric spasms can be observed in suicide shootings and drowning cases. Drowning victims, for example, may clutch underwater weeds or other materials. The cadaveric spasm is significant in forensic investigation because it helps to determine a deceased person's last activity prior to death.

> **Cadaveric spasm**
> A rare form of instantaneous muscle stiffening that occurs at death.

Decomposition

Under normal circumstances, the body will decompose (deteriorate) after death. Two processes contribute to the decomposition of the body: **autolysis,**

> **Autolysis** A process that contributes to the decomposition of the body initiated by lysosome cells that release digestive enzymes.

Photo 14-15. Cadaveric spasm in a hand. Courtesy of National City, California, Police Department.

initiated by lysosome cells that release digestive enzymes, and **putrefaction**, involving the decomposition of proteins by anaerobic microorganisms (putrefying bacteria). Environmental conditions (e.g., temperature and climate), clothing, and body weight can increase or decrease the rate of decomposition. Hot, humid environments accelerate the process, while dry, cold environments slow the process. Very dry climates may cause **mummification** (drying of the body and tissues). Very wet environments may cause **adipocere** (a wax-like, cheesy appearance caused by the slow hydrolysis of fats in decomposing material). The transformation of fat into adipocere occurs best in environments (e.g., sealed casket, muddy lake bottom, wet soil) that are cold, humid, and relatively free of oxygen.

Decomposition of the human body occurs in stages:

- Fresh stage. Few physical signs of decomposition.
- Putrefaction stage. Obvious color changes, bloating, emission of odor.
- Black putrefaction stage. Body cavities rupture, abdominal gases escape, body darkens, bones become apparent.
- Butyric fermentation stage. Mummification begins, adipocere (wax) forms, internal organs consumed by insects.
- Dry decay stage. Skeletonization, no soft-tissue remaining, deterioration of skeletal remains.

Generally, the physical signs of decomposition are observed as follows:

Within 36 hours:

- Discoloration of the skin; the lower abdominal area appears bluish green.
- The eyes appear cloudy around the cornea, with a film appearance over the entire eye (if the eye was open at death). Dry weather may cause a black or brown discoloration of the eye known as *tache noire*.

> **Putrefaction**
> A process that contributes to the decomposition of the body initiated by proteins by anaerobic microorganisms (putrefying bacteria). Environmental conditions (e.g., temperature and climate), clothing, and body weight can increase or decrease the rate of decomposition. Hot, humid environments accelerate the process, while dry, cold environments slow the process.

> **Mummification**
> Drying of the body and tissues which may occur in very dry climates.

> **Adipocere** A wax-like, cheesy appearance caused by the slow hydrolysis of fats in decomposing material. The transformation of fat into adipocere occurs best in environments (e.g., sealed casket, muddy lake bottom, wet soil) that are cold, humid, and relatively free of oxygen.

After 36 hours:

- Discoloration of the body is pronounced.
- Gases forming within the body cause it to swell.
- A very unpleasant odor is released from the body.
- Blisters with fluid and gas appear on the skin.
- Skin slippage occurs (skin disconnects from the body).
- Purging of liquid may occur through the mouth, nose, or anus.

After 3 days:

- The entire body shows signs of decomposition.

Photo 14-16. Fluids from a decomposing body soaked through a mattress, floor, ceiling below, and settled in the ceiling light fixture in room below. Photograph by Todd Griffiths.

Photo 14-17. Fluids from a decomposing body soaked through a mattress, floor, ceiling below, and settled in the ceiling light fixture in room below. Photograph by Todd Griffiths.

Photo 14-18. Fluids from a decomposing body soaked through a mattress, floor, ceiling below, and settled in the ceiling light fixture in room below. Photograph by Todd Griffiths.

Photo 14-19. Fluids from a decomposing body soaked through carpet. Photograph by Todd Griffiths.

EVIDENCE DOCUMENTATION AND COLLECTION AT AUTOPSY

In many jurisdictions, the forensic technician is responsible for taking photographs and collecting evidence at the postmortem examination (autopsy). Other jurisdictions may utilize trained staff employed with the coroner's or medical examiner's office. Still other jurisdictions rely on a sworn officer or investigator to document and collect the forensic evidence. Regardless of the person's title or position, the following protocol functions as a general guide to photography and evidence collection at the autopsy:

1. Photographic equipment and evidence collection supplies should be gathered and organized prior to the autopsy. One should not leave the autopsy room to obtain supplies or equipment. One must be prepared with items such as various-sized evidence bags, tweezers, toothpicks, fingernail clippers, bindles, sterile swabs, plastic bags (in case the victim's clothing is blood-soaked), black permanent markers, pen, notepad, extra latex or vinyl gloves, camera, extra film (if applicable), an extra digital camera memory card (if applicable), and a measuring device. Camera and flash unit batteries should be fresh. It is recommended that a cardboard box be used to remove evidence from the room at the conclusion of the autopsy. A second box or container is used to retrieve supplies and equipment.

2. Full safety gear should be worn: eye protection, particle mask, lab coat, gloves, and shoe protection.

3. The time the autopsy begins as well as the names and titles of all personnel present should be recorded.

4. If x-rays of the victim are available, normal lens views of the x-rays are photographed without a flash. The light emitted from the flash unit would obscure the detail of the x-ray.

5. Prior to the autopsy, the body is sealed in a body bag. An identification tag is located next to the seal placed on the body bag at the crime scene. Photograph the seal and the name tag. Record the seal number.

6. An overall view of the body in the body bag (wide-angle) is photographed. A flash unit is used along with the appropriate camera settings (1/60 shutter and F-8 usually produce good results for indoor flash photography). Adjust the camera settings according to exposure need. The white balance should be set to *flash* if the flash unit is the major light source. Matrix metering (light metering across the entire frame) should be used. The camera settings are typically the same throughout the entire autopsy.

7. After the body is removed from the bag, overall views of the left and right sides of the body are photographed.

8. If paper bags were placed on the victim's head, hands, or feet at the crime scene, they are removed by the medical examiner's assistant. The bags should be collected separately as evidence in the event trace evidence is transferred from the body to the bags.

9. Overall (head-to-toe) and segmented (head-to-chest, chest-to-waist, and waist-to-feet) photographs are taken from the left, right, overhead, and back sides of the body. Segmented photograph requirements vary among agencies. To photograph

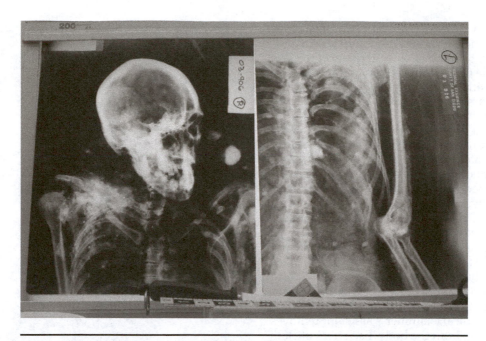

Photo 14-20. X-rays. Courtesy of Chula Vista, California, Police Department.

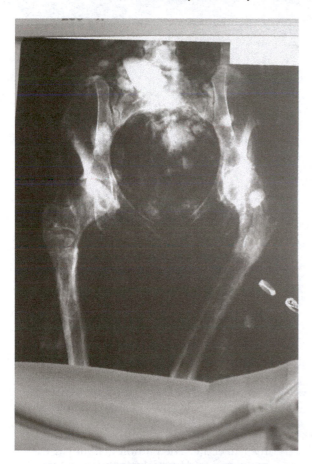

Photo 14-21. X-rays. Courtesy of Chula Vista, California, Police Department.

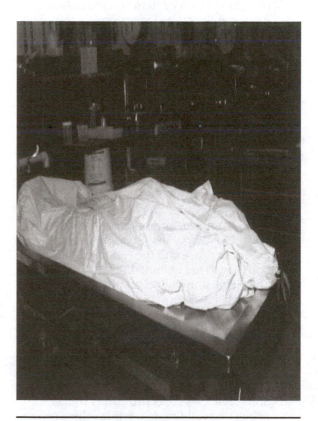

Photo 14-22. Body in a body bag. Courtesy of Chula Vista, California, Police Department.

the body from an overhead view, the forensic technician should use a step ladder or stool to stand slightly above and to the side of the body. To photograph the underside of the body, the medical examiner's assistant will rotate the body onto its side.

10. A close-up view of the victim's face and the front and back of both hands should be photographed.

11. If applicable, gunshot residue should be collected from the victim's hands (if not already collected).

12. Fingernail scrapings or clippings should be obtained from both hands. A separate bindle is unfolded and held under each hand as the nails are scraped or clipped.

13. Head hair samples must be collected from the body (5–10 hairs each from the front, top, back, and sides of the head).

14. The medical examiner's assistant removes clothing, from the body. Each item of clothing is collected separately and placed in a paper evidence bag. If the clothing is blood-soaked and wet, the clothing should be temporarily placed in plastic for transportation purposes. The item is removed for drying at the crime laboratory.

15. After clothing is removed and before the body is washed, the forensic technician repeats overall and segmented photographs of the left, right, overhead, and back sides of the body.

16. Relevant pubic hair, pubic swabs, anal swabs, trace evidence combings, lifts from the pubic area, and oral swabs are collected.

17. If the body is bloody or dirty, it is washed with soap and water by the medical examiner's assistant. After the body is cleaned, the forensic technician should repeat overall and segmented photographs of the left, right, overhead, and undersides of the body. Close-up view photographs of the decedent's face and the front and back of both hands are obtained.

18. Orientation and close-up photographs of all birthmarks, tattoos, scars, and injuries are obtained. Each close-up photograph should be taken without and with a scale, with the face of the camera lens parallel to the injury. The pathologist takes measurements and notes anything remarkable about the body.

19. Fingerprints are obtained from each hand. Some agencies collect 10-prints (fingerprints from all fingers), while others collect major case prints (recording of all friction ridge skin from the fingers and palms).

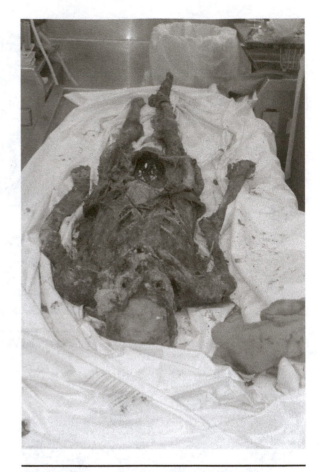

Photo 14-23. Overall, segmented, and close-up photographs at an autopsy of skeletonized remains. Courtesy of Chula Vista, California, Police Department.

20. The pathologist makes the first incision, which is typically Y-shaped, cutting from both shoulders to the mid-chest and down the torso. The major organs are removed, and the pathologist notes everything remarkable about the body. The pathologist collects specimens from the major organs. If injuries to the major organs are relevant to the crime, the pathologist will communicate the relevance to the forensic technician. The forensic technician takes orientation and close-up photographs of the relevant major organ injuries. If the victim was shot and a projectile must be recovered from the body, the pathologist will remove the projectile. The forensic technician should photograph and collect the projectile. The pathologist may use a metal rod to demonstrate the trajectory of a projectile's path through the body. The forensic technician should photograph

Photo 14-24. Overall, segmented, and close-up photographs at an autopsy of skeletonized remains. Courtesy of Chula Vista, California, Police Department.

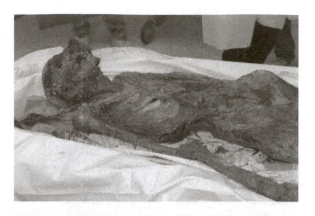

Photo 14-27. Overall, segmented, and close-up photographs at an autopsy of skeletonized remains. Courtesy of Chula Vista, California, Police Department.

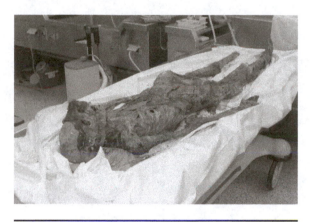

Photo 14-25. Overall, segmented, and close-up photographs at an autopsy of skeletonized remains. Courtesy of Chula Vista, California, Police Department.

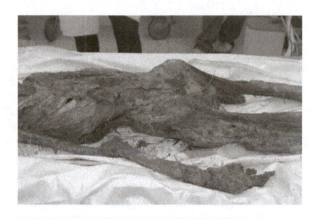

Photo 14-28. Overall, segmented, and close-up photographs at an autopsy of skeletonized remains. Courtesy of Chula Vista, California, Police Department.

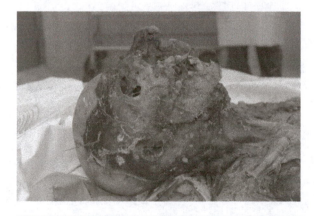

Photo 14-26. Overall, segmented, and close-up photographs at an autopsy of skeletonized remains. Courtesy of Chula Vista, California, Police Department.

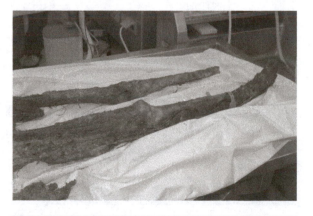

Photo 14-29. Overall, segmented, and close-up photographs at an autopsy of skeletonized remains. Courtesy of Chula Vista, California, Police Department.

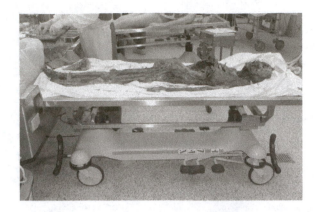

Photo 14-30. Overall, segmented, and close-up photographs at an autopsy of skeletonized remains. Courtesy of Chula Vista, California, Police Department.

Photo 14-33. Overall, segmented, and close-up photographs at an autopsy of skeletonized remains. Courtesy of Chula Vista, California, Police Department.

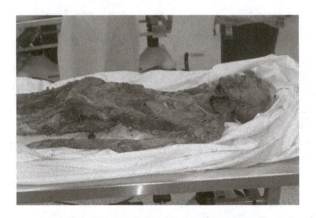

Photo 14-31. Overall, segmented, and close-up photographs at an autopsy of skeletonized remains. Courtesy of Chula Vista, California, Police Department.

Photo 14-34. Overall, segmented, and close-up photographs at an autopsy of skeletonized remains. Courtesy of Chula Vista, California, Police Department.

Photo 14-32. Overall, segmented, and close-up photographs at an autopsy of skeletonized remains. Courtesy of Chula Vista, California, Police Department.

Photo 14-35. Overall, segmented, and close-up photographs at an autopsy of skeletonized remains. Courtesy of Chula Vista, California, Police Department.

Photo 14-36. Overall, segmented, and close-up photographs at an autopsy of skeletonized remains. Courtesy of Chula Vista, California, Police Department.

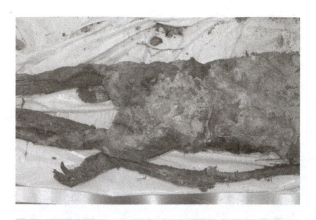

Photo 14-39. Overall, segmented, and close-up photographs at an autopsy of skeletonized remains. Courtesy of Chula Vista, California, Police Department.

Photo 14-37. Overall, segmented, and close-up photographs at an autopsy of skeletonized remains. Courtesy of Chula Vista, California, Police Department.

Photo 14-40. Overall, segmented, and close-up photographs at an autopsy of skeletonized remains. Courtesy of Chula Vista, California, Police Department.

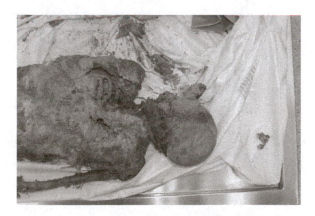

Photo 14-38. Overall, segmented, and close-up photographs at an autopsy of skeletonized remains. Courtesy of Chula Vista, California, Police Department.

Photo 14-41. Overall, segmented, and close-up photographs at an autopsy of skeletonized remains. Courtesy of Chula Vista, California, Police Department.

Photo 14-42. Overall, segmented, and close-up photographs at an autopsy of skeletonized remains. Courtesy of Chula Vista, California, Police Department.

Photo 14-45. Overall, segmented, and close-up photographs at an autopsy of skeletonized remains. Courtesy of Chula Vista, California, Police Department.

Photo 14-43. Overall, segmented, and close-up photographs at an autopsy of skeletonized remains. Courtesy of Chula Vista, California, Police Department.

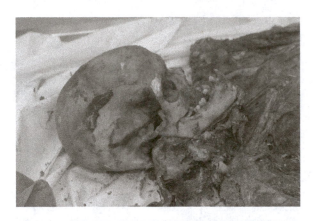

Photo 14-46. Overall, segmented, and close-up photographs at an autopsy of skeletonized remains. Courtesy of Chula Vista, California, Police Department.

Photo 14-44. Overall, segmented, and close-up photographs at an autopsy of skeletonized remains. Courtesy of Chula Vista, California, Police Department.

Photo 14-47. Overall, segmented, and close-up photographs at an autopsy of skeletonized remains. Courtesy of Chula Vista, California, Police Department.

Photo 14-48. Overall, segmented, and close-up photographs at an autopsy of skeletonized remains. Courtesy of Chula Vista, California, Police Department.

Photo 14-49. Overall, segmented, and close-up photographs at an autopsy of skeletonized remains. Courtesy of Chula Vista, California, Police Department.

Photo 14-50. Human organs removed during an autopsy. Courtesy of Chula Vista, California, Police Department.

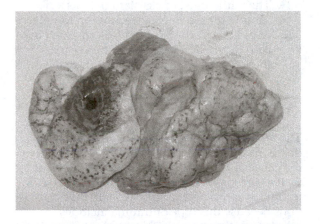

Photo 14-51. Human organs removed during an autopsy. Courtesy of Chula Vista, California, Police Department.

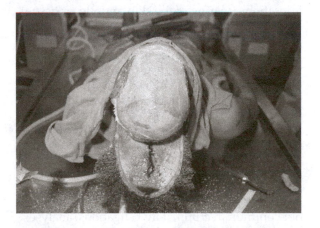

Photo 14-52. Human skull cap and brain. Courtesy of Chula Vista, California, Police Department.

the rod as it is held in place by the pathologist. Side views of the rod should be photographed as well.

21. After the major organs within the torso are removed, the skull cap is removed, and the brain is examined for possible injuries. If injuries are located, the pathologist will summon the forensic technician to photograph the injuries.

22. At the conclusion of the autopsy, two vials of blood are obtained for DNA and toxicology purposes. Additional vials of blood are collected according to the type of criminal investigation or agency protocol. The forensic technician should refrigerate the vials of blood as soon as possible inside the crime laboratory.

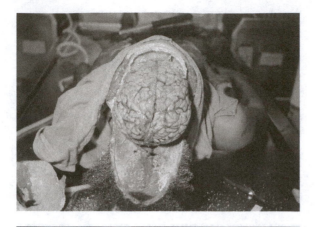

Photo 14-53. Human skull cap and brain. Courtesy of Chula Vista, California, Police Department.

23. The pathologist or assistant obtains a rib sample for the forensic technician to collect as evidence. The rib sample is collected in case future DNA analysis is necessary (beyond the analysis obtained from the blood sample). The rib sample should be frozen (placed in a freezer) inside the crime laboratory as soon as possible.

24. The time the autopsy concludes is recorded, and all evidence is transported directly to the crime laboratory for final packaging and storage. At the crime lab, blood-soaked clothing should be laid out to dry in a secured, sterile room inside the crime laboratory. Later, it is packaged in paper and frozen.

The forensic technician should not describe or present the findings of the autopsy in a written report. Findings are presented in the pathologist's report. The forensic technician's autopsy report should contain the time(s) activities were performed by the forensic technician, the names and titles of the personnel present at the autopsy, and evidence collected by the forensic technician. All other autopsy findings and conclusions are written and presented by the pathologist.

SUMMARY

The forensic pathologist plays a crucial role in death investigations. The pathologist determines the cause, mechanism, and manner of death as well as the classification of injuries. Mechanical trauma is common to criminal death investigations because this type of trauma includes injuries involving sharp objects, blunt force, and firearms. Sharp object injuries and stab wounds are common injuries found in homicidal and suicidal incidents. Blunt force injuries include contusions (bruises), abrasions (scrapes), and lacerations (tearing of the skin, muscle, or tissue). Firearms injuries include entry wounds that are contact, close-range, and distant-range. Determining the distance of the firearm from the victim at the time it was fired is often a crucial aspect of the death investigation. Firearm exit wounds are also important when determining projectile trajectory within the body. Determining the manner of death (e.g., homicide or suicide) may be accomplished through an analysis of injuries.

Other types of trauma include those associated with chemical, thermal, and electrical events. Though these categories of death are not common in criminal investigations, analyses of related injuries are an important aspect of a pathologist's role. Chemical trauma involves deaths related to toxins. Thermal trauma results from hypothermia and hyperthermia as well as burns. Electrical trauma includes low- or high-voltage injuries. Asphyxia-related deaths are common to criminal and suspicious death investigations. The cause of death may be linked to strangulation, hanging, or drowning.

After death, the human body undergoes postmortem changes. Changes are related to body temperature (algor mortis), blood pooling (livor mortis), and chemical breakdown within the muscles (rigor mortis). Decomposition (disintegration of the body due to autolysis and putrefaction) may lead to mummification in dry climates and adipocere in damp climates. Decomposition most frequently leads to discoloration in the body, release of gases and foul odor, skin slippage, and the breakdown of bodily tissues.

When a criminal autopsy is performed, the forensic technician is often required to take photographs and collect evidence during the procedure. A series of photographs are taken before and after the decedent's clothing is removed. The nude body is also photographed after it is washed. Evidence collected includes clothing, head hair, fingernail scrapings, fingerprints, blood, and a rib sample. Other evidence will be collected and preserved by the forensic technician based on directions from the pathologist and case investigator(s). The exact protocol for postmortem examination evidence collection may vary among jurisdictions.

KEY TERMS

Define, describe, or explain the importance of each of the following:

abrasion	cut (slash) wound	paired injury
adipocere	defense wounds	pattern injury
algor mortis	firearm injury	pattern of injuries
antemortem	forensic pathologist	penetrating injury
asphyxia	gross report	perforating injury
autoerotic asphyxia (autoerotic	hanging	perimortem
death)	hesitation wound	petechia
autolysis	hyperthermia death	postmortem
blunt force injury	hypothermia death	postmortem examination
cadaveric spasm	laceration	(autopsy)
cause of death	livor mortis (lividity)	putrefaction
chemical trauma death	manner of death	rigor mortis
chopping wound	mechanical trauma injury	sharp object injury
contrecoup injury	mechanism of death	stab wound
contusion	medical examiner	stippling (tattooing)
coroner	microscopic report	strangulation
coup injury	mummification	

DISCUSSION AND REVIEW QUESTIONS

1. What are the duties of the forensic pathologist?
2. Explain the differences among cause, mechanism, and manner of death.
3. What are the four basic categories of traumatic death?
4. What are hesitation wounds? Which manner of death is closely associated with hesitation wounds?
5. What is a laceration? What type of trauma creates a laceration?
6. What are defense wounds?
7. How does a firearm examiner determine the distance between the firearm at time of discharge and the entry wound on a human body?
8. What is asphyxia?
9. Articulate the biological processes that occur in a drowning.
10. What are diatoms?
11. Define algor mortis, livor mortis, and rigor mortis.
12. Describe the photographic and evidence collection steps taken by a forensic technician at a postmortem examination.

CASE STUDY—BTK Strangler

The BTK ("bind, torture, and kill") strangler Dennis Rader is credited with the murders of 10 people in and around Wichita, Kansas, between 1974 and 1991. Soon after each incident, the BTK killer wrote letters to the police and local media outlets, taunting them by offering intimate knowledge of the killings.

In 2004, long after the trail of the BTK killer went cold, Rader sent a letter to the police, claiming responsibility for a killing not previously attributed to the serial killer. Recently developed DNA technology allowed the police to produce a DNA profile from suspect biological material collected from under the fingernails during an autopsy of the previously unattributed victim.

Police corresponded with the BTK killer (Rader) to gain his trust. The killer sent a message on a computer disk to a local TV station. Authorities analyzed the metadata on the disk's *Microsoft Word* document. The police learned the document was created by a man named *Dennis*, and they located a link to the Lutheran Church where Dennis was a worshiper. The police conducted an Internet search for "Lutheran Church Wichita Dennis" and identified Dennis Rader, a Lutheran deacon, as the suspect.

Police obtained a DNA profile from Rader's daughter and compared it to the DNA evidence retrieved from BTK crime scenes. The DNA comparisons revealed a familial match. Rader was arrested on February 25, 2005, and charged with 10 counts of first-degree murder. He plead guilty to the murders on June 27, 2005.

1. What roles did documentary and DNA evidence play in solving the BTK Strangler murders?
2. How have technological advancements enhanced forensic science capabilities?
3. How did forensic analysis of the evidence produce a link between Rader and his victims?

LAB EXERCISE

Postmortem Photography and Evidence Collection

Equipment and supplies required per student:

- one 35-mm camera (film or digital) and flash unit
- one 24 exposure roll of film (if film camera)
- one photographic ruler
- two toothpicks
- one sterile swab
- three bindles
- three paper evidence bags
- paper and pen

1. Using the techniques discussed in this chapter, students form pairs and alternate roles as a forensic technician and a decedent, photographing and processing each other. The decedent will lie down on a floor or a table. Craft paper or plastic should be placed under a student who must lie on the floor.
2. Obtain the photographs and evidence listed in the check-off sheet presented here. Make notes, including date and time of collection. Write a final report of the processing steps taken.
3. Clothing will not be collected.
4. Mark each check-off box after completion of the accompanying activity. Upon completion of the exercise, submit the check-off sheet, notes, report, and all properly collected, packaged, and labeled evidence and photographs to the instructor.

Photographs   Date: Time:

☐ Overall views

   Left, right, overhead, and undersides

☐ Segmented (medium) views

   Left, right, overhead, and undersides

☐ Close-up view of face

☐ View of each hand, front and back

☐ Orientation view of a mark caused by an injury, scar, or tattoo (Create a mark if none is apparent.)

☐ Close-up view of mark without an L-shaped ruler

☐ Close-up view of mark with an L-shaped ruler

Evidence Collection   **Date:**   **Time:**

☐ Head hair sample
   One hair is enough for practice. Package properly.

☐ Oral swabs
   Obtain oral skin cell samples from an inner cheek using two
   swabs. Package properly.

☐ Fingernail scrapings
   Collect fingernail scrapings using a separate clean toothpick
   for each hand. Package each toothpick separately and label
   properly.

WEB RESOURCES

American Board of Pathology:
  www.abpath.org
American Board of Criminalistics:
  www.criminalistics.com
American Board of Forensic Odontology:
  www.newasfo.com
Forensic Anthropology Center:
  www.utk.edu/~anthrop/index.htm
Armed Forces Institute of Pathology:
  www.afip.org
British Association for Forensic Odontology:
  www.bafo.org.uk/index.php

Bureau of Legal Dentistry (BOLD):
  www.boldlab.org
National Association of Medical Examiners:
  www.thename.org
WinID3 Dental Identification System:
  www.winid.com
International Association of Forensic Nurses:
  www.forensicnurse.org
Forensic Medicine for Medical Students:
  www.forensicmed.co.uk

15

Report Writing and Courtroom Testimony

LEARNING OUTCOMES

After completing this chapter, the reader should be able to:

- explain the importance of effective note taking and detailed report writing,
- articulate how a forensic technician should prepare for court,
- construct a courtroom exhibit.

INTRODUCTION

According to the U.S. Supreme Court, the Sixth Amendment right to a jury trial applies in federal criminal cases and in state cases in which the potential penalty for the crime charged exceeds six months in jail or prison or could result in a fine of more than $500. With the popularity of Hollywood-produced forensic science dramas, many potential jurors enter the courtroom with the belief that they possess broad-based knowledge of forensic science. The jurors, selected through the **voir dire examination** process, often have high expectations of the evidence in the case. *Voir dire* is a French phrase which means *to speak the truth*. The voir dire examination is the process through which prospective jurors are questioned during the jury selection process about their backgrounds and biases (Ortmeier, 2006). Because many jurors entertain preconceived notions about forensic science, the prosecution must explain, through the testimony of the forensic technician and other forensic experts, why evidence is or is not present in a case. The jury's role is to draw conclusions from the evidence presented.

> **Voir dire examination**
> The process through which prospective jurors are questioned about their backgrounds, biases, and suitability during jury selection.

The key to courtroom and testimony readiness is preparation. Success in the courtroom starts with good note taking and report writing during the criminal investigation.

The forensic technician must review notes and reports that were written during the case investigation. Reading the case notes and reports will refresh the forensic technician's memory on specific details of the case. The forensic technician must be prepared and confident while under direct examination by the prosecutor and cross-examination by the defense attorney.

FIELD NOTES

Notes recorded in the field throughout a criminal investigation are critical to effective documentation. One should not rely on memory to recall details of an investigation. Over time, memory fades and numerous criminal cases are investigated. Details of various cases blur, and one can become confused when trying to recall details of a specific case. Notes recorded contemporaneous to the investigation provide a reliable way to produce a report and recall facts. Detailed note taking lays the foundation for the integrity of the final report and lends credibility to one's testimony in the courtroom.

While processing a crime scene, a forensic technician may record a detail in the field notes that later proves to be very significant. For example, making a notation of a distinctive odor such as the strong fragrance of men's cologne is an observation that can only be documented through writing. It cannot be photographed, captured, or measured in any other manner. Likewise, lighting or weather conditions for outdoor scenes are difficult to document other than by means of field notes.

The forensic technician should record notes during each stage of a criminal investigation. Field notes should be recorded during crime scene, vehicle, autopsy, and suspect or victim processing, at search warrant scenes, while processing or analyzing evidence inside the crime laboratory, during any investigative follow-up, and during any other relevant task accomplished during a criminal investigation.

Taking notes throughout a criminal investigation is similar to utilizing an outline for a research paper. The notes form the skeleton of the paper. Notes taken during a criminal investigation form the foundation of the final report (Guffey, 2005).

Events are recorded in chronological order. Task start and end times are recorded as well. A brief description, the assigned evidence number, and the location of each evidence item collected is included in the field notes. Processing methods used and the results of presumptive tests and other analyses are also included. The notes must be detailed, complete, and legible so they can be read and understood by anyone. Many agencies provide forms for recording information, while others provide a simple notepad for field note taking. The field notes should not include information (e.g., the technician's personal opinions) that is not relevant to the investigation or the facts of the case.

Retention of field notes depends on agency policy. Some agencies require that field notes be filed with the official report. Others may allow destruction of field notes after the official report is complete. If allowable, the destruction of field notes may occur under the following conditions:

- The notes are destroyed in good faith, not to conceal pertinent facts.
- The information contained in the notes has been entered into the official report.
- The official report accurately reflects the contents of the notes destroyed.

Without a prescriptive agency policy, it may be wise to retain field notes. However, retained field notes are subject to subpoena by the

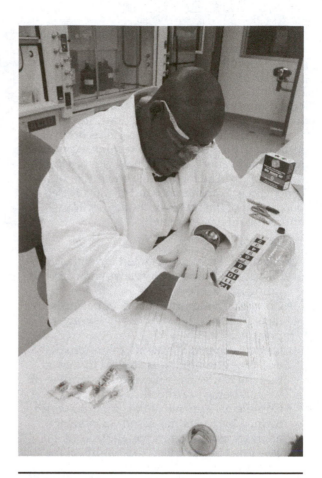

Photo 15-1. Forensic technician writing laboratory notes. Photograph by Chris Nellis.

prosecution and defense attorneys. If the notes are sloppily written and inaccurate, the credibility of the note taker may be questioned.

REPORT WRITING

A report constitutes an official record of the forensic technician's work. It is a reflection of the forensic technician's observations. Although report writing may be viewed as the boring part of forensic technology, it is an essential component of an investigation. The forensic technician's report is the first step in courtroom testimony because it speaks to the tasks performed and the results of tests and analyses.

Many people from various agencies or entities may read a report. Prosecutors and defense attorneys search for elements of the crime, probable cause, possible errors, and conflicting information. A well-written report, one that explains the findings and results of compelling evidence in a criminal investigation, may lead to a guilty plea by the defendant.

A prosecutor or defense attorney often refers to the forensic technician's report during the specialist's testimony in court. Segments of the report may be read aloud. Therefore, the report must be clear, concise, and accurate. Jurors also read reports. If a report is ambiguous or unclear, jurors may dismiss the facts within it. Appellate judges read reports in search of evidence to rule on an appeal. The media may attempt to draw conclusions from a report and create a biased perception of the writer or the agency from which the report originated.

A good report is:

- Accurate. Facts are obtained through a combination of witness interviews and corroborating physical evidence.
- Concise. The complete story or narrative of facts should be told with as few words as possible.
- Clear. Ambiguous statements are avoided and proper grammar is applied to ensure that the reader has a clear understanding of what is being portrayed.
- Complete. Elements of the crime, tasks performed by personnel, results of evidence analyses, and other important facts of the case must be described thoroughly in the report.
- Factual. Assumptions or opinions are not included or inferred in a report. Only factual findings are presented.
- Objective. Forensic technicians and sworn officers should allow the evidence to speak for itself. Remain objective throughout the investigation and the writing of the report.
- Free of grammar and spelling errors. For handwritten forms, legibility is also a must. This adds credibility to the writer and minimizes confusion.

When writing reports, the forensic technician should:

- write in the first person (e.g., "I saw ..." "I performed ..."),
- avoid repetition and jargon (words that are specific to an occupation but not familiar to the general public),
- include detail, keeping the report simple and informative,
- write in paragraphs, use complete sentences, and present events in chronological order,
- write in the past tense,
- not state an opinion,

- provide all information, results of processed evidence, leads, and links to the disposition of the evidence (for example, a forensic technician may write, "I processed the evidence using black magnetic powder, obtaining five latent fingerprint lifts. See latent print examiner Smith's report for latent print comparison details.")
- use the field notes, crime scene sketch, photographs, evidence list, and other pertinent information when preparing the final report. Follow agency policies and procedures regarding specific details of report writing (Guffey, 2005; Parr, 2000).

THE COURTROOM

The forensic technician should review field notes and reports as well as the case photographs and evidence prior to testimony. Reviewing the case will help the forensic technician refresh memory of the investigation and the work performed.

The forensic technician's primary role in the courtroom is to respond to questions related to the evidence presented in the criminal case. The prosecution will ask foundational questions to establish the appearance of the crime scene, identify the evidence collected, and publicize processing results. To be admitted in court, scientific procedures involved in processing evidence must be relevant and reliable. In other words, a new procedure that has not been scientifically tested and validated cannot be used to support forensic evidence in a criminal case.

Along with reviewing field notes, evidence, and case photographs, the forensic technician usually participates in a pre-trial conference with a prosecutor and case investigators. The pre-trial conference is helpful in several ways.

- The prosecuting attorney learns of the forensic technician's qualifications and areas of expertise. The forensic technician should provide a current resume detailing education, training, and experience.
- The forensic technician will learn of the most important aspects of the trial.
- Communication among members of the prosecutorial team is established, specific questions are answered, and technical aspects of the case are clarified.
- Pre-trial tasks are identified.
- Confidence in the case and its investigation is established prior to entering the courtroom (Rutledge, 2007).

CASE #: _____ PROPERTY TAG #: _____ 1 OF _____

LOCATION: _____

DATE OF OCCURRENCE: _____ SYNOPSIS:

DATE/TIME OF CALL OUT: _____ _____

NOTIFIED BY: _____ _____

DATE/TIME 10-19: _____ _____

CASE AGENT: _____ _____

SCENE AGENT: _____ _____

LAB PERSONNEL: _____

SCENE #	LOCATION	DATE AT SCENE	10-97:	10-34:	10-19:
1					
2					
3					
4					
5					
6					
7					
8					
9					
10					
11					
12					
13					
14					
15					
16					
17					
18					

Figure 15-1. Forensic worksheets. Created by Forensic Technician T. Venn. Courtesy of the Chula Vista, California, Police Department.

NOTES

_____ OF _____

CASE #: _____

Figure 15-2. Forensic worksheets. Created by Forensic Technician T. Venn. Courtesy of the Chula Vista, California, Police Department.

SKETCH

ADDRESS: _____

_____ OF _____

CASE #: _____

NOT TO SCALE

CASE NUMBER: _____   _____ OF _____

FROM

ITEM	NORTH	EAST	SOUTH	WEST	BASELINE	DIMENSIONS/NOTES

NOTES: _____

_____

Figure 15-3. Forensic worksheets. Created by Forensic Technician T. Venn. Courtesy of the Chula Vista, California, Police Department.

CASE NUMBER: _____   PAGE _____ OF _____

LATENT PRINT	LOCATION

Figure 15-4. Forensic worksheets. Created by Forensic Technician T. Venn. Courtesy of the Chula Vista, California, Police Department.

CASE NUMBER: _____   _____ OF _____

VEHICLE MAKE: _____ MODEL: _____
COLOR: _____ YEAR: _____ PLATE: _____
VIN: _____ DOORS: _____
DAMAGE: _____
DATE PROCESSED: _____ RELATION TO SCENE: _____
START TIME: _____ END TIME: _____

VEHICLE MAKE: _____ MODEL: _____
COLOR: _____ YEAR: _____ PLATE: _____
VIN: _____ DOORS: _____
DAMAGE: _____
DATE PROCESSED: _____ RELATION TO SCENE: _____
START TIME: _____ END TIME: _____

VEHICLE MAKE: _____ MODEL: _____
COLOR: _____ YEAR: _____ PLATE: _____
VIN: _____ DOORS: _____
DAMAGE: _____
DATE PROCESSED: _____ RELATION TO SCENE: _____
START TIME: _____ END TIME: _____

VEHICLE MAKE: _____ MODEL: _____
COLOR: _____ YEAR: _____ PLATE: _____
VIN: _____ DOORS: _____
DAMAGE: _____
DATE PROCESSED: _____ RELATION TO SCENE: _____
START TIME: _____ END TIME: _____

VEHICLE MAKE: _____ MODEL: _____
COLOR: _____ YEAR: _____ PLATE: _____
VIN: _____ DOORS: _____
DAMAGE: _____
DATE PROCESSED: _____ RELATION TO SCENE: _____
START TIME: _____ END TIME: _____

Figure 15-5. Forensic worksheets. Created by Forensic Technician T. Venn. Courtesy of the Chula Vista, California, Police Department.

CASE NUMBER: _____   PAGE _____ OF _____

ADDRESS: _____

OBSERVATION #		LOCATION:

PATTERN TYPE:

CONTACT/TRANSFER	LOW	MED	HIGH	CAST-OFF	VOID	WIPE	SWIPE	SPURT	GUSH

PATTERN DIMENSIONS:	DIRECTION OF TRAVEL:			

PATTERN LOCATION:	SAMPLE:	TIME:	CONTROL:	TIME:

SEQUENCE OF EVENTS:

OBSERVATION #		LOCATION:

PATTERN TYPE:

CONTACT/TRANSFER	LOW	MED	HIGH	CAST-OFF	VOID	WIPE	SWIPE	SPURT	GUSH

PATTERN DIMENSIONS:	DIRECTION OF TRAVEL:			

PATTERN LOCATION:	SAMPLE:	TIME:	CONTROL:	TIME:

SEQUENCE OF EVENTS:

OBSERVATION #		LOCATION:

PATTERN TYPE:

CONTACT/TRANSFER	LOW	MED	HIGH	CAST-OFF	VOID	WIPE	SWIPE	SPURT	GUSH

PATTERN DIMENSIONS:	DIRECTION OF TRAVEL:			

PATTERN LOCATION:	SAMPLE:	TIME:	CONTROL:	TIME:

SEQUENCE OF EVENTS:

$H = \tan(i) \times D$

H = unknown height above point of convergence (aka: area of origin)

i = known impact angle

D = distance to point of convergence

$\tan$ = tangent function

NOTES:

Figure 15-6. Forensic worksheets. Created by Forensic Technician T. Venn. Courtesy of the Chula Vista, California, Police Department.

#	ITEM OF EVIDENCE	TIME	#	ITEM OF EVIDENCE	TIME
	CASE NUMBER:			PAGE ____ OF ____	
	PROPERTY TAG #:			VICTIM:	
	DATE OF AUTOPSY:				
#	ITEM OF EVIDENCE	TIME	#	ITEM OF EVIDENCE	TIME
	HEAD BAG			BODY BAG	
	LEFT HAND BAG			WHITE SHEET	
	RIGHT HAND BAG			FACIAL HAIR SAMPLE	
	LEFT FOOT BAG			CHEST HAIR SAMPLE	
	RIGHT FOOT BAG			PUBIC HAIR SAMPLE	
	ORAL SWABS			ANAL SWABS	
	FINGERNAIL SCRAPINGS			URETHRAL SWABS	
	HEAD HAIR SAMPLE			VAGINAL SWABS	
	BLOOD			GUNSHOT RESIDUE TABS	
	INKED FINGERPRINTS			MISSLES/FRAGMENTS	
	RIB SECTION				
	CLOTHING			JEWELRY	
	OTHER				

Figure 15-7. Forensic worksheets. Created by Forensic Technician T. Venn. Courtesy of the Chula Vista, California, Police Department.

CASE NUMBER: _____ _____ OF _____

SUSPECT: _____ DATE PROCESSED: _____

DOB: _____ HAIR: _____ EYE: _____

PHOTOS   BLOOD   HAIR   MOUTH   FINGERNAIL   GSR   MAJOR CASE

CLOTHING: _____ COLLECTED: YES   NO

SUSPECT: _____ DATE PROCESSED: _____

DOB: _____ HAIR: _____ EYE: _____

PHOTOS   BLOOD   HAIR   MOUTH   FINGERNAIL   GSR   MAJOR CASE

CLOTHING: _____ COLLECTED: YES   NO

SUSPECT: _____ DATE PROCESSED: _____

DOB: _____ HAIR: _____ EYE: _____

PHOTOS   BLOOD   HAIR   MOUTH   FINGERNAIL   GSR   MAJOR CASE

CLOTHING: _____ COLLECTED: YES   NO

SUSPECT: _____ DATE PROCESSED: _____

DOB: _____ HAIR: _____ EYE: _____

PHOTOS   BLOOD   HAIR   MOUTH   FINGERNAIL   GSR   MAJOR CASE

CLOTHING: _____ COLLECTED: YES   NO

SUSPECT: _____ DATE PROCESSED: _____

DOB: _____ HAIR: _____ EYE: _____

PHOTOS   BLOOD   HAIR   MOUTH   FINGERNAIL   GSR   MAJOR CASE

CLOTHING: _____ COLLECTED: YES   NO

SUSPECT: _____ DATE PROCESSED: _____

DOB: _____ HAIR: _____ EYE: _____

PHOTOS   BLOOD   HAIR   MOUTH   FINGERNAIL   GSR   MAJOR CASE

CLOTHING: _____ COLLECTED: YES   NO

Figure 15-8. Forensic worksheets. Created by Forensic Technician T. Venn. Courtesy of the Chula Vista, California, Police Department.

CASE NUMBER: _____   _____ OF _____

VICTIM: _____   DATE PROCESSED: _____

DOB: _____   HAIR: _____ EYE: _____

   PHOTOS   BLOOD   HAIR   MOUTH   FINGERNAIL   GSR   MAJOR CASE

CLOTHING: _____ COLLECTED: YES   NO

VICTIM / WITNESS: _____   DATE PROCESSED: _____

DOB: _____   HAIR: _____ EYE: _____

   PHOTOS   BLOOD   HAIR   MOUTH   FINGERNAIL   GSR   MAJOR CASE

CLOTHING: _____ COLLECTED: YES   NO

VICTIM / WITNESS: _____   DATE PROCESSED: _____

DOB: _____   HAIR: _____ EYE: _____

   PHOTOS   BLOOD   HAIR   MOUTH   FINGERNAIL   GSR   MAJOR CASE

CLOTHING: _____ COLLECTED: YES   NO

VICTIM / WITNESS: _____   DATE PROCESSED: _____

DOB: _____   HAIR: _____ EYE: _____

   PHOTOS   BLOOD   HAIR   MOUTH   FINGERNAIL   GSR   MAJOR CASE

CLOTHING: _____ COLLECTED: YES   NO

VICTIM / WITNESS: _____   DATE PROCESSED: _____

DOB: _____   HAIR: _____ EYE: _____

   PHOTOS   BLOOD   HAIR   MOUTH   FINGERNAIL   GSR   MAJOR CASE

CLOTHING: _____ COLLECTED: YES   NO

VICTIM / WITNESS: _____   DATE PROCESSED: _____

DOB: _____   HAIR: _____ EYE: _____

   PHOTOS   BLOOD   HAIR   MOUTH   FINGERNAIL   GSR   MAJOR CASE

CLOTHING: _____ COLLECTED: YES   NO

Figure 15.9. Forensic worksheets. Created by Forensic Technician T. Venn. Courtesy of the Chula Vista, California, Police Department.

Technical Review Checklist

Case Notes	Tech Review
Is the correct case number on each case documentation page? (at least one page should include the property tag number)	
Is each case documentation page numbered? (at least one page should include the total number of pages)	
Is each case documentation page marked with the original initials of the note taker?	
Are handwritten notes and observations of a permanent (written in ink) nature?	
Are the notes and observations clear, legible, and understandable?	
Are the cross-outs and additions legible, initialed, and dated?	
Evidence	**Tech Review**
Is the chain of custody properly documented?	
Is the chain of custody current as of this date?	
Is there a description of the evidence packaging and/or sealed condition?	
Analysis	**Tech Review**
Was the requested work performed?	
Were appropriate approved laboratory methods used?	
Is there proper use and documentation of standards and controls?	
Were scientifically valid and appropriate methods used?	
Is the report information supported by the case jacket documentation?	

Administrative Review Checklist

Evidence	Admin Review
Is the evidence sufficiently described?	
Are all derivative items of evidence documented, to include the description and date of recovery?	
Is the disposition of all items documented?	
Results and Conclusions	**Admin Review**
Does the report accurately reference all evidence received and/or analyzed?	
Are the conclusions clearly communicated to the reader?	
Does the report accurately reference the agency's case number and property tag number?	
Is the Spelling and Grammar correct?	
Is the report page numbered? (at least one page should include the total number of pages)	
Is the signature and identification number of the analyst and date of issue present on the report?	

Figure 15-10. Forensic worksheets. Created by Forensic Technician T. Venn. Courtesy of the Chula Vista, California, Police Department.

On the day of the trial, the forensic technician should possess field notes and reports as well as evidence specifically requested by the prosecuting attorney. The case should not be discussed in public areas. The forensic technician should be professional in appearance. The first impression is very important in the courtroom. Some jurors predetermine witness credibility based on personal appearance. The following courtroom attire is recommended:

- A pressed business suit in black, gray, dark navy blue, or neutral color is preferred.
- Shoes should be neutral in color, preferably black, and polished.
- Jewelry should be minimized.
- Women should avoid excessive make-up (Ortmeier, 2006).

Before entering the courtroom, the forensic technician should disconnect cell phones and other electronic devices. Personal items (e.g., brief case, purse) should be kept to a minimum. Food, drink, and chewing gum should remain outside. Evidence may be brought in if specifically requested by the prosecuting attorney.

Inside the courtroom, the forensic technician will be asked to affirm or swear to tell the truth (sworn in) by the clerk or bailiff. The forensic technician should stand erect, and outstretch a raised right hand while reciting the oath.

Once seated, the forensic technician is asked by the clerk to state his or her name. **Direct examination** (questioning by the attorney who subpoenaed the forensic technician) follows. The forensic technician is asked a series of background questions regarding education, training, experience, and current employment. After the forensic technician's credentials are established, the attorney will ask a series of questions pertaining to the crime scene, evidence, and relevant facts related to the forensic technician's role in the criminal investigation (Weston & Lushbaugh, 2008; Neubauer, 1996).

> **Direct examination**
> A series of questions asked by an attorney of the attorney's witness that pertain to a crime scene, evidence, and relevant facts related to a criminal investigation.

After direct examination, **cross-examination** by the opposing attorney(s) may occur. The attorney conducting the cross-examination may attempt to discredit (impeach) the witness. The following should be considered during cross-examination.

> **Cross-examination**
> By the opposing attorney(s). The attorney conducting the cross-examination may attempt to discredit (impeach) the witness.

- Remain objective. Do not purposely show favoritism to either side. Allow the evidence to speak for itself. Do not introduce emotion into the testimony.
- Think before responding. Be careful of leading questions. A *yes* or *no* answer may be sufficient. If the response requires an explanation, explain as necessary. Conversely, avoid volunteering information that was not solicited or providing an explanation that is beyond the scope of the question.
- Correct mistakes. If a mistake is made in the testimony, correct the error immediately.
- Remain calm and avoid sarcasm. If an attorney asks questions rapidly in an attempt to stir emotion, respond with a calm, even tone. One must remain respectful and professional in the courtroom. The forensic technician can slow the questioning process by pausing or reaching for a drink of water (if available).
- The attorney may ask the same question repeatedly or in a different form. Answer each question with the same response. Never

reply with, "I already answered that." The attorney may be trying to elicit contradictory responses.
- The attorney may refer to or quote from a book while asking a technical question. Ask to see and read the passage in the book before responding to the question.
- If the attorney utters a demeaning comment, ignore it. The prosecuting attorney should intervene with an objection. Remain calm and professional.
- If the attorney interrupts during a response, one may ask the judge, "Your honor, may I complete my response?"
- If asked to present statistics on the number of particular cases worked, fingerprints lifted, etc., explain that the exact number is not readily available. If asked to approximate, understate, do not exaggerate the number.
- An attorney may ask for the estimated time it took to perform a certain task. Rather than guessing, verbally retrace the event, approximating the time of each movement to arrive at an estimated time for the entire task.
- If the forensic technician lacks extensive experience, qualifications may become an issue. The forensic technician should remain calm and confident. The prosecuting attorney should not allow the specialist to testify if qualifications are an issue.
- An attorney may compare testimony presented in a previous proceeding (e.g., preliminary hearing) with testimony in the trial. The attorney is searching for contradictions. If the forensic technician cannot recall previous testimony, a transcript of the previous testimony may be requested for review.
- An attorney may ask questions that are out of the forensic technician's scope of expertise. The attorney may be unaware that the forensic technician is not qualified to answer the question. An attorney may also attempt to lure the forensic technician into providing testimony that is outside the scope of the specialist's job description. Regardless of the reason for the question, a forensic technician should not provide testimony outside the scope and nature of the job description or areas of expertise.
- A forensic technician may be asked if the case or testimony was discussed with anyone prior to court. The specialist may respond affirmatively that the case was discussed with case investigators as well as prosecutorial and crime lab personnel.

- A forensic technician may be asked an unreasonable scenario-based question. Often, this type of question is prefaced with the phrase, "Is it possible that ...?" An appropriate forensic technician response may be, "Anything is possible, but that is very unlikely."
- If a lengthy and confusing question is asked, the forensic technician may request that the question be rephrased. One should not respond to an ambiguous or misunderstood question.
- Appear interested in the proceeding. Avoid monotonous "yes" and "no" answers. Sit straight or lean forward slightly.
- Look at and make eye contact with jurors while giving testimony.
- One may demonstrate a sense of humor on the witness stand as long as the humor is appropriate. Humor may help establish rapport with the jurors. While employed as a forensic technician, one of the authors was presenting testimony in a murder case in which the defendants attempted to clean up blood using rags and soiled laundry. Several men's white tube socks were found in the laundry basket of the home. The socks tested positive for blood, and were collected as evidence. During cross-examination, the defense attorney asked the forensic technician, "How do you know those were *men's* white tube socks? Do you have any experience in handling *men's* white tube socks?" The forensic technician replied, "Yes, five years experience doing my husband's laundry." The jury and defense attorney laughed, and the defense attorney responded with, "No further questions."
- Refer to the defendant as "Mr. or Ms. (last name)" or "the defendant" (Guffey, 2005; Rutledge, 2007).

During direct examination or cross-examination, the opposition attorney may object to questions asked by the attorney conducting the examination. The forensic technician should discontinue testimony until the judge replies with a ruling on the objection. If the objection is overruled, the forensic technician may continue with an answer. If the objection is sustained, the forensic technician should not respond. If the forensic technician-witness becomes confused, the judge can be asked to clarify.

It is impossible to prepare for every conceivable question that could be asked of a forensic technician-witness. However, if the forensic technician prepares for court by reviewing field notes, reports, photographs, and evidence, courtroom testimony can be approached with confidence.

COURTROOM EXHIBITS

In addition to presenting courtroom testimony, the forensic technician is frequently asked to explain courtroom exhibits and displays (demonstrative evidence) to the jury. Courtroom exhibits are often used during testimony to help the jury visualize descriptions (e.g., crime scenes) presented through the testimony. Courtroom exhibits may be created by the forensic technician, the prosecutor, or the defense team. The judge must approve of each display before it is admitted for viewing at the judicial proceeding.

Photographic evidence is assigned a court exhibit number and is usually exhibited in the courtroom on a display board. The display board is often placed a few feet from the jury.

For photographic evidence to be admitted in court, the following requirements must be met.

- The photographic image must be a reasonable and accurate representation of the evidence at or very near the time of the incident.
- The photograph must be authenticated by a person who was at the scene and can testify that the photograph accurately depicts the scene.
- The photographer can testify only to the condition of the scene at the time the photograph was taken. Therefore, the forensic technician should record the time photography begins and ends at the scene.
- Photographs cannot be altered. Digital images cannot be deleted, even if a camera misfire results in a badly composed photograph. Traditional film images must contain the same detail as the photographic negative.
- Grotesque or embarrassing images are often inadmissible in court because of their emotional impact on the jury. Overall photographs may be allowed while close-up views are not. Many autopsy photographs are not allowed. The judge determines admissibility.
- Photographs of evidence may be admitted in lieu of actual items if the items are bloody, foul-smelling, or too large to be brought into the courtroom (Fredrickson & Siljander, 1997).

Although display boards with photographs and diagrams are commonly used in the

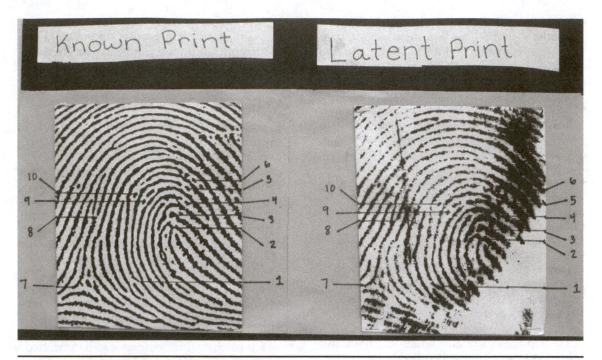

Photo 15-2. Display of a known and a latent fingerprint.

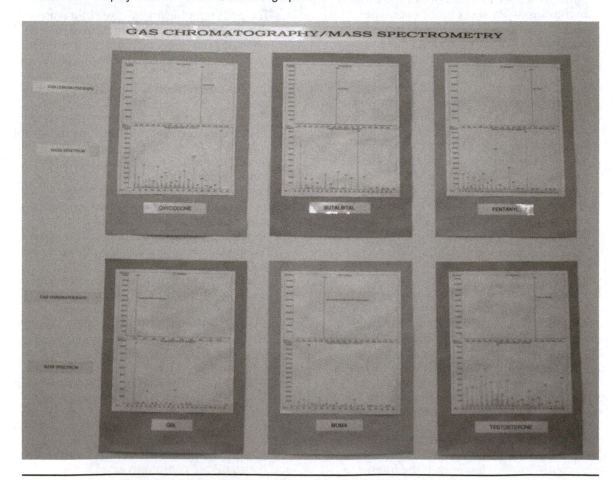

Photo 15-3. Display of a gas chromatography/mass spectrometry printout.

courtroom, other types of exhibits are used as well. Latent fingerprint examiners often utilize computer software programs to compare known to unknown fingerprints obtained at a crime scene. Shoe impression experts and forensic document examiners utilize similar digital imaging software to create comparison exhibits. Images presented via computer software must be original.

Illustrations may be used to compare forensic documents, glass fractures, striation and firing pin marks for firearms comparison, tool and bite marks, and other types of forensic evidence. A video recording of a crime or surveillance may be viewed in court. As with any other exhibit, the video recording must be authenticated by a person with knowledge of the recording's content.

SUMMARY

A forensic technician must record field notes throughout a criminal investigation. The notes provide the foundation for the final report, which documents the details of the forensic technician's observations, tasks performed, evidential findings, and test results. Detailed and well-written reports are indicative of thorough investigations that often lead to guilty pleas rather than trials. The report is a reflection on the forensic technician's professionalism, and is often used to refresh the forensic technician's memory.

In a courtroom, the forensic technician is often asked to present testimony to authenticate

photographs taken and evidence collected. Courtroom exhibits are frequently used to display photographs and diagrams. Display boards, overhead transparencies, and projected views of digital images are commonly presented in court. Regardless of the exhibit used, the forensic technician is often asked to explain the details of the exhibit. Direct examination and cross-examination of the forensic technician-witness will occur. In preparation for court, the forensic technician must review field notes, reports, photographs, and evidence. In court, the specialist must remain calm and dress and behave professionally.

KEY TERMS

Define, describe, or explain the importance of each of the following:

cross-examination   direct examination   *voir dire* examination

DISCUSSION AND REVIEW QUESTIONS

1. What is a *voir dire* examination?
2. Why must a forensic technician take detailed filed notes during an investigation?
3. What are the characteristics of a good report?
4. How should a forensic technician prepare for court?

5. What types of exhibits are displayed in court?
6. Why does a forensic technician testify on photographic evidence?

CASE STUDY—Courtroom Testimony

The following represents testimony presented by a forensic technician during direct examination in a criminal trial.

PROSECUTOR: Good afternoon.
TECHNICIAN: Good afternoon.

PROSECUTOR: Would you state your name and spell your last name for us, please.
TECHNICIAN: Sarah Foster. F-O-S-T-E-R.
PROSECUTOR: How are you employed, Ms. Foster?

TECHNICIAN: I am a forensic technician with the Sunshine Police Department.

PROSECUTOR: And how long have you been a forensic technician there?

TECHNICIAN: Seven years.

PROSECUTOR: What are your duties as a forensic technician?

TECHNICIAN: I respond to various types of crime scenes, including homicides, attempted homicides, and other types of scenes. I photograph and sketch the scenes as well as collect, preserve, and transport evidence.

PROSECUTOR: Let me ask you: What training prepared you for this position?

TECHNICIAN: I hold an associate degree in forensic technology, and I received over 600 hours of training in crime scene processing. In addition, I completed a nine-month internship with the David City, New York, Police Department.

PROSECUTOR: You are also experienced in lifting fingerprints, correct?

TECHNICIAN: Yes.

PROSECUTOR: Could you tell us what a latent fingerprint is?

TECHNICIAN: When one touches an object, oil and residue from the ridges of the skin are deposited on the object. If the print cannot be seen, it is latent, invisible to the unaided human eye. We use different processing techniques, chemicals, and powders, to make the latent fingerprint visible.

The exchange between the prosecutor and the forensic technician continued for some time, revealing how the technician identified, photographed, collected, preserved, and transported fingerprints and other evidence located at the crime scene.

When direct examination of the technician was completed, the defense attorney proceeded with cross-examination. The defense attorney focused immediately on bloodstains collected by the technician at the scene. The bloodstains were subsequently analyzed by a DNA expert who positively identified the defendant as the source of the blood.

DEFENSE: Ms. Foster, please describe the process you followed to collect, preserve, and transport the bloodstain to the crime lab.

TECHNICIAN: I ... (the technician detailed the correct procedure).

DEFENSE: Did the DNA profile of the blood collected at the scene match the DNA profile of my client (defendant)?

TECHNICIAN: I am sorry, but your question calls for an opinion that is beyond the scope of my education, training, experience, and job description.

1. Did the forensic technician present the correct response to the defense attorney's last question? Explain.
2. How should a forensic technician prepare to give testimony in court?

LAB EXERCISE

Courtroom Exhibit

Equipment and supplies required per student (depends on exhibit):

- photographs taken in a previous assignment (film or digital)
- one display board
- two pens or markers
- one compact computer disc

1. Each student will select photos from a previous assignment or photograph a series of images for a courtroom exhibit.

The photographs displayed must be taken by the exhibitor.

2. A display board, overhead transparencies, or a computer software program (e.g., PowerPoint) may be used to present the photos.
3. The exhibit should be thematic and self-explanatory.
4. Each student is allowed 10 minutes to brief the class on the courtroom exhibit.

WEB RESOURCES

Fastone Image Viewer: www.fastone.org/

Justice for Murder Victims: www.vocal-jmv.org

National Association for Court Management (NACM): www.nacmnet.org

National Center for Victims of Crime: www.ncvc.org/ncvc/main.aspx

National Center for State Courts (NCSC): www.ncsconline.org

Supreme Court of the United States: www.supremecourtus.gov

National Institute of Justice: www.ojp.usdoj.gov/nij

The DNA Initiative: www.dna.gov/training/communicating

U.S. Courts: www.uscourts.gov

U.S. Department of Justice: www.usdoj.gov

U.S. Marshals Service: www.usdoj.gov/marshals

Glossary

Abrasion   An abrasion results from the scraping and removal of layers of skin when a blunt force instrument strikes the body.

Accidental whorl fingerprint pattern   A pattern that contains a combination of two separate types of fingerprint patterns.

Achromatic lens   Lens that contains more than one element of transparent material. It concentrates light on a point, yielding photographs with true colors.

Adipocere   A wax-like, cheesy appearance caused by the slow hydrolysis of fats in decomposing material. The transformation of fat into adipocere occurs best in environments (e.g., sealed casket, muddy lake bottom, wet soil) that are cold, humid, and relatively free of oxygen.

Administrative search   is based on a compelling governmental interest embodied in statutory or case law. Under these circumstances, the interests of society take precedence over the privacy interests of the individual. Administrative searches include searches associated with custodial institutions, booking searches, vehicle inventories, fish and game code enforcement, immigration and border inspections, U.S. immigration and customs enforcement, airport and courthouse searches, and driving under the influence (DUI) sobriety checkpoints.

Algor mortis   The cooling of the body after death.

Altered bloodstain pattern   Any bloodstain pattern located at a crime scene that is altered due to environmental conditions, first responder activities, or other actions.

Alternate Light Source (ALS)   An illumination device used to locate evidence that cannot be observed with an unaided human eye.

Amotivational syndrome   A condition created by long-term use of cannabis through which the user experiences indifference, impairment of judgment (makes bad decisions), memory loss, an inability to concentrate, diminished attractiveness, and lack of achievement.

Angular tented arch fingerprint pattern   Variation of the arch pattern that contains ridge incline of 90 degrees or less.

Antemortem   Before death.

Aperture   The opening in a camera lens that regulates the amount of light allowed to enter the camera.

Arterial bloodstain pattern   Created when blood under pressure from a punctured artery of a live person is cast onto a surface. The more severe the damage to the artery, the more blood volume discharged from the artery.

Asphyxia   Death caused by interference with the oxygenation of the brain. Asphyxia can occur as a result of chemical, thermal, or mechanical trauma.

Autoerotic asphyxia (autoerotic death)   An accidental hanging caused by the victim's attempt at sexual arousal. The victim ties a noose or other ligature around the neck and the hands with the intent to gain sexual pleasure from oxygen restriction to the brain during masturbation.

Autolysis   A process that contributes to the decomposition of the body initiated by lysosome cells that release digestive enzymes.

Automated Fingerprint Identification System (AFIS)   A computerized database that stores fingerprints by pattern type and the relationship of the minutiae in the fingerprints. The AFIS computer program does not catalog loops, arches, whorls, bifurcations, or ridge endings. Rather, it utilizes programmed algorithms and identifies relationships associated with the physical features of a fingerprint pattern.

Backspatter pattern   A backspatter (blood particles released toward a weapon) pattern may result when a projectile contacts the body. Backspatter is not as symmetrical as forward spatter because it is traveling in the opposite direction of the projectile. The small droplets located in backspatter do not travel more than four or five feet.

Ballistics   The scientific study of the dynamics of projectiles and bullet trajectory (the path of a bullet).

Baseline sketch method   Sketch method useful at an outdoor scene. Similar to the coordinate method except that the x or y axis is extended by a line. A tape measure or a chalk line can be used to extend the axis lines. For example, if perpendicular sides of a building provide x and y, the axis can be extended from the building's sides. A 50- or 100-foot cloth tape measure works well in this situation because it will lie flat.

Bindle   A bindle is a clean piece of paper that is folded in a manner that prevents damage to or destruction of a trace evidence item.

Blood swipe   Occurs when a bloody object moves along a clean surface (e.g., bloody hair moving across a clean wall or floor).

Blood wipe   Occurs when a clean object moves against a bloody surface (e.g., a hand or cloth moving through a pool of blood).

Bloodstain Pattern Analysis (BPA)   Area of forensic science through which the dynamics or actions occurring in a crime scene are analyzed and interpreted.

Bloodstain Pattern Expert (BPE)   Through detailed analysis of the bloodstain patterns at a crime scene, a

BPE develops a theory regarding the sequence of events that occurred.

Blow-up diagram   A detailed, enlarged view of evidence such as a bloodstain pattern. It is a detailed sketch of evidence within a larger diagram.

Blunt force injury   Wound that causes tearing or shearing of the skin, tissue, or muscles, as well as crushing of bones.

Bounce flash   A technique used to *bounce* (reflect) light from a white- or light-colored surface rather than allowing the flash of light to hit the subject directly.

Bracketing   A photographic term that refers to capturing (photographing) the same subject (object) several times, changing the camera settings each time to obtain various exposures.

Bullet ricochet   Occurs when a bullet in flight strikes and deflects rather than penetrates a surface. Heavy, low-velocity bullets are more likely to ricochet while lighter, high-velocity bullets often disintegrate or expand on impact with a hard object.

Cadaveric spasm   A rare form of instantaneous muscle stiffening that occurs at death.

Camera lens   A transparent material (typically glass) designed to bend light away from (divert) or bend light toward (converge) a point within the lens. A simple lens is similar to a prism that disperses light and colors, focusing the various color frequencies on different points.

Cannabis (marijuana)   The most commonly used illicit drug. Derived from the cannabis plant, which grows naturally in many tropical and temperate regions of the world. The cannabinoid chemical named *delta-9-tetrahydrocannabinol (THC)* inside the plant is responsible for the psychoactive effects.

Casting putty   Used to lift magnetic power-developed fingerprints from textured surfaces.

Cast-off bloodstain pattern   Created when blood is dislodged from a bloody object or weapon as it is being swung. This type of pattern is often observed in beating and stabbing cases.

Cause of death   A conclusion drawn by the forensic pathologist that identifies the injury or disease that led to the biological chain of events resulting in death.

Central pocket loop whorl fingerprint pattern   A plain whorl pattern in which a line drawn between the two deltas does not cross a recurving ridgeline.

Cessation cast-off pattern   Occurs when a bloody object or weapon strikes another object or surface and comes to a complete stop. Blood is dislodged from the object previously in motion and is cast off in the same direction the weapon or object is swung.

Chain of custody of evidence   Establishes who had custody of the evidence, on what date and at what time they came in contact with it, and under what circumstances, and if any tests were conducted on the evidence.

Chemical trauma death   Occurs primarily through the ingestion of toxins such as drugs, alcohol, or poison. Fifty percent of all chemical trauma deaths involve the ingestion of ethyl alcohol (ethanol) contained in beer, wine, or distilled spirits.

Chopping wound   Wound caused by a heavy, sharp instrument, tool, or weapon.

Class characteristics   Physical evidence that possesses the same or similar properties.

Cocaine   Derived from the coca plant grown in the Andean mountains in South America, primarily Colombia. The coca leaves are mixed with gasoline or kerosene to form an alkali that is mashed in a pit. Other chemicals are added and the mash is filtered, producing a paste. The mash paste is dried, yielding a powdered form of cocaine.

Compression   Used to reduce a digital image file size so the image can be stored, processed, and transmitted to a computer or printer.

Concentric cracks   The cracks surrounding bullet holes in a pane of glass that appear in a circular shape around a bullet hole.

Conchoidal cracks   Cracks in glass which originate on the side of the initial impact, curve, then straighten, and end perpendicular to the opposite (inside) edge of the glass.

Conduction   A situation in which heat is transferred through direct contact.

Consensual encounter   Any interaction between a police officer and another that does not involve formal police restraint of the other person's freedom of movement.

Consent search   A search in which a person knowingly and voluntarily waives Fourth Amendment rights after having been given a request-choice by an officer. Consent allows a police officer to conduct an exploratory investigation of the area or property to which the consenting party has possessory rights.

Contrecoup injury   A contrecoup injury to the brain is caused by blunt force trauma. The injury is caused by the brain moving and impacting the inside of the skull opposite the weapon impact site. The injury appears on the side of the brain opposite the impact site.

Controlled Substance Act (CSA) of 1970   Legislation that categorizes each drug into one of five schedules based on the substance's medical use, potential for abuse, and dependence liability.

Contusion   A bruise that results when a blunt force object impacts the body, crushing tissues, and rupturing blood vessels. The skin is discolored but not broken.

Convection   Heat transfer through fluid or super-heated gases.

Coordinate sketching method (rectangular coordinate method)   A measuring technique that uses coordinates from x and y axes to pinpoint evidence items in a crime scene.

Core   The center of the fingerprint.

Coroner An elected official (not necessarily a medical doctor) who oversees forensic pathologists (medical doctors who perform autopsies).

Coup injury An injury to the brain caused by blunt force trauma. The injury results from skull bone pressure against the brain. The injury can be observed on the brain at the weapon impact site.

Crack The rock form of cocaine that can be heated and smoked through a crack pipe.

Criminalist A laboratory analysis person who holds a bachelors degree or higher in fields such as chemistry and biology.

Cross-examination By the opposing attorney(s). The attorney conducting the cross examination may attempt to discredit (impeach) the witness.

Cross-contamination of evidence Occurs when the biological or trace evidence from one evidentiary item contacts and contaminates another piece of evidence, thus destroying the integrity, validity, and credibility of the evidence and its handlers.

Cross-projection (exploded view) diagram is ideal for indoor crime scenes with evidence located on the floor, wall(s), or ceiling. The room sketched is thought of as a box with the floor of the room represented by the base of the box, the walls by the sides of the box, and the ceiling by the top of the box. If the box is unfolded, the walls collapse around the floor and the ceiling connects to one of the walls.

Cut (slash) wound Wound created by a cutting action with a sharp instrument. The wound typically has even, defined edges.

Cutting agents Additives designed to add weight and dilute a drug. Cutting agents include sugar, starch, acetaminophen, procaine, benzocaine, quinine, or other types of additives.

Cyanoacrylate ester fuming A common chemically enhanced fingerprint processing technique. Cyanoacrylate ester is the generic name for fast-acting glue sold under the trade names *Superglue*® and *Krazy Glue*®.

Darkfield illumination A photographic technique used to document bullet holes in glass. The technique highlights the details of the fracture lines and removes distracting features located beyond the glass.

Date rape drug A depressant that is inconspicuously placed into the drink (typically an alcoholic drink) of the unsuspecting victim. The date rape drug is used to incapacitate or lower the inhibitions of the victim, thus overcoming resistance to a sexual encounter. The victim often has no recollection of what happened because the drug produces memory impairment.

Defense wound Wound that often results when victims defend themselves against attacks from sharp and blunt force weapons. The injuries occur when the victim attempts self-defense with arms or legs, blocking the weapon from hitting the body or head.

Delta An area on a ridge nearest the center of type lines in the fingerprint pattern.

Demarcation line An abrupt end to a blood spatter pattern that is indicative of an object blocking the continuation of the blood spatter. A door containing a partial pattern may be moved, leaving a demarcation line on the floor or carpet.

Depressants Drugs that depress (slow) the central nervous system. Depressants are used throughout the world to induce sleep, relieve anxiety, and alleviate stress.

Depth-of-field The distance between the point (foreground) directly in front of a photographic subject and the point (background) immediately beyond the photographic subject that is in acceptable focus when the subject is in perfect focus.

Detailed search A search for evidence that starts at the perpetrator's point of entry (if known) to the crime scene and continues systematically throughout the scene.

Direct examination A series of questions asked by an attorney of the attorney's witness that pertain to a crime scene, evidence, and relevant facts related to a criminal investigation.

Distance determination A calculation of the approximate distance between the firearm at the time of discharge and the impact site of the projectile and GSR. This evidence is critical to determining *near* versus *far* discharge (e.g., suicide versus homicide).

Dominion and control evidence Documentation that links a person to a residence or business.

Double loop whorl fingerprint pattern A pattern with two separate loop formations and two deltas. The two separate loops need not be joined by a sharing ridge. The ridge lines in the loops are not counted.

Double-action revolver Can be operated in a single-action mode or by pulling the trigger. The double-action mode requires a longer and often heavier trigger pull than single action.

Electrostatic lift An electrostatic lift produces static electricity that assists with collecting a print or impression in dust.

Elevation diagram A diagram used to illustrate a vertical plane, such as staircase or the side of a building, outdoor terrain, or slope.

Evidence Any information or item people use to make a decision. Evidence consists of testimony, writings, material objects, and other items presented in a legal proceeding as proof of the existence or nonexistence of a fact.

Exigent circumstance An emergency that requires swift and immediate action.

Expired bloodstain pattern Created when a victim coughs, sneezes, or expels blood from of the mouth. Expired bloodstain patterns may be associated with a homicide or a natural death. The decedent may have blood in the mouth because of a disease or internal hemorrhaging and may expel and deposit blood throughout a scene. Conversely, a victim may sustain a stab wound that results in injury to a lung or some other violent injury may force blood through the mouth.

Exposure   The effect of light on film.

False positive reaction   A presumptive blood test in which the color reaction appears positive but, after confirmatory laboratory tests, the sample is determined to be something other than blood.

Fill flash   Flash used to eliminate undesirable shadows that may obscure an evidence item in the photograph. Fill flash can be used to eliminate shadows under trees, bushes, steps, vehicles, and other environments that require additional light.

Fingerprint classification   The application of a process of individualization to the prints of a human's 10 fingers.

Fingerprint   Created when contaminants (e.g., natural secretions, ink) are transferred from the peaks of friction ridges to a relatively smooth surface (e.g., firearm, bottle, fingerprint card). Using the fingerprints of a human's 10 fingertips (digits), the prints may be classified, providing a unique individualized personal identifier.

Fingerprint identification   The process of comparing questioned and known friction skin ridge prints and impressions.

Firearm injury   A wound inflicted as a firearm's projectile enters and injures the body. The severity of the wound depends on the type of weapon and its ammunition.

Flash synchronization (sync)   Attaches to the hot shoe and a strobe unit. With the strobe unit activated, the photographer presses the shutter release button, and a signal is sent from the camera through the hot shoe and sync cord to the strobe unit, causing the strobe to *fire* a flash of light.

Fleeting targets exception   (to the search warrant requirement) If a police officer has probable cause to believe evidence or contraband is in a vehicle that is mobile and accessible to a roadway, the officer may conduct a warrantless search of the vehicle, including all compartments and containers in the vehicle.

Flow pattern   Created when a large volume of accumulated blood flows from one area to another based on gravity and the contour of the surface. A flow pattern may be observed on a vertical surface (e.g., wall) or on a victim's body as blood flows downward along the contour of the body.

Fly specks   Fly (inspect) activity within a bloody crime scene can produce tiny stains that may be misinterpreted as spatter stains. Flies consume blood within the scene and regurgitate the blood onto other surfaces.

Focal length   The distance between the face of the lens and the point inside the lens at which rays of light passing though the lens face converge. Each f-stop allows half the amount of light into the camera as the f-stop immediately preceding it.

Forensic anthropologist   An anthropologist with specialized forensic training.

Forensic criminologist   An expert in the field of behavioral profiling.

Forensic document examiner   An expert on questioned documents.

Forensic entomologist   An expert in the study of insects with specialized forensic training in postmortem (after death) insect activity in and on a human body.

Forensic entomology   The study of the insect activity associated with a dead body.

Forensic odontologist   A dentist with specialized training in forensic dentistry.

Forensic pathologist   A medical doctor who performs autopsies.

Forensic science   The application of science to conflict resolution in a legal environment.

Forensic technician   A sworn peace officer, case investigator, or civilian employee of an agency who responds to and processes major crime scenes. Many job titles are used to describe a forensic technician: *crime scene specialist, crime scene technician, forensic specialist, forensic evidence technician, forensic science technician, identification technician, and crime scene investigator.*

Fracture match analysis   Comparison of fractured parts of a single item.

Freehand simulation   An attempt to reproduce another person's writing.

Friction ridge   The raised portion of a human's epidermis on digits (fingers and toes), palmar (palms) or plantar (foot sole) skin.

Frisk   A cursory search (pat-down) of a legally detained subject for the purpose of discovering deadly or dangerous weapons that could be used to assault a police officer or other person legally authorized to arrest.

F-stop   (increments of light admission) The *f* refers to a *factor* that represents a mathematical ratio of the focal length of the lens divided by the diameter of the aperture.

Gateway drug   Many law enforcement drug investigators view marijuana as a drug that can lead to use of more potent and dangerous drugs.

Grid search method   Appropriate for large outdoor crime scenes. The grid search is similar to a strip search except it requires a search in four directions rather than two. After the searcher weaves through the scene from two directions (e.g., north–south), the searcher repeats the search from opposite directions (e.g., east–west) and weaves back and forth through the scene in search of evidence.

Groove   The portion of the rifling cut into the barrel.

Gross report   Written report containing information obtained and observations made during the autopsy.

Gunshot Residue (GSR)   Unburned gunpowder released from a firearm when it is discharged. GSR may be located on the shooter's hands, the victim's clothing, or surrounding surfaces.

Hallucinogen   A hallucinogen appears in natural form in some plants and fungi, or it can be produced synthetically (artificially). Synthetic hallucinogens are more potent than the naturally occurring drug. While the term *hallucinogen* may cause one to assume that a user will hallucinate under its influence, not all drugs in this classification produce hallucinations. Most will, however, produce changes in mood, perception, and thought patterns.

Hanging   Can be the result of an accident, a suicide, or a homicide. Most commonly, hangings are accidents or suicides. Complete suspension of the body need not occur for a person to die from a hanging. Asphyxia occurs as oxygenated blood flow to the brain is restricted. A ligature on the neck with minimal pressure applied to arteries servicing the brain can restrict blood flow.

Heroin   A semi-synthetic narcotic derived from morphine.

Hesitation wound   A self-inflicted injury caused by an indecisive suicidal person. The hesitation may be due to fear, anticipation, or uncertainty of the level of force necessary to carry out the suicide.

Hit-and-run   A vehicle collision from which a person involved in a collision flees the scene.

Hot shoe   Attachment connecting a camera with a flash synchronization (sync) cord.

Hyperthermia death   Death caused by exposure to excessive heat.

Hypothermia death   Death caused by exposure to excessively cold temperature.

Impact mechanism bloodstain pattern   Created when an action such as blunt force or a gunshot fragments a blood source (victim), creating a converging pattern of individual blood spatters on nearby surfaces.

Indented writing   An impression on a document resulting from writing on a paper placed on top of the questioned document.

Individual characteristics   Those that are unique to the item. If two people wear shoes with the same class characteristics for a prolonged period of time, each person will create a different wear pattern (individual characteristics) on the soles of the shoes because each person's stride is unique. Additionally, if one walks across a piece of glass, a unique cut may be created in the sole of a shoe, which would be impossible to replicate in the same manner. These markings are examples of individual characteristics.

Initial search for evidence   Search conducted by the forensic technician(s) and crime scene investigator (if one is assigned) to survey the scene to determine and prioritize tasks.

Inner tracing   The ridge traced passes above the right delta and three or more ridgelines lie between the traced ridge and the right delta.

Integrated Automated Fingerprint Identification System (IAFIS)   The FBI's computerized database containing fingerprints of over 50 million individuals.

Laceration   Injury produced by the tearing, ripping, crushing, bending, pulling, stretching, and shearing of skin, muscle, or tissue when a blunt force object is applied to the body.

Land   The portion of the interior of a firearm's barrel not cut away when manufactured.

Large-volume pattern   Indicative of extensive bleeding in a fixed position. A person's body will *bleed* from an open wound while the person is alive. Bleeding is a function of cardiac (heart) activity. When a person dies, the wound no longer bleeds because the heart ceased to function. After death, blood will drain rather than bleed from an open wound.

Latent fingerprint   A fingerprint that is observable after processing with a powder or chemical.

Latent fingerprint examiner   An expert in the identification and comparison of latent fingerprints.

Lens filter   Device placed over a lens to change the composition of the light that enters the camera's lens. Filters do not add color. They subtract (remove) color. Filters are also used to increase or decrease contrast.

Line search method   The line search is used in large, outdoor areas. Instead of reversing directions, a line of searchers walk side by side in one direction only.

Livor mortis (lividity)   The pooling of blood within the body caused by gravity after cardiovascular circulation ceases. When the heart stops, the person no longer bleeds.

Locard Exchange Principle   Principle which proposes that forensic evidence from a crime scene can be linked to a victim and a suspect.

Loop fingerprint pattern   Fingerprint in which the ridge lines enter the pattern area from the left or right side of the finger, recurve, and reverse direction, exiting the pattern area in the direction of the entry point. Three characteristics (requirements) designate a loop fingerprint pattern: sufficient ridge line recurve, a delta, and a ridge count across a looping ridge.

Loop-type tented arch fingerprint pattern   Similar to a loop pattern but it lacks a recurving ridge between the delta and the core of the print.

Loupe   A magnifier with a built-in metric scale used to measure and record the length and width of each selected blood spatter.

Macro lens   Lens used for close-up photography that allows the photographer to obtain close-up and enlarged views of fingerprints, bullet holes, bloodstains or blood drops, tool marks, and other small items of evidence.

Main lighting source   A flash unit is used to create light similar to natural daylight.

Major case prints   The recordings of all of the ridge detail of a suspect's hand, not the fingertips alone. The tips, sides, and lower joints of the fingers are also printed.

Manner of death   The determination made by the forensic pathologist that concludes how the cause of death occurred.

Mechanical trauma injury   Injury resulting from the application of an object such as a sharp or blunt force instrument or a firearm trajectory.

Mechanism of death   The determination of the forensic pathologist that identifies the biochemical or physiological abnormality that caused a death.

Medical examiner (coroner)   Typically a medical doctor who performs postmortem examinations (autopsies) to determine cause, mechanism, and manner of death. In some states, the coroner is elected and not required to possess any medical training.

Medical examiner   A medical doctor trained in pathology who oversees the pathologists in the jurisdiction.

Meet tracing   Less than three ridgelines above or below the traced ridge and the right delta.

Methamphetamine (meth)   A stimulant that remains in the central nervous system much longer than cocaine. Meth's effects are similar to cocaine but develop slowly and last longer. Long-term methamphetamine use results in a psychosis with characteristics similar to schizophrenia. The user becomes paranoid, is preoccupied with delusional thoughts, may have auditory or visual hallucinations, and may pick at skin. Violent, unpredictable behavior is common among long-term meth users.

Microscopic report   Written report containing information obtained and observations made from specimens viewed under a microscope.

Motor Vehicle Collision (MVC)   A situation in which a motor vehicle comes into contact with another vehicle, person, or object.

Mummification   Drying of the body and tissues which may occur in very dry climates.

Narcotic   A narcotic dulls human senses, relieves pain, and reduces tension, anxiety, and aggression.

Negative reaction   A presumptive blood test that produces no immediate color change indicating the absence of blood.

Non-requested writing   A spontaneous or un-dictated writing typically collected from a suspect's home or business.

Normal hand forgeries   With normal hand forgeries, suspects use their own writing style or they may alter their style to deflect suspicion.

Normal lens   Lens with a focal length that is equal to the diagonal measurement of the image area. The image area of a 35-mm camera is 24 × 36 mm, and the diagonal measurement of the image area is 50 mm. Therefore, a normal lens for a 35-mm camera is 50 mm. The photo image angle of a normal lens is 45 degrees, which corresponds to the viewing range of the human eye.

Outer tracing   The traced ridge passes below the right delta and three or more ridgelines lie between the traced ridge and the right delta.

Overhead (bird's-eye) view diagram   An overhead diagram depicting the overall layout of a scene.

Painting-with-light   A process through which one adds light to a timed-exposure photograph.

Paired injuries   Injuries that occur simultaneously (at the same time and in the same manner). More than one injury is produced because of multiple sharp edges on the weapon. For example, a pair of scissors or a fork may produce more than one injury per thrust.

Parole search   Search that may be conducted without a trigger or reasonable (particularized) suspicion, as long as the search is not arbitrary, capricious, or harassing. Thus, a search conducted under the auspices of a properly imposed parole search condition does not intrude on any reasonable expectation of privacy.

Passive bloodstain pattern   Created by gravity and secondary contact with blood at the crime scene. Patterns affected by gravity include drops, blood flow, and a large volume of blood. Patterns affected by secondary contact include those that are created when an object or person contacts blood and transfers it to another object or surface.

Patent print   A fingerprint that is visible to the unaided human eye. A substance or contaminant (substrate) on the individual's fingertips causes the transfer of visible ridge characteristics. Bloody or inked fingerprints are two examples of patent prints.

Pattern injury   A pattern injury is indicative of the object or surface that produced the injury.

Pattern of injuries   A pattern of injuries relates to the distribution of external and internal injuries that suggest a sequence of events or the order in which the injuries were inflicted.

Pedestaling   A technique that allows one to observe and work near a corpse without disturbing it.

Penetrating injury   Injury caused by instruments that enter the body but do not exit.

Perforating injury   Injury caused by instruments that enter and pass through the body, exiting the body at another point.

Perimortem   During death.

Petechia   (plural: petechiae) Pinpoint hemorrhaging often observed in the white area of the victim's eyes. Petechia can occur throughout the body.

Petechial hemorrhaging   The pinpoint hemorrhaging (or rupture) of small blood vessels often observed in the eyes of a victim of an attempted strangulation or other events related to breathing airway obstruction.

Phlebotomist   A medical professional who is trained to extract human blood samples.

Plain arch fingerprint pattern   Fingerprint containing ridge flow that enters the pattern area at one end, flows upward slightly in a wave-like appearance, then flows downward and out to the opposite end of the pattern. Ridge formations (minutiae) may be observed in the center of the print.

Plain-view doctrine   Holds that anything in plain view is not constitutionally protected. There are two elements to the plain-view doctrine. First, the officer must possess legal authority to be in the position from which the observation is made. Second, the officer must have probable cause to believe that the object or property observed constitutes evidence of a crime.

Plain whorl fingerprint pattern   Contains characteristics that include two deltas, at least one complete circuit of ridge flow, at least one recurving ridge line in the inner pattern area if an imaginary straight line is drawn between the two deltas.

Plastic print   A three-dimensional fingerprint that is visible to the human unaided eye. Fingerprints (impressions) in putty, wax, and other substances are examples of plastic prints. Recovery of plastic prints is accomplished through photography or the application of a casting material.

Point of impact   The location at which vehicles collide.

Polar (radial) sketch method   A sketching technique often used at an outdoor crime scene if evidence is dispersed over a large open area. It is also used if no fixed points from which to measure are available. Open terrain, such as a field, mountain range, desert, or other large area lends itself to this method.

Positive reaction   A presumptive blood test that produces an immediate color change indicating the presence of blood.

Postmortem   After death.

Postmortem examination (autopsy)   An examination conducted to determine the cause, mechanism, and manner of death of a human being.

Presumptive blood test   Test used to determine if a substance might be blood. A presumptive blood test does not confirm that a substance is blood.

Probable cause   Involves facts that would lead a person of ordinary care and prudence to believe that there is a fair probability that evidence or contraband will be found in or at a particular location.

Probation search   A search to ascertain if the probationer is complying with the terms of probation.

Projection mechanism bloodstain pattern   Created by blood placed in flight and projected by a force other than an impact.

Putrefaction   A process that contributes to the decomposition of the body initiated by proteins by anaerobic micro-organisms (putrefying bacteria). Environmental conditions (e.g., temperature and climate), clothing, and body weight can increase or decrease the rate of decomposition. Hot, humid environments accelerate the process, while dry, cold environments slow the process.

Quadrant (grid) technique   A method for ensuring that all areas of an impact bloodstain pattern are photographed.

Quadrant (zone) search method   A search that involves dividing the search area into four quadrants (zones). Each quadrant is searched separately, until the entire scene is searched.

Questioned documents   Any document of evidentiary value, including suspect checks, contracts, wills, typewritten and handwritten letters, currency, postage stamps, event tickets, receipts, and virtually any other document of evidentiary value.

Radial cracks   The cracks surrounding bullet holes in a pane of glass which radiate out and away from a bullet hole as jagged, sharp lines.

Radial loop   A loop with ridge lines that enter (start) and exit (end) the pattern area in the direction of the radial thumb bone.

Radiation   Invisible waves that travel at the same speed as visible light. Radiant heat travels in a direct line from the source until it strikes an object.

Receipt and inventory   A list of all evidence items collected as the result of the execution of the search warrant.

Requested writing   Dictated writing (i.e., the suspect is told what to write).

Resolution   Refers to the ability to capture fine details with a digital image. The number of pixels in an image directly affects resolution. More pixels result in higher resolution. Higher resolution equates to more pixels per square inch.

Ridge count   The number of ridge lines between the delta and the core of the loop pattern.

Ridge formation (minutiae)   A characteristic observed in all types of fingerprints.

Rifling   Lands and grooves bored into the barrel during manufacturing which cause the bullet to spin, enhancing accuracy of the bullet.

Rigor mortis (rigidity)   Results from the biochemical changes that occur in the muscles after death. Initially, rigor mortis causes the muscles of the body to stiffen. When the chemicals begin to decompose and deteriorate, the muscles become flaccid (lack firmness).

Roadmapping technique   Utilizes measurements placed strategically throughout the impact pattern; based on the blood spatter chosen for analysis and reconstruction purposes.

Rubber-gelatin lifter   A material made of thick, low-adhesive gelatin designed to lift and collect finger- and footprints, marks, and other trace evidence in dust.

Satellite spatter   Tiny fragments of blood. Satellite spatters are small blood spatter stains created when blood droplets detach from a larger blood drop as it impacts an object.

Search   A search involves a governmental intrusion into an area in which a person has a reasonable expectation of privacy. The purpose of the search is to discover evidence that may be used in a criminal prosecution.

Search incidental (contemporaneous) to a lawful custodial arrest   A search limited to the arrestee and the area within the arrestee's immediate control for possible evidence, weapons, or contraband.

Search warrant   An order issued by a judge and directed to peace officers, commanding a search of a described location for described evidence or contraband.

Secondary mechanism spatter   An alternative reference to satellite spatter because it is produced by a second impact. Satellite spatter can occur in virtually any bloodstain pattern involving blood in flight or dripping blood.

Seizure   Occurs when a person's freedom of movement is restricted or when property is taken into custody by the government.

Semiautomatic pistol   Fires a bullet and automatically reloads a cartridge (ammunition) each time the trigger is pulled.

Sequenced bloodstain pattern   Overlapping bloodstains frequently located at crime scenes. A determination must be made regarding the sequence of the stain patterns. Motion transfer bloodstains (swipes and wipes) are often observed in sequenced bloodstain patterns.

Sequential processing   Involves the use of more than one technique to enhance and develop a latent fingerprint.

Sexual Assault Nurse Examiner (SANE)   A forensically trained nurse. The SANE photographs the victim's external injuries, collects and preserves the victim's clothing, and conducts a search for trace evidence. The SANE also combs genital hair for trace evidence, obtains fingernail scrapings and oral swabs (if oral copulation occurred), conducts a body cavity exam for signs of trauma, and swabs for the assailant's biological material. The victim is provided with alternate clothing upon release.

Sexual Assault Response Team (SART)   Available to assist and counsel the victim and a victim's family.

Sharp object injury   Injury resulting from cutting, stabbing, and chopping wounds.

Shutter   Located within a camera's body, the shutter controls the length of time that light is allowed to enter the camera and expose the film.

Shutter release cable   A cable connected to the camera used in lieu of pressing the camera's shutter release button. Cable is used to prevent accidental movement of the camera.

Single-action revolver   Operates by pulling the handgun's hammer back (cocking) and pulling the trigger to release the hammer. The hammer activates a firing pin that contacts the primer on the cartridge.

Skeletonized bloodstain   The outline of an original bloodstain prior to drying or motion transfer.

Spatter bloodstain pattern   Results when blood is placed in flight because of action upon it. Actions that may create spatter bloodstain patterns include gunshots, beatings, stabbings, satellite (secondary mechanism) spatter, projection mechanisms (cast-off patterns from blood, objects in motion), and arterial and expirated blood (blood forced from a live human body through arterial pressure or coughing action).

Spiral search method   Search that begins at the center of the crime scene and then proceeds outward in a circular fashion to the outer edge.

Stab wound   Wound that punctures the skin; tends to penetrate more deeply than a cut.

Stippling (tattooing)   The embedding of unburned gunpowder and metal particles into the skin around an entrance wound. The tattooing is most pronounced at the point where the bullet entered the body.

Stopping down the lens   Reducing the size of the aperture to improve depth-of-field.

Strangulation   A purposeful act involving the placement of hands or a ligature around a victim's neck, restricting oxygenated blood flow to the brain.

Striations   Fine scratches inside a firearm's rifled barrel that are produced by imperfections created during the manufacturing process.

Strip search method   A strip search involves one or more persons walking in a linear fashion, reversing directions at the outer edge of the scene to search an unsearched strip.

Sufficient recurve   Fingerprint in which a ridge line enters and exits the pattern area at nearly the same point. It does not contain a sharp, right-angle ridge or appendage on the outside of the ridge line.

Telephoto lens   A zoom lens that has a long focal length and captures a close-up image of a distant object or subject. The lens captures a small field-of-view and a shallow depth-of-field. Distant objects are enlarged while near objects do not appear proportionately larger.

Tented arch fingerprint pattern   Similar to a plain arch. However, the top (highest point) of the arch is more pronounced (the peak's ridge flow changes direction abruptly).

Timed exposure   The length of time a photographer chooses to keep the shutter open.

Total station   A surveying instrument used to obtain horizontal and vertical angle measurements, as well as distance and slope measurements necessary to investigate and reconstruct traffic collision scenes.

Trace evidence   Evidence, such as hair or fibers, that may be destroyed or disappear if not collected immediately.

Trace lifts   Method of collecting evidence. Clear packing tape, Handi-Lifts, or hinge lifter used on surfaces where hairs and fibers are not easily observed.

Tracing   A signature or writing.

Trajectory   A bullet's path from the moment of discharge from a firearm until it comes to rest.

Transecting baseline method   An outdoor measuring technique that may be used for situations in which there are no x and y axis lines. Instead, two fixed points are chosen and a line is created between the two points.

Transfer bloodstain pattern   A non-motion or a motion stain pattern that occurs when a bloody object contacts a clean surface (e.g., bloody weapon placed on a clean surface; a bloody shoe pressed against a clean floor).

Triangulation method   A sketching technique that can be used at indoor or outdoor crime scenes. Two fixed points are selected. At an indoor scene, corners in a room are typically chosen. The distance between the two points is measured. Next, a measurement is taken from each fixed point to the evidence item. The sketcher can measure to the center of the evidence item or take measurements to no more than two of the item's sides or corners.

Type lines   The two innermost (closest to the center) ridges of the fingerprint pattern that start out parallel, then diverge, and partially surround the pattern. Some type lines are continuous ridges that surround the pattern area, but most are broken lines that contain but do not completely surround the pattern. In a loop pattern, the delta is located on the side opposite the ridge lines' entry/exit point.

Ulnar loop   A loop with ridge lines that enter and exit the pattern area in the direction of the ulna bone (little finger).

Upthrust tented arch fingerprint pattern   Fingerprint that contains ridges that form an upthrust, with ridge line angles of 45 degrees or more.

Vehicle Identification Number (VIN).   A unique identifier assigned to a vehicle when manufactured and is usually located on the dash near the driver's side.

Vertical illumination (axial lighting)   A photographic technique used to refract (bend) light. The technique is often used for patent (visible) fingerprints observable only when light at a particular angle is reflected from the print.

Viscosity   Resistance to flow.

Void bloodstain pattern (ghost)   Occurs when an object containing a portion of the bloodstain is removed leaving an outline of the voided pattern behind. The outline lacks blood spatter within the area once occupied by the object.

Voir dire examination   The process through which prospective jurors are questioned about their backgrounds, biases, and suitability during jury selection.

White balance   A digital camera locates a reference point in an image that the camera detects as the color white and calculates all of the other colors based on the white point.

Whorl fingerprint pattern   Appears circular, spiral, or oval in shape and contains at least two deltas with a recurving ridge in front of each delta. Each type of whorl pattern (plain, central pocket loop, double loop, and accidental) contains specific characteristics.

Wide-angle lens   Lens with a shorter focal length than a normal lens and covers a photo image angle wider than 60 degrees. The large depth-of-field resulting from the short focal length compensates for inexact focusing, which is ideal for wide, overall views of a scene.

The Forensic Technician's Crime Scene Kit

Basic Supplies and Equipment for Evidence Preservation and Collection

Crime scene barrier tape	Yellow evidence placard numbers and letters
Paper bags (large, medium, and small)	Manila envelopes (large, medium, and coin size)
Gloves (vinyl if latex allergy) and chemical resistant	Permanent markers and pens (black)
Evidence sealing tape	Bindles (see Chapter 4, Figure 4.1)
Sterile swabs	Dropper bottle with distilled water
Presumptive blood tests	Presumptive narcotics tests
Handi-Lifts or transparent tape (trace evidence collection)	Tweezers
Flashlight	Hand-held forensic light source and goggles

Basic Supplies and Equipment for Impression and Fingerprint Evidence Collection

Tool mark casting kit	Shoe impression casting kit
Gel lifters (black and white) and roller	Bio-foam (known shoe impression exemplars)
Black and magnetic powders	Zephyr brush
Magnetic wand	Fingerprint lifting tape (various sizes and types)
Latent print cards (various sizes)	Full sheet white labels and transparency sheets (hand and fingerprint exemplars)

Basic Supplies and Equipment for Sketching and Preparing a Crime Scene Diagram

Graph paper	Pencils, erasers, pens
Straight edge (optional)	Laser measuring device (if available)
GPS system (if available)	Roller tape
Measuring tapes (12, 25, and 100 ft)	

GPS = global positioning satellite

Basic Supplies and Equipment for Forensic Photography

DSLR camera	Flash unit
Hot shoe	Synchronization cord
Lenses: zoom, macro, telephoto	Cable release cord
Tripod (inverse mount capability)	Extra memory cards
Extra batteries for flash unit	L-shaped rulers (standard and shoe impression size)
Rolls of sticky scales, letters, numbers, arrows	Rolls of sticky 12-inch measuring tape
Compass	North indicator and case information cards

DSLR = digital single-lens reflex

Personal Supplies for the Forensic Technician

Hand sanitizer and hand wipes	Hat, sweatshirt or jacket
Energy or protein bars	Bottled drinking water
Sunscreen	Insect repellant
Stash of cash	Toiletries

Forensic Equipment Suppliers (not all inclusive)

Name of Company	Website
Bluestar Forensic Crime Scene Investigation Tools	www.bluestar-forensic.com
Crime Scene Evidence Files (products for the public)	www.crimescene.com
CSI Forensic Supply (formerly known as Kinderprint Company)	www.csiforensic.com
Doje's Forensic Supplies	www.dojes.com
Educational Innovations, Inc.	www.teachersource.com
Evidence Crime Scene Products	www.evidentcrimescene.com
Forensics Source (products: Lighting Powder, Identicator, NIK, Public Safety, EVI-PAQ, ODV, and Projectina)	www.forensicssource.com
Forensic Worx	www.forensicworx.com
Foster & Freeman, Ltd.	www.fosterfreeman.co.uk
Gizmos & Gadgets for the Crime Scene Officer and Investigator	www.csigizmos.com
Law Enforcement Technologies, Inc.	www.lawenforcetech.com
Raysics Quality Forensic Supplies	www.raysics.com
Sirchie Fingerprint Laboratories	www.sirchie.com
Ward's Natural Science	www.wardsci.com

Police and law enforcement link to products and companies	www.policeone.com

References

Acker, J.R. and Brody, D.C. *Criminal Procedure*. Gaithersburg, MD: Aspen Publishers, 1999.

American Society of Crime Laboratory Directors/Laboratory Accreditation Board. 02 Mar. 2009 <http://www.ascld-lab.org>.

American Society of Crime Laboratory Directors/Laboratory Accreditation Board—International. 02 Mar. 2009 <http://www.ascld-lab.org>.

Anderson, Gail S. "Forensic Entomology." *Forensic Science: An Introduction to Scientific and Investigative Technologies*. 2nd ed. James, Stuart and Nordby, Jon. Boca Raton: CRC Press, 2005. 135–59.

Ashbaugh, David R. *Quantitative-Qualitative Friction Ridge Analysis: An Introduction to Basic and Advanced Ridgeology*. Boca Raton: CRC Press, 1999.

Bevel, Tom, and Ross M. Gardner. *Bloodstain Pattern Analysis: With an Introduction to Crime Scene Reconstruction*. 3rd ed. Boca Raton: CRC Press, 2008.

Bodziak, William J. *Footwear Impression Evidence: Detection, Recovery and Examination*. 2nd ed. New York: CRC Press, 2000.

Bodziak, William J, "Forensic Tire Impression and Tire Track Evidence." *Forensic Science: An Introduction to Scientific and Investigative Techniques*. 2nd ed. James, Stuart and Nordby, Jon. Boca Raton: CRC Press, 2005. 377–90.

Burns, Karen Ramey. *The Forensic Anthropology Training Manual*. 2nd ed. Upper Saddle River: Prentice Hall, 2006.

California Commission on Peace Officer Standards and Training. *Regular Peace Officer Basic Course*. Sacramento, CA: POST, 2008.

Chesapeake Bay Division—International Association for Identification. 2003 <http://www.cbdiai.org>.

DiMaio, Vincent, and Dominick DiMaio. *Forensic Pathology: Practical Aspects of Criminal and Forensic Investigations*. 2nd ed. New York: CRC Press, 2001.

DMORT Mass Fatality Assistance. 02 Mar. 2009 <http://www.dmort.org>.

Eckert, William. *Introduction to Forensic Sciences*. 2nd ed. New York: CRC Press, 1997.

Falcone, David N. *Prentice Hall's Dictionary of American Criminal Justice, Criminology, and Criminal Law*. Upper Saddle River: Pearson Prentice Hall, 2005.

Fisher, Barry A. J. *Techniques of Crime Scene Investigation*. 7th ed. Boca Raton: CRC Press, 2004.

Fredrickson, Darin, and Siljander, Raymond. *Applied Police and Fire Photography*. 2nd ed. Charles C. Thomas Publisher, Ltd., Springfield, IL, 1997.

Gaensslen, R. E., Howard A. Harris, and Henry Lee. *Introduction to Forensic Science and Criminalistics*. Boston: McGraw-Hill Higher Education, 2008.

Gammie, Dan. *Field Evidence Technician Course*. California State University, Long Beach, June 1998.

Gardner, Ross M. *Practical Crime Scene Processing and Investigation*. Boca Raton: CRC Press, 2005.

Gardner, T. J., and Anderson, T. M. *Criminal Evidence*. 5th ed. Belmont, CA: Cengage, 2004.

Girard, James E. *Criminalistics: Forensic Science and Crime*. Sudbury: Jones and Bartlett Publishers, Inc., 2008.

Greenfield, Andrew and Sloan, Monica M. "Identification of Biological Fluids and Stains." *Forensic Science: An Introduction to Scientific and Investigative Techniques*. 2nd ed. James, Stuart and Nordby, Jon. Boca Raton: CRC Press, 2005. 265.

Guffey, James E. *Report Writing Fundamentals for Police and Correctional Officers*. Upper Saddle River: Prentice Hall, 2005.

Haglund, William D. "Forensic Taphonomy." *Forensic Science: An Introduction to Scientific and Investigative Techniques*. 2nd ed. James, Stuart and Nordby, Jon. Boca Raton: CRC Press, 2005. 119–31.

International Association for Identification. 12 Apr. 2008 <http://www.theiai.org/certifications/latent_print/index.php>.

James, Stuart H., and Jon J. Nordby. *Forensic Science: An Introduction to Scientific and Investigative Techniques*. 2nd ed. Boca Raton: CRC Press, 2005.

James, Stuart H., Paul E. Kish, and Paulette T. Sutton. *Principles of Bloodstain Pattern Analysis: Theory and Practice*. Boca Raton: CRC Press, 2005.

Joice, Brad. "The Use of Total Stations and Mapping Software to Produce Scale Diagrams." *Journal of Forensic Identification* 58.1 (2008): 15–26.

Keppel, Robert D., Katherine M. Brown, and Kristen Welch. *Forensic Pattern Recognition: From Fingerprints to Toolmarks*. Upper Saddle River: Prentice Hall, 2007.

Laber, Terry L., and Barton P. Epstein. *Experiments and Practical Exercises in Bloodstain Pattern Analysis*. St. Paul, MN: Midwestern Association of Forensic Scientists, 1998.

Leo, William. *Fingerprint Identification*. San Clemente: LawTech Custom Publishing, 2004.

Lightning Powder Co., Inc. *Impression Evidence: Technical notes*. Salem, 2000.

Long, Ben. *Complete Digital Photography*. 3rd ed. New York: Charles River Media, Inc., Hingham, MA, 2005.

Meadows, Robert J. *Understanding Violence and Victimization*. 4th ed. Upper Saddle River: Pearson Prentice Hall, 2006.

Michelson, Richard S. *Crime Scene Dynamics*. San Clemente: LawTech Custom Publishing, 2004.

Miller, Larry S. *Police Photography*. 5th ed. Cincinnati: Anderson Co., 2006.

National Fire Protection Association. *NFPA Fire Protection Handbook*. Quincy, MA: NFPA, 2008.

Nause, Lawren A., and Michael P. Souliere. "Recording a Known Tire Impression from a Suspect Vehicle." *Journal of Forensic Identification* 58.3 (2008): 305–14.

Neubauer, David W. *America's Courts and the Criminal Justice System*. 5th ed. New York: Wadsworth Publishing Co., 1996.

Norwitch, Frank H, and Seiden, Howard, "Questioned Documents". *Forensic Science: An Introduction to Scientific and Investigative Techniques*. 2nd ed. James, Stuart and Nordby, Jon. Boca Raton: CRC Press, 2005. 423–38.

Ogle, Robert R. *Crime Scene Investigation and Reconstruction*. 2nd ed. Upper Saddle River: Prentice Hall, 2007.

Ortmeier, P. J. *Introduction to Law Enforcement and Criminal Justice*. 2nd ed. Upper Saddle River: Pearson Prentice Hall, 2006.

Oxford Essential Dictionary (American Edition) New York. Oxford University Press: Berkley, 2008.

Parr, Lance A. *Report Writing Essentials*. Belmont: Wadsworth, 2000.

Pekala, William and Johnson, Harvey. *Nikon School of Photography Handbook*. NY: Nikon School of Photography, 2006.

Perper, Joshua A, "Time of Death and Changes After Death.," *Spitz and Fisher's Medicolegal Investigation of Death: Guidelines for the Application of Pathology to Crime Investigation*. 3rd ed. Springfield: Charles C. Thomas Publisher, 1993. 14–64

Publishers Group. *Street Drugs: A Drug Identification Guide*. Plymouth: Publishers Group, LLC, 2006.

Redsicker, David R. "Basic Fire and Explosion Investigation." *Forensic Science: An Introduction to Scientific and Investigative Techniques*. 2nd ed. James, Stuart and Nordby, Jon. Boca Raton: CRC Press, 2005. 489–505.

Redsicker, David R. *The Practical Methodology of Forensic Photography*. 2nd ed. New York: CRC, 2000.

Rowe, Walter F. "Firearm and Tool Mark Examinations." *Forensic Science: An Introduction to Scientific and Investigative Techniques*. 2nd ed. James, Stuart and Nordby, Jon. Boca Raton: CRC Press, 2005. 391–419.

Rutledge, Devallis. *Criminal Investigations and Evidence*. Boston: Pearson Prentice Hall, 2007.

Saferstein, Richard. *Criminalistics: An Introduction to Forensic Science*. 9th ed. Upper Saddle River: Prentice Hall, 2007.

Scott, Billie F. *Fingerprint Classification and Interpretation Simplified*. Boston: Pearson Custom Publishing, 2007.

Scott, Marixa. "Improved Results in the Development of Latent Fingerprints on Thermal Paper." *Journal of Forensic Identification* 58.4 (2008): 424–28.

Siljander, Raymond P. and Darin Fredrickson. *Applied Police and Fire Photography*. 2nd ed.

Springfield: Charles C. Thomas Publisher, 1997.

Sorg, Marcella H. "Forensic Anthropology." *Forensic Science: An Introduction to Scientific and Investigative Techniques*. 2nd ed. James, Stuart and Nordby, Jon. Boca Raton: CRC Press, 2005. 99–116.

Southern California Association of Fingerprint Officers. People v. Jennings, 252 Ill. 534, 96 N.E. 1077. *The Print*, 14.4 (1998): 1–2.

Spalding, Robert P. "Identification and Characterization of Blood and Blood Stains." *Forensic Science: An Introduction to Scientific and Investigative Techniques*, 2nd ed. James, Stuart and Nordby, Jon. Boca Raton: CRC Press, 2005. 237–256.

Sperber, N. Personal interview. 20 May 2009.

Spitz, Werner U. "Asphyxia." *Spitz and Fisher's Medicolegal Investigation of Death: Guidelines for the Application of Pathology to Crime Investigation*. 3rd ed. Springfield: Charles C. Thomas Publisher, 1993a. 444–97.

Spitz, Werner U. "Blunt Force Injury." *Spitz and Fisher's Medicolegal Investigation of Death: Guidelines for the Application of Pathology to Crime Investigation*. 3rd ed. Springfield: Charles C. Thomas Publisher, 1993b. 199–251.

Spitz, Werner U. "Drowning." *Spitz and Fisher's Medicolegal Investigation of Death: Guidelines for the Application of Pathology to Crime Investigation*. 3rd ed. Springfield: Charles C. Thomas Publisher, 1993c. 498–515.

Spitz, Werner U. "Gunshot Wounds." *Spitz and Fisher's Medicolegal Investigation of Death: Guidelines for the Application of Pathology to Crime Investigation*. 3rd ed. Springfield: Charles C. Thomas Publisher, 1993d. 311–81.

Spitz, Werner U. "Sharp Force Injury." *Spitz and Fisher's Medicolegal Investigation of Death: Guidelines for the Application of Pathology to Crime Investigation*. 3rd ed. Springfield: Charles C. Thomas Publisher, 1993e. 252–310.

Spitz, Werner U. "Shotgun Wounds." *Spitz and Fisher's Medicolegal Investigation of Death: Guidelines for the Application of Pathology to Crime Investigation*. 3rd ed. Springfield: Charles C. Thomas Publisher, 1993f. 382–412.

Spitz, Werner U. "Thermal Injuries." *Spitz and Fisher's Medicolegal Investigation of Death: Guidelines for the Application of Pathology to Crime Investigation*. 3rd ed. Springfield: Charles C. Thomas Publisher, 1993g. 413–43.

Spitz, Werner U. and Platt, Marvin S. "The Battered Child and Adolescent." *Spitz and Fisher's Medicolegal Investigation of Death: Guidelines for the Application of Pathology to Crime Investigation*. 3rd ed. Springfield: Charles C. Thomas Publisher, 1993, 687–723.

Staggs, Steven. *Crime Scene Photography*. San Clemente, CA: LawTech Custom, 2005.

Sullivan, Wilson T. III. *Crime Scene Analysis: Practical Procedures and Techniques*. Upper Saddle River: Prentice Hall, 2007.

SWGFAST. "Standards for Conclusion." *Journal of Forensic Identification* 54.3 (2004): 358.

U.S. Department of Justice. Drug Enforcement Administration. *Drugs of Abuse*. Government Printing Office, 2005.

U.S. Department of Justice. Federal Bureau of Investigation Homepage. 2009. <http://www.fbi.gov/hq/lab/codis/program.htm>.

U.S. Department of Justice. Federal Bureau of Investigation. *The Science of Fingerprints*. Government Printing Office, 1984.

U.S. Office of National Drug Control Policy. Executive Office of the President. *ONDCP Drug Policy Information Clearinghouse*. Government Printing Office, 2003.

Waters, N. L., and Hodge, J. P. *The Effects of the Daubert Trilogy in Delaware Superior Court*. Williamsburg, VA: National Center for State Courts, 2005.

Weston, Paul B., and Charles A. Lushbaugh. *Criminal Investigation Basic Perspectives*. 11th ed. Upper Saddle River: Prentice Hall, 2008.

Witzke, D. Southern California Association of Fingerprint Officers. Covina, CA, 08 Oct. 2005.

Wolson, Toby. *Bloodstain Pattern Analysis Workshop*. San Diego, CA, Oct. 2000. 16–20.

Wright, Ronald. "Investigation of Traumatic Death." *Forensic Science: An Introduction to Scientific and Investigative Techniques*. 2nd ed. James, Stuart and Nordby, Jon. Boca Raton: CRC Press, 2005a. 43–58.

Wright, Ronald. "The Role of the Forensic Pathologist." *Forensic Science: An Introduction to Scientific and Investigative Techniques*. 2nd ed. James, Stuart and Nordby, Jon. Boca Raton: CRC Press, 2005b. 15–25.

Young, Tina. "A Photographic Comparison of Luminol, Flourescein, and Bluestar." *Journal of Forensic Identification* 56.5 (2006): 906–12.

Index